HOW DOCTORS CARE

THE SCIENCE OF COMPASSIONATE AND BALANCED CARING IN MEDICINE

FIRST EDITION

HOW DOCTORS CARE

THE SCIENCE OF COMPASSIONATE AND BALANCED CARING IN MEDICINE

Dominic O. Vachon, M.Div., Ph.D.

University of Notre Dame

Foreword by

Jean Watson

 **cognella®**

SAN DIEGO

Bassim Hamadeh, CEO and Publisher
Angela Schultz, Senior Field Acquisitions Editor
Michelle Piehl, Senior Project Editor
Jess Estrella, Senior Graphic Designer
Stephanie Kohl, Licensing Associate
Natalie Piccotti, Director of Marketing
Kassie Graves, Vice President of Editorial
Jamie Giganti, Director of Academic Publishing

3970 Sorrento Valley Blvd., Ste. 500, San Diego, CA 92121

Dedicated to my brother,

Ovide J. Vachon Jr.

April 8, 1965 – December 10, 1983

Contents

Foreword

Jean Watson, PhD, RN, AHN-BC, FAAN, AAN

How Doctors Care is a treatise and invaluable manifesto available to the medical and health care professions. It is unlike any other medical text, and serves as a scientific, intellectual, and inspired guide to and for compassionate health care practices and the health care system—now and in the future.

Based upon his vast experience, study, and research, Dr. Dominic Vachon has created a comprehensive study with *How Doctors Care*, indeed, teaching and informing doctors, through both evidence and empirics, as well as philosophy, theory, and concrete methods, as to "how doctors can care." This overarching scientific and ethical-psychological, if not spiritual, training is foundational to humanizing health care for physicians, patients, and organizations alike. Such background findings have profound implications for preserving human dignity, authentic patient-physician relations, patient experience outcomes, as well as practitioner renewal for sustaining a balanced-living for self and others.

Dr. Vachon is a living exemplar of writing what he knows, what he loves, and what he researches, teaches, and practices. For over 20 years, Dr. Vachon has pursued his moral ideals, self-growth, and intellectual passion, tested and expanded through his diverse academic and clinical leadership positions. Toward that end, this work challenges the simplistic conventional mindset of caring, compassion, and empathy as "soft science," dismissive by "sentimentalizing" such phenomena. Instead, this dominant, limited view of caring and compassion is replaced with the hard science of neurophysiological and psychological cutting-edge research not previously compiled for medical students and health practitioners. Not only does this book provide the science of caring and compassion, it also offers a full development of what constitutes optimal, compassionate mental performance informed by philosophical-theoretical and ethical worldviews, as well as spiritual self-awakening.

The model of balanced compassionate caring is an all-encompassing approach that embraces clinician fears, reservations, and tendency to avoid emotions. It provides knowledge and understanding as to why clinicians detach, withdraw, turn away. Why they may be shutting down their heart, their sense of purpose, and why they often default by shutting down their own emotional, inner-subjective lifeworld as an unhealthy solution.

Indeed, Dr. Vachon specifically addresses how to maintain compassion and caring when faced with obstacles from within the unhealthy and dysfunctional US health care system.

For example, systematic chapters are developed to address healthy and dysfunctional types of helping, such as clinician relational attachments or detachments, and to provide concrete directions toward healthy biogenic relations for both.

The model of balanced compassionate caring addresses attitudes and responsibility for a balanced and compassionate medical mindset, offering a better understanding of the wisdom and importance of emotional caring—of compassionate relations for all clinicians. This model offers a solid background of intellectual and experiential issues underlying caring and compassion, such as emotional intelligence, emotional regulation, and mindfulness. It offers relief from unhealthy clinical responses, and addresses and invites the clinical resilience model as both a solution and a counterpoint to burnout and dispirited practitioners.

Dr. Vachon demonstrates his own compassion by providing knowledge and guidance for how clinicians can flourish and survive beyond detachment, and what is commonly referred to as compassion fatigue or burnout. Dr. Vachon refocuses education toward competence training and skills, which shift the mindset from "compassion—not important" to "compassion—as essential."

His background and experiences affirm teaching skills of balanced compassion; skills of clinician-awakening through mindful practices of self-care—for example, centering, intentionality, and self-reflective relational engagements; and generating compassion competencies and literacy informed by an ethical-philosophical experiential ground of scientific and empirical practices.

Dr. Vachon's balanced, compassionate training with *How Doctors Care* invites an awakening of self-awareness, self-reflection, and a spirituality of caring as the ultimate solution for authentic healing. This balanced model embraces Caritas and Love as a core clinician motive for self-growth—honoring, teaching, and practicing self-compassion as a gift to self and ultimately all others. The spirituality and sacred nature of caring is uncovered following an inner awakening of the clinician. Clinician heart-opening generates a spiritual awakening.

The model of balanced compassion, in *How Doctors Care*, elevates hard science evidence and the science of compassion and caring to the foreground instead of the conventional invisible background. As such, this comprehensive work offers a new scientific-spiritual self-awaking to rehumanize patient care—the end goal of all medical education and practice.

When clinicians awake and have the confidence, guidance, and grounding of the science and practice of compassion and caring, there is hope for a new model of healing for medicine and health care. This grounding opens space for organizational self-correcting, for repatterning dysfunctional organizational-economic practices.

As medical education and clinician practices embrace, teach, and incorporate *How Doctors Care: The Science of Compassionate and Balanced Caring in Medicine* into academic-clinical programs, transformation for balanced caring is a hoped-for paradigm for the future of health care—for clinicians, patients, and organizations alike.

Jean Watson

Cautionary Statement Regarding the Use of This Book

How Doctors Care: The Science of Compassionate and Balanced Caring in Medicine is written for the purpose of providing helping professionals with information and research regarding the science of compassionate caring in order to improve patient care and to provide tools for decreasing stress and burnout in the emotionally taxing work of health care. It provides information enabling health care professionals to maintain and cultivate compassionate caring in clinical work in the encounter with patients who are deeply suffering and with patients who are challenging to help. It also describes attitudes, behaviors, and a philosophy of caring that assist the clinician in maintaining balanced compassionate caring within health care delivery systems that vary in terms of corporate culture and organizational health or dysfunction. *While the model and research presented in this book provide a means to increase clinician resilience, improve caring clinician–patient interactions, and buffer clinician burnout, the book is not intended to be used as method to increase compassionate caring in clinicians without also addressing the organizational and systemic factors that can make compassionate caring more difficult to maintain.* A number of the main factors in improving compassionate caring and buffering burnout in clinicians are predicted by the organizational climate within which those clinicians treat patients. It is conceivable that an organization may use this research to demand increased compassionate caring attitudes and behaviors from clinicians without also assessing and improving the organizational and systemic factors that may be making it difficult for clinicians to provide this type of care. While this book may assist clinicians in increasing their resilience and improving their compassionate caring in stressful patient situations and within dysfunctional aspects of health care organizations and society's health care delivery system, it should not be expected that a clinician can fully achieve this when organizations, businesses, politics, and societal expectations negate this effort. *No clinician can be expected to achieve and maintain compassionate caring if an organization, society, or culture make it impossible to do so. Nor is the book intended to be used for deceptive marketing practices that seek to create a veneer of caring.*

Acknowledgments

There are many people who helped make this book possible. First among them is M. J. Murray Vachon, LCSW, my wife. When I came home about 24 years ago and disclosed that I had come to "hate my patients," it was she who lovingly challenged me, saying, "Well, honey, you've got a problem—because your patients need you to love them to get better." It was that remark and the constant support she gave me that sent me back to the drawing board of what it means to live a life of caring in the helping professions. She urged me to recover that compassion and discover what it would take to help me do that. In the years that followed, we spent many hours exploring what it means to live a life of compassion in our helping professions. She supported me in the seemingly endless hours of research and writing for this book. Without her support and advice, this book would never have happened.

I am deeply indebted to Jean Watson, PhD, RN, AHN-BC, FAAN, whose pioneering work in the science of human caring provided me with a whole new intellectual and emotional grounding that helped me recover compassion in my clinical work and ignited this journey to join the study of caring in health care. Jean invited and encouraged me throughout the last 24 years to pursue this science of caring in whatever way it led. She and the many nurses I came to know shared with me the nursing profession's decades of theoretical and empirical work on caring and welcomed me warmly as a colleague. Around that same time, Tom Stella, director of Soul Link, helped me discover the spiritual path I was on and throughout all these years helped me define the practices that would help me cultivate compassion, especially doing solitary retreats in the Colorado mountains every year. I am especially grateful to the Congregation of the Priests and Brothers of Holy Cross at the Holy Cross Novitiate who allowed me to use their hermitage for many retreats for all these years. It was in that hermitage that much of this book was written. Likewise, I am very grateful to the Sisters of the Holy Cross who first hired me in Holy Cross Health System and taught me the organizational factors for sustaining a caring ethic in the business of health care. Susan Tamborini-Czolgosz and Sr. Mary Ellen Vaughan, CSC, were major mentors for me in this work and always supported me throughout these years. Jean Vanier and the community of L'Arche also helped me discover the power of a spirituality of caring and taught me that people who have so-called disabilities are our most wonderful teachers.

Thanks to all the faculty, staff, and residents of the Family Medicine Residency Program at St. Joseph Regional Medical Center in Mishawaka, Indiana. It was with them that I learned more deeply how amazing physicians, nurses, and other clinicians are and also about the difficulties they encounter in their work. I am especially grateful to my boss for over a decade, Marty Wieschhaus who trusted and supported me in applying the new discipline of caring science to residency training. I am grateful to my colleagues of that time who taught me a great deal: Tom Felger, Ted Neumann, Jen Ludwig, Juli Fashner, Kevin Sherbun, Beth Temple, Michelle Cervin, Kevin Ericson, Julie Ortega-Schmitt, MaryAnn Rompola, Betty Swisher, Ed Sheridan, Dan Triezenberg, John McCleerey, Kevin Kaufhold, Elizabeth Weston, Madiha Saeed, and Omer Saeed; to Joseph Schwab, who helped me become part of the wonderful work of residency training; and also Nancy Hellyer, the CEO over many of those years, who taught me how to create and sustain a caring culture in our hospital. Through my work alongside all types of helping professionals, I learned how precious the truly compassionate clinician is and how much we need to support them in this challenging work.

I am very grateful for the tremendous support of the College of Science and the University of Notre Dame in this work in the Ruth M. Hillebrand Center for Compassionate Care in Medicine at Notre Dame. I am especially grateful to Fr. James K. Foster, CSC, Dean Greg Crawford, and Dean Mary Galvin, for their leadership, openness, and unwavering support for this cutting-edge work on applying the science of compassion to health care practice. Thanks to Ruth M. Hillebrand, PhD; the family of John G. Sheedy, MD; and the Reich family, who have endowed the center at Notre Dame. My colleagues here have generously helped me in writing this book. Among them are Kathleen Kolberg, and Bob White, who allowed me to test and improve my material with their students over 24 years. They have been amazing colleagues, listening to my work from its beginning and giving me excellent feedback to make it better. Dr. White particularly helped me refine the balanced compassionate caring model and Dr. Kolberg provided me with excellent information from her incredible knowledge of medical education and practice. I also thank the following colleagues who helped me in many conversations as this work was developing: Bill O'Hayer, Dominic Chaloner, Carry Teshka, Susan Gursky, Kay Ernsberger, Nancy Michael, Tom Merluzzi, Bill Tageson, and George Howard. I am grateful to my assistants over the years who helped with many facets of this book: Rose Carroll, Jaclyn Champagne-Terranova, Elizabeth Moriarty, and Megan Para. My fellow faculty in the Hillebrand Center provided me with insights that helped at several points in writing this book: Mark Sandock, Lynn Damitz, Brandon Zabukovic, Gary Fromm, and Marcus Engel. Thank you to Phyllis Coletta, who provided excellent advice for the book and taught me from her own health care experience. Robert Hamma was very kind to me in guiding me in the process of writing and publishing this book. I am grateful to the many students at the University of Notre Dame who worked with me on my research team and assisted me with various parts of the book: John Vernon, Rebecca Noble, Jen Lewis, Jean

Llenos, Ruby Hollinger, Delaney Weiland, Clare Scantling, Gabriela Moro, Mikhail Heber, Katelyn Walsh, Brooke Gensler, Meredith Balbach, Matthew Gervais, Ivan Leung, Jill Briody, Michael Russell, Matthew Harbrecht, John Mueller, R. J. Weir, and Tom O'Callaghan. Thanks to the Hillebrand Center interns Marisa Lenga and Nicole Wisniewski for their assistance with research and indexing for the book. I am especially very grateful to all the students who engaged so enthusiastically in the Hillebrand Center courses and for how together we discovered more about this awesome phenomenon of compassion in medicine.

The people who helped to train me will recognize the echoes of their teachings in this book. At Loyola University of Chicago, I am especially grateful to Steven Brown, who taught me a great deal about research and gave me expert guidance in my dissertation research on the relationship between empathy and burnout in nurses. His support in what was then an unusual research topic ended up being a defining crossroads that led to this book. Other faculty with whom I worked closely were Kevin Hartigan, Harold Bush, Marilyn Susman, and Donna Rankin. At Notre Dame, I especially thank Susan Steibe-Pasalich, Rita Donley, Patrick Utz, Willis Bartlett, Miguel Franco, Wendy Settle, Len Hickman, Sally Coleman, Joan Schwab, Clint Gabbard, Bob Krieg, Fr. John Dunne, CSC, Rev. Fritz Pfotenhauer, Rev. Richard McBrien, Catherine LaCugna, Vaughn McKim, Fr. Tom Smith, CSC, Fr. John Gerber, CSC, Fr. Bob Antonelli, CSC, Fr. Jerry Wilson CSC, Fr. Tom Tallaraida, CSC, Fr. Ken Molinaro CSC., Fr. Don Dilg CSC, Br. James Blaszak CSC, and Jungian analyst Tom Kapacinskas. May I honor you all by passing on your training to the next generation of healers.

Thank you to the Center for Compassion and Altruism Research and Education (CCARE) at Stanford University, which organized the first Science of Compassion research conference in Telluride in 2011 and then again in San Francisco in 2014. CCARE's vision and bringing together compassion researchers has brought the field to a whole new level. I am very appreciative for the support of Dr. Tom Nasca, CEO of the ACGME, for his enthusiastic interest and ongoing support of this project, and for his vision for what good medical education and practice should be. Thanks to Jane Uygur, for her support and for sharing her research that was very helpful in chapter 16. I am also very appreciative for the collaborative support from Stephen Trzeciak. He was also very generous in sharing his excellent review of the research on the effects of compassionate care and allowed me to use his superb summary table of that work in chapter 5. Thanks to David Addiss, whose parallel work on compassion in global health and his knowledge of this field was very helpful. For over 25 years, I have been fortunate to learn a great deal from Dr. Suhayl Nasr, a master clinician whose compassion and brilliance has helped many people. I am very grateful to Susan Othmer, and Siegfried Othmer, of the EEG Institute in Woodland Hills, California, who taught me about neurofeedback and healing the brain. They taught me not only about brain function and compassion from a neuroscientific perspective but also by the way their discoveries in neurofeedback resulted from the story of their exemplary compassion.

There are many people who had some part of helping with this book over the last 24 years: Mark Walsh, Rajalakshmy Sundarararajan, Rachel Rose, Leslie A. Eid, Carole Blankenbaker, Chantal

Cara, M. J. McGraw, David Acker, Tom Reid III, Jeff Huml, Fr. Marty Devereaux, Fr. Mike Woodcock, Fr. Ed McCarthy, Fr. Peter Dolan, Rajagopala Sarma, Steven Best, Rev. Joseph Czolgosz, Gill Hanlon, David Vanderveen, Jeff Nixa, Sean Allan, Paul Wright, Sr. Laureen Painter, Roger Klauer, Meredith Wierman, Andy Wilhelm, Anton Salud, Tom Petersen, Paul McCauley, Yuri Maracich, Farid Jalinous, Colleen Moore, John Hannan, Sean Kassen, Allison Maddox Slabaugh, Dan Bruetman, Nancy Gulanick, Tony Henke-Wheeler, Mark Fox, Kathy Eggleson, Judith Robert, Rick Vachon, Amy McCord, Phil Shoyer, and Nancy Shoyer. I also want to thank the amazing staff of the Hesburgh Library at Notre Dame, who were excellent in helping me obtain the many articles and books needed for this book, and also the Woodland Park Public Library in Colorado, which provided a great setting and access to research articles for much of this writing.

Thank you to Arjia Rinpoche, director of the Tibetan Mongolian Buddhist Cultural Center in Bloomington, Indiana, and to the Tibetan Buddhist monks of the Tashi Kyil Monastery in Dehra Dun, India. They have been very kind and wise teachers of compassion and meditation, guiding me at critical phases in the book. Thanks also to Jan-Li Lin who assisted me in gaining a deeper understanding of the Buddhist teachings on compassion.

I am deeply grateful to Cognella Academic Publishing for their willingness to publish this book. I especially thank Senior Project Editor Michelle Piehl, Production Editor Chelsey Schmidt, Senior Field Acquisitions Editor Angela Schultz, Senior Graphic Designer Jess Estrella, Associate Production Editor Berenice Quirino, Copyeditor Lauri Scherer, Copyeditor Theresa Winchell, and all the staff at Cognella who were extraordinary in every step of the publication process. Thank you for the great care you took in this book and all that you did to make it better.

All of this work was done out of the desire to respond to the suffering of patients and to give them the best quality care possible. I thank all my clients and patients for the privilege of helping them. They taught me so much about what true compassion means and how it heals. They also taught me from all their experiences, both good and bad, as they navigated the health care system. I hope I have honored them and their experiences by taking what they have taught me in order to improve health care for future patients. They need us to love them as we accompany them in their illnesses and suffering.

Most importantly, I want to thank my family, from whom I first learned compassion. To my parents, Antoinette and Ovide Vachon, to my sister, Madeline, and our brother, Ovide Jr. Our accompanying Ovide Jr. through his four years battling cancer taught me more about love and compassion than anything else. Thank you to M. J., my wife, and our children, Nicholas and Abby, for the tremendous love and support that we share. Thank you for believing in and supporting this work over these years and for putting up with my zeal. Thank you to the Murray clan for your amazing and joyful support throughout the years, always asking me at every family gathering how the book was coming along. Now, we have to find something else to talk about. Thank you to my son's wife, Madhura, and to the Sundararjan and Sarma families for also being so kind and supportive. Finally, I dedicate this book to my brother, Ovide, who died from cancer in 1983. I thank him for being my greatest teacher in this journey of compassion.

"If the science of compassion is not integrated into your practice, you are practicing outdated medicine."

Chapter Sections:

The Dawning of the Compassion-Centric Paradigm of Health Care

Questions to consider before reading this chapter:

1. What is the state of concepts such as "caring" and "compassion" in clinical practice today?
2. What do you think are the problems in how clinicians practice medicine currently?

INTRODUCTION

Despite being initially motivated by compassionate idealism and professing a desire to help others out of compassionate idealism in applications to medical schools and residency programs, empathy declines by the time medical students see their first patients and continues to decline afterward. Physicians in practice often normalize their less-than-empathic behavior as time goes on in their practices. They even discourage their children from becoming physicians. The same often happens in other health professions. Yet we should not be surprised by this. We have set this up to be just as it is. When we trained our young, idealistic aspirants to the health professions, we gave them a sentimentalized theory of compassion and caring that could not sustain the reality of what actually happens in health care. We gave them a simplistic understanding of how to interpret their patients' emotions, much less be able to understand and deal with their own feelings. So as soon as they encountered ongoing suffering in their patients, those simplistic notions of how to manage emotions were inadequate for helping them know what to do with their patients'—much less their own—inner struggles. We made them think that it was going to be possible to maintain the type of caring they felt when they first entered training. As a result, they were not prepared to deal with a society that has very demanding and sometimes irrational expectations and a dysfunctional medical delivery system that would make it very difficult to

1

do compassionate care very well. Nor did we prepare them for how the amount of money involved would complicate the entire enterprise. It was thought that having compassion was the cause of the problem, but we now know that what we thought was the problem is actually the solution to the current crisis in health care.

Loss of compassionate idealism as a survival method

In light of all this, it is no wonder that clinicians start using emotional detachment as a survival skill and become more abrupt with their patients. When you are confronted by working with people who feel very vulnerable in their encounter with their own mortality all day long and you were not trained to manage and deal with that, of course you are going to protect yourself by disengaging from and depersonalizing the very people to whom you promised to devote your life. Go back and read your personal statement in your application to medical or nursing school, and you may see a different person now. In my own experience training physician residents, I had third-year residents who would say to me, "I am not the caring, idealistic doctor I was in my first year. I wish I was. I liked that person. But now after my patients ignore my pleas to take care of themselves, lie to me to get narcotics and benzodiazepines, or get angry at me for things that are not my fault, I don't care as much anymore. I wish I could get out of this now, but it is too late and I am too much in debt to change now." Young doctors feel discouraged and even guilty for getting to that cynical point, compounding the burden they already feel. Nevertheless, we can use that admission of compassionate bankruptcy as their new starting point in reclaiming their compassionate care in medicine and so begin the journey to restoring the compassion and altruism that first drew them to their helping profession.

Using the science of compassion is the key to preventing burnout and doing great patient care

This book is a response to the deficits in training for health care professions and the sentimentalized notions of compassionate care that are not helpful to practicing physicians as they deal with the emotional toll of their work. It will provide clinicians with a rigorous and scientific understanding of compassionate care in medicine that will enable them to deal much more effectively with what they will face in practice, and it will provide the hidden key to preventing burnout and actually improving physician well-being. They will gain an understanding of how their interpersonal skills and the attitudes they hold about their patients have the potential to contaminate or augment the very medicine they are about to deliver. Gone are the days when compassion and caring were considered optional, not essential to good medical practice. Now we know they are essential. Refusing to understand the tremendous advances that have been made in the science of compassionate care in medicine will become equivalent to malpractice in the years to come.

Technically very good medicine is contaminated by uncompassionate delivery

The way the medicine is delivered affects the way the medicine works. If you have the most advanced and expensive IV antibiotic and you deliver it with a contaminated needle, it is likely you have ruined the good that this antibiotic might do. It is the same with how you do your helping work for your patients or clients. The way you treat your patient or client can augment or interfere with the help you have given. Suppose you had the opportunity to see the technically best surgeon you could see but then overheard the surgeon say, "You know, what really matters is the procedure itself, not this washing hands stuff." Would you still want that doctor to perform the surgery? Probably not. You might pick a different surgeon. If that surgeon goes on to explain, "Washing your hands before a surgery is not as important as the procedure itself. What matters is whether you have the manual dexterity and training, not so much whether you fiddled around with something so easy as washing your hands and creating a sterile field for the surgery." Of course, the absurdity of this statement is clear: A simple thing like hand washing for a surgeon is essential for the good work of that surgeon to be brought to a positive outcome. Despite the high level of surgical skill he or she possesses, you would never get a surgery from a surgeon or a hospital that did not practice appropriate aseptic technique. Everyone knows that you might get a technically superb surgery but then die from the infection afterward. Entertaining this kind of thinking is, in fact, ludicrous. No good surgeon, unless it is an exceptional emergency situation, would ever compromise on preoperative practices that could prevent infection. The sterile field is essential to good surgical practice. With the absence of a sterile field, bacteria that the surgery team and their instruments might carry can ruin the technically well-executed surgery. Similarly, a lack of compassionate care will destroy possible benefits of technically well-delivered medicine. It is possible to look back in history and think how unfortunate it was that surgeons

in the Civil War did not know that washing their hands and sterilizing their instruments could have saved so many more lives. So it will be one day when people look back at medicine in the early twenty-first century and marvel at how we thought that the manner in which health care professionals related to patients and the clinician's compassionate mental state were not that important.

Poor relational skills guarantee poor patient outcomes

A physician who does not have good patient relational skills—or "bedside manner," as is commonly said—is like a surgeon who does not wash his or her hands, because the way a doctor relates to a patient can contaminate the medicine that is being delivered to a patient. It is commonly thought that giving the correct diagnosis, the right treatment answer, or the right medical procedure is what is most essential in medical practice, and whether the doctor is crusty, abrupt, arrogant, or not a good listener is irrelevant. If you make patients feel ashamed about their illness, they might not follow through on your brilliant treatment plan. If you convey a lack of confidence in a procedure or drug, that can contaminate the treatment. For example, if you say, "I'm not really sure this drug is going to work. Why don't you give it a try?," many people will not be very motivated to take that drug. How you are with a patient always affects the medical treatment you are providing. You might have the best injectable drug that exists for a particular disease, but if you deliver it with a contaminated syringe or IV, it is likely you will lose all the treatment benefits of that drug. The best-case scenario is that the patient will get some new infection that you have to treat, and the worst outcome is that the disease will be cured but the patient will be killed. You might be a really smart doctor, but if you do not pay attention to *how* you deliver your medical knowledge, you can expect similarly poor results.

Practicing without compassion is practicing outdated medical science

If you think that care and compassion are nice but optional parts of how you help people, you need to know that you are using outdated science. In the past it might have been considered acceptable medicine to be very smart but have lousy compassionate care skills. The thought was that as long as the doctor was smart, we could accept his or her lack of communication ability. But this should now be seen the same way as a doctor using leeches, bloodletting, and the four humors to help patients. At one time this was considered the state of the field, the best medicine available. Now it is considered outdated science. When a healer does not have a compassionate caring attitude and does not express that care concretely to a patient when helping that person, he or she is practicing outdated medicine. This is true not only for medicine but all the helping professions. There is now very clear scientific evidence not only that true caring for the people you serve improves the patient's satisfaction with your care and concrete medical outcomes but also that practicing with a compassionate caring mindset actually protects the clinician from burnout.

Simplistic theories of emotion are taught to clinicians

There have been major advances in our understanding of emotions and emotional regulation, and in neuroscience. Yet the insights from these areas have not yet been incorporated into medical training. We are proud of the evidence-based training of our physicians, nurses, and allied health professionals. They have the latest training in the cutting edges of biology, biochemistry, pharmaceuticals, surgical techniques, and computer technology. Yet either we do not teach the role of emotions in medicine or we teach a primitive, outdated theory of emotions in medicine: erroneous ideas such as thinking that emotional detachment is possible and considered good self-care, that emotions interfere with the practice of medicine, that emotional work always drains the clinician, that emotions always cloud judgment, and that emotions contribute to inefficiency. Without exception, every one of these notions popular in the medical hallways is incorrectly based on a distorted view of science or on an uninformed understanding of emotion in the practice of medicine.

Clinicians set up to fail by lack of training for the emotional intensity and complexity

Put anyone in a race car and have them drive 200 miles an hour and disaster is fairly likely. Race car drivers are trained to handle that high speed. You would never just assume that because a person can drive, he or she can handle driving a race car. Someone might say, "It's just driving; you know how to drive. Right? It's just faster. It's that simple." Similarly, we just expect health professionals to know how to handle intense suffering in their patients or in themselves. "You're a human, and you know about your emotions. Right? Health care just has more emotions. Now just go and see your patients." The reality is that we have set up most of our health care professionals to fail in this work because we have not given them all the training they need to do their jobs well and to handle the increased emotional intensity and complexity of their careers. We justify depersonalized, emotionally distant care because that is what clinicians are forced to do when they do not know what else can be done.

Does caring in a medical application really matter?

How helpers view the role of feelings in caring for their patients and clients is absolutely critical. However, we have a fundamentally flawed notion of the importance of emotions in helping others. If you read applications to nursing school, medical school, social work, psychology, or most any other helping profession, you will almost always read statements like, "I want to help people," "I want to give to others what I have been given," "I want to relieve suffering and cure diseases." Words like *caring*, *compassion*, *making a difference*, and *helping others* are so commonplace that the personal statement has sometimes become a meaningless part of the application. However, if someone wrote in a personal statement, "I don't connect well with people and, frankly, I don't like people very much; but I have the best MCAT score in the country, and I am very good at fixing things," we might have reservations about accepting them into our medical school. We expect to hear the altruistic words from the applicants to the helping professions. But they do not really mean anything except when they are absent from how applicants describe their motivations to help others in medicine.

Caring intentions are not enough

Where we are failing is that we assume that the ability to care for others is a given and not a skill that must be developed like any other ability. For example, we might have a very bright chemistry student who is applying to a graduate program to research and develop pharmaceuticals. The student has the raw ability but does not yet have the particular training and experience to develop and test new drugs. After training, and then gaining experience with development and clinical trials, that student becomes a seasoned professional in the pharmaceutical field. With caring, however, we often assume that a caring intention in an applicant is sufficient for a whole career of helping others without being further developed and refined. We assume that caring is the easy part and further training is not needed. We trivialize it at the same time as we say it is absolutely central to the helping professions. But when you start working with suffering people, difficult people, or ignorant people, you find out that you need to become very sophisticated in how to connect with people who might be afraid of you or resistant to your helping intent. You also find that working with certain people makes you not want to care about them very much anymore. As more than one physician resident has told me after several years of treating patients, "I used to be an idealistic, caring physician; but I don't feel like that anymore." We expect a learning curve when it comes to any skill, such as making furniture or doing open heart surgery. Learning how to deal with people is no different, so why is it a surprise that young helping professionals struggle with this skill and no longer feel very caring in their work? Unfortunately, they are set up for failure because we never explained to them that not only is caring an attitude but it is also a skill that has to be developed and seasoned. We never trained them how to take that desire, which led them into this helping profession in the first place, and then deepen that commitment when they start working with great suffering, injustice, and stupidity. We have treated our own caring attitudes and behaviors as easy things to have and express even though the grueling work of helping others in the world requires a much more sophisticated and seasoned foundation.

Compare similar cases with and without caring methods

Additional examples can help illustrate the point. Consider two helping professionals who are working with the same type of client or patient and yet get very different results. One nurse or physical therapist can get a patient to do all sorts of therapeutic things; another nurse or physical therapist of the same gender, age, ethnic background, and education gets nowhere with the patient. One doctor does a history and physical with a patient who does not disclose very much and as a result makes an incorrect diagnosis, or the lack of some information interferes with treatment; another doctor gets the patient to disclose crucial bits of information that lead to a more accurate diagnosis and more effective treatment. One therapist works with an adolescent having an angry outburst and does not make it any better, maybe even unintentionally escalating it. Another therapist goes into the same situation and deescalates the situation almost magically. Only it is not magic in this example or the preceding ones, because that ability was developed by the practitioner and honed as a particular skill.

It's like we are not teaching clinicians one physiological system

In many ways, we set up our students in medical training for failure and disillusionment as they work with real patients in the real world. This is especially true with medical school. Imagine if we said this to our medical students as they enter medical school: "We don't have enough time to teach you every physiological system, so we have to leave one out and you'll have to do independent study on it on your own time. How about the cardiovascular system? No, a patient would die without that. How about the muscular or skeletal systems? No, that's so important for patients' abilities to function. How about the endocrine system—who really ever uses that? Well, we have an epidemic of diabetes, and thyroid problems can have such pervasive effects. Okay, let's leave out human nature. You're a human, your patient is a human. You can figure most anything out by just figuring out what you would want as a human and assume that for your patient. Because it is so obvious, let's leave that out of medical school." We do not train our future clinicians in the science of human nature. Indeed, this is what we have done. We teach every aspect of the human being in mind-numbing detail, from the intricate memorizing during anatomy and physiology courses to how to interpret the subtle wave irregularities of an ECG. Yet we do not discuss in any real depth what really motivates or discourages patients to take care of themselves and follow through on good medical advice. Studying human nature is not the same as studying psychiatry or psychopathology. This more comprehensive understanding of humans is not what is done in a psych rotation. It is, rather, about the complexities of normal human nature as individuals encounter illness in their own lives.

Other helping professions have similar deficits in training as does medicine

Nearly every helping profession commits the same omission in training. Nursing, by its roots, has been very holistic in training, but with the perceived demands of being technologically proficient, even nursing programs have been deemphasizing their relational skills training and caring theories in their curricula. Pastoral ministers can graduate filled with all kinds of lofty theology, but they may struggle their first years after seminary catching up on what they should have learned about spiritually helping people. Even mental health therapists, who should be able to navigate the thorny complexities of their client situations best of all, are often left feeling powerless, with an armful of empirically supported therapies as they enter professional practice but not knowing how to apply these therapies practically in the complexity of real life.

We should learn from veterinarians

Instead, what happens is that many of these new helping professionals who put words like *caring*, *compassion*, and *helping people* in their applications become very frustrated and eventually discouraged by how difficult it really is to help people. But consider this. Neurologists do not get frustrated by how complex the brain is when they enter the practice of helping patients who have brain pathologies. They come to accept and even be engaged by the complexity of the human brain, and they expect that to be a lifelong truth of their careers. Yet we set up our medical students and other helping professional trainees to think that treating humans medically is a logical, straightforward process, if only it had not been for that pesky human nature. "If only people did not act like people, we could really heal them!" Every helper in the human helping professions can learn a lot about this process from good veterinarians. When a horse kicks or a dog bites as the vet is doing a digital rectal exam, the vet does not take that personally.

Hence, the title of veterinarian Jeff Wells's book, *All My Patients Kick and Bite* (2011). He says, for example, that when someone tells you their pet has "never tried to bite anybody in his whole life," then, "in real-life veterinary practice, the phrase translates to 'This dog is going to try to bite me'" (p. 227). Of course, an animal might get irritated with this kind of procedure. You plan for it. You prepare the animal as best you can, and you protect yourself in case the animal gets angry. Animals just do that. You learn tricks of the trade for how to maximize your ability to work with an animal who might react to you negatively even though you are trying to help it.

"These horses are stupid!"

At a resident physician retreat we had a number of years ago, a horse trainer and I came up with an exercise that we thought would help the residents reflect on their attitudes toward their patients. We had the residents work in teams of two going into the pen with five or so horses. All the residents had to do was approach a horse, put the rope halter on its head, and lead it back. These were domesticated horses used for giving children rides at summer camp. The exercise went terribly as horses became spooked and fled the young physicians. Teen volunteers who took care of the horses giggled on the fence rails as they watched eminently well-trained doctors become totally flabbergasted by these obstinate animals. We heard remarks like, "Something is wrong with these horses." "I did everything right and that horse still did not let me put the halter on." "These horses are stupid!" The residents became so frustrated that they were not able to hear the incredible lesson they had just experienced. These comments were exactly the words they used to describe their patients when they do not do what they want them to do medically. As facilitators of the retreat exercise, we did not expect there to be such a clear parallel with patient care, and we failed to help the residents process the experience well enough to make the insight that how they approached the horse could make all the difference. To add insult to injury, one of the teen girls jumped off the fence rail, rope in hand, and in just a few moments had haltered one of the spooked horses. As any person who works with horses can tell you, horses can sense the emotions and intentions of the humans. They can sense fear, anxiety, lack of confidence, passivity, or ill will in the person. To work with a horse, a person has to have the right balance of assertive confidence with an intention of goodwill to get the best from the horse. The point is that *how* they approached the horse made all the difference in the horse's behavior.

Remember that humans are animals, too

If you have never experienced this with a horse, then watch how a dog picks up on a person who is afraid of it. If you work with animals, you know this, and you work with it. It is just the way things are, whether we like it or not. It is easy to forget that humans are basically sophisticated cortex over animal brain. Time and time again, helping professionals are exasperated by how stupid people can be. Of course, they can be. How come you did not know that? What made you think they would not be?

Who told you that there would ever be perfect conditions to practice medicine?

To get at this question, I offer a story about learning how to do skeet shooting with a 12-gauge shotgun under the capable direction of one of my cousins several years ago. Even though we grew up together working in orange groves in Florida, I missed a number of farm boy lessons. There was a certain delight in the air that the PhD boy was looking fairly stupid. At one point, as my cousin was coaching me, I did not shoot at the flying target because the sun was in my eyes. "Why didn't you shoot?" he asked. I defended myself by saying, "Well, the sun was in my eyes." My coaching cousin heckled me and simply said, "So, what's the problem?" Feeling more stupid, I realized the wisdom of what he said. In reality, there are never perfect conditions to skeet shoot. There will always be sun, wind, or teasing companions. You just expect to encounter these things when you go skeet shooting. It is no different with anything else. Pilots know and accept that they need to be prepared for unexpected wind shifts. There is always a headwind, a tailwind, or a crosswind to manage. There is rarely a perfect day to fly. Our training of helping professionals often lacks this wisdom of accepting unforeseen, challenging circumstances as the norm.

If you do not like problems, maybe medicine is not for you

Patients almost always have something else going on that complicates a seemingly straightforward biomedical problem. There can be situational factors, such as the fact that the clinician has a solution for the patient's problem, but the patient does not have the resources to get the recommended treatment or medicine. Patients have complicating factors like jobs (or no jobs); other people they have to care for, making it hard for them to take care of themselves; being in abusive relationships; or other circumstances that make it hard to handle some medical issue. Then there are the "difficult patients," as we like to call them. What is "difficult" for a particular clinician varies a lot, based on an individual's personality or gaps in training. Some patients get very prickly and touchy when we challenge them about their weight, their smoking, or other negative health behaviors. Addicts get angry when confronted about their drinking or their drug of choice. Very intelligent people can defend their poor health choices behind a barrage of rationalizations. People of influence through money, power, or fame can leverage this to get their way with us. Sometimes people who get sick are not beyond putting some pressure on friends who are clinicians. Patients manipulate and even blackmail health care professionals to avoid a medical situation or to get something they want. There are also things about a clinician that can interfere with treating someone. Some people are more likable than others. It is easy to get tired or beleaguered by something that makes a certain situation more of a hassle. One may like (or dislike) some problems more than others. There is more money to be made (or less money) with some types of problems versus others. Our list of whines is long and noble in clinical care. "So, what's the problem?" If we want the purity of a straightforward problem, the clinical world is really the last place we should be. But if it is the place we want to be, and healing people is really what we want to do, what can we do to make this more possible and us more fulfilled to be doing it?

Paradigm Shift from Techno-Centric to Compassion-Centric Health care: "The Earth Is Not the Center of the Solar System."

"*Moreover, since the sun remains stationary, whatever appears as a motion of the sun is really due rather to the motion of the earth.*"

—Nicolaus Copernicus of Torun (*Six Books on the Revolutions of the Heavenly Spheres*, 1543)

What is the center of your "solar system" of clinical practice?

We are in the midst of a major paradigm shift in the practice of the helping professions, very similar to the shift that happened when it was thought the Earth was the center of the solar system and then the sun was proved to be at the center of the solar system. Likewise, we have been practicing medicine with the notion that compassionate care is an important part of medicine but not the center of its practice. With this orientation, it is not unusual for a clinician to say something like, "I care about my patients and I try to be caring, but a lot of times I just have to get the job done, and I can't do the caring thing." Caring is seen as a helpful and desirable accessory to health care practice, like wearing jewelry or special shoes with an outfit. Everyone likes the idea of compassion and caring in medicine. Organizations and individuals are quick to market themselves in this way or to apologize sadly for how things are now and reminisce about the good old days when it was possible to practice in a way that was more caring. We hear things like, "Well, I'm not a very caring doctor, but I am a very competent doctor; people would rather have a smart doctor than a caring doctor." A distinction is made and generally accepted between the "caring" doctor and the "competent" doctor, yet this is fundamentally absurd when it is examined more deeply, as will be seen in this book. Technology, science, and sometimes the financial "bottom line" are the centers of the solar system of our health care practice.

Trick question: "Which of the planets is analogous to compassion in clinical practice?"

To expand the analogy, for many, compassionate caring can be viewed as a desirable but nonessential planet circling around the central positions of "hard science" and "business necessity." For many, compassionate caring is an important planet and may rank as a Mercury or Venus around the biotechnical sun; for others, compassionate caring is not unlike Pluto, eliciting the question: Is it really the status of a full-fledged planet or not? Is compassionate caring really integral to the solar system of health care? Pick any planet as a way to rank the importance of compassionate caring. Regardless of what one chooses as the "compassion" planet, it will yield the same results: compassionate caring is not the center of the health care solar system. Just as some can imagine a solar system without Pluto, many imagine a health care system in which compassionate caring is like Pluto. But we cannot imagine a solar system without a sun, a star. This is exactly our situation. A solar system is inconceivable without a sun. This is the point: Compassionate caring is actually "the sun," yet it has been viewed in health care work as if it were merely an orbiting planet.

The paradigm shift from biomedical/technical to compassion-centric medicine is already happening

With the tremendous gains of biomedical science in the advancement of medical treatment, we have assumed the biomedical/technological is our center around which everything else must by necessity revolve, to the point that we cannot imagine anything else being the center. In our clinics or surgeries, it is as if the high altar is the drug, the surgical technique, the procedure, or even the computer; the doctors, nurses, and other clinicians are the servants of this centerpiece. It is still hard to see how

our compassionate caring is fully integrated with the biomedical and technological aspects of medicine. Yet the paradigm shift from the biomedical/technical to the compassion-centric is already underway, and the seeds of this shift were planted years ago. Shimon Glick proposed this in 1993, saying, "The foundation on which medicine must be based is compassion, that is where it all starts, and without this basis one cannot be a true physician" (p. 90) and that the compassion paradigm integrates both the humanism and the science in medicine. This paradigm shift can be detected in four major developments: (a) the move from the biomedical to the biopsychosocial model of medicine, (b) the rise of medical humanities programs, (c) efforts to be more patient-centered and less dehumanizing in the delivery of health care, and (d) the development of the science of compassionate caring.

The move from the biomedical to the biopsychosocial model of medicine

The challenging but definite transition from biomedical to biopsychosocial medicine

The tension and seeming opposition between the biomedical/technical and compassionate caring aspects have been noted since the time when there were major scientific discoveries that impacted the success of medicine to cure various ailments. There have been major efforts to integrate these two aspects for decades now. In 1977 George Engel argued for the transition from the narrower biomedical model of medicine to the more integrated and holistic biopsychosocial model now espoused as the ideal way to practice medicine. Yet while everyone knows that the biopsychosocial model is what we should practice, the biomedical model still dominates in clinical practice. It is still not clear how to practice in this fashion consistently and efficiently across all health professions. It is difficult not only to practice but to train well. Medical students are already overwhelmed with what they have to learn on the biomedical side of medicine. It is still not generally clear how to integrate the behavioral medicine, the communication skills, and what exactly it means to be compassionate and caring in medicine. But if we start with compassionate caring as the beginning point and the center of what we do, and if we use what is already known about compassionate caring scientifically, then the training challenges and actual clinical practice problems will improve. Clinicians have a difficult time articulating how the biomedical/technical and compassionate caring/psychosocial aspects of medicine are inseparable and fully integrated. This is the problem we address and resolve in this book.

The biopsychosocial model is more scientific

In 1976 George Engel, who articulated the bio-psychosocial model, wrote an article he titled "Too Little Science: The Paradox of Modern Medicine's Crisis." In it he argued that medicine has focused much scientific energy on the biomedical and technical parts of medicine but has not done the same regarding the psycho-social aspects of illness and in the treatment of patients. He related that this was far from being a new proposal; Dr. Francis W. Peabody, director of the Harvard Medical Service in the 1920s, wrote about it in the *Journal of the American Medical Association*:

> *Disease in [a person] is never exactly the same as disease in an experimental animal, for in [humans] the disease at once affects and is affected by what we call the emotional life. Thus, the physician who attempts to take care of a patient while he [or she] neglects*

> *this factor is as unscientific as the investigator who neglects to control all the conditions that may affect his [or her] experiment. (Peabody, 1927, p. 882; bracketed text added for nonsexist language)*

For a variety of reasons, as we will discuss in detail later in this book, science was not extended into this realm or even thought possible to achieve. Ignoring or minimizing the importance of those psychosocial factors sabotages the assessment and diagnosis process as well as the treatment process in patient care. Engel and others after him have argued for more science; and indeed, much science has developed in the way Engel implored in the following words in 1976:

> *What will render the human dimensions of patient care correspondingly effective will only be the rational understanding that comes from application of the scientific method to human problems. For it is through science that we aggregate the facts that yield the generalizations and principles from which we can make reliable predictions and institute rational actions. Through science we learn how to investigate and expand our knowledge of the unknown. Through science we evaluate outcome and correct errors. Through the scientific understanding of human behavior can our natural attributes of compassion, intuition, and empathy be rendered accessible to the many whose personality characteristics and cultural backgrounds differ from our own range of personal experience? Through scientific inquiry can we learn how to individualize our behavior to meet the needs of each patient? How else can one decide with which patient to be firm and with which to be permissive? Which patient has a need to feel in control and which is content to be passive? Which patient needs to be comforted and which one needs to be educated? Which patient needs permission to stay in bed and which one needs encouragement to get up? (p. 130)*

The biomedical approach to medicine is failing our patients

There has been tremendous progress in the advancement of the biopsychosocial model. While the biomedical/technical is still dominant in actual practice and in training, major changes are underway to treat patients in a more effective, holistic way. These changes have intensified with the research data that connects psychosocial and other factors to illness and disease. McGinnis and Foege (1993) and Schroeder (2007) found that unhealthy behavioral choices account for 40% of early deaths and make up the most significant determinant of health in the United States. Mokdad, Marks, Stroup, and Gerberding (2004, 2005) reported that the leading causes of death have been tobacco (18.1%), poor diet and physical inactivity (15.2%), and alcohol consumption (3.5%). Those who were trained solely with a biomedical/technical model find themselves not as helpful in medical interventions now. They like the biomedical problems better, which makes sense because when we do not know how to deal with a nonbiomedical problem, we try to avoid that type of problem. As Suls, Krantz, and Williams (2013) wrote, "Reluctance on the part of mainstream medicine to adopt the biopsychosocial model is understandable because molecular biology is its hub science" (p. 597). But it would be a grave mistake to say now that those problems are beyond medicine's purview simply because they are beyond the biochemical model. As clinicians, we seek to serve our patients, not our tools. Imagine a car mechanic who says he or she prefers not to work with all the new electrical and computer systems that have come to dominate modern cars. That mechanic will not be doing mainstream car repair any longer. Furthermore,

there is an ethical mandate for physicians to embrace fully the biopsychosocial model:

> The physician's skills should be judged on their ability to produce greater health or to relieve the patient's sufferings—whether they include creating an adequate emotional tone, gathering an accurate history, or distinguishing between what the patient needs and what the patient says he or she wants. In that regard, a clinical skill includes the ethical mandate not only to find out what concerns the patient, but to bring the physician's agenda to the table and influence the patient's behavior. ... To abandon this obligation, in our view, is breaking an implicit social contract between physicians and society. (Borrell-Carrio, Suchman, & Epstein, 2004, p. 580)

The good twenty-first-century clinician can no longer practice in a narrow manner

As we have begun the twenty-first century, major changes have already taken place in health care training in terms of clinicians being more completely trained in the biopsychosocial model of medicine. Schwartztein, Rosenfeld, Hilborn, Oyewole, and Mitchell (2013) argue that

> in the 21st century, physicians have to be "Renaissance" people with expertise in areas as different as psychology, biology, statistics, sociology, economics, culture, and communication skills. With the explosion of medical knowledge and the technologies that make information easily available, physicians must be able to find and evaluate information and to think critically when applying that information to solve their patients' problems. (p. 564)

Not only is it necessary to know areas outside biology and biochemistry, clinicians must also be able to cross interdisciplinary boundaries and integrate that information in order to be more effective within their specialties. Even within a specialty, the clinician has to be able to analyze a medical problem holistically and respond in a way that promotes that solution.

Changes in the MCAT and ACGME Competencies

Two major changes that have arisen as a result have already occurred in physician training. First, the Association of American Medical Colleges (Kirch, 2012) decided in 2012 to revise the Medical College Admission Test (MCAT) beginning in 2015 to include a new test section on psychological, social, and biological foundations of behavior, as well as a new section on critical analysis and reasoning skills. Second, the Accreditation Council for Graduate Medical Education (ACGME, 2017) has mandated six general competencies that must be integrated and concretely assessed in residency training for all physician specialties: Patient Care and Procedural Skills, Medical Knowledge, Practice-Based Learning and Improvement, Interpersonal and Communication Skills, Professionalism, and System-Based Practice. Each of the competencies either directly refers to or implies the move in medicine to emphasize the biopsychosocial and compassionate aspects of medicine in residency training. For the competency of Patient Care and Procedural Skills, residents "must be able to provide patient care that is compassionate, appropriate, and effective for the treatment of health problems and the promotion of health" (ACGME, 2017, p. 9). Under Medical Knowledge, the ACGME (2017) states, "Residents must demonstrate knowledge of established and evolving biomedical, clinical, epidemiological and social-behavioral sciences, as well as the application of this knowledge to patient care" (p. 10). For Practice-Based Learning and Improvement, residents "must demonstrate the ability to investigate and evaluate their care of patients, to appraise and assimilate scientific evidence, and to continuously improve patient care based on constant self-evaluation and life-long learning" (ACGME, 2017, p. 10). With Interpersonal and Communication Skills, "Residents must demonstrate interpersonal and communication skills that result in the effective exchange of information and collaboration with patients, their families, and health professionals" (ACGME, 2017, p. 11). The Professionalism competency requires "a commitment to carrying out professional responsibilities and an adherence to ethical principles" (ACGME, 2017, p. 11). It includes specific mention of the ability to be sensitive and responsive to all facets of diversity in the patient population. Finally, the System-Based Practice competency requires residents "to demonstrate an awareness of and responsiveness to the larger context and system of health care, as well as the ability to call effectively on other resources in the system to provide optimal health care" (ACGME, 2017, p. 12). Medical training is certainly in the process of fleshing out the details of how to train and assess these competencies, but the commitment has been made to the biopsychosocial model in training and actual practice. Parallel developments have been occurring across all the helping professions. The transition from the biomedical model to the biopsychosocial model is a clear indicator of how responding to the actual needs of the patient are guiding the way care is done. In this way it can be considered within the compassion-centric paradigm in medicine because our more holistic response to human suffering can be said to guide the sciences we are utilizing in this healing work.

The rise of medical humanities programs

The second indicator of the paradigm shift for the biotechnical paradigm to the compassion-centric is the concerted effort in the rise of the medical humanities that has been taking place to address the dehumanizing aspects of health care delivery and also the harsh aspects of medical training. In terms of the impact of studying the humanities in medical education, Schwartz et al. (2009) have defined this "broadly as nonmedical subjects that may enhance the training of physicians including literature, visual arts, performing arts, ethics, philosophy, anthropology, history, and sociology" (p. 373). Possible benefits have been thought to be diversifying the medical profession with people of different backgrounds and talents, fostering more open-minded physicians who might relate to their patients better, helping physicians be more comfortable with patients of all types of backgrounds, improving communication skills, improving the ability to listen and empathize with patients, improving diagnostic observational skills, enriching the student's life, providing opportunities for self-reflection in medical training, and promoting the moral and personal development of the student (Schwartz et al., 2009). Despite the challenge of empirical study in this area, the impact of humanities education on medical practice has been found to help cultivate or maintain empathy during medical training, improve professionalism, increase cultural competence and ability to serve diverse populations, and improve self-care and well-being by means of the practice of self-reflection (Schwartz et al., 2009). Extending the general humanities in medical education further and making them more specifically applied to medical practice, medical humanities programs have been developed in the past 40 years in both medical schools and preprofessional programs. While there is no standard definition of medical humanities programs, Shapiro, Coulehan, Wear, and Montello (2009) found that they all share three features. First, one or more of the humanities disciplines is used to explore the nature of illness, the therapeutic relationship, and other aspects of medical practice. Second, the goals of these programs are to increase self-awareness in clinicians and encourage more human practice by helping them understand and reflect on their profession through the humanities. Third, these programs tend to be interdisciplinary and collaborative among all types of scholars, clinicians, and patients. While these programs have often been relegated to the periphery of medical training and been challenged because it is difficult to assess the impact of this approach, many people outside medical humanities programs agree that the goals of training professionalism and more humane practice are high priorities (Campo, 2005; Shapiro et al., 2009). The tremendous scholarship and investment in these programs are another indication of the paradigm shift to compassion-centric medicine that is emerging.

Efforts to be more patient-centered and less dehumanizing in the delivery of health care

The third indication that the paradigm has been shifting is the emergence of health care delivery models that are less dehumanizing and more focused on the patient's needs and experiences. Major examples include the patient-centered model, the relationship-based caring model, the relationship-centered caring model, and Planetree. Many health care organizations seek Magnet Recognition as a sign of high-quality nursing in that organization. As part of that credentialing process, the organization must have adopted and implemented a professional practice model of care that involves selecting a theory of care that guides the total system of providing care to patients. (Tinkham, 2013). A professional practice model of care may also be called a care delivery model, a nursing model, or a model of governance. As Hoffart and Woods (1996) have described it, a professional practice model includes five elements: (a) specified professional values that underlie nursing practice and training; (b) a description of how professional relationships should proceed; (c) the structure and process for how patient care is delivered by the staff; (d) the management approach in terms of the structure and process of how decisions are made and operations are conducted; and (e) how staff are compensated and rewarded for their contributions to patient care, the organization, and their profession. As a profession, nursing has developed a number of theories and models of professional practice (see *Philosophies and Theories for Advanced Nursing Practice* by Butts and Rich, 2011). Other health professions have articulated their own models as well but typically have not explicitly articulated that model unless the health care institution has chosen to adopt a particular one to solidify its patient care culture and/or seek the Magnet Recognition.

Growing expectation to base clinical practice in a model of care

Nevertheless, whether connected to a particular profession such as nursing or as part of an interdisciplinary general effort to improve its patient care, health care organizations are more often now adopting some professional practice model to help their whole staff become more coordinated in providing patient care. Stewart et al. (2003) state that models of care "not only simplify the complexity of reality but will focus our attention on those aspects of a situation that are most important for understanding and effective action" (p. 7). Models of care "guide our perceptions by drawing our attention to specific features of practice," "they provide a framework for understanding what is going on," and "they guide our actions by defining what is important" (p. 7). Common models of practice are the patient-centered medicine approach (Mead & Bower, 2000; Stewart et al., 2003), relationship-centered caring (Tresloni & Pew-Fetzer Task Force, 1994), relationship-based caring (Koloroutis, 2004), and Watson's theory of caring (Watson, 1988, 2012).

Renewed emphasis on "the patient experience"

Major health care organizations and consultants have arisen to help health care institutions assess areas like patient satisfaction, benchmarks for performance, and internal staff surveys. They also provide methods of improving the health care performance by providing top-to-bottom overhauls of individual organizations, from ways staff relate to patients, to how managers supervise and hold their staffs accountable, to how to hire the best staff for the goals of that organization. With the recent addition of payment being at least partially contingent on variables such as patient satisfaction, infection rates, and readmission rates, health care institutions have increasingly sought out specialized health care business consultants to aid them in this process. Beginning in 2006 the HCAHPS initiative (Hospital Consumer Assessment of Healthcare Providers and Systems) collects, publicly reports, and compares information on patient satisfaction and quality across hospitals. It measures how well physicians and nurses communicate with their patients, the responsiveness of hospital staff responding to patient needs, how the staff communicates about medicines, how well staff manage patient pain, how well discharge information was given, and the cleanliness and quietness of the hospital environment. These and other programs are tying reimbursement to patient outcomes or other performance indicators. While there appears to be evidence for improvement in some areas with this method, there are also concerns for negative consequences, such as leading physicians to practice inappropriate patient care because of overfocusing on patient satisfaction scores (Zgierska, Rabago, & Miller, 2014). In any case, the spirit of these programs is to incentivize improvement of patient care by using objective measures, and this has been part of the renewed emphasis in the health care industry to work on what patients actually perceive and experience. Health care organizations now more commonly devote staff and resources to improving the health care culture in connection to the effect on patient care. Reflecting this evolution in the industry, the Beryl Institute emerged as an association of health care leaders dedicated to the improvement of the patient experience. As they define it, the *patient experience* is "the sum of all interactions, shaped by an organization's culture, that influence patient perceptions, across the continuum of care" (Wolf, Niederhauser, & LaVela, 2014, p. 8).

The development of the science of compassionate caring

Jean Watson and the advent of the Science of Caring

The work on caring and compassion has most often been done from philosophical, literary, and spiritual approaches throughout the centuries. In the past several decades, it has become clear that caring and compassion can be studied scientifically. Jean Watson (1985, 1988, 2008, 2012) has been one of the pioneers of caring science, articulating the philosophical and scientific foundations for studying caring as a human phenomenon and practicing caring in clinical practice. She and other nurse theorists have developed a number of theories of caring in nursing practice, and a great deal of empirical research has been generated along these lines in the last 40 years.

The Science of Compassion

There also have been other efforts to study compassion scientifically. In 2012 the first Science of Compassion Conference was convened by Stanford University's Center for Compassion and Altruism Research and Education (Doty, 2012, 2016). Neuroscientists, biologists, and psychologists from around the world presented scientific research on compassion, examining its origins, methods for its measurement, and interventions to increase compassion. Apart from these specific scientific studies of caring and compassion, other empirical approaches have researched the effects of relational and communication variables on patient care. In medicine, psychology, sociology, and anthropology, scientists have examined the impact of therapeutic alliance, nonverbal behaviors, and communication techniques on patient satisfaction and medical outcomes. While the science of compassionate caring in health care is a newer term in the landscape of the helping professions, there already exist thousands of empirical studies that analyze the dynamics of compassionate caring. Various research initiatives often do not even know of similar work being done in other disciplines, specialties, and professions or in other countries. The main problem is that this information has not been generally known nor has it been integrated into training. While there has been the common notion that compassionate caring is a desirable but expendable or optional feature of health care, the evidence is that such thinking is scientifically unfounded and outdated.

WHAT IS HEALTH CARE WITH COMPASSIONATE CARING AT THE CENTER?

Many of the problems in health care can be improved if we begin with compassionate caring as the center of how we conceive of health care. What does health care look like when compassionate caring is at the center of whatever we do rather than conceptually tacked on to (or jettisoned from) the practice of medicine?

The motivation for whatever we do is stated explicitly

First, when compassionate caring is central to health care practice, the motivation for whatever we do is stated explicitly. Ironically, most people going into health care state that caring for patients or wanting to respond to suffering is why they chose health care, but later they distinguish between curing or caring, being competent or caring, being problem-focused or patient-centered, and focusing on the financial bottom line versus the altruistic mission of the organization. When all is going well, there is no tension in these pairs. But when times are tough, these same people will separate out the caring component for the sake of being efficient, getting things done, setting limits on patients, or surviving as either an individual clinician or an organization. They will argue that suspending the caring component is justified and that it is necessary to be "emotionally detached,"

"objective," and "scientific." This is an incredible turmoil for a person in a helping profession, to go into the profession for altruistic reasons and then to say that these values have to be suspended at certain points, and that is just the way health care is. You want to care for patients, and then you have to act in a way that is not caring. As we will see later, this tension or emotional dissonance underlies much of the burnout experienced in health care. After a period of time of being this way, the compassionate foundation of that person's health care career is whittled away, and the clinician starts thinking that the caring values were just idealistic fantasies. Health care centered on compassionate caring explicitly means that your motivation to enter and continue in a helping role is rooted in compassionate caring. That altruistic desire itself is always part of who the person is and what the person is doing. It is not only the reason people go into health care but also why they train so hard to be as competent as they can be, because competence is the most essential part of really caring for your patient. You are competent because you want to relieve suffering and promote the well-being of your patients. Everything you do and everything you are in health care is ultimately for the good of your patients. Your competence in health care is always rooted in your fundamental desire to take care of people.

It enables the optimal and most efficient use of medications, procedures, and technology

Second, having compassionate caring as the center of health care enables the optimal and most efficient use of medications, procedures, and technology. Again, when we look more closely, we can see that compassionate caring is implicit all along in the use of biotechnology. We might think that the surgery or the medication or the test is not about caring, but its very use is an extension of our desire to respond to the illness in a patient. Yet we actually say things like, "I'm good at surgery, but I'm not so good at the caring thing." The choice of doing surgery is rooted in the compassionate caring response to a patient. To act as if they are separable is absurd. The problem is that when people act as if they can separate caring from the technology, a number of difficulties arise. The medicine, procedure, or technology by itself cannot guide how it should be used. We might imagine that it is just the surgery or just the medication that helped a patient, but that is never the case. The right surgery or medication has to be chosen for a patient, and that depends on proper assessment and diagnosis. Have we defined the problem properly? This relies on judging the information from tests, scans, and information from the patient. Things that can interfere with our judgment include not being competent with this particular condition, not taking enough time to evaluate all the data, not making the patient feel comfortable enough so that he or she might give us all the data about his or her symptoms that we need to make the right diagnosis, being in a rush to make a decision, not liking the patient or making a decision out of our misjudging or stereotyping the person, or not considering the overall life circumstance of a person and how this treatment fits into that larger picture of the person's life. Why do we find it easy to separate the biomedical interventions from the compassionate caring dimension so easily? One of the main reasons is that the treatments we have are very good and, in hindsight, seem to be the only agent in curing or managing a medical condition. But

when you look at the context in which that intervention takes place, you see how much of the clinician's judgment is involved—and that judgment is both subjective (a trained subjectivity) and relational (dependent on accurate attunement with a patient). When we analyze our treatment mistakes or failures, it is often related to human factors. Having an attitude and ethic of compassionate caring is a way to optimize those human factors.

The inability of biomedical interventions to guide their appropriate use

Biomedical interventions by themselves cannot guide the course of treatment. Cancer care is a very good example in this regard. When a patient has some type of cancer, there is often a range of treatment options. Depending on the type of cancer and the age and overall health of the patient, we usually have research on how various treatment options might work. If our standard methods are not helping, we might move to clinical trials of experimental methods. Whether this is from the physician, the patient, or the patient's loved ones, we can always find another treatment option or do more of what we have already done. This happens with medical problems in general, and intensive care units are often places where this dynamic unfolds. We can always do something more or try something else, and that may or may not be the right thing to do. But the biotechnology in itself cannot make that decision. There is always something more we can try. If nothing is curative, we might overuse life support technology even when there is little hope of improvement. Biotechnology also can make you think you are not doing anything if you are not choosing some biomedical treatment. Focusing only on biomedical treatments can actually narrow the field of options. This is not a criticism of the use of this technology. It is simply that it is we who have to judge the application and duration of using that technology. We will only get better at biotechnology, but we also have to get better at how we use it. Being compassion-centric ensures that whatever we do is attuned to the patient in a complete way. (This will be discussed further later in the book.)

How *the biotechnology is delivered is always part of the treatment equation*

The third way having compassionate caring at the center of health care makes a difference is that *how* biotechnology is delivered is always part of the treatment equation. Just as a sterile field is necessary for optimum surgery and an IV must be sterile for the delivery of a medication, so too must there be great care for the emotional/psychological field for any procedure or intervention. As we will see later in this book, empirical evidence is now very clear on how the clinician's manner of doing a history and physical, discussing treatment options, and implementing the treatment actually affects the outcomes of all of these; and those outcomes are both actual medical outcomes as well as patient satisfaction. The neuroscience and psychology of placebos, placebo-related effects, and noceboes are very relevant.

Placebo and nocebo effects

The placebo effect occurs when a perceived and/or actual improvement in patient symptoms occurs after being given an inert substance or intervention with the expectation of improvement. Placebo-related effects are similar, but no inert treatment has been given, and improvements occur as a result of

verbal suggestions, for example (Benedetti, 2008). In contrast to the placebo (literally meaning "I shall please"), the nocebo ("I shall harm") effect involves giving an inert substance accompanied by suggesting that symptoms will worsen. The nocebo-related effect involves a person's symptoms worsening after the provider suggests negative expectations, but no inert substance is given (Benedetti, Lanotte, Lopiano, & Colloca, 2007; Benson, 1997). All of these effects have been extensively documented, including the neuroanatomical and neurophysiological pathways for the psychological precipitants (Benedetti, 2008; Benedetti, 2012; Bensing & Verheul, 2010; Faria, Fredrikson, & Furmark, 2008; Mitsikostas, Mantonakis, & Chalarakis, 2014; Murray & Stoessl, 2013; Petersen et al., 2014; Pollo, Carlino, & Benedetti, 2011; Sanderson, Hardy, Spruyt, & Currow, 2013). While the placebo effect is typically thought of in connection with research design for comparing the effectiveness of treatments, what is commonly overlooked is that the placebo and nocebo processes always have some effect in any clinician–patient interaction. How a clinician communicates is having a positive or negative adjunctive effect on any treatment given and any advice offered to the patient. Benedetti has explained also how pharmacological interventions themselves are affected by cognitive modulation. As he explains in a review of mechanisms of placebo across diseases and treatments,

> it is clear that for many types of treatments, whenever a medical treatment is carried out, a complex biochemical matrix is activated by several social stimuli. Such biochemical cascades of events will inevitably contribute to responses observed with drug administration. In other words, drugs are not administered in a vacuum but rather in a complex biochemical

environment that varies according to the patient's cognitive/affective state and to previous exposure to other pharmacological agents (conditioning). (Benedetti, 2008, p. 52)

You are (part of) the medicine

As we shall examine later in this book, there are a number of other ways that clinician attitudes and communication behaviors are affecting the patient both psychologically and physiologically. These include the neuroception process in the polyvagal theory, in which a person rapidly and unconsciously assesses the safety in interacting with a clinician—and the clinician assesses the safety with a patient (Porges, 2011). In a compassion-centric paradigm of health care, clinicians are aware that, in a real way, they are part of the medicine being delivered to the patient or a negative force undercutting the effectiveness of a biomedical treatment. In light of this, there is no such thing as a neutral objective interaction between the clinician and the patient. Instead, the subjectivity of the clinician must be highly trained in order to provide optimum care for the patient.

It provides a scientific rationale for the role of emotions in medicine

A fourth way having a compassion-centric paradigm for health care is a major improvement over the biotechno-centric paradigm in that it provides a scientific rationale for the role of emotions in medicine, and as a result, it makes possible practical ways of managing and using both the patient's emotions and the clinician's emotions for the healing process. In the biotechno-centric paradigm, the foundation includes only the biomedical sciences and does not have a way to include how patient (and clinician) emotions are involved in health care. Because of biochemical reductionism and persisting mind–body dualism, the role of emotions is either explained away or disregarded. They therefore are not utilized in the healing process and instead are considered irrelevant, distracting, or annoying. As a result, a great deal of healing potential for the patient and for the clinician is not accessed. As I will explain in greater detail later in this book, the patient experience is critical for all phases of health care, from the decision to seek help, the assessment and diagnostic process, the creation of the treatment plan, and the way a patient proceeds after that health care interaction. The way a patient perceives and experiences health care—and in particular, each clinician—is a critical variable in each phase. Positive perceptions and experiences are related to seeking health care more promptly and preventively; providing the clinician with more complete symptom information, enabling a better diagnosis; and being more collaborative and invested in the treatment process, which therefore leads to better adherence to the treatment plan. We have become especially aware that a majority of medical problems (Schroeder, 2007) are related to negative health behaviors. Even though patients generally know the right steps to being healthy (e.g., eat healthy, exercise regularly, lose weight, sleep enough, do not smoke or abuse drugs and alcohol), most patients have great difficulty accomplishing these things, and we have a culture with strong hedonistic and materialistic values, making this doubly difficult to manage. So, having the right biomedical answer to a patient problem is only part of the medical solution. Working with patients, considering their perceptions, their psychosocial context, their racial and ethnic background, and their financial situations are part of the patient's medical problem. While the clinician cannot be expert in each of these areas, the best clinicians will be aware of these factors and able to manage them for the healing process. To try to ignore them, as we have seen all too often, leads to poor medical outcomes. A compassion-centric paradigm treats patient perceptions, patient emotions, psychosocial factors, and biomedical factors as all part of helping patients.

The emotional experience of the clinician is central to the effectiveness of that clinician

The clinician's emotional experience is also improved with a compassion-centric paradigm. When health care is seen as essentially a biomedical enterprise, the clinician's emotional experience (like the patient's) is considered not essential, a distraction, or even an interference with patient care. Yet everything about being in health care involves emotions. There is first the desire to be in a health care career and to go through the grueling study and training to become a certain type of clinician. The clinician has to learn how to manage his or her own feelings in working with patients undergoing horrible bodily trauma as well as experiencing mortal danger and indescribable losses. As I will explain further in this book, emotional detachment in a clinician does not occur as often as clinicians think it does. They may be using emotional suppression or distraction, but emotional detachment is not typical; and if it does occur, then the clinician (and the patient) are subject to many negative consequences. Clinicians have to learn how to work with emotionally

difficult patients (and health care organizational stresses) while maintaining their own composure in order to remain effective. Finally, a whole lifetime in a health care career involves the need to take care of one's emotional/psychological life. In the past 40 years, we have learned a great deal about burnout and compassion fatigue in the helping professions and about methods to deal with these in order to survive and maybe find fulfillment in a helping career. To ignore the emotional life of the clinician is to ignore the volumes of data we now have documenting the higher rates of depression, substance abuse, marital problems, and suicide among our helping professionals. To ignore the inner world of the clinician is to ignore all the harm that is done to patients when clinicians have lost touch with their initial compassionate caring desire that brought them into their specialty. A lot of people in health care have thought that dealing directly with the emotional impact of their work would interfere with their performance, so they avoid doing it. The problem is that then they put off working through their strong feelings about various difficult situations, and not dealing with the emotional impact actually does start interfering with their performance. They become insensitive to their own experience, and this can make them become insensitive to their patient's experience. A compassion-centric paradigm of health care begins by assuming that the emotional experience of the clinician is central to the effectiveness of that clinician.

Compassionate caring is more than a feeling

There is certainly a need to present the evidence for the central importance of compassionate care in medical practice to those who are skeptical of this claim. Yet there is also the problem of clinicians who think they know what compassionate care in medical practice is, but what they instead have may be a sentimentalized and simplistic understanding of what it is and how it operates. Such an uninformed understanding of compassionate care can be almost as problematic as someone who discounts its importance. A clinician who separates this caring manner from being integrated with competence may not be very helpful to a patient. "You are very kind to me, but do you know what you are doing?" Good intentions toward a patient can only go so far. Furthermore, the clinician with an overly sentimentalized understanding of caring is vulnerable to the emotional exhaustion of burnout. Compassionate care in medicine is equated and reduced to a feeling with such a clinician. When they have one too many difficult patients and they no longer have that "caring feeling," they can become quickly discouraged and demoralized. If they reduce their compassionate caring to a "caring feeling," then they lose that "caring feeling," and they are in danger of thinking they are no longer engaged in compassionate caring. Compassionate caring is more than a feeling. Clinicians have not been taught this explicitly. Their understanding of compassionate care has no depth and no foundation. The tree with shallow roots is easily blown over.

Compassionate caring cannot be reduced to bedside manner or communication skills

One of the fundamental problems with how we understand compassionate care in medicine is that it can be reduced to simply "bedside manner." Effective communication skills are the tip of the "compassionate iceberg." While those communication skills can be

quite important, they must be built on a deep foundation. Our mistake in clinical training is that we think that cursory attention to bedside manner in training is sufficient. "I was empathic with that patient; it didn't work." I have watched students apply the communication skills in magical "hocus pocus" fashion and be baffled that it did not work; or, they will say that the whole "warm fuzzy" stuff does not make much of a difference anyway. These were students who did not understand what was being communicated both by them and their patient at a deeper level. But when students finally get a sense of what lies beneath those communications skills, they are unable to ignore it ever again. Once you know bacteria exist, you never underestimate their influence. Once you know how compassionate care operates throughout the patient interaction, you cannot ever ignore it again. Our task in health care training is to help our clinicians understand this reality.

Technology's unintended effect on compassion

While caring and compassion are some of the most popular words in medical school applications and health care marketing, they are not actually considered central to the practice of medicine. The priorities in actual practice often become the use of technology and efficient business practice. Compassionate care is considered a priority, but in a distant third sense as long as it does not interfere with the technology or interfere with efficiency. As we will see in the coming pages, an inadequate notion of compassionate care has led to unintended effects on the practice of medicine as well as other helping professions. Rather than joining in the chorus lamenting how awful, materialistic, and depersonalized the delivery of health care is right now, it is important to understand how we arrived at this situation out of our deep desire to alleviate human suffering. From ancient times to the present, humanity has continually sought to prevent, cure, or lessen the suffering that afflicts human beings. Glick (1993) describes technology's unintended effect on compassion in the following way:

> *One factor in the apparent decline of compassion is that while science is indeed neutral regarding the human aspects of medicine, the successes of scientific intervention in medicine have served to award it an ever-increasing role in the physician–patient interaction. The unparalleled advances in science and technology have dazzled the medical profession, have virtually monopolized our emphases and education, and have almost inevitably relegated the human aspects of medicine to a secondary role. (p. 86)*

It was not as if the medical scientists and then health care entrepreneurs plotted alone to drive compassionate care to its distant third place. Everyone participated in this quest to relieve suffering. As Glick puts it, "While society bemoans the qualities of its physicians, the order of priorities favoring technology is a product of society as a whole, and not merely the result of distortion by the medical profession" (1993, p. 87). It was, in a sense, the fault of us all. But the result of this success is that we now have the "problem of technology becoming the overriding operative in the patient–physician relationship" (T. J. Kapacinskas, personal communication, 2011). Everything is seen through the lens of what the technology can do to help this patient. The physician has come to think that he or she has less to offer the patient than the drug, procedure, or surgery that may be prescribed. In fact, many do not imagine they offer more than diagnosis and the prescription.

The physician is simply the problem-solving entity that gathers information to assess the patient and then offers an answer for the problem, usually in the form of a prescription or medical intervention. With computers and electronic medical records, the technology has become even more the centerpiece in the interaction with the patient. Commonly now, the physician's or nurse's hands are on the computer keyboard immediately entering the answers to the clinician's questions. The electronic health record (EHR) has become its own demanding taskmaster. While a very useful tool for having records, test results, and diagnostic scans all readily available, it also demands entry of all required data fields and the answering of all required questions in the institutional templates. In fact, rather than speed up the process, as it was expected to do, many clinicians now report that it has slowed the medical visit process (Babbott et al., 2014). Records are more easily audited, and the physician is often more worried about how well the computer record is kept than what happens in the interaction with the patient. As many residents will tell you, it is more likely they will be critiqued on what they do or do not have in their medical note than what actually happened in the interaction with the patient. No one will really know what happens with the patient except the clinician and the patient. But there is a quite large audience that may see the EHR from other clinicians: your attending physician if you are a resident or your supervisor if you are a nurse, the insurance coders, and potentially attorneys if your records ever become part of a malpractice claim. The medical note is often written for these groups rather than for the patient. Literally speaking, the technology is the centerpiece around which everything else orbits.

Compassion as nonessential auxiliary tool versus central organizing principle of medicine

Let us be clear, however, that we got to this point mostly through good intentions. But now the tools we have created to help our patients have made us doubt that human relational aspects have much to contribute to our interactions with patients. It is easy to see why that would happen. The dramatic results of antibiotics and surgeries are flashy and compelling. So, what is the solution to technology and business efficiency being the dual suns around which we orbit, with compassionate care being relegated to the status of Pluto? Technology and business efficiency are seen as absolutely essential. Our compassionate care is often viewed now as an auxiliary tool, important for patient satisfaction scores and for the business wisdom of how good customer service is good for business but not important as the central organizing principle of medicine in itself. The solution to this predicament is not the elimination or minimization of technology or the removal of any trace of the business realm. It is by situating both technology and the business within a larger model or theory of compassionate care in medicine that then would correct how we approach patient care.

CONCLUSION

We are already in the paradigm shift from the biotechno-centric paradigm to the compassion-centric paradigm. Just as the immune system of the human body fights an infection, various and disparate parts of the health care world have acknowledged that we have fundamental problems in how we conceive of caring for the patient. In many different sectors, there

are very good efforts to humanize the health care delivery system and correct these problems. Many of these reform efforts do not even know about each other, yet their assessment of the problems and their solutions are remarkably similar. In my encounters with these efforts begun independently by physicians, nurses, medical educators, and health care business executives and managers, it has been remarkable to learn of new models of conceiving what is done in health care without even knowing that in another sector, another silo, of health care, very similar programs were being developed. With the accumulation of empirical evidence for the role of compassionate caring in health care, it is clearer that our own version of shifting from the geocentric to heliocentric models of the solar system is occurring. This requires that we reexamine and articulate our fundamental assumptions for the way we do health care. In doing so, I offer this list of 20 major claims that can be made regarding a compassion-centric paradigm of health care. The remainder of this book will provide the thinking and the evidence supporting them.

20 Major Claims of How Doctors Care:

1. Caring does not burn you out. *Not caring* burns you out.

2. A sentimental, feeling-centered notion of compassionate caring is not sufficient to provide effective patient care.

3. Empathy is a distinct from compassion neurologically. Empathy alone can make the clinician vulnerable to burnout. A *compassion mindset* is a means of managing the empathic resonance with patient suffering and a buffer against burnout. Just having empathy is a setup

for burnout; training your compassion mindset is a buffer to burnout and the key to physician resilience.

4. Compassionate caring cannot be reduced to bedside manner and communication skills. It includes the foundations of the desire to respond to human suffering, the manner in which competence in a helping profession is achieved, and the execution of the particular skills of each specialty and discipline.

5. It is impossible to be a smart, competent doctor unless you have integrated compassionate caring into your training and practice. Not having compassionate caring integrated is a sign of serious deficit in the clinician, either personally or because of inferior training.

6. Compassionate caring is absolutely essential to the delivery of biomedical/technical medicine. If compassionate caring is absent or lacking, any procedure or medicine given will be negatively affected or contaminated. No interaction in health care is neutral. The presence of compassionate caring has positive (immediate and extended) effects on the patient (and the provider); lack of compassionate caring has negative (immediate and extended) effects on the patient (and the provider).

7. All aspects of patient care are scientific, including the biomedical, the psychosocial, and the compassionate caring dimensions. The distinction is not between the hard sciences and the soft sciences, but *the hard sciences and the harder sciences*.

8. There is an optimum range of balanced compassionate caring that lies between emotional detachment/underinvolvement and emotional overinvolvement. Both extremes have negative effects on patients and clinicians. Balanced compassionate caring has positive effects both for patients and for clinicians.

9. Learning how emotions are involved in medicine is the key to getting sufficient patient data, making a diagnosis, and implementing effective treatment.

10. Seasoned and expert clinicians achieve superior emotional regulation. Emotional detachment from patients does not occur as often as clinicians think it does; and if it does occur, it is extremely dangerous both to the patient and to the clinician. Suppression of emotions is not the most effective way for clinicians to protect themselves.

11. Long-term maintenance of a compassionate caring attitude, resilience, and well-being can be achieved by training the mind of the clinician regularly using mindfulness, loving-kindness, and other meditation/mind-training techniques.

12. Compassionate caring involves effective challenging and confrontation skills, boundaries in clinician–patient interactions, ability to set limits, effective self-care, and wise stewardship of resources.

13. Compassionate caring is the most effective way of handling difficult patients.

14. Compassionate caring is absolutely essential to successful and effective objective scientific biomedical research.

15. Compassionate caring is critically important to creating and maintaining a successful and effective health care business organization.

16. Taking care of yourself as a helping professional is most effective if rooted in compassionate caring.

17. Compassionate caring can be further learned in any helping professional

because human beings are built for compassion and because of brain plasticity.

18. Compassionate caring is ultimately the best way to steward resources and facilitate efficiency in an organization because it is attuned to the actual needs of patients and the overall goal to relieve suffering in a just and wise manner. It provides the most positive patient experience and is the most satisfying approach for employees and administrators.

19. Compassionate caring evolves in a clinician's career. Expect that there is a growth process in the attitudes and skills of compassionate caring from the beginning to the later years of a helping career.

20. It is possible to recover compassionate caring in your career if you have become burnt out and lost the connection to what drew you into medicine.

QUESTIONS FOR DISCUSSION

1. What kinds of evidence from your experience do you have to support or dispute the message of chapter 1?

2. What do you think needs to happen if we are to fully make the transition to a compassion-centric paradigm of practicing medicine?

REFERENCES

Accreditation Council for Graduate Medical Education. (2017). *Common program requirements*. Retrieved from https://www.acgme.org/Portals/0/PFAssets/Program-Requirements/CPRs_2017-07-01.pdf

Babbott, S., Manwell, L. B., Brown, R., Montague, E., Williams, E., Schwartz, M., ... Linzer, M. (2014). Electronic medical records and physician stress in primary care: Results from the MEMO Study. *Journal of the American Medical Informatics Association, 21*(e1), e100–e106.

Benedetti, F. (2008). Mechanisms of placebo and placebo-related effects across diseases and treatments. *Annual Review of Pharmacology and Toxicology, 48,* 33–60.

Benedetti, F. (2012). Placebo-induced improvements: How therapeutic rituals affect the patient's brain. *Journal of Acupuncture and Meridian Studies, 5*(3), 97–103.

Benedetti, F., Lanotte, M., Lopiano, L., & Colloca, L. (2007). When words are painful: Unraveling the mechanisms of the nocebo effect. *Neuroscience, 147,* 260–271.

Bensing, J. M., & Verheul, W. (2010). The silent healer: The role of communication in placebo effects. *Patient Education and Counseling, 80,* 293–299.

Benson, H. (1997). The nocebo effect: History and physiology. *Preventive Medicine, 26,* 612–615.

Borrell-Carrio, F., Suchman, A. L., & Epstein, R. M. (2004). The biopsychosocial model 25 years later: Principles, practice, and scientific inquiry. *Annals of Family Medicine, 2*(6), 576–582.

Butts, J. B., & Rich, K. L. (Eds.). (2011). *Philosophies and theories for advanced nursing practice*. Sudbury, MA: Jones & Bartlett Learning.

Campo, R. (2005). "The Medical Humanities," for lack of a better term. *Journal of the American Medical Association, 294*(9), 1009–1011.

Doty, J. R. (2012, August 7). The science of compassion. *Huffington Post*. Retrieved from http://www.

huffingtonpost.com/james-r-doty-md/science-of-compassion_b_1578284.html

Doty, J. R. (2016). *Into the magic shop: A neurosurgeon's quest to discover the mysteries of the brain and the secrets of the heart.* New York, NY: Avery.

Engel, G. L. (1976, October). Too little science: The paradox of modern medicine's crisis. *Pharos*, 127–131.

Faria, V., Fredrikson, M., & Furmark, T. (2008). Imaging the placebo response: A neurofunctional review. *European Neuropsychopharmacology*, 18, 473–485.

Glick, S. M. (1993). The empathic physician: Nature and nurture. In H. Spiro, M. G. M. Curnen, E. Peschel, & D. St. James (Eds.), *Empathy and the practice of medicine* (pp. 85–102). New Haven, CT: Yale University Press.

Hoffart, N., & Woods, C. Q. (1996). Elements of a nursing professional practice model. *Journal of Professional Nursing*, 12(6), 354–364.

Kirch, D. G. (2012, March). A word from the president: MCAT2015: An open letter to pre-med students. *AAMC Reporter*.

Koloroutis, M. (Ed.). (2004). *Relationship-based care: A model for transforming practice.* Minneapolis, MN: Creative Health Care Management.

McGinnis, J. M., & Foege, W. H. (1993). Actual causes of death in the United States. *Journal of the American Medical Association*, 270(18), 2207–2212.

Mead, N., & Bower, P. (2000). Patient-centredness: A conceptual framework and review of the empirical literature. *Social Science & Medicine*, 51, 1087–1110.

Mitsikostas, D. D., Mantonakis, L., & Chalarakis, N. (2014). Nocebo in clinical trials for depression: A meta-analysis. *Psychiatry Research*, 215, 82–86.

Mokdad, A. H., Marks, J. S., Stroup, D. F., & Gerberding, J. L. (2004). Actual causes of death in the United States, 2000. *Journal of the American Medical Association*, 291(10), 1238–1245.

Mokdad, A. H., Marks, J. S., Stroup, D. F., & Gerberding, J. L. (2005). Correction: Actual causes of death in the United States, 2000. *Journal of the American Medical Association*, 293(3), 293–294.

Murray, D., & Stoessl, A. J. (2013). Mechanisms and therapeutic implications of the placebo effect in neurological and psychiatric conditions. *Pharmacology & Therapeutics*, 140, 306–318.

Peabody, F. W. (1927). The care of the patient. *Journal of the American Medical Association*, 88(12), 877–882.

Petersen, G. L., Finnerup, N. B., Colloca, L., Amanzio, M., Price, D. D., Jensen, T. S., & Vase, L. (2014). The magnitude of the nocebo effects in pain: A meta-analysis. *Pain*, 155, 1426–1434.

Pollo, A., Carlino, E., & Benedetti, F. (2011). Placebo mechanisms across different conditions: From the clinical setting to physical performance. *Philosophical Transactions of the Royal Society B Biological Sciences*, 366, 1790–1798.

Porges, S. W. (2011). *The Polyvagal Theory: Neurophysiological foundations of emotions, attachment, communication, and self-regulation.* New York, NY: Norton.

Sanderson, C., Hardy, J., Spruyt, O., & Currow, D. C. (2013). Placebo and nocebo in randomized controlled trials: The implications for research and practice. *Journal of Pain and Symptom Management*, 46(5), 722–730.

Schroeder, S. A. (2007). We can do better: Improving the health of the American people. *New England Journal of Medicine*, 357, 1221–1228.

Schwartz, A. W., Abramson, J. S., Wojnowich, I., Accordino, R., Ronan, E. J., & Rifkin, M. R. (2009). Evaluating the impact of the humanities in medical education. *Mount Sinai Journal of Medicine*, 76, 372–380.

Schwartzstein, R. M., Rosenfeld, G. C., Hilborn, R., Oyewole, S. H., & Mitchell, K. (2013). Redesigning the MCAT Exam: Balancing multiple perspectives. *Academic Medicine*, 88, 560–567.

Shapiro, J., Coulehan, J., Wear, D., & Montello, M. (2009). Medical humanities and their discontents: Definitions, critiques, and implications. *Academic Medicine*, 84(2), 192–198.

Stewart, M., Brown, J. B., Weston, W. W., McWhinney, I. R., McWilliam, C. L., & Freeman, T. R. (2003). *Patient-centered medicine: Transforming the clinical method* (2nd ed.). Abingdon, UK: Radcliffe Medical Press.

Suls, J., Krantz, D. S., & Williams, G. C. (2013). Three strategies for bridging different levels of analysis and embracing the biopsychosocial model. *Health Psychology*, 32(5), 597–601.

Tinkham, M. (2013). Pursuing magnet designation: Choosing a professional practice model. *AORN Journal*, 97(1), 136–139.

Tresloni, C. P., & Pew-Fetzer Task Force. (1994). *Health professions education and relationship-centered care*. San Francisco, CA: Pew Health Professions.

Watson, J. (1985). *Nursing: The philosophy and science of caring*. Boulder: Colorado Associated University Press.

Watson, J. (1988). *Nursing: Human science and human care*. New York, NY: National League for Nursing.

Watson, J. (2008). *Nursing: The philosophy and science of caring* (revised ed.). Boulder: University Press of Colorado.

- (2012). *Human caring science: A theory of nursing*. Sudbury, MA: Jones & Bartlett.

Wells, J. (2011). *All my patients kick and bite: Favorite stories from a vet's practice*. New York, NY: St. Martin's Press.

Wolf, J. A., Niederhauser, D., & LaVela, S. L. (2014). Defining patient experience. *Patient Experience Journal*, 1(1), 7–19.

Zgierska, A., Rabago, D., & Miller, M. M. (2014). Impact of patient satisfaction ratings on physicians and clinical care. *Patient Preference and Adherence*, 8, 437–446.

"Compassion is not just bedside manner and being kind."

Chapter Sections:

- ▶ Introduction
- ▶ Misconceptions about Caring and Compassion
- ▶ Definitions of Caring and Compassion in Health Care
- ▶ Theoretical Models of Compassion
- ▶ The Compassionate Mind
- ▶ Psychology of Engaging Suffering
- ▶ Psychology of Alleviating/Preventing Suffering
- ▶ Conclusion

CHAPTER 2

What Is Compassionate Caring in Health Care?

Questions to consider before reading this chapter:

1. What kinds of problems do you experience with how people (either clinicians or the public) use the words *caring* and *compassion* when they talk about health care?

2. Before reading these definitions, how would you define what *caring* and *compassion* mean in health care practice?

INTRODUCTION

Compassion and caring are what we look for in med school applications

The idea of being compassionate and caring in health care is very popular. If you did not use one of these words in your application for training or your self-description in the job interview for a particular helping profession, then you likely used phrases such as wanting to "help others," "do my part to make the world a better place," "relieve suffering," or "give back to others for all that I have been fortunate to have been given." Imagine if in your application you said, "I'm smart, really good at solving problems, driven for excellence, and efficient, but I don't really care about people per se; whether it's a sick person or an organic chemistry problem, it's pretty much the same for me." If there is not some evidence of altruism in the application, it is a deal breaker in terms of being accepted for training or joining a clinical practice. If the applicant is self-centered, we would not accept him or her if we could help it, because we want someone who cares about the patients' needs or at least is willing to care about our organization and the fellow colleagues. Actually, this is even true across all types of work that do not have to do with direct service to people. We want employees who will "care" about the equipment they use, the food they prepare, the furniture they make, and the windows they wash.

Imagining a clinician without compassion and caring makes it obvious that these qualities are fundamentally important in clinical practice

We would be particularly suspicious of a person in a helping profession who does not espouse or mention the values of caring and compassion. We certainly would not want a clinician who bluntly said he or she was "not into caring and compassion" but liked solving problems and making money doing that. There are exceptions (which I will discuss later)—clinicians who are crusty curmudgeons on the surface but are quite committed to other people's welfare on a deeper level; they just avoid the "caring" language. The evidence for the fact that they really do care would be what they are like with people in the long run. But if we do not think clinicians are compassionate and caring, we become fearful that they are not really committed to helping alleviate suffering in people. Other people's needs or suffering would not really matter to them or motivate them to do a good job. Would they be reliable? Would they try hard to figure out a complex medical problem or avoid making a clinical mistake that might hurt a patient? If clinicians do not have these compassionate caring qualities, we worry whether their patients will be safe or feel safe; and we worry what the central motivation steering their behavior really is. Imagining the lack of a caring or compassionate attitude in a clinician makes it clear very quickly that compassion and caring are fundamentally important.

MISCONCEPTIONS ABOUT CARING AND COMPASSION

The notion of compassionate caring has tended to be overly sentimentalized, overly emotionalized, overly feminized, and overly spiritualized. In a discussion of the psychology of caring, we have to consider how these distortions affect the behavior of helping professionals.

Compassion and caring are over-sentimentalized

First, compassion and caring often end up being oversentimentalized concepts in clinical practice. Caring and compassion are idealized as a sort of perpetual state of "being nice" to people. The terms may be used in such a way as to emphasize how "sweet" the helper is. In fact, helping professionals can become irritated with the discussion of caring because it does not match how they experience it in their clinical work. It can be used in such a way that it sounds shallow and superficial, as if their competence in their skill was not as important as customer service techniques. It lacks the connotation of just how hard it is to stay involved with some people, especially when effective care in helping those patients involves challenging them or setting limits. Patients are not as likely to say you were caring when you have to challenge them or put them through a difficult treatment. In short, a nauseatingly oversentimentalized description of caring can keep us from obtaining a more subtle understanding of what caring really is.

Compassion and caring are overemotionalized

Second, caring is often overemotionalized. The focus is on the helper having "a very warm emotion" (Wuthnow, 1991) or on the care recipient being able to perceive some emotional sign of caring in the helper. In deciding whether someone is caring, we often want to determine what kind of feeling state the helper had, and this is difficult to determine. As Wuthnow (1991) puts it, "You really cannot tell if someone else is compassionate or not because the essential quality is interior" (p. 217). The problem is that if we think that caring is mainly a feeling, then when we do not see the warm emotion in the person helping us, we might erroneously conclude that the person is not caring. But sometimes a person helping us is genuinely motivated to care for us but adopts a tough, challenging type of behavior to help us grow. Or if we equate compassion and caring with an intense feeling state in ourselves when we help others, then when we do not have this feeling state, we might mistakenly think we no longer care. Especially at the beginning of a helping professional career, but later as well, some helpers become concerned if that "caring feeling" is not there. There can be times when a patient frustrates or irritates you, but you are internally guided by a desire to promote the well-being of the other, and this genuine desire helps you reframe or tolerate your own negative emotions while you help the patient. To reduce compassion and caring to a particular type of emotion or a level of emotional intensity experienced results in a limited understanding of compassion and caring because these involve motivations, attitudes, cognitions, and behaviors, as well as emotions.

Compassion and caring are erroneously thought to be only feminine qualities

Third, compassion and caring are often overly gender stereotyped. Caring is often imagined as being more in the province of the feminine, and consequently it becomes a more awkward concept for male helpers to incorporate in their work. Clinicians who are confined by their own

gender stereotypes might erroneously think things like "Men should not be too warm and feeling oriented as clinicians" or "As a man, I am not good at that feeling stuff, so I don't dwell on my patient's feelings, much less my own feelings." As we will explore later, empathy is a critical part of caring. More (1994) discussed this problem with regard to empathy:

> In popular culture the term "empathy" is associated with a set of traits frequently connoted as "feminine," especially emotional attunement and identification with the feelings of others. … In contrast, those who enlist "empathy" for the professional work of medicine generally resist these "feminized" associations and instead define empathy through the language of scientific objectivity. Indeed, throughout most of the twentieth century empathy has been interpreted by many psychiatrists and medical educators as a technical, discursively male-gendered practice. It has not been employed to foster "identification," to collapse the interpersonal boundaries separating patient from practitioner. Rather its function has been to contain the professional–patient relationship within limits appropriate to the emotionally neutral, scientific enterprise of modern medicine: a form of controlled intimacy. (pp. 19–20)

Clinicians who are men often receive a dysfunctional pressure to "care in a man's kind of way," which tends to have the qualities of distance, emotional control, and more of a cognitive empathy with another person. They might even avoid the use of the word caring because it connotes the gender-stereotyped sentimentalized and emotional understanding of caring. Clinicians who are women might be mistakenly expected (both by their patients and by their colleagues) to "care" in stereotypical ways. Folbre (2001) has described how societal stereotypes have led to rewarding and punishing men and women to the degree they conform to those stereotypes. "The stereotypic belief that women are better at care work probably encourages women to choose care-oriented careers and discourages men from doing so" (England, Folbre, & Leana, 2012, p. 28). If men do not think they are good at "care work," it is not because there is something essentially different between men and women when it comes to caring. When we subtly and sometimes explicitly excuse or discourage men and boys from "care work," they do not develop those skills. Preference for caring work results from actually doing caring work. Actually doing caring work awakens and trains that capacity; it is experience of it that is lacking. Actual gender differences do not determine the capacity for doing care work. When compassion and caring are confined by gender stereotypes (which can vary by culture as well), our conceptions of compassion and caring will be too narrow. There are many ways to express compassion and caring no matter what a person's gender is. Compassion and caring transcend gender and culture and can be expressed in many different ways.

Compassion and caring are narrowly defined as heroic helping or exaggerated pietism

Lastly, caring and compassion are sometimes overly identified with heroic helping or an exaggerated pietism that either (a) intimidates clinicians into thinking they could never be caring and compassionate or (b) distorts the caring process. In terms of the first, sometimes clinicians have such a lofty sense of what caring and compassion are that they exclude themselves from even trying to be caring and compassionate and justify uncaring behavior in this way: "Well, I am no Mother Teresa, so don't expect me to be very caring!" People can

think that caring and compassion must always look like the heroic helping that they see in the news or in famous helpers. Furthermore, they may put them on spiritual pedestals, imagining that these people are not really human beings. Because only extraordinary people are capable of such caring and compassion, "ordinary" clinicians can comfortably exclude themselves from expecting it in themselves.

Exaggerated pietism explained

Regarding a pietism that distorts the caring process, what I am referring to here is that compassion and caring are forced into a spiritual sentimentalism that distorts how caring and compassion are imagined, and are not really connected to what the suffering person needs. It is more focused on itself. For example, caring might be conceived of as requiring a self-martyring dynamic. For helpers who are Christian, there might be the compulsive helping belief that one should "die on the cross for others" every day. There may be times one does choose to act heroically for others (and lose one's life in the process), which is grounded in one's spiritual beliefs. This heroic self-giving is focused on helping another person, not as an end in itself. But the dysfunctional piety that one must never care for oneself in helping others makes the suffering of the helper primary rather than the needs of the suffering person. This can be the result of a distortion of certain spiritual beliefs or a dysfunctional psychological dynamic in the helper that is justified in spiritual terms. For example, individuals might think that they must make themselves available to their clients or patients at all hours of the day and never take a break. "Laying down one's life" might be interpreted as allowing yourself to do whatever your client or patient wants you to do even if it might be excessive or manipulative. The problem is that "laying down your life" in this case is not really connected to helping the client or patient; it is focused on the expectation that one should suffer when helping others.

Consequences of unbalanced portrayals of caring and compassion

As a result of these unbalanced portrayals of caring and compassion, at least two things result. First, to the extent one has such notions, to that degree is the helper liable to become overly emotionally involved with clients or patients. Such notions include that caring always requires a lot of time, that you will need to "be nice" all the time and ignore your own feelings and needs in helping others, that caring means you will have to let people verbally abuse and take advantage of you and that you will have to accept everything your clients or patients say they need in order that they perceive you as a caring helper. If a clinician misunderstands what compassionate caring is, his or her attitudes and actions will reflect that. Second, to the extent that one defines compassionate caring in an overly sentimental manner, then the danger is that one avoids a deeper reflection and discussion about what constitutes true care in helping others, because the clinician is turned off by that definition. Some clinicians come to dislike the words *compassion* and *caring* because these words have been used by patients to manipulate or punish the clinician—for example, "If you were a caring doctor, you would help me the way I think you should." Helpers also flee continuing education seminars on issues such as caring and compassion because they do not want to hear about sentimentalized notions that do not really help them provide the services they were trained to perform.

Compassion and caring are overused words in marketing

To add to the distorted portrayals of caring and compassion, they are overused words in marketing. Many organizations, from retail stores and car dealerships to hospitals and restaurants, use these words in their marketing. I once saw a nursing home company advertise "Caring professionals wanted." But I thought that as soon as they were hired, their "caring" would not mean much. They would end up making less than fast-food restaurant employees, and they would be expected to take care of a lot of people under pressured and understaffed conditions. I have seen insurance carriers or HMOs express some variant of "We care about you" in their brochures. But when a patient tries to access certain services or needs specialized treatment, it can become a bureaucratic battle to get these approved. Or payment is declined for incidental reasons, and the appeal process is designed to exasperate patients so that they give up trying to get something paid and simply go ahead and pay the part of the bill that was declined. Mutual funds, financial advisors, and attorneys also use the term *caring* in marketing. A number of these groups really might care for you. But the problem is that the words *caring* and *compassion* have been so used in marketing or shallow customer relations programs that we have gotten used to the words not meaning much. They become trivialized as a result. In fact, we are used to the words being used insincerely. Or they become conceived of as a means to an end instead of an end in itself. For example, those in charge of a customer relations or guest relations program in a retail store or hospital know that the perception of caring is good for the bottom line, so they expend a great deal of effort in requiring that staff use certain stock phrases that sound compassionate and caring. Indeed, they sometimes are not as concerned about how the service provider really feels about the customer; it is at times more of a series of techniques they demand their staff use to woo customers into buying more. A company that seems caring and has a caring staff sells more. There are times when a salesperson really does present a product accurately and may be genuinely interested in benefiting your life with this product. Some people in sales can be empathic in the sense of matching your needs with what they sell. But empathy is a neutral skill. It can be used to communicate understanding of a person's needs and respond to that need in an altruistic manner or as a tool to detect a potential customer's vulnerabilities or interests in order to manipulate a sale.

DEFINITIONS OF CARING AND COMPASSION IN HEALTH CARE

Need to define compassion and caring precisely

What is needed is a notion of compassionate caring that is deeper and more realistic than the sentimentalized portrayals and the marketing would convey to us. There has been a great deal of philosophical discussion and scientific research about caring and compassion, yet what we mean by compassionate caring in medicine must be clarified for practical purposes. Compassion and caring are ideas that are highly desirable to patients, but generally these are not well defined. Health care marketing expends a great deal to convey how their organizations and clinicians are compassionate and caring, but these sentimental portrayals tend to be shallow. *Caring* and *compassionate* are terms used interchangeably and imprecisely. Various models and theories may emphasize one term over the other. Because clinicians need a more in-depth understanding of what these terms really mean in practice, it is very important that we define what we mean by them and repossess these words from marketing. Clinicians need more than sentimentality to guide them in what it means to be compassionate and caring. Fortunately, with the dawn of the compassion-centric paradigm in our time and the science of compassion and caring, we now have extensive theoretical and empirical work that has been done on compassion and caring that allows us to accomplish this.

Compassion and caring used interchangeably but should be distinct

Technically speaking, compassion and caring are two different concepts, but they are used either interchangeably or together. They should be considered distinct concepts with some overlap. The approach I will use for practical purposes is to define each term and then integrate the two terms with the notion that even with a great deal of overlap in what we mean by each term, there is a unique and complementary usefulness to using the terms *caring* and *compassionate* together. It is not my intention to summarize all the excellent scholarship on these two concepts; rather, it is to provide a practical entry point into this way of viewing health care. My goal is also to provide the general parameters of what compassionate caring in health care means and how it functions as the foundation for many of the models of caring currently used in health care organizations and training institutions. I will provide a number of examples of these models in the latter part of this chapter.

Practical definition of caring

First, let me examine the idea of caring. For training and practical purposes, I have found the need to develop a definition that conveys its essence succinctly and practically in clinical practice, although the definition may not have all the richness and depth of the wonderful research on caring. The definition I propose integrates a number of different models of caring and provides a practical touchstone in the middle of clinical work. *Caring refers to the sincere desire to promote or attend to the well-being of another and the attitudes, emotions, and behaviors originating from this concern for another person.*

Other definitions of caring

The philosopher Milton Mayeroff, in the classic book *On Caring,* defined caring as helping another person grow or actualize him- or herself. The focus is attending to the other person's needs as opposed to one's own needs. Rather than dominating, manipulating, or possessing the other person, caring means not to impose one's own direction on another person but to "allow the direction of the other's growth to guide what I do, to help determine how I am to respond and what is relevant to such response" (Mayeroff, 1971, p. 9). The person caring discerns what the other person needs and responds in such a way to facilitate his or her growth, not to impede it. Jean Watson, renowned for her work on the science of caring in nursing (1988, 2008, 2012), has summed up the essence of caring as found in the idea of *caritas. Caritas* "comes from the Latin word meaning to cherish, to appreciate, to give special, if not loving, attention to. It represents charity and compassion, generosity of spirit. It connotes something very fine, indeed, something precious that needs to be cultivated and sustained" (Watson, 2008, p. 39). What is implied in both Mayeroff and Watson is the deep sense of the dignity of the human person in caring. As both explain in their work, caring is

much more than an attitude or emotion. Caring involves cognitive, emotional, philosophical, and spiritual components. At its core, caring is a fundamental orientation in the helper to attend to and assist another person in terms of what that person really needs for his or her current situation and well-being. Gadow (1985) defines caring as "a commitment to protecting and enhancing the dignity of patients" (p. 33) and a relationship that protects "the patient from being reduced to the moral status of objects" (p. 34). There is a great deal of work that has been done on the scientific construct of caring, especially in nursing. Watson (2009) and Nelson and Watson (2012) have brought together many of the measures of caring, ranging from caring abilities and self-efficacy from the clinician's perspective to caring behaviors as perceived by either patients or clinicians. Watson (2008) has provided a professional-theoretical map consisting of ten Caritas Processes that facilitate the healing process:

1. Practice of loving-kindness and equanimity toward self and other

2. Authentic presence

3. Instill faith and hope/spirituality

4. Develop and sustain a helping-trusting caring relationship

5. Being present and supportive to the expression of positive and negative feelings

6. Creativity in caring process

7. Engage in genuine teaching-learning experience

8. Create a healing environment

9. Honor/assist basic human needs

10. Opening and attending to the spiritual/mysterious and existential unknowns of life-death

The tremendous work that has been done on caring is beyond the scope of this book, but some of this research will be presented in the course of this book.

Definition of compassion

Compassion is another term often used to describe what we aspire to in health care. We speak of nurses and physicians who are compassionate and of health care organizations that have being compassionate as a fundamental value. The idea of compassion, like its partner, caring, has been heavily discussed over the centuries as a moral ideal in clinical practice. In recent years it has become explicitly researched in neuroscience, biology, and psychology. One of the most succinct definitions I have found and used as an entry point to discussing compassion in training and clinical practice is the one Jinpa (Jinpa, 2012; Jazaieri et al., 2016) and other compassion researchers have used to define compassion as having four elements. First, a person notices or is aware of another's suffering (cognitive/attentional component). Second, this person is emotionally moved by that suffering, giving rise to an empathetic concern (affective component). Third, the person wishes or desires to see the relief of that suffering (intentional component). Fourth, the person responds or acts to help ease or relieve that suffering in some way (motivational component). Goetz, Keltner, and Simon-Thomas (2010) have reviewed the empirical literature on compassion and found three theoretical accounts of compassion. One is that *compassion* is another term for *empathic distress*, in which people vicariously experience the distress of a suffering person. The second is that compassion is a type of love or sadness, or a blend of the two. The third account is that compassion is a unique emotional state that is distinct from sadness, love, or distress. Overall, they found that the research supports the third account. Compassion involves a concern for the well-being of a suffering person and the desire to approach that person in order to help reduce or alleviate the person's suffering (Kim et al., 2009). The term *empathic concern* is sometimes used in the research as equated with compassion (Batson, 2011; Goetz, Keltner, & Simon-Thomas, 2010). Overall, "there is broad agreement that compassion is comprised of a combination of affective, cognitive, and motivational components" (Jazaieri et al., 2014, p. 23).

A study on how patients perceive compassion in clinicians

In an effort to empirically define compassion in health care from the perspective of the patients, Sinclair, Beamer, McClement, et al. (2016) examined how palliative care patients understood and experienced compassion by their health care providers. What emerged was the definition from the patients' perspective that compassion is a "virtuous response that seeks to address the suffering and needs of a person through relational understanding and action" (Sinclair, McClement, et al., 2016, p. 195). The authors used the term *virtuous* mainly because there was a dispositional quality in how the clinicians worked with patients. That is, the clinicians were somehow internally motivated to know the patient as a person and to see the person as a priority in that clinicians prioritized the patient's needs above their own assumptions or health care system priorities, and the clinicians had a sense of beneficence, an attitude of wanting what is best for the patient. Compassion was conveyed by clinicians seeking to understand the patient and his or her needs and conveying this through both nonverbal and verbal means. Patients perceived compassionate clinicians as being actively emotionally resonating with them, showing a willingness to be actively engaged with them, and allowing themselves to show a sense of shared humanity and vulnerability in that engagement. Finally, the defining feature of compassion (as opposed to the clinicians just expressing empathic understanding) was the clinicians' desire to attend to the needs of the patient and acting in any way they were able in response to the patient's suffering.

Study showing sympathy, empathy, and compassion are perceived to be different from each other

There is sometimes a tendency to conflate the terms *empathy* and *sympathy* with *compassion* and *caring*. However, these are distinct from each other. In another very interesting study, Sinclair, Beamer, et al. (2017) found that patients could define and distinguish sympathy, empathy, and compassion. The study was based on the reports of 53 advanced cancer patients. Sympathy was perceived as *"a pity-based response to a distressing situation that is characterized by a lack of relational understanding and the self-preservation of the observer"* (Sinclair, Beamer, et al., 2017, p. 440). It was experienced as an unwanted response that was superficial and was not helpful to the patient. Patients sensed the clinician was focused more on self-preservation and protection than on being patient-centered. Empathy was perceived as *"an affective response that acknowledges and attempts to understand an individual's suffering through emotional resonance"* (Sinclair, Beamer, et al., 2017, p. 443). Rather than the subtle distancing characterizing sympathy, the patients experienced empathy as the clinician engaging patients' suffering in an other-centered way and trying to understand patients, including their emotional experience. Finally, compassion was *"a virtuous response that*

seeks to address the suffering and needs of a person through relational understanding and action" (Sinclair, Beamer, et al., 2016, p. 444). This was perceived as being motivated by the altruistic and genuine love of the clinician and focused on action. It was also preferred over the clinician only showing empathy. Empathy was considered important to understanding their suffering, but compassionate responses included the genuine love for the patient as shown in actions that range from major interventions to small acts of kindness. A clinician can be empathic or sympathetic but not be moved to action. The key to compassion is the movement toward action for the suffering person.

This book focuses on what compassion looks like within the clinician's brain

There continues to be important scientific work defining what exactly compassion is in health care. Certainly, our objective in health care is that our patients experience us as compassionately working with them to alleviate or prevent their suffering. In chapter 5, I will review some of the research on how compassionate caring is conveyed to patients and the impact that this has on patient outcomes. But the focus of this book is on what compassion is within the clinician's mind. It is extremely important to be precise in our language, especially now that we realize that neurophysiologically as well as psychologically, compassionate caring looks different in the clinician's brain than does sympathy, empathy, or emotional detachment. When a clinician is coming from a place of compassion, it is certainly more likely that this will be perceived as compassionate by the patients—but not necessarily. As I will explore more in chapter 6, sometimes we must continue to work from a compassionate stance, but it may not be appreciated or recognized as such by the patient, especially if the patient's perception of the clinician is distorted by past negative experiences or even the illness itself. The crucial point of this book is that what compassionate caring really is in the neurophysiology and psychology of the clinician's body makes a difference, not only in the best care for our patients but also because it protects us better from burnout than does emotional detachment.

Practical definition of compassion

Integrating the research on compassion (Jinpa, 2012; Jazaieri et al., 2016) into a succinct and practical four-step process, compassion is defined as (a) noticing or recognizing suffering, (b) being empathically resonant with that person, (c) desiring to relieve that person's suffering, and (d) acting to attempt to alleviate that suffering in some way. As you will see in the research compiled in this book, compassion is more than an ethereal moral value that is difficult to define. It is a human phenomenon that can be delineated physiologically, neuroscientifically, and psychologically.

Why compassion and caring complement each other in the phrase "compassionate caring"

The terms *caring* and *compassion* are often used interchangeably in the clinical realm, with clinicians favoring one or the other. In philosophical and scientific circles, scholars often have focused on one or the other. If not using one of these terms, then related ones have been used in health care, such as *patient-centered*, *relationship-based*, *values-based*, or *humanistic* medicine. While each term can represent a distinct approach, there is a high degree of overlap among the areas. But it is not unusual for people to say both *compassionate*

and *caring* when describing a clinician or organization. "My doctor/nurse/therapist is so compassionate and caring." "I was treated in such a compassionate and caring way at this hospital." Practically speaking, it seems that there is some way in which the two terms together work as a whole, complementing each other. *Caring* refers to a general attitude that the clinician has in all interactions, while *compassionate* is more focused on responsiveness to pain and suffering. When a patient says that the clinician was compassionate toward him or her, it suggests that there was some way in which that patient was suffering or in distress and the clinician responded to this specific suffering or distress. When a patient goes in for a routine physical or for a follow-up visit after a successful surgery, the term *compassionate* seems too heavy handed or melodramatic. *Compassionate* is reserved for times of crisis, loss, or intense predicaments in a patient's experience. But for the routine physical or follow-up, to say that the clinic treated you in a caring way fits better. That is, the clinician appeared to be concerned about a patient's well-being in a sincere way. It would also describe anyone who came in contact with that patient that day, such as the receptionist, the nurse, the person who drew blood for the lab work, or the billing person. *Caring* would describe the set of behaviors appearing to come from a staff member who seemed genuinely invested in the patient as a person. The patient would feel respected and valued in all matters, whether ordinary or in urgent situations. Caring is the constant backdrop for all that happens. Compassionate would be the responsiveness that occurs when a caring person who is helping the patient notices that there is something that is particularly stressful or difficult for the patient and responds to it. In short, to say that a patient was treated in a compassionate caring way semantically seems to cover what patients expect to experience with health care staff: *that the patient always feels cared for in every interaction, no matter how ordinary or benign; and if some difficulty emerges, the patient can count on that health care provider responding in a compassionate way connoting that the clinician's response is focused on the patient's immediate distress or predicament.*

Various erroneous ways the term compassionate caring is used in health care and what they imply

It is very important in working with any group of clinicians that we define our terms when it comes to compassionate caring. One of the difficulties in using the concept of compassionate care in the field is that it is defined quite differently by health care professionals, which leads to problems in a shared understanding by a staff, which in turn would affect its implementation. For example, *compassionate caring* may be used as an emotional state only when working with a patient. Examples of this in clinician statements would be, "I didn't feel very compassionate toward that patient because he was such a jerk when he was admitted to the ER," "If I feel too compassionate with a patient, I get too worked up and can't do the procedure for the patient as well," or "I can't be compassionate with every patient because it takes so much time and is emotionally draining for me." This implies that compassionate caring is only occurring when the clinician feels empathic concern for the patient and does not exist when that "feeling" is not there. Clinicians might think of compassion as a quantity of positive emotional energy or a forced mental attitude that would be reflected in statements like these: "That patient was so challenging, and I just started running out of compassion to

help him." In this view, compassionate caring is viewed as a finite internal resource, like having a certain amount of fuel in your car. It implies that the clinician brings a certain reservoir of compassion fuel from which a certain amount is spent with each patient. It suggests a kind of internally forced attitude that is difficult to hold past a certain point, sort of like being able to hold a 100-pound bag of cement for as long as possible. As you tire or become strained, you drop it: "I just couldn't hold it anymore." Finally, clinicians may imagine compassion as a trait that they have, like hair color: "I don't have a lot of compassion like some of my colleagues; I send them the patients who need that sort of thing." Compassion is seen as what one is born with and as not changeable. It also is implied that it is not essential for medical practice. But all of these conceptions of compassion are faulty.

Compassion means "being into it" both emotionally and cognitively

When focusing on whether a clinician is coming from a place of compassionate caring in how he or she is working with a patient, compassionate caring has typically been thought of as how emotionally motivated the clinician is to help the patient (e.g., "I felt compassionate toward this patient, but not that patient") or as the clinician's communication skills, a.k.a. bedside manner (e.g., "There wasn't time to do the compassion thing with the patient because it was an emergency situation"). But compassion is a complex cognitive and emotional process that includes the clinician's cognitive investment in the patient and his or her condition. The cartoon below captures what I mean by this. The surgeon comes out of the operating room to report to the loved one on how the surgery did not go well. He praises the performance of the nurses and technicians but confesses that he "just wasn't into it." He could have done better; he had the skills, but for whatever reason, he was not fully motivated. Maybe he was tired or distracted. Maybe something happened in his personal life that interfered with his performance. Maybe he is discouraged by something else and just could not focus as well as he normally does. "Being into it" would mean that the surgeon was very motivated to do the surgery as well as possible and that he had focused himself completely on the need of that patient in this surgery.

"The nurses and technicians did all they could—
I just wasn't into it."

IMAGE 2.1 The risk of "not being into it"

Our motivation to help a patient is what animates our technical expertise

One might argue that surgery is simply a technical expertise and that the emotions behind it have nothing to do with it. But it is quite possible that you could be the best surgeon in the world for a particular type of problem but not be very invested in doing the best job for a particular patient. Just because a clinician is very smart and very technically skilled does not mean that clinician will work very hard for a particular patient. The clinician's motivation might vary from patient to patient for a variety of reasons: one patient she does not know or does not like; another patient is a wealthy VIP who also happens to be married to an attorney. Or one patient reminds him of his dear mother and another patient is a prisoner serving a long sentence. Our levels of investment or motivation to help a particular patient can vary and will be reflected in our performance no matter how smart or technically proficient we are. You could be the best heart surgeon in the world, but if you are not "into" my heart problem, I should go find another surgeon who would be more "into" helping me with my problem, someone who cares about my particular surgery. Your motivation to help me in particular is what animates your technical expertise; otherwise, your competence means absolutely nothing to me.

Compassion is central to the execution of the clinician's cognitive and technical skills

Rather than being a superfluous (or distracting) emotional appendage to the cognitive and performance aspects of clinical work, compassion (or its absence) is central to how well the cognitive and performance processes of clinical medicine proceed. Compassionate caring is the motivating force energizing the optimum execution of clinical judgment and clinical action. It is what directs our attention and impels us to apply what we know to the particular patient who needs us. It is not just feeling concern for our patient's problem and expressing that concern. It is how we demonstrate that concern by how we apply what we know for this patient. If we are kind and concerned toward our patients but do not give them our competence, then that is not compassion. While we may know how to solve medical problems in general, compassion is what drives us to apply this knowledge to the particular person before us. Without compassionate caring, we are "not into" applying our knowledge and experience to this particular patient. Compassionate caring cannot be reduced to bedside manner and communication skills. It includes the foundations of the desire to respond to human suffering, the manner in which competence in a helping profession is achieved, and the execution of the particular skills of each specialty and discipline.

Cartesian dualism underlies misconceptions of compassionate caring

Part of the reason compassionate caring has been considered separate from, and even detrimental to, the cognitive and performance parts of clinical practice is because of the Cartesian dualism that has permeated our thinking. Damasio (2006) has concluded from extensive scientific research that Descartes's error was separating "the most refined operations of mind from the structure and operation of a biological organism" (p. 250). The mind was thought to be distinct from the body. Emotions were thought of as distinct from reason. Instead, they are intimately interconnected. Illustrating this interconnection, McNaughton and Leblanc (2012) summarize some of the research on how individuals who have a damaged prefrontal cortex may have all their problem-solving and intellectual abilities intact but make disastrous decisions when it comes to their relationships, social status, and finances. Damage to the ventromedial prefrontal cortex results in these individuals not being able to use their emotions to make decisions, especially decisions in which the outcome is uncertain. They have flat facial affect and difficulty reacting in emotional situations (McNaughton & LeBlanc, 2012). Damasio (2006) articulates how even human reasoning is itself undergirded by a motivational system making reasoning and our clinical judgment possible.

> *Reason does seem to depend on specific brain systems, some of which happen to process feelings. Thus, there may be a connecting trail, in anatomical and functional terms, from reason to feelings to body. It is as if we are possessed by a passion for reason, a drive that originates in the brain core, permeates others levels of the nervous system, and emerges as either feelings or nonconscious biases to guide decision making. Reason, from the practical to the theoretical, is probably constructed on this inherent drive by a process which resembles the mastering of a skill or craft. Remove the drive, and you will not acquire the mastery. But having the drive does not automatically make you a master. (Damasio, 2006, pp. 245–246)*

The interaction of cognitive and emotional processes for airline pilots is similar for compassionate caring

Damasio (2006) uses the example of the airline pilot who has to land the aircraft at a busy airport in bad weather. On the one hand, the pilot cannot let his or her feelings overwhelm the attention he or she must pay to the details of executing this landing. On the other hand, the pilot must have feelings about the overall responsibility he or she has to do his or her best for the lives of the passengers, the crew, and his or her own family. The feelings are what motivate the pilot to do his or her best in flying. I believe how Damasio articulates the vital interconnection between cognition and emotion applies completely to compassion in health care professionals. As we are using the term *compassionate caring* here, we are referring to an emotional and cognitive state that one enters in doing patient care. This is somewhat like the mental and emotional state that an airline pilot has to enter and sustain while flying the plane. While flying, the pilot has a composed and focused attention. The pilot is focused on executing the necessary tasks but is also in a state of readiness to react to any sudden problems that may arise. He or she is not overly tense the whole flight, but nor is the pilot lackadaisical or halfhearted in flying. The pilot attains this cognitive and emotional state from training, simulation practice, and then experience. At a certain point, the pilot can enter this state of mind easily and sustain it for hours. This state of mind begins to look like a trait after a while because it is habitual. But much training, practice, and emotional investment has preceded getting to that level of habitual or automatic performance.

The compassionate mind is like the pilot's "flying mind"

Compassion operates similarly. With training and practice, the clinician learns how to be in a certain cognitive and emotional state with patients, a *mindset*. This clinician will approach patients in a certain manner, do the routine things with focused attention, and be able to adjust to the "storms" that happen with patient care. *Just as a pilot does not stop being in a "flying mind" when he or she encounters turbulent airspace, so too does the compassionate clinician not stop being in a "compassionate mind" when the patient is difficult or there is an emergency situation.*

THEORETICAL MODELS OF COMPASSION

What is the evidence that compassion is really this mindset? In this section, I will begin presenting some of the newest research and findings on the science of compassion. I will focus on three models of compassion that will provide an overall view of compassion. There are other models, some of which will be presented later in this book. But these provide a way to work through and integrate the information I present later in this book. The first model is the result of a rigorous review of self-report measures of compassion by Strauss et al. (2016). The second model is the appraisal model of compassion based on the review of much of the research literature by Goetz et al. (2010). Third, I will provide a summary of the compassionate mind approach from the work of Paul Gilbert. All of these models are based on research about compassion in general, but it is readily apparent how applicable they are to what we experience in health care. These three models will provide the background for the biology and neuroscience of compassion that I will summarize in chapter 3.

Empirical definition of compassion in self-report measures

Strauss et al. (2016) reviewed all the definitions and measures of compassion and proposed the definition of compassion

> as a cognitive, affective, and behavioral process consisting of the following five elements that refer to both self- and other-compassion: 1) Recognizing suffering; 2) Understanding the universality of suffering in human experience; 3) Feeling empathy for the person suffering and connecting with the distress (emotional

resonance); 4) Tolerating uncomfortable feelings aroused in response to the suffering person (e.g., distress, anger, fear) so remaining open to and accepting of the person suffering; and 5) Motivation to act/acting to alleviate suffering. (p. 19)

In their review, Strauss et al. (2016) noted that compassion functions in a state-like or trait-like manner. Each of these components could fluctuate across various situations such as one's sensitivity to recognizing suffering, being able to empathically resonate with the other person, being able to tolerate the feelings that can arise, or being motivated to help. But there is also evidence that a certain level of compassion can persist over time. There appear to be ways to cultivate compassion in terms of one's motivational states, attitudes, or behaviors. Strauss et al. (2016) note that, at present, all self-report measures of compassion have deficits and that more work is needed. There is the strong possibility, however, that self-report measures cannot fully explicate the phenomenon of compassion. As we will see in the physiology and neuroscience of compassion in chapter 3, there is amazing evidence about how compassion is manifested in studies using fMRI and other physiological measures.

Appraisal model of compassion

In their review of the studies on compassion from evolutionary biology, physiology, neuroscience, and psychology, Goetz et al. (2010) have collected ample evidence that compassion is an evolved emotion that is distinct from other emotions and that this state is what motivates humans to respond in specific ways to the need or distress of others.

Goetz et al.'s description of the appraisal process leading to compassion

Compassion is a complex cognitive and emotional process that is the result of a distinct appraisal process. All emotions result from how a person appraises how a particular interaction with the environment affects that person (Goetz et al., 2010). The compassion process is initiated in response to a negative event or suffering of another person and is shaped by a series of cost–benefit ratios. In contrast, the experiences that precede and generate love are positive, like being attracted to another person, having positive experiences with the person, or feeling loved or cared for by the person. What causes sadness are experiences that have consequences to oneself, such as negative personal experiences or loss of a loved one. As seen in figure 2.1, if the focus of who is the victim in the situation is oneself, then the resulting emotion is sadness, anger, or shame. If the focus is on the other person, the next step in the appraisal process is whether the suffering of the other person satisfies a goal for oneself. Compassion will be most intense to the degree that the outcomes of the suffering of the other person are relevant to oneself or one's goal. So, compassion might be more intense with a victim who is important to one's well-being, such as one's family, relatives, friends, or tribe, or another close social in-group. Feeling similar or emotionally close to the victim intensifies the compassionate response. The other person's suffering might be relevant to one's goals for oneself, and so he or she is happier because of the suffering and feels the emotion of schadenfreude (i.e., "pleasure at the misfortunes of other people" [Van Dijk & Ouwerkerk, 2014, p. 1]). If the person feels a connection with the other and does not feel a selfish benefit to this suffering, he or she moves along the compassion appraisal process to whether the victim is judged to be deserving of help. This might be based on judging that the victim is somehow a good or bad person, whether the victim is considered responsible for his or her suffering, whether the suffering was the result of an uncontrollable event or condition, and whether the victim is warm and trustworthy. If the victim is not considered deserving, the response may be anger, followed by a response of distancing or retaliation. If the person is considered deserving in some way, then the person appraises what might be the costs as well as benefits of helping the victim. The person assesses whether he or she has the resources to deal with this, what the risks are to him- or herself, and whether he or she is being exploited. An important part of this is the coping ability of the person such that the person feels that he or she has the resources and abilities that would outweigh the costs or risks of helping the victim. The more capable one feels of helping, the more likely one is to help. If the person feels too vulnerable, too weak, or unable to help, then he or she is less likely to help and would feel personal distress, fear, or anxiety. The more self-efficacy for the situation and the more emotional regulation the person has, the more likely the person is to approach and attempt to help the suffering person (Goetz et al., 2010).

Application of the appraisal model to clinical practice

This appraisal model from Goetz et al. (2010) applies to all types of compassion in an effort to describe how compassion might be the outcome in the encounter with a suffering person and what might lead to some other response. The challenge in health care, of course, is that we aspire to the ability that all of our actions come from an attitude of compassion in ourselves for our patients. Our professional code is that we respond to all people who are suffering, not just our acquaintances and our in-group. We do not delight in other people's suffering but instead hate that suffering and desire to respond within our capacity. If we delight in the person's suffering because we get more money, then we have moved out of the compassionate mental pathway. (The distinction between being primarily motivated by compassion or by monetary reward will be discussed further in chapter 8.) We then have to deal with the fact of whether we consider many of our patients deserving of help. If they have contributed to their own suffering, are difficult people, or are manipulative, we might not want to help them; or if we do so, we somehow punish them for that. Then we have to navigate whether we have what is needed to help them in terms of resources, time, and skills. We need to feel confident that we can help, and we also have to judge whether we can cope with what will be needed to help this person. Will we be able to maintain focus for hours in a surgery, be able to manage the distress or fear of the patient in order to treat the person, or be as engaged with and invested in every patient for as long as needed? Being a compassionate helping professional requires the mental capacity to navigate each of these steps—having an altruistic motivation, the ability to treat the stranger as well as the acquaintance, helping people no matter how that suffering was caused, having the competence to handle the problems of our specialty, and having the coping ability and emotional regulation to deal with what will be required to attempt to help this patient. All of these are possible but require training and ongoing

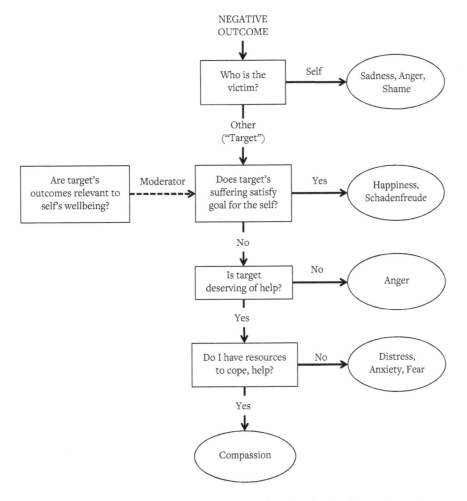

FIGURE 2.1 Appraisal model of compassion displaying how witnessing negative outcomes leads to compassion with moderation of relevance to self (Goetz, 2010, p. 356).

mental conditioning to survive and flourish in this good work.

THE COMPASSIONATE MIND

Dr. Paul Gilbert and Compassion Focused Therapy

Dr. Paul Gilbert is a clinical psychologist and researcher who has also investigated the evolutionary biology and neuroscience involved in compassion. Among his accomplishments is answering the question of how our brains can fall into states of threat, anger, and depression, as well as how our brains respond to compassion received from others (or even from ourselves). Based on this, he founded *compassion focused therapy*, a cognitive behavioral therapy integrating the findings of neuroscience and psychology (Gilbert, 2010). In the fields of the science of compassion as well as the helping professions, his work is also very relevant to understanding what we as clinicians must be able to do to be in a mental state of compassionate caring, what he calls the "compassionate mind" (Gilbert, 2009).

Human brains have three emotion regulations systems

Relying on extensive evolutionary biological and neuroscientific research, Gilbert (2009; Gilbert & Choden, 2014) explains that because our brains are so complex and have so many systems and abilities resulting from millions of years of evolution, our brains need organizing processes or patterns to survive and thrive in the world. There is an older part of our brains that has a variety of desires, dispositions, and emotions that we share with many animals. As we have to deal with life, we are motivated for various goals of detecting and defending against threats, finding food, reproducing, taking care of offspring, and so on. Our brains have to help us detect possibilities for dealing with our needs and motives and then direct our bodies accordingly. Emotions evolved as fast-acting information processors that tell us where we are relative to the goals that are motivating us. The brain organizes and regulates these various emotions and desires according to what we perceive the situation to be and what our response should be. Each one of these systems has evolved to do different things, and without being balanced by the other systems, we can get into a number of problems. The three major emotion regulation systems are (a) the threat-focused and self-protection system, (b) the drive/incentive and resource-seeking system, and (c) the soothing/affiliation and contentment system (see figure 2.2; Gilbert, 2009; Gilbert & Choden, 2014).

Descriptions of the three emotion regulation systems

The *threat-focused and self-protection system* is triggered when a person feels threatened and has to freeze, fight, or flee in order to protect him- or herself. It operates quickly, and when the brain feels threatened, this system has priority over the other systems, such as seeking pleasure or self-soothing. The *drive/incentive and resource-seeking system* has the role of giving us positive feelings to motivate and guide us to obtain the things we need to survive and thrive. We feel pleasurable and energizing feelings as we pursue and obtain what we want (e.g., food, sex, pleasurable experiences, safety, money, status, friendships, closeness, belonging, achievement). If we do not have enough of this system, we are not as successful at attaining our goals. If it is too activated, it can get out of control as we never feel like we have enough. Finally, the *soothing/affiliation and contentment system* is activated when we feel safe, connected, and content, and do not have to defend ourselves or be driven to get something. There is a sense of peaceful well-being, a soothing calmness, a sense of contentment that helps restore a sense of balance in a person. The emotions in this system

> tend to be gentler and slower acting, but when they move through us, they also influence our attention, thinking, and behavior in particular ways, such as opening our attention, softening anxiety, helping us to reason and reflect in more positive, gentler ways, and directing behavior toward slower, calmer actions. (Gilbert & Choden, 2014, p. 63)

This system is also linked to the affection and kindness of affiliation in which the presence of others (e.g., a parent for the baby) is soothing and gives a sense of safety. These three affect regulation systems have to work together to balance each other, and problems emerge when they are in conflict with each other.

Motives organize how our old and new brain work

About two million years ago, as Gilbert explains, our brains gradually became bigger with new

Three Types of Affect Regulation System

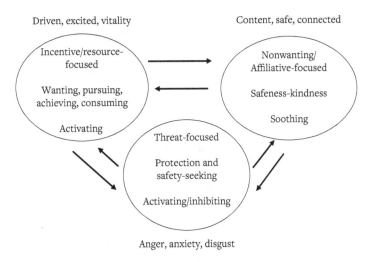

FIGURE 2.2 The interaction between three major emotion regulation systems (Gilbert, 2009, p. 22).

capacities. Humans were able to think, plan, reason, imagine, and fantasize. The human mind was able to be aware of itself and reflect on itself. It became able to think about what was on other people's minds, empathize, and understand what their inner state and motives are. Humans could become aware that they are aware, that is, able to observe their own minds. With that came the sense of being a unique individual. This newer part of the brain allowed for tremendous accomplishments, but these "new-brain capacities can be hijacked and directed by our old-brain passions, motives, and fears. Our planning, reasoning, and imagining can be directed by the emotions and motives of the old brain" (Gilbert & Choden, 2014, p. 43). To deal with this, our brains have the capacity to coordinate all of this by being organized by the motives that we have, those we are aware of, and even those we are not. Our motivation becomes an organizing pattern on the brain that targets the focus of our attention, feelings, thoughts, and behaviors in one particular direction.

Comparing self-focused competition versus a caring mentality in your brain

In terms of a social mentality, Gilbert and Choden (2014) offer the example of *self-focused competition*. Competing directs our attention a certain way so that we can do better than others; it would involve thoughts about how we compare and how we might get ahead; the emotions would be positive when you are winning and negative if you are losing. On the other hand, if we have a *caring mentality*, our attention is focused on the needs or distress of another person; there are feelings of concern for that person—pleasant feelings when that person is relieved and negative feelings if not; our thoughts are focused on how to bring some relief to that person; and our behaviors reflect other-focused actions as opposed to the self-focused competitive mentality in which we concentrate on actions to put ourselves ahead. But it is not possible to do both at the same time. As Gilbert (2009) puts it,

Different patterns in our brain turn different systems on and off. You can't feel relaxed and

frightened or angry and loving at the same time. You can switch between them, of course, but you can't feel them simultaneously. One pattern negates another. (p. 77)

Compassion is a major brain pattern organizer

Compassion is a motivational process that organizes our brains in a certain way. It is a motivational process rather than an emotion. It involves the emotional system of the brain, but it also involves our attention, imagination, thoughts, and behaviors. Compassion is a "major brain pattern generator" (Gilbert, 2009, p. 192) in which we focus our attention in a specific way on the suffering person; we think about ourselves as compassionate and think about how we will be compassionate for the suffering person using whatever competencies we have; we experience certain emotions and engage in an emotional regulation process that enables us to respond to the suffering person. The image Gilbert and Choden (2014) offer is that of a social mentality with compassion as a conductor "of an orchestra

of attention, thinking, and behaving" (p. 46). Gilbert has found that compassion involves two distinct psychologies: (a) the psychology of engaging with suffering and (b) the psychology of alleviating/preventing suffering. The psychology of engaging with suffering "involves the motives, competencies, and preparedness to notice, engage, turn toward, tolerate and make sense of suffering—rather than avoid, deny, be overwhelmed, or dissociate from suffering in self and others" (Gilbert, 2014, p. 19). Second, the psychology of alleviating/preventing suffering "involves the skills and wisdom of knowing (or finding out) what to do about it" (Gilbert, 2014, p. 19). These are the competencies that are action focused. In figure 2.3, the attributes of engagement with the suffering person are in the inner ring, and the skills for alleviating and preventing suffering are in the outer ring. You will notice that all of this is in the context of warmth. In order for compassion to be helpful to others, an emotional quality of loving-kindness, a caring orientation, is needed. This enables the suffering person to perceive the person trying

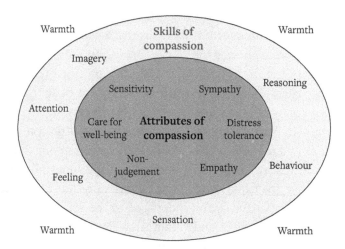

FIGURE 2.3 Multimodal compassionate mind training: The key aspects and attributes of compassion (inner ring) and the skills training required to develop them (outer ring) (Gilbert, 2009, p. 194).

to help him or her as nonthreatening and safe. It tends to calm the person suffering and lower the defenses that people who are vulnerable are likely to have. It also is necessary within the helper because the focus of compassion is the positive desire to alleviate the suffering of the other and its causes (Gilbert, 2009; Gilbert & Choden, 2014).

PSYCHOLOGY OF ENGAGING SUFFERING

As seen in figure 2.3, Gilbert (2009, 2014) has found that there are six interdependent attributes or qualities that are essential for the compassionate response to suffering. Without any one of these, it is more difficult to be compassionate. These are

1. *motivation to care for the well-being of the help recipient,*
2. *attentional sensitivity toward distress and need,*
3. *emotional engagement/sympathy,*
4. *distress tolerance and acceptance,*
5. *empathy, and*
6. *nonjudgment/noncondemning attitude (Gilbert, 2014; Crawford, Gilbert, Gilbert, & Gale, 2011).*

Below I briefly summarize how Gilbert defines each attribute listed above, and I provide examples as I understand that attribute in clinical practice.

Motivation to care for well-being of the help-recipient

The care for the well-being of the other (which sometimes might be yourself when you need

to exercise self-compassion) would be defined as the motivation or genuine desire to care for another who is suffering and promote their well-being. You are motivated and willing to notice, turn toward, and approach the one who is suffering, rather than avoiding or turning away.

Attentional sensitivity toward distress and need

The sensitivity toward distress and need means that you are able to pick up on cues of when someone is in distress or suffering. You have trained yourself to be sensitive and pick up on another's need or to ignore it. There are a number of possibilities about what leads to the ability to notice distress or suffering in another. Here are a few of them. First, a clinician's attachment history and upbringing may be such that he or she does not notice certain emotional and/or behavioral cues that another person is distressed or suffering. This clinician might have been raised in a family that did not attend to the family members' emotional states, or if they did, responded in a berating or negative way. So this clinician either grew up not knowing how to read other people or simply does not notice this because of the conflicted experiences around that. A second possibility is that the clinician has not been trained to notice and be sensitive to cues of distress and suffering. People in health care are exposed to all types of people with all types of problems. A clinician simply might not know how to pick up on those cues. With the emphasis on biomedical training that is common in clinical training, it is quite possible that the clinician simply does not recognize the cues because he or she was never exposed to them and taught what was occurring. Third is the possibility that the clinician is so stressed or busy that he or she is not noticing everything that is going on with another person. Finally, there are times in clinical work that the clinician might become intentionally "hardened" or "calloused" to the signs of distress and suffering in the other. Sometimes, this is thought to be necessary for the work, as when doing a painful procedure on a patient. In order to do the procedure well, the clinician may have been trained to ignore signs of distress for the greater good of the patient's care. (Of course, as discussed in other parts of this book, the ideal would be the ability to tolerate the display of distress in the other and be able to provide a context of safety and support while doing the procedure.)

Emotional engagement/sympathy

Once we have noticed the distress, pain, or suffering of another person, what Gilbert calls sympathy is the ability to allow ourselves to be moved by it. He also calls it emotional empathy, and others might call it empathic resonance. But what it refers to is that we allow ourselves to be emotionally affected by what we see, to become attuned to it and emotionally connected to it rather than being emotionally detached or unmoved by the other's predicament. Of course, compassion does not stop with this, and much of this book is about the fact that simplistic notions of compassion stop with this sympathetic reaction as what compassion is. This is, rather, one of the components of compassionate response, and a very important one. As discussed elsewhere in this book, trying to help without making the emotional connection to what has happened risks a person not being attuned to what is really happening. This lays the foundation for the perspective-taking cognitive aspects of empathy and helps constellate the motivational system for a compassionate response. The trick is to be in the middle between being emotionally detached and emotionally overwhelmed, which is discussed in the balanced compassionate caring model later in this book.

Distress tolerance and acceptance

Complementing the sympathetic emotional connection is the ability to accept and tolerate the emotions that accompany engaging with someone who is in some kind of pain. As discussed in greater detail in this book, true compassion involves the ability to emotionally self-regulate and remain composed in the encounter with distress, pain, and suffering. In working with people who are suffering, it is also "the ability to stay with emotions as they happen" (Gilbert, 2009, p. 200). If I extrapolate this to work in health care, I take this to mean that there are times when, as centered, emotionally composed caregivers, we have to let patients just have their feelings as part of what they need to do to work through a particular situation. For example, if a cancer patient getting a radiation treatment breaks down in tears during the treatment, I need to be able to let that patient cry and to be emotionally present and supportive to that patient. Sometimes people in health care think that they have to fix the patient's feeling immediately, when actually that patient crying at some points is just going be what naturally happens when a person gets overwhelmed and scared in radiation treatment. Distress tolerance means accepting the patient as he or she is right now and not withdrawing or avoiding that patient. As I discuss elsewhere, that supportive accompaniment of that patient through a gesture, a kind look, or an understanding comment can be enormously helpful.

Empathy

Empathy, as Gilbert sets it up in his model, is the ability to understand the perspective of the object of our compassion (including ourselves). As Gilbert (2014) points out, the willingness to engage the distressed person, allow ourselves to emotionally resonate with what is happening in the other, and be able to tolerate the other's distress are all important to the empathic bridging that occurs at this stage. If we do not engage with the suffering, we are not really able to imagine what the person is going through emotionally, cognitively, and experientially. The research literature on empathy is vast, and terms like *empathy* are not always used precisely or consistently. The best definitions refer to empathy having both emotional and cognitive aspects to understanding the other (e.g., Davis, 1994). As Gilbert and others explain, sympathy is an automatic reaction to another person's pain. Empathy actually takes work to understand the other from the other's perspective. As discussed elsewhere in this book, having a sense of what another person is going through both emotionally and cognitively and expressing that to the patient can help that patient hang in with a treatment and actually do what you are recommending he or she do. Knowing that you care helps the patient carry his or her own suffering. Empathy also gives you data—yes, data—about what the person is going through and how he or she sees it. This can be very useful in terms of choosing how to relate optimally with a patient for the goals of treatment.

Nonjudgment/noncondemning attitude

The nonjudgmental quality of compassion refers to the ability to engage with what others are going through without condemning or focusing on being critical. This does not mean one is condoning what is occurring (for example, in situations in which a person makes choices we disagree with) but accepting the individuals as they are and the situation in which they find themselves. Being judgmental both distances us from others, interfering with our understanding, and can make others feel unsafe, with the result that they do not let us engage with them to help them. In medical training, shaming is often used to improve a trainee's performance. Clinicians from this kind of training might think that using this approach with patients is a legitimate way to help them. The reality, however, is that it is not very effective. Patients end up avoiding that type of clinician, getting defensive, or lying to avoid follow-up condemning and shaming comments. Or they fixate on how bad the clinician made them feel rather than really working with their issue. A nonjudgmental/noncondemning accompaniment of patients can actually help patients focus on what they need to do to help their situation.

PSYCHOLOGY OF ALLEVIATING/PREVENTING SUFFERING

Compassion involves two different psychologies: first, the psychology of engaging with suffering discussed above, and second, the psychology of alleviating and/or preventing suffering. It involves the following six skills:

1. *Attention to what is helpful*
2. *Reasoning about what is helpful*
3. *Behavior that is helpful*
4. *Enabling appropriate feeling*

5. *Use of imagery and meditation-like practices to stimulate positive emotion systems*

6. *Sensory work that generates physical reactions contributing to affect regulation and compassion in the helper (Gilbert, 2009, 2014)*

Attention to what is helpful

To be as effective as possible in caring for someone who is suffering, you have to be able to pay attention to what is helpful to others (or even yourself). I am extrapolating this to health care work from Gilbert's work, but for clinicians I think this is the unbiased ability to observe what is helpful or not helpful to your patient. Here are a few examples. Sometimes people in health care recommend treatments that might work for many people but work differently for some patients. I have heard of patients having a negative reaction to a medication and the physician automatically attributing that negative reaction to something else besides the medication or even blaming the patient. Yes, sometimes there are other reasons for the negative reaction, and sometimes patients are doing something that interferes with the treatment. My point in this case is that the physician *automatically* attributed the negative reaction to anything but the medication. That bias kept the physician from really paying attention to what was causing the negative reaction in this particular patient. Are we keenly observant about how this treatment is going for this patient? Another example is the controversy these days about overuse of protocols in delivery of medicine. The problem is that sometimes a protocol is not helpful, or there are confounding factors that might change how a protocol is implemented. The point is that a clinician who is in a compassionate mind will be work to be aware of what is and is not helpful to a patient.

Reasoning about what is helpful

Compassion is more than emotions. Compassionate thinking requires that we use our rational minds to think through a situation, weigh the evidence, and analyze all aspects of our work with a patient. It involves honing our process of clinical judgment, always being mindful of our own biases or limitations as we treat patients.

Behavior that is helpful

Gilbert explains that when we come from a place of compassion in work with patients, we consider how we will show this in our behavior to our patients. This requires an ability to take time to reflect on how to do this for a particular patient. Usually, that means that whatever we do is an extension of kindness, even when we are confronting a patient. Later in this book, I will consider the problem of different perceptions of our behavior by different patients, and I will provide some ways of figuring out how to show compassionate behavior. Finally, Gilbert notes that to be compassionate requires courage to follow through on doing what a patient needs. Whether it be doing surgery, implementing a course of medical treatment, treating a burn patient, or challenging patients to take better care of themselves, a compassionate mind requires courage to do difficult things.

Enabling appropriate feeling

This is the ability to use our feelings first to empathize with a patient's experience and then to use this empathic understanding for the healing process. Also, it is the ability to use our emotions to help alleviate the suffering of the patient. This would involve using our nonverbal (eye contact, voice tone, body posture, touch, etc.) and verbal responses to convey emotions of warmth, support, friendliness, and so on. In chapter 5, I will summarize some of the research on this, and throughout the book the use of emotions in the healing process will be described.

Use of imagery and meditation-like practices to stimulate positive emotion systems

The skill Gilbert is referring to here is that the images we cultivate in our minds and how we train our minds about compassion organize our minds in a compassionate direction. Mind-training practices stimulate emotional reactions and cognitive systems in our brains and bodies, providing a conditioning (like exercise provides conditioning to an athlete) so that we are prepared and able to respond to a patient from a place of compassionate care. Much of this book will present research on the importance of mind-training practices that enable clinicians to respond effectively to patients.

Sensory Focusing

While Gilbert's work has not explicitly discussed this in terms of patient care, I believe there a number of ways to understand sensory focusing in terms of using the sensory modalities to keep ourselves in a compassionate mind. For example, this might involve breathing techniques to center ourselves or maintain composure. Techniques like Heart-Math and mindfulness meditation are ways to calm the body and, in this way, calm our minds so that we can focus well on what is occurring in the patient.

CONCLUSION

The commonly used words *caring* and *compassionate* have been favorites in health care everywhere from applications to medical school to hospital and pharmaceutical advertising. They have been used in overly sentimentalized, overly emotionalized, and overly gender-stereotyped ways that have made them clichéd phrases of little use to clinicians, who have one of the most difficult jobs there is. The words have lost their usefulness because they are distortions of what real caring and compassion are; if clinicians try to rely on these concepts with their sentimentalized definitions, it will create further problems for them. Defining caring and compassion relying on the scientific work of caring and compassion can restore their usefulness and bring us back to the soul of our helping professions as we first imagined them. Caring is defined as *the sincere desire to promote or attend to the well-being of another and the attitudes, emotions, and behaviors originating from this concern for another person.* Compassion is defined as *noticing or recognizing suffering, being empathically resonant with that person, desiring to relieve that suffering, and acting to attempt to alleviate that suffering in some way.* When we use the phrase *compassionate caring* in this book, caring is viewed as the general attitude that the clinician has in all interactions, while compassionate is more focused on the clinician's responsiveness to pain and suffering as it arises. This compassion, however, should not be viewed as simply an emotional response or just good communication skills, a.k.a. bedside manner. As seen with the two scientific models of compassion, compassion is a motivational process that generates a particular pattern in the brain that aligns our attention, cognition, and emotions in a compassionate response to the patient. It is the focused channeling of our competence in response to patient suffering, not simply empathic resonation and expressions of concern. This will be the focus in this book in terms of how this compassionate mind, as Paul Gilbert calls it, provides maximal benefits to our patients but also acts as a buffer against burnout. The next chapter will provide a summary of the newest research on the biology and neuroscience of compassion, followed by an integrative model of the clinician compassion mindset process in chapter 4.

QUESTIONS FOR DISCUSSION

1. What is your reaction to having this scientific understanding of caring and compassion, given how you defined caring and compassion beforehand?
2. How would you respond to someone who says, "Compassion is an emotion and interferes with your clinical judgment"?

REFERENCES

Batson, C. D. (2011). *Altruism in humans*. New York, NY: Oxford University Press.

Crawford, P., Gilbert, P., Gilbert, J., & Gale, C. (2011). The language of compassion. *Taiwan International ESP Journal*, *3*(1), 1–16.

Damasio, A. (2006). *Descartes' error: Emotion, reason and the human brain*. London, UK: Vintage Books.

Davis, M. H. (1994). *Empathy: A social psychological approach*. Madison, WI: Brown & Benchmark.

England, P., Folbre, N., & Leana, C. (2012). Motivating care. In N. Folbre (Ed.), *For love and money: Care provision in the United States* (pp. 21–39). New York, NY: Russell Sage Foundation.

Folbre, N. (2001). *The invisible heart: Economics and family values*. New York, NY: New Press.

Gadow, S. A. (1985). Nurse and patient: The caring relationship. In A. Bishop (Ed.), *Caring, curing, coping* (pp. 31–43). Tuscaloosa: University of Alabama Press.

Gilbert, P. (2009). *The compassionate mind: A new approach to life's challenges*. Oakland, CA: New Harbinger.

Gilbert, P. (2010). *Compassion focused therapy*. New York, NY: Routledge.

Gilbert, P. (2014). The origins and nature of compassion focused therapy. *British Journal of Clinical Psychology*, *53*, 6–41.

Gilbert, P., & Choden. (2014). *Mindful compassion: How the science of compassion can help you understand your emotions, live in the present, and connect deeply with others*. Oakland, CA: New Harbinger.

Goetz, J. L., Keltner, D., & Simon-Thomas, E. (2010). Compassion: An evolutionary analysis and empirical review. *Psychological Bulletin*, *136*(3), 351–374.

Jazaieri, H., Lee, I. A., McGonigal, K., Jinpa, T., Doty, J. R., Gross, J. J., & Goldin, P. R. (2016). A wandering mind is a less caring mind: Daily experience sampling during compassion meditation training. *Journal of Positive Psychology*, *11*(1), 37–50.

Jazaieri, H., McGonigal, K., Jinpa, T., Doty, J. R., Gross, J. J., & Goldin, P. R. (2014). A randomized controlled trial of compassion cultivation training: Effects on mindfulness, affect, and emotion regulation. *Motivation and Emotion*, *38*, 23–35.

Jinpa, T. (2012, July). *Nature, origins and developments of compassion: Perspectives from a Buddhist understanding*. Presentation at the Science of Compassion: Origins,

Measures, and Interventions Conference, Telluride, CO.

Kim, J. W., Kim, S. E., Kim, J. J., Jeong, B., Park, C. H., Son, A. R., ... Ki, S. W. (2009). Compassionate attitude towards others' suffering activates the mesolimbic neural system. *Neuropsychologia, 47*, 2073–2081.

Mayeroff, M. (1971). *On caring*. New York, NY: HarperCollins.

McNaughton, N., & LeBlanc, V. (2012). Perturbations: The central role of emotional competence in medical training. In B. D. Hodges & L. Lingard (Eds.), *The question of competence: Reconsidering medical education in the twenty-first century* (pp. 70–96). Ithaca, NY: ILR Press.

More, E. S. (1994). "Empathy" enters the profession of medicine. In E. S. More & M. A. Milligan (Eds.), *The empathic practitioner: Empathy, gender, and medicine* (pp. 19–39). New Brunswick, NJ: Rutgers University Press.

Nelson, J., & Watson, J. (Eds.). (2012). *Measuring caring: International research on Caritas Healing*. New York, NY: Springer.

Sinclair, S., Beamer, K., Hack, T. F., McClement, S., Bouchal, S. R., Chochinov, H. M., & Hagen, N. A. (2017). Sympathy, empathy, and compassion: A grounded theory study of palliative care patients' understandings, experiences, and preferences. *Palliative Medicine, 31*(5), 437–447.

Sinclair, S., McClement, S., Raffin-Bouchal, S., Hack, T. F., Hagen, N. A., McConnell, S., & Chochinov, H. M. (2016). Compassion in health care: An empirical model. *Journal of Pain and Symptom Management, 51*(2), 193–203.

Strauss, C., Taylor, B. L., Gu, J., Kuyken, W., Baer, R., Jones, F., & Cavanagh, K. (2016). What is compassion and how can we measure it? A review of definitions and measures. *Clinical Psychology Review, 47*, 15–27.

Van Dijk, W. W., & Ouwerkerk, J. W. (2014). Introduction to schadenfreude. In W. W. van Dijk & J. W. Ouwerkerk (Eds.), *Schadenfreude: Understanding pleasure at the misfortunes of others* (pp. 1–13). Cambridge, UK: Cambridge University Press.

Watson, J. (1988). *Nursing: Human science and human care*. New York, NY: National League for Nursing.

Watson, J. (2008). *Nursing: The philosophy and science of caring* (Rev. ed.). Boulder: University Press of Colorado.

Watson, J. (2009). *Assessing and measuring caring in nursing and health sciences* (2nd ed.). New York, NY: Springer.

Watson, J. (2012). *Human caring science: A theory of nursing*. Sudbury, MA: Jones & Bartlett.

Wuthnow, R. (1991). *Acts of compassion: Caring for others and helping ourselves*. Princeton, NJ: Princeton University Press.

CREDITS

"We're hardwired to be compassionate."

Chapter Sections:

CHAPTER 3

Biology and Neuroscience of Compassionate Caring

Questions to consider before reading this chapter:

1. Based on your knowledge before you read this chapter, what happens in the brain when the person is experiencing empathy and compassion?

2. How relevant or helpful to your clinical practice would it be, do you think, to know some biology and neuroscience of compassionate caring?

INTRODUCTION

The new field of the science of compassion is revolutionizing how we understand what is occurring within the clinician and is providing new support for how compassionate caring improves medical outcomes and the patient experience. Human beings are hardwired for compassion, and this has major implications for the practice of medicine. While we highly esteem compassionate caring in health care, we as clinicians have not thought of compassion in terms of our biology. But with the tremendous research on the science of compassion in the past 20 years, we now have critical information from biology, neuroscience, and psychology that has major implications for how we work with patients and how compassion in the clinician is actually critically important to maximizing clinician well-being and buffering burnout in working with patients.

The past 20 years of research on the science of compassion (Seppala et al., 2017) has just begun to be applied to the practice of medicine. While much more research needs to be done, we are already at the stage in which the discoveries in the science of compassion can be applied to medical training and medical practice. In this chapter, I highlight a number of key findings from the science of compassion that will provide the foundation for the rest of this book. First, I will briefly summarize the insights from evolutionary biology that describe how compassion is indeed how we are constructed and how the evolution of compassion facilitated our success as a species. Second, the polyvagal theory of Stephen Porges delineates how the perception of safety is critical for social engagement and the exercise of compassion. While generally applicable to mammals, the polyvagal theory has profound implications for the patient–clinician interaction. Third, the neurobiological framework of the human caregiving system will be described through the selective investment theory, a way to understand how human beings are disposed to be altruistic. Fourth, the recent findings in the neuroscience of empathy will be explained in terms of the complex nature of the mirror neuron system and the neurocognitive process of empathy. Finally, related to the neuroscience of empathy, the phenomenon of compassion as neurally distinct from empathy will be presented.

EVOLUTIONARY BIOLOGY AND COMPASSION

Darwin and compassion as a product of evolution

When it comes to human nature, many people have come to think that humans are innately selfish, competitive, and violent. Darwin's "survival of the fittest" is used as a kind of reluctant admission that we humans were just built that way in order to survive. Yet evolutionary biology itself has found that the evolution and success of humans as a species may very well be because of our ability to care for each other. Paul Ekman found that the negative portrayal of Darwin is quite mistaken and that Darwin actually discussed how natural selection would favor a species that was compassionate. As Darwin wrote in *The Descent of Man, and Selection in Relation to Sex*,

> in however complex a manner this feeling may have originated, as it is one of high importance to all those animals which aid and defend one another, it will have been increased through natural selection; for those communities, which included the greatest number of the most

> sympathetic members, would flourish best, and rear the greatest number of offspring. (as cited in Ekman, 2010, p. 557)

Darwin's explanation for the origin of compassion was that when a person witnesses pain or distress in another person, the witnessing person empathically experiences that distress. Acting to help the other person would be a way to decrease the empathic distress the witness experiences (Ekman, 2010).

> Empathic concern evolved as part of the parental instinct among higher mammals, especially humans. If mammalian parents were not intensely interested in the welfare of their very vulnerable progeny, these species would quickly die out. Humans have doubtless inherited key aspects of their parental instinct from ancestors they share with other higher mammalian species, but in humans this instinct has become considerably more flexible. The human parental instinct goes well beyond nursing, providing other kinds of food, protecting, and keeping the young close—the activities that characterize parental care in most other mammalian species. It includes inferences about the desires and feelings of the child (e.g., "Is that a hungry cry or a wet cry?" "She won't like the fireworks; they'll be too loud.") It also includes goal-directed motives and appraisal-based emotions. (Batson, 2010, p. 25)

Why kindness is most valued from an evolutionary perspective

Giving and receiving care is fundamental to the survival of humans. So, the wonderful psychophysiological caregiving dynamic evident in infants and their parents is interwoven throughout human life. We need each other to survive as a species, not only to reproduce and raise offspring but also to help each other in our needs and distress. According to Keltner's (2009) review and his own work, the research on this is that the capacity to be kind is what is most prized and essential in humans and what makes it possible for humans to survive and thrive. Mate selection tends to favor those partners who are kind, because they are most likely to help with survival of the species: they are most likely to give more of their own resources, more likely to give physical care to their offspring, and more likely to stay for the long haul. Groups characterized by kindness, mutual support, and cooperation are more likely to survive, deal with threats, and promote health among its members. Furthermore, this kindness that is built into our DNA leads us to recognize and treasure those whose kindness will help us get through the challenges of life. As Keltner (2009) puts it,

> so important was the capacity to care to the survival of our species that new data suggest that we have been wired to identify the trustworthy and reliable caretakers among us, and preferentially trust, and give resources to, those vagal superstars. (p. 246)

Especially important for our purposes in this book, this is probably one of the main reasons people in health care are so valued—because it is their kindness, which is extended through their attentive competence, that helps us survive and thrive. It is not so much a superficial economic transaction that characterizes the relationship between patient and clinician—it is a relationship that taps into the primordial compassionate construction of who we are as human beings.

POLYVAGAL THEORY AND IMPLICATIONS FOR PATIENT CARE

Introduction to the physiological impact of clinician bedside manner

Would you believe that you trigger a fight-or-flight stress response in your patient in seconds if you do not make eye contact, or if you have flat, emotionless facial features, talk in a monotone voice, and are not warm in greeting the patient? The answer is yes. Some clinicians would argue that bedside manner is simply customer relations and not absolutely essential to a clinical interaction with a patient. They would argue that it really does no actual harm to the patient to be more detached and emotionally unexpressive. They would argue that while it might increase patient satisfaction to have a warm facial expression, safe hand gestures, an animated voice, and some eyelid lifting, this more positive initial clinician behavior does not make that much of a difference from a human physiological perspective. What matters, they would argue, is that the clinician is focusing on the problem the patient has and getting a solution as efficiently as possible. But this is completely wrong. The stressed patient's response to the clinician with the flat, emotionless face and no eye contact is a neurobiologically programmed reaction based on how the mammalian nervous system evolved to protect itself in dangerous situations and to assess when it was safe to interact with another person. Clinician warmth is not just a social nicety. Clinician warmth is intimately connected to how the human mammal perceives that it is safe to be treated by you. Not to know this is to create problems automatically for a patient that are caused by you being ignorant of the evolutionary construction of human beings.

Polyvagal theory as the neurophysiological foundation of the clinician–patient interaction

Mammals and especially primates have evolved neural circuits that help them assess the risk of a particular situation and whether they should engage in self-protective maneuvers or can safely engage with the other animal. Discovered and researched by Stephen Porges (2011), the polyvagal theory describes how the mammalian autonomic nervous system provides the neurophysiological mechanisms making possible the social behavior of mammals. Mammals must socially engage with each other in order to survive. Mammals need each other to reproduce, nurse, and survive. The success of mammals has depended on their ability to cooperate with each other, which requires a sense of being safe with each other. Neurophysiological processes tie together body states with behavior. Face-to-face interactions are one of the primary means that mammals use to assess whether they can approach each other or should prepare to defend themselves. These processes are key factors in the way patients responds to clinician bedside manner, especially in the first minutes of a clinical interaction. If I have very limited time to teach clinicians about the science of compassion, I make sure to teach about the polyvagal theory because it is the neurophysiological foundation of patient–clinician interaction.

Evolution of a psychophysiological caregiving system in mammals

The human brain is the result of a long evolutionary process building on the reptilian brain (which had its own mode for adaptation and survival). Driven by survival, reptilian behaviors were mainly foraging, feeding, and stalking. They did not spend much time or energy in social interactions such as reproducing and parenting. Reptiles were characterized by a more defensive strategy. They have less metabolic demands, are less oxygen dependent, and can have very low heart rates. Mammals have high metabolic demands, are very dependent on a plentiful supply of oxygen, and cannot live long with slowed heart rates. Also, unlike tortoise young that hatch and do not require parental nurturance, mammal infants are not able to take care of themselves and so need to be nurtured. Thus, a complex psychophysiological caregiving system developed in which the communication systems involve signaling needs (e.g., the baby's needs) and interpreting the signaling (e.g., parent understands what the infant needs and responds). That is, alongside the physiological evolution of the human mammal was also the evolution of a social cueing system for caregiving and body-state regulation. Human physiology, then, is constructed in such a way that certain facial and vocal cues in an infant in distress, for example, trigger a response from the parental caregiver. The parental caregiver, relying on the operation of the vagus nerve, communicates concern and reassurance to the infant by means of the caregiver's sympathetic facial expressions (e.g., oblique eyebrows, lip press) and soothing voice that provide comfort in the infant as the caregiver responds to the infant's needs (Keltner, 2009).

Vagus nerve evolved as the nerve of compassion

Because of who we are as human mammals, we are wired to signal our needs and wired to pick up and respond to others' needs. Our whole physiologies support our abilities to respond to distress and harm in another, and the vagus nerve is what Porges concluded was the nerve of compassion, or what Oveis and Keltner described as "a bundle of caretaking nerves" (Keltner, 2009, p. 232). Keltner (2009) summarizes this wonderfully in the following passage:

The profound vulnerability of our big-brained offspring wired into us an instinct to care. It created in us a biologically based capacity for sympathy. It produced a vagus nerve, loaded with oxytocin receptors, the provenance of feelings of devotion, sacrifice, and trust. It yielded a rich set of signals—empathic sighs, oblique eyebrows, and soothing touch, which trigger vagus nerve response and oxytocin and opioid release in the recipient, giving rise to oceanic feelings of connection. It produced specific cells underneath the surface of the skin that fire in response to the slow, soothing touch of compassion. The selection pressure to take care produced the indescribably beautiful qualities of the offspring themselves, designed, as many have argued to reset the parents' nervous systems toward more caretaking settings. (p. 244)

Overview of the vagus nerve

The vagus nerve is the tenth cranial nerve and a part of the parasympathetic nervous system in the autonomic nervous system. The vagus nerve is a kind of tube or conduit through which various neural pathways go from different areas of the brainstem to the facial muscles, the vocal muscles, the heart, the lungs, the gastrointestinal tract, and the abdominal viscera, including the kidneys and the liver. The vagus is partly an efferent pathway (i.e., sending signals from the brain to the muscles, organs, etc. of the body in response to sensory input), but 80% of the vagal fibers are afferent (i.e., carrying signals from the senses to the spinal cord and brain; Porges, 1995). There are two branches of the vagus nerve, each with its own adaptive behavioral strategy: one a phylogenetic vestige of the more primitive vertebrate system, the unmyelinated vagus coming from the dorsal motor nucleus in the brainstem; and the other the myelinated vagus originating in the nucleus ambiguus of the brain stem (Porges, 2011).

Polyvagal theory and the response hierarchy of mammals

The polyvagal theory proposes that there are three distinct subsystems, which are the three phylogenetic stages in how the mammalian autonomic nervous system developed from the most phylogenetically primitive to the most evolved subsystem in mammals. These three neural circuits are arranged in a response hierarchy that regulates the physiological and behavioral adaptation to life-threatening, dangerous, and safe environments. Each has a different response strategy in order to perform a specific adaptive function. The phylogenetically oldest part of the vagus is the unmyelinated vagus that most vertebrates have (e.g., reptiles, amphibians), and the response to a life-threatening situation is *immobilization with fear*. Here, the animal freezes or feigns death to protect itself. This could be vasovagal syncope or immobility due to shock response in humans. The second subsystem, called *mobilization*, centers on the sympathetic–adrenal nervous system. When this is activated, it is a fight-or-flight mode. This occurs in moderate or even extreme danger. The third system, associated with the myelinated vagus, is the social communication system, the *social engagement system*. Here, people are able to approach and be in close proximity with each other. Humans, as with all mammals, have to be able to use each other to function, such as when nursing offspring, reproducing, helping each other, and cooperating; to do so, they need to be able to turn off their stress responses and feel safe with each other. At its best, it is a kind of *immobilization without fear* state (i.e., a state of still relaxation), which supports the human's health, growth, healing, and restoration (Porges, 2011).

The social engagement system and the indicators of social engagement

The social engagement system is what helps humans get close to each other. In order to survive and thrive, mammals evolved to be able to detect whether the environment is safe, assess whether something is a threat, and communicate with others in their social unit. It is the way humans interact with each other in such a way that they feel safe with each other, can approach and be close to each other, and be able to touch each other. It involves a complex interaction of bodily cues, especially in the face and vocalizations. As Porges (2001) explains it,

> the social engagement system has a control component in the cortex (upper motor neurons) that regulates brainstem nuclei (i.e. lower motor neurons controlling special visceral efferent pathways) to control: eyelid opening (e.g. looking); facial muscles (e.g. emotional expression); middle-ear muscles (e.g. extracting human voice from background noise); muscles of mastication (e.g. ingestion); laryngeal and pharyngeal muscles (e.g. vocalization and language); and head-turning muscles (e.g. social gesture and orientation). Collectively, these muscles both regulate social engagement and modulate the sensory features of the environment. The neural control of these muscles contributes to the richness of both social expressions and social experiences. (p. 124)

The social engagement system includes the neural regulation of the striated muscles of the face and head (facial muscles, middle ear muscles, eyelids, pharynx, larynx, muscles of mastication, head nods). That is, the social engagement system involves facial expressions, voice intonation, and middle ear preparation to engage in listening. Listening is a motor act in which the facial nerve tenses the middle ear muscles so that one can tune in to the voice of another person, even in a noisy place. The same nerve also controls eyelid lifting, which in the listener is one of the signals to the other person that the listener is cueing into him or her and is interested in what that person is going to say. The social engagement system is linked with the myelinated vagus, which is what turns off our defenses, calms and soothes us, and makes our metabolic systems more efficient (Porges, 2012; Dykema, 2006).

Social engagement can only operate if persons feel safe

Porges has described how the social engagement system can only operate when individuals perceive that they are in a safe environment, and that is the only way compassion can occur. The phylogenetically ordered response hierarchy of the vagus nerve comes into play here, in which the newer, more evolved circuits of the autonomic nervous system are used first, and if this does not help the person feel safe, he or she then uses older circuits. If a person does not feel safe, he or she then moves into a mobilization or the fight-or-flight mode; and if the danger is perceived to be extreme, the person moves into the immobilization with fear mode, shutting itself down in the face of perceived extreme danger. This proceeds according to the Jacksonian principle of dissolution, in which phylogenetically newer/higher neural circuits inhibit older/lower neural circuits; if higher circuits are negated, then the lower ones become operative (Porges, 2009).

Neuroception is the neural process of assessing safety

To switch from defensive to social engagement strategies, the human nervous system has to do two things. First, it has to assess the risk in what is encountered in the environment. Second, if the environment is perceived to be safe, it then has to inhibit the primitive limbic structures that regulate whether the person reacts with fight, flight, or freeze responses. The neural process involved in this is called *neuroception*. This process is distinct from perception and is an unconscious process. It appears to involve subcortical limbic structures. Neuroception is the neural process that distinguishes environmental and visceral/bodily features to determine if the organism is safe, in danger, or in a life-threatening situation (Porges, 2007). In the safe situation, the defenses are turned off, allowing social engagement to emerge and the viscera to calm down. Porges states that the temporal cortex appears to be involved in evaluating the intentions of the facial expressions, the quality of the voice, and the hand movements. The temporal cortex then modulates the limbic system through the central nucleus of the amygdala and the periaqueductal gray (Porges, 2009).

Cues that make a person feel safe or unsafe

What are cues that make a person feel safe? Certainly, seeing familiar faces and hearing familiar voices. Warm and expressive facial expressions communicate safety; listening behavior, eyelid lifting, and eye crinkling also provide safety cues; pleasant vocal inflection and rhythm and safe hand gestures communicating warmth promote a sense of safety. Cues that make people feel unsafe are not making eye contact, eyes dropping away, turning the face away, and emotionally flat facial features. A voice that is a monotone also triggers a stressed response, as does the other person not being inviting or warm. A lot of loud background noise also contributes to a perception of danger (Porges, 2011, 2012).

How the clinician appears to the patient in terms of these features triggers automatic visceral responses in the patient. If the clinician turns his or her head away, drops his or her eyes, and talks in a monotone voice without intonation, the patient feels that the clinician is disconnected. The patient then might feel unsafe, that he or she is being judged, or that the clinician does not like him or her. If your clinician does not like you, that feels dangerous. The patient may also think that the clinician is not motivated to engage with him or her. (See figure 3.1.)

With safety comes the possibility of compassion mediated by the vagus nerve

Applying polyvagal theory to compassion, Porges (2012) states, "Compassion is a manifestation of our biological need to engage and to bond with others." Social engagement behaviors such as listening to people and making eye contact actually physically relax the person we are attending to. As the other person perceives these safety cues, the hypervigilance and fears of the person are given up; the vagus communicates that throughout its end points, calming the viscera, the heart, and the lungs. The other person is then able to enter social engagement and be fully receptive to the help of the other person. Mediated by the vagus nerve, the person being helped is soothed and attuned to the help of the other person. The bodily feelings of calmness increase social engagement behaviors and decrease fears of being judged or attacked. Compassion and compassionate behaviors are then able to be expressed in this state of social engagement and immobilization without fear (i.e., state of still relaxation) (Porges, 2012). The vagus nerve is the key nerve in the capacity to

Polyvagal Neural Response of Patient to Clinician in the First Few Moments of a Patient Interaction

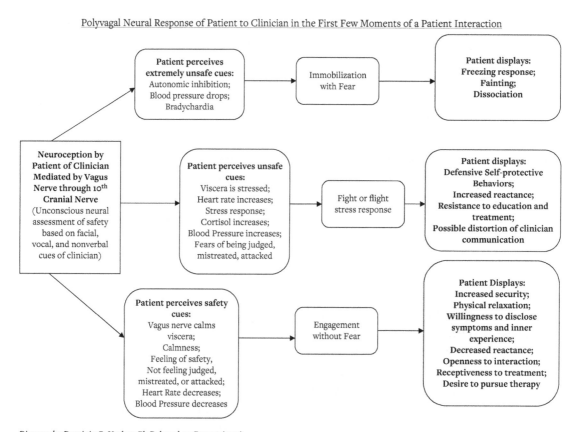

Diagram by Dominic O. Vachon Ph.D. based on Porges (2011)

FIGURE 3.1 Polyvagal neural response of a patient to a clinician in the first few moments of a patient interaction.

experience compassion. Whether a person will feel concerned and motivated to help a suffering person will depend on the subcortical structures and the vagus nerve's ability to handle the feelings that are produced when a person witnesses suffering in another (Simon-Thomas, 2015).

Compassion associated with increased vagal nerve activity

Vagal activity is measured by respiratory sinus arrhythmia (RSA), which is the heart rate variability during the respiratory cycle. When a person inhales, vagal nerve activity is suppressed, which results in acceleration of the heart rate. When a person exhales, the vagal nerve activity increases, which leads to deceleration of the heart rate. RSA is the measure of vagal control of the heart. In four studies, Stellar, Cohen, Oveis, and Keltner (2015) tested whether a compassionate reaction to suffering was related to greater vagal activity and whether compassion was uniquely related to more vagal activity compared to other positive emotions. They found that when research participants experienced compassion, they had more vagal activity as measured by RSA than with other emotional states or when the participants were in a neutral state. Higher RSA was associated with compassion but not with pride or feeling inspired. This adds support to the contention that compassion is a distinct emotion. Higher RSA in response to suffering in videos was associated with a lower heart rate and lower respiration rate. Furthermore, when participants had increases in RSA while watching videos of families with children who had cancer, they tended to have higher self-ratings of compassion-focused emotions, and naive observers rated them as having higher nonverbal and verbal expression of compassion but not higher distress. Overall, compassion is associated with parasympathetic activity through the vagus nerve.

Compassion state associated with optimal emotional regulation

Health care clinicians often imagine compassionate emotion as being in a distressed or overwhelmed emotional state. What is very important to note here is that compassion is associated with greater vagal activity, which calms the heart and respiration of the person encountering suffering in another. *Compassion is associated with decreased personal distress.* In a compassionate state, the negative emotions and distress of the helper are downregulated as he or she approaches the suffering person. If the person encountering suffering has increased personal distress, he or she would tend to withdraw or distance from the suffering person (and would have less vagal control). If clinicians worry that feeling compassion would compromise their judgment or overwhelm them emotionally, they need to know this is not actually compassion. When a clinician enters a state of compassion, he or she is entering an optimally, emotionally regulated state that enables approaching the suffering person, and which is also the best state for objective problem-solving. *The physiological changes in the body during social engagement and compassion are what prepare and enable the helper to engage the suffering person in a soothing and caring manner* (Stellar & Keltner, 2014).

Clinicians also need to feel safety for compassion to occur

While the initial work on the polyvagal theory has focused on the importance of a helper creating a sense of safety for the person who is receiving help, it is also the case that the clinician is also assessing safety for him- or herself. While our focus is on helping patients so that they can engage with their clinician without being stressed by the clinician, the clinician is also a mammal who is assessing safety upon meeting a patient. A clinician may feel stressed by a patient who is threatening to him or her. Clinicians are understandably placed in a fight-or-flight mode when patients are hostile, highly angry, threatening the clinician physically (e.g., attempting to hit the clinician), or threatening the clinician psychologically (e.g., threatening lawsuits or going to the media about the clinician). This will trump the compassionate social engagement process with the patient as well. In these types of situations, the clinician has to take extra steps using safety procedures and boundaries in order to stay in a compassionate frame of mind in working with the patient. I will discuss this further in later chapters of this book.

THE NEUROBIOLOGICAL FRAMEWORK OF THE HUMAN CAREGIVING SYSTEM: SELECTIVE INVESTMENT THEORY

In the introduction to the proceedings of a conference on the integrative neurobiology of affiliation in March 1996, Carter, Lederhendler, and Kirkpatrick (1997) noted that the science of social affiliation and social behavior in general tended to be done in the areas of the social sciences (psychology, anthropology, sociology), evolutionary biology, and psychiatry. But the physiological and neural processes that underlie affiliative behaviors tended not to be researched until the late 1990s. As I will discuss later in this book, in hindsight the separation between the social sciences and the biological sciences, for example, is absurd. Yet we still train medical students and other health professionals with the implicit idea that the social sciences are separate from the other sciences. The research on the physiology and neuroscience of social affiliation exposes our ridiculous assumptions about thinking about social behavior without considering that, of course, this is all embedded in human physiology and the result of a long evolutionary process. Just as our students need to understand basic chemistry in order to understand biochemistry, and biochemistry is needed to understand physiological processes in the body, so too the scientific chain continues such that physiological processes and neural mechanisms would be needed to understand what is happening in social behaviors.

Patient and clinician dynamics are connected to attachment psychology

The nature of human attachment is fundamental to understanding what is happening between a patient and a clinician. If the patient feels safe with the clinician, he or she "attaches" for a period of time to the clinician. The clinician, too, temporarily "attaches" to the patient in response to the patient's need. While we most commonly think of attachment when it comes to infants attaching to their parents, attachment pervades

being human and is considered integral to the human species (Bowlby, 2005a, 2005b). Attachment is a "selective social or emotional bond" (Carter, 1998, p. 780) and is a major component of how we define human love. Bowlby (2005b) defines attachment behavior as

> *any form of behaviour that results in a person attaining or maintaining proximity to some other clearly identified individual who is conceived as better able to cope with the world. It is most obvious whenever the person is frightened, fatigued, or sick, and is assuaged by comforting and caregiving. At other times the behavior is less in evidence. Nevertheless for a person to know that an attachment figure is available and responsive give him [or her] a strong and pervasive feeling of security, and so encourages him [or her] to value and continue the relationship. Whilst attachment behaviour is at its most obvious in early childhood, it can be observed throughout the life cycle, especially in emergencies. ... The biological function attributed to it is that of protection. To remain within easy access of a familiar individual known to be ready and willing to come to our aid in an emergency is clearly a good insurance policy—whatever our age. (pp. 26–27)*

Thus, when a patient attaches to us, the patient (and we) are tapped into a phylogenetically deep dynamic. The very thought of patients "attaching" to clinicians is repellent to many clinicians who associate "attachment" with dependency and burden. They imagine the attachment as not integral to the patient care. They would prefer the patient act like a culture in a petri dish that they can assess and treat with "no strings attached." Given our infatuation with technology as the imagined source of healing as well as our general state of being overworked, patient attachment feels like unnecessary work. Yet taking care of people who are sick or injured is embedded in how humans are constructed. It is disastrous for us to ignore this or to try to work with patients in spite of it. When patients are in need, they seek help, and help comes by attaching to someone who can provide it. Bowlby explains that one of the most important clinical features of attachment is the intensity of the emotion aroused by the relationship. When the relationship is going well, there is a sense of security and joy. When the relationship is not going well or is threatened, emotions like anger and anxiety emerge. When the relationship is broken or ended, there can be grief or a depressed reaction (Bowlby, 1980). We can certainly perceive how this operates in our patient care, just as we can in human life in general.

Neuroendocrinology of social attachment

Beneath attachment behavior, however, is the fact that social attachment (and love in general) has neurobiological mechanisms and neurobiological effects. In other words, social attachment has physiological effects on humans. As Carter (1998) puts it, "Love and social attachments function to facilitate reproduction, provide a sense of security and reduce feelings of stress or anxiety" (p. 780). Social attachment characterizes human beings as a species. In reviewing the neuroendocrinology in social attachment, Carter notes that new social bonds are formed in response to stressful conditions and anxiety. Or the encounter with a threatening situation can strengthen existing social bonds or motivate a person to seek the "secure base" of an attachment figure. With stress comes increased activity in the hypothalamic-pituitary-adrenal (HPA) axis and the release of hormones from the HPA axis such as cortisol; this stimulates the development of social attachments. The stressed individual seeks proximity with others who might calm this stress. Positive social behaviors

and social bonds create stress-reducing or anxiolytic physiological states reducing the activity of the HPA axis. Neuropeptides, especially oxytocin and sometimes vasopressin, are associated with facilitating social behaviors and social bonding. They appear to reduce defensive behaviors, fear, anxiety, and stress; help overcome neophobia (i.e., fear of what is novel or unfamiliar); and facilitate positive social interactions and social bonds. The positive social behaviors may then inhibit HPA activity mediated by oxytocin and vasopressin. These are rewarding states and thus reinforce the social bond, which functions to provide a sense of safety. Negative social interactions increase fear and avoidance, which in turn increase the sense of anxiety and stress and prevent social attachments from forming (i.e., social isolation). This describes some of the neurobiological mechanisms for how social support has mental and physical benefits, while the lack of social attachment and forced separation lead to severe negative mental and physical consequences.

Clinical compassion built on the neurobiology of the parenting/ caregiving system

The compassion that is evident in the helping professions is basically an extension of the neurobiological caregiving system that has evolved to enable humans to rear and nurture their children. As noted earlier in the discussion of the polyvagal theory, mammals have evolved systems to enable the giving and receiving of care. It is this same neurobiological system that is found to motivate maternal care that is recruited to motivate other helping behavior. Social bonds and the interdependence of humans require a motivational system that spurs individuals to go beyond their self-interest for the good of the species. Studying this neurocircuitry and how it is activated in general will provide information for what is occurring in clinicians when they engage in behavior that is often personally costly for the well-being of patients.

Humans have a self-interest system and an altruistically centered system

Why do humans provide costly help to others and, under certain conditions, override their self-centered survival interests? There are remarkable prosocial actions among humans that cannot be adequately explained by a theory of reciprocal altruism (i.e., natural selection favors altruism toward non-kin as long as this altruism will be reciprocated later on). These include caring for offspring; caring for family members; and sacrificing for children, mates, kin, friends, and others to whom one is connected but who are not in one's family. Humans will provide personally costly help for the well-being of offspring and also for taking care of terminally ill partners or protecting fellow comrades in war. Brown and Brown (2006) have concluded that this social exchange self-centered motivational system does not provide a parsimonious explanation for the apparent existence of two contradictory motivation systems in humans, both of which have been evolutionarily adaptive for the human species: the self-centered system and the altruistically centered system. We have one system that is focused on our self-interest but also another system shaped by evolution to suppress that self-interest and to give away our resources to help others reproduce, survive, and grow.

Development of the selective investment theory

Brown, Brown, and Preston (2012) have argued that the traditional assumption common in the social sciences that social behavior can be essentially explained by the person seeking to benefit him- or herself in some way does not explain occasions when a person helps another person at great cost to him- or herself. The common assumption in the social sciences is that all social behavior can be explained in terms of seeking rewards and benefits for oneself and avoiding pain. In this traditional view, connections with others are motivationally based on reciprocity based on self-interest; we stay close to others in order to take care of our own needs better and to survive. Brown, Brown, and Preston found that this could not explain certain behaviors that represented a motivation to give away what one needs in order to help others survive and reproduce. Parenting is the premier example of this phenomenon, in which the costs of rearing their young outweighs the benefits to the parents. Evolution appears to have formed a motivational system that suppresses one's self-interests under certain conditions and prioritizes the well-being of others above one's own needs. In evolutionary terms, this neurobiological system evolved to develop maternal care behaviors. Brown and Brown (2006) developed the *selective investment theory* to explain how humans can desire to give care to others at great costs to themselves for the well-being of others. It is this neurobiological system, this caregiving system, that "is selectively recruited in both humans and nonhumans to motivate many forms of helping behavior, including costly long-term investment in others" (Brown, Brown, & Preston, 2012, p. 77).

Motivation for fitness interdependence

Motivational circuitry, in addition to perceptual and cognitive processes, is required for the occurrence of costly long-term investment.

Brown and Brown argue that social bonds based on fitness interdependence are the mechanism for costly long-term investment. *Fitness interdependence* is a "mutual reproductive dependence," "a state of linked reproductive success between two or more individuals in which increases in one person's fitness result in increases in the fitness of the other or others" (Brown, Brown, & Preston, 2012, pp. 76–77). It includes not only genetically related interdependence but also unrelated individuals "whose interdependence is based on linked reproductive need for a mating partner, food, protection, shelter, and other resources ('mutual-need fitness interdependence')" (Brown & Brown, 2006, p. 6). It is a kind of genetic safety net within which altruism makes sense in order to ensure the reproduction, survival, and growth of interdependent others. There is a "reproductive insurance" in promoting the well-being and fitness of others because we must depend on each other, and what makes you less fit and less strong could affect my condition as well. Fitness interdependence was naturally selected because of its evolutionary adaptiveness, and human neurobiology reflects this. The motivation mechanism that underlies our preference for "fitness-interdependent others" is based on the social bond we have with other humans. In the face of high costs and no possibility of reciprocity, we are motivated to promote the well-being of those with whom we share this social bond. When that bond between humans is activated (e.g., under threat), it amplifies the benefits of altruism to interdependent others and minimizes the costs. Emotions such as concern for others become activated and inhibit the concern for self-interests, and those emotions are experienced as positive. All of this is mediated neurophysiologically. At the genetic level, giving is experienced as rewarding (Brown & Brown, 2006).

Brain circuitry underlying providing costly, long-term investment in others

So, what is this motivational circuitry that organizes our thoughts and emotions to provide costly, long-term investment in others? Selective investment theory identifies the brain regions, neural circuits, and hormones that make up this neurobiological system, which is the result of an evolutionary process that directs parental, especially maternal, care. It is this system, according to Brown, Brown, and Preston (2012), that is selectively recruited for other types of helping behavior. As seen in figure 3.2, the process begins with the perception of need. In rodent maternal models, this takes place in the amygdala, which picks up cues of threat responses, and the subgenual anterior cingulate cortex (subgenual ACC). Then, it is the activation of the medial preoptic area of the hypothalamus (MPOA) that directs the motor actions for the caregiving behavior. In maternal care, the MPOA and ventral bed nucleus of the stria terminalis (vBST) appear to act as a switch for turning on the caregiving motivation. For maternal caregiving behavior to occur, two things need to happen: an increase in approach motivation (i.e., motivation to want to engage in the caregiving behavior) and an inhibition of avoidance motivation (i.e., motivation that would interfere with the helping behavior). When it comes to providing costly resources to someone in need, there is a motivational conflict between providing the valuable resources to the offspring and protecting the self's concerns, leading to avoidance of the offspring's needs (i.e., fearing the costs of providing this help to the offspring in need or seeking rewards for oneself). Caregiving can be trumped by the fears of what it would cost the mother to engage in the caregiving behavior or by prioritizing her own rewards

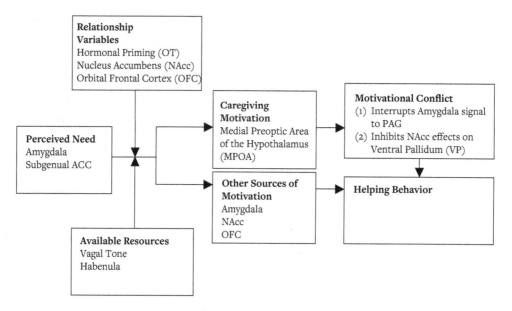

FIGURE 3.2 A biological framework for studying the caregiving systems. Brain regions, hormones, and circuits are described under each variable in the model. ACC, anterior cingulate cortex; OT, oxytocin; PAG, periaqueductal gray (Brown, Brown, & Preston, 2012, p. 78).

to the detriment of the offspring's needs. Both of these must be inhibited for helping behavior to occur.

How the fear-based avoidance response is inhibited

In terms of suppressing its own need for self-protection from the costs of providing resources (e.g., looking after one's own survival vs. protecting offspring), the MPOA appears to inhibit the fear-based avoidance response, thereby allowing the expression of caregiving behavior. The amygdala is activated by the perception of danger or need, and the MPOA interrupts the signal from the amygdala to the periaqueductal gray (PAG). As this decreases defensive behavior and avoidance, it increases the voluntary caregiving responses. In terms of inhibiting the motivation to seek rewards for itself, the MPOA inhibits the reward-seeking motivation of the nucleus accumbens (NAcc) connected

to seeking food, sex, and drugs (e.g., addictive behavior). It does so by disinhibiting the ventral pallidum (VP), which releases the brake on the motor program for the caregiving behavior.

Variables that prime the caregiving brain circuitry

As seen in figure 3.2, Brown, Brown, & Preston (2012) note that there are a number of relationship variables that can prime the caregiving circuit. One of these is the neuropeptide oxytocin, which increases the chances of activating the caregiving neural circuit. While oxytocin does not mediate this circuit, it is released in fitness interdependence situations in both nonhumans and humans (e.g., breast-feeding, birth, sex). Oxytocin release has been found to be triggered in the perception of social cues of closeness and interdependence (Zak, Kurzban, & Matzner, 2005). Increases of oxytocin are associated with positive social interactions, decreasing

HPA axis stress responses, and increasing the likelihood of social attachment and cooperation. Zak, Kurzban, & Matzner (2004) examined the neurobiology of trust and found that social signals of trust increase oxytocin levels in the person perceiving that trust, and in response, the perceiver reciprocated that trust. When there is no signal of trust, there is no oxytocin release and no reciprocated trustworthy behavior (Zak et al., 2005). Zak (2008) reports, "Residing in a safe, nurturing environment may stimulate us to release more oxytocin when someone trusts us—and to reciprocate that trust. Stress, uncertainty and isolation all work against the development of a trusting disposition" (p. 95).

The role of the orbital frontal cortex in facilitating caregiving behavior

The orbital frontal cortex (OFC) also appears to be involved in facilitating caregiving behavior (Brown, Brown, & Preston, 2012). The OFC is involved with mediating complex emotional responses such as social responses. It stores the emotional and visceral aspects of social memories over a person's lifetime. The OFC operates in either facilitating caring behaviors or inhibiting them based on those social memories. An organism's early experiences and the stress or emotional intensity of those experiences come to bear on a current situation. Social conditioning from our society, our families, and our social experiences in general influence how people respond viscerally and behaviorally in future situations (Eisler & Levine, 2002). The OFC thus becomes involved in "helping individuals code, recognize, and discriminate trustworthy, bonded, or interdependent partners" (Brown, Brown, & Preston, 2012, p. 83). So, the OFC aids in evaluating new or old relationships, judging the likelihood of exploitation, making decisions about those relationships, and triggering oxytocin release if a caregiving pathway is chosen.

Internal resources that modulate caregiving motivation

Returning to figure 3.2, we note Brown, Brown, and Preston (2012) add that internal resources a person has can also modulate caregiving motivation. These would include one's developmental history, including one's attachment history. As I will explain in more detail in chapter 8, one's own attachment experiences influence how one perceives and reacts to perceived needs in others. For example, a person who has had a secure attachment history might be less hypervigilant compared to a person who has had a very turbulent attachment experience. The person from the more unpredictable attachment history might be more self-protective and need more assurances of safety before engaging in helping. Other internal resources include individual differences in the person, such as temperament, that influence how need is perceived. The sense of self-efficacy a person has, a confidence that he or she can deal with a particular situation, can also facilitate or impede one's caregiving motivation (Brown, 2012).

Sensitivity to need cues in others

This first step in helping behavior is that the helper is sensitive to cues for need or distress in another person. Relying on rodent data, Brown, Brown, & Preston (2012) argue that it is the medial preoptic area of the hypothalamus and the surrounding vBST that, when activated, release the motor program for helping behavior. In rodent models, this directs maternal behavior by inhibiting the motivation that would interfere with helping behavior and increase the motivation to approach the situation. Response to need cues in others appears to be mediated by the amygdala and the subgenual ACC connected to stress threat responses (Numan, 2006; Moll et al., 2006).

Need in other must be real and the helper not feel exploited

At the perceived need stage, Brown (2012) notes that the caregiving system has to do two things before it proceeds: it has to perceive the need as real and perceive that the caregiver will not be exploited. The results would be disastrous if the caregiving system could too easily be triggered. The potential caregiver is assessing authenticity before proceeding down a helping pathway. This parenting mechanism is recruited when interacting with others in general, and Brown explains that it provides much information about the phenomenon of compassion in all its forms because this mechanism underlies how it functions.

Caregiving mechanism decreases internal stress response

As the hypothalamus releases the brake on helping, it also inhibits stress. Brown explains that the caregiver is not able to relieve the suffering of another if he or she is in a stressed state. The perception of suffering in another causes stress in the caregiver, but the caregiver must find a way to relieve that internal stress in order to proceed. Physiologically, the caregiving mechanism accomplishes this. Brown et al. (2009) explain that in the caregiving mode, stress becomes regulated and the caregiver's own health becomes fortified.

Research on health benefits of caregiving

A number of studies have found that in some situations, caregivers appear to experience health benefits related to giving care to others. In a large sample of caregivers (i.e., over 3,000 individuals) who were providing care for their spouses, Brown et al. (2009) found that caregivers had lower mortality rates if they provided 14 or more hours of care per week to their spouses compared to spouses who did not provide any care. The researchers believe a possible explanation for this effect may be that, in line with the stress regulation dynamic in the caregiving model discussed in the previous section, there is a restorative effect that buffers stress connected to providing help. So, the release of oxytocin and other hormones may have decreased the HPA stress response and facilitated cellular repair and cell nutrient storage. Other studies have found this stress-buffering and health-enhancing effect in helping. Following are a number of examples.

Study on interdependent caregiving spouses and their ill partners

In a sample of 73 individuals who were providing caregiving for their spouses, Poulin et al. (2010) found that the amount of time spent caregiving for a spouse was associated with more positive affect in the caregiver, especially for those spouses who viewed themselves as interdependent with their spouses. The researchers controlled for severity of illness in the spouses (e.g., dementia or functional impairment); thus, the effect was not due to less healthy spouses having poorer quality relationships because of the illnesses. The effect was independent of the severity of spouse illness. Interdependence was defined as having a mutuality of need in which the spouses felt they both needed to depend on each other and that they felt emotional support from the care recipient spouse. Those who did not feel interdependent experienced more negative emotions but not more positive emotions. Poulin et al. (2010) speculated that there are two possible explanations that may overlap. One is that providing care might be viewed in a positive way as an opportunity to provide better care to their spouse than if someone else was, or that it was an opportunity for them to grow as people. Second, the opportunity to provide caregiving may bring about positive emotions of empathy and love over negative emotions. The view of the relationship appears quite significant to the resulting emotions no matter how severe the illness.

Study on giving social support being more beneficial than receiving social support

Brown, Nesse, Vinokur, and Smith (2003) interestingly found that giving social support may be more beneficial than receiving social support. People who gave emotional support to their spouses or who gave instrumental support to their relatives, friends, and neighbors had significantly lower mortality than those who provided less support. Usually, receiving support is associated with lower mortality. Paradoxically, when giving support was controlled, receiving support no longer predicted mortality. Helping behavior directed to others by widowed spouses after the death was related to a faster decline in depressive symptoms in the 8 to 18 months after their partner had died. This effect for helping others was independent of the effect on depression recovery due to receiving support.

Health benefits of caregiving only occur if inner attitude is positive

Do the stress-buffering effects of the caregiver behavioral system occur simply because of the helping of others, or does a person's attitude affect whether the stress-buffering effects occur? The answer strongly appears to be that one's inner attitude toward the people being helped is a critical factor in whether they will experience the stress-buffering health benefits

of helping. In two national studies, Poulin (2014) found that volunteering buffered the negative effects of stress. In his first study, stress predicted mortality for those who had low levels of volunteering, but stress did not predict mortality for those who had high levels of volunteering. However, this stress-buffering effect only occurred for people who had more positive views of others (i.e., low in hostile cynicism). In his second study, Poulin (2014) found that there was less of an association between the number of stressful events individuals had and the psychological distress they experienced for people who volunteered more, but only for those who had a higher perception of the world as benevolent and held positive views of others—that is, believing that people are basically kind and helpful and that human nature is basically good.

Motives for volunteering determined if there were health benefits for the volunteer

Further evidence for the critical factor that motives play in helping comes from a study by Konrath, Fuhrel-Forbis, Lou, and Brown (2012). They looked at the mortality rates four years later of over 10,000 people. The researchers asked if the participants volunteered, and if so, how much they volunteered and why they volunteered. The motives for volunteering included both self-oriented motives and other-oriented motives. Self-oriented motives included learning or understanding motives such as wanting to explore their own strengths, self-enhancement motives such as wanting to feel better about themselves, and self-protection motives such as volunteering being an escape from their troubles. Other-oriented motives included altruistic values such as feeling compassion toward people in need or social connection motives such as people one is close to placing high value on community service. What the researchers found was that volunteers had lower mortality than nonvolunteers, and this was especially the case for those who volunteered regularly and frequently. But when motives were factored in, those with other-oriented motives had significantly less mortality risk, and there was an increased mortality risk for those with self-oriented motives. In fact, those with self-oriented motives had the same mortality risk as nonvolunteers.

Study on health effects of expressing affection

Expressing affection appears to have positive physiological effects. Floyd et al. (2007) exposed three groups to a stressor (watching a video of couples arguing) that would increase their cortisol, indicating a stress response. One group simply sat quietly; the second group thought about a loved one but did not engage in any expression of that affection; and the third group thought about a loved one and wrote a letter to that person expressing their affectionate feelings for that person. What resulted was that the expressing affectionate feelings group had a significantly accelerated recovery from stress than the other two groups. Just thinking affectionate thoughts did not accelerate recovery, but expressing those thoughts made a physiological difference.

NEUROSCIENCE OF EMPATHY

Conception of empathy as a quantity that decreases in medical school and clinical practice

Empathy is considered one of the key factors in therapeutic relationships with patients. Empathy is studied in terms of how it is related to rapport with patients as well as how it relates to patient adherence to a prescribed treatment. It is tracked like a hemoglobin level in medical students, physicians, nurses, and other clinicians. We worry about how much our students have of it at the beginning of medical school and how it seems to decline by the time students start working in clinic (Hojat et al., 2004; Neumann et al., 2011). While there is truth to this, there is a downside to the way we are conceptualizing empathy in terms of having a certain quantity in a clinician or in a relationship with a patient. It suggests that a clinician has to intend to be empathic and add it to the clinical mix of things. It implies that a clinician could have a starting point of zero empathy with a patient and has the option to add it to the clinical relationship if he or she is so inclined and has the time.

Clinicians actually start from a place of automatic emotional resonance

The reality, however, is that the clinician *automatically* starts from a place of empathic resonance and either builds on this initial base or shuts it down. Rather than being an act of deciding whether to engage in empathy, the reality is that empathy is already being engaged; the decision is really about deciding to stop being empathically connected to a patient. This changes everything about what we thought was going on emotionally and cognitively in clinicians when it comes to empathy. *We have thought that we start from a place of emotional detachment or neutrality and then decide to engage a patient in an empathic way. The reality is that we start from an empathic engagement and then, for whatever reason, shut empathy down or refine it for therapeutic use.* Understanding the dynamics of empathy can enlighten us about how we harm ourselves (and our patients) when we are not empathic and how empathy can get out of control if it is not managed well.

Empathy has bottom-up and top-down processing components

Understanding how empathy in the clinician works in terms of evolutionary biology, neuroscience, and social psychology is key to grasping how it is related to helping behavior but also how its mismanagement can be detrimental to the clinician as well as the patient. Decety and Lamm (2006) reviewed the research on empathy and conceptualized it from a social neuroscience perspective that bridges biology, neuroscience, and social psychology. Defining empathy as "the ability to experience and understand what others feel without confusion between oneself and others" (Decety & Lamm, 2006, p. 1146), Decety and Lamm (2011) concluded that empathy appears to consist of (a) an automatic emotion-sharing component that operates in a bottom-up information processing manner and (b) a top-down information processing component in which executive control is used to regulate and modulate this emotion-sharing experience.

Three components of empathy

There are three components of empathy. First, there is the automatic affective arousal and emotion sharing in the perceiver who is observing a person in pain or distress. Second, there is an awareness and understanding of the emotions of that person. Third, the perceiver engages in a process of emotional regulation that determines what the response of the perceiver will be (Decety, 2011). If the perceiver is overwhelmed by the emotional resonance, he or she might withdraw or detach. If the perceiver is able to manage this emotional resonance, then he or she might act to respond and help the person in pain or distress.

Automatic emotion sharing

Empathy is rooted in an automatic emotion sharing between an observer and another person. Human beings are constructed in such a way that there is an unconscious social mimicry or emotional contagion that occurs when one person observes another person who is in pain or distress, for instance. Emotional contagion is an unconscious mimicry and synchrony of facial expressions, postures, vocalizations, and movements that leads the observer's emotions to converge in the direction of the other person's emotions. From an evolutionary biological perspective, this somatic mimicry appears to have survival value in terms of facilitating communication between humans, increasing a sense of affiliation between people, and also preparing others for action in fearful situations. We unconsciously tend to mimic others and synchronize with them, with the result that we "catch" their emotions. This is especially true when the other person is feeling and expressing strong emotions, but it still occurs even when the emotions are not as strong (Hatfield, Cacioppo, & Rapson, 1994).

The discovery of mirror neurons

There is a mirror mechanism in which the motor behaviors observed in another person fire the neurons connected to that action in the observing person. Mirror neurons were discovered first in macaque monkeys. The same neurons that would fire in a monkey when performing a goal-directed hand movement such as grasping an object would also fire when that monkey observed a goal-directed grasping movement in another monkey or a human doing that same action (Di Pellegrino, Fadiga, Fogassi, Gallese, & Rizzolatti, 1992). The observer monkey neurons fired as if it was doing the goal-directed action even though it was not moving at all. It was just watching the other monkey doing some intentional action. What is the function of this mirror mechanism? When the observer monkey sees another monkey grasping for something, the observer monkey is able to predict what the other monkey will do next based on the context of the grasping. The observer monkey is therefore able to infer the intentions of the other monkey's action (Rizzolatti, Fabbri-Destro, & Cattaneo, 2009).

Function of mirror neurons in humans

A similar mirror neuron system has been found in humans in the frontal and parietal areas of the brain and occurs with observed goal-directed motor acts, but also movements that do not have a goal. The human motor neuron system registers both the goal of an observed action in another person and the manner in which that action is performed. The same motor circuits that would be used if the observer were doing the action are activated when the observer sees someone else perform that action, and from that the observer obtains "the direct experiential understanding of the observed actions mediated by the mirror mechanism" (Gallese, Keysers, & Rizzolatti, 2004, p. 397). This mirroring mechanism in the observer helps the observer understand the meaning of the other person's action.

Mirror neurons for emotions

A mirroring mechanism much like the motor mirror neurons appears to be operating for experiencing and understanding the emotions that others have. For example, the part of the insula that is activated when a person experiences disgust is also activated in the observer by the facial expressions of others when they are experiencing disgust. This appears to be true for other emotions (although there are other brain circuits also involved in understanding the emotions of others). The brain circuits that are activated when a person is acting or experiencing an emotion are the same ones that are activated when another person observes those actions or emotions in others. This becomes one of the foundational components of social cognition, in which we are able to enter the perspectives of others and gain insight from what *we are experiencing* as we observe others, not just thinking about them. Gallese, Keysers, and Rizzolatti (2004) comment about this unifying neural hypothesis regarding the mirroring dynamic in social cognition:

> With this mechanism we do not just "see" or "hear" an action or an emotion. Side by side with the sensory description of the observed social stimuli, internal representations of the state associated with these actions or emotions are evoked in the observer, "as if" they were performing a similar action or experiencing a similar emotion. (p. 400)

Facial expression mimicry leads to emotion mimicry

Another example of this tendency toward emotional resonation through a mechanism of unconsciously mirroring the emotions of others is found in the tendency to mimic the facial expressions of others. When unconsciously presented with happy and angry faces in other people, those who were observing them had spontaneous facial muscle reactions that corresponded exactly to those happy and angry faces (Dimberg, Thungerg, & Elmehed, 2000). In another study, when research participants were instructed to create certain facial expressions, this evoked autonomic activity that reflected that particular emotion as measured by heart rate, skin conductance, finger temperature, and somatic activity. They also reported the subjective experience associated with the emotion corresponding to those facial expressions (Levenson, Ekman, & Friesen, 1990).

Intentions, sensations, emotion, and actions become mirrored in the observer

Simply watching the intentional behavior of another person also activates neural circuits in your brain as if you were doing that same behavior (even though you are not). When another person is experiencing something such as a sound or a touch, or is in pain, the same brain regions that are activated in the other person are also getting activated in you as you observe that person. This also happens with emotions. Perceiving particular emotions in another person activates similar brain regions in the observer as in the person who is being observed. It happens as well when a person is imagining the other person in some action or experiencing a sensation or emotion (Watson & Greenburg, 2009). Preston and de Waal (2002) developed the *perception–action model of empathy*, which states that the "attended perception of the object's state automatically activates the subject's representation of the state, situation, and object, and that activation of these representations automatically primes or generates the associated autonomic and somatic responses, unless inhibited" (p. 4). The action, sensation, or emotion of the other becomes represented or mirrored in your brain, although generally you do not lose a sense of yourself in that shared emotion or experience; you maintain a sense of distinction between the person you are observing and yourself.

Pain perception is mirrored

As clinicians, we frequently observe pain in our patients. The expression of pain is important because it signals that the person is in some distress, which can elicit responses from others to help relieve that distress (Decety, 2011). What happens to our brains when we observe pain in others? Research on this question is complicated, but it is clear that perception of pain in another person activates the affective and motivational aspects of the pain matrix in the observer, and less so the sensory aspects (Decety & Lamm, 2011). In a study by Singer et al. (2004), 16 couples were simultaneously scanned by functional magnetic resonance imaging (fMRI) while one partner experienced a painful stimulus from an electrode on the back of the hand and the other partner observed this. The researchers found that certain common areas of the brain's pain matrix were fired in the partner who experienced the shock and in the partner who observed this pain. Specifically, the bilateral anterior insula (AI) extending into the inferior prefrontal cortex, the anterior and posterior rostral zones of the ACC, the brain stem, and the cerebellum were activated in both partners. These areas are associated with the emotional experience of pain as well as the motivational aspects regarding wanting to avoid or end the painful experience. In addition, partners who had higher empathy scores had stronger activations in the posterior rostral zone of the ACC and the left AI. The part of the pain matrix that was not fired in the observer had to do with those parts that are involved in the sensory aspects of the pain experience: the posterior insula/secondary somatosensory cortex, the sensorimotor cortex, and the caudal ACC. When I observe someone else in pain, it is like I am in pain similarly. Singer et al. (2004) conclude that this common neural activation functions to help us understand the emotional importance of a particular pain in another person and what the likely consequences of that pain are. From an evolutionary perspective, understanding and responding to someone in pain only requires that the observer have a subjective sense of how badly the other person feels but not necessarily feel exactly the same sensations.

Common neural areas activated in observing another in pain

Meta-analyses of 39 fMRI studies from different countries using different paradigms have repeatedly found evidence that common neural areas are activated between someone directly experiencing pain and someone who is empathically observing that pain. These are the bilateral AI and the medial and posterior ACC. Studies that involved pictures of body parts in painful situations more strongly activated areas involved with action understanding (anterior inferior parietal cortex and ventral premotor cortex); studies that used abstract visual information about another person's affect state more strongly activated areas that had to do with mentalizing—that is, the inferring and representing of mental states either of one's self or another person (precuneus, ventral parts of medial prefrontal cortex, posterior superior temporal cortex, temporoparietal junction [TPJ], and the temporal poles). Studies that used more vivid picture-based paradigms tended to show activation in the somatosensory areas (Lamm, Decety, & Singer, 2011). In contrast to Singer et al. (2004), when there is a strong visual component in the observation of another person in pain, then the observer will have more activation in the sensory parts of the brain.

Mirroring mechanism facilitates understanding and a response to the other in pain

Human beings as well as social animal species are biologically wired to experience emotional distress in others vicariously. While this experience is not identical to the organism in distress, this mirroring mechanism operates to facilitate understanding of the organism in distress as well as motivates a response to that organism. This may be a response in which the observer is distressed by the distressed person and withdraws or escapes; a response that is other-oriented to attempt altruistically to relieve the distress of the other; or a response in which the observer is both distressed and other-oriented—that is, egotistically motivated to relieve the distress of the other in order to relieve one's own distress, not altruistically (Goubert et al. 2005; Batson, 2011)

Top-down processing of empathy and modulating factors affecting response

Thus far we have considered the bottom-up processes in empathy. But the top-down process profoundly affects how empathy proceeds (or is curtailed) as well as how it is expressed. Cognitive and social factors modulate the empathic concern and personal distress. Factors such as emotional regulation, the relationship between the observer and the person in distress, the disposition of the observer, and the context of the social interaction all affect whether empathic concern and helping behavior result (Decety & Lamm, 2011). First, being able to emotionally regulate is critically important. By the very nature of the bottom-up aspects of emotional resonance, the observer is automatically emotionally aroused in the direction of the person in distress. In order to help the person in distress, the observer has to be able to manage this emotional arousal so that he or she does not become personally distressed (Decety & Lamm, 2011). Clinicians who have empathic concern followed by helping behavior directed at their patients have developed the ability to manage any distress, anxiety, anger, or other negative feelings so that they can remain composed and respond in a way that is helpful to a patient in distress. They may use a strategy to downregulate (i.e., reduce) their emotions, such as cognitive reappraisal. This involves reinterpreting what is happening with a person in distress in such a way that it is less emotionally overwhelming. For example, with a patient who is in a panicked state from injuries in an accident, the clinician might reframe that panic in terms of how it is understandable that a person would be panicked in this situation, and this would help the clinician manage his or her own feelings and yet be engaged with the patient. Clinicians who become overwhelmed by patient distress may either attempt to help the patient in an emotionally imbalanced, confused manner or flee the situation. Some clinicians who anticipate becoming overwhelmed by what their patients are experiencing inhibit the automatic emotional resonance and respond in an emotionally detached or disconnected manner.

Times when a clinician wants to upregulate emotional arousal

There are times when a clinician would like to upregulate (i.e., promote) certain emotions. For example, if a clinician might approach a certain type of patient with indifference or avoid a certain type of patient, he or she might engage in cognitive strategies to increase perspective taking and empathic concern. Or a clinician might want to selectively focus on certain aspects of the patient (Decety &

Lamm, 2006), such as focusing on attending to a severe laceration itself rather than fearful remarks a patient is making. The clinician's arousal is focused on repairing the laceration and modulates the reaction to a patient's hysterical state.

Interpersonal factors affecting top-down processing

Interpersonal factors can affect the top-down processing of empathy. Liking, disliking, or feeling neutral about a particular patient can affect whether we empathically engage or disengage from that patient. How similar or close the observer is to the distressed person can predict whether he or she helps the other person (Decety & Lamm, 2011). For example, Meyer et al. (2013) did fMRI scans on people who were observing friends and strangers going through social exclusion. When watching a friend go through social suffering, the parts of the brain that were associated with direct firsthand experience of being excluded were activated (i.e., dorsal ACC and insula). When watching a stranger being socially excluded, brain regions were activated that were connected to mentalizing—that is, thinking about the mental states, traits, and intentions of others (i.e., dorsal medial prefrontal cortex). While participants reported that they thought both the friend and the stranger were hurt from the exclusion, they felt more badly for the friend. Empathizing with friends elicited a more self-related affective response, while there is less emotional sharing with strangers even though a person might cognitively understand the stranger's experience (Meyer et al., 2013). Judging if another person is fair or unfair affects how much empathy is generated. One study found that empathic brain responses of men who watched someone receiving pain were significantly less empathic to a person who had been playing unfairly in a game. They had more activation in reward-related brain areas associated with a desire for revenge. This effect was not found for women watching the unfair players. While women were similar to the men in rating the unfair players as being less likable and less attractive, women still had activation in the pain-related brain networks indicating empathic responses (Singer et al., 2006). Studies like these highlight how our attitudes toward our patients have direct implications for how we process information about them and what kind of empathy we have toward them. Generally speaking, the more we feel close to another person (e.g., close family member, friend), the more we experience empathic concern and a willingness to help them.

Intrapersonal or dispositional factors affecting top-down processing

Intrapersonal or dispositional factors of the observer can also affect the modulation of empathic responding (Decety & Lamm, 2006). For example, the observer's emotional background state, such as being depressed or anxious, can affect how we perceive and respond to another person's distress. Our prior experience with a certain type of situation can affect our empathic response. Having no experience with a particular type of patient can affect how we react to that patient (e.g., overwhelmed by the case, not having the skills to handle this type of patient), and having a lot of experience can also affect how we react (e.g., we have treated many patients of a certain type, which leads to being less sensitive to future cases). Having had a particular training or experience can heighten our awareness of what is going on with a patient, and

we pay attention to emotional cues in that type of patient that we would normally have missed.

Individual differences in temperament, dispositional empathy, attachment history affecting top-down processing

Individual differences in temperament and dispositional empathy may also modulate empathy, although self-report measures such as self-reported empathy may be challenging to match with underlying neural dynamics. However, empathy as measured by the Balanced Emotional Empathy Scale and the Empathic Concern Scale of the Interpersonal Reactivity Index was found to correlate with stronger activations of the pain matrix when one partner observed the other partner undergoing a painful shock (Singer et al., 2004). Attachment history can also affect empathy. Growing up in a family in which care was unpredictable, the parents were emotionally confusing to the child, and the child's emotional needs were inconsistently met can lead to a more insecure attachment style in that child. Having an insecure base can distort our emotional perceptions of others and oneself throughout one's life. A more secure attachment base, in contrast, allows a person to be able to emotionally regulate better and more effectively attend to the needs of others because the "mental road map" of how to do that has been internalized by that upbringing (Siegel, 2011; Bowlby, 2005b).

The importance of clinician accuracy in assessing patient pain

How clinicians perceive pain in their patients is crucially important in the practice of medicine. In their review of the literature, Goubert et al. (2005) related that underestimations and overestimations of pain in others can have quite negative consequences. If the pain of a patient is underestimated, the patient may not receive adequate care and will likely feel misunderstood. Chronic pain is often underestimated because there are fewer pain signals and cues than with acute pain. People in chronic pain tend to downplay the severity of their symptoms and their emotional suffering either because they want to be perceived as doing better than they are or because they fear being judged and misunderstood by others. They may also worry that they are frustrating others by not having any improvement in their pain, so they may be selective about what they disclose. In short, clinicians must be able to assess patient pain by being willing to assess the pain signals/cues, the contexts that can lead to underestimating or overestimating the patient's pain, and their own biases in evaluating that patient's pain.

Physicians learn to downregulate their pain empathy response

Do physicians downregulate their pain empathy response? Decety, Yang, and Cheng (2010) compared a group of female internal medicine physicians with a matched group of females who were not health care professionals. The researchers compared their event-related potentials (ERP) (EEG changes measuring brain responses to sensory, cognitive, or motor events) when watching body parts be touched by a cotton swab (nonpainful situation) versus being stuck by a small needle (painful situation). The two groups did not differ on dispositional measures of emotional contagion, dispositional empathy, and sensitivity to pain. As expected, physicians reported significantly less pain intensity and unpleasantness than the control group. In terms of the ERP measure, the control group showed reactions to the pain around 120 milliseconds and 350 milliseconds after being presented with

the stimulus, whereas physicians showed less of a reaction to the painful situation. Physicians appeared to have learned how to downregulate their pain empathy response. Comparing the physicians and controls in terms of timing of reactions to the painful situation, it appears that physicians learned how to modulate empathy both at the early automatic emotional sharing phase and at the later cognitive evaluation for pain empathy. The researchers surmised that this downregulation came about because physicians are familiar with needles being used, have less of a negativity toward such painful situations because of their experience, and focus their attention differently (i.e., not on the needle stick as much). In this study, the personality measures do not differ between the groups, so we cannot say that physicians have different empathy levels, for example, than their matched controls. This difference is what the training does to their reactions to painful situations.

The downside to clinicians downregulating their pain empathy response

This is no surprise to anyone in medicine. Of course, we would expect clinicians to habituate to painful situations in patients. But there are a number of concerns. First, what does this mean for the patient? On one hand, patients want a clinician who has emotional composure and is not deterred by painful situations. But if clinicians downregulate their pain empathy response too much, then they will start missing important information about the pain and emotional state of their patients. The tendency to underestimate the pain of a patient will lead to a number of negative consequences for that patient. It is understandable that clinicians would want to downregulate their pain empathy response because it is emotionally challenging to allow oneself to be affected by all that a clinician witnesses in a single day. It is definitely intense work that requires not only experiencing what is occurring in the moment with a patient but also processing these often-powerful experiences after the workday is over. But when clinicians suppress their empathic resonance, they can miss patient cues that can alter the course of treatment. They can miss that a patient is suffering physically, emotionally, and/or spiritually. When clinicians are in touch with a patient's suffering, they get information that can help with modifying treatments, supporting patients, or making referrals to ease that suffering. Also, when clinicians emotionally distance themselves, patients can sense that their emotional experience of the illness is not being noticed by their clinician, and this leads to a sense of being abandoned by clinicians they hoped would in some way emotionally accompany and support them. Most patients do not expect inordinate amounts of support; a simple, sincere recognition of the patient's experience goes a long way in encouraging patients to have emotional strength to bear their illnesses and injuries.

Importance of being precise in using terms such as empathy

Singer (2006) has warned that the way we use the term *empathy* in common lay usage is actually a very complex and multilevel construct that involves an automatic and unconscious affect sharing or resonation with another person's feelings and experience, but there are also complex processes of empathic perspective taking that connect with helping behavior. For the purposes of this book, in line with Singer (2006) and Decety and Lamm (2006), we need to be more precise in how we use the term *empathy*. In medicine, we cannot afford an oversimplified notion of empathy. Making a few distinctions in line with the current research is critical for managing our emotions, empathy, and compassionate caring in a way that is necessary to survive and thrive in health care.

Distinction between empathizing and mentalizing

Singer (2006) suggests we use the term *empathize* to mean to "experience what it feels like for another person to experience a certain emotion or sensation" (p. 856). This is different from the term *mentalize*, which refers to "the attribution of propositional attitudes to another person, that is, the attribution of desires, beliefs and intentions" (p. 856), that is, to infer the other's intentions, beliefs, or mental states. Empathizing, also called affect sharing, occurs when the affect state of another is to some degree induced in the observer by perceiving it in another person, and this occurs without conscious control. It is automatic and unconscious but can be controlled by higher-level cognitive processes. However, the observer is able to distinguish between whether the feeling originated within him- or herself or was induced by observing another person in that emotional state. Mentalizing involves making attributions about the mental states, desires, beliefs, and intentions of another person. (Mentalizing is often referred to as theory of mind.) Singer (2006) argues that empathizing and mentalizing are distinct from each other and rely on different neural circuits. Empathizing involves activation of the AI (associated with processing and feeling disgust), the secondary somatosensory cortex (associated with processing and feeling touch), and pain-related brain circuits. Mentalizing involves the medial prefrontal lobe, the posterior superior temporal sulcus, and the temporal poles.

Clarification on how I use the terms automatic empathic resonance *and* mentalizing/theory of mind *in this book*

Kanske, Böckler, Trautwein, Lesemann, and Singer (2016) use the term *empathy* or *empathize* for the automatic affective sharing in which one's emotional state is isomorphic to another's affective state. But in common usage, clinicians often use the term *empathy* to refer to the cognitive capacity to infer another's emotional and cognitive state rather than the automatic affective sharing. If you read the volumes of research on this, it is very important that you ascertain at the outset how various researchers and clinicians are using these terms. One of the problems in this field is that they use the same terms differently to describe the same phenomena. In order to be clear about what we are referring to, I will use the term *automatic empathic resonance* to refer to this automatic affective sharing, instead of using the terms *empathy* or *empathize* alone. This could be understood as "feeling with" another person, whereby the observer shares in the negative affect of the person suffering. (Some researchers call this a "sympathetic reaction" or "sympathy.") In contrast to this, *mentalizing* or *theory of mind* (ToM) refer to the observer cognitively understanding the other person's mental or affective state. As Kanske, Böckler, Trautwein et al. (2016) put it, the main difference between automatic affective sharing and mentalizing/ToM "is that the former entails embodied sharing of a sensory, affective or bodily state while the latter yields propositional knowledge of another's state" (p. 1384).

Distinction between the automatic empathic resonance and mentalizing brain networks

The empathy and ToM networks have been found to be distinct brain networks. But how do they interact with each other? Are people who are stronger in empathic resonance also strong in ToM, the cognitive perspective taking of another's mental or affective state? Kanske, Böckler, and Singer (2016) found that these two capacities are independent both neurally and behaviorally in that just because you are strong in one does not mean you are strong in the other. Just because you tend to be strong in empathic resonance does not mean you are a proficient mentalizer. But the two brain networks do influence each other. In highly emotional situations, the empathic resonance can inhibit and even harm the mentalizing performance. When a person has high empathic distress, he or she makes more errors in inferring the mental state of the other person. The AI inhibited TPJ activity when there was high negative emotionality.

Instance when empathic resonance overwhelms mentalizing

These findings are very interesting when we apply them to clinicians. When clinicians are worried about becoming emotionally overwhelmed, this describes what is probably going on. In certain very negative emotional situations, one's judgment about what is occurring in the patient can become faulty. The tendency for empathic resonance varies among clinicians; some have a stronger tendency than others. What this means is that clinicians who have a stronger tendency for empathic resonance will have to incorporate methods to modulate this tendency.

Importance of empathic resonance for the salience network

In real life, we need both capacities to work together. If the empathic resonance is too high, then mentalizing suffers. But if the empathic resonance is completely suppressed, there is also a risk. There is a distinct brain network called the "salience network." The brain is continuously barraged by external and internal stimuli. The brain has to have a system to identify what is the most relevant of all these inputs so that it can figure out what to do next. The salience network is activated by what is most subjectively salient, whether that is cognitive, emotional, or homeo-static. It consists of the AI, the dorsal ACC, and subcortical structures (i.e., the amygdala, the thalamus, and the substantia nigra/ventral tegmental area). The insula is the key brain area for bottom-up detection of salient events so that these can be sent on to other parts of the brain for additional processing. When a salient event is detected, the insula then switches to other networks to facilitate attention and working memory. The insula regulates the autonomic reactivity to the salient stimuli and connects with the ACC to help generate a rapid and appropriate behavior in response to the salient stimuli. In short, attention is focused on what is most important, and the working memory and higher order cognitive processes are brought to bear on the situation at hand. Through the salience network, the observer can sort through complex external stimuli very quickly, and the observer's problem-solving ability can focus on what is most important (Menon & Uddin, 2010).

People with psychopathy have deficient empathic resonance but good mentalizing

To get more clear about why the empathic resonance and mentalizing capacities need to work together, it is useful to look at examples when only one of the capacities is working and the other is not. People with psychopathy are described as having little empathy or guilt. They do not have an empathic response to the distress in another person and so have no barrier to inflicting harm on others. In psychopathy,

the ToM mentalizing ability functions, but there is reduced capacity for empathic responding (Kanske, Böckler, Trautwein, Lesemann, & Singer, 2016). They have less physiological and psychological reactivity to emotional material. They have a selective impairment in experiencing fear and sadness. This deficit in experiencing distress emotions leads to a deficit in recognizing distress cues in others. The lack of the emotional contagion, the automatic empathic resonance, leads to a lack of empathy and the appropriate response to someone in distress (Bird & Viding, 2014).

People with autism have deficient mentalizing but intact empathic resonance

People with autism display impairment in their social and communication skills, along with a restricted range of interests and activities. Those with autistic disorders tend to have deficient mentalizing/ToM abilities and difficulty with perspective taking, but the empathic resonance is intact (when controlling for alexithymia). Their empathic response may be intact, but if the deficit in mentalizing/ToM is severe, they might misclassify another person's affective state, leading to an incorrect empathic response. They may have less motivation to seek out and attend to social interactions, which can slow the learning experience of how to associate the empathic resonance with appropriate empathic response. There is also a difficulty with the self-other switch in that they have more difficulty distinguishing their own emotional experience from others. So, they tend to be more affected by the distress of another person but have difficulty distinguishing it from themselves and attributing it to the other person (Bird & Viding, 2014). Alexithymia (which literally means "no words for feelings") is a personality construct in which people have difficulty identifying and describing their feelings; they tend to be externally oriented in their thinking, meaning that they have a pragmatic cognitive tendency and are less disposed to introspective thinking. It has a prevalence rate of 10% to 15% in the general population, and about 50% of people with autism have a severe degree of it. People with alexithymia have difficulties in processing emotions, less empathy, and problems in recognizing emotions in the faces of others (Kajanoja, Scheinin, Karlsson, Karlsson, & Karukivi, 2017; Bird & Viding, 2014). They tend to know that they have an emotion, but they have difficulty in describing what that emotion is. The automatic emotional resonance is intact, but there is a problem in the affective representation system. Because of the difficulty in differentiating their own affective states, they do not learn how to associate the perceptual cues of those states in others.

Implications for clinicians

If we extrapolate, a clinician who has a strong capacity for empathic resonance but a deficient mentalizing capacity is somewhat like the autistic individual who gets emotionally overwhelmed by incoming stimuli but has difficulty inferring and articulating the mental state of another person. The clinician who is strong in mentalizing but deficient in the automatic empathic resonance might have the same risk as a psychopathic person who can infer the mental state of another but not be getting a sense of how the other person actually feels.

Clinicians have to know and manage the levels of automatic empathic resonance and mentalizing capacity in themselves

When we train clinicians using what we know from neuroscience, we must distinguish the automatic empathic resonance from the mentalizing capacity. These are two different capacities that are independent and vary from individual to individual. Clinicians can be high or low in automatic empathic resonance and high or low in mentalizing capacity. The key is to know what the level of each of these is in yourself and work toward a balanced use of both of these. If you tend to be very high in automatic empathic resonance, you have to find ways to manage this so that it does not impair your ability to maintain a sense of emotional separateness and your ability to infer the mental state of the other correctly. If you are too low on automatic empathic resonance, then the risk is that you may miss important emotional information that would guide what you need to do for the patient. If you are high in mentalizing capacity and low in automatic empathic resonance, you might infer the inner state of the other, but you would lack important information about the other person because you are not picking up the emotional state of the person.

The self to other model of empathy

Bird and Viding (2014) have proposed the *self to other model of empathy*. Emotional contagion (automatic empathic resonance) occurs when the observer's affective state matches the affective state of another person, but the observer does not yet explicitly recognize that this is the affective state of the other. There are two input sources in the empathy system from perception of the affective state of another to becoming represented or simulated in the observer in what is called the affective representation system: the *situation understanding system* and the *affective cue classification system*. In the situation understanding system, the observer can ascertain the emotional state of the other because of the situation the other person is in (e.g., black clothes could mean funeral). While this conclusion could be based on the ToM system, it may be the result of stored socioemotional knowledge, which is enough to produce the automatic empathic resonance and becomes represented or simulated in the observer in what is call the affective representation system (located mainly in the insular cortex and the ACC). The *affective cue classification system* refers to perceptual categorization of cues in another person signaling his or her affective state, such as tone of voice, facial expression, or biological motion. This becomes represented in the affective representational system. Sometimes this is mediated by the mirror neuron system. At this point, this is an unconscious process. A critical component in the empathy process is the self–other switch, which tags the empathizer's emotional state as belonging to the other person. The default in the self–other switch is toward the observer; the brain is biased toward attributing the emotional state to itself first. The self–other switch has to process the affective experience (probably located in the TPJ) as belonging to the other person.

ToM/mentalizing in the self to other model of empathy

ToM is the higher-level processing of the other person's situation in which the observer develops a cognitive representation of the mental state of the other. Bird and Viding explain that the ToM is under volitional control and comes into play when there are discrepancies between the situation understanding system and the affective cue classification system; that is, the emotional cues of the person and the situation do not easily match, so the ToM comes into play to cognitively reconcile that information.

How does automatic empathic resonance relate to mentalizing/ToM in clinical situations?

Research is just beginning to articulate how these two routes relate to each other. Say, for example, that a physician has to treat a painful injury in a patient but also needs to infer that the patient is concealing a previous addiction to valium. In such a case, the physician has to prioritize the cognitive control ToM over the automatic empathic resonance (Kanske, Böckler, & Singer, 2016). The automatic empathic resonance helps in situations requiring rapid detection and orientation toward external events that require immediate and appropriate responses to the other person's emotional states (relying on the brain's salience network). When there is a great deal of complexity distraction in a situation, people with a higher capacity for automatic empathic resonance can detect emotions more easily. Hence, in highly stressful situations, people with this higher empathic capacity can more sensitively detect the positive and negative emotions in others, and this facilitates better responses to those individuals (Kanske, Schönfelder, & Wessa, 2013). Mentalizing/ToM is more independent of the external situation, in which the observer relies on more heavily cognitive processes and introspection in trying to understand the other person—that is, relying on the brain's default mode network (Kanske et al., 2016).

Three different pathways leading to altruistic actions

Altruistic actions can result either from the automatic empathic resonance network or from the mentalizing ToM network. In analyzing charitable giving, Tusche, Böckler, Kanske, Trautwein, and Singer (2016) found three distinct psychological mechanisms in altruistic decision-making: automatic empathic resonance, perspective taking/ToM, and attentional reorienting. There were participants whose donating behavior was more influenced by the affective empathy/automatic empathic resonance, and this was shown by more activity in the AI region. There were other participants whose donating behavior was more influenced by the mentalizing/ToM, and the TPJ brain region was more active in that case. Finally, there was a third mechanism for altruistic decision-making in which the donating was connected to what is called domain-general reorienting of attention; the activation, however, was not in the AI or the TPJ but in the posterior superior temporal sulcus. A reorienting response is what occurs when the person has to redirect attention and change behavior when there is a potentially threatening, novel, or rewarding situation in the environment, such as orienting to an ambulance siren while reading (Corbetta, Patel, & Shulman, 2008). While this third mechanism does not directly pertain to the two routes for empathic understanding, the main point is that there is more than one way the brain moves from perceiving a particular situation to a prosocial response.

HOW COMPASSION IS NEURALLY DISTINCT FROM EMPATHY

What does the brain look like in pride versus compassion states?
What does the brain look like in a state of compassion? Recent research has begun to provide an answer to this question. Simon-Thomas et al. (2012) compared fMRI scans of individuals when the emotion of compassion was elicited versus the more self-focused emotion of pride. The researchers presented participants with three types of slides: slides depicting vulnerable suffering and harm to elicit compassion; slides depicting status and achievement, such as graduation, athletic victories, trophies, and medals, to elicit a pride emotion; and also an emotional-neutral group of slides with ordinary objects and unexpressive people in mundane contexts. Pride activated the areas related to self-referent processing and self-reflection, especially the posterior medial cortex. Activation of the left inferior temporal and parahippocampal regions suggests engagement of the participants' autobiographical memory connecting to their own pride experiences. In contrast, compassion activated the midbrain PAG and the anterior region of the right inferior frontal gyrus (IFG)—pars triangularis. The midbrain PAG is an area associated with parental caretaking behaviors and empathy as well as pain regulation; it is the region that is activated during a person's experience of pain and also the perception of another person's pain. When activated, it releases endogenous opioids that inhibit pain signals to the cortex. But it is also involved with parental nurturance. When considered with other research, the PAG shows activation in attachment-related states like maternal love and unconditional love, and also states of empathy for pain in others. It appears that this area along with oxytocin release would motivate, reinforce, and provide resources for parental nurturing behaviors. Activation of the right IFG is related to empathy process in the empathic mirroring of facial expressions, emotion inference, and emotion regulation. It is also involved in the cognitive control of memory processes that could support its role in an emotion simulation system when observing others who are suffering. Overall, the study provides some evidence for the uniqueness

of compassion as an emotional response and how it involves aspects of both the empathy network and the caregiving systems.

Compassion appears to be distinct from empathy

While the research on the neural distinctiveness of compassion is at an early stage, there is evidence that compassion is distinct from empathy, and this distinction may provide the key to managing clinician burnout. What the most recent research seems to suggest is that the emotional toll that results from empathizing with patients all the time is due to the fact that this is empathy without the protective effects of a compassionate approach to working with patients. Compassion, in a sense, helps contain and redirect the empathic resonance with patients that is in fact better for clinicians as well as patients. Klimecki and Singer (2011) have differentiated the constructs of empathy, compassion, and compassion fatigue and found that "a new integrative model arises that can account for mechanisms underlying compassion fatigue. This model suggests that, rather than compassion fatigue, it is empathic distress that underlies the negative consequences of caregivers who are exposed to others' suffering" (p. 370). An approach centered on compassion helps direct the empathy in a way that does not emotionally burden and distress the clinician, such as when a clinician is using an empathic approach without the protective (and ultimately more helpful) features of compassion.

Empathizing can go in two directions; the first is personal distress

As Klimecki and Singer (2011) explain, when a clinician empathizes with the suffering of a patient, this empathy can go in one of two directions within the inner life of the clinician.

In the first direction, the clinician empathically resonates with the patient's suffering and vicariously experiences the negative emotions of the patient. This can often be felt as overwhelming and personally distressing to the clinician. One of the reasons this occurs, according to Klimecki and Singer, is that there is not a clear distinction between the clinician self and the other person. The clinician identifies with the patient's feelings (what Klimecki and Singer call a state of empathic distress) and then tries to reduce that personal distress by withdrawing or distancing from the situation in some way. This withdrawal is not intended to harm the patient; it is a self-protective move on the part of the clinician (see figure 3.3). What I have observed in clinicians is that besides withdrawing from the patient, a clinician might self-protect by emotionally detaching from the patient or becoming explicitly or subtly hostile toward the patient as a way to distance from the internalized empathic distress. If the clinician is not able to manage this empathic distress by a distancing maneuver, then the clinician may become overwhelmed and respond to the patient based on that distress. This may be one of the mechanisms for how clinicians become overinvolved with patients; that is, the clinician helps the patient more to soothe the clinician's own distress than to help the patient in his or her suffering: "I help you so that I can feel better."

The second way empathizing can go is compassion

The second direction of empathy is one that results in feelings of concern or compassion *for* the person suffering. It is other-oriented in that there is not a loss of the self–other distinction, and there is not an identification with that person's suffering. The clinician maintains awareness

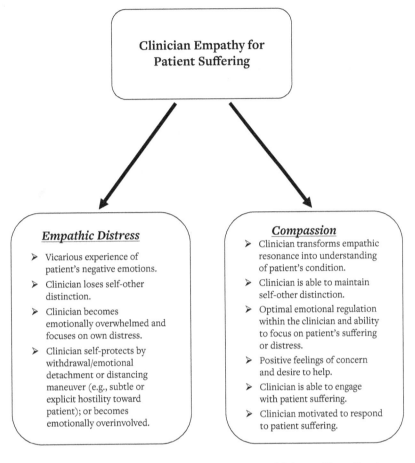

FIGURE 3.3 Two possible pathways in empathizing with patient suffering (adapted from Singer & Klimecki, p. R875).

that it is the other person who is in a state of suffering. The clinician is able to emotionally regulate his or her own negative feelings and focuses on responding with feelings of concern for the patient. "In other words, the compassionate person has the capacity to help because he or she is not overwhelmed by distress, but instead guided by feelings of concern, love, or affection toward the other" (Klimecki & Singer, 2011, p. 377). In short, the clinician has transformed the automatic empathic resonance into understanding the patient's condition and can positively engage with the distressed or suffering patient in the attempt to try to alleviate the patient's suffering.

Experiment revealing distinct neural characteristics of empathy versus compassion

In an ingenious experiment, Klimecki, Leiberg, Ricard, and Singer (2014) sought to show what happens when empathy alone is trained, and then what happens when compassion is trained. The goal was to experimentally test whether compassion training can mitigate the negative emotional transfer in empathy. The researchers sought to determine both whether these had distinct neural characteristics and whether there would be participant reports of less subjective stress with compassion training versus empathy training. Klimecki et al. (2014) constructed a prospective training study in which one group was first trained in empathic resonance and later received compassion training. The participants' reactions and brain activity were measured after empathy training, then later after the compassion training. They were also compared to a control group that received a memory training task for the same amount of time. The task involved watching high- and low-emotion videos from the news or documentaries of people who were suffering from injuries or natural disasters. Measurements included the participants' self-report of their affective states during the study and blood oxygenation levels in repeated fMRI measures. In the empathic resonance training, participants focused on resonating with the suffering depicted. They were instructed to empathize with the other person's suffering and imagine it as if it were their own pain.

How compassion was trained in the experiment

The research participants subsequently received compassion training that consisted of a contemplative technique from a secular compassion training program that is an adaptation of the loving-kindness meditation from Buddhism. The aim of the compassion training was to cultivate feelings of benevolence and friendship in a state of quiet concentration (Salzberg, 2002). It works by extending the caring feelings one experiences with close loved ones to other human beings who are not close to the person. The guided contemplative practices first have the participant visualize a close loved one, then extend these feelings toward themselves, then a close person, a neutral person, a person in difficulty, strangers, and human beings in general.

Results showing distinct brain regions for empathy versus compassion

After empathic resonance training, participants reported increased empathic responses and increased distressing negative affect with both the high- and low-emotion videos. After compassion training, the negative affect returned to baseline levels, and there was an increase in positive affect. Furthermore, there were distinct patterns of neural activity. Empathy training increased brain activations in the anterior insula and anterior midcingulate cortex, which are brain regions involved with empathy for pain. These areas are also involved in self-experienced pain and negative affect. Subsequent compassion training increased activations in a nonoverlapping brain network of the ventral striatum, pregenual ACC, and the medial orbitofrontal cortex. These are networks associated with affiliation, reward, and positive affect. The researchers concluded that

> this suggests that ... the generation of compassion in response to distressing situations is distinct from other emotion regulation strategies, such as suppression or reappraisal, which involve an active down-regulation of negative affect. Thus, the generation of compassion focuses on strengthening positive affect, while not ignoring the presence of suffering or changing the negative reality. (Klimecki et al., 2014, p. 877)

Implications of this experiment for clinicians

In terms of the neurophysiology of empathy and compassion, this study demonstrates a number of important dynamics that will be of major importance for how compassionate caring operates within clinicians. First, it provides evidence that compassion is built on empathy but is distinct from it. There is a way in which compassion functions as a channel or container for the empathic resonance so that it does not lead to overwhelming or distressing the clinician. As Singer & Klimecki (2014) put it,

> *in contrast to empathy, compassion does not mean sharing the suffering of the other: rather, it is characterized by feelings of warmth, concern and care for the other, as well as a strong motivation to improve the other's wellbeing. Compassion is feeling for and not feeling with the other. (p. R875)*

Second, compassion connects to the positive affect, reward, and affiliation brain regions and subjectively adds a positive emotional dimension to the experience of compassion. The negative affect is still experienced, but it is less overwhelming, with the added focus on the positive desire to attempt to relieve the suffering of the other. This positive affective experience is key to clinician resilience and balanced compassionate caring, as I will show in the rest of this book. Third, what is fascinating is that there was a differential pattern of brain activity with a relatively brief intervention. The compassion training was completed in a one-day, 6-hour training session. Participants practiced this an average of 5.7 hours on their own with at least 2 additional supervised training hours (Klimecki, Leiberg, Lamm, and Singer, 2013). This suggests that longer-term brain training with compassion induction elements may be a way to buffer burnout. This also strongly indicates that this compassionate approach can be trained in clinicians.

Growing evidence for the distinct brain regions for affective empathy, cognitive empathy, and compassion

One of the most important findings from the science of compassion is that there are distinct brain networks for the affective and cognitive empathic processes and for compassion.

Additional neuroscientific evidence continues to delineate these distinct and interconnecting neural networks (Asha, Andrews-Hanna, Dimidjian, & Wager, 2017; Lamm, Rütgen, & Wagner, 2019; Marsh, 2018; Preckel, Kanske, & Singer, 2018; Yu & Chou, 2018; Weisz & Zaki, 2018). Preckel, Kanske, and Singer (2018) have summarized much of this research, as seen in table 3.1. The automatic emotional or empathic resonance of bottom-up empathy processing occurs in the empathy for pain matrix brain regions and the mirror neuron network. Top-down empathy processing occurs in brain regions associated with the cognitive process of empathy in which the clinician takes the other person's perspective, that is, infers the thought, emotions, and beliefs of the suffering person which we call theory of mind or mentalizing. As we have seen in this chapter, research has shown how the affect-sharing component of empathy is an independent process from theory of mind/mentalizing, but it is most helpful in responding to another person when both processes are activated and balanced together. A key component in encountering the emotional experiences of others is the ability to differentiate one's own emotional and mental state from the other's emotional and mental state. Being able to differentiate self from the other enables the clinician not to make mistaken inferences based on the undifferentiated blending of one's own and the other's experience. Examples of these mistakes include an egocentricity bias projecting one's own thoughts and feelings onto others, thinking that the other feels and thinks exactly as oneself. The clinician erroneously judges the other person based on the clinician's own emotional or mental state, not being able to accurately judge the distinct emotional and cognitive state of the other person. Another mistake is picking up the emotional and mental state of the other leading to judging oneself based on how another person feels; Preckel et al. (2018) call this an altercentric bias. The TPJ and the SMG appear to be brain regions particularly connected with the capacity for self-other distinction. Finally, compassion is an activation of the brain networks associated with generating positive emotion by activating the reward and affiliation brain networks. The generation of the positive affect within the clinician emotionally regulates and contains the negative affect that emerges in empathizing with the suffering person. Rather than becoming emotionally distressed or overwhelmed in the encounter with the suffering person, the clinician experiences a positive sense of concern and warmth toward the other person connected to a motivation to do something to help the other person in some way (Preckel et al., 2018).

TABLE 3.1 Distinct and Interconnecting Brain Networks for Empathy, Theory of Mind/Mentalizing, and Compassion

Based on Preckel, K., Kanske, P., & Singer, T. (2018). On the interaction of social affect and cognition: Empathy, compassion and theory of mind. *Current Opinion in Behavioral Sciences, 19*: 1–6.

SOCIO-AFFECTIVE AND SOCIO-COGNITIVE PROCESSES	BRAIN REGIONS PRINCIPALLY INVOLVED	NEURAL NETWORKS
Empathy for Suffering/ Automatic Empathic Resonance/ Affect Sharing	Anterior insula (AI) Anterior middle cingulate cortex (aMCC) Dorsolateral prefrontal cortex (dlPFC) Supramarginal gyrus (SMG)	Pain matrix/ Empathy for pain Mirror neuron system Emotional empathy network
Theory of Mind/Mentalizing/ Cognitive Empathy	Temporoparietal junction (TPJ) Superior temporal sulcus (STS) Temporal poles (TP) Posterior cingulate cortex (PCC) Precuneous (PC) Medial prefrontal cortex (mPFC)	Cognitive empathy network, representing or inferring others' mental states/ Perspective-taking
Compassion/Prosocial Behavior	Globus pallidus (GP) Medial orbitofrontal cortex (mOFC) Substantia nigra (SN) Ventral striatum (VS) Ventral tegmental area (VTA) Subgenual anterior cingulate cortex(sgACC) Putamen (PUT) Nucleus accumbens (NAcc)	Networks associated with reward, affiliation, and positive emotion

CONCLUSION

Human beings are built for compassion. From the perspective of evolutionary biology, we can see how our success as a species was built on the capacity to notice the sufferings of others and have the desire to alleviate it. The neuroscience of empathy describes the brain mechanisms that make the sufferings of others have an impact on those around them. The polyvagal theory describes how the perception of safety is critically important for the giving and receiving of compassion. Neurobiologically, the selective investment theory provides a description of how the human caregiving system is structured and what happens as the person acts in terms of self-interest or altruism. What we do in the helping professions is built on these caregiving circuits and processes.

When human beings encounter suffering in others, they may either become personally distressed from that empathic resonance or go into a state of compassion. Compassion is neurally distinct from empathy, and there is now evidence of how this brain state can be achieved and trained. These are just some of the new findings from evolutionary biology, physiology, neuroscience, and psychology that provide us with information clinicians can use to understand themselves and their patients. As we will see in the following chapters, these scientific discoveries of how we are built for compassion offer insight into what are the optimal ways for us to engage the suffering of our patients so that our patients benefit and we as clinicians can successfully live a life of compassionate caring.

QUESTIONS FOR DISCUSSION

1. What is your reaction to reading this summary of some of the research on the biology and neuroscience of empathy and compassion?
2. What would you change in your approach to your clinical work, given what you have read in this chapter?

REFERENCES

Ashar, Y. K., Andrews-Hanna, J. R., Dimidjian, S., Wager, T. D. (2017). Empathic care and distress: Predictive brain markers and dissociable brain systems. *Neuron*, *94*, 1263–1273.

Batson, C. D. (2010). Empathy-induced altruistic motivation. In M. Mikulincer & P. Shaver (Eds.), *Prosocial motives, emotions, and behavior: The better angels of our nature* (pp. 15–34). Washington, DC: American Psychological Association.

Batson, C. D. (2011). *Altruism in humans.* New York, NY: Oxford University Press.

Bird, G., & Viding, E. (2014). The self to other model of empathy: Providing a new framework for understanding empathy impairments in psychopathy, autism, and alexithymia. *Neuroscience and Biobehavioral Reviews*, *47*, 520–532.

Bowlby, J. (1980). *Loss: Sadness and depression.* Vol. III of *Attachment and loss.* New York, NY: Basic Books.

Bowlby, J. (2005a). *The making and breaking of affectional bonds*. New York, NY: Routledge.

Bowlby, J. (2005b). *A secure base: Clinical applications of attachment theory*. New York, NY: Routledge.

Brown, S. L. (2012, July). *Placing compassion in a neurobiological and evolutionary framework*. Presented at The Science of Compassion: Origins, Measures, and Interventions Conference, Telluride, CO.

Brown, S. L., & Brown, R. M. (2006). Selective investment theory: Recasting the functional significance of close relationships. *Psychological Inquiry, 17*(1), 1–29.

Brown, S. L., Brown, R. M., & Preston, S. D. (2012). The human caregiving system: A neuroscience model of compassionate motivation and behavior. In *Moving beyond self-interest: Perspectives from evolutionary biology, neuroscience and the social sciences* (pp. 75–88). New York, NY: Oxford University Press.

Brown, S. L., Nesse, R. M., Vinokur, A. D., & Smith, D. M. (2003). Providing social support may be more beneficial than receiving it: Results from a prospective study of mortality. *Psychological Science, 14*(4), 320–327.

Brown, S. L., Smith, D. M., Schulz, R., Kabeto, M. U., Ubel, P. A., Poulin, M., ... Langa, K. M. (2009). Caregiving behavior is associated with decreased mortality risk. *Psychological Science, 20*(4), 488–494.

Carter, C. S. (1998). Neuroendrocrine perspectives on social attachment and love. *Psychoneuroendocrinology, 23*(8), 779–818.

Carter, C. S., Lederhendler, I., & Kirkpatrick, B. (1997). The integrative neurobiology of affiliation. *Annals of the New York Academy of Sciences, 807*, xiii–xviii.

Corbetta, M., Patel, G., & Shulman, G. L. (2008). The reorienting system of the human brain: From environment to theory of mind. *Neuron, 58*, 306–324.

Decety, J. (2011). Dissecting the neural mechanisms mediating empathy. *Emotion Review, 3*(1), 92–108.

Decety, J., & Lamm, C. (2006). Human empathy through the lens of social neuroscience. *Scientific World Journal, 6*, 1146–1163.

Decety, J., & Lamm, C. (2011). Empathy versus personal distress: Recent evidence from social neuroscience. In J. Decety & W. Ickes (Eds), *The social neuroscience of empathy* (pp. 199–213). Cambridge, MA: MIT Press.

Decety, J., Yang, C.-Y., & Cheng, Y. (2010). Physicians down-regulate their pain empathy response: An event-related brain potential study. *NeuroImage, 50*, 1676–1682.

Dimberg, U., Thunberg, M., & Elmehed, K. (2000). Unconscious facial reactions to emotional facial expressions. *Psychological Science, 11*(1), 86–89.

Di Pellegrino, G., Fadiga, L., Fogassi, L, Gallese, V., & Rizzolatti, G. (1992). Understanding motor events: A neurophysiological study. *Experimental Brain Research, 91*(1), 176–180.

Dykema, R. (2006). How your nervous system sabotages your ability to relate: An interview with Stephen Porges about his polyvagal theory. Retrieved from https://www.sott.net/article/228410-How-your-nervous-system-sabotages-your-ability-to-relate

Eisler, R., & Levine, D. S. (2002). Nurture, nature, and caring: We are not prisoners of our genes. *Brain and Mind, 3*, 9–52.

Ekman, P. (2010). Darwin's compassionate view of human nature. *Journal of the American Medical Association, 303*(6), 557–558.

Floyd, K., Mikkelson, A. C., Tafoya, M. A., Farinelli, L., La Valley, A. G., Judd, J., ... Wilson, J. (2007). Human communication exchange: XIII. Affectionate communication accelerates neuroendocrine stress recovery. *Health Communication, 22*(2), 123–132.

Gallese, V., Keysers, C., & Rizzolatti, G. (2004). A unifying view of the basis of social cognition. *Trends in Cognitive Sciences, 8*(9), 396–403.

Goubert, L., Craig, K. D., Vervoort, T., Morley, S., Sullivan, M. J. L., Williams, A. C. de C., ... Crombez, G. (2005). Facing others in pain: The effects of empathy. *Pain, 118*, 285–288.

Hatfield, E., Cacioppo, J. T., & Rapson, R. L. (1994). *Emotional contagion*. New York, NY: Cambridge University Press.

Hojat, M., Mangione, S., Nasca, T. J., Rattner, S., Erdmann, J. B., Gonnella, J. S., & Magee, M. (2004). An empirical study of decline in empathy in medical school. *Medical Education, 38*, 934–941.

Kajanoja, J., Scheinin, N. M., Karlsson, L., Karlsson, H. & Karukivi, M. (2017). Illuminating the clinical significance of alexithymia subtypes: A cluster analysis of alexithymic traits and psychiatric symptoms. *Journal of Psychosomatic Research, 97*, 111–117.

Kanske, P., Böckler, A., & Singer, T. (2016). Models, mechanisms and moderators dissociating empathy and theory of mind. *Current Topics in Behavioral Neuroscience, 30*, 193–206.

Kanske, P., Böckler, A., Trautwein, F.-M., Lesemann, F. H. P., & Singer, T. (2016). Are strong empathizers better mentalizers? Evidence for independence and interaction between the routes of social cognition. *Social Cognitive and Affective Neuroscience, 11*(9), 1383–1392.

Kanske, P., Böckler, A., Trautwein, F.-M., & Singer, T. (2015). Dissecting the social brain: Introducing the EmpaToM to reveal distinct neural networks and brain-behavior relations for empathy and Theory of Mind. *NeuroImage, 122*, 6–19.

Kanske, P., Schönfelder, S., & Wessa, M. (2013). Emotional modulation of the attentional blink and the relation to interpersonal reactivity. *Frontiers in Human Neuroscience, 7*, 1–9.

Keltner, D. (2009). *Born to be good: The science of a meaningful life*. New York, NY: Norton.

Klimecki, O. M., Leiberg, S., Lamm, C., & Singer, T. (2013). Functional neural plasticity and associated changes in positive affect after compassion training. *Cerebral Cortex, 23*, 1552–1561.

Klimecki, O. M., Leiberg, S., Ricard, M., & Singer, T. (2014). Differential pattern of functional brain plasticity after compassion and empathy training. *Social Cognitive and Affective Neuroscience, 9*, 873–879.

Klimecki, O., & Singer, T. (2011). Empathic distress fatigue rather than compassion fatigue? Integrating findings from empathy research in psychology and social neuroscience. In B. Oakley, A. Knafo, G. Madhavan, & D. S. Wilson (Eds.), *Pathological altruism* (pp. 368–383). New York, NY: Oxford University Press.

Konrath, S., Fuhrel-Forbis, A., Lou, A., & Brown, S. (2012). Motives for volunteering are associated with mortality risk in older adults. *Health Psychology, 31*(1), 87–96.

Lamm, C., Decety, J., & Singer, T. (2011). Meta-analytic evidence for common and distinct neural networks associated with directly experienced pain and empathy for pain. *NeuroImage, 54*, 2492–2502.

Lamm, C., Rütgen, M., & Wagner, I. C. (2019). Imaging empathy and prosocial emotions. *Neuroscience Letters, 693*, 49–53.

Levenson, R. W., Ekman, P., & Friesen, W. V. (1990). Voluntary facial action generates emotion-specific autonomic nervous system activity. *Psychophysiology, 27*(4), 363–384.

Marsh, A. A. (2018). The neuroscience of empathy. *Current Opinion in Behavioral Sciences, 19*, 110–115.

Menon, V., & Uddin, L. Q. (2010). Saliency, switching, attention and control: A network model of insula function. *Brain Structure and Functioning, 214*, 655–667.

Meyer, M. L., Masten, C. L., Ma, Y., Wang, C., Shi, Z., & Eisenberger, N. I. (2013). Empathy for the social suffering of friends and strangers recruits distinct patterns of brain activation. *Social Cognitive and Affective Neuroscience, 8*(4), 446–454.

Moll, J., Krueger, F., Zahn, R., Pardini, M., de Oliveira-Souza, R., & Grafman, J. (2006). Human fronto-mesolimbic networks guide decisions about charitable donation. *PNAS, 103*(42), 15623–15628.

Neumann, M., Edelhäuser, F., Tauschel, D., Fischer, M. R., Wirtz, M., Woopen, C., … Scheffer, C. (2011). Empathy decline and its reasons: A systematic review of studies with medical students and residents. *Academic Medicine, 86*, 996–1009.

Numan, M. (2006). Hypothalamic neural circuits regulating maternal responsiveness toward infants. *Behavioral and Cognitive Neuroscience Reviews, 5*(4), 163–190.

Porges, S. W. (1995). Orienting in a defensive world: Mammalian modifications of our evolutionary heritage; A polyvagal theory. *Psychophysiology, 32,* 301–318.

Porges, S. W. (2001). The polyvagal theory: Phylogenetic substrates of a social nervous system. *International Journal of Psychophysiology, 42,* 123–146.

Porges, S. W. (2007). The polyvagal perspective. *Biological Psychology, 74,* 116–143.

Porges, S. W. (2009). The polyvagal theory: New insights into adaptive reactions of the autonomic nervous system. *Cleveland Clinic Journal of Medicine, 76*(Suppl. 2), S86–S90.

Porges, S. W. (2011). *The polyvagal theory: Neurophysiological foundations of emotions, attachment, communication, and self-regulation.* New York, NY: Norton.

Porges, S. W. (2012, July). *The origins of compassion: A phylogenetic perspective.* Presented at The Science of Compassion: Origins, Measures, and Interventions International Conference, Telluride, CO.

Poulin, M. J. (2014). Volunteering predicts health among those who value others: Two national studies. *Health Psychology, 33*(2), 120–129.

Poulin, M. J., Brown, S. L., Ubel, P. A., Smith, D. M., Jankovic, A. & Langa, K. M. (2010). Does a helping hand mean a heavy heart? Helping behavior and well-being among spouse caregivers. *Psychology and Aging, 25*(1), 108–117.

Preckel, K., Kanske, P., & Singer, T. (2018). On the interaction of social affect and cognition: Empathy, compassion and theory of mind. *Current Opinion in Behavioral Sciences, 19,* 1–6.

Preston, S. D., & de Waal, F. B. M. (2002). Empathy: Its ultimate and proximate bases. *Behavioral and Brain Sciences, 25,* 1–72.

Rizzolatti, G., Fabbri-Destro, M., & Cattaneo, L. (2009). Mirror neurons and their clinical relevance. *Nature Clinical Practice Neurology, 5*(1), 24–34.

Salzberg, S. (2002). *Loving-kindness: The revolutionary art of happiness.* Boston, MA: Shambhala.

Seppala, E. M., Simon-Thomas, E., Brown, S. L., Worline, M. C., Cameron, C. D., & Doty, J. R. (2017). *The Oxford handbook of compassion science.* New York, NY: Oxford University Press.

Siegel, D. J. (2011). *Mindsight: The new science of personal transformation.* New York, NY: Bantam Books.

Simon-Thomas, E. R. (2015, March). Measuring compassion in the body. *Greater Good,* University of California, Berkeley. Retrieved from –http://greatergood.berkeley.edu/article/item/measuring_compassion_in_the_body

Simon-Thomas, E. R., Godzik, J., Castle, E., Antonenko, O., Ponz, A., Kogan, A. & Keltner, D. J. (2012). An fMRI study of caring vs self-focus during induced compassion and pride. *Social Cognitive and Affective Neuroscience, 7*(6), 635–648.

Singer, T. (2006). The neuronal basis and ontogeny of empathy and mind reading: Review of the literature and implications for future research. *Neuroscience and Biobehavioral Reviews, 30,* 855–863.

Singer, T., & Klimecki, O. M. (2014). Empathy and compassion. *Current Biology, 24*(18), R875–R878.

Singer, T., Seymour, B., O'Doherty, J., Kaube, H., Dolan, R. J., & Firth, C. D. (2004). Empathy for pain involves the affective but not the sensory components of pain. *Science, 303,* 1157–1162.

Singer, T., Seymour, B., O'Doherty, J. P., Stephan, K. E., Dolan, R. J., & Frith, C. D. (2006). Empathic neural responses are modulated by the perceived fairness of others. *Nature, 439*(7075), 466–469.

Stellar, J. E., Cohen, A., Oveis, C., & Keltner, D. (2015). Affective and physiological responses to the suffering of others: Compassion and vagal activity. *Journal of Personality and Social Psychology, 108*(4), 572–585.

Stellar, J. E., & Keltner, D. (2014). Compassion. In M. M. Tugade, M. N. Shiota, & L. D. Kirby (Eds.), *Handbook of positive emotions* (pp. 329–341). New York, NY: Guilford Press.

Tusche, A., Böckler, A., Kanske, P., Trautwein, F.-M., & Singer, T. (2016). Decoding the charitable brain: Empathy, perspective taking, and attention shift differentially predict altruistic giving. *Journal of Neuroscience, 36*(17), 4719–4732.

Watson, J. C., & Greenburg, L. S., (2009). Empathic resonance: A neuroscience perspective. In J. Decety & W. Ickes (Eds.), *The social neuroscience of empathy* (pp. 125–138). Cambridge, MA: MIT Press.

Weisz, E. & Zaki, J. (2018). Motivated empathy: A social neuroscience perspective. *Current Opinion in Psychology, 24*, 67–71.

Yu, C. L. & Chou, T. L. (2018). A dual route model of empathy: A neurobiological prospective. *Frontiers in Psychology, 9*, 1–5.

Zak, P. J. (2008). The neurobiology of trust. *Scientific American, 298*(6), 88–92, 95.

Zak, P. J., Kurzban, R., & Matzner, W. T. (2004). The neurobiology of trust. *Annals of the New York Academy of Sciences, 1032*, 224–227.

Zak, P. J., Kurzban, R., & Matzner, W. T. (2005). Oxytocin is associated with human trustworthiness. *Hormones and Behavior, 48*, 522–527.

CREDIT

> "A ship in harbor is safe, but that is not what ships are built for."
>
> —John A. Shedd

Chapter Sections:

---

1   Special thanks to Ruby Hollinger, Jean Llenos, Clare Scantling, and Delaney Weiland for their assistance in developing the clinician compassion mindset model.

CHAPTER 4

The Clinician Compassion Mindset Process

Questions to consider before reading this chapter:

1. How do you know when you are no longer in a state of compassionate caring toward your patient?

2. What do you find that you have to do when you want to be compassionate and you are working with a patient you find difficult or do not like?

INTRODUCTION

Chapters 2 and 3 summarized the most recent research on compassion as a scientific phenomenon in terms of biology, neuroscience, psychology, and the latest thinking on an empirical definition of compassionate caring as it would apply to the practice of clinical medicine. There is a great deal more research that provides much more intricate descriptions of these processes, as well as many questions that are not yet answered. With all due respect to this very complex process, this chapter offers an integrative summary as an attempt to bring these wonderful discoveries to the practical clinical world. With apologies to these researchers for some simplifying of their complex research, it is vitally important that those of us practicing in the clinical world begin to incorporate these discoveries in our own work. This research already offers extremely important information that enables us to understand how compassionate caring can be the central organizing principle for all that we do in health care. Figure 4.1 offers an integrative model called the *clinician compassion mindset process* that provides a way to pull together all the information in these first chapters for practical use.

For all the amazing accomplishments of science and the practice of medicine, it is interesting that there has not been more of an effort to articulate the psychology of optimum mental performance in physicians and other clinicians. Despite our declaration that the biopsychosocial approach is better for our patients than the strictly biomedical model, we still devalue the realm of the psychological in our patients and consider it a distraction from our main purpose. Cassell (1982) pointed this out when he wrote, "so long as the mind–body dichotomy is accepted, suffering is either subjective and thus not really 'real'—not within medicine's domain—or identified exclusively with bodily pain" (p. 640). It actually makes perfect sense that we would minimize it when we reflect on ourselves psychologically in terms of what is happening in our own minds (and bodies) as we work with patients. We have been in need of a full articulation of what constitutes optimal mental performance in the practice of medicine, especially when we are in a compassion mindset. Interestingly, the military has articulated what is needed for the optimum performance of soldiers in combat. One of the premier books summarizing this is *Warrior Mindset: Mental Toughness Skills for a Nation's Peacekeepers*, which describes in detail performance psychology applied to combat. In introducing the book, Asken, Grossman, and Christensen (2010) lay out why they believe this is necessary:

> *Thus, the overriding goal of Warrior Mindset is to … provide military, police and their leaders with a foundation in the psychological skills of mental toughness that promotes optimal response, and especially in high stress missions and operations. Individual officers and personnel will vary in their need for this training. As in all areas of high-level human performance, some officers and individuals are already adept at such skills. We usually want to study these individuals to learn what makes them so effective. But it has been our experience that even these warriors can refine their skills, or come to a better understanding of what they are doing, which will result in even more flexibility and effectiveness in fulfilling their duty. (pp. xiii–xiv)*

When I discovered a similar book titled *On Combat: The Psychology and Physiology of Deadly Conflict in War and Peace* (Grossman & Christensen, 2008), it seemed a strange parallel to this book when I read the table of contents. It has chapters called "Sympathetic and Parasympathetic Nervous System: The Body's Combat and Maintenance Troops"; "Stress Inoculation and Fear: Practicing to Be Miserable"; "Making the Decision to Kill: 'I Killed Someone. But Someone Lived'"; "Relief, Self-Blame and Other Emotions: 'My World Was Turned Inside Out'"; and "A Time to Heal: The Role of Critical Incident Debriefings in Preventing PTSD." It validated for me that we need to articulate our own optimum psychological performance and that we are, in fact, quite behind in doing this.

In medicine, we often think that what it takes to approach and engage a patient with a compassion mindset is something simple enough that clinicians can just pick it up on the fly. In *On Combat*, Grossman and Christensen (2004) warn

> *you do not rise to the occasion in combat; you sink to the level of your training. Do not expect the combat fairy to come bonk you with the combat wand and suddenly make you capable of doing things that you never rehearsed before.* It will not happen. (*p. 33*)

A similar thing is true in medicine. Maintaining a compassion mindset while working with one challenging patient after another in a complicated, dysfunctional health care system requires advanced mental training and rehearsal.

Jimmy Fallon, late-night television comedian, periodically does a game with his guests called the Wheel of Musical Impressions. In the game, the guest on the show is given a random song title that he or she must sing in the style of a random singer. Inspired by this, I created the Clinical Attitude Generator for our Medical

Counseling Skills course. A patient actor picks a student at random, and the student picks a random clinical attitude. The random clinical attitudes include "You are a doctor who is exhausted from working too much, and you use this to play the martyr with patients"; "You are really smart, and you like to show this to patients using a lot of technical words and complicated explanations"; "You are expecting this patient to be difficult"; and "You are preoccupied with a personal problem and it leaks out into your visit with your patient." The student has to demonstrate this attitude verbally and nonverbally within the first two to three minutes of a new patient visit with an improv patient actor. What is fascinating is how students will creatively generate amazing portrayals of those attitudes. They can infuse that particular attitude into the typical elements of a patient visit so that the attitude can be felt from the very moment the student clinician meets the patient. The students learn how there is always a clinical attitude generated and expressed with every patient, and they discover how much the clinical attitude they adopt influences whatever they do.

The term *mindset* captures this dynamic. *Mindset* is defined as "a fixed mental attitude or disposition that predetermines a person's responses to and interpretations of situations" (Mindset, n.d.). Whatever the clinician has to do and whatever the clinician encounters are processed or filtered through this mindset. With a compassion mindset, everything the clinician thinks, feels, and does is generated from this fundamental point of view. This compassionate stance is the way the clinician approaches whatever happens in the encounter with the patient. Figure 4.1 shows the mental steps the clinician goes through if he or she is in a compassion mindset. Each step is appraised through the frame or lens of compassion. Building on

the work of Goetz, Keltner, and Simon-Thomas (2010), the clinician encounters a sequence of mental actions, described as questions the clinician has to navigate from the encounter with a patient to the compassionate response. This happens very rapidly in terms of neurophysiology and cognition, and they can become automatic. But the speed does not mean the steps do not occur. At each step, it is possible to fall out of a compassion mindset. A clinician can become personally distressed by the patient, overwhelmed by the patient, or even disgusted by the patient and treat the patient out of that distressed, overwhelmed, or disgusted mindset. If the clinician remains in this emotional state, he or she may treat the patient out of that mindset. The clinician may avoid or withdraw from the patient as a result. Or the clinician may continue to treat the patient but do so in a hostile or emotionally conflicted manner. But at most steps in the clinician compassion mindset process, there is also the possibility of recovering or resetting a compassion mindset and getting back on the path to providing a compassionate response to the patient. Even if the clinician failed to stay in a compassion mindset, it is possible to reflect and learn from the reasons for compassion failure and apply what he or she has learned to future work with patients. In what follows, I will describe each of these steps.

Note that I am calling this the *clinician compassion mindset process*, not the clinician *compassionate* mindset process. As we have seen in chapters 2 and 3, compassion is a specific mental and motivational state that organizes the clinician's thoughts, feelings, and actions in a particular manner. The adjective *compassionate* might erroneous imply that compassion influences the mindset but is not central to the mindset. Referring to the mindset as a compassion mindset more accurately describes how compassion is the central organizing process for what is happening within the clinician in terms of cognition, emotion, motivation, and action.

DEFINITION OF COMPASSION: NOTICING ANOTHER'S SUFFERING, EMPATHIC RESONANCE, INTENTION TO RELIEVE SUFFERING, AND ACTING TO RELIEVE THE SUFFERING

The clinician compassion mindset process diagram is situated above the scientific definition of compassion, providing what constitutes each component in a clinician who is in a compassion mindset. Jinpa and other compassion researchers (Jinpa, 2012; Jazaieri et al., 2016) scientifically define compassion as beginning with noticing or becoming aware of another person's suffering (cognitive/attentional component), then being empathically moved by that suffering (affective component), which then leads to the person wishing or desiring to relieve that suffering (intentional component), and finally the person responding or acting in some way to attempt to relieve that suffering (motivational component). Noticing another's suffering involves the encounter with a vulnerable patient condition or suffering and the clinician being willing and able to recognize and safely engage with the illness or suffering of the patient. Next, the component of empathic resonance is composed of the largest part of what occurs in the clinician compassion mindset process. As explained in detail in chapter 3, empathic resonance consists of first the bottom-up empathy processing and the top-down empathy processing (also called mentalizing or theory of mind) with emotion regulation. As I will explain further, typically we would

expect clinicians to experience automatic mirror neuron bottom-up empathy processing, but research has found that it is possible that a clinician may bypass that step. In the flowchart, I have noted this is possible. The risk of a clinician bypassing bottom-up empathy processing is that he or she loses useful data about the experience of the patient that can help the clinician be more attuned to the patient's experience and allow the clinician to tailor his or her responses to the patient more precisely. I have created the "Is the clinician aware of and able to understand the patient's emotional experience?" as a kind of fail-safe mental step so that if a clinician has suppressed bottom-up empathy processing, he or she can take the conscious step of briefly pausing cognitively to articulate what the patient might be going through emotionally. This step begins the process of top-down empathy processing with four appraisal questions that might capture what the clinician is doing in this phase in order to remain in a compassion mindset. The first appraisal question is "Does the clinician view the patient as a fellow human being who is ill or suffering?" Second, "Is the illness/suffering of the patient of primary concern to the clinician over self-interest?" Third, "Can the clinician view the patient as deserving of some type of help?" And fourth, "Does the clinician have the ability to cope with the illness/suffering of the patient?" Each of these four appraisal questions can be the occasion of falling out of a compassion mindset in which the clinician becomes personally distressed, overwhelmed, or disgusted by the patient suffering, leading the clinician to avoid, withdraw, become detached from the patient; be hostile toward the patient; or help the patient in an emotionally conflicted manner. But each of the four appraisal questions may be the occasion of the clinician who may initially be inclined to answer those appraisal questions negatively but enters the compassion reset and recovery box, in which the clinician is able to reappraise the patient situation and return to a compassion mindset. Other factors also influence this appraisal process, including intrapersonal situational factors of the clinician, interpersonal factors, and individual differences of the clinician. Following top-down empathy processing, the clinician enters the third component of compassion, generating the intention to relieve suffering; this underlies the appraisal question, "Is the clinician motivated to attempt to alleviate the illness/suffering?" If the clinician does desire to attempt to alleviate the patient's suffering, he or she then enters the fourth component of compassion, which is acting to attempt to relieve the suffering.

ENCOUNTER WITH VULNERABLE PATIENT CONDITION/SUFFERING

The clinician compassion mindset begins with an encounter with a vulnerable patient condition or suffering. The patient may be experiencing an illness, injury, or condition that causes pain or emotional concern. The patient may be suffering in some way from a particular condition. The patient may be vulnerable in some way, perhaps not realizing what is happening or that he or she is at risk for a negative condition. The first aspect of the clinician compassion mindset is to be able to notice what this vulnerability, illness, or suffering is.

In using this clinical compassion mindset diagram with clinicians, when only the term *suffering* was used, some clinicians tended not to perceive the term as applicable to their patients. For many clinicians, *suffering* denotes an extreme condition, and many patient conditions do not

appear to warrant this term from the clinician's perspective. I needed a term that would help clinicians realize all their patients may be facing some difficulty even though clinicians might not call it suffering in the strict sense of the term. To capture a wider sense of what patients can experience, I added the sense of vulnerability that accompanies any patient condition whether the patient has a minor issue or a major one that would warrant the stronger term of suffering.

IS THE CLINICIAN WILLING AND ABLE TO RECOGNIZE AND SAFELY ENGAGE WITH THE ILLNESS/SUFFERING OF THE PATIENT?

This involves three subcomponents:

1. The ability and desire to notice the patient's condition

2. A state of emotional and physical safety with appropriate boundaries

3. An emotionally attentive mental state allowing for therapeutic presence

Ability and desire to notice the patient's condition

The clinician compassion mindset process begins with the clinician being willing to notice and recognize what a patient is experiencing in terms of dealing with a particular patient condition, illness, or injury. This requires the ability to notice or detect when a patient is suffering or in distress in some way, physically and/or emotionally; anxious; discouraged; in pain; or struggling in a major or a minor way. The patient may be in pain or suffering in some way from any number of issues that present in a medical context. At times, the patient cues for difficulty, vulnerability, or suffering are obvious, and at other

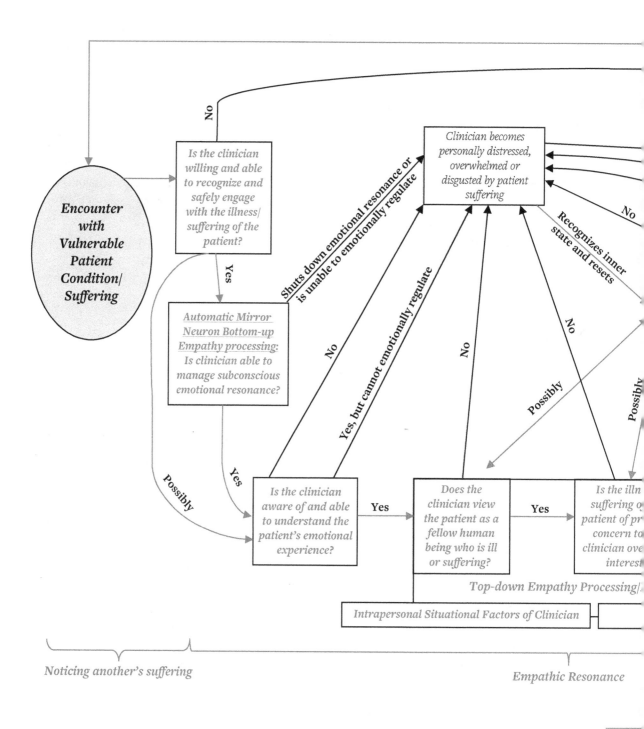

Clinician Compassion Mindset Process™

FIGURE 4.1 Clinician compassion mindset process.

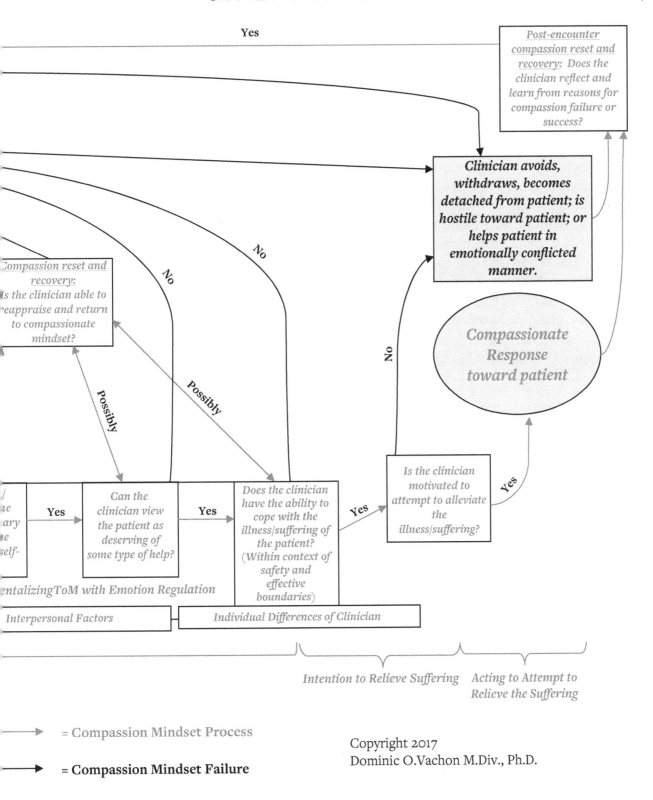

Copyright 2017
Dominic O.Vachon M.Div., Ph.D.

times, the clinician must be able to detect more subtle cues. Clinicians may encounter patients in some phase of experiencing an injury, illness, or problematic condition before assessment and diagnosis, during intervention, or during ongoing care. Compassion is focused on responding to patients as they experience injury or illness or other conditions that place them in a state of vulnerability, either physically or emotionally. At times the patient is not actively in illness or in a state of injury, but the clinician detects the potential for significant problems; in such cases, the clinician's compassionate response will be focused on helping prevent pain and suffering. While the patient may not be in pain or suffering, the clinician may perceive potential suffering in the patient's future and desire to try to prevent the patient from having that suffering.

State of emotional and physical safety with appropriate boundaries

In order for a clinician to be in a compassion mindset, it is necessary that he or she feel a sense of safety both physically and emotionally, as well as not feel taken advantage of as he or she works with patients. Threats to physical and emotional safety include patients or their loved ones who are imminently or actively hostile toward the clinician. Patients or their loved ones may be physically or emotionally threatening for a number of reasons. They may be fearful or under great stress, and this at times can be expressed in physical violence or emotional abusiveness toward the clinician. Patients can be explicitly threatening or more subtly threatening (e.g., threatening lawsuit; insulting the clinician's gender, race, or ethnicity). In order to be in a compassion mindset, the clinician must be able to detect the lack of safety and do

what is necessary to feel safe enough to treat the patient. If the clinician is fearful for his or her safety, it will be difficult for the clinician to focus his or her attention on what the patient needs. Furthermore, if the clinician feels he or she is being manipulated, used, or lied to, the clinician must be able to acknowledge and manage this. The key issue is that if the clinician is dwelling on his or her own safety or is focused on how he or she is being used inappropriately, then that clinician will not be cognitively and emotionally focused on what is needed to help the patient. To manage this, the clinician must either create a safe atmosphere to work (e.g., have security present, use restraints, use sedation, use a de-escalation communication technique, set effective limits) or end the interaction until it can be safely resumed.

Related to having a sense of safety in order to treat a patient is the clinician's ability to set boundaries with patients and their loved ones when necessary. For example, there are times when patients and their loved ones might pressure clinicians to give them a particular test, procedure, or medication even though the clinician judges this to be inappropriate. A patient or their loved ones might be intrusive or inappropriate in some way (e.g., emotionally disturbing, sexually inappropriate, making a request not befitting of the role of the clinician). The clinician must be able to notice threats to good boundaries and assertively maintain them when necessary as they interact with patients and patients' loved ones.

Emotionally attentive mental state allowing for therapeutic presence

In order to be in a clinician compassion mindset, the clinician must be in a state of emotional regulation and composure, along with a focused cognitive attentiveness on the patient. The clinician must be able to devote him- or herself cognitively and emotionally to what the patient is going through without being distracted by personal emotional issues, other problems occurring before this patient interaction, or any mental condition that interferes with the ability to be fully attentive to the patient. To be in a compassion mindset, clinicians learn how to be present with their current patients no matter what has occurred before meeting that patient and to focus their clinical judgment and intellectual resources on the patient in front of them. Any emotional or cognitive carryover from other sources can interfere with assessing and treating a patient accurately. If, for example, a clinician has had a previous patient who was difficult in some way, the clinician must be able to internally monitor and leave behind the way he or she might have been affected by that patient in order to interact and assess the next patient on his or her own terms.

AUTOMATIC MIRROR NEURON/BOTTOM-UP EMPATHY PROCESSING

Is the clinician able to manage subconscious emotional resonance?

As the clinician is noticing and observing a patient in a particular physical and emotional situation, an automatic emotional resonance will become activated in which the clinician's brain will unconsciously mirror the patient's experience. This is done through the mirror neuron system and the perception–action model of empathy explained in chapter 3. Clinicians differ in the degree to which the

automatic emotional resonance is activated, and it is possible for clinicians to suppress this system. To the degree that the clinician automatically resonates with the patient's physical and emotional state, it is possible for the clinician to experience the emotional state of the patient. As clinicians are trained and gain experience, they learn how to manage this automatic emotional resonance and to use this experience as data for the top-down empathy process.

Practically speaking, how is this step in the process experienced? Clinicians who are not very attuned to subtle changes in their emotions, thought process, and physiology may very well miss how they are automatically resonating with the patient experience. Clinicians who are more mindfully aware will notice shifts in their mood, emotional state, or even physical state as they encounter a patient. The fact that a clinician picks up or viscerally senses the patient's emotions is common and not an indication of any problem. In fact, this automatic emotional resonance is used by expert clinicians as a means to gain information about the patient's internal state and to modulate their approach to the patient accordingly. The problem is when clinicians are not aware of the emotional material they are unconsciously picking up and are not managing it effectively. Many times, clinicians will notice their secondary reaction first and then work backward to what the automatic emotional resonance was. For example, a clinician might become more distant and emotionally detached after being with a patient for a short time; this might be in reaction to picking up the patient's intense emotions and experiencing the beginning of feeling overwhelmed or personally distressed by the patient. When clinicians examine their change in behavior (e.g., distancing, getting very controlling of the situation, interrupting the patient), they may become aware that they have "picked up" or "absorbed" some of the patient's experience unconsciously. Expert clinicians will be able to "pick up" the patient's emotional state but remain centered and emotionally regulated in responding to the patient.

Some clinicians will not experience automatic emotional resonance and will bypass this step and go directly to becoming aware of and understanding the patient's experience. As discussed in chapter 3, there is a risk to this because the automatic emotional resonance can give the clinician data about the experience of the patient that helps with responding to the patient in the most effective way. As clinicians habituate to many patient situations and come to suppress the automatic emotional resonance, they have to find ways to stay in touch with the patient's experience as they continue in the compassion mindset process.

When I first meet with patients, it is very possible that I will pick up some of how they feel unconsciously through the automatic mirror neuron bottom-up empathy processing. They may be down or angry or in pain, and I might pick up that experience and feel some of it in myself. However, it is possible that I am not in touch with my automatic empathy processing or I have suppressed it. No matter what, to stay in the compassion mindset, I have to become aware of and able to understand patients' emotional experience. If I do not, or if I get overwhelmed subconsciously by a patient's emotional state, I can easily fall out of the compassion mindset and maybe become emotionally distressed or overwhelmed by the patient, or even disgusted or put off by the patient. If that happens, then I might work with the patient in a detached or hostile way. Or I might treat the person in an emotionally conflicted way, in which I am going through the motions of treating them, but I have a tone of condescension, abruptness, or negativity that the patient might pick up. If I can become aware of the patient's state and remain emotionally centered, I can then move into top-down empathy processing.

IS THE CLINICIAN AWARE OF AND ABLE TO UNDERSTAND THE PATIENT'S EMOTIONAL EXPERIENCE?

Whether automatic emotional resonance has occurred in the clinician or not, the clinician must become consciously aware of the patient's emotional experience in his or her own condition and articulate what that experience is as he or she moves to top-down empathy processing. If automatic emotional resonance has occurred within the clinician, then he or she will need to be able to become aware of this process within him- or herself and understand this as precipitated by engaging with the patient. This requires the ability to differentiate the clinician's self from the patient. That is, even as the clinician can viscerally "pick up" the emotional state of the patient, the clinician is able to maintain emotional separation, meaning that the clinician is aware of what is the patient's emotional material and what is the clinician's emotional material.

If the automatic emotional resonance does not occur within the clinician, the clinician will need to engage in an intentional cognitive process of discerning what the patient may be experiencing and articulate that within him- or herself. The potential advantage of suppressing the automatic emotional resonance is that the clinician does not have to deal with viscerally picking up the patient's experience. The downside, however, is that the clinician could proceed in helping the patient while not really cueing into what the patient is going through. When clinicians do not pick up this information, they lose the data about what the patient is going through that could affect how well clinicians can assess, diagnose, and treat the patient. If clinicians do not experience the automatic emotional resonance, they have to engage their own cognitive processes to discern what the emotional and cognitive state of the patient is. The clinician has to infer how the patient is experiencing their condition and also how the patient is experiencing the clinician. That is, the clinician has to articulate for him- or herself what the perspective of the patient is and what the patient is going through emotionally.

It is possible that a clinician does not become aware of or understand the patient's emotional experience and then falls out of the compassion mindset. The clinician then may act in a distant, detached manner toward the patient and respond in a noncompassionate manner. It is also possible that a clinician becomes more aware of the patient experience but becomes emotionally overwhelmed by what the patient is experiencing. The clinician then might not be able to emotionally self-regulate or may not want to emotionally self-regulate in response to the patient. The clinician may notice him- or herself becoming personally distressed, which then leads to avoiding or withdrawing from the patient. If the clinician is not emotionally self-aware, he or she may instead be disgusted or angered by the patient. This disgust or anger is actually a secondary emotion, which functions as a defense against feeling internally personally distressed by the patient's physical and emotional state.

TOP-DOWN EMPATHY PROCESSING WITH EMOTION REGULATION (ALSO CALLED MENTALIZING OR THEORY OF MIND)

Does the clinician view the patient as a fellow human being who is ill or suffering?

One of the mental steps a clinician in a compassion mindset experiences is either consciously or automatically viewing the patient as a fellow human being, no matter how the patient may be different from the clinician. One of the great qualities of health care is the ethic that we are expected to treat everyone without discrimination. Our profession is to relieve patient suffering no matter who is suffering. If we treat one group over another (e.g., rich people first, only people in our own tribe, people we like over people we do not like), we are considered to have failed the ethical mandate of the helping professions. In this stage of the compassion mindset process, the clinician is able to appreciate the universal human condition having a kinship attitude toward every human being. The common bond of humanity is seen as overriding any difference, such as racial or ethnic background, socioeconomic status, gender, sexual orientation, age, or education. Even if the patient is different from the clinician, the clinician is able to move past that difference and give the patient what the patient needs in terms of health care. If the clinician has difficulty moving beyond that difference, the clinician in a compassion mindset is able to notice the mental block affecting clinical behavior and shift his or her attitude to treating the patient as a fellow human being (*compassion reset and recovery*). The bottom line is that what *every* patient goes through matters to the clinician in a compassion mindset. If the clinician is not able to view the patient as a fellow human being who is ill or suffering, the clinician may fall out of the compassion mindset. As a result, the clinician may become personally distressed, overwhelmed, or disgusted by the patient and then may emotionally detach from the patient, treat the patient in a perfunctory or halfhearted way, or treat the patient in a begrudging manner.

In this step, the clinician also decides whether the patient's suffering matters to him or her. Does the clinician focus on what the patient is going through, or does the clinician focus on what the patient's suffering means for the clinician? Is it about the patient or about the clinician? For example, when a patient is in a medical crisis, does the clinician focus on him- or herself? ("These kinds of cases really upset me." "My shift is about over; I wish I did not have to deal with this.") Does it matter to the clinician that the patient is suffering, or is the focus on the clinician's well-being? This step is based on Goetz et al.'s (2010) "Who is the victim?" If the clinician believes he or she is the victim, then the clinician experiences sadness, anger, or shame. If the clinician believes that the patient is the victim, then one moves further in the compassion process. Because the wording is awkward when applied to clinicians, I have changed the question "Who is the victim?" to "Does it matter to the clinician that the patient is going through this illness/suffering?" My understanding of who is the victim in Goetz's model is who feels like the victim because of the negative event. That is, when something bad has happened, does the clinician focus on what it means for him- or herself or on what it means for the patient? Is it the clinician's own suffering or the patient's suffering that matters to the clinician? An example would be a clinician in the ER who has been overloaded with patients

all night. If another patient comes in—another "hit," as they say—the clinician might feel upset at having to do another case; that is, the clinician feels like the victim when it is really the patient who is the victim. Then the clinician might self-correct and realize that while it is a hassle for him or her, the clinician is not the victim; the patient is.

If the clinician becomes aware that he or she is focusing on how he or she feels rather than what the patient is going through, then the clinician may move in to *compassion reset and recovery*, remind and refocus him- or herself that the patient is going through some hardship, and return to the compassion mindset.

Is the illness/suffering of the patient of primary concern to the clinician over self-interest?

In order to be in a clinician compassion mindset, the illness/suffering of the patient must be the primary concern over any other interest or agenda for the clinician. This has some overlap with the previous question, but it is possible that the illness or suffering matters to the clinician but is not the clinician's primary concern. While it is normal for clinicians to have a number of reasons for helping a patient (e.g., making money, getting research participants, increasing patient numbers), clinicians prioritize the well-being of the patient over other motivations. There may be other concerns or interests involved, but these must be *secondary* to the interests and well-being of the patient if the clinician is to remain in a compassion mindset. Common interests that often supersede or compete with making the interests of the patient primary are financial gain, meeting a patient visit quota, needing patient visits for program requirements or licensing, needing a case study for research or a training program, wanting to work with a particular patient for reasons of prestige, being attracted to a patient, and so on. This also means that clinicians put their own convenience or comfort as secondary to the needs of the patient. Whatever personal desires, agenda, or needs clinicians have, they are able to focus primarily on what the patient needs rather than having their own need be the primary reason for treating a patient in a particular way. This is a major issue in a health care system in which procedures and treatments may be chosen based more on monetary incentives than on what is best for the patient. A clinician might own a particular piece of equipment (e.g., a diagnostic machine), be a partner in a facility (e.g., an outpatient surgicenter), or be invested in a particular treatment approach (e.g., a particular surgical method, infusion center, or specific medical procedure). A clinician in a compassion mindset is able to recognize when recommendations to a patient are primarily based on one's own monetary incentives versus what is best for the patient.

If the answer to the above question is no, then the clinician is no longer on the compassion mindset pathway. The essential clinical qualities for managing this question are self-awareness, honesty, and integrity. If the clinician does realize or admit that the patient's interests are not primary, then the clinician may enter the *compassion reset and recovery zone,* in which the clinician acknowledges the self-interest placed above the patient's needs and either reorders the priorities or continues working with the patient in a noncompassion mindset manner. If the clinician does not realize or refuses to see the patient's illness/suffering as the primary concern, then the clinician falls out of the compassion mindset and becomes personally distressed, overwhelmed, or disgusted by patient

suffering. The most likely reaction is a disgust reaction (e.g., "Why should I bother with this patient?") or a deceitful mindset (either deceitful to the patient or deceitful to him- or herself).

Can the clinician view the patient as deserving of some type of help?

In this step, the clinician considers whether the patient deserves some type of help. For patients who are victims of accidents, crimes, or diseases not the result of the patient's own behavior, the clinician may have no difficulty thinking that the patient is deserving of help. But when a patient has an injury, an illness, or problematic behavior that is seen as the fault of the patient, the clinician understandably may not believe the patient is deserving of help. If so, the clinician may become disgusted or angered by the patient and may distance him- or herself from the patient, become verbally abusive of the patient, or treat the patient in an emotionally conflicted manner (e.g., is rough with the patient while doing an examination or procedure). But the clinician may enter the *compassion reset and recovery zone* and reframe his or her understanding of the patient. The clinician might consider, for example, that the patient has gone through something in his or her life that makes it understandable that he or she would have gotten to this point with the particular injury, illness, or behavioral condition. So, while the patient in one sense does not deserve help, from another perspective the patient deserves some kind of help simply because he or she is a human being who has gone through some type of suffering that led him or her to this point. In order to remain in a compassion mindset, the clinician needs to find some way to understand the patient as a human being who has gone through something or is suffering from something behind the presenting problem or issue. For example, this may be a drug seeker who is suffering from drug addiction, a hostile patient who has PTSD, or a patient who has been raised in generational poverty.

In Goetz et al.'s (2010) appraisal model, they propose the question, "Is target deserving of help?" When I have used this model with clinicians, phrasing the question this way does not always allow the clinician to consider how the patient deserves some kind of help. Clinicians often answer this question of whether the patient deserves help by thinking that even though the patient does not deserve help, they will still help that patient. Clinicians tend to think in absolute terms about deservingness. But phrasing the question as "Can the clinician view the patient as deserving of some type of help?" allows the clinician to consider that the patient may not be deserving of help, strictly speaking, but that the patient is going through something as a human being that has led him or her to this point. For example, if the patient is a drug addict seeking drugs or a person who has shot another person, the clinician might say that this kind of person does not deserve help. But when we say that this person deserves some kind of help, this allows the clinician to consider the person as deserving of some type of humane response. In my own research, some clinicians react negatively to using the term *deserve* because it implies a condescending judgmentalism. Another way to understand this would be that the clinician can understand the patient's difficult behavior in such a way that the clinician stays motivated to give the patient the best care that he or she can provide. If the patient does not follow the clinician's instructions, the clinician can still offer the same quality of care to that patient. If the patient is difficult in some way, the clinician can still be objective in providing

treatment to that patient instead of becoming punishing or vindictive, leading to withholding treatment or managing the patient in a rough manner while treating him or her (e.g., verbally insulting, gruffly placing IV, giving less pain medication to punish the patient). It just means that no matter what, I always try to understand how individuals got to be the way that they are and to acknowledge that they deserve some type of help; at the least, respect from me, or a sincere attempt. I might do the best that I can, refer them, or whatever is appropriate for my role in a realistic and balanced way. In short, the clinician finds a way around the dislike of the patient and still treats the patient well.

Does the clinician have the ability to cope with the illness/suffering of the patient?

In this step of the clinician compassion mindset, the clinician considers whether he or she has the resources, time, and skills to cope with and respond to a particular patient. Does the clinician have the resources to emotionally regulate him- or herself with this particular patient (Goetz, Keltner, & Simon-Thomas, 2010)? Can the clinician tolerate the uncomfortable feelings aroused by this patient and stay open to, connected with, and accepting of this patient? Is the clinician physically able to work with this patient right now (e.g., the clinician is sleep deprived and should not do surgery; the clinician does not have the material resources or team support to respond to this patient)?

If the clinician does not have the ability to cope with the illness or suffering of this patient, the clinician may become overwhelmed, distressed, or disgusted by the patient, which would lead to withdrawing from the patient, detaching from the patient, or helping the patient in an emotionally conflicted manner (e.g., is rough with the patient while doing an examination or procedure). But the clinician may move to the *compassion reset and recovery zone* and examine what it is that is making him or her have difficulty coping with this patient. The clinician may then regain composure, seek assistance, consult other colleagues, or obtain what would help improve the ability to cope with this patient's situation. It could be that the clinician concludes he or she does not have the ability to cope with this situation, but instead of withdrawing or emotionally detaching, he or she will refer the patient. If a patient's situation is beyond the ability of a clinician, it would be inadvisable for the clinician to treat the patient, and the most caring and compassionate thing a clinician could do is help that patient get to a clinician who can help him or her. It may also happen that the clinician does not have the technical ability or skills to help the patient. For example, the clinician may not know how to deal with patients who have suicidal depression. The clinician might then pursue continuing education training to be able to deal with these types of patients more effectively in the future.

If the patient is difficult in some way, does the clinician have the emotional regulation, emotional intelligence, and skills to work in this situation? For example, if the patient is dealing with burns, is the clinician emotionally able to hang in with a patient who is in pain and directing anger toward the clinician or the staff and not take the patient's anger personally? In doing surgery, the surgeon has the emotional endurance to be able to do a complex surgery as well as the emotional composure to manage any problems that may arise. Emotional ability to work with particular types of patients consists of typical emotional-management skills and emotional-management skills necessary for intense

or crisis situations. In terms of typical emotional-management skills, clinicians generally need to know how to respond in very emotional situations with their patients. The particular skills are defined by what is necessary for the type of patient population that you help—for example, children, cancer patients, and chronically ill patients. Also, the clinician needs to have the ability to stay emotionally engaged with his or her patients throughout the course of treatment. For example, a patient needs a surgeon to be emotionally connecting and supportive in preparation and surgery phases, but the surgeon might not be emotionally supportive in the recovery phase. In oncology treatment, the oncologist might be very emotionally connected in the radiation and chemotherapy phase, but when the appointments become more spread out after intensive treatment, patients who are being monitored and patients who still have cancer continue to need the emotional investment, concern, and support from their oncologist. Clinicians in a compassion mindset learn how to maintain a balance of emotional underinvestment and overinvestment with patients over time in working with them. This requires that clinicians be good at self-monitoring in terms of how they are relating to patients and be able to adjust according to the needs of their patients.

Clinicians also need emotional-management skills for intense or crisis situations. When a patient is in crisis, such as after being told bad medical news, the clinician needs to have the emotional-management skills to hang in with the patient as the patient works through the shock of that news, for example. When a patient expresses harsh comments or reactions, likely due to how bad the patient feels when sick or because of the treatment, the clinician is able not to internalize or take personally what the patient said. When the treatment is not going well for a patient or when a clinician is no longer able to do as much for a patient, the clinician continues to do the best he or she can for the patient without abruptly abandoning the patient because the clinician cannot handle his or her disappointment in the challenges of a course of treatment.

The ability to cope with the illness or suffering of a patient is always in the context of safety and boundaries. If the patient is dangerous or attempts to cross boundaries, I do what I need to do to keep safe so that I do not get hurt and also so that I am able to keep trying to respond to the patient in the best way I can. If I am afraid or very angry, I will not be much help to that patient. I do the best that I can in the situation with the desire to try to relieve that patient's pain or suffering or to help in some way; but I am also realistic about what is the best that I can do. A person who is not in a compassion mindset might not even consider how he or she could help or treat a difficult person with respect.

IS THE CLINICIAN MOTIVATED TO ATTEMPT TO ALLEVIATE THE ILLNESS/SUFFERING?

A clinician may empathically resonate with a patient, feel that the patient's suffering matters to him or her, be primarily concerned for the patient above any self-interest, and have the ability to cope with the patient's situation. But the clinician may not be motivated to attempt to alleviate the illness or suffering of the patient. He or she may have the capacity but not want to go any further for a variety of reasons. The clinician may be completely exhausted; so, while the clinician has noticed the patient's vulnerability or suffering and empathically resonated with the patient, he or she does not feel able to move this toward action. The clinician then

avoids, withdraws, or becomes detached from the patient or helps the patient in an emotionally conflicted manner.

If the clinician is motivated to attempt to alleviate the patient's illness or suffering, he or she then finds some way to respond in a compassionate way to the patient. If so, the clinician tries to do something to relieve that suffering, which may range from prescribing medication, doing a procedure, giving advice, assessing, referring, listening, providing emotional support, and so on. Of course, the desire of the clinician is to completely alleviate the illness or suffering of the patient. If it is not possible to completely alleviate the illness or suffering, the clinician tries to alleviate it to the best of his or her ability and what the situation allows.

COMPASSIONATE RESPONSE TOWARD PATIENT

Compassionate responses may vary widely in what those actions are, but what they have in common are responses that are connected to the clinician noticing and being moved by the patient's illness condition or suffering, and then generating a response that truly connects with some aspect of what the patient really needs. This may involve a medical intervention, some advice, emotional support, a referral, or other therapeutic response. A response may appear compassionate but is not if the clinician is not emotionally connected enough with the patient to ensure that the response really matches what the patient needs.

Compassionate response does not necessarily mean that the patient's suffering is fully alleviated. Many times, the clinician's response will be helpful but may not end the patient's illness or suffering because the condition is not possible to cure or fully resolve. Nevertheless, the clinician compassion mindset helps the clinician respond in a way that is a sincere attempt to alleviate the patient's illness or suffering. It may also happen that even though the clinician has been in a compassion mindset, the patient may not notice the clinician's compassionate response or may not perceive the clinician to be compassionate. For example, a drug-addicted patient may accuse the clinician of not being compassionate because the clinician did not prescribe the patient's drug of choice. However, the clinician may have empathized with the patient, understood his or her perspective, understood that the patient is suffering from the terrible condition of addiction, had the ability to deal with the patient's belligerence and insults, but concluded that the most compassionate response is not enabling the patient's addiction but setting a limit on his or her dysfunctional behavior. In such a case, while the patient may accuse the clinician of not having been compassionate, the clinician was actually treating the patient from a compassion mindset.

It is important to note that a compassionate response for a patient includes both the attempt to directly alleviate the medical problem and the way that attempt is implemented. The clinician has applied his or her competence to the fullest extent. The clinician is "into it" in the sense of the cartoon in chapter 2. The clinician has accurately perceived the vulnerability or suffering and been moved by it, and this has generated a motivational process in which clinical judgment is maximized and the emotions of the clinician are optimally regulated toward alleviating the vulnerability or suffering of the patient. If the attempt to alleviate the suffering is kindly and sensitively done but the clinician has not brought to bear his or her full competence on a problem, then we might say that this is not the most compassionate response it could

have been. This is sham compassion because it is delivered in a kind and sensitive manner, but the intervention chosen either is not what is appropriate for the patient or is not the best that the clinician could have done. Likewise, if the attempt to directly alleviate the medical problem is technically correct but executed in a harsh manner, we might consider this a less-than-compassionate response. Indeed, it may not be called a compassionate response at all but an emotionally conflicted response that is partially helpful, yet the way the medical intervention is done is harsh, depersonalizing, or dehumanizing. This would suggest the clinician has fallen off the compassion mindset process at some point for this type of response.

A clinician may be motivated to attempt to alleviate the illness and/or suffering of the patient but may not be able to do so for a variety of external reasons. For example, the clinician may not have the resources at hand to help the patient, such as in a catastrophe like an earthquake or war. Or the desired compassionate response may be blocked by some organizational or systemic barrier. An insurance company may refuse to pay for the surgery, or the organization inhibits or prevents the response because of a particular policy or dysfunction in the organization. In such cases, the compassion mindset is still considered a compassion mindset. What is occurring is that there are external barriers to responding from a compassion mindset. External barriers to compassion might include an organization or clinic overloading the clinician (e.g., not allowing enough time, too large a caseload for the clinician), external distractions (e.g., too many interruptions, such as paging; too noisy an environment; policies rooted in defensive medicine in a litigious society), patient and family members who sabotage the clinician's attempts to help (e.g., patients or loved ones who are continuously obnoxious, family members who interfere with treatment), or other external factors that block a compassionate response (Fernando & Consedine, 2014). Note, however, that the clinician is staying in a compassion mindset even while these external obstacles occur. The clinician is navigating this by continuing to understand the patient and the parties involved, keeping the patient's interests primary, reframing any difficult patient behavior in order to stay engaged, and maintaining emotional stability and internal psychological resources to keep hanging in and dealing with the external obstructions. As I will discuss later in the book, especially when talking about the organizational/business/systemic factors in balanced compassionate caring (chapter 15), there are limits to what an individual clinician can endure or weather over time. Like the Coast Guard rescuer, he or she may be the finest rescuer there can be, but he or she is not likely to succeed in a very severe storm or hurricane. When the societal or organizational factors become too turbulent and obstructive, like a storm at sea, then individual clinicians may get consumed by the organizational hurricane gusts despite being in a compassion mindset. In order for clinicians to be able to fully and continually respond out of a clinician compassion mindset, organizations must create clinical holding environments that sustain and protect the clinician as he or she is in the compassion mindset process.

COMPASSION RESET AND RECOVERY

During the top-down empathy processing phase, the clinician can fall out of the compassion mindset if the clinician does not view the patient as a fellow human being, the illness or suffering of the patient is not of primary concern to the clinician over self-interest, the clinician is not able to view the patient as deserving of some type of help, or the clinician does not have the ability to cope with the illness/suffering of the patient. If this happens, it is still possible to recover the compassion mindset. To do so, the clinician has to reappraise the patient situation. Previous models on compassion have not explicitly referred to the possibility of resetting and recovering a compassion mindset. But in the clinical world, this is a common occurrence. A clinician can, for example, become angry or disgusted with the behavior of a patient and want to be hostile toward the patient. This clinician might then consult a colleague or internally go through a mental process of asking him- or herself what might be underlying this patient's negative behavior. For example, a patient addicted to substances can be quite frustrating to work with and medically complicated. Although tempted to kick this patient out of the clinic and refuse to do anything for the patient, the clinician might instead try to find some way to help this patient improve his or her situation. Or the clinician might at least refrain from being hostile toward the patient, consider how that addiction is imprisoning that patient in some way, and treat the patient with respect and dignity.

Resources to provide skills for compassion reset and recovery

The more clinicians can understand the sources of patient behaviors and reactions, the more they are able to reframe a patient's behaviors and reactions in terms of what these mean. Instead of taking what patients do personally, clinicians can focus on being curious about the problem and strategize what to do about it. In this way, they stay emotionally engaged in helping the patient and can recover the compassion mindset. For example, in their book, *Transforming Negative Reactions to Clients: From Frustration to Compassion*, Wolf, Goldfried, and Muran (2013) offer ways to do this with patients who have personality disorders, substance abuse problems, and depression. *Trauma-Informed Care* by Evans and Coccoma (2014) helps clinicians understand how all types of trauma can influence how patients present and how they interact with clinicians. Hunter and Maunder's (2016) book, *Improving Patient Treatment with Attachment Theory: A Guide for Primary Care Practitioners and Specialists*, is another excellent resource explaining how attachment history influences patients who have cancer, pain, terminal conditions, bariatric surgery, and other medical conditions. Compassionate Care Training (Jazaieri, Jinpa, McGonigal, Rosenberg, Finkelstein, Simon-Thomas, Cullen, Doty, Gross, and Goldin, 2012) and Cognitively Based Compassion Training (CBCT) (Ozawa-de Silva, Dodson-Lavelle, Raison, & Negi, 2012) are both researched mind training approaches designed to help people increase their capacity for compassion to all people, including those we find difficult. Ekman and Krasner (2017) provide a comprehensive list of programs that can help clinicians hone their empathic abilities. These include the Healer's Art curriculum (Remen, O'Donnell, & Rabow, 2008), Nonviolent Communication (Rosenberg & Chopra, 2015), the G.R.A.C.E. compassion practice (Halifax, 2018), Cultivating Emotional Balance (CEB) (Ekman, 2015; Kemeny et al., 2012), the Supporting Provider Resilience by Upping Compassion and Empathy program (SPRUCE) (Ekman & Krasner, 2017), Motivational Interviewing (Miller & Rollnick, 2013), and the Empathetics Program

(Riess, Kelley, Bailey, Dunn, & Phillips, 2012). Balint groups and Schwartz Rounds are two group methods in which clinicians can discuss their experience of patients and thereby reset and recover their compassion mindset for particular types of challenging patients; these two methods will be discussed in further detail in chapter 15.

POST-ENCOUNTER COMPASSION RESET AND RECOVERY

Whether a clinician has responded to the patient from a compassion mindset or not, clinicians who value getting better in their respective specialties will reflect and learn from either compassion failure or success. In terms of when we fail to maintain a compassion mindset, we can examine exactly where we had difficulty and fell out of the compassion mindset. Did we fail to notice the emotional cues of the patient? Did we make assumptions about the patient or the patient's condition and not really understand the patient? Did we minimize the patient's experience or put our own self-interests above the patient's? Can we look at our emotional reactions and behaviors toward patients and recognize how we may have been overwhelmed or put off by a patient? Do we need to work on how we can stay engaged with difficult patients? How is our emotional and cognitive ability to hang in with patients? Are there external factors that are undercutting our ability to respond from a compassion mindset?

Even when we successfully respond to a patient in a compassionate manner, we can still learn from this interaction with a patient. Sometimes we respond very well to certain types of patients, and we can benefit by understanding what enabled us to do this. This is the essence of a technique called appreciative inquiry, in which an individual or group of clinicians examine the best examples of caring for patients to find out what made them the best episodes of a compassion mindset (Hammond, 1998). This allows clinicians to become more conscious of exactly why they are able to be in a compassion mindset so well so that they can continue to do this reliably and even improve or streamline the process for themselves. This is also a very good way to train students, residents, and practicing clinicians, providing exemplars for how to be in a compassion mindset.

Ideally, clinicians have a regular practice of reflecting on their interactions with patients to help them improve their skills and to increase their compassion satisfaction within this work. This practice can be done individually or in groups. Some excellent examples are Schwartz Rounds, Balint groups, and case conferences.

QUESTIONS OF SEQUENTIALITY AND TIME SPAN

While the clinician compassion mindset process can proceed in as linear a fashion as is presented here, the practical reality is that the clinician may be looping back to previous steps as he or she works with a patient. For example, the clinician may be working on the "Can the clinician view the patient as deserving of some type of help?" step, reframing what is going on with the patient to grasp how that patient is suffering. In doing so, this may loop the clinician back to the step of really understanding the patient's emotional experience.

In terms of time span, while the clinician compassion mindset process appears complex and involving a great deal of effort to navigate major appraisal questions, in actuality this mindset process can occur quite quickly. In certain patient cases, the process can proceed within seconds. However, in more challenging patient situations, when the clinician is bouncing up to the *compassion reset and recovery box* to reappraise a particular patient's difficult behavior, it may actually take much more time. For example, if the clinician has difficulty viewing the patient as deserving some type of help, the clinician may need to get the help of colleagues to achieve this. Another example is when the clinician is assessing whether he or she has the ability to cope with the illness or suffering of the patient. When encountering a certain type of patient or situation for the first time, the clinician may have to work on developing that coping ability. He or she may need to develop this ability by seeking further skills training, consulting colleagues, or strengthening internal emotional and cognitive resources to be able to work with certain types of patients. Medical students, residents, and clinicians in the early years of practice may need supervisory support to help them get the knowledge and perspective they need to be able to stay in a clinician compassion mindset process.

Litmus test phrases to help you know if you are in the clinician compassion mindset

How do you know if you are in the clinician compassion mindset? Just as a litmus test gives you a quick way to test for acidity or alkalinity, here are a few sentences that can help you assess if you are in clinician compassion mindset.

Once when we were discussing in class how to spot a clinician compassion mindset among colleagues, a student who was trained as a certified nursing assistant (CNA) said that there were two types of remarks she would hear when

CNAs walked into a room in which the patient had soiled him- or herself. One was, "Now I've got to clean up this patient!" The other was, *"Oh my gosh, how long has the patient been like this? Let's get you cleaned up."* The first statement reflects a clinician disgusted or distressed, but the focus is on him or her having to deal with the soiled patient. The second phrase shows how the empathic resonance of the patient's condition is immediately considered from the point of view of the patient and reflects a positive willingness to help the patient. The focus is on the patient's suffering, not the disgusting nature of the task.[2]

Marcus Engel, who teaches nationally about the patient experience, talks about coming out of a 25-hour surgery he underwent and hearing a nurse named Barb say to him, *"My name is Barb. I get to take care of you for the next eight hours"* (Marcus Engel, personal communication, 2018). The phrase is not "I have to take care of you," "I need to take care of you," or even the more neutral, "I will be taking care of you." The phrase reflects the sense of privilege in taking care of another person that people in a compassion mindset have.

Another story Engel tells is about how bad he felt, disgusted and embarrassed as he was overcome by vomiting and a nurse ran to his side. He apologized, but she said, *"I'm sorry, too, but only because you don't feel well. ... This is nothing! Don't worry about it, okay? I just want to be sure you're all right. I'm here to take care of you. That's what I'm here for, Marcus ... that's ALL I'm here for"* (Engel, 2006, p. 67). The focus is again on the emotional suffering of the patient, not the nurse's own distress.

In my Medical Counseling classes, in which students have to role-play with patient actors in all kinds of situations, sometimes students become overwhelmed or very anxious before going into the room, especially if they know the patient is going to be angry, anxious, or very distressed. They might fear how sad or angry the patient is going to be. They sometimes get paralyzed by all that they have to keep in mind for the role play while doing this in front of 20 other students. Their own fears and distress have overtaken them. When that happens, I say to them: "Yes, that happens when we are with patients who are going through a lot. What I would like you to do whenever you start feeling overwhelmed by the patient, is to ask yourself, *'What is this patient going through? How is their anger or sadness or distress a sign of their suffering? How is this patient suffering?'"* This is a reorienting intervention in which clinicians shift their attention to the emotional suffering of the patient, and the by-product of shifting the attention in the direction of the patient is that it takes the attention off their own internal distress.

Finally, this quote from Fred Rogers (2003) illustrates this same shift in attention that is essential to the compassion mindset:

> When I was a boy and I would see scary things in the news, my mother would say to me, "Look for the helpers. You will always find people who are helping." To this day, especially in times of "disaster," I remember my mother's words, and I am always comforted by realizing that there are still so many helpers—so many caring people in this world. (p. 187)

CONCLUSION

The clinician compassion mindset is a kind of container that internally holds the empathic resonance of the patient's suffering and is directed toward responding to and attempting

---

2   This story is from Jacqueline Johnson.

to alleviate his or her suffering. It is like the chassis or undercarriage of a car or truck; just as the weight of the vehicle and the load is evenly distributed on the chassis and the four wheels, the clinician compassion mindset is a kind of undercarriage holding and distributing the emotional weight of the patient's condition or suffering on an internal mental framework that focuses on the patient's experience of being ill or suffering and not on being personally distressed, overwhelmed, or disgusted by the patient. The clinician compassion mindset process is a series of mental steps, beginning with being able to notice and engage with patients in their illness and/or suffering. The bottom-up empathy processing relying on the automatic mirror neuron network may or may not occur in clinicians; but one way or the other, the clinician must be aware of and able to understand the patient's emotional experience in order to stay in a compassion mindset. Then the clinician moves through the process of top-down empathy processing, in which the clinician views the patient as a fellow human who is suffering and acknowledges that he or she deserves some type of help. The clinician makes the illness/suffering of the patient their primary concern over any other interest. The clinician assesses his or her capacity to cope with and respond to that patient. From there, the intention to help alleviate the suffering in some way translates into action. It is common that clinicians might fall out of a clinician compassion mindset, but there are ways to reset and recover the clinician compassion mindset.

QUESTIONS FOR DISCUSSION

1. Use the clinician compassion mindset process and reflect on a patient case or other interaction when you were helping someone.
2. What parts of the clinician compassion mindset process are most challenging for you? How come?

REFERENCES

Asken, M. J., Grossman, D., & Christensen, L. W. (2010). *Warrior mindset: Mental toughness skills for a nation's peacekeepers.* Millstadt, IL: Warrior Science.

Cassell, E. J. (1982). The nature of suffering and the goals of medicine. *New England Journal of Medicine, 306*(11), 639–645.

Christensen, L. W., & Grossman, D. (2016). 30 questions to ask yourself: You will fight the way you train. In L. W. Christensen (Ed.), *Fighter's fact book 2: Street fighting essentials* (pp. 29–38). Wolfeboro, NH: YMAA.

Ekman, E. (2015). Development, delivery, and evaluation of a pilot stress reduction, emotion regulation, and mindfulness training for juvenile justice officers. *Journal of Juvenile Justice, 4,* 71–91.

Ekman, E., & Krasner, M. (2017). Empathy in medicine: Neuroscience, education and challenges. *Medical Teacher, 39*(2), 164–173.

Engel, M. (2006). *The other end of the stethoscope: 33 insights for excellent patient care.* Orlando, FL: Ella Press.

Evans, A., & Coccoma, P. (2014). *Trauma-informed care: How neuroscience influences practice.* New York, NY: Routledge.

Fernando, A. T., & Consedine, N. S. (2014). Development and initial psychometric properties of the barriers to physician compassion questionnaire. *Postgraduate Medical Journal, 90,* 388–395.

Goetz, J. L., Keltner, D., & Simon-Thomas, E. (2010). Compassion: An evolutionary analysis and empirical review. *Psychological Bulletin, 136*(3), 351–374.

Grossman, D., & Christensen, L. W. (2008). *On combat: The psychology and physiology of deadly conflict in war and peace* (3rd ed.). Millstadt, IL: Warrior Science.

Halifax, J. (2018). *Standing at the edge: Finding freedom where fear and courage meet.* New York, NY: Flatiron Books.

Hammond, S. A. (1998). *The Thin Book of appreciative inquiry* (2nd ed.). Plano, TX: Thin Book.

Hunter, J., & Maunder, R. (Eds.). (2016). *Improving patient treatment with attachment theory: A guide for primary care practitioners and specialists.* New York, NY: Springer.

Jazaieri, H., Jinpa, T., McGonigal, K., Rosenberg, E. L., Finkelstein, J., Simon-Thomas, E., Cullen, M., Doty, J. R., Gross, J. J., & Goldin, P. R. (2012). Enhancing compassion: A randomized controlled trial of a compassion cultivation training program. *Journal of Happiness Studies, 14*(4). doi 10.1007/s10902-012-9373-z

Jazaieri, H., Lee, I. A., McGonigal, K., Jinpa, T., Doty, J. R., Gross, J. J., & Goldin, P. R. (2016). A wandering mind is a less caring mind: Daily experience sampling during compassion meditation training. *Journal of Positive Psychology, 11*(1), 37–50.

Jazaieri, H., McGonigal, K., Jinpa, T., Doty, J. R., Gross, J. J., & Goldin, P. R. (2014). A randomized controlled trial of compassion cultivation training: Effects on mindfulness, affect, and emotion regulation. *Motivation and Emotion, 38,* 23–35.

Jinpa, T. (2012, July). *Nature, origins and developments of compassion: Perspectives from a Buddhist understanding.* Presented at The Science of Compassion: Origins, Measures, and Interventions Conference, Telluride, CO.

Kemeny, M. E., Foltz, C., Cavanaugh, J. F., Cullen, M., Giese-Davis, J., Jennings, P., ... Ekman, P. (2012) Contemplative/Emotion Training reduces negative emotional behavior and promotes prosocial responses. *Emotion, 12*(2), 338–350.

Miller, W. R., & Rollnick, S. (2013). *Motivational interviewing: Helping people change* (3rd ed.). New York, NY: Guilford Press.

Mindset. (n.d.). In *The American Heritage Stedman's Medical Dictionary.* Retrieved from http://www.dictionary.com/browse/mindset

Ozawa-de Silva, B. R., Dodson-Lavelle, B., Raison, C. L., & Negi, L. T. (2012). Compassion and ethics: Scientific and practical approaches to the cultivation of compassion as a foundation for ethical subjectivity and well-being. *Journal of Healthcare, Science and the Humanities, 2*(1), 145–161.

Remen, R. N., O'Donnell, J. F., & Rabow, M. W. (2008). The healer's art: Education in meaning and service. *Journal of Cancer Education, 23,* 65–67.

Riess, H., Kelley, J. M., Bailey, R. W., Dunn, E. J., & Phillips, M. (2102). Empathy training for resident physicians: A randomized controlled trial of a neuroscience-informed curriculum. *Journal of General Internal Medicine, 27,* 1280–1286.

Rosenberg, M., & Chopra, D. (2105). *Nonviolent communication: A language of life* (3rd ed.). Encinitas, CA: PuddleDancer Press.

Rogers, F. (2003). *The world according to Mister Rogers: Important things to remember.* New York, NY: Hachette Books.

Wolf, A. W., Goldfried, M. R., & Muran, J. C. (2013). *Transforming negative reactions to clients: From frustration to compassion.* Washington, DC: American Psychological Association.

"I had no idea there was that much!"
—Anonymous physician after a continuing medical education lecture on the topic

Chapter Sections:

CHAPTER 5

Empirical Evidence for the Impact of Compassionate Caring in Health Care Practice

Questions to consider before reading this chapter:

1. How much research evidence do you think there is regarding how compassionate caring affects patient care processes and outcomes?

2. What do you know about this research?

3. Why do you think you have not heard more about this research?

INTRODUCTION

The scientific work on caring and compassion is taught in a fragmented way

When clinicians become aware of all the research that is already documenting how compassionate caring makes a major difference for health care practice, they are amazed at the quantity and quality of the studies that have been done in the past 20 years. Clinicians certainly have seen individual studies on this, but these instances are often viewed as rarities or as outliers. If you think about the training you have in your particular health profession, it is typical that you would be introduced to numerous studies that scientifically analyzed particular research questions in biochemistry, physiology, biology, pharmacology, and so on. You encounter them grouped together in huge textbooks or journals in courses, whereas studies on empathy or caring appear less often in clinical training—and when they do, they are usually single studies. An article on caring communication is given here or there as a handout that no one reads because they are so exhausted from the rest of the medical school curriculum. Or a summary of the research on the effects of clinician caring communication is presented in a PowerPoint slide, but all the research behind it is not apparent. So, it makes sense that medical students and health care clinicians would not think of the effects of compassionate caring like they do the various classes of antibiotics. This piecemeal approach to compassionate caring creates the perception that there is not a body of work to it. We do not typically have any occasion to present many of the studies together regarding the impact of compassionate caring because we do not teach it that way in medical school. We do not use compassion or caring as a scientific construct in itself. Some exceptions to this would be in communication skills courses, in which the research on particular communication skills is presented as a chapter in a book, or in a lecture on a particular aspect of patient-centered interviewing. (An excellent example is chapter 9 in Roter and Hall's *Doctors Talking with Patients/Patients Talking with Doctors* [2006]: "Consequences of Talk: The Relationship Between Talk and Outcomes.") While this situation is improving, it still is common that communication skills, much less compassionate caring, are taught without much reference to the background research done on them.

Lack of awareness of the research on the effects of compassionate caring

While compassionate caring can be said to be the core reason why we even have health care, we do not typically discuss this in depth, and we proceed as if science does not have much to do with it. There is a sense that while everyone agrees that compassionate caring is a good idea, it is not expected to do much heavy lifting in actual practice. This is due partly to a sentimental and overly emotional conception about compassion as well as to the idea that scientific research cannot be done on compassionate caring. Once, after I had given a continuing medical education lecture to a group of physicians on the research literature on this subject, a surgeon came up to me and said, "I had no idea there was that much!" He went on to say that he expected the lecture to be hokey, but given what he had heard, he added,

"If I had known this, I would have had the rest of my department come." When a resident physician was doing a rotation with me, I noticed he seemed baffled when I referred to some of this research. When I asked him why he seemed this way, he said "I thought you made all of this stuff up." (A less neutral word than *stuff* was used.) Generally, clinicians are not aware of the volume of research in this area, nor do they realize how it is possible to study compassionate caring in a scientific manner. The purpose of this chapter is to give an overview of this research and hopefully to give some sense of how this research is done.

Brief overview of the effects of compassionate caring communication

My intention here is not to replicate the excellent reviews of the impact of medical professional communication skills. Nor will I be able to review all the other areas of compassionate caring's effect on patient care. My goal in this chapter is simply to provide a number of premier examples and a broad sense of the research accumulating on the measurable impact compassionate caring has on patient care. Typically, clinicians know one part or another of what I will present, but not the breadth and depth of it. While this research is in its early stages, it can no longer be denied that compassionate caring is of major importance to the practice of medicine. Many doctors know this and practice this way, but they do so without knowing the empirical evidence.

Compassionate caring should not be reduced to bedside manner/ communication skills

As I explained in chapter 2, compassion in a clinician should not be reduced simply to bedside manner and communication skills. Yes, these are what we think of when we discuss compassionate caring because bedside manner and communication skills are some of the major ways a patient gets indications about whether a clinician is really caring about him or her. But compassionate care is also expressed by the cognitive and emotional investment in the patient's problem, in which the clinician is motivated to do his or her best in applying his or her technical competence and problem-solving ability to respond to that patient's suffering. A clinician's expertise and deep drive to help patients may not be expressed in his or her particular communication style, but that compassionate attention will still be positively affecting the quality of that patient care. The fact that the clinician is focusing his or her competence completely on you and that your problem matters to them will have definite effects on the medical outcome and the patient's perception of quality care. Patients are often able to detect this underlying compassionate care in spite of less-than-optimum communication skills. (In chapter 6, I will discuss the "geode doctor"—rough on the inside, but break it open and it is full of beautiful crystal.) There is also the problem that a clinician may use very good communication skills on the surface, but the patient can pick up that the clinician really does not care about him or her as a person. Acting like you care does not necessarily mean you really do care.

There are three perspectives to studying compassionate caring

There is a methodological sloppiness in discussions about compassion that we should address first. This has to do with the issue of from what perspective we are discussing and studying compassionate caring. There are three perspectives: compassionate caring from the clinician's perspective, compassionate caring from the perspective of the patient, and compassionate caring from an external observer perspective. When we examine compassionate caring within the perspective of the clinician, we are studying how the internal attitudes, thoughts, feelings, and neurophysiology shape how that clinician behaves in working with patients. This is the focus of this book. The second perspective is from the point of view of the patient. From this perspective, a patient is experiencing the clinician behavior and judges whether the clinician cares about him or her, how much the clinician cares about him or her, and how the patient experiences this. The third perspective is from the point of view of an external observer, such as a family member or a researcher, who is judging whether he or she thinks the clinician is caring for the patient, how that caring (or lack of caring) is conveyed, and the effects of that caring on the patient in terms of objective measures like medical outcomes. We would imagine that all three of these are correlated, meaning that if a clinician is in a compassion mindset, then this would be expressed in the clinician's behavior, and patients and external observers would experience it as indeed caring and observe its effects on the patient. But this is not always the case. Sometimes a clinician is coming from a compassion mindset, but the patient and external observer do not perceive it that way. For example, an addict might not perceive the limit setting of the clinician as caring, but the clinician is intending to be compassionate in this limit setting with the goal of addiction recovery as the desired medical outcome. Or sometimes a patient experiences the clinician as caring for him or her, but this is not apparent to an external observer such as a family member or other external observer.

Focus of this chapter versus the rest of the book

This book is mainly about the first perspective from the clinician's internal world point of view, in which we are examining what compassion is like within the clinician and what happens within the clinician when he or she is regularly (or not regularly) in a compassion mindset when working with patients, and how to be balanced in that caring. However, this chapter on the effects of compassionate caring on the patient is a digression from the main focus of the book because this chapter focuses on the second perspective of the patients and the third perspective of the external observer. But given that the reader may not know the research on the second and third perspectives, it is important that at least a summary of it be presented because, in the end, what we hope for is that the first perspective of the inner world of the compassionate clinician will make a difference in how the clinician is perceived by patients and what difference the compassion mindset makes from the external observer perspective (i.e., what others beside the patient observe and objective measures like medical outcomes).

Construct of compassionate caring (C^2) is studied in multidimensional ways

The construct of compassionate caring usually does not appear as the single, independent variable in patient care research. It is a scientific construct that is viewed in a multidimensional way. One common research route is to isolate particular communication skills or communication styles as a means to communicate compassionate caring (let us call it C^2 for short). These skills or styles would be considered ways of operationalizing C^2. Sometimes this research might isolate behaviors that convey C^2. These may be behaviors that are explicitly intended as part of a communication style (e.g., open vs. closed posture, greeting the patient by name, using a patient-centered interview format), or they may be behaviors that a clinician does in providing care that are not explicitly part of communication (e.g., attire, washing or not washing hands, how the clinician talks to other clinicians). Other research will focus on training clinicians in a particular philosophy of patient care, such as patient-centered medicine, and examining the effects of this on outcomes. Another research route is to try to get at the underlying attitudes of the clinician, such as empathy and C^2, and examine how this affects patient care.

What follows in this chapter are first a few exemplary research studies among thousands of others. Next, I present two models describing how empathy and communication skill have therapeutic effects on patients. Then, I provide an overview of major theoretical and empirical work on caring within the nursing profession. Finally, I present an overview of *compassionomics* "as the brand of knowledge and scientific study of the effects of compassionate care on health, healthcare, and healthcare providers" (Trzeciak, Roberts, & Mazzarelli, 2017, p. 92).

A SELECTION OF REPRESENTATIVE STUDIES ON THE RELATIONSHIP BETWEEN COMPASSIONATE CARING VARIABLES AND PATIENT OUTCOMES

Patient nonadherence is typically low

In a review of 50 years of research, DiMatteo (2004) found that adherence ranged from 4.6% to 100%; median adherence was 76%, and the average was 75.2%. In a review of 30 years of research, Zolnierek and DiMatteo (2009) reported that no matter what the setting, disease, or prognosis, 30% to 50% of patients can be expected to be nonadherent. So, the average rate of nonadherence was 24.8%. In general, then, the odds of your patient not doing what you recommend can range from 1 out of 4 to 1 out of 2.

Meta-analysis on the effect of communication skills on patient adherence

What difference do clinician communication skills make for patient adherence to treatment? Zolnierek and DiMatteo (2009) conducted a meta-analysis of 106 correlational studies and 21 experimental interventions of physician communication effects on treatment adherence. The physician communication variables included nonverbal and verbal communication, effective questioning, transmission of information, expressions of empathy and concern, partnership, and participatory decision-making. Of the 106 correlational studies, 104 studies showed a strong positive relationship between physicians' communication and patient adherence. Using meta-analysis statistical techniques for the strength and direction of the treatment effects, the researchers found that, overall, there was a 19% higher risk of patients being nonadherent if their physician had poor communication than if he or she had good communication. The odds of patient nonadherence were 1.47 times greater with a poor physician communicator, and the odds of patients adhering to treatment recommendations were 2.16 times better with a physician who is a good communicator (effect size d = 0.39). This finding is so clear that the others noted that it would take over 28,563 studies with nonsignificant results to nullify this finding (fail-safe n >

540 tolerance level). When the researchers analyzed the 21 experimental studies examining the effect of training physicians in some communication skill on patient adherence, all of the studies showed positive results. Calculating the effect size for those studies, there was a 12% higher risk of patients being nonadherent if their physician was not trained versus physicians who had been trained. The odds of a patient being nonadherent were 1.27 times higher when they had untrained physicians, and the odds of a patient being adherent were 1.62 times higher with a trained physician (effect size d = 0.24). It would take over 550 studies to nullify the findings of these 21 studies (fail-safe n > 115 tolerance level). Often it is assumed that effects due to variables such as communication would not be as powerful as various medical interventions. However, the effect sizes for these communication studies exceed those for many medical interventions, such as using Plavix for reducing the risk of cardiac events, Tamoxifen for prevention of breast cancer, and preventing blood clots with low-dose Warfarin.

Study on caring behaviors being related to fewer malpractice claims

A number of studies have measured some type of caring behavior and related it to some outcome. First, a study by Levinson, Roter, Mulloly, Dull, and Frankel (1997) in the *Journal of the American Medical Association* found that several characteristics of physician–patient communication predicted which primary care physicians would have a malpractice claim brought against them and which would not. No-claims primary care physicians "used more statements of orientation," that is, "educating patients about what to expect and the flow of a visit" (Levinson et al.,

1997, p. 553). No-claims primary care physicians laughed more "and used humor more and tended to use more facilitation," which means "soliciting patients' opinions, checking understanding, and encouraging patients to talk" (Levinson et al., 1997, p. 553) Finally, no-claims primary care physicians spent an average of 3.3 minutes longer in routine visits than did primary care physicians who had a malpractice claim brought against them (the average was 18.3 minutes for no-claims versus 15.0 minutes for claims primary care physicians).

Study on the relationship between empathic understanding and effects on patients

Second, Squier (1990) reviewed studies from the medical and psychotherapy literature examining the relationship between empathic understanding by medical professionals and patient adherence to treatment regimens. Squier found that expressed empathy in the clinician (a) "facilitates the sharing of emotional concerns about the illness"; (b) reduces tension in the patient; (c) "enhances motivational processes directed toward getting better"; (d) is related to "increased satisfaction with the care provided"; and (e) is strongly related to patient "commitment to a treatment plan and the adherence to the therapeutic regimen" (1990, pp. 330–331). The demonstrated emotional investment by a helper toward a client or patient has clear health results. The "soft," difficult-to-measure factors have hard empirical results.

Review study on nonverbal and verbal behaviors related to favorable patient outcomes

In an extensive review of nonverbal and verbal communication studies with primary care physicians, Beck, Daughtridge, and Sloan (2002) found that many nonverbal and verbal behaviors were correlated with short-term outcomes such as patient recall and satisfaction, intermediate outcomes such as patients adhering to treatment, and long-term outcomes such as the resolution of symptoms and the patient's quality of life. In terms of nonverbals, behaviors such as leaning forward and nodding, but not too-intense eye contact, were related to positive outcomes. Positive outcomes were also related to when physicians had a more direct listening posture, with uncrossed arms and legs and even a kind of mirroring of arm positions with the patient. In terms of verbal behaviors, better patient outcomes were associated with empathic expressions by physicians who convey how they appreciate the patient's situation. Positive outcomes were associated with giving reassurance, encouragement, and support; encouraging patients to ask questions; and letting patients guide the conversation in the last part of the visit but also giving clear explanations to the patient. Patients do better with a friendly and courteous approach with an openness to what the patient says and wants to ask the physician. Joking and laughing decrease tension in patients. Outcomes are better when physicians have a less controlling voice tone. Asking both open and closed questions about psychosocial issues and discussing patients' feelings and life situation are associated with positive outcomes. Having sufficient time in an appointment is also related to better outcomes. Other positively related behaviors are letting patients know what physicians are doing in a physical exam, taking time to do the history, sharing medical data such as lab results, and discussing the possible effects of treatment. Better outcomes are also associated with the physician taking time to do health education, talking to patients at their level, allowing the opportunity to discuss and clarify what is said, and summarizing what has been covered in the appointment.

Nonverbal and verbal behaviors are related to unfavorable patient outcomes

In that same review by Beck et al. (2002), unfavorable outcomes were associated with certain nonverbal and verbal behaviors as well. More negative outcomes are related to when physicians are not conveying a good listening posture and not facing the patient; this would include leaning back or listening with crossed arms. Touch that conveys physician dominance or is too frequent is related to poorer outcomes. In terms of verbal behaviors, negative outcomes are associated with physicians interrupting patients, not giving patients feedback after getting information from the patient, or doing too much biomedical questioning. Emotional tone toward what patients say was related to poorer outcomes. This would include when physicians *passively* reject or accept what the patient says and being irritable, nervous, or antagonistic with patients. Patients are negatively affected by physicians being too directive and dominant and not really showing interest in what patients are saying. Unfavorable outcomes are also associated with physicians who give their opinions while doing the physical exam or who give too much feedback near the end of the appointment.

Caring and communication skills related to greater efficiency

When clinicians think about caring and communication skills, there is often the concern that caring communication is inefficient. Caring communication has been found to actually save resources and time in the long run. When clinicians communicate well with patients, they obtain better data, which leads to more accurate diagnoses, which in turn leads to better treatment. As Carol Montgomery (1994) puts it, "Because authentic caring empowers clients … it never promotes unnecessary dependency or over-treatment, and is ultimately the most cost-effective method of helping" (p. 40). While this can be convincingly argued theoretically, there is some research evidence that communication skills can actually improve efficiency. Mauksch, Dugdale, Dodson, and Epstein (2008) reviewed research from 1973 to 2006 that focused on communication and quality-enhancing relationship skills associated with improvement in efficiency. The skills had to either improve the quality and decrease the visit length or improve the quality without increasing the visit length, and they had to manage the time without compromising the quality. Nine studies fit these standards. The researchers found four skills with ongoing influence in patient visits and three sequentially used skills at certain points in the visit.

Communication skills used in an ongoing way related to efficiency

With regard to communication skills used in an ongoing way with patients, Mauksch et al. (2008) first list *rapport building and relationship maintenance*. Having a warm greeting with eye contact and brief nonmedical interactions lasting even less than a minute (such as asking about some important event in the patient's life) are associated with better outcomes and efficiency. Second, *mindful practice*, in which clinicians are mindful of patient cues or their own thought process, improves efficiency. The mindful clinician is emotionally present and curious, which prevents premature closure on issues as well as guards against physician cognitive bias or dominance of the agenda by the clinician. Third, the skill of *topic tracking* is one in which clinicians use summarization to give their impression of what has been discussed, describe the interaction to make the communication process transparent, and align the goals of the patient and the clinician. This fosters a more efficient and organized way of managing multiple issues and also makes resolving them more likely. Fourth, efficiency and the therapeutic relationship are enhanced with the skill of *acknowledging emotional or social cues with empathy*. Patients are more likely to disclose illness beliefs and treatment preferences, which leads to making a better treatment plan, and patients do not have to keep restating their concerns. Noticing and exploring these cues can focus more effective discussion and increase patient self-efficacy, which helps with treatment adherence.

Sequentially used communication skills related to efficiency

In terms of sequentially used skills (i.e., skills used at specific times in the course of a patient visit), Mauksch et al. (2008) first list that *using up-front and collaborative agenda setting* made it more likely to prioritize the most important concerns and decreased the likelihood of patient issues surprising the clinician later in the visit. Second, *exploring the patient's perspective* can improve adherence, decrease patient anxiety, and identify knowledge gaps without increasing the visit length. This is especially indicated when working on health behavior change, the patient gives clues about underlying feelings or thoughts, there are psychosocial problems interfering with patient functioning, there are family or cultural factors affecting the patient's beliefs and behavior, the clinician is trying to increase the self-management of the patient, or symptoms are medically unexplained. Third, *co-creating a plan in a participative decision-making manner* that makes the goals explicit and clarifies each person's role leads to better outcomes and patients being more satisfied. Patients are more likely to follow through on recommendations because the plan matches their readiness to change as well as their financial and social resources. Patient problems tend to resolve faster, and physicians are less likely to order unnecessary tests or referrals.

Review study on the significant effects of patient–clinician relationship on medical outcomes

Kelley, Kraft-Todd, Schapira, Kossowsky, and Riess (2014) conducted a rigorous systematic review and meta-analysis of only randomized controlled trials (RCTs) on the influence of the patient–clinician relationship on health care outcomes. The researchers reviewed only RCTs using objective or validated subjective medical outcomes. They excluded studies that examined the outcomes of patient satisfaction, the comprehension of medical advice, or adherence to treatment. They found 13 such studies from 1998 to 2011. Their meta-analysis found that there was a small ($d = 0.11$) but statistically significant effect of patient–clinician relationship on health care outcomes ($p = 0.02$). While a small effect size, they point out that effect sizes in medicine are usually small "because there are many factors that influence health outcomes (e.g., severity of disease, ancillary treatments, comorbidity, psychosocial stressors, natural course of illness, regression to the mean, etc.)" (Kelley et al., 2014, p. 5). A small effect size can translate into a large clinical impact. To put this in perspective, the researchers cited Rutledge and Loh (2004), who report that there are many important variables that have a small effect size but are clinically significant. For example, the effect size for the influence of aspirin use over five years is only 0.03, but this translates into cutting the risk for a myocardial infarction (MI) in half compared to placebo users. The effect size for the influence of selective serotonin reuptake inhibitors (SSRIs) on the risk of an MI is 0.05, and this translates to those who use SSRIs being half as likely to suffer an MI as the placebo group. Thus, the fact that there is a significant effect size comparable to other health care studies is notable. Furthermore, Kelley et al. (2014) argue that it is quite possible that the effect is stronger than the numbers suggest. They note that the studies reviewed were trials that had the therapeutic relationship as one component among other interventions and that there may have been insufficient emphasis on the relationship variables. Also, clinicians were restricted to one intervention method, whereas in actual practice, a clinician would attempt to pick the best method for the particular patient. Finally, greater contact between patients and clinicians could also increase that effect size.

Summary of seven of the randomized controlled studies

The 13 RCT studies Kelley et al. (2014) reviewed encompassed a variety of patient populations, interventions, clinicians, and outcomes. Given that the gold standard of randomized clinical studies was used, it is helpful to summarize seven of the studies that pertain to purpose of this chapter. Brief physical activity counseling for overweight and obese patients led to a better body mass index and abdominal girth in the experimental group after a five- to six-month follow-up compared to the control group (Bolognesi, Nigg, Massarini, and Lippke, 2006). Clinicians trained in enhanced communication prescribed significantly fewer antibiotics for lower respiratory infections compared to the no-training group without compromising patient satisfaction or patient recovery (Cals, Butler, Hopstaken, Hood, and Dinant, 2009). The experimental group of asthma patients had improved asthma outcomes with nurses trained in the implementation of individualized asthma-focused clinical and communication skills (Cleland, Hall, Price, and Lee, 2007). Somatizing patients who worked with general practitioners trained in a specific communication technique reported significantly improved health outcomes than the control group in terms of bodily pain, mental health, physical functioning, vitality, and social functioning (Aiarzaguena et al., 2007). Patients with osteoarthritis who were treated by general practitioners trained on relationships and communication in working with such patients had better overall pain relief, decreased stiffness, increased physical functioning, and better perception of treatment than the control group (Chassany et al., 2006). In a sample of underserved and African American patients with hypertension, those patients who had uncontrolled blood pressure at baseline had significantly larger reductions in systolic blood pressure compared to the group that received minimal intervention if they worked with physicians who received patient-centered communication skills training (Cooper et al., 2011). Finally, in another study, patients with type 2 diabetes who worked with physicians trained to provide a brief health lifestyle counseling had significantly higher levels of physical activity and lost more weight compared to the minimal intervention group (Christian et al., 2008).

Neumann et al. study on outcome-relevance of empathy

In a review of studies on the outcome-relevance of empathy, Neumann et al. (2012) found a number of positive effects in patient care. They noted, however, that the studies used different definitions and measurements of physician empathy. With that caveat, they found that physician empathy was related to better patient reporting of their concerns and symptoms, better diagnostic accuracy, and improved patient education and patient participation; patients were more able to receive illness-specific information; patient compliance/adherence and satisfaction increased; patient enablement, the ability of the patient to cope with a prescribed treatment, was increased; and patients had reduced depression and experienced an increase in their quality of life.

Effects of empathy on severity and duration of the common cold

Can empathy affect the severity and duration of the common cold in patients? Who would have believed that the answer is yes! Rakel et al. (2009) conducted an RCT in which 350 participants who had a cold went to either a standard physician visit or an enhanced physician visit. The participants rated their physicians on various aspects of the practitioner–patient interaction on the Consultation and Relational Empathy (CARE) questionnaire, which measures a number of aspects related to empathy. More specifically, participants rated their physician on the following ten areas: (a) making the patient feel at ease, (b) how well the physician allowed the patient to "tell their story," (c) how well the physician really listened to them, (d) how well they felt the physician was interested in them as a whole person, (e) how well the patient felt their concerns were fully understood by the physician, (f) how well the physician showed care and compassion versus being indifferent or detached, (g) how well the physician conveyed a positive attitude and approach, (h) how clearly the physician explained things, (i) how well the physician helped the patient take control of his or her health, and (j) how well the physician made a plan of action with the patient in a participative way. The researchers found that higher empathy in physicians predicted a significantly shorter duration of a cold and less severity of symptoms. No other patient or physician variable accounted for this. Interestingly, this relationship with decreased cold severity and duration was only found for patients who gave their physicians perfect scores on the CARE measure. Rakel et al. (2009) surmised that empathy is experienced as an "on or off" phenomenon; either the patient feels the clinician is empathic or not. There is no dose-related effect because patients either feel that empathic connection or do not feel it. Specifically, patients who gave their doctors perfect scores have a 0.91-day shorter duration of having a cold and had a 16% reduction in cold severity. Interestingly, patients had double the response in the immune biomarker IL-8 in the 48 hours after intake. The authors explained that inflammatory-immune cytokines such as IL-8 indicate an active immune response to a virus. It is possible that the positive emotions the patient experienced with the clinician are what led to the shorter duration of the cold and the increased immune response.

Effects of communication variableson malpractice claims

What difference do certain communication variables have on malpractice claims? Levinson et al. (1997) compared primary care physicians who had no malpractice claims against them versus primary care physicians who had two or more malpractice claims. The researchers analyzed the communication behaviors in at least 10 audio recordings for each of the physicians. What they found is that physicians who had no malpractice claims used significantly more facilitation statements (e.g., confirming patient understanding, asking patients for their opinion, paraphrasing, and interpreting) and gave more orientation about the flow of the visit (e.g., instructions and directions about the medical visit process, transitional statements like "Get up on the table, take a deep breath"), and gave more information about the therapy (e.g., "You will need to take the antibiotic for 10 days for it to work") than physicians with claims. They also used significantly more humor and laughed more. On the average, no-claims physicians tended to talk more than claims physicians, and their visits tended to be a little longer (i.e., 18.3 vs. 15.0 minutes). The same study was done comparing two groups of surgeons, but these differences were not found with them. It is unclear why this was the case, but the researchers speculated that there may be different critical times for communication differences to show with surgeons (e.g., breaking bad news or informing patients of poor outcome) or different expectations.

Surgeon tone of voice predicts malpractice history

Lest surgeons come to believe they are off the hook, Ambady et al. (2002) found that surgeon tone of voice was related to malpractice history in a study of 65 orthopedic and general surgeons. The researchers compared no-claims surgeons with surgeons who had two or more malpractice claims. They extracted two 10-second audio clips of the surgeon's speech from the first and last minutes of the visit with two different patients. Controlling for content, surgeons who had dominant voice tones and a lack of concern/anxiety in their voice tones tended to have previous malpractice claims. Dominance in voice tone is characterized by being loud, deep, unaccented, moderately fast, and clearly articulated. This voice tone may come across as having a lack of empathy and understanding for the patient. Hence, such surgeons tend to be sued more. Concern or having some anxiety in the voice tone is associated with showing concern and empathy. Those who lack this tone also tend to be sued more.

Failure to provide C² related to poor medical outcomes in chronic pain patients

Ekstrom (2012) has provided examples of how failures of compassion can lead to poor medical outcomes in how physicians approach working with patients who have persistent pain. While there are certainly patients who may fabricate symptoms for ulterior motives such as seeking drugs, deceptively trying to get financial compensation, or trying to meet unconscious or conscious needs for attention, Eckstrom (2012) explains how there are many more patients who are immediately discounted when the patient's pain is difficult to discern. Patients in this situation often encounter a no-win situation, in which the clinician biased to view the patient as lying will construe any patient behavior as "evidence" of malingering. If a clinician does not appraise the patient's situation as involving pain, suffering, or distress, he or she will not feel moved to act to respond compassionately toward it.

Ekstrom (2012) tracks how such a clinician will not take any ownership of the problem and will refer without thinking more rigorously about the symptoms. So begins a cycle of circuitous referral patterns taking months to work through. As the patient becomes more panicked and distressed, the clinicians respond with more suspicion, especially with patients who may be more assertive or adamant. Ekstrom (2012) relates how there have been numerous cases like this, which have led to inappropriate procedures and tests, unnecessary expenses, poor medical decisions, escalation of pain, increased neurological damage, and iatrogenic effects—and this may all lead to actually producing a permanent disability. In addition, the experience of alienation and self-doubt created by being treated as a liar has been found to be connected to the high rate of suicides of people with severe chronic pain. Clinicians who begin with a more compassionate view of the patient will begin by considering and being open to the patient's suffering, actually caring that the person is suffering, and making reasoned referrals and follow-up, rather than just getting the person out of the clinic with a lack of emotional supportiveness. In short, we should not consider only examples of how caring behaviors affect outcomes. We should also consider when uncaring behaviors and attitudes negatively affect outcomes.

MODELS EXPLAINING HOW EMPATHY AND COMMUNICATION SKILLS HAVE THERAPEUTIC EFFECTS

Overview of compassionate caring causal pathways to patient effects

Why do these seemingly amorphous variables like empathy, caring, and communication skills have the positive effects that they do? The scientific importance of compassionate and caring communication is easily lost in medical training. So much time is spent on the physiological and biochemical causal pathways for injuries and disease, while relatively little time is spent on the causal pathways for communication dynamics on outcome, much less the influence of C^2. Once medical professionals become aware of these causal pathways and how they dramatically influence the processes of assessment, diagnosis, and treatment, then communication skills and C^2 can no longer be minimized. The research on this has steadily improved over the past 30 years, but there are major research challenges.

Two types of research on clinician communication and patient outcomes

What is the state of the research on the relationship between clinician communication and health outcomes? Street, Makoul, Arora, and Epstein (2009) provide a good overview. They report that there are two types of research in this area. The first is RCTs of interventions focused on changing clinician communication and decision-making and observing the effects on health outcomes. Griffin, Kinmouth, Veltman, Grant, and Stewart (2004) conducted a rigorous review of all RCTs and found only 35 such trials had been done by the end of 1999. While there have been more RCTs since then, it is still useful to consider their findings. There were 25 studies that focused on a health outcome relative to a communication intervention, such as having physicians use more patient-centered communication or having patients ask more questions. Of these, only 11 (44%) showed significant positive outcome results. The researchers found that typically there were research design flaws, outcomes were measured differently, and samples were small. The second type of research consists of correlational cross-sectional and descriptive studies of physician communication behaviors and various health outcomes. These studies are far more numerous, and while many document positive results, a number have mixed or nonsignificant findings.

Reasons for inconsistent findings in the research

Street et al. (2009) provide four reasons for the inconsistent findings of these two types of research. First, most of the research is correlational, so the causal explanations are not clear. The exact processes and pathways between the communication behaviors and the outcomes are not specified. Possible explanations are not tested against each other. Second, it is very difficult to know what elements of various communication behaviors are connected to the specific outcomes. Sometimes a communication intervention is related, for example, to better patient satisfaction but does not affect the health outcome. Third, this research does not typically situate communication behaviors within wider social determinants of health or other physiological or individual variables. Communication variables might directly explain or mediate the relationship between clinician behaviors and outcome, or one communication variable may be moderating a relationship of another variable that may more directly explain the outcome. Fourth, this research has major measurement challenges. Variables such as shared decision-making can be defined differently by different researchers and operationalized differently as well. Patients may

perceive a clinician action differently than an outside observer. Street et al. (2009) explain that the stage of the research we are at now requires us to develop theoretical explanations for the relationship between communication and outcome. Also, patient outcomes are affected by a complex array of factors, so the effort to identify the influence of a single clinician–patient interaction on outcome is not as likely the major factor as is the cumulative effect of all the communications patients experience over time with their clinicians, other health providers, and personal social support groups. In terms of understanding the mechanisms of how compassion and caring leads to better outcomes, I will offer two theoretical models that delineate the causal pathways: Street et al.'s (2009) model linking patient–clinician communication with health outcomes and Neumann et al.'s (2009) effect model of empathic communication on the clinical encounter.

Overview of Street et al.'s model of how communication affects health outcomes

Street et al. (2009) have described a model of the causal pathways that link patient–clinician communication with health outcomes. They have found seven clinician–patient communication processes by which communication affects health outcomes: (a) facilitating "access to needed care"; (b) "patient knowledge and shared understanding"; (c) "enhancing the therapeutic alliance (among clinicians, patient, and family)"; (d) "enhancing patients' ability to manage emotions"; (e) "improving family and social support"; (f) "enhancing patient empowerment and agency"; and (g) "higher quality decisions" (pp. 297–298). I will summarize each of these below.

Description of the seven pathways by which communication affects health outcomes

1. *Facilitating access to needed care*: This refers to communication that clinicians engage in to help a patient realize their condition and what they must do to follow up on getting the appropriate care. Clinicians assist patients in becoming aware that they have a problem that requires medical attention and help patients navigate the health care system in terms of getting referrals, knowing where to go for certain services and treatments, and deciding whether any tests are needed. Clinicians might have to advocate for the services the patient needs and communicate with other professionals to coordinate care. If there are barriers to access to care, clinicians may need to coach the patient about how to proceed and help solve whatever problems arise.

2. *Patient knowledge and shared understanding*: To achieve optimum health outcomes, clinicians have to help patients understand their condition and the treatment options. Clinicians have to ascertain how patients view their medical condition based on the patient's beliefs, culture, values, and personal experiences that influence their perception of the situation. So, the clinician uses communication to help patients be as fully informed as possible about their medical situation and facilitate a process in which they have a common understanding of what is happening and what the next steps are. This enables the clinician to give care that meets a patient's expectations, increases the likelihood of the patient adhering to the treatment, and helps the patient cope with the illness.

3. *Enhancing the therapeutic alliance*: When there is a sense of being cared for by the clinician and a sense of trust between the patient and the clinician, the direct result is that the patient may have an increased sense of emotional well-being that helps the patient cope with the stress of his or her situation. Indirectly, this will help the patient be more committed to the treatment plans and be more satisfied with the overall care, and there will be better continuity of care. Any communication that improves the therapeutic alliance ends up having direct and indirect healing effects for the patient and improves health outcomes.

4. *Enhancing patients' ability to manage emotions*: While medical staffs do not often view helping patients manage their emotions as a primary concern, doing so has direct and indirect effects on medical outcomes. Any time a patient has a significant health concern, there will be a number of negative emotions that will become stirred up. It is understandable that a patient will become fearful, worried, sad, angry, anxious, and upset when confronted with health problems. Those emotions are actually very important because without them people would not seek medical attention. (When people do not have emotional reactions to their symptoms, they do not seek help.) So, the emotions are not "in the way"—rather, they are just a natural part of the clinical presentation. Helping patients manage their emotions is very important so that they can do what they need to do regarding their situation and their suffering. Street et al. (2009) list at least three ways this has direct or indirect benefits to a patient. First, when clinicians give clear and very good explanations about the health problem and what to do about it, it gives patients a sense of

control, which helps them navigate the uncertainty, be hopeful, and learn what they need to do to get through the health issue. It not only calms the negative emotion, it helps direct the emotion to its intended end. A patient, then, who is very anxious about a symptom will be calmed by an explanation but will also be encouraged to manage that anxiety to take what control there is to respond effectively to the problem. Second, when a clinician helps patients articulate and explore their emotions, patients becomes clearer about what is happening to them, and this helps them feel some emotional relief. Validating patients' emotions provides support and encouragement for them. Third, good clinician communication gives patients a sense of hope and confidence to stay motivated and find the energy to deal with their problem. With that emotional support, patients gain the ability to keep moving forward on their problem, do the best that they can, and find meaning in what they are going through. Directly, helping patients manage their emotions helps them experience some relief and support in the midst of a difficult situation. Indirectly, it helps patients engage their situation and channel that emotional reaction into dealing directly with the situation. If patients do not manage those emotions well, it will detract from their ability to take care of themselves, which is certain to lead to a poorer outcome.

5. *Improving family and social support*: Patients who have the support of their family and others have better medical outcomes. There is actually a great deal of research examining how this occurs. Street et al. (2009) mention three ways. One is that feeling connected and supported by others, and having the opportunity to process feelings and problems, provides emotional support. Second, experiencing social support has physiological effects on patients, countering the autonomic hyperreactivity and immunosuppression that occurs in the stress response. Third, having good social support networks results in better instrumental support, in which patients are more likely to have help with things like financial problems, logistical issues, and daily activities. Clinician communication augments better health outcomes when it encourages or facilitates better social support for a patient. The clinician can help the patient and/or the loved ones ensure that they have a good social support network, both for emotional support and for instrumental tangible support with basic needs. A clinician might also help a patient with negative social support, such as addressing dysfunctional family dynamics that undercut the patient or people in the patient's life who negatively affect his or her progress (e.g., drug-addicted friends might prevent the recovery of an addicted patient). The clinician being supportive of the patient and/or loved ones is also part of that social support. Knowing that your clinician really cares about you is another part of that social support. When patients feel supported, they tend to feel better and more motivated to do what needs to be done in response to their health problem. As a result, medical outcomes are better.

6. *Enhancing patient empowerment and agency*: As implied in the above pathways, good communication skills by a clinician increases a patient's sense of agency, a sense of accepting what has happened and being actively engaged in taking care of him- or herself. Clinicians who use a collaborative decision-making process empower patients and increase patients' self-efficacy throughout the process of

dealing with the health concerns. Giving patients clear information and explanations with a focus on involving them in the decision-making process in a collaborative way gives patients a sense of control, autonomy, and ownership in dealing with the problems. Patients who are passive and do not understand what is happening or why will not be motivated to do what they can to respond to their situation after they leave the clinic or hospital. A communication style that facilitates empowerment and agency is one that is a critical factor in achieving the best health outcome possible.

7. *Higher quality decisions*: When communication is very good, patients get very good information in a way that they can understand. The clinician understands and works with the perspective of the patient and/or the loved ones to achieve a common understanding of what is occurring and what the options are. In making decisions, the clinician helps the patient understand what the evidence for treatments is and what the risks and benefits of various courses of actions are, and then works to get a mutually agreed-upon course of action. Imagine if the clinician were not good at communicating his or her diagnosis or explaining it well; or that the clinician was not aware of the perspective of the patient and/or loved ones; or that the clinician did not take time with a patient to achieve a common understanding of the problem and the options. Medical outcomes will certainly suffer because the medical decisions made will not be very good. Decisions are much better with good communication skills.

Communication processes have direct and indirect pathways to improving health outcomes

Figure 5.1 delineates the direct and indirect ways that communication improves health outcomes (Street, 2013). Good patient–clinician

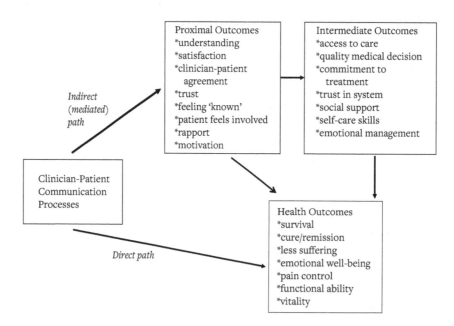

FIGURE 5.1 Communication pathways to improved health outcomes adapted from Street, 2013.

communication can have direct effects on health outcomes in terms of decreasing negative emotions such as fear and anxiety, increasing positive emotions such as hope and self-worth, or gaining a sense of resolve or meaning that helps individuals better "carry their suffering." Good communication can also directly help patients physiologically in terms of improving pain or other symptoms. Communication also causally leads to health outcomes indirectly through proximal outcomes and intermediate outcomes. Good communication skills can lead to the proximal outcomes of patients feeling a sense of trust, rapport, and safety with that clinician. This in turn increases patient motivation to take care of themselves better and to adhere to the recommended treatment, which then contributes to a better outcome (Street et al., 2009).

Overview of the Neumann et al. model of how empathy is related to better patient outcomes

Neumann et al. (2009) have provided another theoretical model explaining the mechanism for how clinical empathy is related to better patient outcomes. Building on Squier's (1990) initial model of empathic understanding and adherence to treatment regimens, Neumann et al. (2009) have proposed the *effect model of empathic communication* in the clinical encounter shown in figure 5.2. Neumann et al. (2009) conducted a review of the theoretical and empirical research literature on empathy to create this model. The research literature on empathy is vast, and studies on the effects of empathy use a variety of definitions, measures, and methods to examine its effects. In order to create a comprehensive model, the researchers reviewed the study of empathy across disciplines. They found studies that

approach empathy as an affective event and others as a cognitive event or a combination of these two approaches. There were also studies that examined empathy as a behavior, a social and emotional competence, in which the clinician interacts in such a way with a patient that the understanding of the patient experience is expressed and perceived by the patient to be empathic. There are studies that have found neurophysiological indicators of empathy in terms of the building blocks of clinical empathy that are summarized elsewhere in this book. Overall, Neumann et al. (2009) found that clinical empathy has strong and specific positive effects on patients' health outcomes and that "being empathic is a necessary clinical procedure that enables the clinician to accurately fulfill core medical tasks, such as 'anamnesis, diagnosis, education, information, and therapy'" (p. 343; includes subquotation from Adler, 2007, p. 7).

Definition of empathic ability used in the model

Because empathy is studied in such varied ways, Neumann et al. (2009) used Mercer and Reynolds's (2002) definition of clinical empathy because it combines the affective, cognitive, behavioral, and moral dimensions of empathy, which all appear essential for empathic communication. Clinical empathy is defined as "a complex, multidimensional concept. Empathy involves an ability to:

a. *understand the patient's situation, perspective and feelings (and their attached meanings);*

b. *communicate that understanding and check its accuracy; and*

c. *act on that understanding with the patient in a helpful (therapeutic) way." (p. S11)*

Description of effect model of empathic communication focusing on cognitive/action-oriented effects

In the *effect model of empathic communication* in the clinical encounter, Neumann et al. (2009) diagramed the established, theoretical, and hypothesized causal pathways for the effect on clinician empathic communication on short, intermediate, and long-term outcomes (see figure 5.2). Solid lines are based on empirical and theoretical studies, while the dotted lines are hypothesized relationships. When patients experience empathic communication, they tend to disclose more information about their symptoms and concerns (arrow 1), which then has cognitive/action-oriented effects and affective-oriented effects. In terms of the cognitive/action-oriented effects, with the patient disclosing more information, the clinician is able to obtain more detailed medical and psychosocial information (arrow 2), which provides the basis for a more accurate assessment of medical and psychosocial issues and therefore a more accurate diagnosis (arrow 3). This more accurate assessment and understanding leads the clinician to understand better what the patient's individual needs are in terms of what therapy is indicated for the condition, the psychosocial considerations of using that therapy, and what kind of communication with the patient would work best (arrow 4). This leads to the clinician being able to optimize the specific medical and/or psychosocial therapies (arrow 5). The clinician is able to support the patient better because the therapeutic action is tailored to what the patient actually needs both medically and psychosocially, which in turn leads to better long-term outcomes (arrow 7). This is further enhanced by the fact that the clinician's better understanding of the patient's

individual needs leads to better communication in terms of illness-related information, patient education that is tailored to who the patient is, and in a patient participative style (arrow 6) that in turn also contributes to better long-term outcomes. These outcomes include health status, the psychological state of the patient, increased enablement of the patient, and the patient being better able to self-manage what is needed.

Description of effect model of empathic communication focusing on affective-oriented effects

In terms of affective-oriented effects, clinician empathic communication can cause positive emotional reactions in the patient directly resulting from clinician empathy (arrow 8) or as a result of the patient becoming more disclosive of his or her concerns in response to clinician empathy (arrow 9). Either way, the patient has more positive emotional reactions of feeling valued and understood, validated, and accepted. These possible positive patient emotional reactions can affect long-term outcomes in direct and indirect ways. Indirectly, these positive patient emotions can improve short-term and intermediate outcomes such as patient satisfaction, trust, and increased adherence to prescribed medical regimens (arrow 10).These positive emotional states can enhance cognitive processes (arrow 11) in that with this increased sense of trust and being understood, a patient is more likely to be active and engaged in discussing and making decisions about his or her health care. The patient will be more likely to hear and accept what the clinician is saying and to realize he or she needs to follow through with what has been decided. There is also the possibility that the patient's positive emotional reactions to

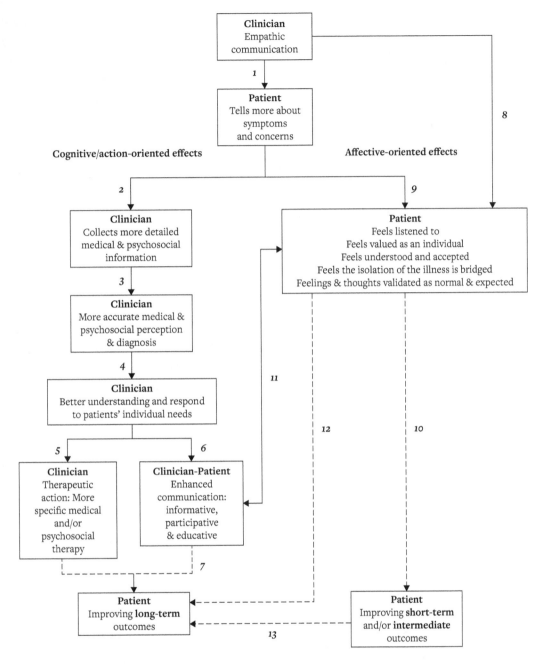

FIGURE 5.2 Effect model of empathic communication in the clinical encounter (Neumann et al., 2009).

clinician empathy has direct effects on long-term outcomes such as in palliative care or with psychosomatic conditions (arrow 12). Finally, the patient's positive emotional reactions lead to better short-term and/or intermediate outcomes, which then would help with improving long-term outcomes (arrow 13; Neumann et al., 2009).

Neurobiological mechanisms that might account for empathy's beneficial patient outcomes

What might be the neurobiological mechanisms that account for empathy's beneficial effects? Decety and Fotopoulou (2015) have argued that social baseline theory (SBT) and the free energy principle (FEP) are two mechanistic explanations that together help explain how physician empathy results in so many positive physical and mental outcomes for the patient. Social baseline theory (Coan & Sbarra, 2015) proposes that the human brain is most attuned and adapted to its social ecology so that social proximity to other people is what is expected. Social proximity is the brain's baseline assumption in that "the human brain *expects* access to relationships characterized by interdependence, shared goals, and joint attention" (p. 87). Anything that violates this expectation is a threat to the person and results in increased physiological and cognitive effort to prepare to deal with the situation. Social support leads to improved emotional self-regulation and decreased hormonal stress response. Clinician empathy would signal a compassionate caring attitude leading to decreased stress in the patient and conserving the internal resources of the patient. The clinician him- or herself becomes a resource to the patient psychologically but also with positive physiological consequences. The free energy principle (Firston, 2010) postulates that biological organisms minimize the free energy of their internal states by the brain optimizing its predictions of the outside world by constantly comparing those predictions against what actually occurs in the physical and social environment. In this way, the organism maintains bodily homeostasis by making optimal inferences about the outside world with its ambiguous cues. This neurobiological process explains how clinician empathy (a) provides cues that make the patient feel safe, (b) optimizes the use of internal resources, and (c) facilitates specific physiological and psychological processes as a result (Decety & Fotopoulu). Overall, rather than clinician empathy being an optional adjunct to the care of patients, these neurobiological theories strongly make the case that clinician empathy is necessary for optimal patient care.

THEORY OF HUMAN CARING AND EMPIRICAL RESEARCH IN THE NURSING PROFESSION

Parallel work on caring and compassion has been occurring across disciplines and professions

While the science of compassion is relatively new in terms of studying compassion from the perspectives of evolutionary biology, physiology, neuroscience, psychology, and other sciences (Seppala et al., 2017), there has already been very significant work on the related concept of caring for about 40 years. One of the problems in the health professions, and the helping professions in general, is that we do not typically read each other's work. As a result, we often work parallel to each other on the same issues without knowing it. What is fascinating in health care is to witness how this parallel work ends up providing greater validity to the overall study of C^2 as we discover similar dynamics even though we use different language and approaches to describing the same phenomena of caring and compassion. Even in medicine, it is not uncommon to go to conferences and discover very similar work on caring and compassion variables even though the specialties did not know another specialty was working in a similar way. While I have made it a practice to learn of all the parallel work on caring and compassion, I am fairly certain there are other lines of inquiry in various disciplines like anthropology, sociology, and diverse specialties in medicine or helping professions that are relevant.

Legacy of caring research in the profession of nursing

The profession of nursing has probably the longest track record of generating theory and empirical research on the phenomenon of caring. The book by Alligood and Tomey (2010), *Nursing Theorists and Their Work*, is an excellent summary of caring theory, with its roots in Florence Nightingale's work through many nursing theorists and researchers. A collection of research instruments on caring can be found in Jean Watson's (2009) *Assessing and Measuring Caring in Nursing and Health Sciences*. In it are measures from various theoretical streams, such as the Caring Ability Inventory (Nkonho), the Caring Efficacy Scale (Coates), the Caring Behavior Checklist and Client Perception of Caring Scale (McDaniel), and the Caring Factor Survey (Nelson, Watson, and InovaHealth). An international compendium of research on Jean Watson's theory of human caring can be found in *Measuring Caring: International Research on Caritas as Healing* (Nelson & Watson, 2012).

Jean Watson and caring science

In terms of research on the phenomenon of human caring, Jean Watson (1985, 1988, 1999, 2009) is one of the pioneers of both developing theory and empirical measurement of caring in the nurse–patient interaction. While developed in the profession of nursing, it is recognized internationally for being one of the first scientific approaches to understanding human caring theory and practice, which

is called caring science. Caring, or *caritas*, according to Watson, is the central theoretical construct about which we formulate conceptual-theoretical systems trying to get at this phenomenon within the research paradigm of caring science. Unlike many other research efforts, Watson recognized the importance of doing research based on theory rather than studies focused on the relationships of particular variables loosely categorized as exemplifying care. She developed the theory of human caring focused especially in nursing and then articulated the scientific methodology to explore and test this theory. While it is very difficult to study *caritas*/caring in its full complexity, especially because of it subjective and phenomenological nature, she and other nursing researchers developed research tools that have been successful in studying it. As Watson (2009) explains,

> measuring caring within this context takes on a different meaning and may allow researchers to be more explicit so that the manifest key indicators of empirical caring still contain and honor the nonmanifest field that is emergent and unseen behind the observable empirics, as we remind ourselves that the empirical objective evidence of caring measurements are not the phenomenon itself, but only an indicator. The empirical indicators cannot be understood by themselves but must be located back into the conceptual system or model from which they were derived. In other words, the part that becomes objectively present in the manifest field must be placed within the context of the whole nonmanifest field from which it emerged. The findings can then be interpreted/reinterpreted within an authentic theoretical–conceptual context and not stand alone as isolated evidence, void of context and meaning. It is through such efforts to connect research traditions, designs, methods, measurements, and findings that new interpretations, new knowledge, and new theories can be generated. (pp. 9–10)

Watson's scientific approach to caring has yielded a great deal of research affirming the positive outcomes related to caring behaviors, attitudes, and processes.

Research on compassion is more than patient–clinician communication variables

It is important to note in terms of the scientific construct of compassion or caring that it is a variable used in examining not just the patient–clinician relationship but also other dynamics. For example, what is the effect of clinicians having more or less caring/empathy/sympathy on their level of burnout or personal well-being? Or what does brain functioning look like when a person is in a compassionate state versus an emotionally detached, objective state? What is the effect of an organizational culture that is characterized by C^2 compared to one that is not on variables such as employee turnover, burnout, number of medical errors, patient satisfaction, or productivity? In the next section, this wider perspective on the construct of compassion is presented.

THE NEW FIELD OF COMPASSIONOMICS

Thought experiment on compassionate behaviors having no effect on patients

In my experience teaching research on the effects of C^2 on patients, even when all of this research is presented, there can still be an old habit of minimizing the influence of factors like caring, empathy, and communication skills. This is probably due to many decades of not knowing about this research. Or it can be due to uninformed suspicion about this type of research and the denigration of what is erroneously called "soft science." I will address this directly in chapter 7, on health care as an objective subjective science. But when I have only a small amount of time with a clinician or a class, I ask them to do a thought experiment and apply the null hypothesis to this material. The null hypothesis would be, "My clinical communication skills have NO EFFECT on ANY patient outcome variables." That means that how I communicate with a patient as we work through a medical problem will make NO DIFFERENCE on what the health outcomes will be. So, I might use good patient-centered communication and motivational interviewing coming from an internal attitude of genuinely caring about my patients; or, I might be abrupt with patients, hit them hard with the truth of their behavior in the most shaming, off-putting way with an internal attitude of dislike for them. According to the null hypothesis, I would then expect that either of these approaches to a patient will make no difference in the outcome. Are you really prepared to say that the *manner* in which you deliver health services has absolutely no significant effect on the patient and the patient outcomes?

Compassionomics as the scientific study of the effects of compassionate care

Trzeciak, Roberts, and Mazzarelli (2017) have proposed a scientific framework for testing whether and how compassion variables have measurable effects. They argue that either compassionate care has a significant beneficial effect on patients and health care providers or it does not (i.e., the null hypothesis). They reviewed the research in health care with the overarching hypothesis "that the provision of healthcare in a compassionate manner is more effective than healthcare provided without compassion, by virtue of the fact that human connection can confer distinct and measurable benefits" (Trzeciak, Roberts, and Mazzarelli, 2017, p. 93). Specifically, they articulated four research hypotheses with regard to the beneficial effects of compassionate health care. First, compassionate health care is beneficial to patients in terms of clinical outcomes. Second, it benefits health care systems and payers in terms of financial sustainability. Third, providing compassionate care benefits health care providers by lowering burnout and promoting their well-being and resiliency. Fourth, in social networks of health care providers, there is an emotionally contagious effect of performing compassionate behaviors; and this in turn can amplify the effects on the first three hypotheses. Trzeciak et al. (2017) have proposed the term *compassionomics* "as the brand of knowledge and scientific study of the effects of compassionate care on health, healthcare, and healthcare providers" (p. 92).

List of outcome measures and potential mechanisms of action explaining the effect of compassionate behaviors

Trzeciak et al. (2017) reviewed over 200 empirical papers that related to "compassion" or "compassionate" related to the above four hypotheses with the goal of finding all of the potential outcome measures and potential mechanisms of action for how compassionate health care is beneficial in those four hypotheses. They found 45 potential outcome measures and 50 potential mechanisms of action. These are listed in the table from their article, as shown in table 5.1 with their permission. Note that they have sorted these measures and mechanisms of action by hypothesis: compassionate health care as beneficial to (a) patients, (b) health care systems and payers, (c) health care providers themselves, and (d) these compassionate behaviors having a mutually positive contagious

effect among the health care providers. Note also how varied the mechanisms of action are. They included physiological, neurological, psychological, systemic, and other processes that mediate or explain how those compassionate behaviors actually do affect the outcomes. A more detailed analysis and presentation of this information is also available in Stephen Trzeciak and Anthony Mazzarelli's book, *Compassionomics: The Revolutionary Scientific Evidence that Caring Makes a Difference* (2019).

Challenges of doing experimental research on the effects of compassionate behaviors

The work by Trzeciak et al. (2017) is a landmark study in that it has summarized to date how C^2 is beneficial to patients, clinicians, and health care organizations. Their integrative paper amplifies the fact that C^2 definitely is part of evidence-based medicine. But while there appears to be a great deal of supporting data, the authors point out that most of these studies are observational and correlational. The causality is inferred between the compassionate behaviors of health care providers having an effect on patient outcomes, with the patient's experience of that compassionate care being the mediating variable. Trzeciak et al. (2017) argue that more experimental research designs are needed to test various compassionate behavior interventions. Along with many other researchers, they point out that there are number of challenges to this research. One is that terms to describe these dynamics are not used consistently; for example, *empathy* and *compassion* are used interchangeably, but they appear to be distinct constructs that operate differently. Another is that we are far from a consensus on what are the best instruments and methods to study compassionate care. Furthermore, experimental study

TABLE 5.1 Potential Mechanisms of Action and Outcome Measures for Compassionate Health-care. These Mechanisms and Outcome Measures are Supported by More Than 200 Publications in the Scientific Literature. [HCP = Health Care Provider] (Trzeciak et al., 2017).

HYPOTHESIS	DOMAIN	MECHANISMS OF ACTION	OUTCOME MEASURES
Compassionate healthcare is beneficial for patients	Physiological	Reduces stress-mediated disease pathophysiology for patients Reduces systemic inflammatory pathophysiology for patients Improves autonomic nervous system activity (parasympathetic activity over sympathetic activity) for patients	Enhanced: - immune function - wound healing - neuroendocrine function Fewer cardiovascular events
	Pain and analgesia	Modulates nociception for patients	Reduced patient experience of pain (and/or lower analgesic requirement)
	Nonspecific treatment factors	Effect modifier for therapies Stronger placebo effect	Enhanced efficacy of therapeutic agents
	Clinical quality	Increases HCP commitment (i.e. "go the extra mile") to ensure optimal outcomes for patients Higher quality standards for HCPs Higher HCP diligence and meticulousness regarding quality Better therapeutic alliance (e.g. better patient trust in HCPs) Better patient self-disclosure (versus concealment) in medical interviews Better history-taking, information gathering and listening by HCPs Better HCP diagnostic accuracy	Higher quality of care Fewer medical errors Improved patient safety Better HCP alignment on the priorities of patients (patient-centeredness)
	Patient behavior and belief modification	Better patient adherence to a prescribed treatment plan Better patient enablement, engagement, and activation Better patient self-care Better recovery expectations for patients Better patient self-efficacy	Better disease prevention Better control of disease progression Better functional status in response to therapy (i.e. relief of impaired function) Shorter recovery time

HYPOTHESIS	DOMAIN	MECHANISMS OF ACTION	OUTCOME MEASURES
	Psychological	Stress buffering Antidepressant effects Attenuates somatic disease effects on psychological and emotional well-being	Reduced patient anxiety Better patient psychological adjustment to serious and/or chronic disease Reduced patient distress Reduced depressive symptoms for patients Positive affect and emotions for patients
	Experience	Better communication between HCPs and patients Protects dignity and respect for patients Prevents emotional harms to patients	Better patient experience (satisfaction) Better patient perception of HCP clinical competence Reduced patient concerns Reduced patient suffering
	Subjective health	All of the above	Better patient-reported outcome measures (PROMs) Better patient quality of life Improved patient well-being
Compassionate healthcare is beneficial for healthcare systems and payers	Financial performance	Better patient experience Practice differentiator (raises reputation of healthcare system and HCPs, and increases referrals) Builds patient loyalty (prevents voluntary disenrollment from HCP practices) Better performance in Value-Based Purchasing programs from payers (i.e. based on patient experience) Cost avoidance through: - higher quality of care (more efficient, less re-work) and fewer medical errors - better clinical outcomes - reduction in discretionary resource use (less unnecessary testing, therapies, and referrals to specialists) - fewer hospital admissions (and réadmissions)	Revenue growth for healthcare systems Lower costs for healthcare systems Higher financial margins (or avoidance of financial loss) for healthcare systems Lower healthcare spending by payers Better financial sustainability for payers

(Continued)

HYPOTHESIS	DOMAIN	MECHANISMS OF ACTION	OUTCOME MEASURES
		- lower hospital length of stay	
		- better patient self-care and adherence to therapy	
		- better patient self-disclosure in medical interviews	
		- better HCP teamwork	
		Lower HCP absenteeism	
		Lower employee turnover for HCPs	
		Promotes culture of professionalism	
		Fewer medical malpractice lawsuits	
Providing compassionate healthcare is beneficial for healthcare providers	Psychological and neurobiological	Activates pleasure centers in the brain ("helper's high") for HCPs	Better provider experience among HCPs
		Promotes neurobiological concordance between HCPs and patients ("mirror neurons" and autonomic nervous system activity)	Lower burnout among HCPs
			Promotes resilience among HCPs
		Shifts self-focus perspective to other-focus perspective	Promotes well-being for HCPs
		Stress-buffering for HCPs	Better self-esteem for HCPs
		Promotes HCP perception of time affluency	Reduces HCP depressive symptoms
			Reduces HCP anxiety
			Promotes positive affect for HCPs
	Physiological	Down-regulates systemic inflammation for HCPs	Promotes longevity for HCPs
		Improves autonomic nervous system activity (parasympathetic activity over sympathetic activity) for HCPs	Lowers risk of cardiovascular events for HCPs
			Enhances immune function for HCPs
	Professional	Promotes HCP compassion satisfaction (vs. compassion fatigue)	Better professional satisfaction among HCPs
		Generates high esteem for HCPs among their peers	Promotes career longevity for HCPs
		Better practice environment	
Compassionate healthcare behaviors are contagions among healthcare providers	HCP social networks	HCP group affect/emotion contagion	Compassionate emotional culture in a healthcare system
		Amplification of positive emotions and behaviors in and among HCPs (e.g. "broaden and build" theory; "elevation" theory)	
		Leadership behavior contagion	

will be very complex because it is not as easy as examining the relationship between individual health care provider and effect on the patient. The entire practice environment affects outcomes as well. For example, the compassionate emotional culture of an organization can affect patient outcomes as well as the well-being of the clinicians. Thus, study designs have to take into account the multifactorial influence of various compassionate or noncompassionate variables that can interact or negate each other (e.g., an uncaring organizational culture trumps the individual caring clinician in affecting patient outcome). Also, patients interact with many different health care providers, and differing care provider behaviors can make it difficult to know if things are as simple as focusing on an individual clinician's behavior having a particular effect on a patient (Trzeciak et al., 2017).

CONCLUSION

While the focus of this book is on explicating what the clinician compassion mindset is and how to maintain a balanced C^2 approach to help sustain that mindset, this chapter has summarized representative studies that demonstrate scientifically how compassionate behaviors and approaches have definite positive effects on patients and outcomes. Patients are more satisfied with the health care provided, more likely to follow the clinician's advice and treatment regimen, and even less likely to sue their clinicians when they perceive something has gone wrong. The outcomes also include actual medical outcomes. Two models were provided to explain how C^2 and clinician empathy actually do result in these outcomes. Preceding the current work on the science of compassion has been nearly 40 years on the theory and practice of human caring in the nursing profession. The caring science approach of Jean Watson has moved the research to be more theoretically grounded, and there are a number of other theories as well. This work has led to the new field of *compassionomics*. While much solid research has been conducted, much more rigorous study must be done.

QUESTIONS FOR DISCUSSION

1. What is your assessment of the current state of the research on the impact of C^2 on patients and patient outcomes?
2. How would you explain the importance of compassionate caring practice to other clinicians?

REFERENCES

Adler, H. M. (2007). Toward a biopsychosocial understanding of the patient-physician relationship: An emerging dialogue. *Journal of General Internal Medicine, 22,* 280–285.

Aiarzaguena, J. M., Grandes, G., Gaminde, I., Salazari, A., Sanchez, A., & Ariño, J. (2007). A randomized controlled clinical trial of a psychosocial and communication intervention carried out by GPs for patients with medically unexplained symptoms. *Psychological Medicine, 152,* 40–46.

Alligood, M. R., & Tomey, A. M. (Eds.). (2010). *Nursing theorists and their work* (7th ed.). Maryland Heights, MO: Elsevier.

Ambady, N., Laplante, D., Nguyen, T., Rosenthal, R., Chaumeton, N., & Levinson, W. (2002). Surgeons' tone of voice: A clue to malpractice history. *Surgery, 132,* 5–9.

Beck, R. S., Daughtridge, R., & Sloan, P. D. (2002). Physician-patient communication in the primary care office: A systematic review. *Journal of the American Board of Family Practice, 15*(1), 25–38.

Bolognesi, M., Nigg, C. R., Massarini, M., & Lippke, S. (2006). Reducing obesity indicators through brief physical activity counseling (PACE) in Italian primary care settings. *Annals of Behavioral Medicine, 31*, 179–185.

Cals, J. W., Butler, C. C., Hopstaken, R. M., Hood, K., & Dinant, G. J. (2009). Effect of point of care testing for C reactive protein and training in communication skills on antibiotic use in lower respiratory tract infections: Cluster randomized trial. *British Medical Journal, 338*, 1112–1115.

Chassany, O., Boureau, F., Liard F., Bertin, P., Serrie, A., Ferran, P., ... Marchand, S. (2006). Effects of training on general practitioners' management of pain in osteoarthritis: A randomized multicenter study. *Journal of Rheumatology, 33*(9), 1827–1834.

Christian, J. G., Bessesen, D. H., Byers, T. E., Christian, K. K., Goldstein, M. G., & Bock, B. C. (2008). Clinic-based support to help overweight patients with type 2 diabetes increase physical activity and lost weight. *Archives of Internal Medicine, 168*(2), 141–146.

Cleland, J. A., Hall, S., Price, D., & Lee, A. J. (2007). An exploratory, pragmatic, cluster randomised trial of practice nurse training in the use of asthma action plans. *Primary Care Respiratory Journal, 16*(5), 311–318.

Coan, J. A., & Sbarra, D. A. (2015). Social baseline theory: The social regulation of risk and effort. *Current Opinions in Psychology, 1*, 87–91.

Cooper, L. A., Roter, D. L., Carson, K. A., Bone, L. R., Larson, S. M., Miller, ... Levine, D. M. (2011). A randomized trial to improve patient-centered care and hypertension control in underserved primary care patients. *Journal of General Internal Medicine, 26*(11), 1297–1304.

Decety, J., & Fotopoulou, A. (2015). Why empathy has a beneficial impact on others in medicine: Unifying theories. *Frontiers in Behavioral Neuroscience, 8*, 1–11.

DiMatteo, M. R. (2004). Variations in patients' adherence to medical recommendations: A quantitative review of 50 years of research. *Medical Care, 42*(3), 200–209.

Ekstrom, L. W. (2012). Liars, medicine, and compassion. *Journal of Medicine and Philosophy, 37*, 159–180.

Firston, K. J. (2010). The free-energy principle: A unified brain theory? *Nature Reviews Neuroscience, 11*, 127–138.

Griffin, S. J., Kinmouth, A., Veltman, M., Grant, J., & Stewart, M. (2004). Effect on health-related outcomes of interventions to alter the interactions between patients and practitioners: A systematic review of trials. *Annals of Family Medicine, 2*, 595–608.

Kelley, J. M., Kraft-Todd, G., Schapira, L., Kossowsky, J., & Riess, H. (2014). The influence of the patient-clinician relationship on healthcare outcomes: A systematic review and meta-analysis of randomized controlled trials. *PLoS One, 9*(4), 1–7.

Levinson, W., Roter, D. L., Mulloly, J. P., Dull, V. T., & Frankel, R. M. (1997). Physician-patient communication: The relationship with malpractice claims among primary care physicians and surgeons. *Journal of the American Medical Association, 277*(7), 553–559.

Mauksch, L. B., Dugdale, D. C., Dodson, S., & Epstein, R. (2008). Relationship, communication, and efficiency in the medical encounter. *Archives of Internal Medicine, 168*(13), 1387–1395.

Mercer, S. W., & Reynolds, W. J. (2002). Empathy and quality of care. *British Journal of General Practice, 52*, S9–S13.

Montgomery, C. L. (1994). The caring/healing relationship of "maintaining authentic caring." In J. Watson (Ed.), *Applying the art and science of human caring* (pp. 39–42). New York, NY: National League for Nursing Press.

Nelson, J., & Watson, J. (Eds.). (2012). *Measuring caring: International research on caritas as healing.* New York, NY: Springer.

Neumann, M., Bensing, J., Mercer, S., Ernstmann, N., Ommen, O, & Pfaff, H. (2009). Analyzing the "nature" and "specific effectiveness" of clinical empathy: A theoretical overview and contribution towards a theory-based agenda. *Patient Education and Counseling, 74*, 339–346.

Neumann, M., Scheffer, C., Tauschel, D., Lutz, G., Wirtz, M., & Edelhäuser, F. (2012). Physician empathy: Definition, outcome-relevance and its measurement in patient care and medical education. *GMS Zeitschrift für Medizinische Ausbildung, 29*(1), 1–21.

Rakel, D. P., Hoeft, T. J., Barrett, B. P., Chewning, B. A., Craig, B. M., & Niu, M. (2009). Practitioner empathy and the duration of the common cold. *Family Medicine, 41*(7), 494–501.

Roter, D. L., & Hall, J. A. (2006). *Doctors talking with patients/patients talking with doctors* (2nd ed.). Westport, CT: Praeger.

Rutledge, T., & Loh, C. (2004). Effect sizes and statistical testing in the determination of clinical significance in behavioral medicine research. *Annals of Behavioral Medicine, 27*, 138–145.

Seppala, E. M., Simon-Thomas, E., Brown, S. L., Worline, M. C., Cameron, C. D., & Doty, J. R. (2017). *The Oxford handbook of compassion science.* New York, NY: Oxford University Press.

Squier, R. W. (1990). A model of empathic understanding and adherence to treatment regimens in practitioner-patient relationships. *Social Science and Medicine, 30*(3), 325–339.

Street, R. L. (2013). How clinician-patient communication contributes to health improvement: Modeling pathways from talk to outcome. *Patient Education and Counseling, 92*, 286–291.

Street, R. L., Makoul, G., Arora, N. K., & Epstein, R. M. (2009). How does communication heal? Pathways linking clinician-patient communication to health outcomes. *Patient Education and Counseling, 74*, 295–301.

Trzeciak, S. & Mazzarelli, A. (2019). *Compassionomics: The revolutionary scientific evidence that caring makes a difference.* Pensacola, FL: Studer Group.

Trzeciak, S., Roberts, B. W., & Mazzarelli, A. J. (2017). Compassionomics: Hypothesis and experimental approach. *Medical Hypotheses, 107*, 92–97.

Watson, J. (1985). *Nursing: The philosophy and science of caring.* Boulder: Colorado Associated University Press.

Watson, J. (1988). *Nursing: Human science and human care.* New York, NY: National League for Nursing.

Watson, J. (1999). *Nursing: Human science and human care, a theory of nursing.* Boston, MA: Jones and Bartlett.

Watson, J. (2009). *Assessing and measuring caring in nursing and health sciences* (2nd ed.). New York, NY: Springer.

Zolnierek, K. B. H., & DiMatteo, M. R. (2009). Physician communication and patient adherence to treatment: A meta-analysis. *Medical Care, 47*(8), 826–834.

CREDITS

"The pessimist complains about the wind; the optimist expects it to change; the realist adjusts the sails."

—William Arthur Ward

"The meeting of two personalities is like the contact of two chemical substances: if there is any reaction, both are transformed."

—Carl Jung

Chapter Sections:

CHAPTER 6

Overview of the Helping Process

The Problem and Challenge of Clinician and Patient Perceptions

Questions to consider before reading this chapter:

1. Describe a time when you thought you were being caring and helpful to a patient and the patient did not receive it that way. Why did that happen?

2. Do you think communication skills are the main factor in whether you are perceived as compassionately caring by your patients? Why or why not?

3. How do you work with a patient who is responsible for his or her problem but does not want to take responsibility for the solution?

INTRODUCTION

One of the important skills for a clinician to have in order to maintain a compassion mindset when working with patients is the ability to navigate how patients are perceiving the clinician and for the clinician to be aware of how he or she is perceiving the patients. Perception of what the other person is intending is a central component of the helping process and the clinician compassion mindset. The clinician must be concerned about how he or she is being perceived by a patient so that the help intended for the patient is either immediately or eventually perceived as such. The clinician must also be self-aware in terms of how he or she might be perceiving (or misperceiving) the patient. In this chapter, I will begin with an overall model of the helping process and then examine this interplay between the patient and the clinician perceptions. What influences how patients perceive that their clinicians really do care or do not care about them? I will present some of the research on how communication skills alone are not enough to ensure the patient perception of compassionate caring. I will examine some of the factors that influence both the clinician's perception of the patient and what patient perceptions affect the patient's receptiveness to help from the clinician. Finally, I will present four models of helping based on the attributions clinicians make about their patients' behaviors and outcomes.

AN OVERALL MODEL OF THE HELPING PROCESS

At its most basic level, the helping process consists of a helper providing some type of helping action to a recipient or helpee. Helping actions are those behaviors that are concrete responses to the helpee's need or desire. Whether it be providing surgery or giving a hungry person food, helping actions are, on the surface, one-way interactions between at least two human beings. More deeply, they are interactions between two subjectivities that mutually affect each other, building on all previous interactions in that relationship. Skovholt (2005) describes the cycle of caring as the model that describes helping relationships beginning with an *empathic attachment phase* with the patient, then the *active involvement phase*, and ending with the *felt separation phase* (see figure 6.1).

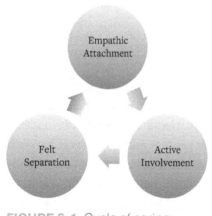

FIGURE 6.1 Cycle of caring (Skovholt, 2005).

Patient brings expectations based on past experience to the helping episode

The therapeutic relationship begins with the clinician making an optimal professional attachment with the patient that creates a safe and trusting relationship. *Empathic attachment* involves entering the world of the patient understanding the patient's perspective and the complexity of his or her situation. There is either an implicit or explicit contract or understanding of what will happen in this relationship in terms of helping the patient. The clinician is expected to facilitate an attachment with the patient that is positive no matter whether the patient has positive or negative attachment styles. As I will explain further in chapter 8, early relationships in a person's life create a psychological template for later relationships in that person's life, influencing how he or she approaches those relationships. Typically, the person's earlier experiences set up positive or negative expectations in the present helping interaction. The patient brings concerns or ingrained fears either consciously or unconsciously into the current helping interaction. We expect the patient to have problems and that the patient may respond to us in negative or conflicted ways. The patients are the ones who are sick, and we—at least when we are in the role of helper—are expected to respond therapeutically.

Role of the clinician is to form an optimal level of attachment with the patient

No matter what the patient's attachment style is, clinicians are expected to form an optimal level of attachment with the patient in which the clinician experiences the world of the patient without being overwhelmed by it. Our professional code is that as clinicians, we know ourselves well enough and have worked through our issues sufficiently that we are always attaching in a positive therapeutic manner. This requires a great deal of training, skill, and experience to become connected to a patient, both getting a deep sense of his or her condition and maintaining emotional regulation so as not to be distressed by what the patient is going through. There has to be a balance between not caring enough (i.e., professional underattachment) and caring too much (i.e., professional overattachment). It is very common when clinicians are just learning how to connect with patients that they become overwhelmed or distressed by the pain or condition of their patients (Skovholt, 2005).

Active involvement in helping involves sustained caring for the patient

In the *active involvement phase*, the clinician builds on this optimal connection with the patient (recall the polyvagal theory and the need for safety in compassion) and becomes involved with the problem the patient brings to him or her. The length of time needed for helping a patient will vary from a few minutes in one visit to many visits over many years. This depends on what the need of the patient is and the role and capacity to help that the clinician offers. Integral to the success of this professional helping relationship is that the clinician provides consistent and sustained caring for the patient. As Skovholt (2005) puts it,

> *the core of the helping professions is the work of the practitioner when he or she makes a series of optimal professional attachments and then separations with people in need. At the heart of these professional attachments is the essential ability to care that must be maintained throughout the process of helping. An inability to care is a dangerous sign of burnout, ineffectiveness, and incompetence.* (p. 82)

The felt separation phase of working with patients

When the goal of the helping has been achieved as dictated by the role of the helper and the expectations for a particular patient situation, the patient and clinician end the helping relationship. This may be initiated by either party when either party has perceived that the goal has been met or that the relationship with this particular clinician is not what the patient needs or desires for whatever reason. If there has been a good connection between patient and clinician, there is typically an experience of loss at this point of felt separation. In any attachment dynamic, there is a loss for both parties even though the ending of a helping relationship is expected. The patient has (hopefully) had the benefit of this clinician who has accepted the patient as he or she is and accompanied the patient through some predicament or hardship. So, there are typically emotional features of the separation that may include sadness at no longer seeing this caring clinician, gratitude, or even anger that they can no longer work together. The clinician must be psychologically healthy enough to be able to end the therapeutic relationship when it is optimal for the patient. The clinician must also be psychologically able to attach and separate repeatedly with patients. This can be emotionally satisfying or depleting because of the emotional investment or attachment that occurs in every positive helping relationship (Skovholt, 2005). The clinician will also experience various emotional reactions to the ending of the helping relationship, such as compassion satisfaction, some sadness at parting from a person in whom he or she has been invested, or discouragement if the clinician was not able to help the patient well.

THE INTERPLAY OF PATIENT AND CLINICIAN PERCEPTIONS IN THE CARING PROCESS

A story about red hamburger meat

I was on my way to my clinical practice late on a very sunny day and decided I should get a quick, early dinner (a burger and fries) from a fast-food restaurant. As I left the drive-through, I began to eat the burger and noticed that the meat was quite reddish pink, and I was concerned that I would get sick from poorly cooked meat. A bit irritated, I drove back to the restaurant and went inside. I indignantly told the worker what was wrong with the burger and was getting ready to provide the uncooked evidence. The worker took my word for it and did not even look at the burger. I went away and again began to eat the burger. But again, it was not fully cooked! At that point, I could not believe it had happened again, and I began to speculate about the incompetence of that restaurant. At that point, I took off my new prescription sunglasses and looked at the burger and saw that it was fully cooked! I did not realize that my sunglasses made any meat look red inside. (I actually tested it.)

Patients and clinicians each have their own lens in perceiving the same action

We each look at the world through different lenses. This is a common metaphor used to describe how people can view the same thing and see it differently. Street, Makoul, Arora, and Epstein (2009) use the metaphor of how "achieving a shared understanding can be difficult because clinicians and patients often understand health and illness through different lenses" (p. 297). We can, of course, extend this metaphor to how patients and clinicians might view any action that comes from the clinician or from the patient in different ways as well. I offer the diagram in figure 6.2 to represent this reality in the work of caring for patients. This is actually a regularly occurring frustration in the helping professions—and in reality, all human interactions. How often have you as a clinician been surprised by how your actions or words were interpreted negatively in some instances, whereas those same actions have been perceived positively by many other people? Or how many times have you heard patients say the same thing about their clinicians: that one clinician interprets their words or actions positively but another interprets them negatively? For instance, you ask two patients to explain how they understand your explanation of their illness (the teach-back method). One patient thinks, "Wow, that doctor really wants to make sure I understand what is going on. I appreciate that he or she is taking the time to make sure I understand." But the other patient thinks, "Wow, this doctor thinks I am an idiot! How condescending to quiz me on whether I understood!" Another example of this would be when a patient comes in with a thick notebook of all his or her medical history, including scan and lab reports. One physician thinks, "Oh great, a professional patient whose identity is wrapped up in being sick. This is not going to go well!" Another physician thinks, "This is great. I can have all the medical history at my fingertips, and I can get a quicker assessment going right away." Or another physician might think, "I often see people with severe chronic illnesses have notebooks like this. They have been burned so many times by the health care system, and they have to help each of us see the big picture. I will try to be better for this patient than he or she has experienced at the hands of the fragmenting and depersonalizing health care system."

The "Problem of Perception" in Caring for Others

Helper) ← Action → (Patient

Helper's Lens   Patient's Lens

Copyright D. Vachon, 2010

FIGURE 6.2 The "Problem of perception" in caring for others.

Accepting the reality of adjusting to patient perceptions

From the point of view of health care professionals who really are committed to being compassionate caring clinicians, it is really frustrating that one's internal caring attitude may not come across that way. But like the William Arthur Ward quote at the beginning of the chapter says, "The pessimist complains about the wind; the optimist expects it to change; the realist adjusts the sails." As clinicians, we will be far more content in our work if we know and accept the reality of the challenge of communicating that we really care for our patients. It's like sailing. The waves are always different, the wind always shifting. To sail from one point to another means constantly readjusting the trim to stay in a more or less direct route to our goal. In this case, the goal of helping a patient requires many subtle and expert maneuvers to convey that we care, which maximizes the best medical outcomes for our patient. In the next section, I provide the caring matrix as a graphic representation of the possibilities of how we

might appear to patients and what attitude we actually have.

THE CARING MATRIX OF CLINICIAN APPEARANCE OF CARING AND ACTUAL INTERIOR ATTITUDE

When we imagine the possibilities of what results when a clinician may or may not appear to care and may or may not actually really care, we get a 2 x 2 matrix of four possibilities (see figure 6.3).

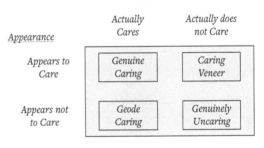

Caring Matrix
(Copyright D. Vachon, 2010)

Interior Attitude

	Actually Cares	_Actually does not Care_
Appears to Care	Genuine Caring	Caring Veneer
Appears not to Care	Geode Caring	Genuinely Uncaring

Appearance

FIGURE 6.3 The caring matrix.

Description of the caring matrix

First, in terms of what is the appearance of caring for the patient, the patient perceives either that the clinician _appears to care_ or that the clinician _appears not to care_. Second, in terms of the interior attitude of the clinician, either the clinician _actually cares_ or _actually does not care_. In the top left cell, if the clinician actually cares and the patient perceives that the clinician really does care, this is called _genuine caring_. This is where the clinician really is in a compassion mindset, and that is apparent in the clinician's actions under most circumstances. If the patient perceives that the clinician appears to care, but the clinician actually does not care in that situation, this is called a *caring veneer*. The clinician might have gone through very good communications training or learned the AIDET model, but he or she does not really care. It is "fake caring," and the hope is that the patient will "buy it." If the clinician appears to the patient not to care, but actually does care, this is called *geode caring*. With a geode, the exterior may look rough and unremarkable, but when it is broken open, there are beautiful crystals lining the inside. There are physicians who may come across as crusty, with seemingly poor bedside manner, but they actually are rooted in a deeply caring attitude. Finally, there are clinicians who appear not to care and actually do not care, which is called *genuinely uncaring*.

Noncaring interactions negatively affect the helpee and the helper

In a noncaring interaction, the helper might be somehow negative in the encounter. He or she might be rude, impersonally detached, or hostile toward the client or patient. The helper has thereby decided not be fully present to the other person, which that person can detect. That person may become more defensive or uncooperative as a result. The helper gets limited information about the client or patient as a result, and the effectiveness in problem solving is drastically reduced because the client or patient becomes more closed to the helper as a protective measure. The client or patient may go away with something pertaining to his or her problem (e.g. advice, a diagnosis and treatment recommendation, a prescription), but a number of things may happen. First, the likelihood of the client or patient following through on the helper's recommendations at all is reduced. Research has found that a lack

of empathy is related to patients less likely to follow through on treatment recommendations (Squier, 1990). Second, being treated in a condescending or impersonal manner may make the client or patient feel worthless and negatively affect the patient's motivation to care for him- or herself. But the helper does not walk away unaffected either. The helper derives little satisfaction from the interaction. Also, if the patient or client has become more irritable or uncooperative as a result of how the helper approached him or her and treats the helper negatively, the helper may become resentful or defensive. The clinician "was just trying to help" but does not see how he or she made the patient become that way. The helper then takes this resentment and defensiveness to the next appointment because he or she expects that the next person might be a difficult client or patient, too.

Same clinician behavior can be perceived as caring or not caring

One of the challenges in researching and in training health professionals in caring attitude and caring behaviors is that patient perceptions about caring vary a great deal. In spite of the best of caring intentions, the same behavior can be perceived as caring by one patient but as uncaring by another (Quirk et al., 2008). This has led to some clinicians being so frustrated and discouraged about trying to be perceived as caring that they get to the point that they do not care about caring any more. As explained in chapter 2, researchers have found that the perception of caring by a patient is more likely to occur if the clinician develops the underlying abilities of discerning the patient's perspective and responding in a way that is attuned to the patient's perspective (Quirk et al., 2008). What is key is that the clinician has the motivation to attend to the emotional experience of his or her patients and to develop the capacity to be able to read patients and respond in a way attuned with their perspective. Typically, patients do not directly state what their emotional experience is but instead give clues about their emotional state and perspective. This only comes to the fore when a clinician picks up on this and invites some exploration of the patient's experience. When the clinician either misses this clue or ignores it, the patient often will display the clue again, especially if it is causing concern or tension in him or her (Suchman, Markakis, Beckman, & Frankel, 1997).

Patient satisfaction does not always increase with clinician communication training

Having had communication skills training is not a guarantee that patients will be more satisfied with their clinicians. In a randomized controlled trial with groups of physicians and other clinicians using a high-quality and commonly used communication skills program, there were no differences between the groups in terms of patient satisfaction. This and other experiments do not always show a link between patient satisfaction and communication skills training (Brown, Boles, Mulloly, & Levinson, 1999). Salmon and Young (2009) have noted, along with others, that too much emphasis on communication may actually detract from a clinician's helpfulness to patients. As they put it,

> whereas current consensus emphasises types of communication, such as breaking bad news, providing information or attending to psychological cues, we suggest focussing on its

> functions, such as hope or feeling cared for. This will complicate teaching because a single type of communication, such as providing information, can serve different, conflicting functions. (p. 335).

Study showing how patients perceive the same communication behavior differently by different specialties

The same communication behavior done by different types of physicians can be perceived quite differently by patients. In a study of 1,265 patients who worked with 65 surgeons and 59 primary care physicians, patient satisfaction was assessed after times when physicians self-disclosed some experience that was medically or emotionally relevant to the patient. When surgeons used self-disclosure, patients tended to report more feelings of warmth and friendliness, more reassurance and comfort, and more satisfaction with the visit than when primary care physicians did the same. The researchers speculated that the expectations patient have for each specialty and the emotional state they are in affect how they perceive physician self-disclosure. Surgical patients may be in a more emotionally vulnerable state with a relatively short and intense connection with the surgeon compared to primary care patients who have more chronic ongoing issues that are less acutely distressing to patients (Beach et al., 2004).

Caring and compassion should not be reduced to communication skills

With the goal of understanding what patients perceive as caring in their doctor, Quirk et al. (2008) found that "the most important element of caring may not be a set of behaviors nor even an attitude but a set of abilities that include awareness of the patient, taking the patient's perspective, and reflecting on the patient's responses" (p. 364). The researchers found that if physicians used "cookbook caring behaviors" but did not attune these to the patient's perspective, those caring behaviors could actually be viewed as uncaring, despite the caring intent of the physicians. While what is considered caring by a patient is subjective, the key to maximizing the likelihood that one is perceived as caring is getting a sense of the patient's perspective either directly or intuitively; this directs how to communicate with the patient in such a way that meets the needs and preferences of the patient. The physician notices and explores the cognitive and affective responses of the patient, notices emotional clues, and chooses words carefully in responding and "titrating the 'dose' of information provided" (Quirk et al., 2008, p. 364) according to what the patient can handle best.

Behaviors that enable awareness of patient perspective

Quirk et al. (2008) found 13 behaviors that captured this quality of the physician's ability to be aware of the experience of the patient, understand the patient's perspective, and then attune his or her response to that patient. In table 6.1, these 13 behaviors are listed and organized for teaching purposes under the mnemonic CARE.

Whether the clinician genuinely cares does matter

A critical question, however, is whether the quality of care in terms of things such as empathy, expressed concern, humor, and so forth necessarily means there is some emotional investment in the client or patient on the part

TABLE 6.1 Themes and Categories of Caring Behaviors from Focus Group Data Quirk et al., 2008)

Communicate effectively

Listening requires asking and using intuition

Give information in appropriate doses (inform as needed)

Choose words carefully and check for meaning

Be direct and straightforward but not abrupt

Be consistent in your verbal and nonverbal behaviors

Exhibit a soft but confident tone, slow pace, and comfortable appearance

Arrange to meet health care needs

Help the patient move forward with the next steps (follow-up)

Act quickly and decisively while preserving patient autonomy

Respectful

Know the patient but focus on the problem

Offer hope but be realistic

Apologize after an error

Empathic

Offer measured empathy

Carefully craft empathic statements

of the helper. That is, does expressed quality of care necessarily mean you are to some extent emotionally involved with the client or patient? Do you really have to feel the connection? Do you have to care genuinely for the person? Can you fake it? Based on some evidence I review below and my own experience both as a giver and a receiver of help, care that is not genuine by a clinician is picked up by clients or patients. Most people can pick up nonverbally and intuitively whether a remark is genuine. People can tell when there is little feeling in a response by a helping professional. They can hear it when a statement sounds mechanical or cliché. In fact, when people detect this, they are suspicious of the clinician's intent, even if the content of the statement is ostensibly a caring one: they feel uncared for and as if the helper thinks they are stupid. I have observed clinicians make a good effort at "faking care," but what eventually happens is that over time clients or patients do figure out what the helper's intentions really are.

Authentic caring matters more than polished communication skills

Salmon and Young (2009) point out that *patients perceiving the clinicians as authentically caring about them can matter more to patients than the clinicians having polished communication skills*. Sensing that a clinician genuinely cares about the patient is the most important factor in an effective patient–clinician relationship. A patient may sense this when a clinician shares his or her own vulnerability, such as in the spontaneous appearance of the clinician's own emotions or in self-disclosing some personal challenge, but only after carefully considering the appropriateness of sharing this with a patient (Malterud & Hollnagel, 2005). In a study of what economically and socially marginalized HIV-positive patients considered good doctoring, this authenticity can be revealed in physicians who communicated respect by not acting aloof or superior and by working with patients in a way that respects their autonomy instead of being controlling or forcing decisions as well as the patients being able to share anything they need to with the physician, trusting that the physician will accept in an understanding way where the patient is at and working from there; trusting the physician's motives and expertise; and having confidence that the physician will stay engaged with them

no matter what. The care of physicians was also revealed when they were generous with time and provided important and useful information. That caring attitude also shows when a patient notices that a clinician tolerates the way that patient is challenging and yet the physician still hangs in with them. A physician who goes beyond expectations also conveys that genuine caring (McCoy, 2005).

Communication skills are viewed through the lens of whether the patient can rely on the clinician

Wright, Holcombe, and Salmon (2004) interviewed 39 women who had breast cancer who represented all phases of treatment, from diagnosis through follow-up at two years. What mattered most to the patients was that they considered their doctor expert, that they had a caring relationship with that doctor, and that their doctor respected them as autonomous individuals. This mattered to the patients more than the doctor's specific communication skills. In fact, if they were confident in their doctor, they would rationalize or discount the doctor's poor communication. What the authors found was that when patients are in a vulnerable or dependent state, they will seek and view the doctor as an attachment figure who has the potential to make them feel safe. Particular communication skills like offering patients choices or providing a lot of information are viewed differently by various patients; for some, this causes them to gain confidence, whereas others feel a loss of confidence in the doctor. Rather than focusing on particular communication skills, the researchers recommend that research on patient–clinician communication focus on the function those skills serve rather than as ends in themselves. While communication skills are very important, they are perceived through the lens of whether a patient can trust and rely on that clinician.

Trust in the clinician from expertise and how information is given

The patients' main concern was whether they could trust the expertise of the physician. This trust was created by observing the technical skill and efficiency of the doctor; what other staff or patients said positively about the doctor; and for many, simply being a doctor. In terms of giving information about the illness or treatment, it was not so much how much information that was given but what kind of information was given and how it was given. Patients gained trust with physicians whom they perceived as being frank and answering questions honestly and without hesitation. Many wanted only certain aspects of the prognosis, with appointments ending on a positive note. The researchers concluded that patients want information more for the purposes of maintaining hope and trust, and not so much for being better informed for its own sake (Wright et al., 2004).

Clinical communication skills are not enough to convey a genuine and caring relationship

Along with this, patients wanted a genuine and caring relationship with their doctor in which they were recognized as an individual by their doctor and in which they recognized their doctors as unique individuals. Patients felt recognized as individuals nonverbally by eye contact, vocal intonation, smiling, and touch, and verbally often by brief nonmedical conversation. Patients did not seem to perceive this because of how a doctor might form a relationship by talking about emotional issues. A doctor doing something that he or she did not have to do, something outside the typical physician role, had a powerful impact on patients (e.g., sitting down with them and reassuring them when everyone knows how busy a doctor is). Patients liked what the researchers called idiosyncratic behavior by the physician, characteristics about the physician that they found likable and unique. Feeling respected by the physician was also a common desire among patients. They appreciated when physicians treated them as human beings on the same level of eye contact and language. They also wanted to feel that they had a choice, but not so much that they had to have options laid out in detailed fashion and fully share in decision-making; they preferred instead that they would be given recommendations directly and clearly, and that physicians recognize that the patient has the option not to follow them. Wright et al. (2004) note how this does not mean a return to medical paternalism; rather, they argue that patients are seeking to feel safe with a trusted expert who genuinely cares about them. Clinical communication skills in themselves are not enough and can be perceived quite variedly (Wright et al., 2004). Communication skills are tools to help convey to patients that they have a good physician they can rely on and feel safe with, both by the physician's expertise and the physician's implied personal commitment to a patient.

Clinician emotional response and biomedical response can both provide security and comfort

From an attachment psychology perspective, "'Attachments', or 'attachment relationships', are emotional bonds that lead an individual to see proximity to a safe or powerful person (the 'attachment figure') when threatened" (Salmon & Young, 2009, p. 332). People who become ill or are injured feel vulnerable and fearful as their life is threatened in some way. This precipitates intense attachment needs as the ill person seeks someone with the power or expertise to help them feel safe, secure, comforted, and helped in their distressed condition. In health care, patients seek this mainly in the clinicians' technical or biomedical care. In modern health care, we typically make distinctions between the biomedical, technological, or skill aspects of the medical care and the emotional aspects of the medical care. But this is not a clear distinction. We train clinicians in interpersonal and communication skills to respond empathically and supportively to the patient's condition, attending to any psychosocial clues that may accompany the illness or injury. In this way, we hope to provide a sense of safety, relief, and support. But the clinicians' biomedical expertise itself provides security and comfort (Salmon & Young, 2009), so we should actually not draw such a hard line between the emotional response and the biomedical response to patients' situations.

Are we promoting caring veneer in simulation and standardized patient training of clinicians?

Wear and Varley (2008) have noted that the problem of using simulation and standardized patients in medical education is that they only verify that the medical student can perform communication skills on the surface, without really showing whether the student actually cares about the patient, coupled with that fact that the student knows this is not a real patient. As Wear and Varley (2008) explain,

> if students are too busy concentrating on how to act as if they care (because someone is evaluating them for those very behaviors), the idea of developing genuine, empathic connections with patients may not be a high priority for their professional development. (p. 154)

The students care about impressing the evaluators but not necessarily about the well-being of the simulated patient (because they are not actually sick). Testing students on their external communication behaviors only gives the message that the external is all that matters if that is where we stop in their training. The fact that medical training does not try to work more with the internal attitudes of the medical student gives the message that this is not that important or is somehow easy to do. Wear and Varley (2008) point out that while there are many benefits to using simulated patients, the downside of such a training is that it can make medical students think that "communication with patients is an 'exterior' set of behaviors, not necessarily from the heart" (p. 154). Compassionate caring requires practicing interacting with a patient when the stakes are high for the patient; it also means that as a clinician, you have to learn how to manage all the emotions that will surface from within you as well as how to respond to that patient while juggling all of this internally.

Study on the relationship between physician surface acting and patient satisfaction

What effect does it have on patients when physicians regulate their displayed emotions to hide their actual feelings with a patient? Yagil and Shnapper-Cohen (2016) conducted a study to ascertain if "surface acting" by a physician had an effect on patient satisfaction. Their sample consisted of 46 patients across a number of specialties (i.e., surgery, orthopedics, gynecology, otolaryngology, pulmonary, urology, nephrology, and GI), with 5 patients for each of these physicians. The researchers developed a scale to assess how frequently physicians engaged in surface acting, that is, suppressing their genuine emotions from being displayed to the patient. The items were the following: "I pretend, in order to cope with patients properly," "I put on a 'mask' to present the emotions I am required to display in my job," "I fake a good mood," "In my job I act as if I am 'on stage,'" "In my work I put on a 'matter-of-fact mask' to hide the various emotions I experience," "I play a role and make an effort so that patients will not see what I am truly feeling," and "There is a gap between what I feel and what the patients would say they see and feel regarding my emotions" (Yagil & Shnapper-Cohen, 2016, p. 1695). The researchers also asked patients to report their level of distress and how long they had known their particular physician.

Distressed patients tended to be less satisfied with surface-acting physicians

What Yagil and Shnapper-Cohen (2016) found was that the more physicians regulated their emotional display, the lower the patient satisfaction, but only when the patients reported their distress to be high. The researchers speculated that when physician emotional display is filtered, the emotional cues are vague to the patient; therefore, the distressed patient will feel more uncertainty with that physician and be less satisfied. A physician who is more genuine in his or her emotional interaction gives more certainty to a distressed patient. Likewise, a less-than-genuine emotional expression by the physician may be experienced as inauthentic by the patient and thereby decrease trust.

The stronger the relationship, the more distressed patients need physician genuineness

In terms of length of the relationship between patient and physician, the stronger the relationship, the more patient satisfaction is negative when the physician is surface acting. The researchers explained this by noting that patients tend to focus more on the instrumental outcomes of their appointments and have lower expectations of the emotional tone of their physician. In stronger relationships, patients have higher expectations of the physician responding in a genuine emotional way. The researchers added that the more patients know their physicians, the better they are at detecting when their physician has an inauthentic emotional expression. In short, genuine emotional expression by physicians is what is most helpful to distressed patients.

Study on increasing clinician attention to quality of care

When clinicians are motivated to be fully attentive to their patients, the quality of care dramatically improves. While this is obvious, we repeatedly have to deal with the negative effects of clinicians not being fully attentive to patients in our health care system. Organizations use all kinds of methods to increase the motivation to be fully attentive. What we prefer is for clinicians and health care staffs to be internally motivated and disciplined to be this way with all their patients. Human nature being what it is, this does not always happen. So, organizations find ways to motivate attentiveness. In a study by Rheineck-Leyssius, Kalkman, and Trouwborst (1996), anesthetists and nurses were given an explicit written instruction on preventing and treating postoperative hypoxaemia in the recovery room and were told that they were being studied (the Hawthorne effect). Baseline rates for the team were gathered before this intervention occurred. As you would expect, the rates of severe hypoxaemia significantly decreased after the intervention. Two months after the intervention to decrease hypoxaemia, the rates were examined again. The rates returned back to the levels they were before the study intervention. The improvement was not sustained.

How clinical attention to patients varies

This may seem like an obvious study, but it highlights that our levels of attention and motivation fluctuate dramatically. As clinicians, we get into a routine operating mode, and unless we are doing something to maximize our attention, we slide in quality, and it is completely due to our level of attention to the potential problem. Managers use every method they can find to improve this, such as using periodic inspections, rewards for good outcomes, punishments for deficiencies, and appeals to clinicians to do the best for their patients, as if they were the clinicians' loved ones. But clinicians are not the only ones trying to influence this. Our patients know this about us. Like the cartoon earlier in this book, they know we are not always "into it" and will work to increase our level of attention to their problem. I had a patient once tell me that she preferred seeing me in the morning rather than late in the afternoon because she noticed I was sharper in the morning. I have heard patients who implement their own interventions to increase the clinician's level of "caring about their problem." One patient said, "I always try to get a new doctor to smile or laugh when I first meet them.

If I can get them to notice me and like me, I know I am going to get better care." We can be the smartest clinicians around in the most prestigious institutions, but our patients know that neither of these factors matter if we are not focused on them as individuals with particular problems.

HELPER'S PERCEPTION OF THE NEED FOR HELP

Influences on the helper's perception of the need for help

The helper perceives that the help recipient has some need or is in a state that requires assistance. The helper perception can be an accurate or inaccurate perception of the other's need. There are times when helpers somehow misperceive that another person needs help. For example, a person may see a handicapped person who is moving him- or herself from a wheelchair to the driver's seat of a car. The handicapped person might do this alone frequently and not require anyone's help. If someone offered help, he or she might say, "No thank you, I'm fine." But the "helper" might perceive a need based on some assumptions. The helper may be wrong in assuming that anyone moving out of wheelchair is in some hardship and *needs* assistance. This erroneous assumption is based on one of two things: past history or the helper's own issues. In terms of past history, the helper probably has encountered people with handicaps who genuinely could not perform some task by themselves and either asked for assistance or were in a situation in which it was expected that help would be given. Thus, the helper imagines this is a similar situation and offers help without verifying it was indeed the same type of situation. Another source of making erroneous assumptions about someone else's need for help comes from the helper's own issues, either conscious or unconscious. Conscious personal issues include those that come from personal experience or training. The helper may have been told while growing up, "When you see a handicapped person, you should help them," just like a boy may be told, "You should always open the door for a girl." It is just an automatic response for some people, and they can tell you why they are helping another person when asked. Unconscious personal issues are those that motivate the helping response but about which the helper is unaware. People can sometimes automatically assume another person needs help because of a compulsive tendency to assist others. Adult children of alcoholics often discuss this phenomenon in which the helping response is cued by any expression of a wish or any exertion in another. Whether it be someone saying he or she is thirsty or witnessing someone struggling to open a jar, the compulsive helper launches into action. Thus, the perception of the need for help is influenced by the helper's own judgments, based on conscious expectations or unconscious influences.

Failing to notice the need or suffering of another person

While the above focuses on the perception of need when there is not a real need for assistance, it also is the case that helpers misjudge another person's need in the opposite direction—that is, they fail to pick up that another person needs help. Again, the same forces operate. In terms of conscious influences, one possibility is that the failure to perceive that another person needs help may be due to lack of training to recognize that another person needs help. Some people are raised not to be particularly attuned to noticing other people's needs. Either through neglect of their own

needs by their parents or by simply lacking someone to teach them how to be sensitive to needs in others, these individuals are not aware of, much less affected by, other people's needs. On a professional level in terms of training, one person might interact with a person who is not going to work and sleeps all the time and conclude that this is a lazy person not deserving of any special attention. Another person trained to assess for clinical depression might interact with the same person and recognize the need to rule out a diagnosis of depression or, if needed, help get treatment for a person who may be experiencing a major depressive episode. A second possibility in the failure to recognize needs in others can be personality factors that incline a person not to notice needs in others. Third, lack of awareness of needs in others can be due to situational factors such as being overwhelmed with so many stressors that a person does not notice needs in others. A parent who is dealing with job stress, financial problems, and difficulties in a romantic relationship might be unaware of his or her child's needs. It is simply the result of having too many demands to be able to process incoming information and demands; some items get priority and others do not. A variant of situational forces interfering with the perception of others' needs occurs with "burned out" helping professionals. After long periods of dealing with very difficult needs in others, coupled with neglecting their own needs, these helpers simply detach from others as a defense mechanism. They can walk by others' needs in the nursing home or the homeless shelter and not seem to notice. If you point it out to them or remind them of their job, they can then notice the needs. But as a way to survive feeling overwhelmed with others' needs or being emotionally exhausted in their work, they learn how to detach from others.

Unconscious forces interfering with the helper noticing the needs of others

Unconscious forces can also operate in the failure to notice needs in others. While there certainly can be unconscious aspects to the above scenarios, there are situations in which people have a psychological block to noticing the needs of others. For example, individuals may have experienced past trauma to the extent that they need to block an awareness of others' needs. That is, if they did notice certain needs somehow similar to what their own trauma was, this might trigger a reexperiencing of the unbearable pain of their own trauma. Of course, the opposite can also occur. At times, people who have experienced trauma are exquisitely attuned to pain in others. Also, the attachment history and childhood of the helper may influence the perception of others' needs. For example, clinicians can have upbringings that either lead them to minimize the needs of others or to be hypersensitive to the needs of others. (This will be further discussed in chapter 8.)

Multicultural and gender influences of helper perception

A person's culture will influence the perception of other people's needs or suffering. Culture also influences the expectations for helping—that is, how one should respond or not respond to another person's needs. Emotional cues can vary across cultures. Depressive symptoms can manifest differently, and a clinician has to be mindful of this in order to notice it accurately. Emotional expression can be modulated by cultural norms as well as how one is expected to respond in such situations. For example, what are the attitudes about crying or expressing anger? Along with this is how clinicians must be aware of how their gender socialization affects the perception of others' needs. In health care, I have witnessed clinicians treat patients differently in terms of their gender even though they had the same symptom or problem. The same is true regarding racial and ethnic differences; some clinicians may assess and treat patients with similar problems differently based on race or ethnicity.

Jean Watson's description of the actual caring moment

Jean Watson (2012) has offered a very helpful model of what occurs in what she calls an actual caring moment, or a transpersonal caring moment (see figure 6.4). Using the insights of phenomenology and transpersonal psychology, she describes an actual caring moment as the intersection of two phenomenal fields that represent two individuals in the caring episode. Throughout their lives, all people are in a continual state of becoming something new as they journey through life, and they can be affected in a positive or negative way by all their encounters with others. Both the patient and the clinician have unique and independent life histories with a past, a present, and a future as they meet at this point in time, represented by the intersection point. As their life paths intersect, with the clinician caring for the patient, both the clinician and the patient are affected by that intersection in this moment of caring. Whatever they each experience in that interaction with the other will now influence each of them as they leave that moment. What happened in that moment now becomes part of their life histories. If the interaction is positive, both the patient's and the clinician's lives are enhanced in some way. In the encounter, each person has the opportunity to choose how to be in that moment and how to react to what happens in that encounter. If there is a true connection between them—that is, one in which the spirit of each person is present to the other—then the event expands the limits of openness and has the ability to expand the human capacities of the patient as well as the clinician. As the caring episode ends, each takes with them the impact of that experience. For the receiver of the care, this might mean a new energy or perspective that helps them deal with their problem. For the caring clinician, this might mean learning from the patient and experiencing personal growth and satisfaction from that encounter.

RECEPTIVENESS TO HELPING BY THE HELP RECIPIENT

Ways patient receptiveness to help is affected

In order for a helping action to be helpful, it must deal with how that helping is perceived by the help recipient. If the person receiving help is not receptive or open to the helper's action, then this interferes with the helping action and its potential healing effect. As with the helper's perception of the person needing help, the receptivity by the help recipient is influenced by conscious and unconscious dynamics based on past history of the help recipient, current situational dynamics, and the type of problem or pathology the help recipient has.

The effect of the patient's past history on receptiveness to help

The patient's past history can improve or impede receptiveness to helping. If the patient has had positive experiences being helped in the past, then he or she is more likely to be open to future offers of help. If experiences of being helped by parents, caregivers, teachers, and other helpers have been characterized by trust, competence, and unconditional love, then the help recipient has more faith in the offer of help. If, however, the help recipient has been harmed or deceived by previous helpers, he or she becomes less able to be open to offers of help. The helper may be the most competent and effective helper there is, but he or she will still have to deal with the fact that the help recipient perceives the helping action in a suspicious or defensive manner based on past experience. Later in this chapter, I will devote a special section to the role of a patient's

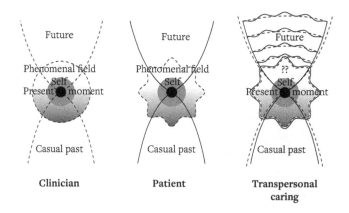

FIGURE 6.4 Actual caring moment/transpersonal caring moment diagram (Watson, 2012, p. 72).

attachment history affecting the receptiveness of the patient to the clinician's help.

Current situational dynamics that influence patient receptiveness to help

Current situational dynamics can improve or worsen the receptivity of the patient. The manner and the context of the helper's actions can influence receptivity. Take, for example, the helping action of starting an IV. The nurse who demonstrates a caring manner is more likely to enhance receptivity than the nurse who treats the patient gruffly or in a depersonalized manner. A prime example of these dynamics is found in person-centered therapy, founded by the Humanistic psychologist, Carl Rogers. It was theorized and researched that certain core conditions expressed in therapy would improve the openness of clients to both the actions of the counselor and the willingness to look at themselves. These core conditions are empathy, genuineness or congruence, and unconditional positive regard (Meador & Rogers, 1984). How attentive the helper seems both nonverbally and verbally can create more receptiveness. The helper's knowledge of and respect for the help recipients' culture also enhances receptivity. When a helper shows sensitivity and interest for a help recipient's racial or ethnic background, sexual orientation, or religious preference, the help recipient is more likely to engage in an open way with the helper.

Other situational factors affecting patient receptiveness to help

Added to this are other situational considerations that facilitate or block receptivity. Help recipients are more receptive if they are in a safe environment. Safety is perceived when care is given by helpers who are appropriately trained and credentialed. Safety is also enhanced by some agreement of privacy or confidentiality. How the room or facility is set up as well as the dress of the helpers also can contribute to receptiveness.

The patient's problem or pathology can affect receptiveness to help

The help recipient's problem or pathology can also negatively affect receptivity to help. The most dramatic example is a person who is suffering from a psychotic episode. If a person is suffering from delusions or hallucinations, this will no doubt affect how a helping action is perceived. In fact, it may be perceived in a hostile manner, thus increasing the defensiveness of the patient. A number of disorders have as one common feature the help recipients' denial of a problem and therefore a lack of receptiveness to helping. Examples include people dealing with alcohol or drug addiction, bulimia, anorexia, gambling compulsions, and sexual addiction. The competently trained helper plans on how to deal with the denial and resistance. A number of medical problems can make receptivity to help problematic. Individuals who are experiencing delirium or changes in mental status because of some medical or psychiatric problem may not be receptive to help.

People with problems or illness often regress psychologically

Just having a problem or an illness can negatively affect receptivity. When people are not feeling well, they tend to regress emotionally.

Especially when a person is encountering a life-threatening situation, he or she can become so emotionally upset as to make it very difficult to receive help. Firefighters, police officers, lifeguards, and emergency room staffs are very aware that they must be careful of people in a state of panic. If they are not careful, they can be harmed by the very people they are trying to help.

Times when people are "overly" receptive to help from others

People can also be overly receptive to help from others. Certain personality types seek out ways to be helped. The prime example in this case is the dependent personality; such individuals have difficulty making decisions on their own and prefer to rely on the guidance of others. By temperament and by upbringing, some people can be overly reliant and overly trusting of others. There are some types of personalities that appear overly receptive but in fact are unlikely to follow through with the treatment they need. One example is the histrionic personality who can very quickly appear receptive to help, but such intentions are typically shallow and fleeting (Millon & Davis, 1996). Other examples include a drug addict after a crisis or an arrest who may express an intention to enter recovery and actually even want to recover but who will face the challenge of staying in recovery when the crisis is over.

Certain psychopathologies are connected to dysfunctional help seeking

There are certain types of psychopathologies that are reinforced in their seeking of help. In the factitious disorders, individuals feign symptoms in order to be in the sick role, deceptively leading to excessive clinical interventions. According to the fifth edition of the *Diagnostic and Statistical Manual of Mental Disorders* (DSM-5), these individuals take "surreptitious actions to misrepresent, stimulate, or cause signs or symptoms of illness or injury in the absence of obvious external rewards" (American Psychiatric Association, 2013, p. 325). People who suffer from borderline personality disorder tend to deteriorate when they feel in any way abandoned or rejected. They may become suicidal or engage in some self-destructive behavior as a way of gaining help and thereby feeling cared for by others. In fact, mental health professionals who work with this type of individual have to learn how not to reinforce negative attention-seeking behavior. Linehan (1993) has formulated dialectical behavior therapy as a way for therapists to continue helping people with borderline personality disorder without unintentionally reinforcing their pathology. More generally, there are times when individuals unconsciously as well as consciously become sick in order to gain attention or achieve certain goals, such as causing family cohesion with the illness in an otherwise dysfunctional family.

Attachment history of patient affects perception of clinician and receptiveness to help

The attachment history of patients lays the foundation for their perceptions and expectations of all relationships. Clinicians can be more effective in helping patients if they try to understand the needs, fears, and expectations patients may have based on their attachment histories. Thompson & Ciechanowski (2003) and many other clinical experts have made the case that such an understanding assists clinicians in establishing a therapeutic alliance that matches their patients' concerns and expectations. This in turn leads to better clinical relationships, more successful adherence to treatment, and increased patient satisfaction. Patients with dismissing attachment styles present as compulsively self-reliant because their histories have led them to expect that the people who care for them will be unavailable or reject them. Clinicians may have difficulty connecting with them because these patients tend to be emotionally distant and minimize their problems, or they may tend to reject help offered because they fear relying on others. Patients with preoccupied attachment styles come from backgrounds in which their caregivers were inconsistent in responding to their needs, and such patients tend to express more intense attachment needs in a clinical situation. They tend to be perceived as "compulsively care-seeking" (Thompson & Ciechanowski, 2003, p. 221) and come across as dependent, needy, and lacking self-confidence. This can feel burdensome to clinicians, who might respond by being more controlling or distancing; this in turn can fulfill these patients' expectations that more powerful caregivers may be inconsistent in helping them, thus making them more anxious. Patients with fearful attachment styles come from backgrounds in which they were mistreated and tend not to trust others or themselves. They desire connection but fear it at the same time. In relationships with clinicians, they can alternate between intensely seeking help and rejecting that help. Clinicians can become exasperated being treated like this and then distance themselves or become angry, which in turn becomes the patients' fearful attachment a self-fulfilling prophecy that they will be harmed by those who care for them (Thompson & Ciechanowski, 2003). While such attachment styles can appear frustrating and overwhelming to clinicians, there are actually

very good strategies for being successful with these types of patients. Thompson and Ciechanowski (2003) and Hunter and Maunder (2016) are two resources, along with many others, who provide clinicians of all different specialties with effective approaches to these insecure attachment styles.

HOW THE CLINICIAN ATTRIBUTES PATIENT RESPONSIBILITY AND THE APPROPRIATE HELPING RESPONSE: FOUR MODELS OF HELPING

Patient responsibility for the problem versus patient responsibility for the solution

Brickman et al. (1982) argued that people differ in terms of how they conceive of helping others. They theorized that people differ in terms of how they attribute responsibility for the cause of the problem and how they attribute responsibility for the solution of the problem, resulting in four models. In terms of the *cause of the problem*, people can be seen as being responsible for the cause of the problem or not responsible for the cause of the problem. In terms of the *solution for the problem*, people are seen to be either responsible for the solution of the problem or not responsible for the solution (see table 6.2). This results in four models of helping when responsibility for the cause of the problem and responsibility for the solution are placed along the axes of a 2 x 2 matrix. In the *moral model*, people are seen as responsible for the cause of the problem and as responsible for the solution to the problem. Helping in this model consists of giving exhortations and reinforcement for the desired behaviors. In the *compensatory model*, people are not considered responsible for the problem, but they are considered responsible for solving it. Helping in this case consists of providing resources for people to help themselves. In the *enlightenment model*, people are seen as responsible for causing their problems but are either not able or not willing to come up with the solutions. Helping such individuals consists of providing discipline in the form of guidelines or rules to solve their problems. Finally, in the *medical model*, people are considered not responsible for the problem and not responsible for the solution. Because people are not considered able to solve their problems on their own, helping consists of offering expert help.

The moral model

In what Brickman et al. (1982) called the *moral model*, patients are considered to have high responsibility for causing the problem and a high responsibility for the solution of the problem. In terms of causing the problem, patients are viewed as having created or worsened the problem because of their lack of willpower, noncompliance, stubbornness, or willfully chosen poor choices. Patients are seen as having had control of the cause and also as having control for solving the problem. The responsibility lies totally with the patients, who are expected to work hard and strive to solve the problem. The clinician's tone with such patients is exemplified in such statements as, "It's up to you." "You have

to decide to help yourself." The role of the clinician and others in a patient's life is to exhort, support, and "cheerlead" the person as he or she strives to solve the problem. The positive side of this is that it encourages patients to hold themselves responsible for what is happening to them, and they might push themselves very hard as a result. The downside is that they might hold themselves responsible for things that they should not; or if the treatment fails, they might think it was their fault when it really was not.

The compensatory model

The second model is the *compensatory model*, in which patients are not considered responsible for causing the problem but are considered responsible for the solution. Patients are seen as having to compensate for some handicap or unfortunate event imposed on them through no fault of their own. Such patients are seen as suffering because of what happened to them or deprived because of a lack of resources they deserve. Patients are seen as being worthy of help, but the main responsibility regarding whether this will be successful lies in their own effort. Patients need to be assertive to get access to the resources needed. Those who help them are seen as peers, collaborators, or attendants helping them get what resources they need or helping empower or educate them. Others who support them are seen as mobilizing resources at the service of such a patient rather than a

TABLE 6.2 Helping Models (Based on Brickman et al. 1982)

Responsibility for the cause and the solution to the problem	Patient considered responsible for causing the problem	Patient considered **not** responsible for causing the problem
Patient considered responsible for the solution to the problem	**Moral** **Model**	**Compensatory** **Model**
Patient considered **not** responsible for the solution to the problem	**Enlightenment** **Model**	**Medical** **Model**

paternalistic directing of a passive patient. The tone is more one of partnering with a patient and asking, "What do you need to get through this, and how can I help you get it?" The positive aspect of this model is that it does not focus on blaming patients for what happened, and all of their motivation can be directed to working on the solution rather than losing energy berating themselves or dealing with the judgments of others. Patients are seen as good and worthy, not deficient. The downside of this model is that if patients have numerous problems or one problem after another, they can feel a great deal of pressure to succeed at handling each one. The expectation is that people should be able to conquer each obstacle; when that is not possible because there are so many, it can make people feel like a failure for not being able to be the "hero" in the eyes of others (or their own).

The enlightenment model

Third, the *enlightenment model* is based on the assumption that patients are responsible for their problem but not for the solution. In this model of helping, patients are seen as responsible or guilty for whatever problem or suffering they are now experiencing and must be enlightened about the nature of their problem and agree to submit to the course of action that will be required to deal with it. This view of human nature is negative, and the solution involves submitting to "authorities" who provide a stern or sympathetic discipline. The solution to the problem lies externally with the individuals; the solution occurs only in submitting to that outside authority or power. This view of helping is often used in alcohol or drug addiction treatment, in which addicts admit they are powerless and give over control to a higher power and/ or the community of recovering addicts. The

positive side of this model is that this approach works well in a situation in which people feel they are not able to control their behavior on their own. For example, it has worked very well for many people recovering from alcoholism using Alcoholics Anonymous. The downside can be that "it can lead to a fanatical or obsessive concern with certain problems and a reconstruction of people's entire lives around the behaviors or the relationships designed to help them deal with these problems" (Brickman et al., 1982, p. 374). Complete compliance to the external program or method is often required, which may necessitate changes that are not actually necessary for success. Furthermore, this model puts a great deal of power in the control of external agents, who could abuse this influence (Brickman et al., 1982).

The medical model

Finally, the fourth helping model is called the *medical model*. This is based on the assumption that patients are not considered responsible for the problem or the solution. Patients are viewed not so much as a person but as a physiological system that can become sick or malfunction. Treatments such as medicine and surgery are directed to that physiological breakdown and do not fully consider who the patients are. Patients are viewed as weak or incapacitated, as victims of outside forces beyond their control. Their job, then, is to accept this and rely on experts to get better. There is an expectation that patients will try to get well, but it treats patients as more passively compliant rather than as active partners who are encouraged to take the lead on improving the situation. The focus is on relying on external agents who are the only source of knowledge about how to proceed in getting better and the only valid judges of whether things are better. This is what the traditional medical model was, and it might be more descriptive to call it the *paternalistic biomedical model*. Nonetheless, the advantage of this model is that patients can seek help without being blamed for the problem, which makes it easier for them to accept treatment. When a patient has difficulty taking responsibility for the solution, this model also works in taking control of the patient's life. The downside is that this approach can foster dependency so that when that external control is gone, patients do not follow through. Being more passive in the treatment, a patient does not engage in what he or she needs to do or participate in figuring out what he or she needs to do. This model relies very much on the perspective of the external expert to decide what and how to proceed (Brickman et al., 1982).

The patient and the clinician may assume conflicting models of helping

There are several important considerations for clinicians when it comes to these four helping models. One is that the clinician needs to be aware not only of his or her helping model assumptions, but also of what the patient's assumptions are. If you as the clinician believe the patient is not responsible for the problem/illness and your patient does think he or she is to blame, then you will be working at cross purposes with each other. Your patient will be feeling guilt or shame about the problem or illness, and you will be thinking that "these things happen, so let's just move forward." Or you will be thinking that the patient needs to take an active role in solving the problem, but your patient is more passive in response. "Well, doc, I need you to fix me up." So it is very important that both you and your patient make the same assumptions about responsibility or, at least, that you are aware that there is a difference between the two of you on this and that this may create some conflict. The other consideration is to be aware of the patient's significant other's view, which may be different from yours and your patient's. For example, if both you and your patient view this illness as genetically caused or out of your control but the loved one believes it is the patient's fault, this tension could be an impediment to progress for the patient (e.g., the partner is angry for the patient causing this problem, and as a result of punishing the patient for this, the partner comes across as unsupportive to the patient, who is trying to improve the problem).

Causes and solutions are often more complex than a single model of helping would imply

Second, the causes of problems and/or illnesses are often complex. It is important, therefore, to be careful of global assumptions. Typically, there is a mixture of causes and a mixture of factors involved in responding to a problem/illness. For example, a certain medical condition may just run in a family's gene pool. Almost everyone in the family gets high blood pressure when they are young, even with healthy habits. There is currently a tendency in American culture to believe that everything is preventable or should be preventable and to quickly assume a person could have done something to prevent the problem/illness. But there are quite a number of things that are not in our control, either in causing the problem/illness or in treating it. When it comes to stress, I have seen clinicians be quick to land on stress being a causal factor for a problem and to offer the advice rather easily: "You need to get rid of some of the stress in your life." But say that with a straight face to a mother who has a chronic illness with a couple of children who have major problems all while having financial problems, a minimum wage job, and an ex-husband who does not pay much child support. Or say a person has been raised in an abusive family and used food for comfort as he or he was growing up, or the parents were very bad in the diet they promoted in the family and that was really all the person knew until he or she reached adulthood. Many times, people are doing the best that they can, and we need to be careful about assuming they were completely responsible.

Consider your patterns and personal issues in which helping model you choose

Third, we need to ask ourselves if we always make the same assumptions about every patient, both in terms of responsibility for causes and for dealing with the problems/illnesses. Maybe I always scold one type of person but let another person off very easily, and the only difference is gender, race, culture, or whether I like the second person more. If we only use one helping model all the time, chances are we are not fully paying attention to what is actually going on in our patients' lives and discerning what they really need. The point of presenting these four helping models is not so much to argue here for which is better, but to be aware of your assumptions and think through how you are approaching the patient, who also has his or her own assumptions of responsibility for the cause and the solution to the problem.

Attributions we make about patients are the linchpin of the clinician compassion mindset process

While you may find that no single one of the above helping models is satisfactory for your practice, the key issue is "attributions." To what are you attributing anything about a patient? Whenever you encounter a particular patient behavior, you are consciously or unconsciously making an attribution; that is, you are making an inference about why a particular event, behavior, or outcome has occurred. Bernard Weiner has done a great deal of work on intrapersonal and interpersonal theories of motivation from the perspective of attribution theory (Weiner, 1995, 2000). For our purposes, I will focus on how the emotions that arise from our attributions about a patient's behavior lead to particular responses from us as the helper, using Weiner's theory (Weiner, 2000; Rudolph, Roesch, Greitemeyer, & Weiner, 2004). For example, if a clinician is meeting with a person who is obese, the clinician will engage in a process (sometimes conscious, sometime automatic) of ascertaining the perceived controllability or responsibility of the patient's obesity. If the clinician attributes the obesity to a controllable patient cause in which the patient is responsible for the obesity (e.g., the patient is thought to be self-indulgent, lacks willpower), that clinician might then become angry and react in a hostile or detached way with the patient. If the clinician attributes the obesity to an uncontrollable cause for which the patient is not responsible (e.g., the obesity is the result of medical side effects like steroids in cancer treatment, genetic factors, the result of hypothalamic damage), then the clinician might experience a more sympathetic emotional response and respond to the patient in a more prosocial way, such as being emotionally supportive. This is the linchpin of the compassion mindset: What are the attributions we are making about patients, either consciously or subconsciously, and are we able to be mindful of our attributions with their consequent emotions? The clinician must always manage these attributions and emotions, as we saw in the clinician compassion mindset process in chapter 4. Whenever we become aware of an attribution or negative emotion that knocks us out of the compassion mindset, we then need to move to the reset and recovery box and reappraise the patient and the patient's situation to help keep us in a compassion mindset.

CONCLUSION

The helping process in the helping profession is a continual cycle of empathic attachment, active involvement to help the person in need, and then separation when that helping episode is completed. It is a complex process that is heavily dependent on the mutual perceptions of the patient and clinician. These perceptions are influenced by many different factors, and as clinicians it is important that we are mindful of these so that we may accurately perceive our patients and effectively provide what we can for their situations. The patient perception of the clinician's inner attitude is very important to the effectiveness of the interaction. But a genuine compassionate caring attitude in the clinician is not by itself a guarantee of successful outcome because of the factors that influence the help recipient's receptiveness to that offer of help. The navigating of this process by clinicians varies by the models of helping clinicians have of the helping process. Next, we delve more into the subjective nature of this helping process and examine how the clinician's trained subjectivity is essential to the helping process.

QUESTIONS FOR DISCUSSION

1. What are examples from your own experience of the caring matrix?
2. What is a situation in which you were involved where you had to deal with challenging patient perceptions of you as you attempted to help the patient?
3. Select one of your experiences helping a patient, and describe the model of helping you used and your perception of its effectiveness.

REFERENCES

American Psychiatric Association. (2013). *Diagnostic and statistical manual of mental disorders* (5th ed.). Arlington, VA: Author.

Beach, M. C., Roter, D., Rubin, H., Frankel, R., Levinson, W., & Ford, D. E. (2004). Is physician self-disclosure related to patient evaluation of office visits? *Journal of General Internal Medicine, 19,* 905–910.

Brickman, P., Rabinowitz, V. C., Karuza, J., Coates, D., Cohn, E., & Kidder, L. (1982). Models of helping and coping. *American Psychologist, 37*(4), 368–384.

Brown, J. B., Boles, M., Mulloly, J. P., & Levinson, W. (1999). Effect of clinician communication skills training on patient satisfaction: A randomized, controlled trial. *Annals of Internal Medicine, 131,* 822–829.

Hunter, J., & Maunder, R. (Eds.). (2016). Improving patient treatment with attachment theory: A guide for primary care practitioners and specialists. New York, NY: Springer.

Linehan, M. M. (1993). *Cognitive-behavioral treatment of borderline personality disorder.* New York, NY: Guilford Press.

Malterud, K., & Hollnagel, H. (2005). The doctor who cried: A qualitative study about the doctor's vulnerability. *Annals of Family Medicine, 3,* 348–352.

McCoy, L. (2005). HIV-positive patients and the doctor-patient relationship: Perspectives from the margins. *Qualitative Health Research, 15*(6), 791–806.

Meador, B. D., & Rogers, C. R. (1984). Person-centered therapy. In R. J. Corsini & D. Wedding (Eds.), *Current psychotherapies* (3rd ed., pp. 142–195). Itasca, IL: Peacock.

Millon, T., & Davis, R. D. (1996). *Disorders of personality DSM-IV and beyond* (2nd ed.). New York, NY: Wiley.

Quirk, M., Mazor, K., Haley, H., Philbin, M., Fischer, M. Sullivan, K., & Hatem, D. (2008). How patients perceive a doctor's caring attitude. *Patient Education and Counseling, 72,* 359–366.

Rheineck-Leyssius, A. T., Kalkman, C. J., and Trouwborst, A. (1996). Influence of motivation of care providers on the incidence of postoperative hypoxaemia in the recovery room. *British Journal of Anaesthesia, 77*(4), 453–457.

Rudolph, U., Roesch, S. C., Greitemeyer, T., & Weiner, B. (2004). A meta-analytic review of help giving and aggression from an attributional perspective: Contributions to a general theory of motivation. *Cognition and Emotion, 18*(6), 815–848.

Salmon, P., & Young, B. (2009). Dependence and caring in clinical communication: The relevance of attachment and other theories. *Patient Education and Counseling, 74,* 331–338.

Skovholt, T. M. (2005). The cycle of caring: A model of expertise in the helping professions. *Journal of Mental Health Counseling, 27*(1), 82–93.

Squier, R. W. (1990). A model of empathic understanding and adherence to treatment regimens in practitioner-patient relationships. *Social Science and Medicine, 30*(3), 325–339.

Street, R. L., Makoul, G., Arora, N. K., & Epstein, R. M. (2009). How does communication heal? Pathways linking clinician-patient communication to health outcomes. *Patient Education and Counseling, 74,* 295–301.

Suchman, A. L., Markakis, K., Beckman, H. B., & Frankel, R. (1997). The patient-physician relationship: A model of empathic communication in the medical interview. *Journal of the American Medical Association, 277*(8), 678–682.

Thompson, D., & Ciechanowski, P. S. (2003). Attaching a new understanding to the patient-physician relationship in family practice. *Journal of the American Board of Family Practice, 16,* 219–226.

Watson, J. (2012). *Human caring science: A theory of nursing.* Sudbury, MA: Jones & Bartlett.

Wear, D., & Varley, J. D. (2008). Rituals of verification: The role of simulation in developing and evaluating empathic communication. *Patient Education and Counseling, 71,* 153–156.

Weiner, B. (1995). *Judgments of responsibility: A foundation for a theory of social conduct.* New York, NY: Guilford Press.

Weiner, B. (2000). Intrapersonal and interpersonal theories of motivation from an attributional perspective. *Educational Psychology Review, 12*(1), 1–14.

Wright, E. B., Holcombe, C., & Salmon, P. (2004). Doctors' communication of trust, care, and respect in breast cancer: Qualitative study. *British Medical Journal.* doi.org/10.1136/bmj.38046.771308.7C

Yagil, D., & Shnapper-Cohen, M. (2016). When authenticity matters most: Physicians' regulation of emotional display and patient satisfaction. *Patient Education and Counseling, 99,* 1694–1698.

CREDITS

- Figure 6.1: Adapted from Thomas M. Skovholt, "Cycle of Caring, from 'The Cycle of Caring: A Model of Expertise in the Helping Professions,'" Journal of Mental Health Counseling, vol. 27, no. 1, pp. 86. Copyright © 2005 by American Mental Health Counselors Association (AMHCA).

- Table 6.1: Mark Quick et al., "Themes and Categories of Caring Behaviors from Focus Group Data, from 'How Patients Perceive a Doctor's Caring Attitude,'" Patient Education and Counseling, vol. 72, no. 3, pp. 362. Copyright © 2008 by Elsevier B.V

- Figure 6.4: Adapted from Jean Watson, "Dynamics of Human Caring Process, Including Nurse-Patient Transpersonal Dimension," Human Caring Science: A Theory of Learning, pp. 72. Copyright © 2012 by Jones and Bartlett Learning.

- Table 6.2: Source: Brickman et al. (1982).

"I have little patience with scientists who take a board of wood, look for its thinnest part, and drill a great number of holes where drilling is easy."

—Albert Einstein

"Body and soul are not two different things, but only two different ways of perceiving the same thing. Similarly, physics and psychology are only different attempts to link our experience together by way of systematic thought."

—Arthur Fine

"In the summer of 1608, no one had a telescope; in the summer of 1609, everyone had one."

—Albert van Helden

Chapter Sections:

CHAPTER 7

Health Care as an Objective Subjective Science

Hard Science and the Harder Sciences

Questions to consider before reading this chapter:

1. What parts of clinical practice involve the subjectivity of the clinician?
2. What is your opinion regarding the subjective parts of medical practice?
3. What is it like to do clinical practice in the biopsychosocial model?

INTRODUCTION

Fears of subjectivity in medicine

Subjective is often a despised word in medicine. Yet the best practice of medicine requires an ability to work with the subjectivity of the patient and also an ability to work with the clinician's own subjectivity. In their training, which is based heavily on biology and chemistry, clinicians inherit a suspicious attitude toward the subjectivity of the patient while imagining themselves as mostly objective beings simply applying the scientific facts learned in their training. This suspicion of the subjective becomes mixed with the discomfort with emotional material and a view that the psychological is not real or not connected to what is happening in the body. It becomes an excuse and a means to disregard the psychosocial factors or at least to suggest that these factors are not as important. The word *subjective* is used as a way to end discussions by implying that if something is subjective, then it is inherently false. This inherited attitude is not typically discussed or examined, even though the subjective is a central part of medicine.

Purpose of this chapter

In this chapter, I will examine how this automatic denigration of the subjective is completely unscientific and has contributed to practicing medicine in a narrow and noncompassionate way, causing problems for patients as well as for the clinicians themselves. I will then outline how grounding our work in a theory of compassionate caring resolves many problems we struggle with in health care. Finally, I will provide a succinct overview of the use of levels of analysis/explanation that can facilitate the use of the biopsychosocial model as a way to provide holistic compassionate caring.

THE PARADOX OF SUBJECTIVITY IN MEDICINE AND THE OBJECTIVE SUBJECTIVITY OF CLINICAL JUDGMENT

The usefulness of the patient's subjective report in assessment and treatment

Clinicians are suspicious of their patient's subjectivity, but imagine if you did not have your patient's subjective report. If you work with unconscious patients, you are very hampered in treating them. If they arrive unconscious, you may not know the history of the presenting problem. You do not know any other history about them. You do not know if they are in pain. Pain is subjectively experienced, but pain is the body's way of communicating that something is wrong at a particular location in the body. As a clinician working with someone in pain, the patient's report is absolutely essential in assessment. When did the pain begin, what is its duration, is it intermittent or constant, where is it, does the pain radiate, what is the quality of the pain, how bad is the pain,

what are the other symptoms related to it, and what makes it worse or better? As you palpate the abdomen, you not only get the verbal report but also the nonverbal report of pain (Fortin, Dwamena, Frankel, & Smith, 2012). Based on the clues you pick up from the patient, you ascertain the truthfulness of the report, the degree of suffering, the personality of the patient, and whether this is a person with a low tolerance for pain or a person with a high tolerance who is minimizing how much pain he or she is really in. As you treat the person, the patient's subjective report tells you whether you are on the right track. If you mistake what the origin of the pain is, the patient's self-report lets you know that something else is going on. This is an example of how important subjectivity is when it comes to patient pain. With any medical condition, a comparable stream of issues requiring the patient's subjectivity is necessary.

The subjectivity of patient-centered interviewing is more scientific

Robert Smith (2002) reviewed and summarized the research and presented how patient-centered interviewing is not only more humanistic but also more scientific than doing only doctor-centered interviewing. Doctor-centered interviewing focuses on the clinician gathering information identifying a disease without eliciting or considering patient concerns or nonmedical data that may be relevant but are ignored or discounted without investigation. This approach has been found to be related to poor health outcomes, poor patient satisfaction, and frustrated clinicians (Fortin et al., 2012). Patient-centered interviewing begins with a wider approach and getting a more complete sense of what is happening to a patient, including his or her thoughts, feelings, and concerns. From there, the clinician refines what the nature of the medical problem is and engages in doctor-centered interviewing and the physician exam to confirm this. While incorporating much more patient subjectivity, it actually is more scientific. Patients tell you more when you ask them to tell you what is going on. Doctor-centered interviewing actually elicits less data than patient-centered interviewing (and it is biased in terms of the clinician's initial impressions). The patient-centered approach has been found to be less biased by the clinician and more accurate in terms of what the actual problem is. Better data means a more accurate diagnosis, which means that the treatment is more likely to fit what the real problem is. This means better medical outcomes. Imagine not letting a patient tell you about his or her problem and the risk you incur by restricting this data flow.

The importance of subjective reports of patient emotional and personal material

Patient-centered interviewing is also more scientific because it elicits emotional and personal material that adds data regarding the medical problem. It may help with clarifying the origin of the problem. An approach that is inclusive of the subjective produces more complete information that is reliable and valid. Also, it may provide helpful information about this person's life context, mental status, and personality that helps a clinician become clear about causal pathways and decide what treatment and what manner of giving the treatment might work best. A biopsychosocial approach is more effective in diagnosis and treatment than a biomedical approach (Smith, 2002). Overall, Fortin et al. (2012) reviewed the research and found that the more subjective, inclusive patient-centered approach has been found to be related to more

accurate diagnoses, improved health outcomes, increased patient adherence, increased patient satisfaction, and decreased malpractice claims and doctor shopping.

Research on how patient history leads to the best diagnosis

In current medical practice, many believe that objective indicators such as laboratory tests are doing most of the diagnostic work for clinicians, but it is the ability to take a good history and really think through that history that leads to the best diagnoses. In residency training, we have found more wishful thinking by residents that scans and lab tests can now do most of the diagnostic work, but this is not the case. Sometimes a physician who is overreliant on objective measures will end up making mistakes on diagnoses that have to be fixed by the next physician. Lab results can be the outcomes of quite diverse medical conditions, and it is the history and the thinking through of the differential diagnosis that leads to the best diagnoses. The research bears this out. Roshan and Rao (2000) studied the relative contributions of the patient history, physical examination, and further investigations to formulate a medical diagnosis. They found that the patient history led to the diagnosis in 79% of the patients, the physical exam led to the diagnosis in 8%, and further investigations led to the diagnosis in 13%. Peterson, Holbrook, Hales, Smith, and Staker (1992) found that history led to the final medical diagnosis in 76% of the patients, physical exam in 12%, and lab investigation in 11%. The confidence of internists in the correct diagnosis on a scale from 1 to 10 was at 7.1 after the history, 8.2 after the physical exam, and 9.3 after the laboratory investigation (Peterson et al., 1992). Hampton, Harrison, Mitchell, Prichard, and Seymour (1975) found that reading a referral letter and taking the history produced a diagnosis that agreed with the final one in 82% of the patients.

The problem of evaluating the subjectivity of your colleagues' advice

The importance of subjectivity does not stop with the patient report. Let us suppose you are in doubt about accepting the "subjective" report of your patients as part of the scientific practice of medicine. So, you consult your more "objective" colleagues. Yet you are confronted with the problem of their subjectivity as well. You are still at the mercy of your clinical colleagues' subjective perceptions. Can you rely on them? How do you know? You know that one of your colleagues tends to be very careful before making any diagnostic claims and that another of your colleagues tends to come to diagnostic conclusions too quickly, leading you to be cautious about accepting that colleague's judgment. Over time, you get a sense of your colleagues also trained in the science of medicine. You might sense if they are under a lot of personal stress that is affecting their medical judgment. You would weigh that against the advice they give you while in that state. You know if a particular colleague tends to be dismissive when a person of a certain gender or certain racial/ethnic background describes his or her symptoms; perhaps you know the colleague is overly attentive and accepting of certain other patients and that the wealth or fame of a certain patient may have clouded this colleague's clinical judgment. The fact is that we must deal with subjectivity, if not of our patients, then of our colleagues, and in the end, we have to confront our own subjectivity. But rather than follow the extreme skeptic who becomes paralyzed about believing anything, there is a way we keenly judge the reliability and validity of this subjectivity and can proceed quite effectively and successfully.

Lab tests and scans can never be the final word on a diagnosis

The physician who claims to be an objective person might enter at this point and claim superiority to both the rose-colored and dark-colored spectacled clinicians. The argument here is that with the proper lab tests and scans, all of this can be clear. The reality, however, is that this does not work as well as we would like. Patients have complex diseases, and our lab results and scans require thoughtful detective work to sort out what exactly is going on with a patient. Our overreliance on lab results can result from the fantasy that an "objective" lab result would make it easier to grapple with the subjectivities of our patients, our colleagues, and ourselves. Our best diagnostic work comes when we help a patient feel comfortable telling us what is going on, not fearful of our judgmental responses or gruff manner. We get better data when we help people feel safe with us.

> *For when expression of human understanding on the part of the physician is not forthcoming and the patient does not feel understood, then trust and confidence may be impaired and with it the patient's capacity and willingness to collaborate—critical if the physician's scientific aims are to be accomplished. (Engel, 1992, p. 11)*

The importance of training clinician subjectivity to evaluate patient subjectivity

We also do better diagnosis when our trained subjectivity evaluates the patient's subjectivity. I notice how patients are talking about their symptoms and the way they are suffering, and this may give me clues as to how to understand their symptoms. So-called objective clinicians might say that they will not consider a patient's subjective report nor their own subjective appraisal. But there are ways patients talk about their symptoms that give clues about what the underlying problem is. Is it a dull pain or a sharp pain? They are losing a great deal of weight, but they say their appetite is good and they do not feel depressed. No scan or lab test can give you that information. Or the clinician has an educated guess—an intuition, if you will—that a certain test is a false negative or a false positive. On one hand, our subjectivity can be unexamined and untrained to the point that we cannot tell what our distortions are. Because it is not trained, we could take the easy way out and just say that it is impossible to train our subjectivity. On the other hand, we can make a practice of always checking our perceptions. We can so train our subjectivity that we can gather even better data about what we are seeing in our patients.

What does it mean to develop and rely on trained subjectivity with appropriate safeguards?

The subjective is at times the only way to gain the information you need. As Smith (2002) puts it, "Human medicine is the only scientific field in which the subject literally tells the scientist what the problem is" (p. 1). What we strive for is an objective way to navigate subjectivity, but this can only be done through the subjectivity of the clinician. This is what I call a "trained subjectivity." While we like the comfort and directness of objective indicators such as lab results and vitals, clinicians must learn how to manage their own subjectivity in

order to reach the best clinical solutions using those lab results, vitals, and scans. This is not unlike what judges in Olympic sports have to learn. In ice skating and gymnastics, we rely on judges who each have a thorough knowledge of the performance of that sport and who have learned how to rate a performance of an athlete. If any judge has been found not to assess well or is always biased, we would no longer use that judge. Maybe the person has an attention problem and cannot focus on a whole performance or has a memory problem and cannot recall a whole performance long enough to make of rating of it. Or maybe a judge has an "ax to grind" and has been found to rate certain types of athletes more highly or poorly than is appropriate (e.g., an athlete from a particular state or country or of a particular race or ethnic background, or an athlete who reminds the judge of someone who bullied him or her as a child). Or we discover that a particular judge is moody and his or her ratings reflect more how the judge feels on a particular day, or the judge cannot rate reliably when he or she is hungry or tired. As a safeguard, we use a panel of judges when the stakes are high in order to guard against bias. There are two methods we use to assure an accurate assessment of the performance—judges who have proven themselves able to be reliable and trustworthy, and a panel of such proven individuals with the expectation that expert ratings should be similar. The same is done in teaching and judging musical performances. It would be nice if these activities could be judged like we do for running or swimming, in which we can use sensors and computers to determine who finished first, second, and so on. But that is simply not the nature of the more complex sports or of music. We have, thus, developed generally reliable ways to judge these activities that include safeguards to detect when subjectivity is not accurately assessing the situation.

Trained subjectivity is a reliable tool in clinical diagnosis

Practicing medicine relies on training human subjectivity to be a reliable method of diagnosing and treating human patients. The subjective is a necessary part of medicine. Medicine cannot proceed without it. For example, we provide radiologists with many years of advanced training to be able to name what they see in X-rays, CTs, PET scans, and MRIs reliably. Radiologists might claim this extensive training makes them objective, but it really is not objectivity. It is a subjectivity that has been trained and found to be reliable in diagnosis.

The influence of the subjective in radiology

There have been a number of studies, in fact, that together show how the subjectivity of the radiologist has to be considered and managed in interpreting scans. Having a photograph of the patient attached to a chest radiograph increased the ability to detect labeling errors (i.e., the wrong patient) from 12.5% to 64% (Tridandapani, Ramamurthy, Galgano, & Provenzale, 2013). Having a photograph attached to the scan during interpretation improved how radiologists scanned and interpreted radiographs without increasing interpretation time (Krupinski, Chung, Applegate, DeSimone, & Tridandapani, 2016). John Leonidas (2007), a pediatric radiologist, wrote how interruptions of radiologists while reading scans can affect their conclusions; and the psychological pressure of another clinician "breathing on

their necks makes most radiologists give in" (p. 317). While Ryan et al. (2015) did not find that having patient photographs improved interpretation of CTs in their study, they speculated that this may have been because the reporting style requirements were more stringent at their institution. They used standardized templates that increased the content of the reports, and the radiologists were aware that they were in a reporting-based study. Yet the researchers still found that when photographs were attached, the radiologists did report more negative, normal, and qualifying statements. Overall, even with diverse findings, note how the subjectivity of radiologists is potentially compromised by things such as reporting procedure, the presence of other clinicians, being interrupted, or something as simple as a photograph of the patient being attached. Krupinski has reviewed the factors involved in medical image perception, including image quality and color, as well as psychological factors influencing interpretation, such as fatigue, time of day, and visual search strategies. For example, one source of errors is called "satisfaction of search" which is "once an abnormality is detected and recognized, it takes additional diligence to look for other possible abnormalities within an image" (Krupinski, 2010, p. 6).

Research on interpretation in radiology

In a guest editorial introducing research on medical image perception in the *Journal of Medical Imaging*, Krupinski (2016) discussed how radiologists have to deal with complicating factors in image interpretation:

> Image interpretation is more than just looking for predefined features and calling them out as they are found. The appearance of

lesions and other abnormalities change as a function of technology used to acquire the images, how the images are displayed, and the simple fact that there is so much variation in the basic anatomy within which these targets are embedded that looking for and finding feature x does not always lead to detection and the right diagnostic interpretation. But what makes one radiologist better than another or a given radiologist less error prone on one day than another? How can two experts look at the same image and come up with different interpretations? How can we optimize image presentation in order to optimally educate trainees to ensure the most accurate image interpretation and thus patient care? (p. 1)

Because of this, the Medical Image Perception Society was formed to bring researchers together to examine the processes affecting the perception in medical images. The society has formed a collaboration of physicians, psychologists, physicists, engineers, and statisticians studying factors such as the effects of different types of visual search strategies, how memory of previous images affects later interpretation, image quality, how to train radiologists, and preventing errors. As Krupinski (2016) put it succinctly, "Medical images need to be interpreted because they are not self-explanatory" (p. 3).

Trained subjectivity is also what we call clinical judgment

This trained subjectivity is central to what is done is medicine—we call it clinical judgment. Kathryn Montgomery (2006) examined clinical judgment in depth in her excellent book, *How Doctors Think: Clinical Judgment and the Practice of Medicine.*

Young physicians have their budding clinical skills and the profession's goal of exercising a cool, rigorous, scientifically informed rationality for the good of the patient. They have not become scientists, not by going to medical school and completing a residency, but they have acquired crucial intellectual and behavioral skills and a rational clinical method. They have absorbed a commitment to objectivity: Close observation, the suspension of judgment until information is gathered, skepticism about information they have not acquired or witnessed themselves, and, when results don't make sense, skepticism about their own procedures. They have learned a careful, rational method that enables them to sort through what once were bewildering signs and symptoms and now make medical sense of them. As they gain a capacity for clinical reasoning, they can begin to diagnose and treat an array of diseases with a fair degree of reliability. Their commitment to objectivity and their mastery of clinical method, both essential to clinical reasoning, enable them to do what is best for the sick people whose care is their responsibility. This is not science but clinical judgment. (Montgomery, 2006, pp. 158–159)

Montgomery reminds us that the goal of medical education is the training of clinical judgment, not the mere memorization of information. She explains that clinical judgment is an intellectual capacity that is the result of years of dealing with the uncertainty that is part of clinical medicine. Clinicians learn how to navigate patient care situations in which they do not have all the information they would like to have to diagnose and treat the person; yet they become expert at how to provide excellent care because they have developed the clinical judgment to discern the best course of action for each patient.

There is no clear division between the subjective and the objective in medicine

In medicine, we like to think that there is a neat and clear division between the subjective and the objective. There is no clear division. Everything we do is fraught with subjectivity, and we should quit pretending it is not. But this is a misplaced worry. In our training and practice of clinical judgment is this trained subjectivity that actually works very well when we clinicians are investing our energies and paying attention to what we are doing with patients.

The absurdity of not wanting to get more subjective information from the patient

In a conversation I had with a trial attorney about "defensive medicine," he remarked that he did not understand why physicians would not want to have a longer conversation with patients before beginning various treatments or procedures. As he explained it, there is an element of "guesswork" in medicine, by which clinicians are really basing what they think about diagnosis or the likelihood of success of a particular treatment on probability. Having a further conversation with patients gives clinicians more information about what is going on with patients physically, allowing clinicians to gain more confidence about their approach; and they also can understand more how patients are viewing what they are doing, which would allow clinicians to clarify unrealistic expectations or possible negative outcomes. Why would clinicians want to go so quickly with major medical issues without really talking to the patient more?

Physicians are not scientists

In medicine, we are attached to saying that what we do is science, and with that we present ourselves as wearing the cloak of objectivity. What is meant when clinicians claim they are practicing the science of medicine? Physicians are, strictly speaking, not scientific in how they practice medicine. If they were as scientific as they could be, they would insist on more information before making a diagnosis or recommending a treatment. They would run repeated tests because of the chance of false positives and false negatives. They would want to parse out each variable in a complex clinical situation in order to understand what is wrong with the patient before proceeding. This would take time and resources that are not often possible in the real world of medical practice; but if you are strictly scientific, that is what the physician would do. Instead, the physician must act quickly without having the luxury of knowing everything about the patient's condition. Yet, physicians really believe they are practicing the science of medicine. Montgomery (2006) argues that the science of medicine is more a commitment to an ethos or a way of being than it is actually being a scientist. Physicians know that they have to become comfortable practicing in a less than precise way with uncertain conditions. But they do so by developing a practical and flexible reasoning process that is rational and careful. This is what they mean by being "scientific." Furthermore, it is understandable how physicians would seek guidance for their own emotional regulation from that rational method that is so helpful in solving medical problems. The commitment to be thorough and objective in their clinical judgment enables physicians to develop the confidence that they can make a difference in tragic and uncertain situations. By viewing themselves as rooted in a rational and efficacious clinical method, they are emotionally able to enter miserable and painful circumstances that most people would find overwhelming and distressing. But physicians feel bolstered by the power of their scientific clinical judgment to make a difference in the suffering of their patients (Montgomery, 2006).

Our commitment is to a rational process, not a fantasy of unachievable objectivity

The desire to claim that medicine is an objective science is really how medicine has expressed its commitment to work with patients in a rational manner. It is also the way medicine has tried to find a way that it can cope with the hard work that it is. Hence it adopts the attributes of science as its "coping method," but doing so creates a number of the problems that we now have in medicine. Imposing the attributes of what enables good laboratory science onto the way in which one works with patients does not fit the nature of clinical medicine. We have erroneously equated our rational process of clinical judgment to be the same as being a scientist, when these are really two different things. Our clinical judgment is our use of science and our experience of what happens in actual practice to interpret what we see before us in a particular patient. That is a subjective process that clinicians conduct in a rational manner, what I call a trained subjectivity. The downside, however, of erroneously imagining ourselves as scientists is that it mistakenly leads us to denigrate our patients' subjectivity and to make us uncomfortable with our own subjectivity and emotions (Montgomery, 2006).

WHY A THEORY OF COMPASSIONATE CARING MATTERS

Theory affects your clinical perception

Your theory of what is going on clinically affects how you perceive a clinical situation. If you were a surgeon or a nurse during the American Civil War and you were doing amputations, you would not see anything wrong with using the same saw to cut off the limbs of different wounded soldiers. Health care professionals of that time did not know about bacteria as a cause of infection, so they would not "see a problem" with unsterilized surgical instruments. Bacteria was not part of a scientific explanation of what went on in treating war wounds. Their theory about wounds and wound care did not include bacteria, so their approach did not factor it in. But surgeons and nurses today would know that they have to sterilize the instruments before amputating, which would decrease the likelihood of infection; and they would make sure to give an antibiotic if infection was likely to occur. Health professionals now know that bacteria exist, and that awareness completely changes how they treat wounds and other injuries.

Biomedical theory does not have a place for the role of compassionate caring

This is similar to what is happening with compassionate caring in medicine. Our core biomedical theory of how to help patients medically does not include how compassionate caring is involved. We like compassionate caring as part of our clinical service, but it is not considered fundamental to what is happening clinically. In the Civil War, cleaning surgical instruments would be seen as a good thing to do, but not absolutely essential to prevent infection. With germ theory, that completely changed. Now that we know that things like compassionate caring and psychosocial factors are intimately part of what is going on with helping patients get better, medicine has to change its theory of how we explain this. But the problem is that mainstream medicine prefers a biological explanation that does not include things that are intertwined with subjectivity, such as caring or the roles of psychosocial factors in the onset, maintenance, and treatment of diseases or injuries.

How theory is not understood among people applying science to their lives

Many people are not aware of the role that theories play in everyday science. When I ask medical trainees to explain what a theory is and to give me examples of theories that we use all the time, there is usually a long pause. Then they will start giving examples such as atomic theory, quantum theory, or the theory of evolution. That long pause is not because these trainees were not very smart; they were very smart. Why is there always a long pause to answer this simple question? That long pause is because they get so used to practicing science that it is easy to take for granted and thus forget the theories on which science is based. Certainty about atomic theory clouds the realization that it is a theory that is used when it comes to understanding chemistry. Another use of the word *theory* is to label something as not a fact. For example, when we criticize or cast doubt on something someone says, we might say, "Well, that's your theory" or "That's theoretical," implying it is not based on fact. But that is not the way we are using the word *theory* in this case. Theory is absolutely essential to the progress of science. A bunch of facts without a theory is just a bunch of facts. A theory helps explain how facts and observations are connected to each other. It helps explain things such as how water can be solid, a liquid, or a gas and still be water, H_2O. If it is a really good theory, it helps you explain other related things and supports making predictions and testing

the theory itself. The success of the current theories of chemistry and biology has made the study of theory and the philosophy of science relegated to being a brief portion of the lectures or the introductory chapters of a textbook, if at all. Thus, it is easy to forget that atomic theory and evolutionary theory were major shifts in perception. In physics, there tends to be more of an awareness of theory because physics is still in an early phase in the understanding of quantum theory. The long pause in knowing what theories are scientifically is that we feel fairly certain that they are the right theories to use. The danger of taking these theories for granted because of their recent successes in explaining and predicting various phenomena has tended to make people intellectually lazy and unable to examine assumptions. When we are not aware of our assumptions, we are no different than Newtonian physicists on the eve of Einstein's quantum theory. We think we have explained everything, but it turns out that there is something that explains everything even better than we had imagined.

Anomalies and theory evolution

One of the classics in the history and philosophy of science is Thomas Kuhn's *The Structure of Scientific Revolutions*. Kuhn has explained how in conducting normal science in an existing paradigm, scientists will encounter anomalies or unexpected results, findings that do not fit in the existing theory being held. The first approach to handling anomalies is to blame the scientist for making a method error or blame the measurement error on the tools one is using. He explains that to question one's assumptions, to change the rules of how problems are solved, is initially resisted. When these anomalies occur again and again, this is the prelude to another paradigm, another way of looking at the phenomena and how to study them.

> New theories arise from work conducted under old ones, and they do so only when something is observed to have gone wrong. Their prelude is widely recognized anomaly, and that recognition can come only to a group that knows very well what it should mean to have things go right. (Kuhn, 1998, p. 312)

This is what occurred in the shift from Newtonian physics to Einstein's quantum physics, Ptolemaic astronomy to Copernicus's and Kepler's heliocentric proposals, and the history of theory about electricity and the atom.

> That pattern—discovery through an anomaly that calls established techniques and beliefs in doubt—has been repeated again and again in the course of scientific development. Newton discovered the composition of white light when he was unable to reconcile measured dispersion with that predicted by Snell's recently discovered law of refraction. The electric battery was discovered when existing detectors of static charges failed to behave as Franklin's paradigm said they should. The planet Neptune was discovered through an effort to account for recognized anomalies in the orbit of Uranus. … In the mature sciences unexpected novelties are discovered principally after something has gone wrong. (Kuhn, 1998, pp. 311–312)

Compassionate care as secondary add-on in the practice of medicine

Something has gone wrong in medicine. We are both enamored of our biomedical accomplishments and becoming increasingly worried about the dehumanized approaches resulting. We attempt to add caring and compassion to balance this in the same way as we would add sugar to change the taste of salty water. But because compassionate caring is the added feature, it is condemned to be always in a secondary status, easily jettisoned when problems occur. If we start with compassionate caring as the center of our work, an integrated approach to medicine emerges that still has all the biomedical benefits. But first, let me take you through some key information about scientific theories and how they operate in our daily lives.

What is theory and the example of the geocentric theory

What is a theory, and why should we care? Theory comes from the Greek word *theoria*, meaning looking at something, contemplating something, or considering something. Theory as we use it in science is a way of viewing, contemplating, or considering what one is studying (Rychlak, 1985). More formally, a theory is "a coherent set of hypothetical, conceptual … and pragmatic (predictive) principles forming the general frame of reference for a field of inquiry. From this coherent entity, the theoretician deduces principles, formulates hypotheses, and then undertakes the actions necessary to validate these hypotheses" (Rychlak, 1985, p. 11). The way you imagine what you are seeing, the model you have in your head, affects how you perceive things in the world. The classic example of the role of theory in science is the evolution of the geocentric theory (model) of the solar system to the heliocentric theory. Ptolemy's geocentric theory assumed that the Earth had to be in the center of the solar system. All explanations about the courses of the planets had to cohere with this fundamental assumption. When astronomers had Ptolemy's model in their heads, they did not consider that the sun could be the center of the solar system. It was not considered possible and was not even worth considering.

The resistance to changing one's theory

The geocentric theory had tremendous staying power, not to mention that there were ecclesiastical prohibitions against reconsidering the basic assumption about the Earth being the center of the solar system. But religion was not the only barrier to reconsidering the assumptions. It was the science of the day. This assumption was not questioned, and if it were questioned, the astronomer was sure to be banished from the scientific community and even declared a religious heretic. Even without political and religious prohibitions against reexamining our scientific assumptions, there is the human tendency to keep with one's first assumptions and to explain away any anomalies in order to preserve one's pet theory. Scientists are notorious for doing this. Yes, the almighty objective scientist has historically time and time again fallen prey to this tendency to remain with and defend one way of looking at things (their theory) rather than changing theories to account for the data better. Physicist Max Planck once said, "A new scientific truth does not triumph by convincing its opponents and making them see the light, but rather because its opponents eventually die, and a new generation grows up that is familiar with it" (as cited in Kuhn, 1996, p. 151). The history and philosophy of science has many such examples in the evolution of science. One thing that regularly occurs is that a scientific paradigm gains ascendancy in a certain branch of science with particular assumptions that are not questioned as that paradigm is explored and tested. Anomalies, discoveries that do not fit well with the model or theory being tested, are explained away as measurement error or an error of some sort by the scientist. The history of science is filled with examples of dogmatic, rigid behavior of scientists who more likely would die holding a particular theory than question its fundamental assumptions; and this is even before religion is thrown into the mix.

Geocentric theory and the use of epicycles to protect that theory

Back to the example of the geocentric theory, for hundreds of years, astronomers kept explaining their observations with the assumption of the Earth's fixed central position. Rather than reexamine this assumption, they explained any unusual finding of planetary positions by showing how it occurred by adjusting their model of the solar system all while keeping the Earth at the center. Ptolemy developed the clever model of epicycles to explain and predict planetary position. Rather than following smooth, somewhat circular paths around the Earth, his model accounted for planetary observations by using epicycles; that is, as the planets would orbit around the Earth, they would each also have a circular path within that orbit. Geocentric astronomy held the power of prominent position of the time. To put it in another way in contemporary terms, research grants would only go to proposals with the geocentric assumption at that time. Heliocentric proposals would be categorically rejected.

How the heliocentric theory became dominant

Copernicus worked out a different model in the sixteenth century with the Earth revolving around the sun, rotating on its tilted axis relative to the sun. This heliocentric theory could account for the movements in a much more parsimonious way than the cumbersome epicycles in the geocentric theory. The geocentric theory never quite could account for all the movements of the planets unless all sorts of geometric gymnastics were used. The heliocentric theory was simpler; it accounted for the planetary movements more easily, and it generated other predictions that verified this model of the solar system. It took the invention of the telescope by Galileo and the discovery of the moons orbiting around Jupiter to move the field into more serious consideration of the heliocentric theory of the solar system. Later, Isaac Newton definitively proved the heliocentric theory. Despite not being the popular or ecclesiastically endorsed model at that time, there is no doubt today of the heliocentric model of the solar system. But there were centuries of great scientists who were equally certain that the Earth was the center of the solar system and who explained away any discrepant findings in order keep the original theory.

Theory can be proposed and only later substantiated with evidence

In the past several decades, there have been a growing number of researchers alluding to this overarching idea of compassionate caring as a scientific phenomenon that underlies not only health care dynamics but human relationships in general. The difficulty measuring it has led some to mistakenly conclude it does not exist in such a form. But this is a poor way to conduct scientific research. Indeed, it is not unusual to have a theory that has been developed that has no empirical evidence for it until years after it has been proposed. One such example that dramatically demonstrates this is Einstein's general theory of relativity, which included a theory of gravity and a theory of space and time. His theory of gravity accounted for the calculation of the shift of the perihelion point

(the point of closest approach to the sun) more exactly than did Newtonian theory. But this had only been hypothesized, not empirically tested. Furthermore, his wave theory of light predicted that the gravitational influence of the sun would bend the path of starlight more than could be predicted with Newtonian theory. British astronomers Arthur Eddington and Frank Dyson tested this prediction with the solar eclipse of 1919, and it was empirically confirmed. Einstein had developed his theory from 1905 to 1915 without the benefit of empirical testing (Baierlein, 1992). Now, of course, we take this theory for granted. But for people who think that the empirical observations always come first in scientific revolutions, it is a demonstration that scientific progress does not come about so neatly. We are seeing the same dynamic in this field of compassionate caring in health care.

The measurement problem and the hard and soft sciences

Before we can discuss how compassionate caring can be so central to health care in a scientific sense, we have to deal with the measurement problem. Some scientists would argue, "If we cannot measure it, it does not exist. If we cannot measure it, it is not a valid part of medicine." We have to deal with the fact that until very recently, medicine has not considered things such as the mind, the psychological factors, the social factors, the phenomenon of caring, and the like to be real, or, at least, these are considered less real than the "hard sciences." We technically all profess to follow the biopsychosocial model for practicing medicine, but our actions in medicine still say that the biomedical model is more valid, "more real," to us. For decades the medical humanities and the social sciences have vied for a place at the table, and there has been some progress on this. But this will not be solved until we confront the erroneous philosophical and scientific thinking that has led to distinguishing the "hard" sciences from the "soft" sciences. They are called hard because we know how to measure them and soft because the scientific constructs are more difficult to define and involve the subjective. Furthermore, they are probably called soft because things like feelings are involved, and the machismo of the "hard" sciences denigrates the vagueness and emotionality of the "soft" sciences. But anyone who makes this distinction does not understand philosophy of science and does not understand that a narrow observational method does not get to dictate what phenomena are acceptable to science. We should never use the terms *hard* and *soft* sciences again. If people insist on some distinction, then it should be called the "hard" sciences and the "harder" sciences. It is, in fact, possible to have a science of the subjective sources of data in the patient's life.

Must have the right instrument to measure the phenomenon

Scientists are often portrayed as skeptics. Scientists want evidence for their claims, and they can be portrayed as initially doubting other people's findings. "What is it?" and "How do you know?" are two of the most powerful questions in science. However, there is a type of scientist who could be thought of as engaging in "methodolotry" (playing off the idea of idolatry). In others words, if a scientist said, "If it cannot be measured, then it does not exist," we would quickly see the mediocrity of this scientist. At one time, it was not possible to see distant galaxies, and one could have easily contested the theory that there are thousands of galaxies light years away.

If scientists had simply stopped this type of research because of the inability to verify that there are distant galaxies, we would never have found out that these exist. As the instruments from the basic telescope to the Hubble were developed, the evidence was gained. Because a thing may be difficult to measure should never be used as a reason not to investigate some phenomenon. At one point in our medical history, we did not know germs existed. Once we had the instruments to confirm the existence of bacteria, we understood why sanitary practices decreased infection. But bacteria existed all along. Our lack of knowledge about them did not prevent them from existing. The same is true with compassionate care in medicine. Because it is difficult to measure is not sufficient reason to deny the impact that it has.

Limits of logical positivism in applying to studying human beings

What has plagued scientific study of human beings is that we have expected to use the same methods to study all aspects of human beings as we did for the chemical and biological sciences. George Engel, who articulated the biopsychosocial model in medicine in 1977, was an early critic of this approach. As he said,

> *advances in science depend on developing means and techniques of inquiry that are appropriate for the phenomena under investigation and the conditions and circumstances under which such can be studied. Viruses are not to be studied with the naked eye at absolute zero. By the same token scientific study of human phenomena requires human means and human circumstances.* (Engel, 1992, p. 5)

Part of the problem is that the philosophy of logical positivism has dominated psychosocial research. Logical positivism argues that the truth or falsity of any scientific proposition must be established by empirically observable conditions. This is called the principle of verification. In the social sciences, this was the philosophical foundation for operationalization or operational definitions in which an object or variable is defined by the operations, or objective measures. The advantage of this was that it provided objective means of substantiating scientific propositions. One of the problems, however, is that this is very difficult to use when it comes to human beings. It favors observations that are external to the subject, and the observer is in this way neutral and detached from the object of study. This method works very well in the natural sciences but does not work well with human beings, who have a subjective perspective that is not easily measured externally. Human beings have perspectives in which various events or experiences mean something to them that cannot be determined unless you ask them what they perceive and what something like a symptom or an illness means to them (Goldenberg, 2006). On top of that, those subjective perceptions or individual meanings then affect their behavior. If a scientist of human nature only allows external objective indicators to be the only acceptable data, then the perspectives of the persons are not allowed. To use a crude analogy, using a pair of binoculars is not sufficient to study the existence of distant galaxies. You need the right instrument to study them—powerful telescopes. The method of the natural sciences is not sufficient to study all aspects of human nature.

Other problems with logical positivism

Two other problems emerged with logical positivism. One is that it became more evident that all observations are theory laden. Our theoretical assumptions and beliefs "color" our observations such that pure objectivity is not possible. Observations are always interpretations. Secondly, scientific theories are undetermined by the data, meaning that "any given body of evidence may support numerous, even contradicting, theories" (Goldenberg, 2006, p. 2624). What this means is that as you study more complex aspects of human beings, the theoretical assumptions and interpretations you have require much more effort to achieve scientific validity. To study them, your method for study has to fit what kind of phenomenon you have, and you have to find ways to test and validate the evidence for your findings.

What is required to study the phenomenon of compassionate caring

The phenomenon on which we are focusing in this book is that of compassionate caring, but in discussing the science of compassionate caring, this will include the psychosocial aspects of being human. In terms of a theory of compassionate caring, we need a theory that includes the multiple levels on which compassionate caring operates, such as the biological, neurophysiological, psychological, and sociological. A mechanistic reductionistic paradigm fails to explain compassionate caring fully. The theory must be able to explain how the multiple levels operate together, rather than only one. Finally, because subjectivity is an integral part of the helping, healing process, the theory of compassionate caring must include a way of integrating both the subjective and objective components of helping, healing interactions. In terms of the theoretical model, "we must have a model adequate to the characterization of our data—no more, but no less" (Rychlak, 1985, p. 67). Furthermore, the methods we use for studying the phenomenon must be adequate for the full understanding of that phenomenon. Shimon Glick (1993), who echoed and amplified the pioneering work of George Engel, affirmed that such a model was needed and what it should be:

> The only model that can satisfactorily meet, not just the demands imposed by compassion, but those required by the exactitude of science, is the biopsychosocial model. A failure of compassion will inevitably lead to poor science in medicine because it ignores data critical to the patient's care. (p. 91)

Furthermore, Glick (1993) stated that "it is impossible to provide scientific medicine without humanism, or compassionate medicine without an adequate base" (p. 90).

The biopsychosocial model integrates both the objective and subjective aspects of patient care

The biopsychosocial model was articulated by George Engel in 1977. While the biomedical model accounts for the causes, course, and treatment of disease solely by biological and physiological variables, "The biopsychosocial model proposes that biological, psychological, social, and structural processes operate in a matrix of nested and inextricably connected subsystems that influence all aspects of mental and physical health" (Suls, Krantz, & Williams, 2013). Engel's critique of the biomedical model was based on the fact that illness can result from the interaction of causal factors at the biomolecular, individual, and social levels. Biochemical problems can cause an illness, but a psychological factor may also cause biochemical and health problems. Psychosocial factors can affect how susceptible a person is to an illness, how severe that illness becomes, and the course of the illness for that person. Also, simply knowing the biological problem does not give any sense of what the symptoms mean to the patient and what kind of suffering it creates for the patient; the clinician has to have the attitudes and skills to obtain and process that information from the subjective report of that patient. Furthermore, even the success of biological treatments is affected by psychosocial variables, including dynamics such as the placebo effect. The relationship the patient has with the clinician will affect the medical outcomes, at the very least in terms of how that relationship influences a patient to be adherent to the treatment recommended. Engel was very aware of the influence of the subjectivities of both the patient and the clinician. In scientific studies, patients are affected by how they are studied, and scientists are affected by the people they are studying (Borrell-Carrio, Suchman, & Epstein, 2004).

Predominant emphasis on molecular biology as the hub science prevented serious consideration and training regarding psychosocial variables

There is the temptation to disregard anything regarding theoretical models as not helpful in practice, but I think I have made the case that our perceptions are affected by our implicit theories, our expectations for how things work. Taking this biopsychosocial model seriously is critical because, as Stewart et al. (2003) note, models of practice give us a framework to understand what is happening with a patient. Models guide our perceptions and our actions by hinting at what we should look for and what is important in helping people in medicine (Stewart et al., 2003).

As Suls et al. (2013) note, "Reluctance on the part of mainstream medicine to adopt the biopsychosocial model is understandable because molecular biology is its hub science" (p. 597). Premedical and medical training has emphasized this model without spending a lot of time examining how other factors play major roles in the causes, courses, and treatments of illness. By the time this kind of discussion regarding the role of psychosocial factors takes place in a person's training, it is literally much too late. The fact that it is brought up in an adjunctive way with probably a relatively small amount of teaching time conveys to the new clinician that the other factors such as the psychosocial ones are ultimately less important.

Medicine prefers simple biomedical causes, but this is not the reality

On paper and more frequently in training, we now espouse the biopsychosocial model in practicing medicine over the biomedical model. Yet the reality is that while more elements of the biopsychosocial model are used in patient assessment and treatment, the biomedical model still has the dominant position. Medicine prefers to have a simple, linear cause for a patient's symptoms, and its favorite type of cause is biological. All other causes or combinations of causes are not as popular because they are seen as less scientific (Montgomery, 2006). If you doubt this, sit in on most medical rounds and notice what happens when a cause is not primarily biological or a set of causes includes psychosocial factors. It will be instantly clear to you that there is a pecking order to which are the favorite types of causes and the favorite types of treatments. Other types of causes and nonbiological treatments for medical problems

are often viewed as less than valid. But as Montgomery (2006) explains, causal complexity is more of a challenge in biology than in other sciences, such as physics. This is particularly true of human biology. These biological organisms called humans "have reasons as well as causes for their behavior" (p. 71). This is much less precise than work in chemistry and physics because there are social factors that are intertwined with all the other aspects of a complex biological system. In addition, these biological organisms are affected as well by the fact that they know they are being observed and examined (by their clinicians). The very act of engaging these humans also introduces other variables that can influence what occurs within these "biological organisms" beyond simple biomedical causes.

Seven phenomena that biomedically centered medicine cannot handle well

Interestingly, medicine is in a situation not unlike the geocentric theory of the solar systems was. Just as the astronomers who used the geocentric theory of their time explained away or ignored findings that did not fit what the geocentric theory would predict, so too is biomedical medicine demonstrating theoretical inadequacies. Kirkengen et al. (2016) list seven phenomena that biomedically centered medicine cannot handle well. First, sicknesses are unevenly distributed (from a solely biological point of view) in that these are caused by individual choices and lifestyles as well as by social conditions such as poverty. Second, there is a problem of comorbidity or multimorbidity in patients. From a biomedical point of view, different diseases or medical problems in a patient will each be biomedically classified by its own etiology, course, and prognosis instead of being organized systemically. Third, as we fragment the body further, Kirkengen et al. (2016) note that an "epidemic of risks" is occurring in which there are an unlimited and unmanageable number of risk factors for particular diseases. Fourth, medically unexplained syndromes are clear indicators of the limits of biomedical approaches. Chronic pain syndromes, somatization, and other complex illnesses are very frustrating to clinicians who are biomedically focused. Fifth, especially in patients with multiple and chronic diseases, medications accumulate in their bodies, leading to adverse consequences that are listed as one of the top 10 causes of death in Western countries. Sixth, overdiagnosis and overtreatment are some of the consequences of an emphasis on technology and medications. Preventive measures involve early screening but may actually increase sickness and suffering rather than better health and longevity. Finally, while research studies typically control for placebo and nocebo effects, we still do not understand these phenomena, which show up in the majority of medical treatments.

Overemphasis on objectivity and value neutrality negatively affects the practice of medicine

Kirkengen et al. (2016) argue that the overemphasis on objectivity and value neutrality have helped create these problems. By focusing on objectifying the body in a physiological way, other causal factors from society, culture, and the person's life are seen as "outside" the core of medicine. Human care is viewed as lower in rank than technological treatment, in which the biological frame of reference "has become a hypervalue, itself 'beyond' criticism, rendering all other kinds of knowledge either less relevant or less reliable" (Kirkengen et al., 2016, p. 498).

Viewing the patient as a set of body ailments ends up disregarding major factors involved in that person's life. "The main challenge is to acknowledge that the patient is an experiencing and interpreting subject, a human being in the same way as the professional herself or himself" (Kirkengen et al., 2016, p. 498). Everything that is identified as nonnatural, such as the mental, social, spiritual, emotional, relational, and personal aspects of a person's life, is separated out of the purview of medicine. Yet the meaning of health and illness are subjectively perceived by the patients, and this impacts the quality of the suffering, how patients should be approached, and the clinician's ethical obligations. Furthermore, evidence-based medicine has moved from being a tool to the goal of treatment. Evidence-based medicine is based on the "average" patient and is the result of a highly controlled, randomized study that excludes the other variables that would confound a pure research study. To apply evidence-based medicine uniformly without regard to particular factors in a patient's life will result in poor care for many patients.

Patient subjectivity affects DNA expression

The very subjectivity of patients, the fact of how they appraise what everything means to them, is intimately involved with the biological. In fact, the neurological, immunological, and endocrine systems are tied into what a person's environment is and how they appraise that environment and themselves in connection with it. Kirkengen et al. (2016) note that based on years of research in psycho-neuro-endocrino-immunology, genetics, and epigenetics, there is clear evidence that "*human* biology is saturated with *human* meaning; experience is inscribed in the body down to sub-cellular level" (p. 499). Getz, Kirkengen, and Ulvestad (2011) synthesized new scientific knowledge of how biographical information of the human affects biomolecular processes in the body. First, they reviewed the work on the science of epigenetics, which "is concerned with the way experiences enable contextual 'programming' of genetic material" (Getz et al., 2011, p. 2). Epigenetics focuses on relatively stable temporary changes in the genetic expression of the DNA without changes to the DNA itself. The mechanisms that block or trigger gene expression include histone modification, non-coding RNA, and DNA methylation. Research studies have shown how a person's experiences and interpretations of those experiences affects what part of the DNA is expressed under various situations; these processes appear as early as conception and go on throughout a person's life. The authors note how this relates to the increase of lifestyle-related diseases.

Patient subjectivity impacts human physiology and bodily processes

Second, Getz et al. (2011) reported that for the past 10 to 20 years, research at the interfaces of microbiology, immunology, endocrinology, psychology, and neuroscience has shown how experience and interpretation impacts human physiology. A pregnant mother's psychosocial stress can affect the fetus through the hypothalamic-pituitary-adrenal (HPA) axis and other epigenetic effects. The traumatic experiences in a pregnant woman's own childhood can be reflected not only in her adult life but then also in the HPA regulation of the fetus. Psychosocial stress can also create a risk for the pregnancy. Negative experiences, like chronic debilitating caregiving, can damage the chromosomes' telomeres, whose function is to protect the chromosome ends from fusing with nearby chromosomes or from deterioration. Negative emotional and relational experiences have been found to negatively affect the immune systems. This can occur with inflammatory response and altered cytokine balance. Social threats such as "losing face," experiencing unfairness at work, and experiencing loss or powerlessness negatively affect the immune system. Emotions have physiological correlates, affecting cortisol and cytokine levels. Negative relationship experiences can lower the antibody response in vaccines.

Additional evidence that patient subjectivity affects bodily processes and diseases

Allostatic overload is the long-term overtaxation of a human's physiological adaptability. Intense or persistent threats to the integrity of the person and his or her existence lead to physiological wear and tear. This can occur in any situation with severe chronic stress, such as poverty, trauma, war, and other conditions in which there is a serious loss of control and mastery over one's life. Both psychosocial and physical stressors cause changes in the immune system, cause chronic low-grade inflammation, create autonomic dysfunction, disrupt the endocrine system, and lead to telomere shortening, causing accelerated cell aging. Allostatic overload leads to chronic metabolic disturbances, which contribute to major diseases. These include diabetes, cardiovascular disease, chronic obstructive pulmonary disease, obesity, depression, osteoporosis, immunological and inflammation-driven diseases, pain syndromes, chronic fatigue, and adverse pregnancy outcomes (e.g., premature birth, low birth weight). These disturbances also contribute to mental disorders such as depression, anxiety, substance dependence, and other psychiatric conditions. Severe negative childhood experiences such as physical, emotional, and sexual abuse negatively affect the developing brain structures, depending on the age of the child and how long such experiences last. Throughout a person's life, the brain appears to be affected positively or negatively by respectively positive or negative relational experiences. Positive relational experiences such as psychotherapy and strong social support can lead to changes in the brain and lower the risk of dying from a number of negative physical conditions.

Mind–body dualism is outdated in medical science

The bottom line is that the separation we have had between the natural sciences and the social sciences is no longer clear, based on the advances in biomedical understanding of how our subjective experiences are deeply interwoven into what happens to us biologically. The parallel tracks of mind–body dualism are no longer valid. As Getz et al. (2011) argue,

> an integrated medical theory about human beings must take as its starting point that every individual is conceived with a given biological predisposition, which gradually becomes shaped by experience, understanding, interpretation and action, influenced by physical environment factors and woven into relationships with significant others in a society with culturally constituted values. We hardly need more empirical detail to claim with authority that (and suggest an explanation as to how) all these factors affect people's health-related development. (p. 5)

A theory of medicine that continues to treat mind and body separately is very much outdated. This kind of research provides the kind of material that will help clinicians have the evidence they need to be able to make the shift to the biopsychosocial model from the biologically reductionistic biomedical approach.

Biopsychosocial model requires compassionate engagement with patients

One of the major barriers to implementing this change in the theory of medicine is the lack of training in the biopsychosocial model in terms of the importance of psychological and social factors and the mechanisms of interactions with, for example, the biological. But Ronald Epstein (2014) notes that utilizing the biopsychosocial model requires clinicians to engage with patients more deeply in terms of their experiences, emotions, and suffering; this in turn requires clinicians to have the capacity to be self-aware, engage in compassionate action, and have resilience in doing this work. To accomplish this, Epstein finds that there are eight "leaps" clinicians have to make. One is that in working with patients in a more holistic way, clinicians are pushed to move from a fragmented way of looking at themselves to looking at themselves in a whole way. The former mode of compartmentalizing your life in medicine will be more clear to you, and you will move toward thinking about all of it in a more integrated way. Second, it requires changing your thinking from looking at that patient in a more detached way to one in which you engage with patients in terms of trying to understand their experience. This requires a willingness to be humbly open to what another human being's life is like. Third, clinicians have to move from an objective stance to an emotionally resonant one. As we will discuss in more depth later, this requires learning how to find the right balance in terms of how you manage the empathic response to patients. Fourth, as you exercise your skills with a patient, another shift required is moving from a detached concern with the patient to being fully present in a caring and tender way with the patient and to be steady in terms of doing your work for the patient and doing it well (Coulehan, 1995). Fifth, clinicians doing this type of work make a transition from focusing on self-protection and having rigid notions of what they and others are like to being able to suspend their notions about themselves and others so that they can see the real truth in both the other and themselves. Sixth, clinicians move from a stance of just maintaining well-being to seeking to be resilient. One can approach work in terms of focusing on avoiding burnout by maintaining work–life balance, taking time off work, and so on. Of course, this is very important to do. But this is a type of focus on personal well-being that is self-focused and self-protective. Epstein points out that in order to experience joy, fulfillment, and meaning in the work, one has to be engaged with the work, which means one is fully present to experience what is going on at work. For this, more than maintaining well-being is required. What is needed for this deeper engagement is the capacity for resilience. But he warns that resilience is more than adaptability in the face of adversity. Resilience also means that the "clinician responds to challenges with growth, maturation, and perseverance … managing the unexpected, preparing to be unprepared, 'meeting each new guest at the door, laughing'" (Epstein, 2014, p. 283).

Seventh, clinicians need to move from focusing on empathy with patients to compassion with patients. As you will see later in this book, while empathy is an important tool for helping patients, the clinician has to imbed this empathy in compassion. Neurocognitive research has shown how clinicians who are in this more compassionate mindset are less distressed by purely empathic resonance and more able to act to help with less emotional cost to themselves. In fact, this compassionate mindset enhances the clinician's sense of reward and fulfillment as well as resilience. (Much of the reset of this book will explain the mechanisms for this compassionate mind.) Finally, Epstein (2014) notes that when clinicians work with the biopsychosocial model, they tend to move from an individualistic sense of mind to more of a "shared mind." That is, clinicians become much more aware of the mutual influence everyone has on each other and gain more of a sense of shared thinking and awareness among everyone in their team or group and even wider community (Epstein, 2014).

Theory of compassionate caring is necessary to describe how this is helpful to patients

In the biomedical approach to helping patients, caring and compassion are not integral to explaining how assessment and treatment occur. But we now know that a strict biomedical approach to helping patients is not adequate to assess them fully and to treat them most effectively. A biopsychosocial model is a more accurate way to understand human beings and how illness develops, progresses, and might be treated. In order to do this, we must have an approach that can deal with both the objective and subjective aspects of the patient. A clinician must have a theory of compassionate caring in order to articulate the patient-clinician dynamics that make healing possible. Furthermore, this theory of compassionate caring can be scientifically described and measured.

Consequences of neglecting the role of compassionate caring in medicine

To neglect the role of compassionate caring in medicine is scientifically short sighted. Because it is difficult to measure and study, it can be tempting to try to ignore it altogether. But we now possess the tools to measure and study it. We have a great deal of evidence that caring for patients solely out of a technocentric biomedical model leads to deficient assessment and treatment of patients. Theoretically, neglecting the role of caring in medicine leads to making technology operate alone at the center of the medical solar system, and a technocentric biomedical theory of the helping process is not sufficient to treat patients. As a result of the lack of scientific recognition of the role of compassionate caring in medicine, medical training is incomplete because it does not provide those in training with a thorough understanding of what is involved in human illness (the biopsychosocial model) and what is necessary to treat human illness—a compassionate caring approach that integrates the biomedical and the psychosocial in assessment and treatment of patients.

Empathic dialogue with the patient is the key to solid data collection

Compassionate caring relies heavily on the interaction between the clinician and the patient. The communication process between them is the route to gaining complete data to assess the patient and also to facilitate the healing process. Engel (1992) captured this necessity in the following passage:

> Once the foundational character of dialogue is acknowledged, the essential complementarity of the human and the scientific premised by the 20th century paradigm becomes apparent. This is inherent in the fact that dialogue as a means of data collection and processing is itself regulated by conditions that determine human relationships. Accordingly, completeness and accuracy of the data are correspondingly enhanced by optimizing those human circumstances which are most likely to facilitate dialogue. The physician has no alternative but to behave in a humane and empathic manner, that is, to understand and be understanding, if the patient is to be enabled to report clearly and fully. Only then can the physician proceed scientifically; to be human and empathic is not merely a prescription for compassion, as medical educators would like us to believe; it is a requirement for scientific work in the clinical realm. (p. 8)

Try assuming that medicine could be practiced using only objective labs, scans, and physical symptoms

Let us suppose that we take the biomedical argument to its extreme, in which we consider only "objective" lab tests, scans, and physical symptoms to be valid data for practicing medicine scientifically. In this biomedical model, the patient's report is considered irrelevant or suspect. Let us then imagine this extreme and test the null hypothesis: Dialogue with the patient does not contribute at all to the scientific practice of medicine. The ridiculousness of this claim becomes quickly apparent. Without the patient relating the history of the current illness, we would lose very relevant data for assessing our patients. It is the patient report and the nonverbals we observe that provide information that helps guide our subsequent testing and help us interpret what we observe physically. We might observe intense agitation and depressive symptoms with no physical findings. Is the patient making the symptoms up? Is the patient seeking attention? Or might this patient have tinnitus, a medical condition no one denies but no lab test can delineate better than the patient's description? Imagine if your patient refused to talk about his or her symptoms. You would label the person a difficult patient and probably decline to treat him or her. In short, if you grant that dialogue is at least somewhat helpful to your clinical reasoning, you must then admit that it is part of the scientific process. No exceptions.

There are two modes of observation in patient care: biological empirical and relational

Engel (1992) pointed out how we have two modes of observation when it comes to patient care: the traditional biological empirical mode and the relational mode, in which dialogue is a major component. Engel (1992) explained how

> in clinical practice the physician always operates in both modes at the same time, making observations while engaging in dialogue and vice versa. The two processes thus not only are complementary and supplementary with respect to the results achieved, they are also interdependent in operation. Information being obtained in one mode may not be accessible in the other but may be clarified, elaborated, verified, or refuted by access to the other mode, sometimes simultaneously. Anxiety verbally denied may be verified by demonstrating tachycardia and cold sweaty hands. The meaning of "OK" in response to "How are you?" may be questioned if a gesture of helplessness is observed to accompany it. A patient's report of "palpitation" may be elaborated through direct examination or electronic recordings. Accordingly, the two modes constitute not alternative, but a single integrated means for data disclosure, clarification and interpretation in the clinical realm. (p. 8)

Levels of explanation tool using the analogy of letters on a page

When clinicians are using both of these modes of observation and still feel uneasy with how the psychosocial data fits coherently and seamlessly with the biomedical data, it can be useful to use a philosophical tool called the levels-of-analysis approach (Bube, 1971; Collins, 1981), which is also called the levels of explanation approach (Fodor, 1965; Myers, 1987; Myers & Jeeves, 1987; Schoen, 1985). Collins described the idea of levels of analysis using Bube's example of how one might analyze language. Let us say you are looking at a page of text. You can analyze it from any number of perspectives. At one level, you can look at the page in terms of individual letters. You can describe what kind of letters they are (e.g., Greek, Arabic, English) and even count them, finding out how many there are of each letter. Another way of analyzing the page is to look at phonetics or words. The letters do not necessarily make up words; they could be just random letters. But then you notice these letters *do* make up words. You can notice what the words are, count them, and so on. At another level, you notice that these are not simply random words on a page but that they make coherent statements. At another level, you notice that all the statements actually relate to each other and that not only does each sentence have meaning but together all the statements have a larger meaning. As Collins (1981) says, "Each of these perspectives is more complex than the one lower, and each higher perspective embraces all of the lower levels" (p. 23). Each level is true by itself and can stand alone as a way of analyzing the text. But if you reduced everything to individual letters (reductionism to the letter), you would be missing the fact that they make up words, sentences, and paragraphs with meaning. You could say, "I can explain everything on this page in terms of analyzing the individual letters, and without letters you could not have words, sentences, and meaning." In one sense, you would be absolutely correct. But the words were chosen to convey some meaning, so it would also be true to say that you can analyze the words on the page in terms of an intended meaning. While you cannot have words without letters, just counting the letters does not tell you that they mean something because of the ways they have been arranged.

Understanding human beings using the levels of explanation approach

When it comes to human beings, you can analyze them in the same way: atomic particles, atoms, molecules, organic compounds, cells, tissues, organs, organ systems, and so on. Or put another way, when a human being does something, you can explain that action using any number of explanations that are simultaneously true. You can explain the human in terms of physics, chemistry, organic chemistry, physiology, psychology, social psychology, sociology, culture, politics, and spirituality (or philosophy of life)— and the list could go on. Let us say, for example, that I want to explain the behavior of a person who helps another person. I could explain that behavior in psychological terms, such as the helper perceived another person as being in some distress. The helper experienced some empathic resonance with the person in distress, and this triggered a helping response. But I could also explain this using neuroscience. I could track what parts of the brain fired when observing and

interpreting the distress, then what part of the brain fired for a compassionate response. I could also use chemistry to explain the whole sequence. I could use sociology as well to explain how social and cultural factors explain this behavior. Or perhaps this person is someone who aspires to be kind based on spiritual/religious beliefs or, if the person is agnostic or atheistic, perhaps he or she had some humanistic ethical code that motivated the action.

Each level has unique explanatory power

From one perspective, you could explain a certain behavior using just one level of analysis. Each level is true by itself. Each level is simultaneously occurring as the other levels are. But when I omit a level, I lose explanatory power. Therefore, while I can explain the behavior using only neurophysiology or chemistry, I would lose explanatory power if I did not have the psychological level. Each level is legitimate in its own right. But what happens at one level can affect what happens at another level (Vachon & Agresti, 1992). If the person has a brain injury or a depletion of some critical mineral or chemical, then the psychological perception might be affected so that the person did not experience empathy. Or maybe the person has a hedonistic philosophy of life and does not value or believe in helping other people. This person might observe the distress, but because the person views life as essentially each individual just focusing on increasing his or her own pleasure or avoiding pain, that belief interferes with the empathic process, and the person distances him- or herself from the person in distress.

What happens when all the tests are negative?

Because of the overemphasis on the biomedical model, physicians have tended to rely more on lab tests or scans than their own judgment, leading to an overuse of tests and diagnostic procedures. While patients feel dehumanized in the process, it is important to note that "physicians feel bewildered, inept, frustrated, and angry when sophisticated instrumentation fails to yield answers and patients persist in feeling ill and making demands in the face of the laboratory demonstration of 'no disease'" (Engel, 1978, p. 170). It is interesting that many clinicians accept the idea that when the tests are all negative, there is nothing wrong, and the words "it's all in your head" are offered to the patient as the clinician ends the consultation. If the clinician were indeed being scientific about what is going on, the sheer number of times this occurs should raise suspicion for the scientifically trained clinician. Furthermore, it is inappropriate to conclude another disease process in another field of medicine is proved by the fact that the tests in your own specialty are negative. It is incredible in a time when psychiatry and psychology are receiving little time in medical education that clinicians are diagnosing these types of problems so often.

What a clinician expects to see changes what he or she sees

What we expect to see changes what we see. If I expect that a patient who presents a binder of medical records is going to be a "difficult patient," then that is what I will see. If I see a patient who complains of severe chronic pain who has made the rounds of specialists and this person is not well dressed or well groomed, not well educated, from an impoverished background (and add that the person is a different gender and/or ethnic background than I am), then what are my assumptions about the presenting complaint? I might expect I am seeing a drug seeker who is exaggerating the symptoms to get what he or she wants. But what if I see a patient who complains of severe chronic pain who has made the rounds of specialists and this person is well dressed, is well educated, and has resources (and add that the person is the same ethnic background and gender as I am), would my assumption now be that this patient may very well have an undiagnosed condition that is in the early stages and is diagnostically difficult? Would I begin by considering that this patient's distress may be due to an undiagnosed condition rather than assuming the person is a malingerer? Of course, there are clinicians who would just assume both of these patients are malingerers. Such clinicians might begin with that assumption, and no evidence would change their minds. There is the opposite situation that is no less problematic. If I assume that everyone who presents with severe pain is truthful and being discriminated against by clinicians who are not as smart as I am or just do not care to work hard at the diagnosis, then I am equally biased. It does not matter whether they are rose-colored or dark-colored glasses; either one of these ways of viewing a patient is distorting what the clinician is seeing.

Attending to patient cues

Clinicians generally are not well prepared to pick up on patient cues and either miss them completely or consciously avoid them (Levinson, Gorawara-Bhat, & Lamb, 2000). Clinicians are often reluctant to investigate a patient cue because they fear that it will take too much time and put them behind or that other problems will surface, such as psychosocial issues, which are often considered secondary in a medical visit. The consequences of not investigating these cues are that important diagnostic material can be missed (e.g., medical symptoms the patient is afraid to disclose) or that the ignored psychosocial issues will undermine the treatment (e.g., fear of taking medications, depression, chaotic family system). Investigating these cues requires first being able to recognize the cue suggesting a patient need or problem that would require active listening to investigate. Second, the clinician has to have a willingness to explore the cue and feel prepared to do so. Third, the clinician has to make a choice about pursuing the cue. This choice is weighed against how important the cue seems, how much time the clinician has, and how the clinician feels about investigating it (Cocksedge & May, 2005).

Therapeutic responsibility to attend to patient cues but find a balance of if and when to pursue them

From a patient-centered and biopsychosocial perspective, there would seem to be a therapeutic responsibility to notice and explore patient cues; clinicians who see numerous patients a day have to quickly decide whether to pursue such cues. Not pursuing them is not necessarily an indication of lack of caring. Some cues are not critical and can wait. Some patients have so many underlying issues that a clinician has to pace how far they pursue these and whether doing so will be useful in the long run. The clinician may also have pursued several patient cues earlier in the day, spent extra time and energy on them, and now is very behind and still needs to see many patients who have been waiting. It is easy to judge clinicians in

terms of what they should do, but the reality is that clinicians cannot work through every problem. Some clinicians handle this by never learning how to recognize cues or by ignoring all of them. This would be unprofessional and definitely uncaring. It would be like addressing a patient's sore throat but pretending you did not hear that the patient said he or she was having chest pain because you did not want to deal with it. This would be irresponsible, and you certainly would not want to send a family member to such a clinician. But well-trained and compassionately caring clinicians have another problem: They notice more of what is going on with a patient and are generally motivated to help patients, but they have limits regarding what they can realistically do. A helping professional of any specialty can go down the street and spot all sorts of problems. Whatever your specialty is, your ability to notice those particular problems is much better than that of the layperson. What helping professionals have to learn is a way of preserving their compassionate desire while at the same time not getting overwhelmed and depleted; and they need to do this by not falling into pathological guilt but also by not becoming completely impervious and closed to the suffering of others.

It is possible to improve emotion recognition ability, but the training method matters

Research has shown that students going into medicine can improve their ability to recognize patient emotion cues. But the method of training matters. Blanch-Hartigan (2012) compared five training conditions and a control group. They were consciousness-raising condition, an instruction condition, practice alone, practice with feedback, and finally, a comprehensive condition that integrated all the components of the other conditions. The comprehensive training led to the most improvement in emotion recognition accuracy, and the most effective training component was practice with feedback.

Practice with feedback improves emotion recognition best

What was interesting was that the students in the practice with feedback condition felt less confident in the emotion recognition task, but they were actually the most accurate compared to the other conditions. Blanch-Hartigan noted that the feedback made the students feel inadequate, but that actually made them attend better and learn better than the students in the other conditions. Based on previous research, it turns out that medical students and physicians are poor self-assessors of their abilities, especially with regard to their communication skills (Blanch-Hartigan, 2011; Davis et al., 2006; DePaulo, Charlton, Cooper, Lindsay, & Muhlenbruck, 1997). Often, men tend to overestimate their ability and women tend to underestimate (Blanch-Hartigan, 2011). In training, then, it is very important to remember that clinicians tend not to be able to assess themselves accurately and that training should help them become acutely aware of their actual performance in emotion recognition.

HOW BIOMEDICAL EXPLANATIONS AFFECT OUR PATIENTS' BEHAVIOR

Patients now expect biomedical explanations from their clinicians

Because the biomedical model of medicine has been the dominant model in medical practice, patients expect that their physicians will emphasize biological explanations of their illnesses. The biopsychosocial model, with its understanding of the interaction of biological and psychosocial factors in the onset, course, and treatment of illness, has been promoted more recently as the more accurate model of treating illnesses; however, most physicians are not yet adept in using this model, and patients have not routinely expected it in their care. When they do have a clinician who is more proficient in using the biopsychosocial model, they may be surprised at the interaction between their physiology and stress, health behaviors, mental health, and social factors. Some patients actually can become resentful about the clinician's investigation of things such as the patient's stress or health behaviors because they have expected a biomedical explanation of their sickness and a biomedical solution. The tremendous advances of biomedicine have led to clinicians approaching patient problems mainly in this model, and patients have come to expect to be viewed in this biomedical fashion.

The biomedical model has limited not only the clinician's perspective but also the patient's perspective

While medicine is trying to learn how to practice the biopsychosocial model more fully for the sake of higher quality health care, our patients have been influenced by the biomedical model and reductionism to see themselves in this way. Patients can view themselves in such a reductionistic way that when clinicians investigate other areas of their patients' lives, the patients become annoyed. "Just give me the inhaler, and don't ask me about my smoking!" Not only do we have to help clinicians understand how the biological and psychosocial levels interact in causing, maintaining, or treating medical problems, we also have to help patients understand how they need to view themselves in a systemic and holistic way. Many clinicians are frustrated by how patients just seek medications and procedures but are not taking better care of themselves, such as by exercising, eating better, and sleeping better. Patients are compartmentalizing their lives just as we have compartmentalized them in medicine for years. For some patients, rebuffing biopsychosocial interventions can be an excuse not to accept that they need to change some negative health behavior. For others, they may genuinely not understand how their lifestyle and habits can affect their illnesses.

Patients dehumanize themselves and become more passive with biomedical care

But what are the consequences of patients expecting the clinician to approach them from an almost solely biological explanatory point of view? Expecting to be viewed as a system of interacting parts inadvertently fosters a mechanistic dehumanization (Haslam, 2006), both by the clinician and the patient. Patients come to view themselves as they imagine they are viewed, and then behave accordingly. Modern medicine tends to

> dehumanize patients with its lack of personal care and emotional support; its reliance on technology; its lack of touch and human warmth; its emphasis on instrumental efficiency and standardization, to the neglect of the patient's individuality; its related neglect of the patient's subjective experience in favor of objective, technologically mediated information; and its emphasis on interventions performed on a passive individual whose agency and autonomy are neglected. (Haslam, 2006, p. 253)

Patients can come to imagine themselves as things, as biomedical machines, and respond more passively to let the clinician work on them as a car would "allow itself" to be worked on by a mechanic. The patient's subjectivity would not be essential in that situation or would even get in the way of the clinician "fixing me up."

How patients perceive clinicians when they know the clinicians are biomedically focused

Some research actually has examined how patients perceive their clinicians when they know the clinicians are biomedically focused. Lebowitz, Ahn, and Oltman (2015), for example, researched how patients viewed mental health clinicians (psychiatrists, psychologists, and social workers) who were more biologically or more psychosocially oriented in explaining the patient's mental disorder. The researchers found that patients viewed biologically oriented clinicians as competent and effective when the patients construed the mental disorder as mainly biologically caused. However, if the patients construed the mental disorder as having a more psychosocial explanation, they perceived biologically oriented clinicians as less competent, less effective, and less favorable. While one would think that having clinicians be more biologically focused would be seen as more legitimate, be more scientific, and absolve the patient from blame, patients who have a sense that the psychosocial is more involved will lose confidence in those clinicians.

Biologically oriented clinicians are viewed as less warm and kind

This finding makes sense and may seem obvious. If a patient thinks the clinician is not explaining the illness correctly, he or she views the clinician as less competent. But the surprise in this study is that the patients viewed the biologically oriented clinician as always less warm no matter whether the mental disorder was principally biological or psychological, and patients always thought the psychosocially oriented clinician was warmer. The researchers noted that clinicians who are mainly biological in their understanding of patient symptoms come to be viewed as less warm, less kind, more likely to dehumanize patients, and more robotic and machinelike themselves. The dehumanized, objectified patient comes to view his or her clinician in a dehumanized, objectified way as well; the negative result of all of this, the researchers explain, is that the therapeutic alliance is drastically weakened. The therapeutic alliance has been found to be the engine, the fulcrum, for effective and successful mental health treatment. Both warmth and competence are needed for the therapeutic alliance. If warmth is automatically expected to be less when a patient views the clinician as very biologically oriented, then the results will likely suffer even if the clinician is technically competent (Lebowitz et al., 2015).

The kinds of explanations we prefer affect how we assess patients and how empathic we are

The kind of explanations we favor (biological, psychosocial, or a combination) tends to bias the way we think about patient problems and even how empathic we are with them! How a clinician explains things that are happening to a patient can affect how much empathy the clinician feels for that patient. Lebowitz and Ahn (2014) presented clinical vignettes of patients with mental disorders to mental health clinicians, including psychiatrists, psychologists, and social workers. Patients whose symptoms were explained biologically evoked less empathy from all the clinicians than if the symptoms were explained psychosocially. This decrease in empathy was found even when the explanations were a mixture of biological and psychosocial factors but the biological predominated. Those who were MD clinicians, and thus had more biomedical training, tended to have less empathy than those with less biomedical training. But all the clinicians, MD or not, expressed less empathy with biological explanations. Furthermore, the type of explanation affected what type of therapy would be thought to be more effective. When presented with cases with explanations that were more biological, all clinicians thought that psychotherapy would be less effective than medication. Neither of the explanation types induced more personal distress in the clinicians for social phobia, depression, or obsessive–compulsive disorder. The difference in empathy ratings did not appear to be due to the possibility that the psychosocial explanations were more distressing than the biological ones.

Why clinician empathy may be less with biological explanations

The authors speculated that biological explanations decreasing empathy may result because the suffering of the patient is portrayed mechanistically, a mechanistic dehumanization, rather than as a human being suffering. Another possibility is that patients who have mental disorders are perceived as categorically different than people who do not have mental disorders because they have permanent or immutable genetic and neurobiological anomalies (i.e., essentialism and neuroessentialism). There is something wrong with their DNA or their brains, and they become perceived as the out-group distinct from normal people (Lebowitz & Ahn, 2014).

CONCLUSION

One of the doubts clinicians may have about compassionate caring is that subjectivity is involved. Medicine imagines itself as very scientific, and this seems to suggest that it is completely objective and the subjective is considered unscientific. The purpose of this chapter is to show how medicine's understanding of objectivity and subjectivity is erroneous. It is possible to have a trained subjectivity that is objective. In order to practice good medicine, the subjectivities of the patient and the clinician are integral and unavoidable. The biopsychosocial model is the most accurate way to understand human beings and how the predisposition, onset, course, and outcome of all illnesses are the result of the interactions of biological, psychological, and social factors. In order to accurately assess and treat patients, clinicians must gain data from objective sources such as labs, vitals, and scans but also from the subjective report of patients processed through the trained subjectivity of the clinician. The only way to achieve this data from both sources is to have clinicians who are grounded in a compassion-centric approach to the patient.

QUESTIONS FOR DISCUSSION

1. After reading this chapter, how would you explain the role of subjectivity in clinical practice?
2. What are the limits of biomedically based clinical practice and the advantages of practicing in the biopsychosocial model?
3. What is scientifically required to be able to study the phenomenon of compassionate caring in health care?

REFERENCES

Baierlein, R. (1992). *Newton to Einstein: The trail of light.* New York, NY: Cambridge University Press.

Blanch-Hartigan, D. (2011). Medical students' self-assessment of performance: Results from three meta-analyses. *Patient Education and Counseling, 84,* 3–9.

Blanch-Hartigan, D. (2012). An effective training to increase accurate recognition of patient emotions cues. *Patient Education and Counseling, 89,* 274–280.

Borrell-Carrio, F., Suchman, A. L., & Epstein, R. M. (2004). The biopsychosocial model 25 years later: Principles, practice, and scientific inquiry. *Annals of Family Medicine, 2*(6), 576–582.

Bube, R. H. (1971). *The human quest: A new look at science and Christian faith.* Waco, TX: Works Books.

Cocksedge, S., & May, C. (2005). The listening loop: A model of choice about cues within primary care consultations. *Medical Education, 39,* 999–1005.

Collins, G. R. (1981). *Psychology and theology: Prospects for integration.* Nashville, TN: Abingdon Press.

Coulehan, J. L. (1995). Tenderness and steadiness: Emotions in medical practice. *Literature and Medicine, 14*(2), 222–236.

Davis, D. A., Mazmanian, P. E., Fordis, M., Van Harrison, R. R., Thorpe, K. E., & Perrier, L. (2006). Accuracy of physician self-assessment compared with observed measures of competence: A systematic review. *Journal of the American Medical Association,* *296,* 1094–1102.

DePaulo, B. M., Charlton, K., Cooper, H., Lindsay, J. J., & Muhlenbruck, L. (1997). The accuracy-confidence correlation in the detection of deception. *Personality and Social Psychology Review, 1*(4), 346–357.

Engel, G. L. (1977). The need for a new medical model: A challenge for biomedicine. *Science, 196*(4286), 129–136.

Engel, G. L. (1978). The biopsychosocial model and the education of health professionals. *Annals of the New York Academy of Sciences, 310*(1), 169–181.

Engel, G. L. (1992). How much longer must medicine be bound by a seventeenth century world view? *Psychotherapy and Psychosomatics, 57,* 3–16.

Epstein, R. M. (2014). Realizing Engel's biopsychosocial vision: Resilience, compassion, and quality of care. *International Journal of Psychiatry in Medicine, 47*(4), 275–287.

Fodor, J. A. (1965). Explanations in psychology. In M. Black (Ed.), *Philosophy in America* (pp. 161–179). Ithaca, NY: Cornell University Press.

Fortin, A. H., Dwamena, F. C., Frankel, R. M., & Smith, R. C. (2012). *Smith's patient centered interviewing: An evidence-based method* (3rd ed.). New York, NY: McGraw Medical.

Getz, L., Kirkengen, A. L., & Ulvestad, E. (2011). The human biology: Saturated with experience. *Tidsskrift for Den Norske Legeforening, 131,* 683–687.

Glick, S. M. (1993). The empathic physician: Nature and nurture. In H. Spiro, M. G. M. Curnen, E. Peschel, & D. St. James (Eds.), *Empathy and the practice of medicine* (pp. 85–102). New Haven, CT: Yale University Press.

Goldenberg, M. J. (2006). On evidence and evidence-based medicine: Lessons from the philosophy of science. *Social Science & Medicine, 62,* 2621–2632.

Hampton, J. R., Harrison, M. J. G., Mitchell, J. R. A., Prichard, J. S., & Seymour, C. (1975). Relative contributions of history-taking, physical examination, and laboratory investigation to diagnosis and management of medical outpatients. *British Medical Journal, 2,* 486–489.

Haslam, N. (2006). Dehumanization: An integrative review. *Personality and Social Psychology Review, 10*(3), 252–264.

Kirkengen, A. L., Ekeland, T. J., Getz, L., Hetlevik, I., Schei, E., Ulvestad, E., & Vetlesen, A. J. (2016). Medicine's perception of reality—a split picture: Critical reflections on apparent anomalies within the biomedical theory of science. *Journal of Evaluation in Clinical Practice, 22,* 496–501.

Krupinski, E. A. (2010). Current perspectives in medical image perception. *Attention, Perception, and Psychophysics, 72*(5), 1205–1217.

Krupinski, E. A. (2016). Medical image perception: Understanding how radiologists understand images. *Journal of Medical Imaging, 3*(1), 011001-1–011001-3.

Krupinski, E. A., Chung, A., Applegate, K., DeSimone, A. K., & Tridandapani, S. (2016). Impact of patient radiographs on radiologists' visual search of chest radiographs. *Academic Radiology, 23*(8), 953–960.

Kuhn, T. S. (1996). *The structure of scientific revolutions* (3rd ed.). Chicago, IL: Chicago University Press.

Kuhn, T. S. (1998). The function of dogma in scientific research. In J. A. Kourany (Ed.), *Scientific knowledge: Basic issues in the philosophy of science* (2nd ed., pp. 301–315). Belmont, CA: Wadsworth.

Lebowitz, M. S., & Ahn, W. (2014). Effects of biological explanations for mental disorders on clinicians' empathy. *Proceedings of the National Academy of Sciences of the United States of America, 111,* 17786–17790.

Lebowitz, M. S., Ahn, W., & Oltman, K. (2015). Sometimes more competent, but always less warm: Perceptions of biologically oriented mental-health clinicians. *International Journal of Social Psychiatry, 61*(7), 668–676.

Leonidas, J. C. (2007). Please wait until I finish. *Radiology, 242*(1), 317.

Levinson, W., Gorawara-Bhat, R., & Lamb, J. (2000). A study of patient clues and physician responses in primary care and surgical settings. *Journal of the American Medical Association, 284,* 1021–1027.

Montgomery, K. (2006). *How doctors think: Clinical judgment and the practice of medicine.* New York, NY: Oxford University Press.

Myers, D. G. (1987). *Social psychology* (2nd ed.). New York, NY: McGraw-Hill.

Myers, D. G., & Jeeves, M. A. (1987). *Psychology through the eyes of faith.* San Francisco, CA: Harper & Row.

Peterson, M. C., Holbrook, J. H., Hales, D. V., Smith, N. L., & Staker, L. V. (1992). Contributions of the history, physical examination, and laboratory investigation in making medical diagnoses. *Western Journal of Medicine, 156,* 163–165.

Roshan, M., & Rao, A. P. (2000). A study on relative contributions of the history, physical examination and investigations in making medical diagnosis. *Journal of the Association of Physicians in India, 48*(8), 771–775.

Ryan, J., Khanda, G., Hibbert, R., Duigenan, S., Tunis, A., Fasih, N., ... Sheikh, A. (2015). Is a picture worth a thousand words? The effect of viewing patient photographs on radiologist interpretation of CT studies. *Journal of the American College of Radiology, 12*(1), 104–107.

Rychlak, J. F. (1985). *A philosophy of science for personality theory* (2nd ed.). Malabar, FL: Krieger.

Schoen, E. L. (1985). *Religious explanations: A model from the sciences.* Durham, NC: Duke University Press.

Smith, R. C. (2002). *Patient-centered interviewing: An evidence-based method* (2nd ed.). Philadelphia, PA: Lippincott Williams & Wilkins.

Stewart, M., Brown, J. B., Weston, W. W., McWhinney, I. R., McWilliam, C. L., & Freeman, T. R. (2003). *Patient-centered medicine: Transforming the clinical method* (2nd ed.). Abingdon, UK: Radcliffe Medical Press.

Suls, J., Krantz, D. S., & Williams, G. C. (2013). Three strategies for bridging different levels of analysis and embracing the biopsychosocial model. *Health Psychology, 32*(5), 597–601.

Tridandapani, S., Ramamurthy, S., Galgano, S. J., & Provenzale, J. M. (2013). Increasing rate of detection of wrong-patient radiographs: Use of photographs obtained at time of radiography. *American Journal of Roentgenology, 200,* W345–W352.

Vachon, D. O., & Agresti, A. A. (1992). A training proposal to help mental health professionals clarify and manage implicit values in the counseling process. *Professional Psychology: Research and Practice, 23*(6), 509–514.

"Saviors, Martyrs, and Wolves in Helper's Clothing."

"If you lack self-awareness you can't change. Why should you? As far as you're concerned you're doing everything right."
—Jim Whitt

Chapter Sections:

- Introduction
- The Varieties of Motivations in Helping Professionals
- Attachment History and Helping Styles
- Dysfunctional Helping and Attachment History
- What to Do with the Issues of Your Own Attachment History
- Malignant Motivations Underlying Helping Behavior: "The Wolf in Clinician's Clothing"
- Pathological Altruism
- Pathological Certitude
- Codependency
- The Pathology of Emotionally Disconnected Helping or Not Helping at All
- Fears of Compassion
- Money and Compassion in the Helping Professions
- Conclusion

CHAPTER 8

Healthy and Dysfunctional Types of Helping

Questions to consider before reading this chapter:

1. How do you know when a clinician's helping style is healthy or dysfunctional?
2. How does a clinician's attachment history affect his or her way of working with patients?
3. How does money affect the clinician's compassion mindset?
4. What have you noticed in your own or another clinician's helping style that impresses you as being healthy and balanced or worries you as being problematic?

INTRODUCTION

Your motivation is what sustains you in the hard times and focuses you in the good times. What your motive is relates to what is going to fulfill you or discourage you in your practice. When things are going well, our motivations can fade to the background. But when things are not going well, we ask ourselves why are we doing this and why we should keep doing it. If the motivation is not very deep, you cannot expect it to carry you in the hard times. So you either have to revisit and rework your motivation or change your work. The main argument of this book is that a compassionate motivation is what is most likely to sustain you, and taking care of the positive aspects of this motivation is one of the most important practices you need to have. At the same time, it is important that we engage in self-awareness practice to become aware of and manage any dysfunctional aspects that may be present in how we do our work.

A story about why you would want to work with people in pain all day

"Why do you want to work with people in pain all day?" That was the question someone asked one of our interns about why he had chosen his particular helping profession. He was taken aback by the question because the motivation for helping work is not usually put so crassly. We are used to the more noble question, "Why do you want to help people, become a doctor, etc.?" When it is put in terms of why do you want to work with people with burn injuries, addictions, bunions, anxiety, heart attacks, and tumors, it sounds different. I imagine the intern thought, "Wow, when he puts it that way, it sounds kind of sick—what is it in me that is attracted to and somehow comfortable with this type of work?"

Why on earth would you put yourself on this quest?

The journey to becoming a physician as well as many other helping professions requires incredible drive and motivation. To achieve this goal, individuals sacrifice other endeavors, delay many of their other life goals, willingly endure endless hours of study and work, and put themselves through incredible stress. While there are many ways to help human beings, helping professions, especially the medical ones, attract very driven people who are willing to compete vigorously to achieve this professional status. Focusing on medicine, being a physician meets the desires for prestige, financial reward, sense of control and mastery over nature, and a desire to help others. Especially in the application process, many will try to argue that altruism is the primary motivation, a selfless desire to use one's talents and emotional energy for the welfare of others. But psychologically we know that when we are in the presence of Herculean efforts to achieve something, that is an indication that an intense and, in large part, unconscious motivational machinery has been constellated by this goal of becoming a doctor (or whatever your profession may be). This is not only true of these helping professions, but also of any profession that offers so many rewards, such as high prestige, economic reward, power, mastery,

competence, and a sense of meaning. Whether it is becoming a fighter pilot, a firefighter, a politician, a minister, or a CEO, attaining these goals requires tremendous psychological machinery to be engaged. Bottom line—these are not easy; why on earth would you put yourself through this?

Psychological factors are involved if we choose our specialty freely

On one hand, this may sound cynical and ignoble, especially when we put medicine and other helping professions on the proverbial pedestal, but it is not meant to be. Nature uses what it has to survive and thrive. As I have described in this book, we humans are built for compassion. We are designed for interdependency and are most fulfilled when we care for each other as humans. But when you choose a particular helping profession, there is an added dynamic in play. Why colons, hearts, knees, brains, feet, kidneys, or eyes? We make fun of each other's specialties and have all kinds of jokes about our colleagues' choices of helping work. While good in moderation, the jokes and jabs can work against us because making fun of or deriding another's helping work can discourage others from doing it. This is not a good thing, because we need all the different specialties. (We are witnessing the effects of this not-always-playful bullying with the tremendous shortage of certain specialties these days.) Whether it is surgery, primary care, therapy, or other health care interventions, wanting to work intensely with people who are suffering from various illnesses and problems is not for everyone. Each of us feeling passionate about a particular health problem is very important, and it takes a complex set of psychological factors to create the motivation for a particular work.

How clinicians stop reflecting on their motivation as their career unfolds

Motivation to choose a clinical profession is mostly discussed at the beginning of a person's career, especially in the application period. In fact, it is asked so often that applicants become fatigued by their own answers and apologize for sounding rote or cliché before even answering the question. But as the training and application to internship or residency is done, the open discussion of motivation dramatically decreases. It is as if it is no longer considered as important and also as if it remains the same from what your reasons for entering the profession were at the beginning. The reality is, however, that the motivation will grow and evolve (or wither and devolve) over the course of a career. Most importantly, what your motivation is and how you take care of that motivation will be major factors in how you survive, thrive, or burn out in this profession.

Your career satisfaction or fulfillment is connected to your motivation

Your sense of satisfaction or fulfillment is tied to what your motivation is. It is possible you have a complex set of motivations, which determine what will satisfy that set of motivations. But to keep it simple, let us imagine you have just a single motivation. If I am motivated to help other people because I want to "fix" people but I work with people who have chronic, progressively deteriorating medical conditions, I will not be very happy doing palliative care unless I redefine what "fix" means. If I want to practice medicine in order to become wealthy and I end up in a specialty, location, or era in which I will not be able to accrue the wealth I hoped for, that will affect how good I feel doing that work. What you want in your work affects what will please you or discourage you in that work.

Situations in which motivation is not aligned with choice of specialty

What complicates this dynamic is that clinicians may pick specialties or work situations based on lifestyle considerations such as monetary compensation, call coverage, work schedule, ability to take time off, and so on. It is possible that a clinician picks a specialty or work situation that is not aligned with one's deeper clinical motivation. On one hand, the lifestyle consideration is very important to taking care of oneself. On the other hand, there are risks if the type of work does not provide the compassion satisfaction that comes with choosing maybe another specialty with different lifestyle characteristics. Furthermore, clinicians may be blocked from pursuing certain specialties because of very limited available slots, intense competition, financial needs, personal circumstances, and so on. In such cases, it is critical that the clinician enter a personal reflection process to find a specialty or a way of doing a specialty he or she is "stuck with" that activates the clinician compassion mindset process.

Motivations to do clinical work evolve

Motivations typically need to grow and deepen from where they begin. I may enter health professions training with a global motivation to help people without much sense of what type of pain or suffering to which I am interested in devoting my life. But as you go through the first years and do your clinical rotations, it becomes clearer in what way you want to help people and what you are capable of doing. There is usually an interplay between what you imagine you would like to do and finding out if you have the ability to do it and whether you will get the opportunity to do it. Most students do not know their specialty at the beginning of their training, but it unfolds as time goes on. The motivation can become refined like gold tested in fire (e.g., you discover that you are able to help people with a technique you did not even know existed at the beginning of medical school), or it can completely change and you realize you do not really like a particular profession. Being in touch with what that motivation is becomes more critical as time goes on.

How initial idealistic motivations can become displaced

A common dynamic is that the initial desire to be helpful to patients gives way to just wanting to survive as time goes on. Grueling training, scut work, being in debt, and not seeing your loved ones (or being able to have loved ones) can hammer at this initial desire to the point that it no longer has as much positive power. Or perhaps that motivation to respond to suffering seems less meaningful now as everyone around you seems less motivated by it, or your idealistic motivation to help others just gets you more work and more hassle. Your work becomes the living example of the proverb "No good deed goes unpunished." Eventually, the initial motivation takes a figurative backseat to some other motivation. Then you pick your specialty based on how well it will give you sane hours, the money you need or expect, and the lifestyle you want. This can take care of those needs, but if the motivation to help others has been left

too far behind, then we have a problem when it comes to what will fulfill you in this profession.

Internal motivations to help others

Are you externally or internally motivated? Does your desire to help others come from what is gained externally or from internal sources? Internal motivations are not necessarily altruistic. As I notice suffering in another person, my motivation influences what happens next. I can be motivated to protect myself from that distress and withdraw from it, or I can be motivated to respond to it for the sake of the other. Compassionate caring would be an example of an altruistic internal motivation. The very desire and movement to respond to suffering is not done for reward or gain. When a person is motivated from a desire to relieve others from suffering, this organizes and directs their cognitive and emotional resources toward some response to the other's suffering. If I am motivated to protect myself, that intention organizes my cognitive and emotional resources to withdraw or distance myself. If the response to the other's suffering is motivated by a desire to relieve my own distress, we would not call this compassionate caring or altruistic, because it is focused on oneself, not the needs of the other.

External motivations for helping and their risks

Being externally motivated means that you focus on external events or things to keep you going. The common examples would be things like money or prestige. As I will discuss later, these external motivators can undercut or supersede a compassionate motivation. But there are other, less obvious external events that can also impair a compassionate motivation. If I become dependent on the success of my efforts to relieve another person's suffering, this can create problems. In other words, if my attempts to relieve the suffering of another person do not result in actually relieving that suffering, I can be tempted to think that my efforts were in vain and I should not have bothered to try. For example, maybe I work hard to help alcoholics stop drinking or drug addicts stop using, but very few of them actually stop. Because my compassionate caring efforts meet with little success, I can understandably become discouraged and stop trying to help them. But this would be an example of when I need an external event to occur (change in an addict) in order for me to want to keep going. I rely completely on success to sustain my compassionate motivation. This is very confusing to most American or Western minds because we easily slide from the "attempt to relieve the suffering" to the "expectation that we can relieve the suffering." Because of our scientific advances, there are many more ways to relieve suffering than ever before in human history. But with that has come the irrational cognitive belief that because we *can* relieve suffering fairly often, we *should* be able to relieve suffering all the time. (And even if we do not make that error, our patients can have the expectation that we should be able to relieve suffering all the time.) Our health care ancestors would not make this error, because they met with failure more often than we do. They did not expect to be able to relieve suffering all the time, but that did not mean they would have stopped trying. Our own successes can confuse us when we are not able to relieve or conquer some problem. Armed with evidence-based medicine and the tracking of medical outcomes, our focus can become whether we succeeded or failed.

Compassionate caring focuses on doing the best one can to alleviate suffering

Clinicians who have been in practice for some time realize that all they have control of is doing the best they can in every situation; fervent and passionate attempts cannot be dependent on whether the suffering is actually relieved. Someone then says, "Well, you have to have some success, otherwise you would not want to keep trying or it is a waste of time!" Compassionate caring deeply desires success, but it is motivated to continue trying to respond to suffering even when it meets with failure. This is the tricky ground. What do you need to do to keep this compassionate caring going in the absence of successes and patient appreciation? It requires understanding what a compassionate attitude truly is, training ourselves to attain this in ourselves, and then doing what needs to be done to maintain this compassionate mind.

Defining what is in your control and being realistic about the outcomes

Perhaps phrasing a different way will make this more palatable and less daunting. Another way to say this is that we have to be realistic about outcomes, and we need to make sure what our definitions of what constitutes "success" are. For example, I do not have control over whether my patient will follow my recommendations or adhere to a treatment regimen. I should therefore not stake my professional self-efficacy on whether a particular patient follows my advice. Depending on your type of practice, you may only see a patient for 15 minutes every so often. On one hand, we have to be realistic enough not to expect that our rapid advice in brief visits can surmount all the negative health behavior advertising and culture along with dysfunctional family systems and incredible stresses our patients have. On the other hand, what I do have control over is whether I tried to make an emotional connection with this patient and used the best health behavior change skills that I should have as a clinician of that specialty. Have I done the best that can be done in terms of my caring investment and skills? Indirectly, your patient rates of adherence will be higher than if you did not use your caring investment in this patient and your skills. But you want to be careful in staking your professional self-esteem on what those rates are if you did the best that you could and the outcome still turned out badly.

THE VARIETIES OF MOTIVATIONS IN HELPING PROFESSIONALS

The motivation of altruism

People have a variety of motivations to help others. Rather than being purely one motivation or another, helper motivations are more likely combinations of the following. The first is the altruistic motivation. Human beings have an empathic sensibility, and with that empathic perception comes concern for other human beings in some type of suffering. Evolutionary scientists have argued that the capacity for empathy and altruism in human beings were qualities that increased their survivability. In the altruistic motivation, the helper is somehow moved by the perception of human suffering and desires to respond to it in a way to relieve this suffering. Batson (2011) defines altruism as "a motivational state with the ultimate goal of increasing another's welfare" (p. 20). This is contrasted with egoism, which is "a motivational

state with the ultimate goal of increasing one's own welfare" (Batson, 2011, p. 20).

Three possible self-benefits of empathy-induced helping and the existence of true altruism

A long debate in the study of altruism is whether empathic concern for a person in need produces an altruistic motivation to respond to that need, as opposed to the possibility that empathically induced helping is not altruistic but self-serving in some way. That is, the claim is that helping always has a selfish component to it, and therefore there is no such thing as true altruism. Indeed, empathy-induced helping can be rooted in benefiting oneself. Batson (2010) notes three possible self-benefits of empathy-induced helping. The first is *aversive-arousal reduction*. Here the motivation to help another person is to reduce the helper's own distress that arises in witnessing someone else's distress. The helper helps the person suffering so that the helper him- or herself can feel better. Second is *punishment avoidance*. In this type of helping, the helper helps in order to avoid "empathy-specific material, social, and self-rewards" (Batson, 2010, p. 20). In other words, the helper helps another person in order not to feel guilty or ashamed about not helping. Third, *reward seeking* is the kind of helping that is done in order to gain "empathy-specific material, social, and self-rewards" (Batson, 2010, p. 20). Helping is done in this case to obtain some reward such as money, admiration, or prestige. Researchers have carefully examined whether empathy leads to altruistic motivation or to a self-benefiting or egoistic motivation for the helping. After more than 30 experiments testing the empathy–altruism hypothesis, there is now significant evidence that empathy-induced altruism does indeed exist (Batson, 2010).

Other motivations may be mixed in with the altruistic motivation

While we now have evidence that altruism can truly exist and that this is possible in ourselves, the reality is that there may be a variety of motivations operating underneath our helping behavior. A specific altruistic behavior can actually be the result of quite different mixtures of motivations. Burton (2012) gives an example:

> A combination of fear of humiliation, a rigid upbringing that requires strict adherence to religious precepts, and a desire not to stand out as different, might produce the same "altruistic" behavior as someone with an empathic "pureness of generosity" that approaches saintliness. (p. 132)

Browne (2003) discusses how many different motivations can enter into a health care professional's (HCP) mental state when working with residents in long-term care facilities and rehab hospitals. He summarizes his view beginning by referring to Jean-Jacques Rousseau.

> Rousseau ... argued that for citizens to fulfill their function as citizens they must aim at the general good and scrupulously exclude influences that may get in the way of that aim. HCPs have to do something similar to act as professionals. HCPs sometimes dislike their colleagues, jobs, and those under their care; or fear litigation and the disapproval of others. They also often see that they can make their lives easier by refusing to respond to the requests for help from residents. Who in healthcare has not seen decisions driven by these factors to the cost of the resident? Following Rousseau, HCPs must put all this aside. Citizens must enter the voting booth with a firm commitment to the good of the public; HCPs must enter team deliberations with a

> firm commitment to the good of the patient. (Browne, 2003, p. 90)

In short, it is very important as health care professionals that we are aware of how a number of motivations, both conscious and unconscious, may be driving our helping work. It is normal to have a variety of motivations as human beings. The critical task is that we regularly make ourselves aware of which motivation is dominating what we do.

Helping others based on duty

Besides altruism, the motivation to help others can be based on duty. Rather than focusing on the empathic experience of another's suffering, helping out of duty focuses on what should be done when another person is suffering. It is often based on the conception of the fundamental dignity of human beings. That is, human beings are considered worthy of help in and of themselves. No matter if that suffering person is poor, alienated from society, or unconscious; this approach argues that human beings should be helped because human beings by definition should be treated in a dignified manner. This could be based on a religious principle that humans are made in the image of God and therefore should be treated in a certain way, or it could be based on a more humanistic philosophy of the fundamental worth of human beings.

Helping motivated by external self-interests

The motivation to help can be based on some type of self-interest. In this motivation, we help others because in some way we benefit from helping them. In reality, some type of self-interest is almost always involved no matter what the main motivation for helping is. But if this motivation is dominant, the reason the helper helps someone is that he or she gains from it or gets some personal need satisfied from helping others. This is distinct from the sense of satisfaction one gets from helping others that is a by-product of compassionate caring (called compassion satisfaction). With compassion satisfaction, the clinician is not helping in order to have a sense of self-satisfaction but to relieve suffering in another person, which incidentally makes one feel a sense of fulfillment. Thus, one type of self-interest is one in which you are helping *in order to feel good about yourself* or so that others will have a higher opinion of you. Another type of self-interest is when your primary motivation is being paid for your helping. The more people you help, the more you get paid. You fix people's cars, do surgery on people's bodies, or provide psychotherapy as a way to make a living. Helping is simply your job. If this is the principal motivation, it does not necessarily mean that the outcome of helping is negative; but as I will argue later, it does limit the total effect of the helping and, paradoxically, limits the potential benefits to you in the life of being a clinician.

Helping motivated by internal self-interests

The motive to help can be one of self-interest or taking care of one's own feelings or inadequacies. For example, when people witness suffering, those primarily motivated by this type of self-interest may become very distressed at what they see happening. Their desire to help comes from taking care of their own distressed feelings. While some argue that altruism has some element of this, the motivation to take care of one's own distress in witnessing suffering is actually quite different.

In altruism, one might be emotionally moved to respond, but the focus is on helping the other person. In helping out of the personal need to take care of one's own feelings, the focus is on one's own well-being, not the person who is helped. Related personal needs can be motives such as helping others as a way to deal with low self-esteem or personal inadequacy on the part of the helper. In this case, helping others allows the helper to feel better about him- or herself primarily; the helping of others is secondary. Helping others can also be a way to protect oneself or manipulate others in the "strings-attached helper." "Being helpful" can be a way to gain emotional currency with others. When you help someone, it might be a way of making a person feel indebted to you; and if they feel indebted to you, they might give you favors as well, or at least not harm you. It also can be a way of manipulating others. "I did all this for you, and now all I'm asking is that you do this for me." Helping can also be a response to guilt. The "guilty helper" seeks to help others as a way to undo past wrongs, whether realistic or not. Related to this is the "compulsive helper" who does not exactly know why he or she helps but cannot refrain from doing so. If the individual does not help others, he or she does not feel quite right. The thought "I ought to be helping" dominates the act of helping, not so much for the satisfaction of helping as for avoiding the discomfort of not doing something for others. Finally, some people are motivated to help others as a way to neglect or put down themselves. The "masochistic helper" is one who is primarily motivated to help others not so much to be helpful to them as to confirm or accentuate their own perceived worthlessness. These are individuals who tend to neglect their own needs in order to help others, eventually creating more suffering for themselves.

Helping motivated by power, status, and narcissism

Another type of self-interest is one based on helping others out of some personal need such as power or status, or a compulsive need to help others. In this motivation, one's desire to help others comes from responding to one's own needs. Some people help others primarily out of a need to dominate others or to gain status in the community, such as in the "power-hungry helper" and the "narcissistic helper." Helping is a means to collect power over others for power-hungry helpers and reinforce their view of themselves as invincible and above the rest of weak humanity. The narcissistic helper is motivated to help others because of how it makes him or her seem greater in other people's view. A related dynamic is found in the "pseudo-heroic helper," whose interest is not so much power or narcissism as the need to be seen as a great rescuer.

Helping that originates from severe psychopathology within the clinician

In its worst scenarios, the personal need primarily driving the helping can be rooted in severe psychopathology that is sadistic or sexual in nature, such as in the "sadistic helper" and the "predatory helper." The desire to help others is actually a cover for these motives or an attempt to deal with the clinician's own inner turmoil. A prime example of the sadistic helper is the parent who has Munchausen by proxy syndrome (also called factitious disorder by proxy) who gets the personal need of inflicting suffering and keeping his or her child in the sick role. The "predatory helper" uses the trappings of a helping profession to seek out his or her needs,

whether sexual or otherwise. These helpers are actually quite antisocial in nature. They may be able to help others quite well, but their helping is in fact a ruse to satisfy their own distorted needs for love, sex, or companionship that originate in unresolved pathology usually rooted in childhood. But they are never satisfied with only one victim; they instead are continually looking for the next desirable object to prey upon. The "delusional helper" is motivated to help others out of a psychotic belief that he or she is some sort of messiah or on some mission that, while noble and heroic, is actually quite disconnected from the well-being of others. Examples of the delusional helper include medical staff who kill patients secretly and without the consent of the patients. Later in this chapter, I will discuss this further with the concept of pathological altruism (Oakley, Knafo, Madhavan, & Wilson, 2012). Before discussing pathological altruism, however, let us discuss how any type of helping that we do is influenced by our attachment history.

ATTACHMENT HISTORY AND HELPING STYLES

Helping involves not only what is being done but how it is being done for the patient

Helping is a complex process, and many things can go wrong. Certainly, the task at hand shapes the form of the helping to a large extent. Someone is lost, and helping the person means giving him or her directions. Someone is distressed and needs to talk about a problem in order to calm down and get perspective on what to do. A person has a well-defined tumor, and the helping task involves a surgeon to remove it. But the helping task also includes the way that helping task is done. When a person asks someone for advice for a particular problem (e.g., financial advice), the person giving the advice might do this in an abrupt and impatient manner and not check to see if the person being helped understands. Or the helper might give the advice in a condescending manner and subtly shame the person being helped for not knowing better. In a more positive manner, a person giving advice might have an attitude of genuine concern for the person being helped and offer advice as he or she would to a good friend who needs help. He or she would be supportive and understanding of how a particular problem could arise and offer advice in a way that is encouraging to the person being helped.

Clinicians can be described by their helping style over time

Over time, the way a person tends to help others will have a pattern or follow a particular helping style. People who encounter a particular helper a number of times will end up being able to describe that helper's style in terms of how the helper came across and how the helper's manner made them feel. Furthermore, the reason a helper decides to help enters the process. He or she has a motive or purpose in deciding to help another, and so motives are intertwined with the helper's psychology. Helpers can have simple reasons to agree to help someone, and their reasons can be complex. Reasons for helping can be multi-layered, including conscious and unconscious reasons for helping others and helping them in a certain manner or style.

How you were cared for influences how you care for others

It is hard to give what you did not get. If you are dedicating your life to caring for others but you did not receive good caring in your own life, you will encounter internal tensions in trying to provide good caring to others. Put another way, what you think is important in caring for others and how you think that should be done is learned from your own experience of being cared for, especially when you were a child. How you were cared for influences how you care for others later on.

Examples of two different upbringings for clinicians

Contrast the following two backgrounds. In one, you were given what you needed in your upbringing in terms of basic needs. But your parents considered your needs a nuisance or interruption for them and what they wanted to do. Whenever you had some need, you were made to feel badly about that need. If you needed emotional support, this need was shamed, and you were told that you should not feel certain ways and should be able to handle your feelings yourself. You were given help but always with the message that something was wrong with you when you needed to depend on your parents. In the second example, you are likewise given what you needed for your basic needs, and this was done in such a way that you felt your parents really did want to care for you and that caring for you was one of the most important things they could do. When you had some need, they responded without making you feel badly about that. If you needed emotional support, you could count on your parents to be available and to provide a safe, accepting place to work out your difficulty. You were supported and guided in your problems. You learned that challenging things often happen in life, and you were taught how to navigate these as a way to prepare you for eventually handling these issues on your own.

How we experienced being helped in our childhood creates the script for how we care for others as adults

How do you think an upbringing in each of these cases would affect you as an adult in terms of how you relate to others and the manner in which you help them? How would you view and respond to the needs and issues of other people who temporarily need to rely on you? What do you think would be the emotional tone for you to help someone, given each of those backgrounds? If you have children, would you give them an upbringing the same as what you received? We are taught how to care for others largely influenced by what our experience was in receiving care. In a very real way, we internalize the pattern of how we were cared for, and this becomes the script we have for how we should think, feel, and behave in giving or receiving care later on. If we are receiving care, we expect that it will go a certain way, and we think and feel accordingly. If I was made to feel badly about having needs, I might want to avoid getting help in the future. If I was made to feel that needing others is part of life and was given what I needed in a safe and supportive way, I would tend to have that same attitude when I need help later on.

Humans have biological mechanisms both to signal need and to perceive another's need

Human beings—who are so vulnerable and helpless, especially in infancy—need a lot of care to help them survive and thrive. From an evolutionary perspective, we have mechanisms in our biology that will lead us to be very interested in taking care of our offspring. We need the ability to perceive and attend to what the infant's needs are and to respond to those accordingly. If we happen to be the infant, we need mechanisms in which we would attach to our caregivers and be able to signal what our needs are. These mechanisms for giving and receiving care as parent and child become the foundation for all other types of giving and receiving care in our lives. These mechanisms become recruited for how we select and relate to our romantic partners, how we function cooperatively (hopefully) in our communities, and how we treat others when they are in distress or suffering. It is these mechanisms that undergird how we help each other in health care.

Definition of attachment style

With the focus on problem solving and the general business of health care practice, it would seem to be a stretch to say that my early attachment history would affect how I perceive patients and how I react to their requests for help. But there is a large amount of evidence that has documented that this is true (Salmon & Young, 2009). The innate parameters of the attachment style are "gradually shaped and altered by social experiences with attachment figures, resulting eventually in fairly stable individual differences in *attachment style*—a systematic pattern of relational expectations, emotions, and behaviors that result from a particular attachment history" (Mikulincer, Shaver, Gillath, & Nitzberg, 2005, pp. 817–818).

Further explanation of attachment style as a representational model

Helping generally involves one person who has an ability or a resource and another person who is in need of that skill or resource. The helper is in a position of power, and the helpee in a position of vulnerability or suffering in some way. This is caregiving at its most basic level and is the story of every human being. It is impossible for humans to raise themselves. At birth and in early childhood, humans are completely dependent on parents or other caregivers to help them survive. As humans grow, they become interdependent. It is impossible not to need someone else at some point. A single human life contains millions of helping episodes. At one moment, you are the helper. At the next moment, you are the one in need of help. Whenever someone helps another person in a certain manner, the decision to help and the way that help is done taps into the psychological and sociological history of that person. Everything from early childhood experiences of caregiving by his or her parents to experiences in the community and school to the person's current situation influences that decision to help and the way that helping is done. Each of us carries all of these experiences together, and these influence how we view ourselves and others. As Bowlby (2005a) succinctly puts it, "Each of us is apt to do unto others as we *have been* done by. The bullying adult is the bullied child grown bigger" (p.166). Bowlby and attachment theorists call it a *"representational model."* Bowlby explained this as an internalized and unconscious representation of one's experience with a significant attachment figure. The overall style of those interactions with that attachment figure are internalized and influence the person's later interactions with others. As Bowlby (2005a) explains:

> Briefly put, attachment behaviour is conceived as any form of behaviour that results in a person attaining or retaining proximity to some other differentiated and preferred individual, who is usually conceived as stronger and/or wiser. Whilst especially evident during early childhood, attachment behaviour is held to characterize human beings from the cradle to the grave. It includes crying and calling, which elicit care, following and clinging, and also strong protest should a child be left alone or with strangers. With age the frequency and the intensity with which such behaviour is exhibited diminish steadily. Nevertheless, all these forms of behaviour persist as an important part of man's behavioral equipment. In adults they are especially evident when a person is distressed, ill, or afraid. The particular patterns of attachment behaviour shown by an individual turn partly on his [her] present age, sex, and circumstances and partly on the experiences he has had with attachment figures earlier in his [her] life. (p. 154; bracketed text added for nonsexist language)

The interplay between the attachment behavioral system and the caregiving behavioral system

For human beings to have succeeded and to continue succeeding as a species, two biologically evolved innate behavioral systems work together: an *attachment behavioral system*, in which the infant/child has a number of behaviors to ensure attaching to the parent and signaling to the parent when he or she is in need or distress; and a *caregiving behavioral system*, in which the parent responds to the need of the dependent infant/child. That attachment behavioral system is activated by any perceived threat that makes the infant/child seek proximity to the caregiver for protection. These proximity-seeking behaviors include "crying and calling, which elicit care, following and clinging, and also strong protest should a child be left alone or with strangers" (Bowlby, 1977, pp. 203). These signals of need activate caregiving in the parent to respond positively to the distress, need, or suffering of the infant/child and to promote the growth and development of the infant/child. When the caregiver responds optimally, the caregiver becomes the "secure base" that provides safety, support, and reduction of distress. The infant/child experiences this as relief and security, and the helping episode by the caregiver becomes a positive mental representation of the interaction between signaling a need and having a positive response. Repeated experiences of caregiving string together to become a representational model or an attachment working model of one's self in relation to the caregiver. Over the course of infancy, childhood, and adolescence, these themes of internalized experience become an attachment style, "a systematic pattern of relational expectations, emotions, and behaviors conceptualized as residues of particular kinds of attachment history" (Gillath, Shaver, & Mikulincer, 2005, p. 123).

How attachment experiences affect the child

When there are positive experiences of the attachment figures being available and responsive, the infant/child gains a sense of security and connectedness and comes to feel more confident in seeking the support of others to respond to distress. He or she is able to explore the world more confidently and to form warm, positive relationships with others. If the attachment figure is not available and reliable, the infant/child does not gain a sense of security. If the attachment figure is unpredictable, insensitive, frightening, cold, or rejecting, the infant/child comes to expect that he or she cannot count on others for comfort and support and has to figure out other ways of managing this distress over time (a secondary attachment strategy). This

might be done by developing attachment anxiety (constant concern or worry that others will not be available if needed, excessively demanding attention) or by developing attachment avoidance (distrusting that others can be reliable, withdrawing and keeping emotional distance from others, excessive striving for self-sufficiency and self-protective independence) (Gillath et al. 2005; Fraley & Shaver, 2000).

Categorizing attachment styles

There are a number of categorization systems of attachment styles building on the work of Bowlby (2005a, 2005b) and Ainsworth, Blehar, Waters, and Wall (1978). Bartholomew (1990) developed a four-category scheme that is widely used in this research. It is built on the fact that there are two dimensions to attachment styles; one dimension is that based on their attachment experiences, people come to have a positive or negative view of others. In relation to those experiences, people internalize either a positive or a negative view of themselves (see figure 8.1).

Brief descriptions of the four attachment styles

The *secure person* develops an attachment style that has a positive view of oneself and of others. Based on their positive experiences of relying on others, such individuals tend to be comfortable with closeness in relationships, and they have internalized a sense of self-worth. The *preoccupied attachment style* is one which the person has a positive view of the other but a negative view of him- or herself. Such individuals are anxiously attached to others, believing that they can get safety and security if they can get others to respond the way they hope. They are very dependent on gaining other people's acceptance and validation. In the *fearful attachment style*, the person views him- or herself and others in a negative way. Because such individuals have had negative experiences earlier in their lives, they expect to be rejected or abandoned. They therefore avoid intimacy and connection with others out of this fear, even though they desire intimacy. The *dismissing attachment style* is one in which the person has a negative view of others but a positive view of him- or herself. Such individuals have experienced being failed by others in their early upbringings and as a result avoid closeness with others. As a defense, they deny the need to have close relationships, and they maintain a positive sense of self-worth by achieving this avoidance of close relationships (Bartholomew & Shaver, 1998).

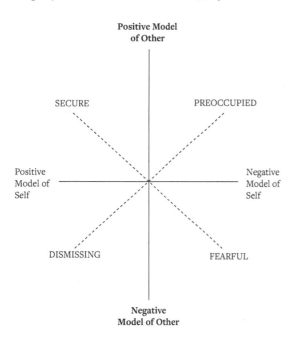

FIGURE 8.1 Two-dimensional four-category model of adult attachment (Bartholomew, 1990).

Other resources that are available on this topic

A great deal of research has been conducted on the way these attachment styles affect future romantic relationships, friendships, parenting, health care utilization, and psychopathology (Cassidy & Shaver, 1999; Hunter & Maunder, 2016; Mikulincer & Shaver, 2016). Most clinicians who read the above descriptions will immediately be reminded of patients and the way they behave, as discussed in chapter 6. The focus here is to describe how a clinician with a particular attachment style tends to work with patients.

Characteristics of secure caregivers

Secure caregivers in all forms (not just clinicians) have internalized positive models of good caregiving and are able to pull from this to respond to others in need. They are comfortable with being close to others and have an interdependent view of relationships. They can see others as being potential sources of comfort and support and also that others are deserving of the sense of security, comfort, and support. They tend to be more motivated to be compassionate to others who are suffering or in need and able to provide care for them. They are able to handle the temporary dependence and distress of a person in need and are comfortable with the emotional closeness that can occur in such interactions. They have a greater capacity to help more people than insecure caregivers have. Because of their sense of security in their own lives, they are able to focus on another person's needs and not see that as a threat to themselves. They tend to have a sense of confidence and control in being able to respond effectively to the distress of another person and manage their own distress and related emotions (Gillath et al., 2005).

Insecurely attached caregivers

Insecurely attached caregivers tend to feel less empathy and compassion toward distressed persons. Anxiously attached or preoccupied caregivers have part of their psychic energy consumed by their own unsatisfied attachment needs, and this diverts energy from focusing on what the person in distress needs. They tend to have poor self–other differentiation and will tend to have an increase in their own distress in response to another person's distress. It is easy for them to become emotionally overwhelmed. As a result of their own internal distress, they can also become overinvolved and intrusive in their caregiving because they experience the distress more intensely, since it is combined with their own distress and their own psychological issues. Even though they can appear very activated and sympathetic in helping a suffering person, their seemingly compassionate responses tend not to be effective because they are responding to their own distress more than to the actual needs of the suffering person (Gillath et al., 2005).

Avoidant caregivers

Avoidant caregivers (e.g., the dismissing type) tend to have a negative view of others and to be uncomfortable with closeness, thus they will not be as responsive to the suffering of another person and will not be as compassionate or altruistic. Because they have not experienced emotional relief and warmth from others when distressed, they are less likely to help others. Consequently, they engage in deactivating strategies in which they emotionally detach from the suffering of others. Avoidant caregivers often have a deep-seated sense of weakness and vulnerability from that lack of reliable responsiveness to their own suffering. When they encounter others who are suffering, it can remind them of their own

past suffering, and they tend to manage this by distancing themselves emotionally from the suffering of others and suppressing the reminders of their own vulnerability. To feel less vulnerable, they defend themselves psychologically by detaching emotionally, adopt an attitude of disdainful pity for the suffering person, or have an air of condescension and superiority to the person suffering. This psychological defense can lead them to think they are immune to adversity, and they tend to blame others for their misfortune. They may have hostile attitudes in which they show contempt and even enjoyment in the bad misfortune of others (Gillath et al., 2005).

DYSFUNCTIONAL HELPING AND ATTACHMENT HISTORY

In his seminal article, "The Making and Breaking of Affectional Bonds," Bowlby (1977) makes a number of points that are useful in the discussion of healthy and dysfunctional helping. As he explains how parental caregiving in relationship to the child's attachment behavior are critically important in the mental health of the child, he states, "The roles of the care-giver are first to be available and responsive as and when wanted and, secondly, to intervene judiciously should the child or older person who is being cared for be heading for trouble" (Bowlby, 1977, p. 204). Of paramount importance is that the parents provide the child with a secure base and encourage the child to explore their world from this secure base. While this is directed toward what constitutes healthy parenting and developing, these ideas provide ways to evaluate the caregiving as we are focusing on it here in terms of helping in the helping professions. Like good parenting, it is also the case that healthy helping behavior is characterized by being "available and responsive as and when wanted." *Dysfunctional helping* would be characterized by not being available and responsive in the way in which someone in need requires or by providing help when it is not needed. Dysfunctional helping is also characterized by ways in which helpers are not "secure bases" for the people they help. That is, our job as helpers is to act in such a way that a person in need can rely on us and trust us. When we act in ways in which we are not reliable, we create additional problems for our clients and patients. Our job is to help people in the way that they need help, and so "intervening judiciously" means that we have to be very clear about what our clients and patients need and keep that distinct from our own needs. Dysfunctional helping would involve inserting our own needs into how we assess the persons in need. *Healthy helping* typically means that we intervene and provide what others need, not that we take over their lives after the helping episode is done. Dysfunctional helping would involve laying demands on a client or patient during or after the intervention is completed that have nothing to do with the person's problem.

Clinician's early affectional bond echoes later in relationships and patient care

In reflecting on healthy and dysfunctional helper styles, it is necessary to consider how one's early experiences of caregiving have contributed to those styles. Bowlby uses the term *affectional bond*, and he focuses on early caregiving experiences with parents and how these create representational models that later influence how a person behaves in adult affectional bonds such as marriage and parenting.

But the way one connects and cares for someone who needs help can also be considered an affectional bond, especially because of the emotions that are commonly stirred in helping dynamics. Therefore, it is very important that helpers become aware of their own caregiving histories because of the likelihood that personal issues may affect how care is given in a professional role. The following statements by Bowlby (2005a) are thus relevant to the helper:

> Many of the most intense emotions arise during the formation, the maintenance, the disruption, and the renewal of attachment relationships. The formation of a bond is described as falling in love, maintaining a bond as loving someone, and losing a partner as grieving over someone. Similarly, threat of loss arouses anxiety and actual loss gives rise to sorrow; whilst each of these situations is likely to arouse anger. The unchallenged maintenance of a bond as a source of joy. Because such emotions are usually a reflection of the state of a person's affectional bonds, the psychology and psychopathology of emotion is found to be in large part the psychology and psychopathology of affectional bonds. (p. 155)

Entering into a helping relationship with a person in need is a type of affectional bond. Those being helped are in the more vulnerable position or at least in a place of need. Being in need will stir their emotions, depending on their situation and their developmental history of what they have come to expect when they are in a state of need. For people in need, then, the helping interaction is most certainly a kind of affectional bond. As I argued above, being a helper also stirs some emotional tone such as caring, resentment, fear, superiority, or sympathy. It is not surprising that the way helpers help others will reflect patterns or styles that are influenced by more than the task and specific situation.

Overview of Bowlby's four dysfunctional helping styles

There are many ways in which professional and (everyday) helpers can be dysfunctional in how they relate to those they are helping. While the above ideas from Bowlby have indirect but critically important relevance for a discussion of what can make helping dysfunctional, Bowlby also describes four pathological patterns of attachment in adulthood that often appear in clinicians. They are *compulsive caregiving, compulsive self-reliance, compulsive care seeking,* and *angry withdrawal* (Bowlby, 1978; Ainsworth & Bell, 1970; West & Sheldon, 1988). I will summarize each of these and speculate on what it would mean when this pattern is manifested in a health care clinician.

Compulsive caregiving

Compulsive caregiving is an attachment pathological pattern that can create problems for a clinician who has it as well as for his or her patients and coworkers. As the terms suggests, this is a person who cannot help but help in every situation of need. In close relationships, this person sets up the relationship to be always in the giving role, never the receiving role. If this person ends up in a receiving role, he or she becomes very uncomfortable. It is compulsive because it is not freely chosen but automatic, causing anxiety if he or she does not help. This person tends to care for other people even when people in need do not want help or are not seeking help. As Bowlby (1977) puts it:

> *From early childhood, the person who develops in this way has found that the only affectional bond available is one in which he [she] must*

always be the care-giver and that the only care he [she] can ever receive is the care he [she] gives himself [herself]. (p. 207; bracketed text added for nonsexist language)

In analyzing case histories, Bowlby found compulsive caregiving occurring in individuals who had "intermittent and inadequate mothering during early childhood" that would end with total loss (we would now add the same possibility for poor fathering) and in individuals who as children were pressured to take care of a parent with physical or mental problems as well as the rest of the family. Bowlby (1980) adds:

> *In some such cases the child is made to feel that he himself [she herself] is responsible for his [her] parent's being ill and therefore has an obligation to act as caregiver. In others, whilst not held responsible for the illness, he [she] is none the less made to feel he [she] has a responsibility to care for his [her] parent.* (p. 222; bracketed text added for nonsexist language)

As these individuals grow up, they tend to seek out roles in which they continue this pattern of seeking love and approval by taking care of others to the detriment of their own needs. They place the highest priority on the needs of others, and they give care whether they have been asked or not. They tend to have feelings of self-sacrifice and martyrdom (West & Sheldon, 1988). They will tend to interpret relationships from this lens, causing communication problems and dysfunctional helping (Lapsley, Varshney, & Aalsma, 2000).

What compulsive caregiving looks like in clinicians

Clinicians who have compulsive caregiving patterns would have a number of problems in a clinical setting. They would have difficulty staying focused on what their helping task is and become easily swept away in trying to solve other problems of patients even if not requested. Some patients would welcome this kind of rescue, but others would find it intrusive, especially if it was not requested. Practicing medicine this way would be a clear pathway to emotional exhaustion and burnout. Coworkers can be irritated with this because compulsive caregivers can look like "super helpers," making other helpers feel inadequate even if they know it is compulsive, or coworkers can become irritated because compulsive caregivers take too much time with patients, do not get their work done in time, and add to the workload of others. Compulsive caregivers may tend to be inefficient, not only with time but also in the use of resources. Also, significant others of compulsive caregivers can grow weary of their loved one always helping others and neglecting them or being constantly guilt ridden for not helping both others and their loved ones.

Compulsive self-reliance

Compulsive self-reliance is the opposite of compulsive caregiving. These are helpers who insist on "keeping a stiff upper lip" and doing everything for themselves no matter what. Bowlby (1980) found that people who have compulsive self-reliance have gone through the loss of a parent in childhood and were then left to take care of themselves or are from backgrounds in which the parent was critical and unsympathetic toward a "child's natural desires for love, attention, and support" (p. 224). The expression of feelings is disparaged, with the result that the child suppresses his or her feelings and inhibits normal attachment behavior. Bowlby (1980) says that such children tend to

> grow up to be tough and hard. They may be competent and to all appearances self-reliant, and they may go through life without overt sign of breakdown. Yet they are likely difficult to live and work with, for they have little understanding either of others or of themselves and are readily aroused to smouldering jealousy and resentment. ... Even when they do not become psychiatric casualties themselves they can often be responsible for the breakdown of others—spouse, children or employees. (p. 225)

Further description of compulsive self-reliance

These are individuals who avoid seeking help and avoid closeness or affection with others. They tend to be uncomfortable with others needing them. They tend to "switch off" their attachment feelings, especially because if they let themselves have these feelings, it would stir up their own feelings of vulnerability and resentment at not having gotten their own needs met (West & Sheldon, 1988). They will tend not to trust close relationships and even mock their necessity. They are actually afraid of relying on others for fear of being failed (again) and cover this fear with an apparent disdain for needing others. They would be inclined to avoid others relying on them and any situation that might lead to rejection (Bowlby, 2005a; Lapsley et al., 2000).

What compulsive self-reliance looks like in clinicians

While seemingly at odds with being in a helping profession, compulsive self-reliance is regularly found in helping professionals. Compulsively self-reliant clinicians tend to be emotionally detached in relating to patients. They are more biomedically focused and not interested in distressed emotions of their patients. On one hand, they help their patients, but they are not very empathic, nor do they like having patients being needy with them. When a patient needs emotional support or health behavior change counseling, such clinicians tend to avoid this terrain. Their view is that they had to rely on themselves, so other people should have to rely on themselves, too. Such clinicians have an air of condescension, disgust, or avoidance with patient complaints or expressions of pain. Coworkers could become irritated because the compulsively self-reliant clinician's habitual avoidance of emotional support of patients would fall to them if they become involved in the care, leading to a feeling of being dumped on. Colleagues might think less of that clinician because compulsively self-reliant clinicians can come across as so uncaring. Furthermore, compulsively self-reliant clinicians do not tend to be very connecting or supportive with their colleagues, which can be demoralizing, especially if such a clinician is supervising other staff.

Compulsive care seeking

Compulsive care seeking is a pattern in which such persons live with constant anxiety that their attachment figures will not be available and responsive to them. These individuals often come from backgrounds in which they had an anxious attachment with their caregivers and were fearful of losing those attachment figures. This attachment style then permeates their adult relationships, in which they are always trying to find someone to make them feel secure. Any stressful situation can set off their insecurity, and they tend to seek care from their attachment figures frequently and urgently. They are focused on what problems they have and how they can receive care from others. They come across as dependent and yearn for attachment figures who could assume responsibility for major parts of their lives (West & Sheldon, 1988).

What compulsive care seeking looks like in clinicians

One would not expect to see compulsive care seeking in clinicians because patients are seeking care from them. It is hard to know how often this occurs, but it can be apparent in the early part of clinicians' careers as they transition from training to independent practice. Their faculty and other trainers become aware of a lack of confidence and a greater-than-average dependence on the clinical faculty, always needing reassurance or more support than usual. There is a kind of clinging behavior and a fearfulness of independent practice even though they spent years working toward this level. They may hide this from their patients and unsympathetic faculty, but they can experience a great deal of inner turmoil about this and seek certain people who can serve as secure bases for them. If this pattern becomes apparent to patients, the patients may become concerned with the lack of confidence and decisiveness in their clinicians.

Angry withdrawal

Finally, another pathological attachment pattern in adulthood is called *angry withdrawal*. These are individuals who, when they are in need, experience anxiety about not having attachment figures, but this is accompanied by anger. One can imagine how this pattern emerged from early childhood. The caregivers might not have been available, which caused both anxiety and anger. Or maybe the individuals tended to get their needs met more when they were angry, thus reinforcing the presence of anger with the experience of needing another person. This would carry over into adulthood and manifest in a number of ways. When their attachment figures (e.g., spouses, friends) are not available, these individuals can become both upset and angry. Even when the attachment figure responds, it can be difficult for these individuals to let go of their anger. They may feel a generalized anger toward an attachment figure in adulthood without even knowing why they have this anger. Or anger may become part of the relationship because that is what helped get their needs met when they were children. When frustrated, they tend to withdraw instead of talking about the anger directly, but their resentment is palpable (Lapsley et al., 2000; West & Sheldon, 1988).

What angry withdrawal looks like in clinicians

Clinicians with an angry withdrawal pattern are quite possible. One can certainly see it in medical students, residents, or others in training when it comes to how they react to frustration and their needs not being met. On one hand, we expect there to be many unmet needs and frustrations in training. But these individuals have an intensity that is higher than the average frustrated clinician in training. They would be people for whom working things out is always accompanied by an inordinate amount of anger, and they have difficulty self-soothing. The anger may persist far beyond the offending incident. In clinical practice, these clinicians relate in this way to whomever is in a kind of attachment figure role, such as management, hospital administration, mentors, and loved ones.

Using the knowledge of attachment styles to manage yourself, not to shame yourself

It is very important not to engage in armchair psychological analysis and judge others in a way that is unfair. Everyone has bad days, and there are intensely chaotic and difficult situations and

systems in health care that can bring out the worst in us. As Bowlby (2005a) says, "Our role is not to apportion blame but to trace causal chains with a view to breaking them or ameliorating their consequences" (pp. 175). But there are certain patterns in how we "lose it," and that becomes an invitation for us to examine what is happening in us and articulate what our dynamic is if it falls in one of these categories. The main problem is when clinicians are unconscious of these pathological patterns. Having such patterns just happens to us humans. The positive difference comes from naming and addressing these rather than being possessed by unhealthy dynamics that take over our lives. Attachment psychology is helpful because it keeps us from dealing with current circumstances using old scripts from our childhood.

WHAT TO DO WITH THE ISSUES OF YOUR OWN ATTACHMENT HISTORY

What if you have a more insecure attachment history? Are you doomed to unhealthy helping dynamics? Absolutely not. First, becoming aware of your attachment history and how it influences all relationships in your life, including your clinical ones, is the most important first step. Becoming conscious of what is unconscious will help you with the most problematic patterns. Second, there are ways to increase your internal sense of security that will enable you to function more effectively in your clinical work. While the research is young on this intervention and how it might be done for health care professionals, it is very clear that this has enormous potential. This has been used for years in helping people in psychotherapy with all types of relational problems. Health care professionals have discovered this individually for some time and sought a number of means to address how issues in their own attachment histories are negatively affecting clinical care and self-care.

Naming your primary attachment style and the one to which you regress

In my work with students, I have introduced them to the importance of the patient's attachment history in receiving care and the clinician's attachment history in providing care. In a training setting with very achievement-oriented personalities, there is a tendency for such students to overestimate how secure their attachment histories really are. To help them "save face," I encourage them to reflect on what attachment style they typically have and what attachment style they regress to when they are especially stressed and overwhelmed. The reality is that no one ever has a perfectly secure attachment history. There are always subtle, problematic patterns from our past that echo forward and influence how we perceive and act in our relationships. Furthermore, the health care system is so stressed and dysfunctional that even securely attached clinicians need to become aware of how they regress when they are pushed to their limits.

Ways to boost a secure attachment style in yourself

Attachment researchers have found that boosting a person's attachment security can help that person function as if he or she had a more secure attachment style. This can be done explicitly or implicitly. In an *explicit attachment priming intervention*, participants are given the description of a secure attachment relationship and then asked to recall a relationship in their past that fits that description. They are then asked to visualize it, recall a specific time with that person, what that person would say, and how they feel with that person (Bartz & Lydon, 2004). In an *implicit attachment-security priming procedure*, participants would be incidentally shown pictures of people enjoying close attachment relationships or involved in some caregiving actions. Doing so makes people feel more safe, calm, and loved (Norman, Lawrence, Iles, Benattayallah, & Karl, 2015).

Insecure attachment style clinicians have too much threat reactivity

Insecure attachment styles are associated with an increased threat reactivity; that is, they are more vigilant and predisposed to view things in a threatening way (Norman et al., 2015). When people have experienced repeated threats in their lives, there is a way in which the brain moves through the world overprepared for more threats; what is called *threat reactivity*. While being able to notice and respond to actual threat is important for survival, when people have too much threat reactivity, it can interfere with functioning because of increased anxiety. This is important in clinical practice for two reasons. One is that this can help us understand how some of our patients go through the world. Second, if we tend to view things in a threatening way, we become more focused on protecting ourselves (unnecessarily) and less on responding in the best way possible to our patients.

Research on how to decrease threat reactivity in a clinician

Using an *explicit attachment-security priming intervention* asking participants to recall a past vivid example of a healthy secure relationship, Norman et al. (2015) found that this could decrease threat reactivity as measured by the amygdala activation. What this means is that reminding ourselves of positive, secure attachment relationships can help with modulating threat appraisals. We approach situations in a more centered and calm state rather than a self-protective fearful state.

Implicitly priming your secure attachment leads to greater compassion

Using interventions that enhance a person's sense of attachment security (no matter what their attachment style has been) has been found to improve the ability to respond compassionately to others. Mikulincer et al. (2005) found that using an *implicit attachment-security priming intervention* led to participants having greater compassion and a willingness to actually help a distressed person. This occurred even when there was no egoistic reason to help, such as gaining empathic joy or mood relief for helping. It even improved the willingness to help an acquaintance beyond a family member.

MALIGNANT MOTIVATIONS UNDERLYING HELPING BEHAVIOR: "THE WOLF IN CLINICIAN'S CLOTHING"

One type of dysfunctional helping about which health care organizations and training programs must be vigilant is the one in which people use the mantle of helping in a manipulative, deceptive way to get their own needs met. While this type may have the common feature of helping professionals taking advantage of their position in order to meet their own needs or to harm the patient, there are quite a number of causes. These range from severe psychopathology (e.g., antisocial personality disorder, delusional disorder, pedophilia) to some personal agenda that clinicians are seeking to meet by deceptively using the persona of the caring helping professional. One might argue, probably correctly, that anytime individuals deceptively use or abuse a patient for their own needs, this in itself strongly indicates psychopathology as well as criminal intent. Unfortunately, there are many stories of this occurring: sexual predation and abuse, stealing from patients, emotional manipulation of patients for personal gain, injuring or killing patients for some perverted cause, or intentional harm rooted in sadism. When such instances are exposed, they become headlines and instill a great deal of fear in patients. Less obvious but still harmful are clinicians who deceive patients into thinking they need more treatment than they really need. Clinicians may exaggerate or fabricate diagnoses in order to bill more, or they may "double dip" by ordering more tests and procedures from surgicenters, labs, testing facilities, or other treatment facilities they also happen to own. While this is disturbingly common, it can vary from full insurance fraud to more subtle fraud by using the veil of expertise and complexity to recommend and bill for things that are only known in the mind of that clinician.

PATHOLOGICAL ALTRUISM

Background for the concept of pathological altruism

In the medical world as well as in other helping professions, altruism is one of the most common reasons clinicians report for why they entered their profession and why they keep doing it. When people discuss the nature of this altruism, it is common that they interject whatever bias, whether Pollyannaish or cynical, into the discussion. On one extreme are people who believe that there is no such thing as altruism and that every seemingly altruistic behavior has some selfish motivation. On the other side are those who do think altruism exists and yet have difficulty explaining how altruism goes awry or has aspects that benefit the giver. As I have discussed, there is a way in which the medical world both exalts altruism but also considers it embarrassingly soft, not scientific, and not essential to the successful practice of medicine. As we have seen, there is indeed a science to this, and it is vitally important for work in health care. But doubt about altruism also was not helped by the early psychoanalytic position that altruism was a pathological defense mechanism and arose from masochistic impulses. Despite the general rejection of considering altruism a pathological defense mechanism, there was a nagging awareness that sometimes altruistic behavior was not a healthy altruism. Beginning with Nancy McWilliams first mentioning "pathological altruism" in 1984 when she distinguished it from "healthy humanitarianism," a whole area of study regarding pathological altruism has emerged, relying on psychology, neuroscience, and biology to study, describe, and explain it. An extensive discussion of the research on pathological altruism can be found in the book *Pathological Altruism*, edited by Oakley et al. (2012).

Definition of normal altruism

Seelig and Rosof (2001) argued that the early psychoanalytic school was too simplistic in its merging of altruism and masochism. They thought that there were primitive and pathological forms of altruism, in which "the individual projects his own desires into the object and uses the object as a narcissistic extension of the self to satisfy those needs, often erroneously believing that the motivation is altruistic" (Seelig & Rosof, 2001, p. 956). They articulated five types of altruism with the range from normal to pathological altruism: protoaltruism, generative altruism, conflicted altruism, pseudoaltruism, and psychotic altruism. They describe the component of a mature or normal altruism as follows:

> *Normal altruism, as we are defining it, should be clearly distinguished from a pathologically narcissistic and/or masochistic involvement with an object. Those capable of normal altruism recognize and respect the autonomous wishes of the object and enjoy enhancing the object's pleasure or success. Mature parental altruism requires the ability to distinguish between what the child wishes and what the child actually needs. This normal parental altruism assists in the parent's ability to tolerate the inevitable aggression of the child when the parent thwarts the child's wishes for a good reason that is evident to the parent but not the child. We are suggesting also that this normal form of mature adult altruism is the developmental heir of the earlier infantile protoaltruism. (Seelig & Rosof, 2001, p. 957)*

I include this quote for how certain health care clinicians will read it if they substitute themselves for parent and the patient for the child. One of the distortions of altruism is that the altruist always does what the other person wants; but here it is noted that a mature altruism is focused on what the other person really needs, not wants, and that this does not always meet with gratitude.

Definition and examples of pathological altruism

In the past 15 years, tremendous research has been done on altruism and when it is pathological. Oakley et al. (2012) have developed this current definition of pathological altruism:

> Pathological altruism is defined as "any behavior or personal tendency in which either the stated aim or the implied motivation is to promote the welfare of another. But, instead of overall beneficial outcomes, the 'altruism' has irrational (from the point of view of an outside observer) and substantial negative consequences to the other or even to the self." (p. 3)

The authors add that a more simplified working definition of a pathological altruist would be

> a person who sincerely engages in what he or she intends to be altruistic acts, but who harms the very person or group he or she is trying to help, often in unanticipated fashion; or harms others; or irrationally becomes a victim of his or her own altruistic actions. (Oakley et al., 2012, p. 4)

As the authors explain, a con artist who is raising money for orphaned children with the intention of getting that money for him- or herself is not a pathological altruist. But a person who felt compelled to give to the con artist might be a pathological altruist. One example of this pathology might be malignant altruism, in which a person tries to control or manipulate someone they have helped into feeling that the person helped should appreciate the helper in the way that the helper expects. Another would be animal hoarding, in which someone wants to save animals but fails to provide good care for the animals and is in denial about the effects on the animals, others, and themselves. A parent of an unwanted child who overprotects or spoils the child as a way to hide his or her guilt is another example. A pseudoaltruist is a person who creates a crisis situation in order to intervene and help someone. Suicide attack martyrdom, in which a person will kill others in the name of some moral cause

or justice, is another example of pathological altruism (Oakley et al., 2012). For the purposes of this book, I will summarize two types of pathological altruism than can occur among people in health care: pathological certitude and codependence.

PATHOLOGICAL CERTITUDE

Pathological certitude (Burton, 2012) is the belief that one is acting in the best interest of the other person when the helper is actually not acting in the best interest of the other person, but he or she is not open to correcting the initial belief in the helping of that person. Burton (2012) gives the example of a colleague's description of an oncologist who was very aggressive with the most terminal of cancer patients:

> I have known Dr. X for years and have no doubt about his clinical skills and his utter dedication to his patients. Medicine is his life; he's available 24/7, and, when all fails, he even attends his patients' funerals. And yet, I dread working with him. Driven by a personal, unshakable ethic of what a good doctor must do for his patients, he wears his mission on his rolled-up sleeves, his full-steam-ahead attitude challenging and often shaming those of us who favor palliative care over prolongation of life at any cost. He has the intense, uncompromising look of someone with a calling. (p. 131)

Such doctors will insist on treatments with staunch conviction, even though the treatments may cause harm to the patient and indirectly to the patient's loved ones. These doctors operate out of a deep conviction of what is best for their patients, motivated by "an excessive sense of obligation to help others" (Burton, 2012, p. 132). But they disregard contradictory evidence even after the fact. Burton points out that in terms of neurobiology, feeling certain or correct is a mental sensation that functions independently of rational thinking, such as love or anger. He says it is not a conscious choice or a thought process. He explains that such a feeling is useful from an evolutionary perspective because it helps you move toward action in spite of the fact that you really do not know what the correct answer is; otherwise, you might be paralyzed from acting at all. This feeling is also a rewarding sensation that what you are doing is the right choice. The problem is that in terms of the way our brain processes information, there is a hidden layer of processing that comes from our genetic predispositions, personality traits, and past experiences that influences how we perceive incoming information. But we may not be aware of these, in spite of the fact that having a moral conviction about something can be intensely rewarding in itself. It becomes very important to reflect on what we are doing and be mindful of what is actually going on rather than acting solely out of the moral conviction that you alone know best what the patient should have. Burton (2012) argues that in order to guard against this, one should treat one's altruistic actions like writing a prescription for a drug:

> *Believing that you are helping isn't enough. You must know, to the best of your ability, the potential risks as well as benefits. And, you must understand that the package insert as to the worth of the medication (your altruistic act) was written by your biased unconscious, not by a scientific committee who has examined all the evidence. (p. 136)*

Again, we see in pathological certitude the common feature in dysfunctional helping: that our own needs or issues are distorting our perception of the patient or interfering with the patient's healing process.

CODEPENDENCY

When dysfunctional helping is discussed, the concept of codependence is often identified as a common type of dysfunctional helping. Books such as *I'm Dying to Take Care of You* and *Recovery from Rescuing* are examples of this. The concept of codependence, while a popular notion, has been problematic because of inconsistency in how it has been defined. There are elements similar to Bowlby's notion of compulsive caregiving. Even though it is a controversial psychological concept, it is important to examine this as a disparaging term, so often hurled at people who are thought to be "helping too much."

Lack of agreement in defining codependency

While the term *codependency* is often used to describe certain types of dysfunctional caring behavior in familial relationships as well as in the helping professions, there is not agreement about exactly what the psychological construct of codependency is (Stafford, 2001). Definitions for codependency vary widely, and it has been difficult to develop measures to assess it. A thorough discussion of this construct is beyond the scope of this book. However, codependency does refer to unhealthy or dysfunctional dynamics in helping others, and while we do not have agreement on which of those dysfunctional characteristics constitute codependency, there does seem to be a way is which helping relationships that appear to be caring are actually not based in a genuine caring motivation; instead, the helping is contaminated with the dysfunctional needs and goals of the caregiver. The term *codependency* emerged from substance abuse treatment literature (Cermak, 1986; Stafford, 2001) and has often been applied to the helping professions. It has tended to be a construct that has become inconclusive of any dysfunctional caring behaviors and as a result has not proved of reliable use in the helping professions. Among some health care clinicians, there have been occasions in which all caring behaviors have been construed as somehow codependent (Van der Wal, 1996). My purpose here is to discuss how codependency defined widely is still a very distinct phenomenon from genuine compassionate caring.

Core characteristics of codependency

In a review of the eleven most cited definitions of codependency, Dear, Roberts, and Lange (2004) did a thematic analysis and found four core elements across definitions: *external focusing*, *self-sacrificing*, *interpersonal control*, and *emotional suppression*. *External focusing* is defined as the tendency to focus one's attention on the opinions, behaviors, and expectations of others; an over-concern for how others view the person; and an excessive need for their approval. *Self-sacrificing* is defined as the tendency to neglect one's own needs and focus on meeting the needs of others; another person's needs are more important than one's own. *Interpersonal control* is defined as having an entrenched belief that one has the capacity to fix the problems of others and to control their behavior. Finally, *emotional suppression* is defined as the tendency to deliberately suppress one's emotions or to have limited conscious awareness of the them until those feelings become overwhelming. There is also commonly the notion attached of *enabling*, in which an individual inadvertently reinforces the addiction of a loved one (Whitfield, 1984).

Research on codependency

Dear and Roberts (2005) tested the validity of the Holyoake Codependency Index (Dear & Roberts, 2000) and found support for a number of these factors across several different populations: external focusing, self-sacrifice, and reactivity. The reactivity factor emerged (Dear, 2004), which is described as the tendency to perceive one's quality of life to be contingent on another person's problematic behavior and to be overwhelmed by the other person's problematic behavior. The aspects of interpersonal control and emotional suppression were not found in their particular measure, but one may argue that they may still be part of the syndrome. In fact, Dear and Roberts (2000) found that different aspects of codependency are more salient among certain types of individuals in certain family situations. In another study to develop a revised measure of codependency called the Composite Codependency Scale (Marks, Blore, Hine, & Dear, 2012), the researchers did find three dimensions of interpersonal control, self-sacrifice, and emotional suppression; but external focus did not emerge as a distinct factor in their sample.

Description of codependent helping in clinicians

While certain types of caring behavior appear to be centered on the needs of others, the *need* of the caregiver is actually driving the helping behavior in codependent helping. Such helping professionals are actually more controlling and tend to stifle the independence and autonomy of their patients. They tend to take over the responsibilities of others and do not allow patients to take responsibility for themselves. They tend to have low self-esteem, and thus the actions of others are seen as a reflection on them; and they rely on others for a sense of self-worth. Typically, these behavior patterns have their roots in the caregiver's dysfunctional family of origin (Davidhizar & Shearer, 1994). Other behaviors mentioned in connection with codependency in helping professionals are perfectionism and unrealistic demands on oneself; such individuals may become overachievers, caretakers, and workaholics. They have difficulty setting limits on the demanding behaviors of others and have great difficulty taking care of themselves. They tend to make themselves indispensable to others and may give or "care too much" to the point of exhaustion. There is constant need for validation from others so that they feel good about themselves. They can be manipulative, either from adopting a victim role, a rescuer role, or a persecutor role, in which they blame others for failures. They often engage in denial about what is occurring and may use ignoring, pretending, or lying to support whatever illusion they may have—for example, an unrealistic optimism that everything will be fine. They may engage in "people pleasing" and have poor boundaries. They are often in turmoil, dealing with feelings of shame, worthlessness, and the need for others' approval. There is also a tendency to blame themselves inordinately (Herrick, 1992).

Herrick's questions to self-assess codependent caring

Herrick (1992) offered these questions as a way to self-assess if one's caring is healthy or unhealthy:

> 1. *Do you help others at your own expense? 2. Do you have trouble identifying your needs and expressing your feelings? 3. Is taking care of yourself your last priority? 4. Do you feel taken advantage of by others? 5. Do you feel best when helping others? 6. Are you unhappy in your current job or current relationship? 7. Are there times when you feel you don't have enough energy for either yourself or others?* (p. 13)

Implications for clinical practice

As you may have gathered from the descriptions of codependency, its definition has become very broad and nonspecific. For our purposes, it does not matter so much what to call this dysfunctional dynamic in helping; what matters, rather, is to focus on how it is dysfunctional. It is very useful in a discussion of what compassionate caring is to examine *examples of what it is not* as a way to become more clear about how we define and demonstrate compassionate caring. It highlights that if it is our need for another person to be a certain way, we have made our need primary over the need of the other person. In compassionate caring, our focus is on attempting to alleviate the suffering of another. But what the patient does or what the outcome turns out to be is not in our control. This does not mean we are lesser people because we do not have control of all that happens and people do not do what we want them to do. We simply do the best that we can according to our roles and the appropriate boundaries of that role. If our behavior taps into the patterns described above, then that should be a warning sign that we have fallen out of the compassion mindset and need to examine how our own issues are interfering with a healthier helping process.

If we are to be consistent and criticize clinicians who appear to "care too much," we also must consider the fact that emotionally disconnected clinicians also have a problem.

THE PATHOLOGY OF EMOTIONALLY DISCONNECTED HELPING OR NOT HELPING AT ALL

Emotionally disconnected or detached helping is excused or more accepted

What is interesting to notice in the curbside analyses of dysfunctional helping behavior is that we are quick to point out and pathologize codependent helping, but the emotionally detached or unfeeling helping style is not as criticized and pathologized. We are quick to pass judgment on the helper who goes out of his or her way to help people all the time, but we often excuse the more detached helping style in the hallways of medical practice. Idealism or passion about helping others is at times portrayed as problematic. "Really wanting to help other people" can evoke amateur psychological interpretations about "*needing* to help." Early psychoanalytic theory viewed altruism as negatively motivated as a defense mechanism to suppress internal aggressive impulses or as a masochistic behavior (Ricard, 2015). There are remnants of this thinking still. Feminist critiques of the concept of codependency have revealed a gender bias in our society that tends to pathologize relational needs and overvalue independence and self-reliance (Malloy & Berkery, 1993). Many researchers note that the human person needs relationships and mutual empathy in order to grow and to be happy in life. Indeed, the central finding of the science of compassion is that human beings are designed to rely on each other in order to survive and thrive. As a result, it would be appropriate to pathologize habitual emotionally disconnected helping as least as much as we pathologize codependent or compulsive types of helping.

Four ways clinicians become emotionally disconnected and detached

It is important to note that there are at least four ways a clinician can become habitually emotionally disconnected or detached in caring for patients:

1. The result of stress and burnout

2. Adopted attitude related to how the clinical work is imagined

3. Training to be disconnected or detached in caring

4. Clinician attachment history

Emotional detachment as a consequence of prolonged stress and burnout

Emotional detachment can be the result of stress and burnout. Clinicians can become emotionally detached because of what they experienced in their helping work. For example, if a clinician is experiencing a great deal of emotional stress in working with patients and has an inadequate sense of how to handle this, then emotional detachment becomes a way to manage this in a self-protective manner. Emotional detachment may also be an indication of burnout. Burnout certainly is a dysfunctional state in the clinician, in which he or she has become emotionally exhausted, feels cynical and tends to treat patients in a depersonalized way, and experiences a lack of fulfillment in the work (Maslach, Schaufeli, & Leiter, 2001). This is a condition that develops over time, which I discuss elsewhere in this book. The key here is to regularly monitor one's emotions in practice and be able to use them as information either for what we need to do with a patient or with ourselves. If we do not pay attention to the information emotions have for us, then we are at risk for prolonged stress and burnout. As Austen (2016) puts it,

> we often lack the tools to interpret troubling emotions, or we do not believe ourselves capable of doing so, meaning that we opt instead for a predominantly detached response. This real or perceived inability to process emotional resonance is the most important driver of our over-detachment because it is the most amenable to change. By promoting strategies to better interpret emotional resonance arising from patients' traumas, we can provide a buffer

facilitating a shift back towards the ideal balance of true empathy and clinical detachment. (pp. 376–377)

Detachment due to stress and burnout is the topic of much of the rest of this book. Chapter 10 will delve deeper into how to focus on emotional management rather than detachment, and Chapter 11 will present an overall model for the balance between overinvolvement and detachment. In this chapter, I will focus on the clinician who approaches helping other people in a more mechanistic, emotionally disconnected manner and has always done so in this manner, but not because of stress and burnout.

Emotional detachment due to adopted clinical attitude

Second, clinicians might approach their patients in an emotionally disconnected manner because they do not even consider that emotional connection is necessary for clinical care. They view working with patients as equivalent to changing tires on a car. Patients are viewed as objects, and emotional connection or expressiveness is not considered necessary to work with objects. Just as a tire does not need to be greeted or "made comfortable" before being changed, so do they view patients: "Just do the procedure and that's all you're supposed to do." This approach is common, especially with clinicians who have mainly an economic view of their work. "It's a job, nothing more." "It's a way to make a living." As we have seen earlier in this book, such an approach to patients is known to be negative for patients and even for the clinicians. While the adopted attitude is egosyntonic (i.e., the clinician experiences no internal conflict about it), there is something dysfunctional in doing clinical work but not realizing that patients need to be treated differently than mundane objects for effective clinical outcomes.

Emotional detachment due to training philosophy

Third, emotionally disconnected helping can arise because some clinicians are trained to help patients in an emotionally detached way from the beginning of their careers. As discussed in chapter 7, clinical detachment is thought to be more scientific and, incidentally, more self-protective of clinicians in this emotionally difficult work because of the mistaken way we apply a narrow understanding of scientific objectivity to medical practice. The detached helper is thought to be doing what is necessary in order to survive the hard work of caring for lots of people. Throughout the history of medicine, we have tried to find a palatable blend of terms that preserves the care for the patient with the ideal of clinical detachment. Lief and Fox (1963) proposed the term *detached concern*. Even Sir William Osler, whose work reformed medical training with patient-centered principles, himself would lapse into detachment language.

> *Now a certain measure of insensibility is not only an advantage, but a positive necessity in the exercise of a calm judgment, and in carrying out delicate operations. Keen sensibility is doubtless a virtue of high order, when it does not interfere with steadiness of hand or coolness of nerve; but for the practitioner in his [her] working-day world, a callousness which thinks only of the good to be effected, and goes ahead regardless of smaller considerations, is the preferable quality. (Osler, Hinorhara, & Niki, 2001, p. 23; bracketed text added for nonsexist language)*

Yet Osler balances this with almost the opposite in this statement:

> *Cultivate, then ... such a judicious measure of obtuseness as will enable you to meet the exigencies of practice and courage, without, at the same time, hardening "the human heart by which we live." (Osler et al., 2001, p. 23)*

In another place, Osler (1904) gives some of the rationale for a more emotionally engaged approach to patient care:

> As the practice of medicine is not a business and can never be one, the education of the heart—the moral side of the [person]—must keep pace with the education of the head. Our fellow creatures cannot be dealt with as [a person] deals in corn and coal; "the human heart by which we live" must control our professional relations. (pp. 349–350; bracketed text added for nonsexist language)

In short, many clinicians have been taught that being emotionally detached is the right way to practice medicine, and their teachers were sincere in thinking that this was the right way to do it. It was the best thinking we had at the time. But we know now that when we practice this way, it has negative consequences for both our patients and us.

Iatrogenic effects of medical training

Besides the explicit training that leads to the adoption of a clinically detached attitude and approach, the grueling experience of being trained can emotionally blunt the young clinician who spends the rest of his or her career to some degree emotionally damaged by what happens to a person in medical school. In training, students must suppress personal needs and ignore their own feelings to survive. Many students take an emotional beating in terms of feeling inadequate, which is made worse if the medical school culture is shaming or cruel. In a very dramatic study, Marcus (2003) collected almost 400 dreams of medical students and residents and tracked how these showed the emotional turmoil that marks their psychological journey to becoming physicians. He argues, "There is no immunity from empathic, masochistic suffering, nor from death and sadistic

education and training experiences. Medical school is a traumatic, invasive, painful, near lethal emotional illness. No one needs a second dose of it" (Marcus, 2003, p. 378). Reiser (1993) notes that there are lessons in the technical aspects of medicine, but there are also lessons in how those facts are taught to students in terms of emotionally disconnected teaching methods by faculty. Landau discusses the way that faculty teach anatomy and the dissecting of cadavers has been thought of as the method for developing the desensitization considered essential for the practice of medicine. He remarks that it could actually be called the process of "deempathization":

> As the students progress from normal human biology and physiology to pathology and then intimate and responsible contact with patients, it is not unusual for them to be disturbed and to personalize one disorder or another. Additional desensitization or deempathization becomes essential in order to face and care for sick patients without alarming them. This is accomplished by multiplying the students' encounters with patients and by gradually increasing their responsibility. The scientific diagnosis of the patient requires the object evaluation and integration of all available information. Sound therapeutic decision necessitate the detached assessment of the diagnosis with consideration of all facets of the patient's life situation. It is not easy to find a place for empathy in this scenario. (Landau, 1993, p. 108)

In short, emotional detachment may be one of the iatrogenic conditions of some types of medical training.

Consider using the phrase "a Necessary Inhumanity" instead of "clinical detachment"

Richardson (2000) argued that maybe we should resurrect the phrase "a Necessary

Inhumanity" instead of "clinical detachment." She was referring to how William Hunter, a surgeon-anatomist in the eighteenth century, recommended dissecting dead bodies as a way to develop "a Necessary Inhumanity." Surgeons needed to be quick and accurate in doing surgery because there was no anesthesia, transfusion, or antibiotic. Richardson (2000) points out that "clinical detachment" does not simply mean one thing but rather is "a spectrum of sensibility which can range from extreme cruelty to conscious empathy" (p. 106). Her concern is that an uncomfortable phrase like "a Necessary Inhumanity" is preferable to "clinical objectivity" or "clinical detachment" because it may remind us of the dangers of those terms that make us feel comfortable being distanced from the patient over too long a period of time and encourages an inhumane attitude. As she puts it,

> the notion of a "Necessary Inhumanity" could be valuable because the questions it prompts might help serve as an effective calibrator: how necessary in these circumstances? For how long? And with what effect? Resurrecting and knowingly re-embracing the term "inhumanity" now might mean an increased awareness of its dangerous potential, which in turn might mean there'd be less of it about. (Richardson, 2000, p. 106)

Emotionally detached because of attachment history

The fourth way an emotionally disconnected or detached style can result is from the clinician's attachment history. This may have come about because they were raised in an emotionally detached way in their families or they became emotionally disconnected as a way to protect themselves emotionally in the family. As described in detail earlier in this chapter, the way clinicians practice echoes their own psychological issues and becomes reenacted in their patient care. The way they were "cared for" in childhood becomes the way they "care for" their patients and themselves—in a way in which emotions are avoided or suppressed. This is not an intentional or even conscious process, and many detached clinicians are not even aware that they are emotionally detached or even alexithymic. If clinicians remain unaware of this dynamic, both they and their patients can suffer as a result.

Emotional overinvolvement with patients

The extremes of emotional involvement with patients range from being overinvolved on one side to being emotionally disconnected, detached, or uninvolved on the other. I would define overinvolvement with patients as being more invested in, or doing more for, a patient than is good either for the patient or for the clinician. For clinicians who aspire to be compassionate and caring, it is not always easy to find the boundary between being optimally emotionally engaged with a patient and becoming overinvolved. Larson (1993) characterizes it as a state of overarousal in which a person feels engulfed by the work:

> The overaroused position is characterized by emotional involvement at a high pitch and strong emotions—both positive and negative. Positive feelings can include a sense of excitement, exhilaration, and getting something important accomplished. This intensity of feelings is exciting, but it is also exhausting. You think, "Nobody can do it as well as I can" or "Why aren't all the others more involved?" (p. 37)

In overinvolvement, there is a positive sense of intense motivation to help others but also of internal distress while being consumed by a case or the work in general. While it may seem like a clinician in this state is "in touch" with his or her feelings because of the emotional intensity of it, the clinician is often "out of touch" with the data of his or her emotions. As Larson (1993) puts it, "Being close and helpful without being distressed requires that we know ourselves and respect our own feelings. When we misinterpret, don't know, or cover up our genuine feelings and reactions, we risk the hazards of overinvolvement" (p. 47). The overinvolved clinician needs to pay attention to how he or she is doing more for a patient than is needed or is internally consumed with what is happening to a patient. Self-reflection and mindfulness are very helpful in examining one's own intense reactions or behaviors. For example, "What is going on with me that I am so upset at this patient for not following my advice?" "Why am I making exceptions for this patient that I would never make for other patients?" "How come I can never stop thinking about my work and patients when I am away from work?" "Why am I taking things so personally at work?" "Is my self-worth tied up with 'successes' at work?"

Ways overinvolvement can occur

There are a number of ways that overinvolvement can occur. Certainly, our attachment histories can echo forward into our patient care. Maybe we were cared for in an engulfing way, and it is our expectation that this is the way one should care for others. The reverse also happens, in which we always go to the extreme in caring for others because we did not experience feeling genuinely cared for in our own lives; overinvolved helping is a compensation for the lack of help we experienced. At times, particular patients or situations can tap issues in us that impel us to act in an overinvolved way, what we would technically call personal countertransference. A patient reminds us of a dynamic with a current or past loved one; the patient situation taps into feelings of distress or helplessness because it reawakens a past trauma in our own lives. As a result, we are more involved than we need to be or should be. In addition, then, to the empathic resonance we experience with our patients, we are adding an emotional dimension that impels us to do more or feel more than what the patient actually needs from us.

Overinvolvement as a reflection of workaholism

Overinvolvement can also be related to a dynamic of workaholism, in which our self-worth is completely wrapped up in our work. Medical training is so consuming that one can define the overwork of medical school and residency as the new normal in a clinician's life. This actually begins long before entering a health profession. To be accepted into medical or other health profession training, there is a tremendous pressure to have the best grades, the best research experiences, and the best volunteer sites. This easily cultivates an identity that is defined by work successes and by perfectionism.

Overinvolvement is bad both for patients and for clinicians

Overinvolvement is a dysfunctional helping dynamic that is bad both for patients and for clinicians. In chapter 10, I will lay out more of the negative consequences of overinvolvement. Because overinvolvement is out of touch with what the situation actually requires, clinicians in this state are not paying attention to what is going on in themselves and what is going on with their patients because there is another emotional dynamic that is driving them. The key would be to become conscious of what that dynamic is so that you control it rather than the unconscious dynamic owning you. Maybe you tend to be driven to work very hard. This can be useful as long as you know when and how to turn off that drive.

Overinvolvement negatively affects our colleagues

Another consequence of overinvolvement is how it negatively affects colleagues. Because we are motivated by compassionate caring, it is understandable that we would want to affirm others for their heroic or exemplary work and to have that done for ourselves. But if a clinician is always "overdoing it," this can be demoralizing to colleagues, just as it is demoralizing to have colleagues who are habitually uninvested in quality patient care. It is also a negative influence on the culture of the work group and on those in training because it makes others who are actually doing good, compassionate work feel inadequate. I am not speaking here of exemplary clinicians whose excellence at work inspires others to do the same. If we are truly compassionate and collaborative, we want to be with other colleagues who nudge us to be better than we would be if left to ourselves. What I am referring to here is the kind of overinvolvement that has elements of grandiosity to it. Moore (2003) describes this well:

> Very simply, "grandiosity" means you have larger fantasies and wishes for yourself than your real life can support, so they either make you manic, running around trying to keep up with their demands, or they make you depressed because your desires are so high and unachievable that it soon seems useless to try to do anything at all. (p. 69)

There is the grandiosity of the clinicians who manically run around reminding everyone of how important and indispensable they are to the patients and the institution; and then there is the grandiosity implicit when colleagues act as if they are burdened by carrying the whole world on their shoulders.

FEARS OF COMPASSION

There are times when clinicians have fears related to positive emotions in general or to particular aspects of compassion. Paul Gilbert, who developed compassion-focused therapy, noted that some people have fears about positive emotions in general. For a variety of reasons, these individuals become uncomfortable when they feel happiness or pleasure. Compassion is connected to positive emotions, and this can be challenging for people who are fearful of positive emotions. For example, the experience of another person's kindness can activate negative attachment memories related to being neglected, abused, shamed, or harmed in some way. To feel safe and not overwhelmed by these memories, people who fear positive emotions will shut down the soothing system that is activated by another person's compassionate response to them. They will become fearful, uncomfortable, and even try to avoid such a situation (Gilbert, 2010). As Gilbert, McEwan, Matos, and Rivis (2010) put it, "It is not just the absence of compassion that is important but also the fear of compassion. This means that people may actively resist engaging in compassionate experiences or behaviors" (p. 252). What can emerge are three types of fears related to compassion: fears about receiving compassion, fears about expressing compassion, and fears about being compassionate toward oneself (Gilbert et al., 2010).

Fears about receiving compassion

Some people are fearful about receiving compassion from others. They may feel it is a sign of weakness to receive care from someone else. They might have concerns about having to depend on another person's help. They may feel they do not deserve to be helped or should not accept help. Receiving care from others makes them feel sad, uncomfortable, empty, or even suspicious about the motives of the other person being helpful to them (Gilbert et al., 2010). If clinicians have any of these fears, imagine how risky it is for a person in a highly challenging profession to be reluctant to accept compassion for themselves.

Fears of expressing compassion

Fears about expressing compassion can take the form of believing that others should not need help from someone else or that some people do not deserve compassion from others. Some people imagine that helping others is not holding them accountable and that these individuals should be disciplined or punished instead of shown kindness. They might think that expressing compassion will make others soft, too dependent, or too vulnerable. There can also be a fear that being too compassionate to others will make people want them more, take advantage of them, or potentially drain them (Gilbert et al., 2010). While on the surface this seems less likely in helping professionals, it certainly occurs among clinicians. When clinicians have concerns or fears about what happens if they offer compassion to their patients, you can understand how that would encourage a more detached emotional approach with patients as well as a minimalist approach to patient care.

Fears of self-compassion

Fears about expressing compassion or kindness toward themselves can involve such individuals

not feeling like they deserve it. Being kind to themselves might make them feel uncomfortable or sad. Like the fears for expressing compassion to others, there can be a fear of becoming weak if one is kind to oneself. There might be the attitude that one should always be tough and critical of oneself (Gilbert et al., 2010). With clinicians, who must be able to be kind to themselves in order to recover from the emotional toll of this work, imagine the risk if a clinician is not able to be kind and compassionate toward him- or herself.

Implications for patient care and for clinician self-care

With each of the above fears, you can imagine how the person with that particular fear learned that fear in his or her upbringing and experience. There are so many ways these fears result. Such fears are quite relevant in terms of understanding why some of our patients may resist our help even though there is no logical reason for it. I recall one patient a group of us treated who would lose his temper every time we said we "cared" about him. We discovered that he had undergone severe abuse by people who "should have cared about him." When we physicians, nurses, and psychologists cared about him, it tapped right into that unresolved trauma. When we stopped using the word *caring*, things went much better. For our purposes in this chapter, my focus in on dysfunctional helping. With that in mind, imagine if you are a clinician with one or more of these fears. Gilbert et al. (2010) investigated what these fears were like in students and therapists and found that while therapists had significantly fewer fears than the students (as we would expect and hope, given that they are helping professionals), there were a number of things that were found in the therapist group.

Fears of receiving compassion from others were correlated with fears of being self-compassionate. Fears of receiving compassion and being self-compassionate were correlated with being cold and critical toward oneself and with depression. Therapists with these fears tend to have anxious attachment styles, in which there is a fear of abandonment but also a fear of affiliation with another person. While there generally were not fears about expressing compassion toward clients, think of the implications for clinicians who have difficulty receiving compassion or being compassionate toward themselves. In professions as stressful as health care, surviving this work requires that we be able to accept help from others as well as be compassionate to ourselves; fears of receiving compassion and self-compassion in clinicians can put them at risk for burnout and for not recovering from that burnout.

MONEY AND COMPASSION IN THE HELPING PROFESSIONS

In a discussion about compassionate caring and health care, there is often a tendency not to discuss money at the same time. In fact, the discussions are often held separately, or there is a quick statement about money and compassion being uneasy partners. Many people think compassion and money are like oil and vinegar: you can mix them up together, but after a while they separate, one going to the top and one to the bottom. Clinicians fantasize about providing compassionate care for their patients unencumbered by having to think about billing systems and coding and how much prescription drugs cost. "Just let me do my job and let somebody else worry about the money." Often clinicians who volunteer to go on medical mission trips in developing countries report feeling a renewal of their love for their profession because for several weeks to several months they could just focus on taking care of people and not worry about filling out forms or billing (Campbell et al., 2009). Clinicians often find it burdensome to have discussions about the financial aspects of health care operations. Those with financial responsibility for a health care organization fantasize about the smooth flow of six-minute patient visits and efficient use of the surgery facilities to maximize cash flow. At their worst, they imagined health care as an assembly line with a minimum of interruptions to the productivity. Patients who need "extra" time are seen as threats to productivity. Such clinicians would prefer a minimum of any activity that is not codable for billing. Of course, patient satisfaction scores are important, and so cordial customer service is expected. But this is seen in shallow terms not much different than what is expected in fast-food service. Clinicians can see financial issues as interfering with compassion. Financial people can see compassionate care as interfering with finances.

Money is necessary to sustain a compassionate career

The relationship between money and compassionate care is complex, and it is important not to be simplistic in discussing this relationship. People in health care need to make money, but this does not automatically mean that they are not compassionate because they want to make a living by doing this work. While people may idealistically think that people in health care should not worry about making money, no one would be able to continue working in health care for any length of time if he or she were not able to take care of basic own needs like food, shelter, transportation, providing for the needs of their loved ones, and so forth. A sentimentalized view of compassion in health care imagines that the clinician gains nothing personally from helping people who are suffering. But compassionate caring requires that a helper have a stable foundation from which to help the other person. If the helper is chronically hungry, has no shelter, or no way to take care of his or her own health and well-being, that helper will not be able to focus on any other person's needs because his or her own needs would eventually predominate. This is not meant to discount the role of helping or gestures of great generosity. But a helper who does not take care of him- or herself is doomed to have a very short career in health care. Money is part of taking care of oneself.

Money can interfere with compassionate caring if self-interest is the primary motivation

On the other hand, there is a certain point at which money begins to interfere with compassionate care. Not having enough money trumps compassion; so does making too much. There are several ways this can occur. First, the focus of helpers' attention changes based on whether compassionate care is primary or making money is primary. Clinicians need to make enough money so that their own needs do not interfere with focusing on a patient's needs. In this case, compassionate caring is what guides a clinician's mental focus, and how much money he or she is making has to be adequate so that this attention is not disrupted by the clinician's ongoing lack of self-care. However, if patient care is viewed *primarily* as making money, that clinician's focus is now compromised by his or her own self-interest. Such clinicians may push their treatment, their procedures, or their surgeries on a patient even though such approaches might not be necessary or another approach might be better. If clinicians have just spent a huge amount of money for the medical technology in their clinic, they may become biased in the direction of using that technology when it is not actually necessary for the patient but helps pay for the new equipment. If clinicians' focus is making money, they may be tempted to rush people through appointments and ignore any patient need that lengthens a visit. While they may still be aware of the patient's needs, they are motivated to downplay what those needs are if that affects their primary goal of making as much money as possible.

Money can interfere with compassion if it is perceived as excessive or suspect

There is a point at which money interferes with compassionate care because of how it is perceived by patients and others. Patients who are suffering prefer a clinician who will be compassionately invested in relieving their suffering. They prefer someone who intrinsically desires to help them and who does not harbor hidden agendas for helping them. Generally, most patients understand that you have to make a living and that you need a good income to compensate for how many years and how much money it took to train you and for the long hours and emotional costs of this work. But a certain point is reached at which that assumption of your altruism is threatened because of how the amount of money you make is perceived. Whether you are intrinsically motivated or not, patients begin to wonder what your primary motivation is. While they desire your service, they may find themselves on guard regarding your motivation. Most patients are reluctant to voice these thoughts because of their vulnerability. If I, as the patient, complain too loudly about how much you make or question your motives about where you are referring me, you may decide not to help me or may help me in a halfhearted way in order to punish me for criticizing you. While this is a popular topic in our society, along with how exorbitant CEO salaries are considered, patients are reluctant to voice this too loudly when they are in need. Many decide to squelch such talk because they are in need and vulnerable. But such a clinician can walk away never having to be challenged. "None of my patients seem to be complaining. If they don't want my care and don't like how much I charge, they don't have to come and see me." What if you were one of the few specialists in that area, and the only other specialists are partners in your practice?

Money can usurp compassionate motivation

The helper's motivation can be usurped. As the old saying goes, "Money changes people." You enter a helping profession because it seems to be a great use of your talents and you care about people, so why not do something that you love and are good at and make a living at the same time? But as you go forward in your career, how much you make can affect how you view your own compassionate motivation. Making too little money can be just as dangerous as making a lot of money when it comes to how it might affect a clinician's compassionate motivation.

The dangers of making a lot of money

Making a lot of money has its own dangers. Most people going into health care intend to be primarily based in a compassionate caring attitude for their whole careers. Practically every personal statement I have ever read of people applying to medical, nursing, mental health, and ministry training programs has been some version of how everything in that person's life has inspired them to be in that particular helping profession with a desire to "help people for the rest of my life." Either we assume the best in most people entering into health care or we have an awful lot of people lying to us (and maybe to themselves). Many people in training observe the corrupting influence of making a lot of money and vow, "That will never happen to me." Being at the lowest rung of the health care hierarchy, working long hours studying and in patient care, and going into a lot of debt because of the training, there is a sense in which one cannot imagine money could change you for the worse because of what you had to endure. For some, this can, in a sense, purify their motivation because they have mainly passion for their profession, and this keeps them going. For others, this can be experienced as of victimization or oppression, and this lays the foundation for an entitlement that may last their whole careers. They figure they deserve to have very high compensation, but there does not seem to be a limit to what that might be. "I suffered so much in my training and in my early practice, I deserve to make a lot later on." In any case, if you happen to be in a very lucrative position, the initial amazement about how much money you can make begins to shift into an expectation of how much you ought to make and how much that ought to increase over the years. But then the danger is that you have made your compassion mindset contingent on the amount of money you are making. The intrinsic motivation for the work has subtly dwindled as the focus has moved to the quantity of money.

How making a lot of money can change your perceptions and thinking

Especially as you experience the emotional costs of the work, this shift can feel justifiable. You become habituated to the level of income, your standard of living will often rise to the level of your income, and it may even begin to feel commonplace and normal to have that level of income. In research on people's perceptions of their own social class, most people underestimate what class they are in (e.g., many wealthy people consider themselves middle class) (Rampell, 2011). Any change in that income level will be felt as a violation. A person whose income goes down from $200,000 to $100,000 might sound as insulted and panicked as a person whose income goes down from $20,000 to $10,000; but realistically, those two situations are quite different in terms of ability to have a comfortable life. Furthermore, it may not matter that people in other professions that might have the same or greater emotional toll and risk do not make the same as you do. To resolve any cognitive dissonance about making a lot of money, many people move to a stance that they deserve to make this amount compared to other professions with similar personal costs. This is not something new to human beings or unique to the health care professions. It is as old as money itself. People who make more begin to believe they should make that amount and that they deserve it. We humans also tend not to stay satisfied with our current levels either. The lack of fulfillment and satisfaction people feel in their lives leads some people to think that making more money or having more power would somehow make them feel all right. But the link between wealth and happiness is an illusion (Kahneman, Krueger, Schkade, Schwarz, & Stone, 2006).

Making too little money can trump the compassion mindset

Making too little money can be a threat to sustaining the compassion mindset. We make a grave error when we think of health care in terms of money versus compassion. Folbre and Wright (2012) point out that in paid and unpaid care work, the "love versus money" type of analysis is too simplistic to capture the complex dynamics of care work. Money (or compensation) is absolutely critical for clinicians to be able to sustain the compassion mindset. Most of the time when money is discussed as a threat to compassion, it is done from the point of view of people who are perceived to be making a lot of or "too much" money. But making too little money also brings with it particular dangers. I am not speaking here about the common perception most people have that they should be making more than they are. Rather, I am speaking here of objectively comparing levels of income across helping professions. Certain helping professions make significantly less than other helping professions. If you happen to be in one of those helping professions, you have to contend with the knowledge that what you are doing is monetarily not as valued in our society as other professions in the top quartile of income. Without getting into whether this is just or unjust, how a profession is valued in terms of monetary income can contaminate a compassionate motivation in an insidious way, just as making a lot of money can. You enter that profession believing that your abilities can be well used in a particular kind of service to other people. You have no doubt about the intrinsic worth of your profession. But then a number of things begin to happen. First, if you are not able to make enough money to pay your training debts or to support yourself (or your family), resentment may begin to build. The resentment might be against a society that would value other professions significantly more than yours or a resentment of the work itself. When people make too small an income, they can begin to question the worth of their work or resent that they are drawn to a particular kind of helping work. No matter what kind of resentment it is, those negative feelings are in danger of being brought to the helping work itself. Rather than having a centered, caring focus on the people you are helping, your own resentment or discouragement can begin to interfere with your performance. "Why should I care about these people? No one really cares about what we do." "I don't get paid enough to do this." And so begins the slide toward cynicism and emotional detachment from the work.

How people can erroneously equate worth of a profession with its income

As if being paid too little was not bad enough for one's own compassionate motivation, there is the problem of how others, including your patients, perceive the low-income status of your particular helping profession. In a kind of "blame the victim" dynamic, patients can be subtly influenced to devalue your profession because society devalues it. Fill in the blanks with what you have heard patients or clients say about a lower income helping profession: "It's not like you are a _____; you're just a _____." People can tend to disrespect a profession based on what is paid for it versus the inherent worth of that work. There are ways that such helping professionals and those served in those helping professions try to compensate for this and protect the dignity of those professions. People who recognize this often go out of their way to express gratitude to these helping professionals. There will be special appreciation days for them, or the virtues of that profession will be extolled in the media, for example. Helping professionals of those occupations often rely on regularly reminding themselves of the inherent worth of their work. They also rely on their colleagues in the same helping profession to provide support and focus on the compassionate ideals of their particular work.

The problem of making money from other people's problems

The issue of money in health care can be awkward and unsettling because it is "making money off of other people's tragedies and misfortunes." The nature of compassion is such that we desire that human beings truly care about each other without conditions, that as clinicians we would express our compassionate response no matter what the compensation was. We would like it if all human beings operated this way; and we would like it if all professions, not just health care, espoused an ethic of compassion,. However, there are lots of people and certain parts of the health care industry (e.g., pharmaceutical companies, health care organizations, medical device manufacturers, and insurance companies) that are making a lot of money from other people's problems. In fact, in the United States, for example, there are ways in which certain types of health care businesses are looking for ways to maximize profits at the expense of patients. This is one of the major moral problems of our time. Unfortunately, clinicians get confronted with this often because they are the one part of the health care industry that has face-to-face interactions with patients. Those face-to-face interactions can actually help clinicians stay honest about their financial intentions—that is, unless they restrict who can see them by not serving people who live in poverty or who have complicated medical conditions with poor reimbursement. Many clinicians (and patients) become irate that the parts of health care that do not interact with patients directly can so blatantly seek profit over compassion. As a clinician, when you are face-to-face with a suffering person, it keeps your priorities clearer. The further removed you are from the suffering of another person, the easier it is not to be motivated by the compassion mindset.

Overemphasis on money can objectify patients and clinicians to the detriment of both

Helpers are affected by the people they try to help. In our society at this time, helping continues to be viewed as a one-way interaction in which we expect the care recipient to be changed but not the helper. The mechanistic scientific paradigm of helping has now been joined with the cordial but detached paradigm of the business transaction. The people who are being helped are viewed either as the passive recipients of technical expertise or as "customers" who need to have the service or product delivered to them in such a way that they will come back with their business or spread the word to others. Often lacking is the sense of specialness to enter another person's life to the extent that it might be changed; also often lacking is the sense that in helping another person, the helper's life might be changed. As many managed care companies would portray it, an objective health professional applies a standardized and empirically validated treatment to an objective patient. This is not intended maliciously. The intent is to have a cost-effective and helpful outcome. Caring language is added like an overcoat. The helping interaction is viewed as providing a service that you have paid for as part of the managed care policy. No one has said to the helping professional not to do this in a caring manner; but the helping service is precisely delineated in terms of what is considered an accepted service or procedure as well as how much time it should take and the most money that you can expect from doing the service (provided the health professional and the patient have followed all the rules for delivering the service and filing a claim for the service). With such pressures, it becomes understandable that both the helper and the help recipient would be objectified. But there is much more going on in a helping interaction than can be objectively described. In fact, the subjective dimensions of the patient and of the helper are actually very important parts of what helps people in the long run. As Carl Jung (1933) describes the relationship between two people, "The meeting of two personalities is like the contact of two chemical substances: if there is any reaction, both are transformed. ... You can exert no influence if you are not susceptible to influence" (pp. 49).

Study on ratings of physician empathy with private insurance

Do patient ratings of physician empathy differ with different financial incentives? Neumann et al. (2010) surveyed over 300 cancer patients in Germany on this question. They compared physician empathy ratings for physicians paid by private health insurance (i.e., fee for service) versus physicians paid by statutory health insurance (i.e., capitation). Private health insurance patients rated their physicians higher on physician empathy compared to those who had statutory health insurance. Patients with private health insurance reported speaking more often with their physician while they were in the hospital, although the length of time for each consultation was no longer on average compared to statutory health insurance. Those with private insurance tended to perceive less stress in their physicians, which in turn positively influenced their ratings of physician empathy. Time spent with the patient and being perceived as less stressed led to higher ratings of physician empathy. The authors noted Braddock and Snyder's (2005) explanation of what may be occurring:

> In terms of adverse effects of time pressure, the physician working under the perception of inadequate time may exhibit signs of stress or annoyance that, while not directed at the patient, can nonetheless be perceived so. Patients may question whether the physician really cares if the physician seems annoyed, rushed, or inattentive. These same feelings in the physician may over time lead to burnout, clinical syndrome that is underrecognized in clinical practice. (p. 1059)

Socioeconomic status affects compassionate response

How does your socioeconomic status relate to the likelihood of performing prosocial compassionate actions toward others? Significant research has found that individuals in lower socioeconomic classes showed more sensitivity and compassion to other people's needs, including strangers and people in distress. They exhibited less entitlement, less self-importance, and less narcissism. They tend to assist and share with others more than people in higher socioeconomic classes (Piff & Robinson, 2017). In a series of studies, Stellar, Manzo, Kraus, and Keltner (2012) found that individuals from lower classes had more dispositional compassion; reported more compassionate responses to other people in distress; and had greater heart rate deceleration, a physiological indicator of being oriented toward and engaging others in the social environment. Piff, Kraus, Coté, Cheng, and Keltner (2010) found that individuals from lower classes were more generous and gave more support to charitable organizations than individuals from higher classes. Lower-class individuals experienced more compassion, which was related to more prosocial action in response. It is paradoxical that individuals with fewer resources, reduced feelings of personal control, and more stress and threats in their lives would be more generous. The researchers found that lower-class individuals expressed more concern regarding others' well-being and showed more trust in interpersonal situations, whereas higher class individuals were less trusting of strangers and prioritized self-interest over concern for others.

Power can decrease compassionate response

Power also affects our compassion and response to suffering. Van Kleef et al. (2008) found in their experiments that participants with higher power respond with less distress to another person's distress, had less compassion toward someone in distress, and had more autonomic emotion regulation in the presence of another person's distress. In terms of possible explanations, the researchers were able to rule out that these differences were due to higher-power people feeling less distress because they had higher positive baseline states or to higher-power people being less accurate in decoding distress cues in others. It appears that a motivational explanation was operative: People with more power had less of a desire to establish a relationship and invest emotionally with the other person. Also, the people disclosing their distress felt less socially connected to higher-power listeners. It seemed that higher-power people buffered themselves against the other person's distress by engaging a parasympathetic process as measured by RSA reactivity. The authors found that there were no differences in attention paid to others; rather, people with more power were not as motivated to respond to people in distress. As we gain power over time as clinicians, it is therefore important to check ourselves to see if increased power has negatively affected our compassion.

The lessons of the power of pharmaceutical marketing

Does how you get paid for your clinical work affect the way you practice? There is some research on this question, which I will briefly describe. But before getting to that, let us consider some relatively small things like, for example, letting pharmaceutical representatives buy you lunch and whether that affects the way you practice. DeJong et al. (2016) found that even receiving one meal from a pharmaceutical representative changed the prescribing habits of physicians; and the more meals they received, the more it affected their prescribing rates. In a review of 49 studies examining the relationships between physicians and pharmaceutical representatives/industry, Fickweiler, Fickweiler, and Urbach (2017) found that most physicians did not believe those interactions influenced their own prescribing behavior, but they did think their colleagues were more likely to be influenced than they themselves were. My point here is not only that pharmaceutical marketing techniques really do influence physician prescription patterns, and physicians do not even realize it; my bigger point

is that this same lack of awareness with anything related to financial arrangements might also be influencing us. The question is not, "Does the way I get paid influence my medical practice and my compassion mindset?" It really is, "How does the way I get paid influence my medical practice and my compassion mindset?"

Physician altruism is not a uniform constant

Godager and Wiesen (2013) examined whether there is a range of physician altruism in terms of the weight placed on patient benefit versus the physician's own profit. Using behavioral data from Hennig-Schmidt, Selten, and Wiesen's (2011) study comparing the provision of health care services with fee-for-service versus capitation incentives, the researchers examined how 42 German medical students weighted the patient's health benefit with their own profit. While a laboratory experiment, what is interesting is that the researchers discovered a significant heterogeneity of altruism. They found that 44% put higher weight on the patient's benefit, 26% placed more weight on their own profit, and 29% put equal weight on the patient's health benefit and their own profit. This means that whatever incentive system is used should not assume a "uniform amount" of physician altruism. Whatever system is used has to attempt to constrain less altruistic clinicians while at the same time not impeding the services of the more patient-centered physicians.

Clinician motivations are a combination of extrinsic and intrinsic motivations

In care work, there is typically a combination of extrinsic and intrinsic motivations in the care provider. Folbre and Wright (2012) point out that the "love versus money" dichotomy is too simplistic an approach to understand unpaid and paid care work. Extrinsic motivations consist of those in which the work is performed to obtain an external reward or avoid a penalty or punishment. The rewards might consist of direct payment, social approval, or future rewards such as reciprocity in response to the service provided. Extrinsic negative factors might be that it is the only job one can get, the best of the choices available to the person, or what one was pressured into doing. Intrinsic rewards are rooted in the sense of pleasure or sense of accomplishment that results from doing the care work. There can be an enjoyment in the labor process or the activity in itself, or there may be prosocial intrinsic motives. These would include following the norms for caring that are part of one's identity; acting out of values related to a sense of calling to care for others, a sense of moral duty, or a sense of deep personal meaning; or a satisfying desire to impact the well-being or happiness of the other person. Overall, for any care provider there is typically a combination of sources of motivation.

How is the physician who is the "double agent" motivated in the end?

There is a delicate balance between extrinsic incentives in health care and the intrinsic motivations to provide that care. Extrinsic incentives can be more salient, but in the end, the system works better if the clinician's intrinsic motivation for compassionate caring is in the driver's seat. For example, Mitchell, Hadley, Sulmasy, and Bloche (2000) found that physicians reported financial incentives to reduce medical services to patients with capitated insurance plans, compensation incentives with a gatekeeper arrangement,

a health plan that discouraged the provider from telling patients of the financial arrangement with the plan, the perception that referrals are contingent on what the physician charges, or that physicians would lose contracts if their costs were high. The physicians reported incentives to increase services if they were paid on a fee-for-service basis or their salary had bonuses or incentives to increase services. However, in the end physician attitudes determine how much they will weight those incentives against the best interests of the patients. Physicians can be perceived as "double agents" in health care. There is an asymmetry of information between the patient and the physician. Typically, the physician is paid by some type of insurance. The patient would like to view the physician as his or her agent in terms of getting information and the best treatment possible. Yet the insurance provider would like the physician to be economical in the choice of health services to reduce the costs of claims. The insurance company might incentivize the clinician one way or another accordingly (Blomqvist, 1991). If there is little intrinsic motivation, the clinician may be governed by what the current mix of incentives can provide for both the patient and the clinician. But the stronger the intrinsic motivation, the more the patient's best interests are safeguarded.

Directly caring for people changes our perspective on health care and life

Folbre and Wright (2012) comment that, ironically, "research has shown that here is little about the actual *doing* of care work that is in itself inherently interesting or pleasurable, independent of the prosocial aspects of the work such as helping others" (p. 22). The intrinsic prosocial motivation is what is most critical either in attracting people to care work or in what gets developed or increased as people do this work. There is also evidence that as people provide care, especially direct care, it increases their empathy and preference to be caring (England, Folbre, & Leana, 2012). The experience of being involved in the nitty-gritty details of caring for people ends up changing us to the point that we look at it very differently than people who do not do caring work or avoid caring work. The intrinsic prosocial motivation to care for people becomes more developed, but not in the abstract. We think of particular people with cancer, particular people with dementia, particular people with cardiac problems, and so on. This sounds obvious, but understanding this dynamic will reveal the huge internal tensions that arise in the business of health care and how the clinicians and other direct care staff get penalized because of how this powerful, emotionally engaging process with patients ends up widening their perspective on health care and life. Those who do not experience this can minimize what is occurring between patient and clinician as simply transactional, simply reduced to the action: operating on a patient, debriding a wound, doing a physical exam, delivering a baby, giving chemotherapy, and so forth.

> A preference for caring developed as a result of caring activities, which might be called endogenous altruism, can also be costly. An emotional attachment to their students, patients, or charges may discourage workers from demanding higher wages or changes in working conditions that would benefit them but that might adversely affect care recipients. By contrasts, owners, employers, and managers in care industries are less likely than care workers to come into direct contact with care recipients and may be more likely to engage in cost-cutting strategies without experiencing negative emotional consequences themselves. Owners and managers often seem to depend on their workers' willingness to sacrifice for their clients—expecting workers to respond to cutbacks in staffing levels, for instance, by intensifying their efforts or agreeing to work overtime. These aspects of prosocial motivation many be good for care recipients, as least in the short run, but they penalize workers who develop caring preferences. (England et al., 2012, pp. 32–33)

The intrinsic motivation to provide compassionate caring is the most important ingredient in providing high-quality health care. Yet having that intrinsic motivation creates tensions with systems that have a more extrinsic approach and takes for granted that the intrinsic motivation is a given.

Intrinsically motivated staff are always preferred by organizations and fellow clinicians

Everyone knows that health care is better when the clinician really cares about the patient. Health care managers and executives know that when their clinicians have a true caring attitude and an intrinsic prosocial motivation, everything will go better, from the quality of the services to employee satisfaction and engagement (England et al., 2012). The patient care will be better, outcomes will be better, patient safety will be better, staff turnover will be lower, and morale will be better. That internal attitude is so important that health care institutions spend millions of dollars trying to instill this attitude beyond the surface-acting level. Health care certainly has its customer service protocols (e.g., AIDET) so that the clinicians and the rest of the staff will at least perform the outside caring behaviors that will improve the patient experience. But the gold standard we all want is a staff with genuine caring attitudes for the patients and for each other. When health care staff have sick loved ones or are sick themselves, it is quite telling who they will "pull strings" to get as their clinicians—typically those who are intrinsically motivated to give the best care possible. The key to taking care of an intrinsically motivated, caring staff is to be careful not to undermine that intrinsic motivation.

Loss aversion as undercutting intrinsic motivation

But the way compassion, the intrinsic prosocial motivation, is rewarded is very critical, and subjectivity is very involved in it. To look at "only the numbers" is a sure way to undercut the very thing you want to reward. There are a couple of psychological dynamics that occur that decrease intrinsic motivation. One is called "loss aversion," in which the brain is more sensitive to losses than to equivalent gains. Generally in health care, it is thought that intrinsic motivation exists on its own in clinicians, and this motivation would remain constant even if the extrinsic rewards decrease. But if you have been paid one amount and then that is decreased in a way that seems punitive, what results is that the reward circuitry activity in the brain is reduced (Tom, Fox, Trepel, & Poldrack, 2007). The withdrawal or decrease of the extrinsic reward suppresses the reward circuitry underlying the positive intrinsic motivation. In our terms, the compassion mindset has been disrupted by the way the changes in external reward are perceived.

The motivation crowding effect

In economics and psychology, research has discovered what is called the motivation crowding effect, in which "external intervention via monetary incentives or punishments may undermine and, under different identifiable conditions, strengthen intrinsic motivation" (Frey & Jegen, 2001, p. 589). We have all probably heard of studies showing that when individuals are rewarded for an activity they find interesting—for example, they are paid for performance—it will undercut the intrinsic motivation and the performance. The extrinsic rewards are thought to "crowd out" the intrinsic motivation. However, there are times when "subjects who are paid a fixed positive amount, independent of their performance, do not display reduction in intrinsic motivation" (Gneezy & Rustichini, 2000, p. 793). In care work, this would mean that staff who are paid well "up front" would reciprocate what the employer has offered. If an extrinsic reward such as money is perceived as controlling or punitive, it will actually undercut the intrinsic motivation of the staff (England et al., 2012). It is perceived as an attack on the competence and autonomy of the worker. However, if the extrinsic reward "acknowledges" the skill and intrinsic motivation of the staff, it sends the message that they are "trusted, respected, and appreciated" (England et al., 2012, p. 34). The intrinsic motivation is strengthened.

Recap of how intrinsic motivation is crowded in or out from external interventions

The bottom line is that intrinsic motivation is "crowded out" if the external interventions are perceived to be controlling; the self-esteem and the self-determination of the staff person are insulted, and the intrinsic motivation decreases for that staff person. Intrinsic motivation is "crowded in" when the staff person perceives that the external intervention is supportive. The staff person's motivation is acknowledged, and his or her competence is affirmed; this encourages the self-esteem and self-determination as the staff person feels more freedom to act as he or she sees fit and maintains a high quality of effort.

Study on how keeping our professional norms salient helps curb self-interest

Physicians have to balance the health benefits of the patient, their own profit, and the medical cost paid by the third-party payers. Kesternich, Schumacher, and Winter (2015) created an experiment with 266 German medical students in an analog study of the effect of professional norms on how the students made decisions in a number of cost-dispersion scenarios. The experimenters varied whether the scenario was framed as a medical decision-making or a neutral decision-making situation, whether the receiver was a student or a charity that served patients, and the salience of the medical professional norms (e.g., one group read a modern version of the Hippocratic oath). What resulted was that those for whom the professional norms were more salient were significantly more likely to give up some of their own benefit and give more to the receiver in a medical situation, but not in the other situations. Interestingly, in that situation, they were less concerned with efficiency. The authors concluded that the reminder of the norms in medical situations tended to restrain the self-interests of student aspiring to be physicians but did nothing regarding factoring in the costs or efficiency of the medical care.

Promoting work discretion and flexibility strengthens intrinsic motivation

According to England et al. (2012), the quality of care work depends on the extent to which staff are supported and allowed to be flexible and creative in responding to the unpredictable nature of the people who are sick. Intrinsic work motivation is built on the freedom and sense of personal control care workers feel to do their jobs. This work discretion leads to increased feelings of agency on the job, resulting in greater learning, creativity, innovation, and efficiency. Excessive control and scripting by management tends to undercut the intrinsic work motivation. When intrinsically motivated staff have a sense of trust and common shared purpose with other staff, they support each other spontaneously and can keep the collective goals as primary. As they collaborate better, there is less danger of diffusion of responsibility decreasing the quality of care.

Factors that undermine clinician intrinsic motivation

Folbre and Wright (2012) concluded that intrinsic motivations can be undermined by institutional barriers to good care, economic stress, poor working conditions, and not being able to give good-quality care because of inadequate training. Intrinsically motivated workers hate being part of organizations that treat patients badly. If the organization systemically makes it impossible to give good care, intrinsically motivated people are scandalized by that. If they are not able to do a good job because they do not have the institutional resources to do a good job or do not have the training they need, this also undercuts their motivation. If the organization does not pay them well, they do not like to feel as though the organization is taking advantage of them. Furthermore, if they are not able to take care of people important to them in their personal lives (including themselves), it is too difficult to pursue an intrinsic motivation at the expense of others they deeply care about (Nelson & Folbre, 2006).

The dangers of what we incentivize and measure

In health care today, there is a major emphasis on measurement of every aspect of health care delivery. We have to be very careful, however, that we do not inadvertently undercut the clinician compassion mindset by rewarding particular measures and not the factors that tap into the caring quality of the interactions with patients. When we reward certain performance-based measures but not the more difficult-to-measure compassionate caring variables, we can easily cause our most caring staff to focus less on the most important factors leading to our best results with patients. They will instead focus on meeting the specified targets that are rewarded (England et al., 2012). Clinicians are frustrated by compensation and quality of care being driven by patient satisfaction scores and certain performance or quality measures that may not be the best care for the patient. In a study of the impact of patient satisfaction scores on physicians and clinical care, Zgierska, Rabago, and Miller (2014) found that many physicians thought that such scores are a poor way to evaluate the quality of medical care, that they could promote inappropriate medical practices, and that too much focus on patient satisfaction survey results could take away from administrative efforts to improve medical outcomes. A number thought that patient satisfaction surveys can be perceived as a conflict of interest, and others experienced them as a punitive tool. About half of the physicians (48.1%) reported that focusing on patient satisfaction ratings had led them to practice inappropriate patient care (e.g., inappropriately prescribing an antibiotic or opioid pain medication, ordering an inappropriate test). It had led to unnecessary hospital admission by 33.6% and unnecessary procedures by 17.6%. Most of the physicians, 77.9%, said that patient satisfaction surveys negatively affected their job satisfaction. A third considered quitting (28.2%) or leaving medicine (28.2%).

Every incentive system and measure can potentially strengthen or undermine intrinsic compassion-centered motivation in the clinician

This is by no means arguing that we should get rid of patient satisfaction surveys or other measures we use in health care. These are very important tools for improving the patient experience and the quality of medical care. It is also not an argument for or against a particular incentivizing compensation system. But it is an argument that any patient satisfaction survey, measure, or compensation model can be implemented in such a way that it strengthens or undermines the clinicians' intrinsic compassion-centered motivation. This is true whether it is a fee-for-service, capitation, or value-based approach. This is true whether it is a capitalistic, socialized, or other system of universal health care. Any system can be manipulated and abused for self-interest. We have many examples of this. The intrinsic compassion-centered motivation is the ultimate promoter, regulator, and guardian of the best health care. Organizations and practices must be mindful of how they care for this type of motivation so as not to undercut the very thing we all value the most in our clinicians.

Moral injury and the clinician's intrinsic compassion-centered motivation

As we consider the ways in which the compassionate intrinsic motivation of the clinician can be undermined, there has been more of an awareness of how the dysfunctions of the current health care system are insulting and offensive to intrinsically motivated clinicians. Recently, the term *moral injury* has been applied to what clinicians are experiencing. Moral injury is a term that has been used to describe what soldiers in wartime experience. Litz, Stein, Delaney, Lebowitz, Nash, Silva, and Maguen (2009) define morally injurious experiences as

> Perpetrating, failing to prevent, bearing witness to, or learning about acts that transgress deeply held moral beliefs and expectations. This may entail participating in or witnessing inhumane or cruel actions, failing to prevent the immoral acts of others, as well as engaging in subtle acts or experiencing reactions that, upon reflection, transgress a moral code. (p. 700)

Talbot and Dean (2018) argue that physicians also experience moral injury because they are not able to provide the healing and high-quality health care they know is possible. Physicians have to satisfy insurance companies and their business organizations in terms of profit-driven motives. They have to work with EHRs that are more tailored for productivity and reimbursement than for patient care; so much time has to be spent on meeting the requirements that the EHR demands and this competes with time working with the patient. They have to deal with times when patients are not able afford medications and treatments that would help those patients. Patient satisfaction measures and the fear of litigation lead to testing and treatment that may not be necessary or appropriate, yet are experienced as necessary to protect from lawsuits or from unsatisfied unrealistic patients whose ratings can damage the reputation of a clinical practice or organization. Physicians are pulled in many different directions including their patients, their business organizations with the need to be profitable, governmental requirements, insurance companies, and their internal understanding of what very good health care should be for their patients. Not being able to give that health care because of having to attend to all these competing demands violates the compassionate intrinsic motivation of physicians and clinicians in general. As Talbot and Dean (2018) articulate this:

> Navigating an ethical path among such intensely competing drivers is emotionally and morally exhausting. Continually being caught between the Hippocratic oath, a decade of training, and the realities of making a profit from people at their sickest and most vulnerable is an untenable and unreasonable demand. Routinely experiencing the suffering, anguish, and loss of being unable to deliver the care that patients need is deeply painful. These routine, incessant betrayals of patient care and trust are examples of "death by a thousand cuts." Any one of them, delivered alone, might heal. But repeated on a daily basis, they coalesce into the moral injury of health care. (paragraph 10)

In short, as we will examine in further detail in chapter 9, the compassion-centered intrinsic motivation of clinicians must be cared for by society, health care organizations, and clinicians themselves.

CONCLUSION

To survive and thrive as a clinician, it is critical that we are aware of and continue to reflect on our motivations for doing clinical work. One of the main reasons for this is that our motivation for helping others is our touchstone for what keeps us going in this work. If the motivation is not fulfilled in the work, that disconnect becomes a risk factor for dissatisfaction and burnout. What we imagine in health care is that the desire to be compassionately caring is what drives us and what keeps us doing it. Typically, other motivations are part of the clinician's psychology. A number of those things can taint or undercut this altruistic motivation. The attachment histories of clinicians will influence the clinician compassion mindset process from the moment of noticing another person's suffering, how it affects the appraisal process, and the actual helping actions. There are ways in which the clinician's attachment history can set the stage for a healthy helping style or a dysfunctional helping style. The more dysfunctional the helping style, the more likely that the compassion mindset process will be undercut as other motivations related to the clinician's attachment psychology predominate. The key here is to be aware of one's attachment psychology and manage how it is manifested in one's clinical work. Later in the chapter, I also presented some of the common pathologies that are known to undercut the compassion mindset. Malignant motivations most often rooted in personality disorders in clinicians are clearly opposite to the compassion mindset. Other pathologies are not as clearly pathological because they can appear positive at first. These include pathological certitude, codependency, and emotional overinvolvement with patient care. Emotionally disconnected or detached care may seem benign and even positive for a number of reasons, but upon closer analysis, it turns out to be negative for both the patient and the clinician. Another concept called fears of compassion may also describe what is healthy or unhealthy in a clinician, including fears of expressing and receiving compassion or fears of being compassionate toward oneself. Finally, the issue of money was examined both in terms of how too much or too little compensation can trump the compassion mindset and how the intrinsic motivation for the compassion mindset can be enhanced or nullified by the way organizations and other situations are experienced by clinicians.

QUESTIONS FOR DISCUSSION

1. How would you describe the motivations you have for being in a health profession and how those motivations influence each other in your psychology?

2. How would you describe your particular vulnerabilities in terms of falling into dysfunctional helping patterns, considering your attachment psychology, your tendencies to be disconnected or overinvolved, and your own fears of compassion?

3. How would you describe how money and other compensation interact with your own clinician compassion mindset?

REFERENCES

Ainsworth, M., & Bell, S. (1970). Attachment, exploration and separation: Illustrated by the behavior of one-year-olds in a strange situation. *Child Development, 41,* 49–67.

Ainsworth, M. D. S., Blehar, M. C., Waters, E., & Wall, S. (1978). *Patterns of attachment: Assessed in the strange situation and at home.* Hillsdale, NJ: Erlbaum.

Austen, L. (2016). Increasing emotional support for healthcare workers can rebalance clinical detachment and empathy. *British Journal of General Practice, 66*(648), 376–377.

Bartholomew, K. (1990). Avoidance of intimacy: An attachment perspective. *Journal of Social and Personal Relationships, 7,* 147–178.

Bartholomew, K., & Shaver, P. R. (1998). Methods of assessing adult attachment: Do they converge? In J. A. Simpson & W. S. Roles (Eds.), *Attachment theory and close relationships* (pp. 25–45). New York, NY: Guilford Press.

Bartz, J. A., & Lydon, J. E. (2004). Close relationships and the working self-concept: Implicit and explicit effects of priming attachment on agency and communion. *Personality and Social Psychology Bulletin, 30*(11), 1389–1401.

Batson, C. D. (2010). Empathy-induced altruistic motivation. In M. Mikulincer & P. Shaver (Eds.), *Prosocial motives, emotions, and behavior: The better angels of our nature* (pp. 15–34). Washington, DC: American Psychological Association.

Batson, C. D. (2011). *Altruism in humans.* New York, NY: Oxford University Press.

Blomqvist, A. (1991). The doctor as double agent: Information asymmetry, health insurance, and medical care. *Journal of Health Economics, 10,* 411–432.

Bowlby, J. (1977). The making and breaking of affectional bonds: I. Aetiology and psychopathology in light of attachment theory. *British Journal of Psychiatry, 130,* 201–210.

Bowlby, J. (1978). Attachment theory and its therapeutic implications. *Adolescent Psychiatry, 6,* 5–33.

Bowlby, J. (1980). *Loss: Sadness and depression.* Vol. III of *Attachment and loss.* New York, NY: Basic Books.

Bowlby, J. (2005a). *The making and breaking of affectional bonds.* New York, NY: Routledge.

Bowlby, J. (2005b). *A secure base: Clinical applications of attachment theory.* New York, NY: Routledge.

Braddock, C. H., & Synder, L. (2005). The doctor will see you shortly: The ethical significance of time for the patient-physician relationship. *Journal of General Internal Medicine, 20,* 1057–1062.

Browne, A. (2003). Helping residents live at risk. *Cambridge Quarterly of Healthcare Ethics, 12*(1), 83–90.

Burton, R. A. (2012). Pathological certitude. In B. Oakley, A. Knafo, G. Madhavan, & D. S. Wilson (Eds.), *Pathological altruism* (pp. 131–137). New York, NY: Oxford University Press.

Campbell, C., Campbell, D., Krier, D., Kuehlthau, R., Hilmes, T., & Stromberger, M. (2009). Reduction in burnout may be a benefit for short-term medical mission volunteers. *Mental Health, Religion and Culture, 12*(7), 627–637.

Cassidy, J., & Shaver, P. R. (Eds.). (1999). *Handbook of attachment: Theory, research, and clinical applications.* New York, NY: Guilford Press.

Cermak, T. L. (1986). Diagnostic criteria for codependency. *Journal of Psychoactive Drugs, 18*(1), 15–20.

Davidhizar, R., & Shearer, R. A. (1994). Is adapting to others codependency or flexibility? *Today's OR Nurse, 16*(5), 41–43.

Dear, G. E. (2004). Test-retest reliability of the Holyoake Codependency Index with Australian students. *Psychological Reports, 94,* 482–484.

Dear, G. E., & Roberts, C. M. (2000). The Holyoake Codependency Index: Investigation of the factor structure and psychometric properties. *Psychological Reports, 87,* 991–1002.

Dear, G. E., & Roberts, C. M. (2005). Validation of the Holyoake Codependency Index. *Journal of Psychology, 139*(4), 293–313.

Dear, G. E., Roberts, C. M., & Lange, L. (2004). Defining codependency: An analysis of published definitions. In S. Shohov (Ed.), *Advances in psychology research, 34*, 63–79. Huntington, NY: Nova Science.

DeJong, C., Aguilar, T., Tseng, C-W, Lin, G. A., Boscardin, W. J., & Dudley, A. (2016). Pharmaceutical industry-sponsored meals and physician prescribing patterns for Medicare beneficiaries. *JAMA Internal Medicine, 176*(8), 1114–1122.

England, P., Folbre, N., & Leana, C. (2012). Motivating care. In N. Folbre (Ed.), *For love and money: Care provision in the United States* (pp. 21–39). New York, NY: Russell Sage Foundation.

Fickweiler, F., Fickweiler, W., & Urbach, E. (2017). Interactions between physicians and the pharmaceutical industry generally and sales representatives specifically and their association with physicians' attitudes and prescribing habits: A systematic review. *BMJ Open, 7*, e016408. doi:10.1136/bmjopen-2017-016408 1–12

Folbre, N., & Wright, E. O. (2012). Defining care. In N. Folbre (Ed.), *For love and money: Care provision in the United States* (pp. 1–20). New York, NY: Russell Sage Foundation.

Fraley, R. C., & Shaver, P. R. (2000). Adult romantic attachment: Theoretical developments, emerging controversies, and unanswered questions. *Review of General Psychology, 4*(2), 132–154.

Frey, B. S., & Jegen, R. (2001). Motivation crowding theory. *Journal of Economic Surveys, 15*(5), 589–611.

Gilbert, P. (2010). *Compassion focused therapy.* New York, NY: Routledge.

Gilbert, P., McEwan, K., Matos, M., & Rivis, A. (2010). Fears of compassion: Development of three self-report measures. *Psychology and Psychotherapy: Theory, Research and Practice, 84*, 239–255.

Gillath, O., Shaver, P. R., & Mikulincer, M. (2005). An attachment-theoretical approach to compassion and altruism. In P. Gilbert (Ed.), *Compassion: Conceptualisations, research and use in psychotherapy* (pp. 121–147). New York, NY: Routledge.

Gneezy, U., & Rustichini, A. (2000). Pay enough or don't pay at all. *Quarterly Journal of Economics, 115*(3), 791–810.

Godager, G., & Wiesen, D. (2013). Profit or patients' health benefit? Exploring the heterogeneity in physician altruism. *Journal of Health Economics, 32*, 1105–1116.

Hennig-Schmidt, H., Selten, R., & Wiesen, D. (2011). How payment systems affect physicians' provision behaviour: An experimental investigation. *Journal of Health Economics, 30*, 637–646.

Herrick, C. A. (1992). Codependency: Characteristics, risks, progression, and strategies for healing. *Nursing Forum, 27*(3), 12–19.

Hunter, J., & Maunder, R. (Eds.). (2016). *Improving patient treatment with attachment theory: A guide for primary care practitioners and specialists.* New York, NY: Springer.

Jung, C. G. (1933). *Modern man in search of a soul.* New York, NY: Harcourt Brace Jovanich.

Kahneman, D., Krueger, A. B., Schkade, D., Schwarz, N. & Stone, A. A. (2006). Would you be happier if you were richer? A focusing illusion. *Science, 312*(5782), 1908–1910.

Kesternich, I., Schumacher, H., & Winter, J. (2015). Professional norms and physician behavior: *Homo oeconomicus* or *homo hippocraticus. Journal of Public Economics, 131*, 1–11.

Landau, R. L. (1993). "... And the least of these is empathy." In H. Spiro, M. G. McCrea Curnen, E. Peschel, & D. St. James (Eds.), *Empathy and the practice of medicine* (pp. 103–109). New Haven, CT: Yale University Press.

Lapsley, D. K., Varshney, N. M., & Aalsma, M. C. (2000). Pathological attachment and attachment style in late adolescence. *Journal of Adolescence, 23*, 137–155.

Larson, D. G. (1993). *The helper's journey: Working with people facing grief, loss, and life-threatening illness.* Champaign, IL: Research Press.

Lief, H. I., & Fox, R. C. (1963). Training for "detached concern" in medical students. In H. Lief, V. Lief, & N. Lief (Eds.), *The psychological basis of medical practice* (pp. 12–35). New York, NY: Hoeber Medical Division.

Litz, B. T., Stein, N., Delaney, E., Lebowitz, L., Nash, W. P., Silva, C., & Maguen, S. (2009). Moral injury and moral repair in war veterans: A preliminary model and intervention strategy. *Clinical Psychology Review*, 29, 695–706.

Malloy, G. B., & Berkery, A. (1993). Codependency: A feminist perspective. *Journal of Psychosocial Nursing and Mental Health Services*, 31(4), 15–19.

Marcus, E. R. (2003). Medical student dreams about medical school: The unconscious developmental process of becoming a physician. *International Journal of Psycho-Analysis*, 84, 367–386.

Marks, A. D. G., Blore, R. L., Hine, D. W., & Dear, G. E. (2012). Development and validation of a revised measure of codependency. *Australian Journal of Psychology*, 64, 119–127.

Maslach, C., Schaufeli, W. B., & Leiter, M. P. (2001). Job burnout. *Annual Review of Psychology*, 52, 397–422.

Mikulincer, M., & Shaver, P. R. (2016). *Attachment in adulthood: Structure, dynamics, and change* (2nd ed.). New York, NY: Guilford Press.

Mikulincer, M., Shaver, P. R., Gillath, O., & Nitzberg, R. A. (2005). Attachment, caregiving, and altruism: Boosting attachment security increases compassion and helping. *Journal of Personality and Social Psychology*, 89(5), 817–839.

Mitchell, J. M., Hadley, J., Sulmasy, D. P., & Bloche, J. G. (2000). Measuring the effects of managed care on physicians' perceptions of their personal financial incentives. *Inquiry*, 37, 134–145.

Moore, R. L. (2003). *Facing the dragon: Confronting personal and spiritual grandiosity*. Wilmette, IL: Chiron.

Nelson, J. A., & Folbre, N. (2006). Why a well-paid nurse is a better nurse. *Nursing Economics*, 24(3), 127–130.

Neumann, M., Bensing, J., Wirtz, M., Wübker, A., Scheffer, C., Tauschel, D., ... Pfaff, H. (2010). The impact of financial incentives on physician empathy: A study from the perspective of patients with private and statutory health insurance. *Patient Education and Counseling*, 84(2), 208–216.

Norman, L., Lawrence, N., Iles, A., Benattayallah, A., & Karl, A. (2015). Attachment-security priming attenuates amygdala activation to social and linguistic threat. *Social Cognitive and Affective Neuroscience*, 10(6), 832–839. doi: 10.1093/scan/nsu127

Oakley, B., Knafo, A., Madhavan, G., & Wilson, D. S. (Eds.). (2012). *Pathological altruism*. New York, NY: Oxford University Press.

Osler, W. (1904). On the educational value of the medical society. In *Aequanimitas* (pp. 345–362). Philadelphia, PA: Blakiston's.

Osler, W., Hinorhara, S., & Niki, H. (2001). *Osler's "A way of life" & other addresses with commentary & annotations*. Durham, NC: Duke University Press.

Piff, P. K., Kraus, M. W., Coté, S., Cheng, B. H., & Keltner, D. (2010). Having less, giving more: The influence of social class on prosocial behavior. *Journal of Personality and Social Psychology*, 99(5), 771–784.

Piff, P. K., & Robinson, A. R. (2017). Social class and prosocial behavior: Current evidence, caveats, and questions. *Current Opinion in Psychology*, 18, 6–10.

Rampell, C. (2011, January 11). Why so many rich people don't feel very rich. *The New York Times*. Retrieved from https://economix.blogs.nytimes.com/2011/01/11/why-so-many-rich-people-dont-feel-very-rich

Reiser, S. J. (1993). Science, pedagogy, and the transformation of empathy in medicine. In H. Spiro, M. G. M. Curnen, E. Peschel, & D. St. James (Eds.), *Empathy and the practice of medicine* (pp. 121–132). New Haven, CT: Yale University Press.

Ricard, M. (2015). *Altruism: The power of compassion to change yourself and the world*. New York, NY: Little, Brown.

Richardson, R. (2000). A necessary inhumanity? *Journal of Medical Ethics: Medical Humanities*, 26, 104–106.

Salmon, P., & Young, B. (2009). Dependence and caring in clinical communication: The relevance of attachment and other theories. *Patient Education and Counseling*, 74, 331–338.

Seelig, B. J., & Rosof, L. S. (2001). Normal and pathological altruism. *Journal of the American Psychoanalytic Association, 49,* 933–959.

Stafford, L. L. (2001). Is codependency a meaningful concept? *Issues in Mental Health Nursing, 22,* 273–286.

Stellar, J. E., Manzo, V. M., Kraus, M. W., & Keltner, D. (2012). Class and compassion: Socioeconomic factors predict responses to suffering. *Emotion, 12*(3), 449–459.

Talbot, S. G. & Dean, W. (2018, July 26). Physicians aren't 'burning out.' They're suffering from moral injury. *STAT.* Retrieved from https://www.statnews.com/2018/07/26/physicians-not-burning-out-they-are-suffering-moral-injury/

Tom, S. M., Fox, C. R., Trepel, C., & Poldrack, R. A. (2007). The neural basis of loss aversion in decision-making under risk. *Science, 315*(5811), 515–518.

Van der Wal, D. (1996). Codependency: A concomitant field of interest in research into the phenomenon caring. *Curationis, 19*(4), 40–42.

Van Kleef, G. A., Oveis, C., van der Löwe, I., LuoKogan, A., Goetz, J., & Keltner, D. (2008). Power, distress, and compassion: Turning a blind eye to the suffering of others. *Psychological Science, 19*(12), 1315–1322.

West, M., & Sheldon, A. E. R. (1988). Classification of pathological attachment patterns in adults. *Journal of Personality Disorders, 2*(2), 153–159.

Whitfield, C. L. (1984). Co-alcoholism: Recognizing a treatable illness. *Family and Community Health, 7,* 16–25.

Zgierska, A., Rabago, D., & Miller, M. M. (2014). Impact of patient satisfaction ratings on physicians and clinical care. *Patient Preference and Adherence, 8,* 437–446.

CREDIT

"Unrealistic Difficult Patients and the Titanic of a Healthcare System."

"The test of a first-rate intelligence is the ability to hold two opposing ideas in mind at the same time and still retain the ability to function. One should, for example, be able to see that things are hopeless yet be determined to make them otherwise."

—F. Scott Fitzgerald

Chapter Sections:

- ▶ Introduction
- ▶ Dehumanized Health Care
- ▶ External Barriers to Compassion
- ▶ Increased Incivility in Society and Abuse of Health Care Professionals
- ▶ Malpractice Claims and Defensive Medicine
- ▶ Epidemic of Negative Health Behaviors in Society
- ▶ Breakdown of Community
- ▶ Economic Reductionism and the Commodification of Compassion
- ▶ The New World of Electronic Health Records
- ▶ Impact of Technology and Electronics on Health Care Relationships
- ▶ Compartmentalization of the Helping Professions and Loss of Compassion
- ▶ Is Health Care in "*Titanic* Time" or "*Apollo 13* Time"?
- ▶ Conclusion

CHAPTER 9

The Societal Factors That Make Compassionate Caring More Difficult

Questions to consider before reading this chapter:

1. What are the external societal factors that make a compassion mindset difficult for you to maintain?

2. How should we prepare clinicians in terms of what they will face in a health care career in the twenty-first century?

INTRODUCTION

Every historical period and culture present unique challenges to the clinician compassion mindset

Compassionate caring does not exist in a cultural vacuum. While suffering has always been part of life, every historical period has its own problems and ways that it can worsen (or theoretically improve) the suffering of that time. The response to that suffering also shifts with the passage of history. In some periods, certain societies are noted for their increase in compassionate response, and at other times, they are marked by a decline in that compassion. Every period of history has a unique set of forces or dynamics that pose unique challenges for those who dedicate their lives to compassionate response. To maintain a compassion mindset as a clinician, it is important to consider the historical and cultural context that enables or impedes compassionate caring. To deal especially with the dynamics and situations that make compassionate response difficult, it is important that clinicians be able to articulate what those challenges to compassionate caring are. In this chapter, I will describe some of these external societal challenges that we must manage in order to maintain a compassion mindset amid situations that can demoralize even the most resolute of caring professionals. The hope would be that we can create a more compassionate caring world in the new millennium.

Helping professions explicitly dedicated to respond to all suffering

If you are reading this book, in one way or another you are either in a particular health care profession or preparing to be in one. In doing so, you are declaring explicitly that you want to live a life of compassion—that is, you know there is suffering, you are moved by it, and you want to do what you can to try to relieve that suffering. While human beings are built for compassion, those who choose helping professions or vocations are centering their whole life's work on the attempt to relieve or prevent suffering. Ideally, that is the way all humans should be, not just helping professionals or full-time caregivers. But among this group is often a desire and a commitment to respond to all suffering, not just the suffering of one's own loved ones, communities, or tribes. In medicine, there is an explicit code that we help everyone, friend and stranger. While we live out our heart's desire to help others, we therefore also have to prepare ourselves for an ordeal.

Health care professionals go where the hardest things are

Many people probably warned you or currently advise you to get out of this work or change how you are doing it. Sometimes we need to heed that advice, and other times we need to ignore it (or challenge that person to get on the compassion bus with us!). It can be a hard life and can take a terrible emotional toll. Health care is hard work now, but it has always been hard. As health care professionals both now and throughout history, we always go where there are hard things. We go to help people who suffer from disasters, plagues, wars, political turmoil, poverty, racism, diseases, accidents, and human evils. That is what we do. Of course, we're going to complain, because we are right there where the suffering is. There has always been burnout, compassion fatigue, and dark nights of the soul. But when we have the compassion and the capacity, we do not want to turn away. We have to take care of ourselves, but compassion is what we were built to do, and that is the source of our deepest fulfillment.

The need to prepare ourselves for the hard journey of health care and responding to suffering

Let us take a few pages to complain about what we have to face in our health care professions and what we may have to deal with in the near future. This chapter will not be comprehensive. You will have more to add, and there are major works and research on this topic in many fields, including anthropology, sociology, political science, and history. My hope is that you articulate what the historical challenges are for yourself, decide what piece of that you want to handle (because we cannot help everyone), and prepare yourself for what you have to face. When I decide to do a long hike up a mountain, I have to anticipate what I am going to face in terms of weather and climbing conditions. I have to plan for the supplies I need. I have to assess the risks and have a realistic appraisal of my ability to do this journey. Did I condition myself well enough for it? If I get into trouble, how will I seek help? Do I have an unrealistically optimistic expectation of the journey, or have I prepared myself for setbacks? The bottom line is, if I really want to take this journey, it helps me to know what I may face along the way. In this historical period of health care, what do we need to prepare ourselves to face on this journey?

DEHUMANIZED HEALTH CARE

An external force that is constantly a challenge for clinicians trying to sustain a compassion mindset is the way in which our health care is experienced as dehumanizing and depersonalizing for everyone. Patients often complain that they feel reduced to mere objects in a health care business, more as consumers than as patients. Interestingly, health care clinicians also complain that they feel depersonalized and not able to do the healing work that they want to do in the way they would like to do it. Clinicians often feel like pawns in a dysfunctional health care system; they can feel reduced to being mere functionaries, servants of electronic medical records, governmental regulations, and insurance billing requirements. Science and technology are imagined as being the source of healing, with clinicians simply getting the test results and following protocol guidelines. Clinicians are frustrated at being cast as the passive purveyors of evidence-based protocols mandated by systems or have been unwitting participants in the "creeping normalcy" of depersonalizing forces in health care (Gabbert & Salud, 2009). Even patients depersonalize the clinicians as servants of the technology. They think all the answers can be found in the scans, the labs, and Google, and that all their doctor needs to do is keep up with the latest advances.

Research on patient and physician ratings of compassionate care in our society

Interestingly, patients and physicians view the health care system similarly. In a survey of 510 physicians and 800 patients who were recently hospitalized conducted by the Schwartz Center for Compassionate Healthcare, Lown, Rosen, and Marttila (2011) reported that "only 53% of patients and 58% of physicians said that the US health care system generally provides compassionate care" (p. 1774). Nearly half of both patients and physicians think the system needs work in terms of compassionate care. When patients and physicians were asked to rate what compassionate care is like at the individual level, "78% of physicians said that most health care professionals provide compassionate care, but only 54% of patients said that they do" (Lown et al., 2011, p. 1774). At the individual level, then, physicians think they are doing a very good job with compassionate care but only half of patients think so. There are two possible reasons for this. One is that physicians actually are trying to be compassionate in their care, but patients are not picking this up. The other is that physicians overestimate the quality of their compassionate care, and the patient assessment is a more accurate appraisal.

Strong general agreement about the importance of compassionate care

While there is a discrepancy in how patients and physicians judge the quality of the physician's compassionate care, both patients and physicians are in general agreement about the importance of compassionate care. Most of the patients (85%) and most of the physicians (76%) believe that compassionate care is "very important" to achieve successful medical treatment. In terms of what makes a difference in a patient living or dying, most physicians (71%) and most patients (81%) think that good emotional support and communication can make a difference, and far fewer physicians (23%) and patients (19%) think that physician scientific knowledge and medical skills were the only factors in helping a patient live or die.

Patients, physicians, and clinicians in general all want the same thing

In light of all the criticisms of physicians for being too biomedically focused and not emotionally supportive enough, it is astounding that when patients and physicians are asked to rate the importance of various elements of compassionate care for patients, they are largely in agreement. Looking at table 9.1 of Lown et al.'s (2011) result, the rank ordering of each compassionate behavior is very similar. In many ways, patients and physicians want the same thing. We can safely assume other health professionals would also rate these similarly. The bottom line is that we all want the same thing in health care: We want it to be compassionate. But both patients and clinicians are very unhappy with the way things are. While nurses and other clinicians were not surveyed in this research, their perspective would be very similar. It would be one thing if patients wanted compassionate care and physicians did not think it was as important, but the fact is that physicians think compassionate care is important, too. That is why these results are so astounding. We all think compassion is important, and we all want it to be that way, even if we have excuses or rationalizations for why it cannot be that way.

Patient fears about hospitals and health care

Sweeney (2017) interviewed 1,080 adults, asking, "If you were a patient in a hospital, what would your greatest fear be?" In this qualitative study, she found that 96% had some significant fear about hospitals or health care.

The top 11 fears were as follows: "1. Infection; 2. Incompetence; 3. Death; 4. Cost; 5. Medical mix-up; 6. Needles; 7. Rude doctors and nurses; 8. Germs; 9. Diagnosis/prognosis; 10. Communication issues; and 11. Loneliness" (Sweeney, 2017, p. 195). Three of the top fears are explicitly about the clinicians themselves in terms of incompetence, rude doctors and nurses, and communication issues. A fourth fear, medical mix-ups, is related to mistakes that are due to things such as human error; communication failures among staff; and staff working in a stressful, complex health care delivery process. This means four of the top fears are connected to the clinicians themselves.

Haque and Waytz's analysis of the causes for dehumanization in health care

It may be helpful at this point to consider what the causes of this dehumanization are, relying on the excellent work of Haque and Waytz (2012). They state that dehumanization in medicine results from "structural and organizational features of hospital life, as well as from functional psychological demands intrinsic to the medical profession" (p. 176). They explain that the dehumanization is essentially "a diminished attribution and consideration of other's mental states" (p. 177), denying their experience in feeling pleasure or pain and their agency—that is, their ability to plan or make choices. Neurologically, what occurs is a deactivation of the medial prefrontal cortex, which is associated with mentalizing (Harris & Fiske, 2006; Haque & Waytz, 2012). This means we stop inferring and representing within ourselves what the mental states of others are. Haque and Waytz concluded that there are six possible causes of dehumanization:

TABLE 9.1 Patients' and Physicians' Views on the Importance of Compassionate Care (Lown et al., 2011, p. 1774)

ELEMENT OF COMPASSIONATE CARE	PATIENTS RATING THE ELEMENT 9 OR 10 (%)	PHYSICIANS RATING THE ELEMENT 9 OR 10 (%)
Show respect for you, your family, and those important to you[a]	87	89
Convey information to you in a way that is understandable[b]	87	89
Communicate test results in a timely and sensitive manner[a]	85	76
Treat you as a person, not just a disease[a]	85	86
Listen attentively to you[b]	84	86
Always involve you in decisions about your treatment[b]	82	78
Gain your trust[b]	79	85
Consider the effect of your illness on you, your family, and the people most important to you[b]	74	65
Comfortably discuss sensitive, emotional, or psychological issues[a]	73	65
Express sensitivity, caring, and compassion for your situation[b]	67	70
Spend enough time with you[a]	66	70
Strive to understand your emotional needs[b]	62	60
Give you hope, even when the news is bad[b]	57	57
Show understanding of your cultural and religious beliefs[a]	51	61

Source: Authors' analysis of Schwartz Center for Compassionate Healthcare national telephone survey of 800 patients and 510 physicians, conducted between September 23 and October 29, 2010.
Notes: For each element, respondents were asked, "On a scale of 1 to 10, how important is a doctor's ability to...," with 10 defined as "absolute top priority and needs maximum attention." To test the maximum number of elements in the patient sample, we employed split sampling. Thus, we asked 415 patients about some elements, and 386 patients about other elements. This does not sum to the total number of patients (800) because of weighting and rounding. We asked all 510 physicians about all of the elements. [a]n is 415 patients. [b]n is 386 patients.

1. *Deindividuating practices:* The medical culture tends to have practices that take away individuality by subsuming people as anonymous members of a particular group. This occurs both with the caregivers and with the patients. Like soldiers in the same uniforms who can feel less personal responsibility for

what happens in war, clinicians in their white coats and scrubs can feel less individual responsibility for what happens with patients. Patients become deindividuated by making them all dress in skimpy hospital gowns. Haque and Waytz (2012) recommend changing medical practices that take away individuality, such as doing away with white coats or other uniforms and instead having clinicians wear idiosyncratic yet professional clothing.

2. *Impaired patient agency*: As a consequence of their illness or injury, patients have impaired capacities to think, plan, make decisions, and act. Because their thought process is diminished, patients are more helpless, dependent, and passive. Decisions and actions are made for the patient, and it may in fact be more difficult to know of the patient's personal experiences and preferences. Haque and Waytz (2012) suggest that medical environments institute ways of reminding both clinicians and patients of the patient's ability to plan, make decisions, and act. Ways to do this can include clinicians remembering to treat patients as partners in clinical decisions and also being mindful of the personal and professional lives of their patients that are not obvious in a clinical setting.

3. *Dissimilarity*: Dehumanization can result from how patients are dissimilar to the professional care providers. Haque and Waytz (2012) focus on physician–patient dissimilarity, but the same dynamic can occur between patients and nurses, aides, therapists, and administrators. Haque and Waytz describe three ways this can happen. First, there is a dissimilarity in illness; the patient is ill and may seem less fully human compared to the caregivers. That is, there is

a way in which ill people are not viewed as normal, and there is a tendency to dehumanize others when they appear different than the norm. Second, dissimilarity between caregivers and patients is heightened by the fact that patients are labeled by their illnesses. Labeling someone as a "diabetic" as opposed to "a person with diabetes" predisposes caregivers to view him or her as the disease itself rather than a person who has the disease. Dehumanization occurs because labeling people as their disease makes them appear less than fully human. Third, the power asymmetry between a caregiver and a patient also can contribute to dehumanization. People who are ill and in need of care have lost power over their lives and are seeking physicians, for example, to help them regain that control. Dehumanization of patients tends to occur because they are seen as having less power. Having power can itself change the thinking of people who have that power. People with power do not have to consider what people with less power think and feel, and gradually the people with power become accustomed to overlooking what patients are experiencing. To reverse these dehumanizing dynamics, Haque and Waytz suggest that training and clinical practice include reminders of how patients and clinicians are both mortal and what all humans are like when they become vulnerable and suffer. They also suggest that organizations try to match the racial, ethnic, and gender demographics of caregivers with those of their patients, thereby improving perceptions of similarity. Finally, they urge organizations to resist labeling their patients by their injuries or diseases.

Haque and Waytz (2012) label the next three causes as *functional causes*, meaning that they are psychologically intrinsic to effective medical practice and result as understandable by-products of the way medicine is practiced.

4. *Mechanization:* From one perspective, biomedical reductionism can be very helpful in medicine. Objectifying people into their component parts can greatly facilitate medical problem solving. Analyzing a person's symptoms and clinical findings by searching for the specific source of the problem within the various physiological systems helps with diagnosis and treatment. The injury or disease is explained by referring to organs, blood levels, biochemistry, and so on. Treatment interventions focus on particular body parts, organs, or biochemical dynamics. While looking at people in this mechanized fashion can be very useful for diagnosis and treatment, habitually viewing people in this way can understandably lead to a more dehumanized view of the person. Haque and Waytz (2012) recommend finding ways to remind clinicians of the patient as a person. Some ways to do this include clinicians at rounds always mentioning something about the patient's personal history or current life. In surgical procedures, the team might be told something about who this person is or how he or she came to need this surgery.

5. *Empathy reduction:* Haque and Waytz (2012) review research that documents a decline in empathy as physicians go through medical school as well as a decline in pain empathy, in which physicians are not as emotionally affected by the perception of pain in others. They argue that this increased cognitive control of emotional responses may be necessary for the higher level of medical problem solving necessary for the practice of medicine. This regulation of emotional responses to patients can be helpful because it allows physicians and other clinicians to do things that ordinary people would find unpleasant or disgusting. They also explained that complex problem solving may require suspending empathy for the purposes of efficient problem solving and high-pressure situations. Dehumanizing patients may be a way to manage emotionally stressful situations and cognitively manage the situations in the most efficient way possible. Haque and Waytz recommend training clinicians to be able to learn the respective benefits and limitations of empathic versus more cognitively objective approaches and to learn how to switch back and forth between the two approaches. (One of the main purposes of this book is to propose the clinician compassion mindset model that integrates these two approaches rather than making them opposed to each other.) The other means of dealing with the problem of empathy reduction is to do a better job of selecting clinicians who can exercise both sets of skills well. Haque and Waytz suggest assessment and interview methods that can identify candidates for training who are potentially capable in both skill sets.

6. *Moral disengagement:* Because physicians are required to perform procedures that inflict pain or make patients feel uncomfortable, they must learn how to disengage from the fact that they are inflicting some harm for the sake of helping the person in the long term. Dehumanization can understandably result, because physicians and other clinicians learn how to minimize the pain and discomfort they witness in

their patients. The problem is that becoming accustomed to doing this may extend this emotional detachment further than is required. Haque and Waytz (2012) suggest practices that decrease the psychological distance between patients and clinicians, such as changing the depersonalizing hospital gowns. In medical specialties dominated by technology—such as in pathology and radiology, in which there may not even be direct patient contact—they suggest putting a picture of the person in the record. They cite Turner and Hadas-Halpern's (2008) study in which radiologists gave more accurate diagnoses and patient outcomes improved when there were photographs of the patient's face with the scans.

EXTERNAL BARRIERS TO COMPASSION

Fernando and Consedine (2014) note that our research on compassion has tended to neglect studying the barriers to compassion in medicine. The general view by clinicians and patients alike is that compassion is a simple behavior that can be turned on when it is expected. But as the researchers note and as we have seen in earlier chapters,

> as a prosocial behaviour, the expression of compassion results from a complex interplay of multiple variables involving the individual (e.g., personality type), the specific situation and the environment where the compassionate act takes place. Because of this complexity, compassion can be easily disrupted. (Fernando & Consedine, 2014, p. 388)

We have tended to focus on internal psychological variables such as compassion fatigue, stress, and burnout. Thus, Fernando and Consedine examined what physicians feel are barriers to being compassionate with patients.

Barriers to physician compassion

In developing the Barriers to Physician Compassion questionnaire, Fernando and Consedine (2014) found that the four major impediments to being compassionate in their clinical practice were (a) physician burnout and overload; (b) external distractions (e.g., multiple interruptions in patient care, culture of defensive medicine and fear of lawsuits, excessive documentation); (c) difficult patients/families; and (d) complex clinical situations (e.g., cultural and communication barriers with patients, personal emotional reactions interfering with compassionate response). Overall, these external barriers can undercut the effort to be in a compassion mindset and require a great deal of individual effort and (ideally) organizational support to overcome these barriers, as we will discuss at length in the components of balanced compassionate caring in later chapters.

Inspired by this notion of barriers to clinician compassion, I offer a number of societal factors and trends that may also be considered threats to maintaining the compassion mindset and which we must prepare for in the years to come. At this point, let us consider

- Increased incivility in society and abuse of health care professionals
- Malpractice claims and defensive medicine
- Epidemic of negative health behaviors in society
- Breakdown of community
- Economic reductionism and the commodification of compassion
- New world of electronic health records

- Impact of technology and electronics on health care relationships
- Compartmentalization of the helping professions and loss of compassion

INCREASED INCIVILITY IN SOCIETY AND ABUSE OF HEALTH CARE PROFESSIONALS

One of the major challenges of this time that clinicians are more frequently facing is an increasing rudeness in our society as well as physical and emotional abusiveness from patients and their loved ones. Clinicians are not the only ones experiencing this, and it is one of the most frequent topics of discussion among teachers, food servers, customer service staff, receptionists, cashiers, firefighters, paramedics, police officers, and anyone who dedicates their work to others. Simply ask any one of these people about how their clientele treats them and you will open the floodgates on stories of incredibly entitled and rude behavior they have experienced. It is one of the most demoralizing realities of our time and a major threat to all these professions. Add to this an increase in self-centeredness and ingratitude that is very common in service work. We not only have a barrier to compassion in practice, we also have a major threat to the future of helping professions. Why would people want to go into the work of serving others if they most often would be met with rude, threatening, and ungrateful behavior?

Emergency rooms as war zones

In health care, it is the emergency room staff who can tell you endless stories of extremely rude and dangerous actions done to health care staffs.

Emergency Departments have been described as "distilleries of human fear and anxiety" resulting in the demonstration of aggressive and violent behaviour. Furthermore, Sweet (1991) compares working in the ED's in North America to working on the frontline of a war zone. (Chapman & Styles, 2006, p. 246)

The epidemic of drug abuse, including opioid abuse, has led to the threat of verbal and physical abuse, even death, of clinicians. Clinicians of all types now have to deal with the increased likelihood of being the target of verbal or physical attacks, not only in emergency rooms but in practically any unit of a hospital or any type of clinic.

Research on workplace violence against nurses

Speroni, Fitch, Dawson, Dugan, and Atherton (2014) surveyed nurses with over 10 years of experience regarding whether they have encountered workplace violence in the past year. The results were staggering. In a sample of 762 nurses, 76.0% had experienced some type of patient physical or verbal violence. Among emergency room nurses, 96.7% reported some type of workplace violence. The major causes were patients with dementia (49.9%), drug-seeking patients (47.9%), and patients under the influence of alcohol (45.0%). For nurses working in the emergency department, 77.2% of the incidents were related to drug-seeking behavior, and 70.7% were related to patients/visitors intoxicated by alcohol or 69.6% by drugs. Over their whole careers in a sample of 595 nurses, 63.7% experienced physical violence and 25.4% verbal violence. Nurses and other clinicians now regularly have to prepare for the likelihood of some type of physical or verbal violence, which as we saw in chapter 3 makes it very difficult for clinicians to stay in a compassion mindset if they do not feel safe with a patient. Furthermore, this study shows the toll the epidemic of drug abuse is having on our clinicians.

Rudeness negatively affects clinical therapeutic performance and teamwork

There is a way in which people who are not in service or health care work can minimize the impact of uncivil patients and customers. While we would expect some of this type of behavior in anything that is human, the tremendous increase in this incivility and threatening behavior is a societal crisis that threatens the emotional infrastructure of our society. Not only is it an emotional burden to the service providers, it also actually threatens the quality of health care itself. Riskin et al. (2017) conducted experiments on the effects of rudeness on NICU physician and nurse teams. Compared to the control group, exposure to mild rudeness actually interfered with the quality of the therapy plan, the procedural and skill performance, and the general therapeutic score (e.g., diagnostic errors, plan execution errors, general performance). It also significantly interfered with teamwork processes such as workload sharing, helping among team members, team member communication, and general teamwork performance. Similar results have been found in other studies (Rafaeli et al., 2012) showing how customer verbal aggression negatively affects the employee cognitive processes (e.g., attention, memory, problem solving).

Types of disrespectful behavior in health care

Leape et al. (2012) published their findings from a Harvard Medical School working group on professionalism and argue that "disrespectful behavior is the 'root cause' of the dysfunctional culture that permeates health care and stymies progress in safety and that it is also a product of that culture" (p. 845). They identified six types of disrespectful behaviors that occur in health care. First, *disruptive behavior* consists of inappropriate action and words that "interfere with, or has the potential to interfere with, quality health care delivery" (College of Physicians and Surgeons of Ontario, 2008, p. 5). The Joint Commission on Accreditation of Healthcare Organizations (2012) revised the term *disruptive behaviors* to "behaviors that undermine a culture of safety" (p. 13). Examples include verbally and physically aggressive actions such as angry outbursts, swearing, throwing objects, abusive language, shaming, bullying, insensitive comments, inappropriate joking or comments, violations of physical boundaries, and sexual harassment. The second type of disrespectful behavior is *demeaning and humiliating treatment of nurses, residents, medical students, or any subordinates*. This is an abuse of power that is very difficult to confront because of fear of retaliation by the physician. Not only might physicians engage in this type of disrespect, but nurses may do this to their subordinates, such as other nurses, residents, and students. Residents might do this to younger residents, interns, and students. The third type of disrespectful behavior is *passive–aggressive behavior*, in which the physician (or other clinician) employs passive resistance to what is expected of him or her. Examples include declining to do expected tasks or performing those tasks in such a way as to annoy others, such as administrators, colleagues, and even patients. This may include delaying needed actions, making others look bad, and being very critical of their organization or others. People who engage in passive–aggressive behavior intend psychological harm because of their hidden anger, but they will pretend to be innocent, complain about being unfairly treated, and inappropriately blame others. The fourth type of disrespectful behavior is *passive disrespect*. In contrast to passive–aggressive behavior, this behavior is not based in malice or anger; rather, it may be a reflection of a person's burnout, frustration, apathy, or related state. Examples include not working collaboratively, not doing patient documentation in a timely way, arriving late to meetings, and not participating in organizational improvement or safety efforts.

Dismissive treatment of patients

The first four types of disrespect mainly concern disrespect to other health care staff, although all of them can occur toward patients and their loved ones as well. The fifth type of disrespect is focused on patients: *dismissive treatment of patients*. Examples include talking to the patient in a condescending way, ignoring the patient with others such as loved ones or other clinicians present in the room, putting the patient down in some way, or communicating being annoyed with the patient. Clinicians subtly or bluntly demean the patient, discount how the patient feels or thinks, or do not take what the patient says seriously. This kind of behavior can also occur toward other health care staff.

Systemic disrespect

Finally, the sixth type of disrespect is *systemic disrespect*. This characteristic of health care systems is so common that it might not be recognized as disrespectful. The main example Leape et al. (2012) offer is how it is expected for patients to wait for just about any service

they receive in health care. The message here is that the patient's time is not as important as the physician's or other clinician's time. Systemic disrespect of patients also occurs when patients are repetitively asked for information that has already been given or when staff do not treat patients in a courteous manner, fail to apologize for mistakes, or discount the need of patients to get the information they need for their care. However, Leape et al. point out the physicians and other clinicians also get systematically disrespected when they are overscheduled. Health care organizations many times do not give them the time they need to see their patients, instead expecting assembly-line behavior. But when a patient needs more time or there is an unexpected patient issue that must be addressed, the clinician is just expected to "deal with it." Leape et al. point out that this is a kind of disrespect to both the clinician and the patient. The later patients are just expected to accept it and wait. With greater emphasis on improving the patient experience, health care organizations often work to improve this or at least notify patients, if they can, or apologize. Systemic disrespect can also occur toward other staff such as nurses and residents in terms of overwork, poor or unsafe working conditions, and even being routinely understaffed.

MALPRACTICE CLAIMS AND DEFENSIVE MEDICINE

One major external barrier to compassion physicians and other clinicians face is the increase in litigiousness in our society and the costly impact this has on the practice of medicine as well as personally for clinicians. In a survey of 1,500 hospitalists, 25% had been sued for medical practice. For those who had been in practice for 20 or more years, 55% had been sued. The hospitalists estimated that the perceived need to practice defensive medicine amounts to 37.5% of health care costs (Saint, Vaughn, Chopra, Fowler, & Kachalia, 2018). In a study of 1,214 orthopedic surgeons, 96% reported practicing defensive medicine by making specialist referrals, admitting to the hospital, or ordering lab tests and scans in order to avoid lawsuits. The surgeons estimated that defensive medicine accounts for 24% of all ordered tests. The researchers estimated that defensive medicine accounts nationally for $2 billion in the specialty of orthopedic surgery (Sethi, Obremskey, Natividad, & Jahangir, 2012). Reschovsky & Saiontz-Martinez (2018) estimated that defensive medicine accounts for 8% to 20% of Medicare costs. Cost varied by specialty, with family physicians having the most defensive medicine costs (probably in part because they see a high number of Medicare patients). In terms of personal consequences to physicians, in a sample of 7,164 American surgeons, Balch et al. (2011) assessed factors that were independently associated with having had a medical malpractice suit in the previous two years. They found increased likelihood of burnout and depression as well as increased suicidal ideation in the prior year. The overall quality of life for those who had been sued was poorer than for those who had not been sued. They had significantly decreased career satisfaction and were less likely to recommend that their children go into medicine, much less become a surgeon. The highest rates of malpractice claims were in the following surgical specialties: neurology, 31%; cardiothoracic, 29%; general surgery, 28%; colorectal, 28%; and obstetrics/gynecology, 28%. No matter what the outcomes of the lawsuit are, physicians live more emotionally burdened and stressed during the litigation process, as well as lose practice time and deal with concerns about

their reputation. Patients and their families are also undergoing similarly stressful lives during the process. The average time for completing a malpractice suit is 19 months (Jena, Chandra, Lakdawalla, & Seabury, 2012).

EPIDEMIC OF NEGATIVE HEALTH BEHAVIORS IN SOCIETY

The United States is ranked as one of the lowest on most measures of health status compared to the 30 developed nations of the Organisation for Economic Co-operation and Development (Schroeder, 2007). These are measures such as maternal mortality, life expectancy from birth, and infant mortality. In terms of the relative contributions to premature death, 40% are due to behavioral patterns, 30% to genetic predisposition, 15% to social circumstances, 10% to inadequate health care, and 5% to environmental exposure. Schroeder (2007) points out that while immunization and antibiotics were the major forces in improving the public's health in the twentieth century, the key to improvement in the twenty-first century "is more likely to come from behavioral change than from technological innovation" (p. 1222). The four unhealthy behaviors that cause most of the chronic diseases and conditions leading to a great deal of suffering and early death are lack of physical activity, poor nutrition, excessive alcohol, and tobacco use (Centers for Disease Control and Prevention, 2017). Our behaviors related to obesity, alcohol use, and smoking account for 70% of US health care costs (National Association of Health Underwriters, 2015). Also, those who live in poverty are disproportionately affected by the determinants of health status that are within our control, including social factors, personal behavior, access to and quality of health care, and environment (Schroeder, 2007). But our political and economic systems appear quite resistant to systemic change.

Clinician emotional reactions to the negative health behavior epidemic

In every health care setting in which I have worked or consulted, clinicians are alarmingly concerned about the epidemic of negative health behaviors. But that concern often becomes so overwhelming in a number of ways that it can undermine the clinician compassion mindset. One way it is so frustrating to clinicians is that it is all under the behavioral control of the patients. Clinicians are flabbergasted that their patients will not heed the warning signs and change their health behaviors. It seems the rational thing to do, and yet so much of our population is not rational about this. Add to this the clinician frustration at the tremendous economic marketing machinery that has mentally conditioned our society to keep pursuing these negative health behaviors. Clinicians become angry at their patients and at the big business that trains their consumers to keep doing these self-destructive behaviors. Poverty intensifies these frustrations because those who live in poverty are especially affected by societal forces, fewer economic resources, lack of political power, and psychological stress related to poverty. When clinicians become frustrated by the lack of behavioral change in their patients and by the societal and political factors that block improvement, they may become angry. That anger, of course, is a secondary emotion—secondary to feeling helpless in the face of enormous, preventable suffering. When that happens, it is easy to see why clinicians might take out their anger on patients

or just avoid helping them, restricting their practices to easier problems. It is also a reason clinicians may slide into emotional detachment; they just treat the patients in a perfunctory way and never try to help them change their behaviors.

New attitudes and skill sets required for twenty-first-century health care

In light of this epidemic, clinicians of the twenty-first century have to be better in general than they were in the twentieth century with regard to truly implementing the biopsychosocial model and having the skills to promote health behavior change. A number of clinicians have entered the twenty-first century wishing they did not have to abandon the solely biomedical model that became comfortable and straightforward. But as clinicians, we do not get the luxury of having the disease fall into our preferences. Just as certain bacteria mutate and require us to find new antibiotics to fight them, we must adapt to treating the new forms of illness that have emerged. Our first task is to accept that this is the new reality, grieve that "things aren't like they used to be," and then form ourselves into what our patients need us to be. Our second task is to become more comfortable and skilled at being political advocates for change of the dysfunctions of our current society and the health care system.

BREAKDOWN OF COMMUNITY

As sociologists and others have documented, there has been a breakdown in our sense of community. The causes are many and beyond the scope of this book, but several that do pertain can be highlighted. In our modern society, we relocate more than we ever have, and as a result we can be less tied to our communities. We know our neighbors less than ever before. Our families have changed. The modern person imagines his or her family as smaller than before and may define it differently as well. Many have come from smaller families in the first place and have fewer relatives or are more disconnected from them. We may grow up some distance from those relatives, and we have less family support than we had in previous times. Families have increasingly had to weather separations and divorces and then learn how to be a new family or have a wider sense of one's family. The idea of a marriage commitment is much less popular; single-parent households are much more common. We may all debate how this came to be and whether it is good or bad, but the fact remains that we are learning to deal with how a fragmented sense of community and family affects all of us—and in particular, we have to deal with that in our clinics and offices.

Breakdown in community means people have fewer family and friends to rely on when they get sick

We cannot assume our patients will have someone to take care of them as often as we used to do so. We cannot assume that there is someone in a patient's family who will help in a health crisis. As a society, we are so busy with work and other activities that it is harder for loved ones to stop or decrease work to care for a loved one. While we have the Family and Medical Leave Act in the United States, allowing us to care for loved ones during sickness, it still is often difficult to manage an illness with the demanding expectations of employers. As clinicians,

we therefore encounter patients who more and more do not have as strong a family or community safety net to care for them in difficult times. While we might be able to perform our medical procedures and prescriptions, we wonder how it will go for people in the long run, recuperating and following through on what they need to do. Often people reveal to us during their appointments the fact that there is limited help for them while they are sick. Sometimes, they expect us to help them with that, especially when they have limited resources. In any case, witnessing this takes a toll on our compassionate sensibilities because of the increased suffering this can mean. We have to prepare for this and work on how we will keep our own spirits up in the process.

Are we becoming more or less caring as a society?

Folbre (2001) notes that it does appear that the importance of close, personal relationship has declined because of economic developments in our society. There are higher rates of divorce, and this affects how we view and manage personal commitments. People are more focused on their jobs than on where they live. They are less loyal to particular companies. Our society does appear more materialistic. But she cautions against making generalizations about altruism. She notes that it is possible that we are in the transition to new forms of community and different ways of being altruistic. However, she presents a strong case for concerns about "competitive pressures that penalize those who devote resources to the care of dependents, such as children and the elderly" (Folbre, 2001, p. 33). At the very least, we as clinicians are accompanying our patients in a time of great change in community and family networks, with a future that is not yet clear in terms of what we will be like.

Decline in trust by age, socioeconomic status, ethnicity, and residence

The Pew Research Center (2014) asked people from 1987 to 2012, "Generally speaking, would you say that most people can be trusted?" In 2012, only 19% of millennials endorsed that statement. Gen Xers were at 31%, the boomers at 40%, and the silent generation was at 37%. Since 1987, there has been a decrease in trust, with silents at 42%, boomers at 42%, and Gen Xers at 36% in 1991 when they were first asked this question. When first surveyed around 2006, millennials were at 20%, then had an increase to about 28% in 2008, and then sharply back down again to around 19% from 2010 to the present. While the decrease in trust has been not very much for boomers and Gen Xers, it is a 12% decline for silents, who are now in the elderly years and use health care probably the most of any of the generations. The millennials started out not feeling very trusting and have generally stayed at the same level. Analyzing all the reasons for this is beyond the purpose of this book. The main concern is that most of our patients do not feel like they can trust others in American society. This is even worse for people who are low income and who are minorities. Among African Americans in 2007, only 20% were in the high trusting zone, 14% were in the moderate zone, and 61% in the low zone. Among Hispanics, only 12% rated in the high trusting zone, 24% in the moderate zone, and 53% in the low zone. Among people who made less than $30,000, it was 26% high trusting zone, 19% moderate zone, and 48% low zone. People in large cities trust less than people in rural areas. For people in large cities, it was 23% high trusting

zone, 24% moderate zone, and 46% low zone; for people in rural areas, it was 43% high zone, 23% moderate zone, and only 30% low zone (Pew Research Center, 2014). As clinicians, not only do we face a breakdown in community network support, we also have to deal with a decline in trust overall.

ECONOMIC REDUCTIONISM AND THE COMMODIFICATION OF COMPASSION

Denigration of caring in the "bottom-line paradigm" of business

As with the culture of individualism, the business paradigm is a primary value in our society in that everything we do is put through a cost–benefit analysis. In itself, a cost–benefit analysis is not bad as long as costs and benefits are defined widely. Instead, they are defined narrowly. Costs tend to be seen in monetary terms with less of an emphasis on what business decisions cost in human terms. For example, when a company needs to downsize to improve profitability, what it costs the organization in terms of employee loyalty and suffering does not often weigh heavily in the equation. Benefits are also seen in economic terms. The bottom line is the key measure of outcome. Profit must always be maximized, and it is expected to grow each year; otherwise, we think something is wrong with the organization. It has become common for people to criticize how much CEOs of major companies receive in terms of salary and stock options, but this thinking applies to anyone who invests. Many people invest in mutual funds or stocks with the expectation that the investment will grow. If it does not grow by a certain amount in a certain time, many are tempted to change the investment. Many expect consistent short-term gains each quarter, and this becomes the measure of the company, not its long-term gains. In terms of caring, very few investors ask about *how* the company is making a profit or *how* the company is contributing to the human community. "Business is business." We have come not to expect businesses to worry about any other values than their profitability. Caring is seen as superficial and unessential. In fact, many executives sound like emotionally detached helping professionals: "I can't think about how people feel because it will cloud my judgment of what needs to be done." A tough-mindedness that puts the profitability of the company first is hailed as virtue. Of course, not all companies work this way, but many do. What is interesting is how often the lessons from exemplary companies are ignored. As we have seen in innovative and courageous companies in the United States and other countries, those who put an emphasis on the well-being of their employees and the quality of their products do succeed in a major way, even though short-term profitability may be sacrificed for the longer-term gain.

Excessive commodification of health care service will likely deprofessionalize all health care professions

To strategically plan for the future of physician training, the Accreditation Council for Graduate Medical Education (ACGME) engaged in an extensive study of all the possible scenarios that may occur in health care by 2035. While forecasting one scenario is not possible, they were able to establish the common themes across all of those "alternative futures" and what that implies for the future of health systems, medical training, and accreditation. They concluded that there will be an increase in the "commoditization"

of health care services and that "there will be profound societal pressures to deprofessionalize all of the health care professions, not just physicians" (Nasca & Thomas, 2015, p. 140). As a profession, medicine must demonstrate that it is dedicated to the public good and that it is worthy of the trust given by patients and the public (Swick, 2000). It is a moral enterprise that commits itself to be competent and altruistic for the sake of the public good. As a profession, it must act in a way that ensures quality of care and "that patients' interests should always come before personal or pecuniary interests" (Wynia, 2009, p. 884). Thomas J. Nasca, CEO of the ACGME, has explained that this commitment to the principles of professionalism

> is jeopardized by the movement to govern physician actions by rules and regulation and assess professional commitment based solely on normative expectations; physicians' role as providers of a volume of service; and the healing relationship with patients redefined as a commercial contract between service provider and consumer (often with structural economic conflicts of interest). These and other factors threaten to devolve medicine back to a guild. Replacement of trust by a commercial contract substantially changes the individual patient-physician relationship and the social contract as well, (Nasca, 2015, p. 1801)

In all the future scenarios of medicine in 2035, commoditization of medicine will parse health care into standardized tasks and services that will be delivered mainly on the basis on efficiency and lowest cost. These tasks will increasingly be distributed to lower-priced health care providers, automated technologies, and self-care approaches. The negative consequence of this will be that more complex medical conditions will be missed. When health care is perceived as being a conglomeration of disparate tasks for patients, then medical problems that can only be treated by more integrated and systemic assessment will not be spotted and treated effectively. In short, the "commodification" of health care threatens to reduce all health care providers to a set of health care tasks in which cost and financial interest direct care more than the commitment to professionalism (Nasca & Thomas, 2015).

Patients and clinicians in a continual war of attrition with insurance companies/third-party payers

The current health care system is built largely on this constant battle to get paid for services rendered. The more insurance companies restrict what is approved for patient care, the more profit they make. A huge insurance bureaucracy is built to require maximum effort by health care providers and patients in order to get payment. It is difficult to talk directly with those having the power to approve care. Providers have to work the system, starting with waiting on the phone for a long time, then talking to the lowest ranking person with the power to deny or approve services but who is not a clinician trained to take care of patients. Waiting to talk to a manager takes more time, and appeals take even longer. In all of this, it is amazing how often a fax or letter is "lost" in an insurance company. It is a war of attrition for providers and patients in terms of wearing them down so they finally give in to what the insurance company prefers. In my own practice, for my patients and myself, it often amounted to how much perseverance, time, and experience could be sustained in order to have clinical care approved or to work through disputed claims. The insurance company usually has the advantage in terms of time and shrewdness. How long can a patient or a clinician stay

on the phone before the patient (if he or she has the physical capacity) has to go to work or do other things or the clinician needs to get back to seeing patients? How long can clinicians and patients last in a continual emotional war of attrition with those who control payment for services?

The complexity of motivations and incentives in health care interactions

In a normal purchase of a service such as getting your car repaired, the customer pays the mechanic for the particular service needed. The mechanic does not have to consider pleasing anyone else, just the customer. The mechanic is motivated to take care of the customer, and the customer gets what he or she paid for. As things are currently, the motivational aspects in health care for patients, clinicians, health care organizations, and insurance companies are split. The insurance company is motivated by maximizing profit, so it regulates what is paid for and how much is paid. The patient needs and wants the best care that someone else usually has to pay for because it is too expensive for the patient to pay for him- or herself. The clinician is between the patient and the third-party payer and has the motivation to give the patient quality care, yet he or she has to balance what the insurance company will actually pay for that care. The requester of services (i.e., the patient) does not typically pay for the services; therefore, the motivation of the clinician can become bifurcated. As a clinician, I want to help my patient, but in the back of my mind there is the awareness that someone else is paying for this health care. In fact, the patient's motivation is split as well (if he or she has private insurance, Medicare, Medicaid). The patient would like the best quality health care and, especially if he or she has insurance through work, feels like he or she has paid for it. But that sense of having "paid for it" is weird because the patient typically does not pay directly for health care and, in fact, could generally not afford to pay for it. Deductions from the paycheck are part of a probability game. The insurance company is betting it can make enough money to cover those who get sick and have enough left over for profit. The patient is betting that the premiums paid, as costly as they are, will be worth it because he or she could never afford health care services for serious illnesses or injuries. In short, the giving and receiving of health care and the paying and the being paid do not coincide with the straightforward relationship of a patient paying a clinician directly for a particular service.

Only patients and clinicians have to pay the emotional costs for the business of medicine

This complexity of motivations complicates the patient–clinician relationship. The insurance company may deny payment, which makes the patient feel betrayed because he or she needs the service and "sort of" paid for it. The clinician may want to provide the service but cannot because he or she will not be paid for it. But imagine that suffering patient is seated before you on the exam table. While other parties are involved who are not in the exam room, only you and the patient are emotionally taxed by what health care service has been denied. You as the clinician are not doing this "directly and on purpose" to the patient, but both you and the patient have to sort this out emotionally. That wears on both patients and clinicians. This system is stressful to everyone except the third-party payers, pharmaceuticals, and medical device manufacturers. As a clinician,

I have to deal with the denial my patient receives, explain why I think that happened, process what that means emotionally for the patient, and then figure out how I am still going to help my patient now that he or she cannot get that particular treatment. This is one of the major challenges we face as clinicians who want to stay in a compassion mindset yet get frustrated at what we may not be able to do for our patient and the fact that it is out of our control.

If you want to know what health care is really like, don't talk to healthy people

In all my years of working with patients, one thing is very clear to me when it comes to assessing health care: If you want to know what is really going on in health care, don't talk to healthy people—talk to people who have chronic health conditions! People whose care is more episodic care do not understand the systemic challenges patients who are sick for long periods of time face. Here are just a few of them: Care fragmented across various specialties without good coordination and communication among those specialists. Copays for every visit. Insurance denials of payment for various treatment components that require time to appeal. Waiting for everything. The need to fight the insurance company while feeling sick. Medication reactions lead to discontinuing the medication, but the remainder of the prescription cannot be returned for reimbursement. Documents lost or delayed. Repeated requests for the same information already given. Providers who do not want to see you again if your problem is too complex. Needing a loved one to stay with you in the hospital to prevent errors and relay information to the next shift, who did not read the notes on you. Snap judgments made about you based on how you look or the fact that you have all your notes about your illness in a binder. Certain severe illnesses get you casseroles from the neighbors; other severe illnesses get no sympathy or understanding. Judgments made if you know too much about your illness or what medications work best for you. Delays in getting appointments. The receptionist not relaying your messages to the clinician. This list goes on. The point is that when you have a chronic or severe illness, you will experience all the dysfunctions of our health care system and what it is like to be sick in our society.

Importance of finding a way to accompany patients while dealing with one's moral distress

If you are a clinician who is paying attention to what patients are going through, you have to deal with the moral distress or the outrage of what very sick people have to endure. When you take the time to ask what your patients are going through, there will often be two parts to the answer. One part will be what they suffer because of the illness. The other part will be what they suffer as they go through the health care system to get care. We might call that the iatrogenic aspects of the care. The longer a clinician practices, the more he or she will understand how the health care system can be brutal for patients even while it strives to make them better. As I have discussed before, emotional detachment is an understandable temptation because it is easier not to hear what many patients have to go through at the hands of the health care system, pharmaceuticals, third-party payers, and general society itself. To stay in a compassion mindset, the clinician has to find a way to accompany these patients

and not become overwhelmed by the injustices and dysfunctions in health care.

THE NEW WORLD OF ELECTRONIC HEALTH RECORDS

Patient–physician dynamics have changed with the use of electronic health records (EHRs). While it is relatively early in the use of EHRs, let us consider where we are in terms of what it means for the compassion mindset and how patients perceive it. Many clinicians and patients complain about the entry of information to the EHR as a distraction from the clinician–patient relationship. Let us explore what we know so far about it.

Positive and negative impact of EHRs in patient care

The advantages of EHRs have included having more complete medical records and improvement in the following areas: patient adherence to guidelines, information exchange, medical error prevention, patient safety, medical management, chronic disease management, health care quality, decision-making, efficiency of care, and patient access to records and communication with providers (Asan, Young, Chewning, & Montague, 2015; Duke, Frankel, & Reis, 2013). However, there have been concerns that EHR use has decreased eye contact and nonverbal presence, interfered with physician attention to the patient, and negatively affected physician–patient communication (e.g., rapport building, psychological discussion) (Asan et al., 2015). Psychosocial discussion and emotional responsiveness suffer with increased EHR use. Keyboarding can interfere with the dialogue, physicians can appear disengaged or uninterested to the patient, and the visit may take longer (Margalit, Roter, Dunevant, Larson, & Reis, 2006). Haider et al. (2018) conducted a randomized controlled study comparing physicians using only a notepad in the interaction with patients to physicians using a stationary computer accessing patient information and typing notes with an effort to minimize disruption in eye contact. Overall, patients gave higher compassion, professionalism, and communication skills scores to the physicians who interacted without the computer.

EHRs can be successfully integrated in patient-centered communication

In a systematic review of the impact of EHR use on the patient–physician relationship, Alkureishi et al. (2016) found interesting and seemingly contradictory findings across 53 studies. On one hand, they found a number of negative communication behaviors when using the EHR, including interrupted speech in the physician or the patient, low rates of sharing the screen with patients, multitasking, and gaze shifting to the computer. Paradoxically, there was no change in patient satisfaction or patient perceptions of the patient–physician relationship or communication. Five studies showed a positive impact, mostly in countries other than the United States. However, it appears this can be improved with clinicians being trained to share the screen with the patient and use the computer screen to improve discussion, patient involvement, and shared understanding. For example, actively sharing the computer screen instead of passively sharing the screen or blocking sight of the screen can improve patient–physician interaction (Asan et al, 2015). Duke et al. (2013) and others have proposed models for integrating the EHR in patient-centered communication.

The consumption of time by EHRs and increasing administrative demands

While it does seem possible with training and intentional planning to be patient-centered using EHRs, the central issue appears to be the sheer volume of EHR tasks that need to be done. Sinsky et al. (2016) conducted a study to ascertain the proportion of time in ambulatory care that was spent on direct clinical face time, EHR and desk work, administrative tasks, and other tasks. The researchers studied 57 physicians in four states from the specialties of family medicine, internal medicine, cardiology, and orthopedics. They did 430 hours of observation with a total of 23,416 tasks recorded. What they found was that during the office day, almost half of physician time (49.2%) was spent on EHR and desk work. (Within that type of task, 38.5% of the time was used for documentation and review tasks, 6.3% on test results, 2.4% on medication orders, and 2.0% on other orders.) Direct clinical face time accounted for 33.1% of the total time. (This was a total of 27% of time seeing patients in the exam room and 6.1% with staff without the patient present.) Other administrative tasks accounted for 1.1% of their time (0.6% on insurance-related tasks and 0.5% on scheduling). Other tasks accounted for 19.9% of physicians' time (6.3% personal breaks, 2.9% transit time, 5.5% of time that was closed to observation, and 5.2% for other tasks). When physicians were in the exam room with a patient, direct clinical face time amounted to 52.9% of the time, and 37% was spent on EHR and desk work. After-hours data were collected on 21 physicians who reported that they spent one to two hours of their personal time every night mostly on EHR tasks. The bottom line is that about two hours of the day is spent on

EHR and desk work for every hour of providing direct clinical face time with patients.

EHR demands possibly related to career dissatisfaction and burnout

It appears that much of the career dissatisfaction for physicians (as well as other types of clinicians) relates to the increased EHR demands and not having as much time with patients (Sinsky et al., 2016). Many of my colleagues have noted that they have not been able to achieve the same levels of productivity and patient care that they had before EHR, despite its advantages. This frustration with documentation demands has intensified in recent years, and we are reminded of Shanafelt et al.'s (2015) findings that burnout and satisfaction with work–life balance decreased from 2011 to 2014. In that relatively short amount of time, physicians with one symptom of burnout went from 45.5% in 2011 to 54.4% in 2014. The percentage satisfied with their work–life balance went from 48.5% to 40.9% in that period. One of the major needs of our clinicians in this time is that we find ways to decrease the documentation burden, because it takes clinicians away from what they do best and from that which provides them the most satisfaction. The use of scribes and innovative improvements in work flow have helped improve this, but much work remains, especially because compensation is tied to that documentation.

Clinicians more externally pressured to do good EHR than to do good patient care

Much of our stress related to EHR and documentation in general is that there are very complex documentation requirements laid on clinicians in order to receive payment from insurance companies, Medicare, and Medicaid. Coding of medical conditions and procedures is one of the most important tasks in health care organizations. Many clinicians complain that EHR and complex documentation attends to the needs and requirements of third-party payers, but not so much to the needs of patients. Insurance companies are extremely exacting, and even the smallest error becomes grounds for delaying or decreasing payment. What is ironic is that clinicians get more oversight, reminders, and reprimands for documentation problems than they do for actual medical care or communication with patients. Can you imagine what it would be like if we got as many calls about improving patient–clinician communication and genuine caring for patients as we do calls about missing EHR information and rejected insurance claims?

The future of EHR and documentation stress for clinicians

It is indeed a time of major transition for clinicians integrating EHR demands into their interactions with patients as well as a time when clinicians are seriously questioning why so much documentation is necessary. Master clinicians have frequently complained to me that they have not been able to reach the previous levels of productivity they had before EHR and the new documentation requirements. While the next generation of clinicians who have grown up with electronics may have some advantage in comfort with using EHR, the fact remains that the sheer quantity of time it demands will need to be addressed and reformed in the years to come. We certainly will not be able to go backward; EHR is here to stay. The keys will be good training in how to use EHR and the reduction of outside documentation demands.

IMPACT OF TECHNOLOGYAND ELECTRONICS ON HEALTH CARE RELATIONSHIPS

The other factor that will affect how our patients relate to us and what they expect from us will be how electronic communication and media impact the relational capabilities of our patients (not to mention of us). I separate this from the use of EHRs because the wider issue is how technology and electronics will change how we relate. On one hand, we have the best means for communication and the greatest tools for accessing information humanity has ever had; but on the other hand, we do not fully know what the effect will be on the way we have relationships with each other. We also do not know how this will affect raising our children. I will highlight a few of the most pertinent possibilities and how this might affect expectations about health care practitioners.

Speed and efficiency of electronic communication has changed patient and provider expectations

The speed and efficiency of electronic communication and media have already affected expectations about health care. People experience relative ease and quickness with cell phones, texting, and email. There is an increased expectation that everyone is electronically connected and that a response should be rapid. In the workplace, we have the new problem of our staffs never getting a break from work because of this constant access, so it has become a new stressor. From the patient perspective, the

bar has been raised in terms of response time. People have become used to quick response times, so any time waiting for a response can be perceived negatively. In health care, clinicians can feel the pressure of this expectation and feel judged by it. From an information perspective, people now have rapid access to huge amounts of medical information, and so patients can press for answers more quickly as their anxiety rises from the possibilities they read about in their internet searches.

The effect of constant electronicinterruptions on patients and clinicians

The dynamics of relationships themselves are becoming different because of electronic communication and media. People are growing up now with frequent interruptions in their encounters with others to the point that this can feel normal. People regularly check their phones for messages and take calls during appointments. On a practical level, clinicians more and more are having to ask patients not to take calls during appointments. Patients are generally accustomed to their doctors getting paged during their appointments, but the patient being "paged" is a more recent issue for clinicians. On a deeper level, giving one's full attention to another person is rarer now and generally requires some imposed barrier to getting interrupted.

The positives and negatives of patients having internet research: More informed but self-doctoring

One of the major changes that will affect how patients relate to their clinicians is our relatively new reliance on computers and smartphones for information and directions. This reliance is changing our behavior and our expectations in health care interactions in several positive and negative ways. First, when patients have medical questions, they often consult the internet for information even to the point of surmising what diagnosis they have and how it might best be treated. On one hand, this provides health care information and education to everyone and encourages personal engagement in taking care of one's health. But on the other hand, clinicians have to deal with patients who are overconfident with their own internet research; they are not always able to discern valid sources of information nor do they have the knowledge to assess their own condition accurately. Clinicians are at times put on the defensive as some patients challenge them with their own internet research. Sometimes, this can be helpful; at other times, it can alienate the clinician.

Ability to ask for help is changed when you can "do it yourself"

Second, our ability to ask others for help is dramatically changing. We use search engines such as Google to get answers for our questions, even on very personal issues. On one hand, there is the benefit for everyone to have access to good information and to get help with issues around which there may be stigma or shame. The problem can be that we lose the ability to ask others for help. The tremendous usefulness and ease of using internet search engines can make asking others for help much less preferred than just "doing it yourself." As we have whole generations who have handled their own questions with their computer or smartphone, the ability to ask another person or rely on another person becomes less familiar and less comfortable. The problem is not that we can get answers on our own, but that when we have to rely on another person (e.g., an urgent medical situation, not being able to see our own blind spots in our self-care), we may find ourselves very uncomfortable in that situation because we have to do it so much less than we ever have before. The illusion of self-sufficiency that comes with being able to do things ourselves can make the experience of relying on others feel riskier when we do not often have to ask for help.

Overreliance on electronics can lead to the loss of the ability to find truth through dialogue

Third, this perceived ability to answer our own questions with search engines and find our own directions with our GPS devices can inadvertently lead to losing the ability to find the truth in our lives that only comes from people sharing their problems with each other. And these answers can be found quickly, which makes us impatient when things take more time. Now that we will have whole generations who have solved their problems and reassured themselves electronically, there is a loss of a sense of how talking through your situation, processing your thoughts and emotions, can lead people to a much better awareness of themselves and provide better solutions, despite how wonderful search engines and GPS devices are. As we have more people who have less experience with the benefits of verbally processing with another person what is going on in their lives, we may all lose the awareness that this ability is helpful. Getting advice that fits what is going on in our life is better when we find a trusted, expert consultant. People make better decisions when they have another person help them analyze their situation, whether it be investment decisions, taxes, household repairs, parenting, or health care. But being able to consult another person openly and honestly takes courage because of how vulnerable it can make us feel to lay out our situation to another person. Consciously processing our thoughts and emotions is very healthy for us. Will our society forget this just like it forgot that too much sugar and not enough vegetables is bad for us? Will our society wake up and self-correct just as we are doing now with the importance of good nutrition?

How the loss of the ability to find truth through conversation affects both patients and clinicians

This is affecting both patients and clinicians, and will become a major problem in the years to come. On the patient side, it is very common that people may not be aware of (or want to be aware of) what their weaknesses or their blind spots are. A patient may be engaging in a negative health behavior (e.g., poor diet, smoking, not getting enough sleep) or a negative psychological dynamic (e.g., not caring about his or her body, working too much). It can be very important for a person to learn the truth about him- or herself, but this is very difficult to achieve by oneself. The problem with having a blind spot is that by definition, you cannot see what your problem is. You need to rely on another person to help you "see what you cannot see in yourself." Yet there is a growing reluctance to be open to this kind of conversation. Clinicians increasingly report that a number of their patients tell them they are being intrusive by engaging in these discussions or that it is none of their concern; "just fix my problem." This ability to talk through tough issues also relates to the fact that people in our society are getting weaker on conflict-resolution skills. Successful conflict resolution relies on the knowledge that actual mutual conversation with

the other person helps people understand and resolve their conflicts. On the clinician side, this lack of experience and confidence in the value of consulting another person about oneself or the value of processing a problem with another person leads clinicians not to engage in this type of conversation either. If clinicians do not think talking through a problem is a good idea leading to more accurate assessments, they are not likely to engage in this with another person. They also might not even know it could be helpful. The newest cohorts of clinicians in training face the problem that they may have come to value self-sufficiency in solving their own problems but do not really value, much less understand, how relational skills are needed to help patients discover hard truths about themselves. It is hard to give something you have not gotten yourself. The bottom line is that our use of electronics to solve our problems is leading us to forget the tremendous usefulness and importance of discovering insights about ourselves through conversations with trusted others.

Deficits in interpersonal skills resulting from overuse of electronics

Fourth, with each passing year, more and more people are doing most of their communication through messaging or on the phone. Many people are actually feeling more comfortable discussing things through electronic communication. Or their means of entertainment and self-soothing is through electronics (e.g., watching many hours of shows and movies, browsing websites, Facebook, texting). While there are wonderful benefits to having easy access to electronic entertainment and being able to communicate when you are unable to be with another person physically, the overuse of electronics seems to be leading to new issues. My colleagues and I have noticed how children and adults are becoming less physically and emotionally expressive in person. There is a passivity in watching hours of video that does not require learning or practicing reading, or using facial and other nonverbal cues. In schools, children and adolescents have a flatter affect in classes. With the high intensity and polish of electronic entertainment, everyday interactions are less stimulating. The ability to interact effectively with others is becoming more difficult. Many in business organizations have noted such difficulties in their employees, including deficits in interpersonal skills either with customers or with coworkers. The ability to connect with a wide range of people consistently is less common in workers today, not so much because of their lack of good intention, but because they do not have as much practice at it as we did when we had less time devoted to electronic engagement. Managers are losing their ability to manage their staffs effectively using good communication skills. Our electronic emphasis with its associated satiated effects and encouragement of passive, distant interaction will have dramatic effects on patient–clinician interactions.

Technology—the new god in our modern religious pantheon

It was never our intention to have technology become more primary than relationships. Technology was intended to make our lives better and easier. We have welcomed its use to improve our connection with each other and our ability to ease suffering. It makes sense that we would appreciate it so much and that it is one of the things we most value in modern life today. While it is a seemingly value-neutral tool, what we do with it reflects our values and our vices. As history unfolds with the progress provided by

technology, the uses of technology reflect the best and worst of our human natures. Whatever is good and bad about us gets amplified through technology. Yet there is a way in which technology is the new deity in our modern religious pantheon. While technology appears quite separate from religion and spirituality, the central place it has taken in our minds and in our lives has certain religious characteristics. It is to some degree worshipped and respected because of what it has done for us and what we think it will do for us. Even when something about technology goes awry, we have the expectation and the hope that technology can be used to correct itself. Many times, we now think that Technology (with a capital "T") will save us. It is our new messiah.

How it makes sense that we encourage technological progress

But the very thing that indeed does make our lives better creates certain problems that require attention. On one hand, our life challenges, sufferings, and necessities become the "mothers of invention." But as we gain a solution to one of these, it seems to create a new challenge, and we have to adjust to it. Take, for example, the manufacture of things. Technology has allowed us to make more things more easily for more people, requiring fewer people to make them. Certainly, I could go on to describe the eventual obvious problem that if we do not need many humans to make things, what are all the humans with nothing to do going to do? But instead I want to focus on how we have come to believe technology is more reliable than humans. Employees have to be trained and wooed to continue working for a particular business. They can make mistakes, get sick and miss work, or leave the company after a time. When they are unreliable or become problems to manage, we are relieved to have some technology to make up for human deficiencies. Many times, it saves us money to have technology rescue us from having to rely on so many people for our goals. Many employers complain of having difficulty finding motivated and reliable employees to do both skilled and unskilled labor. If, however, we can find a technological way to pursue goals without relying on so many people, we will, of course, pursue it.

Hard to compete with a device that gives you everything you want

I had the opportunity to speak with an excellent musical performer after his show. The show was tightly orchestrated, with no time gaps between songs, and there were constant "wow" moments with fireworks, amazing video backdrops, and circus-like acts with singers hovering over the audience. I told him that while the show was excellent, it had a kind of manic effect in which one stimulating act was immediately followed by another stimulating act. There was no place to "take a breath" between acts, to savor what had just happened and then prepare psychological space to be open to the next act. The celebrity agreed that this was a very different way of doing a show compared to even 10 years ago. Then he said, "Now, when you do a show, you have to compete with them having a device in their hands that can give them everything that they want." The celebrity added that success for him is being able to hold the attention of the audience members so that they would never look down at their device. What results is the enjoyment of a continuously stimulating experience, which can be a good thing. But when we *train* ourselves to think that we must be continuously stimulated

in order to be happy and to dread "downtime" or "boredom," we may lose the ability to understand how important it is to pause and reflect on our present moment. Could it be that our society's current embrace of mindfulness meditation is our mind's way of self-correcting our seeking of continuous stimulation?

What are the consequences when electronics become our patients' principal self-soothing coping method?

"You have to compete with them having a device in their hands that can give them everything that they want." The words jolted me into recognition of what we are all doing. We have devices in our hands that can do anything we want. Anything we want to see or hear from anywhere around the world—in moments. If we are bored, something to stimulate us. If we are anxious, something to calm us. If we are lonely, instant connection with someone no matter how far away. If we are at some difficult crossroads, something to distract us from agonizing over the discernment that is necessary to make good choices for ourselves. In short, these devices have become major ways of soothing ourselves. In moderation, there is no problem. But when one method of self-soothing predominates, we lose the ability to use other coping methods. So, one of the questions of our time is, if electronics become the main way we soothe ourselves, how will that affect other things in our lives, such as our relationships, our ability to stop and reflect on our lives, and so forth? While we have evolutionarily preferred to be soothed, calmed, or stimulated by other people, we now can rely on entertainment technology to substitute for people. If we are bored, anxious, or discouraged, we can find digital means for meeting these uncomfortable internal states when the people we want to help us are not available. But then it is an easy jump to go to technology first to meet our uncomfortable internal states because it is so accessible and reliable. We do not yet know what this all means. We are in the middle of it as a society.

Twenge's research on the effect of electronic screen time

We may get some sense of how the impact of electronic screen time is affecting us by examining the iGen (i.e., the internet Generation). Twenge (2017) defines them: "Born in 1995 and later, they grew up with cell phones, had an Instagram page before they started high school, and do not remember a time before the Internet" (p. 2). Twenge notes that iGens are spending an hour less in face-to-face contact with their friends compared to people in the GenX and millennial generations. As she explains the consequences, "An hour a day less spent with friends is an hour a day less spent building social skills, negotiating relationships, and navigating emotions" (Twenge, 2017, pp. 71–72). The iGens tend be alone more in their leisure time. They may be interacting with friends through social media, texting, and video chatting, or they may be on the internet, gaming, or some form of electronic screen entertainment. No matter what, it does mean that this somehow affects how they think, how they relate, how they manage their emotions, and even how they look at what matters in life.

iGen's trends in terms of emotional safety and what makes a life a happy one

Twenge has gathered evidence that iGens tend to be less happy, more depressed, and more lonely than other generations. As a whole, they seem more concerned with physical safety in terms of driving, preferring marijuana over binge drinking, and having more concerns about sexual and physical threats. This concern about being safe appears to extend to emotional safety. As Twenge (2017) puts it, "Wanting to feel safe all of the time can also lead to wanting to protect against emotional upset—the concern with 'emotional safety' somewhat unique to iGen" (p. 153). The more time that is spent on social media, the more likely the teen is to be more individualistic and not value community involvement much. In terms of life goals, most iGens are placing more importance on extrinsic life goals such as money and fame and less importance on intrinsic ones such as meaning, learning, and helping people. When asked to rate various life goals, 82.3% of first-year college students reported that "being very well off financially" is "essential" or "very important," but only 46.8% said that "developing a meaningful philosophy of life" was. "Integrating spirituality into my life" was endorsed as essential or very important by 42.8% (Twenge, 2017).

Will all of this affect the desire to go into the helping professions?

We should be very careful about making generalizations at this point about the iGens. The research is at the early stages, and attitudes may shift as this generation grows older. Furthermore, while the impact of electronic screen time may be more evident in an age cohort that has experienced this their whole lives, all the other generations have become quite electronically connected as well. It is therefore logical to think that what has been said about the impact on the iGens is also occurring with other generations to some degree. For the purposes of this book on compassion in health care, one question is how the greater values of financial success, materialism, and individualism will affect who goes into helping professions and/or how caring will be construed with a background like this. If it is true that iGens are more concerned with emotional safety and are reluctant to experience emotional upset, then it would seem that entering into the emotional work of the compassionate professions will be more challenging. They will either not want to enter into the work the same way or need training and support to make the transition into becoming more comfortable with the normal emotional challenges that come with the compassion mindset process.

Compassion and altruism are highly ranked

In terms of the outlook for how compassion is ranked, however, there are other data that seem to contradict this materialistic and emotionally guarded approach to life. In the 2015 American Freshman Survey (Eagan et al., 2015), 77.5% of first-year students said "helping others who are in difficulty" is essential or very important. They also rated themselves as very strong in empathy and ability to tolerate others. When asked about a list of qualities being "a major strength" or "somewhat strong" in themselves, 77.0% said this of their "ability to see the world from someone else's perspective," 80.3% about of "tolerance of others with different beliefs," and 86.4% of their "ability to work cooperatively with diverse people." In terms of "helping others who are in difficulty," 77.5% said this was considered "essential" or "very important" in their lives. This would suggest that they highly value empathy and helping others as well as believe that they are very good at it. Yet when asked about specific things they might do, only 36.1% said there was a very good chance that they would participate in volunteer or community service work. In terms of objectives they consider essential or very important, only 35.8% chose this rating for "participating in a community action program," 46.9% for "helping to promote racial understanding," 26.9% for "influencing the political structure," and 48.5% for "influencing social values." The question becomes, is the self-assessment of those abilities inflated or a need to help with practical follow-through? Also, is there a disconnect between loving the idea of empathy/tolerance/compassion and the desire to turn this into action? (Twenge, 2017).

How electronics help patients and loved ones with enduring health care

What has happened with waiting times in clinics and hospitals is interesting in terms of how electronics have filled the gap. There are both positive and negative consequences. On one hand, now patients and their loved ones have a new way to manage wait times. They can stay entertained without having to read three-year-old *National Geographic* magazines in the waiting room, the exam room, or the hospital room. They can keep connected to work and not fall behind. They can keep loved ones informed about the latest in their diagnosis or medical procedure. If they are in pain, the electronics can provide a helpful distraction. Waiting in health care can be an irritation; electronics prove a very helpful solution.

How electronics can interfere with things that patients need to do for themselves

On the other hand, electronics can interfere with important things for which a patient or loved one needs to be present. An obstetrics nurse related her deep concern that a new mother breast-feeding her baby for the first time was looking at her smartphone instead of the baby. Or that mothers breast-feeding their babies (and fathers feeding babies, too) would be engaged with the smartphone instead of engaging with their babies (something we know is absolutely essential to the healthy development of that baby's brain). There are stories, too, of patients who are in distress and their loved ones in the hospital room with them are more engaged with their smartphone than with noticing the emotional pain of their loved one. Sometimes it is important just to reflect on what it means that you are at the doctor's office again for a problem you may have the power to change. That time in the waiting room or in the exam room can provide the cognitive space to reflect on what is going on with your body and what your response to that is. But if what you want is distraction, and the device in your hand can give you that, maybe you will not be able to reap the benefits of just "sitting with" what is going on in your life. In a culture that has normalized not reflecting on our lives, we can be locked into not improving it by leaving the internal emotional pain too quickly. As clinicians, we witness our patients lose life skills when they confine themselves to a distracting, emotion-focused coping method and lose their problem-focused coping skills. Our patients need to have time to mull over what is going on in their lives in order to make better choices for their health.

Technology can come from a desire to decrease suffering, but there are unintended consequences

In almost every aspect of our lives, there is a way in which the technological solutions we have found may become preferred over relationships with other people. It was not our intention to put technology over other humans. It is just that it becomes easier after a while to rely on that technology rather than on another human being. Naturally, this affects the way we perceive health care. We would rather have more technology because it makes things easier. If I can google my problem and find a solution on my own, that is much better than going to a costly health care appointment. If we can get an answer to what a patient's problem is by using a technological solution without having to navigate the patient's self-report, subjective perceptions, and culture, then it makes sense that we would prefer to have that technological solution. This is not a criticism of technology. It helps us, and this help comes from the desire to decrease our suffering and other people's suffering as well as obtain what we desire more easily. The problem is that because technological solutions can seem more reliable and easier than relying on other humans, we have to be aware of how we may be losing other important skills or subtly avoiding other people and relationships.

The fantasy that technology could help us avoid the interpersonal hassles and make health care less emotionally taxing

Human beings can be interpersonally difficult in health care (and everywhere else). Their illnesses can be complex, and it often takes a lot of detective work integrating both the patient's self-reported history with biomedical indicators to find the answers to what they need. Patients, by definition, are not feeling well, and people who are sick often regress psychologically. Sick people are not alike, either, when they get sick. Their psychological histories, their characters, their pathologies, and their motivations can all make that patient more challenging to treat. Because technological solutions have been so effective, it is understandable that we would rely on the hope that technological solutions could help. We fantasize that a lab test or a scan can be the objective indicator so that we do not have to go through all those interpersonal hassles and that it would provide the clear answer to the patient's problem. Because technology has solved so many problems before, we imagine that we could use it to avoid the interpersonal challenges of treating patients. We hope for this because it would preserve intact our desire to help people while also being less emotionally taxing. Inadvertently, however, our fantasy of having scans and labs do our medical thinking may lead us to lose our skills with physical exams and the best data we can get through expert conversation with our patients. Perhaps this tendency will self-correct as we get through our initial infatuation with the recent technological advances. It would seem useful for us to consciously reflect on how electronics are affecting all of us rather than be unconsciously swept down a path of training our minds that we would later regret.

COMPARTMENTALIZATION OF THE HELPING PROFESSIONS AND LOSS OF COMPASSION

Caring is considered a self-depleting action

Currently, caring is often considered a finite resource. Like money, food, oil, or other resources, caring is seen as something that is spent or used up, after which there is nothing left. The business paradigm dominates how we imagine caring. Helping professionals use phrases like "I don't have much left to give today," "I've totally spent myself with that last patient," "It cost me a lot to work with that client," and "My salary doesn't make up for the crap some people put me through." Of course, the word *burnout* has also shaped our imagination about caring being a finite resource. Caring is seen as the candle, the lightbulb, or the wood that is burned for the clients and patients but then is expended and disappears. Many people just read the title of Maslach's (1982) first book on this subject, *Burnout: The Cost of Caring*, and erroneously concluded that caring inevitably causes burnout. Caring got the blame for burning people out even though Maslach and Leiter (1997) themselves argued that the environment in which the helping takes place is a critical factor, a case they lay out well in the book *The Truth About Burnout*. What has emerged, then, is that helpers of all types imagine caring as a self-depleting action. It is seen as a dangerous or risky attitude to care about someone. Phrases like "setting good boundaries" and "pacing yourself" reflect a defensive or protective stance in helping people. The act of caring itself is not generally expected to return anything to the helper. Like the ozone or crude oil, caring is seen as being burned up for others and as not being a renewable resource. Hopefully, this book contributes to correcting this view of compassionate caring.

Compassion is expected in health care but not in most other work

Helping in our society has often been reduced to being a particular type of job. Society demands and expects helping professionals to be altruistic, or at least to act in an altruistic manner. While overly monetarily focused attitudes can often corrupt the compassionate caring motivations of clinicians and health care organizations, society still expects some level of caring and ethics from those who make their living helping others. But other professions—for example, many nonservice businesses—are not held to this same standard. There is no general expectation that these businesses should include the compassionate ethics of being helpful to others. The response might be, "Well, that's just business. I am here to make money. I didn't go into this to help people. But you guys in the helping professions, you have to help others." Our society takes advantage of the care workers by "free riding" on the sacrifices of those who do paid and unpaid care work (England et al., 2012). People who express a desire to help others and society tend to make less money in our society (Fortin, 2008). People who believe in the mission of an organization are more likely to donate their labor, with the result that the rest of society can free-ride on those who dedicate themselves to the public good (François, 2003). As Folbre (2001) puts it,

> we must stop assuming that norms and preferences of caring for others come from "outside" our economic system and can therefore be taken as a given. We must start thinking about care as a propensity that can be defended and developed—weakened and wasted— by economic risks and rewards. (p. 210)

One of the most important priorities in the near future is to increase how we economically value compassion and caring, especially as we face major shortages in certain clinical specialties, the teaching profession, and other service needs in the coming years.

People think clinicians should be able to take patient abuse

While this ebbs and flows over the years across various helping professions, there is a fair amount of respect still for those who choose to make a career of helping others. Especially if you happen to be in need of medical help, there is relief and gratitude for the emergency medical technician or trauma surgeon who was there to help at 3:00 a.m. But there is also the problem that the general public believes health care staffs should be willing and able to take the abuse directed toward them. There is the perception, because health care is so expensive, that health care staffs are highly paid and therefore should just accept what is dished out to them. "That's what you get the big bucks for, Doc!" Unfortunately, this kind of thing is often said to clinicians who have made themselves open to seeing patients and are not making much income. Patients do not realize the tremendous variability in income levels across the medical professions. There are, for example, some very high-income clinicians who avoid emergency situations and protect themselves against high-need and very complex patients. There is also the perception that health care personnel are supposed to able to withstand supernormal amounts of rude patient behavior. For example, some patients reason that because of what they have heard about the grueling medical training, the long hard hours of residency, and stories of rude doctors, this means physicians are "toughened up." I heard a story of a patient who was confronted about his emotionally abusive treatment of a young doctor and said, "He's a doctor—I figured he was supposed to be able to take it."

Society values individual gain and achievement, with caring as a desired but expendable quality

People generally like it when someone expresses care for them. They also generally like caring for others, but this caring is considered "extra." A number of authors have presented strong arguments for how our society has moved away from collective community values to individualism. Personal gain is put above the good of the community or others. At times, people will include their families in this and try to construe that as being community values, but it is really just an extension of the personal gain model. That is, "I take care of my family and myself, and something else like the government will have to take care of the people outside that." An almost medieval clan thinking has reemerged, a kind of fortress mentality. At times those who are less fortunate are even blamed for their poverty or illnesses. "I got where I am through hard work; why can't they do the same?" Of course, there are times when a person is responsible for his or her hardship, but the huge number of times when the person is not responsible for the misfortune is overlooked, such as in racism, structural barriers in poverty, or the economic disadvantages in developing countries in terms of access to resources. This is not to say that the focus on individual gain prevents charity. It is just that the charity to the less fortunate is put into this individualist model as well. In the individualist model, help to others comes out of one's accumulated surplus and is almost a condescension when it is offered to the "less fortunate." This does not mean that some focus on individual gain and achievement is wrong. Competition and the drive for personal success do have positive contributions. The difficulty is not with the value of individual gain but with the fact that this value is primary.

Major study on the trends of emerging adulthood

Smith, Christoffersen, Davidson, and Herzog (2011) conducted a major national sociological study of 18- to 23-year-olds, which they called "emerging adulthood." The study began in 2001 when the sample was 13 to 17 years old with a telephone survey of 3,290 youths, followed by interviews of 267 adolescents in 45 states in the United States. In 2005, the researchers did another telephone survey and interviewed 122 of the same participants. The researchers did a third series of telephone surveys and interviews with participants in 2007 and 2008, which included 230 in-depth interviews. From this they were able to identify major themes that characterize this age group and that reflect on our society as a whole.

Trends in consumer materialism and effects on altruistic attitudes

Smith et al. (2011) found that most of the emerging adults were very positive about consumer materialism. Regarding shopping and buying things, 65% said this gave them much pleasure, and 54% said that being able to afford more things would make them happier. How much they owned was a sign of how well they were doing in life for 47% of the emerging adults. The researchers noted that few had any concerns about a lifestyle centered on material consumption. The researchers were careful not to interview the emerging adults in a biased way but later in the interviews pushed them regarding whether they saw anything problematic with mass consumerism. Most did not. The vision for growth, self-improvement, and transcendence "does not concern self or morals or social justice, but rather material lifestyles and personal consumption" (Smith et al., 2011, p. 73). There was a dominant attitude that there are limitless resources in the world and that technological advances would take care of any limitations that might occur. Of those interviewed, 61% were very content with mass consumerism. Another 30% expressed some concerns about mass consumerism but said that there was nothing that could be done about it. The researchers noted three assumptions of liberal individualism in the group that could not imagine this would change. Those were (a) "everyone, including the rich, has fairly earned their money through hard work"; (b) "no person or society has the right to impose any external restrictions on any other individual"; and (c) "people are naturally driven by self-interested acquisitive motives, which ultimately cannot be denied or deterred" (Smith et al., 2011, p. 80).

Less focus on attending to the needs of others

Smith et al. (2011) noted in their in-depth interviews of emerging adulthood a pervasive sense that those interviewed doubted anyone could really change society or make a positive impact on the world. The researchers found that the participants were very individualistic and focused more on their own needs than the needs of others. Being focused on consumerism was strongly correlated with being less interested in politics or civic engagement. The typical view was that

> they seem to believe that humans share very little in common with each other, that you can't count on any common features or interests across people that binds them together or gives them a basis on which to work out disagreements. (Smith et al., 2011, p. 220)

There was a dislike for words like *responsibility*, *duty*, and *obligation*. The majority did not have an idea about what might be the common good. Helping others, such as by improving society in some way or being involved politically, was viewed as a personal and optional choice. Instead of thinking of the good life as transcending oneself, seeking some higher purpose, or transforming oneself in some way, the good life was much more about having a happy life, which might be having family and friends, having enough money to buy what they wanted, having the ability to travel or have other enjoyable experiences, or pursuing a particular career or some educational goal or other interests. About 25% mentioned wanting to help others or have some positive influence. Only 9% spoke of religious goals as defining the good life.

Narrow public view of compassion in society and the field of global health

While people in our society tend to think of themselves as compassionate, there tends to be a narrow view of compassion. People are very ready to help in dramatic tragedies, rescues, epidemics, and disasters. However, the compassionate response tends to be episodic and short term. What is often lacking is a long-term response to human suffering and also one that is preventive in supporting the efforts of public health. In this we suffer from the oversentimentalized conceptions of compassion, in which the compassionate response is tied to the initial intense emotional reactions, and later help is not imagined as part of the compassionate response or the public fatigues into compassion collapse (see discussion of this in chapter 10). David Addiss has discussed the challenge of integrating compassion in global health. Even though they seem logically joined, they are not necessarily conceived in this way. He notes that one of the challenges in global health efforts is that it can be difficult to stay connected to the compassionate motivation that led many global health clinicians and staff into the field. The compassion response tends to take long periods of time, and the compassion often takes place at a distance from where the suffering is occurring (e.g., the central office for a particular health effort is located in another country). Also, the compassionate response is done through bureaucratic and organizational mechanisms (e.g., proposals, logistics, budgets) that feel removed and emotionally different than serving suffering people face-to-face, especially if such mechanisms are focused on prevention efforts (Addiss, 2016a, 2016b). These same challenges to sustaining compassionate response exist in nonacute, nondramatic human needs and prevention efforts in health care.

IS HEALTH CARE IN *"TITANIC TIME"* OR *"APOLLO 13 TIME"*?

We are in an *"Apollo 13 time"* in health care, especially in the United States. We have a health care system that ranks 37th in the world despite spending the most on health care (Murray & Frenk, 2010; Voelker, 2008). We face a societal epidemic of negative health behaviors that is out of control. Our patients and our clinicians complain of astoundingly dehumanized aspects in our health care system, especially for certain patient populations. Almost half of patients and physicians find that we are deficient in compassionate care in our health care system. Despite the fact that both the general public and clinicians like to think of our society as compassionate, there are many sectors of our society that are not compassionate in terms of access to and quality of health care. On top of that, the suicide rate among physicians is among the highest of all the professions in the United States. We face a time of great transition, as there is deep concern for how our connection with electronics will change our brains and our relationships. The community and family ties that bound us together for support are breaking down, and it is not clear if another type of community and family support will emerge. This is within a society that has come to view itself mainly in economic terms, and even compassion is entered into the accounting balance sheet as a liability or reduced to being simply customer service. While compassion and caring are the primary features of health care marketing, compassionate caring is treated as a nonessential component in many health care organizations. Huge sectors of health care–related businesses, such as insurance companies, pharmaceutical companies, and medical device companies, strive for the maximum profit the market can bear but do not have the intrinsic profit-regulating mechanism that arises in clinicians who are face-to-face with suffering patients. Finally, our political system is in gridlock, in which every attempt at reform is sabotaged by those who profit from the system not changing and from the fears we all have in terms of facing change. This depressing paragraph encapsulates many of the societal factors that will be challenging for all of us in terms of maintaining a compassion mindset versus becoming overwhelmed and shutting down over the distressing societal conditions. Our society is also our patient who needs our compassion mindset. For those of us dedicated to compassion, in the words of Gene Kranz, NASA flight director for *Apollo 13*, "Failure is not an option!"

CONCLUSION

In this chapter, I have reviewed a number of societal factor and trends that are the context for clinicians who provide health care. Each of these factors presents new challenges to clinicians, and their overwhelming nature could easily undermine and deactivate the clinician compassion mindset. There are actually a number of other societal factors that could have been added to this chapter. Clinicians will need attitudes and skill sets to weather the challenges of these factors in individual patient care. They may also deal with the challenge and moral distress caused by these factors by becoming advocates for change in our society. In the next part of this book, we turn to how we can maintain balanced compassionate caring in light of not only our patients' suffering but also society's suffering.

QUESTIONS FOR DISCUSSION

1. What other societal factors would you add to this chapter?
2. What is your reaction to the societal threats to the compassion mindset listed in this chapter?
3. What kinds of attitudes, action, and self-care are needed to deal with the challenges of twenty-first-century health care?

REFERENCES

Addiss, D. G. (2016a, September-October). Who is my neighbor? Compassion in the age of globalization. *Health Progress*, 19–22.

Addiss, D. G. (2016b). Globalisation of compassion: The example of global health. In S. Gill & D. Cadman (Eds.), *Why love matters: Values in governance* (pp. 107–119). New York, NY: Lang.

Alkureishi, M. A., Lee, W. W., Lyons, M., Press, V. G., Imam, S., Nkansah-Amankra, A., ... Arora, V. M. (2016). Impact of electronic medical record use on the patient-doctor relationship and communication: A systematic review. *Journal of General Internal Medicine, 31*(5), 548–560.

Asan, O., Young, H. N., Chewning, B., & Montague, E. (2015). How physician electronic health record screen sharing affects patient and doctor non-verbal communication in primary care. *Patient Education and Counseling, 98,* 310–316.

Balch, C. M., Oreskovich, M. R., Dyrbye, L. N., Colaiano, J. M., Satele, D. V., Sloan, J. A., &Shanafelt, T. D. (2011). Personal consequences of malpractice lawsuits on American surgeons. *Journal of the American College of Surgeons, 213,* 657–667.

Centers for Disease Control and Prevention. (2017). Chronic disease overview. Retrieved from https://www.cdc.gov/chronicdisease/overview

Chapman, R., & Styles, I. (2006). An epidemic of abuse and violence: Nurse on the front line. *Accident and Emergency Nursing, 14,* 245–249.

College of Physicians and Surgeons of Ontario, Ontario Hospital Association. (2008). *Guidebook for managing disruptive physician behavior.* Toronto, Ontario: Author.

Duke, P., Frankel, R. M., & Reis, S. (2013). How to integrate the electronic medical record and patient-centered communication into the medical visit: A skills-based approach. *Teaching and Learning in Medicine, 25*(4), 358–365.

Eagan, K., Stolzenberg, E. B., Bates, A. K., Aragon, M. C., Suchard, M. R., & Rios-Aguilar, C. (2015). *The American freshman: National norms fall 2015.* Los Angeles, CA: Higher Education Research Institute, UCLA.

England, P., Folbre, N., & Leana, C. (2012). Motivating Care. In N. Folbre (Ed.), *For love and money: Care provision in the United States* (pp. 21–39). New York, NY: Russell Sage Foundation.

Fernando, A. T., & Consedine, N. S. (2014). Development and initial psychometric properties of the barriers to physician compassion questionnaire. *Postgraduate Medical Journal*, 90, 388–395.

Folbre, N. (2001). *The invisible heart: Economics and family values*. New York, NY: New Press.

Fortin, N. (2008). The gender wage gap among young adults in the United States: The importance of money versus people. *Journal of Human Resources*, 43(4), 886–920.

François, P. (2003). Not-for-profit provision of public services. *Economic Journal*, 113, C53–C61.

Gabbert, L., & Salud, A. II. (2009). On slanderous words and bodies-out-of-control: Hospital humor and medical carnivalesque. In E. Klaver (Ed.), *The body in medical culture* (pp. 209–228). Albany: State University of New York Press.

Haider, A., Tanco, K., Epner, M., Azhar, A., Williams, J., Liu, D. D., & Bruera, E. (2018). Physicians' compassion, communication skills, and professionalism with and without physicians' use of an examination room computer: A randomized clinical trial. *JAMA Oncology*, 4(6), 879–881.

Haque, O. S., & Waytz, A. (2012). Dehumanization in medicine: Causes, solutions, and functions. *Perspectives on Psychological Science*, 7(2), 176–186.

Harris, T., & Fiske, S. T. (2006). Dehumanizing the lowest of the low: Neuroimaging responses to extreme outgroups. *Psychological Science*, 17, 847–853.

Jena, A. B., Chandra, A., Lakdawalla, D., & Seabury, S. (2012). Outcomes of medical malpractice litigation against US physicians. *Archives of Internal Medicine*, 172(11), 892–894.

Joint Commission on Accreditation of Healthcare Organizations. (2012, March). CAMH Update 1. *Comprehensive Accreditation Manual for Hospitals*, 1–14.

Leape, L. L., Shore, M. F., Dienstag, D., Mayer, R. J., Edgman-Levitan, S., Meyer, G. S., & Healy, G. B. (2012). A culture of respect, part 1: The nature and causes of disrespectful behavior by physicians. *Academic Medicine*, 87, 845–852.

Lown, B. A., Rosen, J., & Marttila, J. (2011). An agenda for improving compassionate care: A survey shows about half of patients say such care is missing. *Health Affairs*, 30(9), 1772–1778.

Margalit, R. S., Roter, D., Dunevant, M. A., Larson, S., & Reis, S. (2006). Electronic medical record use and physician-patient communication: An observational study of Israeli primary care encounters. *Patient Education and Counseling*, 61, 134–141.

Maslach, C. (1982). *Burnout: The cost of caring*. Englewood Cliffs, NJ: Prentice-Hall.

Maslach, C., & Leiter, M.P. (1997). *The truth about burnout: How Organizations cause personal stress and what to do about it*. San Francisco, CA: Jossey-Bass.

Murray, C. J. L., & Frenk, J. (2010). Ranking 37th: Measuring the performance of the US health care system. *New England Journal of Medicine*, 362(2), 98–99.

Nasca, T. J. (2015). Professionalism and its implications for governance and accountability of graduate medical education in the United States. *JAMA*, 313(18), 1801–1802.

Nasca, T. J., & Thomas, C. W. (2015). Medicine in 2015: Selected insights from ACGME's scenario planning. *Journal of Graduate Medical Education*, March, 139–142.

National Association of Health Underwriters. (2015). *Healthcare costs drivers white paper*. Retrieved from https://nahu.org/media/1147/healthcarecost-driverswhitepaper.pdf

Pew Research Center. (2014, March 7). Millennials in adulthood: Detached from institutions, networked with friends. Retrieved from http://www.pewsocialtrends.org/2014/03/07/millennials-in-adulthood

Rafaeli, A., Erez, A., Ravid, S., Derfler-Rozin, R., Treister, D. E., & Scheyer, R. (2012). When customers exhibit verbal aggression, employees pay cognitive costs. *Journal of Applied Psychology*, 97(5), 931–950.

Reschovsky, J. D., & Saiontz-Martinez, C. B. (2018). Malpractice claim fears and the costs of treating Medicare patients: A new approach to estimating the costs of defensive medicine. *Health Services Research*, *53*(3), 1498–1516.

Riskin, A., Erez, A., Foulk, T. A., Riskin-Geuz, K. S., Ziv, A., Sela, R., ... Bamberger, P. A. (2017). Rudeness and medical team performance. *Pediatrics*, *139*(2), e20162305.

Saint, S., Vaughn, V. M., Chopra, V., Fowler, K. E., &Kachalia, A. (2018). Perception of resources spent on defensive medicine and history of being sued among hospitalists: Results from a national survey. *Journal of Hospital Medicine*, *13*(1), 26–29.

Schroeder, S. A. (2007). We can do better: Improving the health of the American people. *New England Journal of Medicine*, *357*, 1221–1228.

Sethi, M. K., Obremskey, W. T., Natividad, H., &Jahangir, A. A. (2012). Incidence and costs of defensive medicine among orthopedic surgeons in the United States: A national survey study. *American Journal of Orthopedics*, *41*(2), 69–73.

Shanafelt, T. D., Hasan, O., Dyrbye, L. N., Sinsky, C., Satele, D., Sloan, J., & West, C. P. (2015). Changes in burnout and satisfaction with work-life balance in physicians and the general US working population between 2011 and 2014. *Mayo Clinic Proceedings*, *90*(12), 1600–1613.

Sinsky, C., Colligan, L., Li, L., Prgomet, M., Reynolds, S., Goeders, L., ... Bilke, G. (2016). Allocation of physician time in ambulatory practice: A time and motion study in 4 specialties. *Annals of Internal Medicine*, *165*, 753–760.

Smith, C., Christoffersen, K., Davidson, H., & Herzog, P. S. (2011). *Lost in transition: The dark side of emerging adulthood.* New York, NY: Oxford University Press.

Speroni, K. G., Fitch, T., Dawson, E., Dugan, L., & Atherton, M. (2014). Incidence and cost of nurse workplace violence perpetrated by hospital patients or patient visitors. *Journal of Emergency Nursing*, *40*(3), 218–228.

Sweet, V. (1991). Violence in the emergency department: California's response to tragedy ... the death of Deborah Burke. *Journal of Emergency Nursing*, *17*(5), 273–274.

Sweeney, C. E. (2017). The patient empathy project: A study of patient fears. In D. L. Zimmerman & D. G. Osborn-Harrison (Eds.), *Person-focused health care management: A foundational guide for health care managers* (pp. 193–201). New York, NY: Springer.

Swick, H. M. (2000). Toward a normative definition of medical professionalism. *Academic Medicine*, *75*(6), 612–616.

Turner, C. W., & Hadas-Halpern, I. (2008, December 3). The effects of including a patient's photograph to the radiographic examination. Paper presented at the Radiological Society of North America, Chicago, IL.

Twenge, J. M. (2017). *iGen: Why today's super-connected kids are growing up less rebellious, more tolerant, less happy ... and completely unprepared for adulthood and what that means for the rest of us.* New York, NY: Atria Books.

Voelker, R. (2008). US healthcare system earns poor marks. *JAMA*, *300*(24), 2843–2844.

Wynia, M. K. (2009). The risks of rewards in health care: How pay-for performance could threaten, or bolster, medical professionalism. *Journal of General Internal Medicine*, *24*(7), 884–887.

"What We Thought Was the Problem Is Actually the Solution!"

Chapter Sections:

- ▶ Introduction
- ▶ Emotional Detachment: Protective Function versus Costs to the Clinician and Patient
- ▶ The Role of Emotional Intelligence in Medical Care
- ▶ Clinician Emotional Regulation Rather Than Emotional Detachment as the Optimal Internal Attitude of the Physician in Patient Care
- ▶ Mindfulness Meditation to Train Optimal Emotion Regulation
- ▶ The Important Role of Positive Emotions in the Clinician
- ▶ Compassion as Buffer against Burnout
- ▶ Conclusion

CHAPTER 10

Compassion, Emotions, and Resilience

Questions to consider before reading this chapter:

1. What is your opinion about the use of emotional detachment in clinical practice?
2. Are emotions important in the practice of medicine? Why or why not?
3. What do you know about meditation practices and their relevance to clinical practice?

INTRODUCTION

Typical medical training offers simplistic advice about emotional work with patients

In the training of nurses and physicians, the warnings against empathy and emotional involvement tend to be crude and simplistic. Part of becoming a physician, nurse, or other health care clinician involves an incredible transition into dealing with human pain. This includes other occupations such as the mental health professions, paramedics and disaster workers, police, and firefighters. Yet it is highly unlikely that the trainings for these helping occupations provide an in-depth analysis of compassionate caring for people in pain for this transition or any guidance in terms of the helper's management of personal feelings. If lucky, the person in training would have a supervisor or a mentor who might convey some of this. Most common are the repetition of one-liners that are sincerely intended to be helpful. "Don't get emotionally involved with your patients." "Don't let your idealism get in the way of the job that has to be done." "Don't let your feelings get the best of you." "If you keep that up, you're going to burn yourself out." "Sometimes you have to push your feelings aside." Somewhere in the training or in the early stages of the career, caring is often cast as dangerous. The solution is obvious, it seems: Do not care as much. Distance yourself. Ignore or suppress the feelings. Be realistic about the world.

Popular understandings of caring reveal underlying assumptions about caring

With the popular sentimentalized understandings of caring and the warnings given about emotional involvement in our training, caring too much elicits concerns about the welfare of the practitioner. Christina Maslach (1982), one of the leading researchers on burnout, wrote a book whose title captures this commonly held notion: *Burnout: The Cost of Caring.* Maslach and others (Maslach, 1982; Maslach, Schaufeli, & Leiter, 2001) have done excellent research on how burnout occurs and how to prevent it. Yet many times health professionals have not read any of this material and simply focus on "caring" as the cause. Indeed, if a clinician has a sentimentalized, shallow sense of compassionate caring, he or she will burn out. Under the popular conceptions, caring practice seems impossible. It is useful to examine how it seems impossible for helping professionals to care because this will show how they imagine caring practice. For example, a common idea is that it will take too much time. It is imagined that you would have to take extra time to hear the patient's story or that being more caring will take more time than being less caring. But with understaffed organizations and external pressures to survive financially, more time with clients or patients appears to be a nonessential luxury. Another common idea is implicit in a statement like "I don't have anything left in me to keep caring." What is implied is that caring is a finite resource, like money or gasoline in the car. What is imagined is that if you care for others, it will cost you emotionally, and you will not get enough back to energize you. Therefore, it is thought you should limit how much caring you do, sort of like not eating too much dessert or not spending too much money at the mall.

EMOTIONAL DETACHMENT: PROTECTIVE FUNCTION VERSUS COSTS TO THE CLINICIAN AND PATIENT

The protective function of emotional detachment

Understandable how clinicians would become calloused or distant

Before we go on to attack these popular notions of caring, it is important to acknowledge the partial truth that is in them. Helping professionals do not intend to lose a sense of caring as they go through their career. In fact, many have heard the dangers of becoming calloused and distanced from clients or patients, and many of us think we will somehow be the exception. Hauerwas (1986) captures this well in the following quote:

> How can anyone be present to the ill day in and day out without learning to dislike, if not positively detest, our smallness in the face of pain. People in pain are omnivorous in their appetite for help, and they will use us up if we let them. Fortunately the physician has other patients who can give him [her] distance from any patient who requires too much. But the problem still remains how morally those who are pledged to be with the ill never lose the ability to see the humanity that our very suffering often comes close to obliterating. (p. 80; bracketed text added for nonsexist language)

It is very easy to blame helping professionals such as physicians for what feels like uncaring distance. It is therefore very important as we continue arguing for a deeper and better understanding of compassionate caring that we acknowledge that helping professionals who witness a lot of pain must develop ways to cope in order to survive. As Hauerwas (1986) explains,

> the fact that medicine through the agency of physicians does not and cannot always "cure" in no way qualifies the commitment of the physician. At least it does not do so if we remember that the physician's basic pledge is not to cure, but to be present to the one in pain. Yet it is not easy to carry out that commitment on a day-to-day, year-to-year basis. For none of us have the resources to see too much pain without that pain hardening us. Without such a hardening, something we sometimes call by the name of professional distance, we fear we will lose the ability to feel at all. (pp. 78–79)

Feeling tricked into entering a helping profession

There are times as a caregiving career begins that helping professionals may feel as if they have been duped. They compete, study, and work hard, sacrificing other things in their lives such as relationships and leisure, all in the name of becoming some "helping noun," whether that be nurse, physician, social worker, physician assistant, psychologist, lawyer, police officer, minister, therapist, firefighter, or teacher. The goal and the idealism drive this self-sacrifice in the hopes of contributing to humanity and making a good living at it, too. But then when someone becomes a "helping noun," it is as if he or she sometimes feels tricked into it. "I didn't know it would be like this—what was I thinking?" Each of these professions can be idolized in some way. All of them promise a certain prestige and honor in our society. The attraction is enhanced if there is substantial financial reward. Having to compete for it increases the attraction, and much time and money is invested. A commitment is made to a profession before even knowing what it is really like. But by the time people find out how hard that profession really is, they have invested

a lot of years of study, gone into debt, and made promises to their family, and they feel as if there is no other way than actually going through with that career and finding a way to tolerate it and, hopefully, somehow thrive. They have already invested so much that it is hard to start another path, especially in medicine, where there can be enormous debt by the time one begins practice. It is as if society conspired to lure people into a helping profession, and then they feel stuck in it and resign themselves to just surviving, at least until another option is available.

The ordeal of training makes us have less empathy for the losers

Even if one does not feel this societal seduction to do these difficult works, the aspiring and the training itself can change us and how we will look at those we trained so hard to serve. Spiro (in Spiro, Curnen, Peschel, & St. James, 1993) described this for physicians:

> We doctors are selected by victories: We reached college because we were bright and competitive in high school, and we reached medical school through competition and hard-edged achievements. We are taught that hard work brings all the answers—and all the rewards. Residencies teach the same tough message. Residency training quenches the embers of empathy. Isolation, long hours of service, chronic lack of sleep, sadness at prolonged human tragedies, and depression at futile and often incomprehensible therapeutic maneuvers turn even the most empathic of our children from caring physicians into tired terminators. No wonder we have little empathy for the defeated, the humble, the dying, those who have not made it to the top of the heap, and even for the sick. Our energy gets us into medical school and after that little time remains for contemplation. (p. 10)

Whatever your profession, what Spiro writes about physicians is probably true in some way about yours.

Patients regress when sick, and we have to protect ourselves from them

But the witnessing of pain or tragedy is not the only thing that requires the helping professional to defend him- or herself by hardening. People we serve can be dangerous, too. McCue (1982) warns that pain and sickness strip away "the social graces that ordinarily make human interactions enjoyable" (p. 459). You may expect a rewarding and satisfying helping encounter but instead have to protect yourself from patients who are very distressed, fearful, self-focused, manipulative, ungrateful, or in some way very difficult. People who confront their mortality are not in a secure place, and their anxiety is contagious. It is not easy to stay centered in this, nor is it easy to deal with decisions that may inflict pain on them as a way to facilitate healing for them. Even if the patient injury or illness is not severe, patients can be very demanding, and we still have to respond to them. The following quote from an anonymous general practitioner humorously describes this:

> *A family doctor's life is awash with contrast: on the one hand he [she] is feted and revered as a pillar of the community, often an elected mason and sometimes president of the cricket team; on the other hand he [she] is at the beck and call of the lowliest of his [her] patients who would demand his [her] presence in the middle of the night to attend to a life-threatening runny nose. (as cited in Wilkins, 1992, p. 17; bracketed text added for nonsexist language)*

Institutional and environmental pressures

Additional factors in the defensive hardening of the helping professional are institutional and environmental pressures. The organization of which you may be a part is interested in its own survival. Just like a patient who has lost all of his or her social graces because he or she is facing death, so do institutions behave in ways that ensure their survival. There are statements heard like, "If we don't get a good bottom line, we won't be able to keep caring for people." Talking about caring for people is a luxury when the focus feels like it must be seeing as many people as possible in order to have good income. This, of course, is so much a current issue with the advent of managed care and insurance companies that have an incredible amount of power in terms of how much time is spent on a person and what will be considered allowable in terms of policy coverage. For health professionals, this means having one part of themselves that has an ideal way of facilitating healing and another part of themselves that somehow has to justify or accept lower standards of care. It is very hard for a patient or a clinician to confront a managed care company that may not pay for certain services or treatment. You never see them face-to-face. But it is very easy for a patient to take out that anger on the nurse, physician, mental health professional, or administrator because he or she actually has contact with these people. The insurance company is shielded by a well-designed defense against patient or clinician confrontation. So, too, are the pharmaceutical companies and the medical device companies. Given that helping professionals get this displaced anger from patients or have their own anger around this issue themselves, we can understand why they might become emotionally hardened and detached.

The costs of chronic emotional detachment

Detachment does not end up being satisfying

Listing all the good reasons we have for becoming more impersonal in our helping may help us feel less guilty, but to stop there does not take care of that part of us that thinks we should care more deeply for others, that we would not want for ourselves the kind of doctor we are to many of our patients. We have established that excessive detachment is a mode of self-protection. If you experience delight in the exercise of your helping role within this detachment, then there is no problem (at least for you). But even when we think we are practicing detachment, there is still frustration with all the hassles, even resentment of the client or patient. "Why am still feeling something if I am detached?" There can be a fatigue, a restlessness or impatience to get through the day. Detachment does not seem to work very well. It implies that there is a suppression of feelings going on because of the resentment, numbness, or depression we feel. If detachment really worked, it would not seem to take a toll on how we function at work or on our personal lives.

Emotional detachment has psychological costs for the clinician

If decreased caring for clients or patients is related to self-protection, it appears to take some energy to block off or suppress our feelings. Newton (2013) notes that clinician detachment requires disconnection from internal affective empathy processes and the clinician engages in role-playing behavior. This takes a great deal of energy because the clinician has to put on a certain front while possibly feeling very negative internally. Given the way caring is conceived and the way the structures for training and for providing help are constructed, emotional detachment is often the easiest defense against emotional exhaustion. But there is a definite cost to using a detachment defense, and we must assess the cost of this approach. It appears that such a defense that blocks the feeling function has detrimental effects in at least four ways.

Emotional detachment leads to decreased gratification

First, a major cost of dulling one's emotional connection with others is decreased gratification. It is next to impossible to suppress negative feelings and not also diminish the capacity to feel the positive feelings, such as a sense of personal accomplishment or gratification in providing effective help. If you detach to avoid the negative, that also means you are cutting yourself from the positive. To allow yourself to savor satisfaction in some aspect of helping means that you are open to letting yourself react positively; but if you are emotionally open to the positive, it means that your emotional door is also open if something goes wrong in your interaction with a client or patient. Also, the degree of positive satisfaction is great because you are emotionally aware of just what an accomplishment it is for a patient or client to overcome some ordeal; you know there are rarely guarantees when you help someone, and it is frankly exhilarating to use your skill to somehow outmaneuver illness, evil, or some other difficulty. Some would say a more stoic approach in which one is unperturbed by success or failure is the safest approach. While this seems a good coping style, one must ask why one would go through the grueling training involved in medicine in order to encounter pain and suffering in patients on a daily basis. What was your motive to get into this whole business? A friend of mine once asked one of the interns regarding his career choice, "So, why do you want to listen to people in pain all day?" The intern was a bit stunned by the question because it sounded odd that one would aspire to work with people in pain as a way of life. Guggenbuhl-Craig (1982) says that physicians, for example, are gripped by the battle against sickness and death. At least initially, there is some passion, conscious or unconscious, driving the healer to get into this battle. So, to numb this passion in order not to feel negative feelings is undercutting the very means by which one could feel satisfaction and personal accomplishment. Research has found that people who use emotional suppression experience less positive emotion. One might say this is acceptable because there would be less negative emotion. But the reality is that people who use this emotion regulation method long term experience greater negative emotion. Over time, they also have a decrease in well-being (Gross & John, 2003).

Suppressing negative feelings has negative consequences

Second, to suppress negative feelings means that negative and positive feelings are not processed, and the result is emotional withdrawal at an unconscious level. In our society we tend to imagine that feelings are distinct from thoughts; we attempt the keep the cognitive domain separate from the affective domain. Furthermore, we put feelings down as things that get in the way of good thinking; in fact, pushed to the logical extreme, we are at times at a loss to know how feelings are useful. But in Darwinian evolutionary theory, emotions were selected because they were adaptive. Later we will discuss more about the adaptiveness of the emotional life, but for the current argument, suffice it to say that if the emotional life is ignored, there are major consequences. Wuthnow (1991) explains this cost in the following way:

> Detachment is relatively easy when the people one cares for are experiencing little pain or trauma themselves and when one's relationship with them is brief or highly structured. In other situations, the trauma is simply too acute. One may try to detach by suppressing one's feelings, but sooner or later those feelings have to be faced. It becomes necessary to acknowledge that your caring has affected you emotionally. Detachment then requires working through those feelings, rather than simply denying them. (p. 208)

Detachment in an emergency situation is useful and probably critical to managing the situation effectively. But Wuthnow (1991) found in his interviews with rescue workers that some of the common consequences of ongoing detachment were not being able to "display emotion as readily as they once did," "not caring about themselves," and one day acting out emotionally by outbursts, emotional withdrawal, drinking alcohol, and having disruptions in relationships. As he says, "Suppression simply drove the feelings underground that needed to surface and be dealt with for true detachment to occur" (p. 209). A large amount of research has established that suppression of emotions actually increases the physiological stress response and does not make people feel that much better (Gross, 1998, 2002). Suppression has negative effects on cognitive processes. Emotional suppression actually impairs recognition and recall memory for material presented during the suppression period. This suggests that the emotional suppression interfered with the encoding of information. Furthermore, while it leads to the inhibition of emotional expressive behavior, emotional suppression does not change the inner negative emotional experience. It also leads to an increase in cardiovascular activation, which means activation of the sympathetic nervous system (Gross, 1998; Richards & Gross, 1999, 2006). While emotional detachment may be useful in some overwhelming situations, long-term use of this approach is more psychologically costly to clinicians (Shiota & Levenson, 2012).

Clinicians need time and space to "metabolize" or process strong emotions

It is understandable that a helper would become emotionally overwhelmed at work and thus employ detachment to cope. But once feelings are turned off, it is not always a simple thing to turn them on again at home. The emotions unconsciously exert pressure to be dealt with, and when they are not, various psychological and even physical symptoms arise from suppressing them. I have observed clinically on a number of occasions that when individuals suppress their negative emotional reactions to survive—for example, some past trauma—they later have to go through what they suppressed in order to arrive at a fully functioning emotional life again. Suppressing the feelings only means that those feelings will have to be dealt with later under hopefully better conditions. But it is hard for helpers to fully process their difficult emotions on the way home from work, especially when there are emotional challenges possibly going on at home or with their partner who also has to switch gears emotionally from his or her work. I find it helpful to use a concept that I have heard object relations and analytic psychotherapists use in this regard. They speak of the need to "metabolize" or digest difficult experiences that a person has had. That is, psychologically, helpers have to face the pain they witness in others and break it down, so to speak, or get perspective about what happened. But metabolizing takes time and conscious effort, and it also takes a comfortability with one's emotional reactions. With our current condescension to "feeling talk," it is not surprising that there is little formal training in emotional management. Emotional detachment is just easier.

Examples of how emotional processing is beneficial

It is widely known that processing one's emotions is essential to self-care, resilience, and recovery after difficult experiences. In psychotherapy, for example, part of the healing process occurs when people are able to put into words what they have been experiencing and thus gain a new perspective, which in turn provides relief or enables them to know what they need to do next to get better. In terms of how we are constructed as humans, Stern (1985) and other developmental psychologists have concluded that one of the biggest developmental jumps in a child's life is the one from when emotions cannot be expressed except crudely to when they can be captured verbally. In health care, we now know that techniques such as critical-incident stress debriefing (CISD) are very important for trauma workers to participate in after traumatic events. CISD is a type of psychological first aid that consists of seven steps: introduction of CISD team members; reviewing the facts of the event; discussion of what their thoughts were during the incident; expressing and listening to others' emotional reactions; reporting of cognitive, emotional, behavioral, and physical symptoms; CISD treatment team providing information normalizing participants' reactions; and finally, transitioning back to their lives. This process facilitates important self-care, support, and recovery from the secondary traumatic stress that trauma workers encounter (Mitchell, 1983, 2008; Harrison, 2017). The use of Schwartz rounds, in which the entire health care team discusses their emotional experience in difficult cases, has been found to be very beneficial in terms of decreasing clinician stress, improving clinician ability to cope with the psychosocial demands of clinical care, improving teamwork, increasing support among staff, and increasing clinician compassion toward patients and their loved ones (Lown & Manning, 2010; Palmer, 2017). In short, not processing feelings appears to result in a wide range of problems, from depression and emotional tantrums to drug abuse and suicide.

Emotional detachment leads to problems in personal relationships

A *third cost to chronic emotional detachment is that personal relationships suffer when one's emotional reactions are suppressed at work.* While occasional use is fine, long-term use of emotional suppression can backfire in the development of long-term relationships. Ongoing use of emotional suppression has been found to lead to decreased social support, decreased closeness to others, decreased satisfaction in social relationships, and worse interpersonal functioning (Gross & John, 2003; Srivastava, Tamir, McGonigal, John, & Gross, 2009). Emotional suppression decreases emotional expression, but it decreases both positive and negative emotionally expressive behavior. Therefore, people who suppress their emotions will not show the social signals that could be helpful in relating to that person (e.g., signaling that the person needs social support), and also, they would be less responsive to facial cues in their partners (Gross, 2002). Having an emotionally suppressed emotion regulation style negatively affects relationships because it leads to missed opportunities in the development and maintenance of close reciprocal relationships.

Patient care suffers from clinician emotional detachment

The fourth cost is that patient care suffers from the helper's emotional detachment. In *The Wound and the Doctor*, Bennet (1988) describes one way this occurs. Being busy is mildly intoxicating. At optimum levels of work, the healer's subjective experience is that he or she enjoys the sense of competence and the experience of his or her mind working efficiently. But at higher levels of busyness, there is less time or capacity to attend to other cues in the client or patient. Bennet explains that patients will sense their emotional needs being overlooked and will push harder or communicate the empathic failure; in turn, this mentioning of emotional issues related to the medical condition can be perceived by the physician as demanding. To use a computer image, when one is too busy or detached, it is as if too much RAM (random access memory, what is needed to run a computer program) is being devoted to running the "busy" and "detach" programs. That means there is less computer memory available to run the program of catching all the emotional data a client or patient is conveying to us, which might help provide a more effective treatment. Studies have found that emotional suppression impairs memory encoding, which would suggest that clinicians who regularly use this method will not recall important patient information. Emotional suppression consumes energy in a finite amount of cognitive resources in the clinician (Richards & Gross, 1999). The detached clinician is actually in a self-protective mode, and the energy required for that defense takes away energy from patient care.

Four adaptive functions of emotional expression

Kennedy-Moore and Watson (1999) reviewed the research on expressing emotions and found that there are four adaptive functions of emotional expression. *First, they found that arousal regulation is one benefit.* They explain that bodily arousal signals that something important is happening and that the body is preparing physiologically to respond. Emotional behavior can help facilitate the return of emotional arousal to baseline levels; inhibiting or suppressing emotional expression requires physiological work, and the strain of not expressing emotion may harm one's health (Pennebaker, 1992). *Second, emotional expression enhances self-understanding because recognizing and interpreting one's inner experience provides information and meaning about the experience.* Kennedy-Moore and Watson found that nonexpression essentially "blindfolds" people because they will not be able to initiate appropriate coping efforts if they do not recognize when they are distressed and why. *Third, emotional expression is adaptive because it facilitates coping efforts and emotional processing.* When a person works through emotions and makes sense of them, he or she can then draw on the information gained from the emotions to motivate adaptive responses and thereby lessen distress. Nonexpression of emotions requires energy; individuals become preoccupied with trying to hold the feelings that can intensify their distress and interfere with other coping efforts. As Kennedy-Moore and Watson (1999) put it,

> just as someone with both hands tightly clasped over his [her] mouth to keep from making any sound doesn't have free hands to do anything else, someone who is using all her [his] energies to avoid expressing can't implement any other coping strategies. (p. 299; bracketed text added for nonsexist language)

Fourth, emotional expression leads to increased intimacy with others and therefore makes social support more likely. The ability to express both positive and negative feelings is what constitutes a genuine interpersonal connection. Maladaptive nonexpression makes social support less possible and also breaks down the emotional communication that is essential in close relationships.

Problems with excessive emotional expression and description of adaptive emotional expression

Kennedy-Moore and Watson (1999) point out that maladaptive, excessive, and inappropriate emotional expression can also interfere with arousal regulation, self-understanding, emotional processing, coping, intimacy, and social support. They conclude that balance is critical in emotional behavior: "balance between indiscriminate venting of feelings and deadening emotional silence; balance between following one's own impulses and considering the impact on others" (Kennedy-Moore & Watson, 1999, p. 301). They find that adaptive emotional expression has three characteristics. First, it "enhances an integration between experiential and cognitive response systems" (Kennedy-Moore & Watson, 1999, p. 301), in which people are able to label and interpret their emotional experience and then be able to accept and feel comfortable with their emotions and their expression. Second, adaptive emotional expression is flexible such that a person has "the capacity to express a variety of emotions in a variety of ways" (Kennedy-Moore & Watson, 1999, p. p. 303) which allows a person to respond appropriately to a particular situation. Third, adaptive emotional expression is characterized by interpersonal coordination so that a person can be able to express his or her feelings so that they can be understood. This means that a person must be able to communicate clearly, taking into consideration other people's perspectives and relevant social norms.

Consequences of repressive coping styles

Kennedy-Moore and Watson (1999) reviewed studies on repressive coping styles and found that repressors have a "greater risk of physical illness and exacerbation of health problems such as cancer, asthma, and hypertension" (p. 88). They said that repressors can seem to be functioning very well, but they may have difficulties in their interpersonal relationships because of a lack of assertiveness, inadequate empathy, and deficiencies in accurately recognizing and predicting their own and others' behavior. Furthermore, repressors' preoccupation with denying their distress interferes with their ability to experience and enjoy their lives fully.

In conclusion, chronic emotional detachment in a helper has negative effects for the patient or client and the helper. You might ask, however, does greater emotional involvement by the helper actually help patient/client outcomes? The research is already able to provide evidence that this is true, and we will take this up in the next section.

THE ROLE OF EMOTIONAL INTELLIGENCE IN MEDICAL CARE

Medicine's suspicion of emotions

Medicine, like many sciences and disciplines, has tended to be suspicious of emotions. The excess of emotion is used as an argument for emotion's general threat to rational thinking. It is as if the human being under normal conditions is a thinking, nonemotional being, and when emotions emerge, they are viewed as lapses from the rational process. The view in the past was that emotions did not have functional value, and dwelling on them was the unfortunate quality of the sentimental clinician or the clinician who had lost his or her balance. Medical training is now beginning to correct this view and provide in its training a more up-to-date understanding of emotion and its important function in normal life. Not only is this important for how the clinician manages his or her own emotions, it is extremely important for understanding what patients are going through and what they need from their clinicians when they are suffering.

Definition of emotional intelligence

Emotional intelligence is defined as "the ability to perceive and express emotions, to understand and use them, and to manage emotions so as to foster personal growth" (Salovey, Detweiler-Bedell, Detweiler-Bedell & Mayer, 2008, p. 535). Salovey et al. explain that emotional intelligence consists of *four competencies.*

First competency: Perceiving emotions accurately

The first is the ability to perceive emotions accurately. Emotionally intelligent people are able to read and interpret emotions in themselves and in others and to express emotions appropriately. This is an information-processing skill in which people "who can quickly and accurately appraise and express their emotions are better able to respond to their environment and to others" (Salovey et al., 2008, p. 536). Extending Salovey et al.'s work on this ability, emotionally intelligent clinicians are able to identify patient emotions correctly and use this emotional material as data for the healing process. Seeing how a patient is feeling can give clues about the patient's illness and how to proceed in terms of treatment and follow-up. Clinicians need to be able to identify emotions in themselves in order to attend to their own needs or issues in patient care. Clinicians need to train their subjectivity to be able to assess the quality of the emotional expression in their patients (as well as themselves). Clinicians are able to use this material, for example, to help judge if a patient is honest about what is occurring, how a patient is suffering, and what the quality of the patient's motivations is.

Second competency: Facilitating problem solving and creativity

The second competency of emotional intelligence is the ability to use emotions to facilitate particular cognitive approaches in problem solving and creativity. Researchers have documented how people can harness their emotions to make positive outcomes more likely or help them solve problems more effectively. Particular moods and emotions can facilitate being able to think of a wide range of actions and possibilities, be creative, and match one's thought process to what is most needed in the situation at hand. People rely on the ability to harness their emotion to motivate themselves to act in a certain way. Again, extending Salovey et al.'s work, clinicians use their emotions to assess patients and their medical conditions. The frustration of not knowing what is happening in a patient, the desire to help a patient to the best of one's ability, or even the fear of making a mistake all can be used to energize one's problem-solving thought process in a particular way. Clinicians need to be able to discern which of their own emotions can facilitate problem solving and which interfere with it. Often, health professionals erroneously imagine that emotions always interfere with their thought processes. Certain emotions and moods can certainly interfere with clinician performance. A negativistic, irritable doctor would have a lower quality of thinking because the negative emotions would likely bias the thinking in a narrower direction, considering fewer options or settling for one option too quickly. A lack of emotions in a clinician would likely be a disaster. Imagine if a physician had no emotional energy in any direction in caring for a patient. That doctor would not be particularly "moved" to think in any particular direction. Who would you rather have as your doctor if your case were a complicated one: a doctor who was neutral about your situation or a doctor who is "bothered" by not having an answer and is "challenged" by your case or "moved" by your suffering to find the best response to your situation? Who would you rather have running your code blue if you had a cardiac arrest: the doctor who was not attached to any particular outcome or the doctor who wants to succeed in bringing you back? In patient care, this ability to use emotions to facilitate thinking is critical for patient care as well. A clinician with this ability can "read" patients and understand what motivational pathway to stir up or encourage to help patients do what they need to do to take better care of themselves.

Third competency: To understand, analyze, and use emotional information

The third competency is to understand, analyze, and use emotional information. This is the ability to understand how various emotions are related to each other, what causes certain feelings, and what can result from these feelings. It involves the ability to make sense of complex emotional states and how emotions are likely to transition from one emotional state to another emotional state and the actions that these can evoke. Imagining this competency in the clinical world, emotions in clinicians and patients or their families are rarely simple. An emotionally intelligent clinician can understand how a patient who over several weeks has lost the ability to work or function might move from feeling discouraged to taking this anger out on his or her loved ones and the physician. You would understand how a patient might both be resentful about needing your help and yet pulls for your reassurance and soothing because he or she feels so vulnerable.

Fourth competency: The ability to manage and regulate emotions in yourself and others

The fourth competency is the ability to manage and regulate emotions in yourself and others. An emotionally intelligent person must be able to be open to his or her feelings, both positive and negative. On this openness is built the ability to do what is needed to bring about the kind of emotional state that person desires. The skill of emotional regulation provides the capacity to maintain a certain mood, employ strategies to repair one's mood, and seek out or avoid activities in accord with one's goals. It involves "an ability to engage, prolong, or detach from an emotional state depending on its judged informativeness or utility" (Salovey et al., 2008, p. 535). The ability to reflect on one's emotional experience is crucial because this helps a person learn about what causes and accompanies his or her emotions, analyze how this occurs in various situations, and as a result, be able to achieve effective emotional regulation, which in turn relates to greater well-being. This ability then enables a person to help others improve or repair their emotional states.

Clinicians should seek emotional regulation, not emotional detachment

Applying this to the clinician's situation, emotional regulation is one of the most crucial competencies for practicing medicine. Commonly, clinicians have been instructed to extol the virtue of emotional detachment or "detached

concern," as Lief and Fox described it (1963, p. 12), but are not explicitly aware that the skill of emotional regulation is the key emotional competency. Emotional detachment is a subset of emotional regulation and can be part of an overall emotional repertoire. But as we saw earlier, emotional detachment as a heavily utilized emotional regulation maneuver has negative consequences to both the clinician and the patient; it should therefore be used sparingly. *Therefore, rather than training clinicians to be emotionally detached, we need to teach them about emotional regulation: the skill of managing their own emotional experience to take care of their patients and of themselves.* Emotional regulation is essential for the formation of a compassionate and balanced, caring helping professional. Maintaining a caring attitude entails being aware of one's own emotional state as it interacts with the patient's emotional state. With the emotional labor involved in interacting with patients, clinicians have to be aware of what they are feeling, apply emotional maneuvers to maintain specific emotional states required in a particular clinical interaction, and be able to adjust emotionally and maintain composure in difficult situations. Within this composed, emotionally regulated state, the clinician then has a firm base to help the patient attain better emotional regulation. While the main goal for the patient is addressing his or her medical problem, the way a clinician emotionally relates to a patient has direct effects on the patient's emotional state. For example, in an emergency situation, a clinician's confident, engaged, and composed demeanor helps patients allow themselves to feel they are in "good hands." If a clinician is anxious, depressed, or angry while interacting with a patient, the patient often becomes more tense and fearful. Emotional regulation within the clinician has therapeutic effects on the patient's emotional state.

Clinical work normally requires cognitive and emotional components

Clinicians are taught a variety of things about their emotions. Given that training for the health professions is rooted in science, clinicians often carry over a notion that this scientific training enables them to be "objective" in stressful situations. Having an emotional reaction is considered tantamount to "losing control" over one's emotions. The goal is to be mindful of those emotions and manage them for the clinical process. Everyone would agree that clinical work requires a great deal of cognitive energy. A clinician is assessing a patient condition, accessing his or her memory of medical facts and experience in order to apply these to this patient situation. This is done while also managing electronic health records and other technology, handling interruptions such as pages or curbside consults, and moving from one patient to another as quickly as possible. It requires a great deal of emotional management to navigate these cognitive tasks because one could easily become very frustrated while going through these tasks and then take out that frustration on others.

Cognitive work has emotional consequences

Clinicians would like to imagine that the energy expended for this cognitive effort can be separated from their emotions; that all conditions being equal (e.g., no patients being particularly difficult), ideally one should be able to go through the day addressing one problem after another almost like a computer processing information. It is work, and one would be tired, but clinicians would normally try to minimize the emotional costs by staying in this cognitive mental mode as much as possible. This is a remnant of the mind–body dualism that would suggest it is possible to be detached from emotions while performing cognitive tasks. Yet research has begun to find that it is not so simple. Mental fatigue weakens emotional regulation. Grillon, Quispe-Escudero, Mathur, and Ernst (2015) experimentally tested this by subjecting one group to the mentally demanding task of copying text but omitting the letters *a*, *e*, and *i*, and then having participants perform complicated calculations. (These are commonly used techniques for studying cognitive depletion in the research literature.) The control group only had to copy text without any omissions and to perform simple calculations. Then all participants were exposed to emotionally negative pictures and instructed either to respond naturally to the pictures or to reduce the emotional response that was evoked by the pictures. Emotional reactivity was measured by the startle reflex with eye blink electrodes under one eye. Those who were cognitively fatigued with the mentally demanding tasks were less able to downregulate their aversive state compared to participants who were not mentally fatigued.

Cognitive tasks in clinical practice can lower threshold for emotional reactivity

The implication of this study for clinicians is that if you want to reduce your emotional reaction to negative events, this will be much more difficult to do as you go through the typical executive cognitive operations required in clinical work. Clinicians prefer to be as emotionally regulated as possible going through the day and try not to be emotionally taxed. But this requires a great deal of cognitive energy to accomplish. Thus, when a clinician is tired, it is just easier not to try to reduce his or her emotional reaction. But that creates problems for everyone, including the clinician. Patients and fellow staff may have to deal with the clinician's emotional negativity, and the clinician will regularly feel unhappy at work if he or she cannot find a way to maintain emotional regulation.

Two ways to fix the emotional costs to cognitive work in clinical practice

There are at least two ways to fix this. First, you could structure your work so that you do not get seriously cognitively fatigued. Like any grueling work, you find a way to pace yourself with a moderate caseload and short periods of rest. (This is generally considered unrealistic in today's medical environment, but that is because we have structured our system this way. Certain organizations do achieve this, but there are, of course, consequences for the business side of the organization.) Second, the other way of fixing this is improving the emotional regulation strategies one uses to deal with negative emotional events. (This is where broaden-and-build theory, compassion cultivation, and other practices come in, which I will discuss in this and later chapters.)

Emotional intelligence leads to increased patient trust and satisfaction

In a study with 39 physicians from 11 different specialties working with a total of 983 outpatients, emotional intelligence (as rated by nurses), the experience of the physician (i.e., being older), and the ratio of patient's follow-up visits significantly predicted the patient's trust.

In turn, patient trust was significantly related to the patient–physician relationship and in turn predicted the patient's satisfaction with the physician. The relationship between trust and patient satisfaction was mediated by the patient–physician relationship. Higher emotional intelligence helps establish trust that in turn allows the patient–physician relationship to develop. Emotional intelligence is a necessary capacity for competency that, when combined with medical knowledge, makes the best physicians (Weng, 2008).

Emotions have been thought to be more primitive than higher-order cognition

In Western culture and in the culture of medicine, emotions have often been viewed as the opposite of rationality. They have often been seen as a threat with the possibility of overwhelming our rationality and negatively affecting our decisions and actions. Emotions are thought to be more primitive and the exercise of reason as more evolved. Emotions have been thought to be found in the limbic system in the evolutionarily older part of the brain, compared to the neocortex, where higher-order cognition is located. Hence, emotions have often been devalued as primitive and separate from the reasoning parts of the brain. However, the latest neuroscience has debunked this view that the cognitive functions and the emotions are so distinctly processed in the brain.

Neuroscience shows how intertwined emotional and cognitive processing are

McNaughton and LeBlanc (2012) note three advances in the field of neuroscience that challenge this notion. First, they cite Damasio's (1994) work showing that the older and newer parts of the brain are not as different as was once thought. Second, "input from the subcortical emotional systems to the cognitive systems is stronger than input form the cognitive systems to the emotional ones, suggesting a primacy for emotional processing over cognitive processing" (McNaughton & LeBlanc, 2012, p. 77). Third, brain structures found in the limbic system, such as the hippocampus, are actively involved in cognitive processes such as memory. Attention and decision-making are influenced by emotion systems. Also, brain structures responsible for cognitive functions are actively involved in processing emotions. McNaughton and LeBlanc reviewed research on the amygdala as an example of the interconnectedness of emotional and cognitive processing. The amygdala is known for the processing of emotional information, especially fear. However, damage to the amygdala negatively affects the ability to process social cues and emotional facial expressions, decreases the normal ability to remember the emotional aspects of a story, and decreases the ability to recall emotional information several weeks later. The researchers also note that the prefrontal cortex has a role in processing emotions. While the prefrontal cortex is involved in planning, decision-making, and social behavior, damage to the prefrontal cortex impairs a person's ability to react to emotional situations and results in flat affect. Such individuals tend to make decisions that are detrimental to themselves and do not learn from their mistakes. McNaughton and LeBlanc (2012) summarize these findings: "Patients with damage to the ventromedial prefrontal cortex are unable to use their emotions as an aid to decision making, particularly when the outcomes of the decision are uncertain" (p. 79). The explanation for this is the somatic marker hypothesis, in which past events that have emotional outcomes are used to guide decisions in future situations in which there is insufficient information or uncertainty. The past emotional reaction becomes a somatic marker, in which the physiological reaction that constitutes the emotion is tagged for future use. When a later situation generates a similar set of bodily changes, these help direct the thoughts and behaviors of the person in a way that will maximize the probability for the best outcome when it is not possible to rely on a logical analysis (Damasio, 1994).

It is scientifically ignorant to separate cognition and emotions in the brain

Emotions play an integral and regular role in cognitively processing information, making decisions, and memory. In their review of recent neuroscience research, McNaughton and LeBlanc (2012) provide numerous examples of how it is scientifically ignorant to separate cognition and emotion from each other in the brain. In terms of attention and perception, emotions are involved in determining what we attend to and how we process that information. We tend to attend to emotionally significant information with a rapid way of interpreting the information we gain from another person's facial expressions. Our interpretation of various situations reflects our current emotional states. When we are anxious, we tend to interpret unclear social situations or facial expressions in a threatening way. Emotions affect what we remember. We tend to remember events in more detail the more emotionally arousing the event is.

Information that elicits our emotions tends to be noticed more, and it increases the likelihood we will remember what we observed and experienced. We tend to remember negative events more than positive events. Emotions can help us remember certain events better but also interfere with our ability to remember previously learned information. Emotions affect our decision-making. An emotion can provide information, such as when our emotional reaction to a problem cues us that we need to deal with that situation. Emotions can bias our decision-making, such as anxiety influencing decisions in the direction of low-risk options with low rewards, while being sad biases decisions in a high-risk direction hoping for high reward. People tend to regret more when their actions lead to negative outcomes than when not taking an action leads to a negative outcome (the action effect); but they feel more regret if their inaction a second time leads to a negative outcome (the inaction effect). Cognitive and emotional processes are intertwined and integral to each other, but our medical training operates more with a cognitive approach and does not address how emotional processes are involved or how to manage these (McNaughton & LeBlanc, 2012).

Compassion fade and the loss of positive affect leading to less helping behavior

As health care providers move on in their careers and report decreased empathy and sensitivity to their patients, many will attribute this at least partly to the sheer number of people they have to help. When confronted with one suffering person or a few, the empathic sensitivity remains engaged. But as the number of patients increases along with a decrease in the amount of time available to help them, the compassionate attitude deteriorates, or at the least, it becomes more difficult to sustain. This is reminiscent of a phenomenon termed the *collapse of compassion* in the general population. The collapse of compassion is a phenomenon in which the degree of compassion decreases as the number of people suffering increases. A number of experiments have documented this collapse of compassion, in which people experience more distress and make more contributions when they consider one identified victim, but that distress and willingness to help quickly deteriorate as the group of victims becomes bigger (Slovic, 2007). This has also been called *compassion fade*, in which both the compassionate behavior and affect decrease as the number of individuals in need increases (Västfjäll, Slovic, Mayorga, & Peters, 2014). This effect can take place with just the addition of a second victim. Västfjäll et al. (2014) presented research participants with either a description of a single, poor, hungry child or a description of two children and asked them for their willingness to make a donation. Willingness to donate dramatically decreased with the addition of a single other child, and the positive affect associated with willingness to donate with one child also significantly decreased. Both self-report and physiological measures showed an increase in negative affect as the number of victims increased but did not predict the decrease in willingness to donate. *It was the decrease in positive affect (i.e., feeling positive about making a donation) that led to a decrease in willingness to donate as soon a single child victim was added.* The researchers found that compassion fade could be reversed with *entitativity* (perception of group as a pure entity vs. perceiving a group as a collection of individuals). Portraying the victims as a family of two children or eight children elicited more positive affect and willingness to donate than if the victims were portrayed as unrelated individuals (Västfjäll et al., 2014).

Collapse of compassion was related to better emotion regulation—how can that be?

Cameron and Payne (2011) found that what drives this collapse of compassion is the result of the way an emotion regulation process is directed toward protecting oneself from anticipated negative emotions. When people had the expectation that they would have to help eight victims versus one victim, compassion decreased. But when they were told they were not expected to help, compassion toward the eight victims was greater than for one person. The increased negative emotions that arise with the expectation that one would have to help many individuals drives the decrease in compassionate response. It is an emotion regulation strategy in which the person decreases compassion as a way of regulating increased negative emotions that would come with considering multiple victims. In a follow-up study, the researchers found that the collapse of compassion occurred only with people who could regulate their emotions well. But people who were not as good at regulating their emotions did not show this collapse of compassion effect. Furthermore, people who were good at regulating their emotions did not decrease their compassion in a reactive way; that is, they did not have an increase in negative affect and then reactively downregulate their emotion. Rather, those who were good at emotion regulation did so proactively; in anticipation of seeing multiple victims, they proactively avoided any emotions.

Discovery that detached emotion regulation led to collapse of compassion

To find out if removing the emotion regulation could reduce the collapse of compassion, Cameron and Payne (2011) had one group adopt "a detached and unemotional attitude" and view one or eight children from Darfur, "objectively" focusing on the "technical aspects" (p. 9) of what they observed. Those in the other group were told to let themselves experience and focus on their emotions without trying to get rid of them. What emerged is that those in the detached emotion regulation group demonstrated the collapse of compassion effect. They experienced more emotion toward one victim and less toward the eight victims. But those in the group told to let themselves have feelings did not have the collapse of compassion effect; they had just as much emotion toward one victim as with eight.

Emotion regulation can be used for prosocial or self-centered goals

I am certainly not proposing that no emotion regulation be used while doing patient care. What is important to note, however, is that the purpose of your emotion regulation is what is key. If you are making a decision to employ a detached emotion regulation strategy, what is your intention? Most commonly, a detached emotion regulation strategy is used to protect oneself proactively from feeling anything negative in working with suffering people. As Cameron and Payne (2011) state, "emotion regulation may be used in the service of either prosocial or antisocial goals" (p. 12). Emotion regulation can be used for the benefit of others, but it can also be used to avoid engaging people who are suffering. With the proactive internal shutdown of potential emotional reactions to patients, the willingness to help the multitude of patients is undercut. The empathic emotional machinery that can make a clinician so motivated to apply his or her medical abilities to one patient in distress can be turned off as we encounter more patients, with the result that the clinician is less motivated, less engaged with the patient, yet still delivering the minimum of good patient care.

Emotional detachment was adopted to help more people, but it leads to less helping

How does emotional detachment come about? Emotional detachment as a clinician emotion management strategy comes about because clinicians are trying to defend themselves from the very taxing emotional work they must do. We should be very careful about judging these clinicians because, frankly, they are often doing the best that they can. They were not taught more beneficial emotion management strategies in their training, and after training is over, there seems to be less time to work on developing these more beneficial emotion management strategies. While it is understandable how the detached emotional management strategy becomes the default option, it is important to know that this detached emotional management strategy appears to lead to a collapse of compassion in health care. In good faith, many clinicians adopted an emotionally detached style in order to survive how hard patient care was, possibly with the hope of lasting longer and helping more people. However, it ends up being harmful to patient and to clinicians. But the intent

of emotional detachment was the hope that clinicians would be able to help more people and last longer in the process. Yet neither of these result from using detachment.

CLINICIAN EMOTIONAL REGULATION RATHER THAN EMOTIONAL DETACHMENT AS THE OPTIMAL INTERNAL ATTITUDE OF THE PHYSICIAN IN PATIENT CARE

What emotional detachment would mean for patient care

Emotional detachment and Lief and Fox's (1963) more agreeable version of "detached concern" have been promoted as the ideal way clinicians should manage their emotions with regard to the emotionally difficult aspects of patient care. But as we have seen above, emotional detachment is bad for both the clinician and the patient. It reflects a fear about having overwhelming negative emotions and a dominant simplistic notion of emotions that is found in the culture of medicine. It can also be argued that emotional detachment is not really possible, and if it were, it would be exceedingly dangerous for both the patient and the clinician. If emotional detachment is fully achieved in a clinician, he or she would not be affected by the suffering of the patient. This would sever the motivation to respond to relieving the suffering of the patient and also allow the clinician to disengage from how the patient experiences treatment. At its best, it would mean the clinician is emotionally neutral about what happens to the patient. At its worst, it would mean the clinician is able to maltreat the patient with no remorse. As one physician said, "I would like to be emotionally detached from patients, but we all know that if you really could do that, we would become Nazi doctors."

Emotional detachment and Nazi doctors

In *The Nazi Doctors: Medical Killing and the Psychology of Genocide*, psychiatrist Robert Jay Lifton examined the psychology of the Nazi physicians who performed medical experiments in the concentration camps and also supervised the killing process. One of the main roles of the physician in places like Auschwitz was to select who among the arriving Jews would go directly to the gas chambers and who would live for a time working in the death camps.

> *Perhaps the single greatest key to the medical function of the Auschwitz self was the technicizing of everything. That self could divest itself from immediate ethical concerns by concentrating only on the "purely technical" or "purely professional" (das rein Fachliche). Demonstrating "humanity" meant killing with technical efficiency. (Lifton, 1986, p. 453)*
>
> *The Auschwitz self depended upon radically diminished feeling, upon one's not experiencing psychologically what one was doing. I have called that state, "psychic numbing," a general category of diminished capacity or inclination to feel. (Lifton, 1986, p. 442)*

Lifton (1986) recounts a story of a Jewish physician who survived Auschwitz who described to him

> *how, at a certain point, he and a few other prisoner doctors were overwhelmed with moribund patients, with suffering people clamoring for relief. They did what they could, dispensed the few aspirin they had, but made a point in the process of offering a few words of reassurance and hope. He found, almost to his surprise, that his words had effect, that "in that situation it really helped." He concluded that by maintaining one's determination to try to heal,*

> *even under the most extreme conditions, "I was impressed with how much one could do." (p. 504)*

Paradoxically, offering emotional support rather than emotional detachment had a positive effect on the patients, but even the Jewish physician who was overwhelmed by all the patients did better when he offered support. Notice, too, the way in which this is reflective of the clinician compassion mindset described in chapter 4.

Clinicians need a more accurate understanding of emotions

Physicians, nurses, therapists, and helping professionals in general tend to rely on an outdated understanding of emotions when it comes to their own emotional experience in helping patients and clients. Helping professionals will use phrases such as "emotional detachment," "being objective," and "keeping my feelings out of it." What is needed in training and practice is a more accurate understanding of what a helper is doing with his or her emotions.

Emotional regulation or emotional management is the key

One of the biggest errors made is that helpers might claim they are being emotionally detached or emotionally neutral in urgent or very stressful situations. Rather than calling this the skill of emotional detachment, it is much more accurate to say that the helper has developed the skill of emotional management. If physicians and nurses were truly emotionally detached, they would respond to a code blue in a manner no different than doing morning rounds on their patient. Instead, they channel their increased arousal in the emergency situation into performance. While not overwhelmed with emotion as untrained people would be in this kind of situation, they channel their heightened arousal into intensified thinking and acting while remaining composed in the emergency. Rather than being indifferent to the situation, they are highly motivated and passionately driven to save that patient's life. They look calm and collected, but their energy is highly focused. This is the skill of emotional regulation or emotional management. It is the same skill we hear test pilots and astronauts achieve in their highly dangerous feats. At least two factors lead to test pilots' and astronauts' ability to accomplish these things. One is that they are constitutionally able to achieve this level of emotional regulation. Second, their emotional regulation ability was trained with numerous hours of simulation scenarios, and they learned from experience.

Impossible to be above or outside the realm of emotions

A more accurate understanding of the function and process of emotional response is needed in which we understand the evolutionary importance of emotions and their essential nature in clinical work. We have imagined that there are times when we do patient care that we are above or outside the realm of emotions. This is impossible. Furthermore, what actually happens when a clinician is able to maintain composure in difficult patient situations or endure years of emotional stress in clinical practice is that this clinician has learned the skill of emotion regulation, the ability to manage emotions and use them for the healing process. When I hear clinicians say that they "push emotions aside," I think what they are saying is that they have learned how to manage their emotions, not that they have really detached from them. They are not precise in their description of what is actually going on emotionally. Emotional regulation is the ideal we strive to achieve in ourselves and in our training of new clinicians, not emotional detachment.

Overview of the modal model of emotion

The field of the science of emotions is complex, with a number of competing theories being researched. Many questions remain, and volumes have been written explaining what we do know. There are a number of different theories of emotion and a growing amount of research on emotion, especially in the area of emotion regulation (Gross, 2014). The *modal model of emotion* has been proposed as a way to capture the common features in the various scientific approaches to emotion. As Gross (2014) describes it, "According to the model, emotions involve person-situation

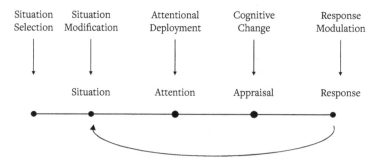

FIGURE 10.1 The process model of emotion regulation (Gross, 2014, p. 7).

transactions that compel attention, having meaning to an individual in light of currently active goals, and give rise to coordinated yet flexible multisystem responses that modify the ongoing person-situation in crucial ways" (p. 5). Put another way, "emotion is an automatic orienting system that evolved to guide adaptive behavior" (Decety & Fotopoulou, 2015). Adapting Gross (2014) to a clinical situation, as seen in figure 10.1, the emotion process begins with a psychologically relevant situation. It can be an external event (e.g., code blue, being double booked on your appointments, a patient who is crying) or an internal event (e.g., being tired, wondering if you made a mistake). A person then attends to the event in some way, which leads to the person's appraisal or assessment of what that situation means with respect to his or her goals. The emotional response that is generated by this appraisal is accompanied by changes in one's physiology, behavior, and experience. As Gross (2014) explains, this emotional response will often lead to changes in the original situation. Picking an example from the clinical world, imagine a physician is talking with a patient who suddenly starts crying. The physician notices this, pauses, and feels very concerned or worried about the patient. He or she considers what might have caused this patient to start crying and responds by asking the patient what led to the crying. The patient's emotional state is highly likely to shift as a result of the physician's asking about it.

First core feature of emotion regulation is activating an intrinsic or extrinsic goal to modify emotion generating process

Gross (2014) defines emotion regulation as "shaping which emotions one has, when one has them, and how one experiences or expresses these emotions" (p. 6). Emotion regulation has three core features. The first core feature is that emotion regulation activates an intrinsic or an extrinsic goal in the attempt to modify the process of generating emotions. In intrinsic emotion regulation, one regulates his or her own emotions (e.g. the clinician tries to dampen feelings of anger or sadness); in extrinsic emotion regulation, one tries to regulate emotions in another person (e.g., the clinician tries to soothe an anxious patient). Typically, people want to downregulate the so-called negative emotions such as sadness, anxiety, and anger by diminishing their intensity or duration. But people often want to upregulate positive emotions such as love or joy by either increasing their intensity or duration. But this depends on what the person's goals are. Sometimes people want to upregulate negative emotions such as "promoting a focused, analytic mindset; fostering an empathic stance; and influencing others' actions"; or, they may want to downregulate positive emotions for the purposes of "maintaining a realistic mindset; being mindful of social conventions; and concealing one's feelings from others" (Gross, 2014, p. 9).

Second core feature of emotion regulation is finding a strategy to achieve your goal: five types of strategies

The second core feature of emotion regulation is that it is a strategy to achieve whatever goal a person has. One engages processes that would alter the emotion trajectory. An example would be a clinician who wants to try to look calm even though he or she is very upset with a patient. These processes can vary from being very intentional and calculated to being automatic or unconscious. As Gross (2014) explains, there are five types of emotion regulation strategies that correspond to each point on the modal model of emotion. The first strategy is *situation selection*. A person takes actions to make it more or less likely to be in a certain situation. Thinking of clinical examples in our case, this might be avoiding certain types of patients or particular colleagues who tend to upset you. Or it might be scheduling particular patients who make you feel more fulfilled, or making a time to meet a colleague who makes you laugh or allows you to vent about how you are feeling. The second type of emotion regulation strategy is *situation modification*, in which you try to change the external situation in some way. Thus, with a patient who has felt difficult for you to manage, you bring another clinician with you to change the situation dynamics, with the hope that either the patient will be less difficult in the presence of another person or that the situation is easier to manage with the help of another clinician. The third type of emotion regulation strategy, called *attentional deployment*, involves shifting your attention in some way to influence your emotions. For example, with a patient who is irritating to you, you might internally distract yourself by thinking of something that you enjoyed last weekend or externally distract yourself by focusing on typing on the computer while the patient is talking so that you are not as focused on him or her. The fourth type of emotional regulation strategy focuses on the appraisal step in the emotion generation process that Gross calls *cognitive change*. This involves reappraising the situation to alter what it means to you emotionally, either by you changing how you think about the situation (e.g., this difficult patient is an opportunity for me to get better at my relational skills; it is understandable that this patient would be difficult because of his or her life circumstances); or it changing how you think

of your capacity to handle the challenge of this situation (e.g., you remind yourself that you have been trained well to handle this type of patient, or you recall that this type of situation always tends to work out in the long run and so you do not need to get worked up about it). Finally, the fifth emotion regulation strategy is *response modulation*, in which you influence the physiological, behavioral, or experiential consequences of your emotional response. This might include trying to diminish, prolong, intensify, or curtail the emotional experience you are having, its expression, or the physiology of that emotion (Gross, 1998). You might use exercise or a relaxation technique to calm yourself physically. Other choices might include using alcohol, drugs, food, and so on to change how you feel after a difficult situation. Another way is by using emotional suppression, in which you inhibit your negative or positive emotional experience. As noted elsewhere in this text, there are problems with emotional suppression, but it is important to note that it is an emotion regulation strategy and is often used in the health professions.

Third core feature of emotion regulation is that it changes the emotion dynamics for a particular outcome

Returning to the core features of emotion regulation, the third core feature is that emotion regulation changes the emotion dynamics so that there is a particular outcome. Compared to a situation in which one would not employ emotional regulation, emotion regulation might increase or decrease the latency or rise time of the emotion, its magnitude, or its duration, or offset the emotional response as it is manifested physiologically, behaviorally, or experientially (Gross, 2014). Every type of emotion regulation strategy has particular consequences in terms of what occurs physiologically, cognitively, experientially, and even socially; these consequences can have advantages and disadvantages. For example, if you use alcohol after work to deal with your negative emotions, you may succeed in calming yourself physically and emotionally, but then your mind may not be as sharp. This could interfere with how you relate to your partner or family. If you use alcohol all the time, then this strategy can create new problems such as relationship problems, work impairment, and addiction.

Two most studied emotion regulation strategies: suppression and reappraisal

In terms of emotional regulation strategies, two of the most studied strategies to downregulate emotion are suppression and reappraisal. Suppression is "a behaviorally oriented form of emotion regulation in which a person decreases emotion-expressive behavior while emotionally aroused" (Gross, 2014, p. 10). It is a response-focused emotion regulation strategy. You already are experiencing the emotion and try to diminish that response after it is already in process. Reappraisal is "a cognitively oriented form of emotion regulation in which a person tries to think about a situation in a way that alters the emotional response" (Gross, 2014, p. 10). It is an antecedent-focused strategy in which you reevaluate the situation in order to decrease its emotional relevance to you.

How clinicians get trained in emotion regulation techniques

There is little formal training in medical school and residency programs in terms of learning effective emotional regulation techniques for dealing with the emotional aspects of working in health care. Clinicians tend to rely on what they have learned from their families of origin or what they have sought to learn on their own. Most often, these techniques are learned informally in training (e.g. the hidden curriculum) from role modeling by senior clinicians, from attendings, or from peers. Because of the lack of formal training in emotions in medicine and the suspicion of emotions inculcated in clinicians by a misunderstood appeal to "scientific neutrality" (see chapter 7), clinicians will often use emotional suppression to regulate their emotions. It is very important to understand the limits of using emotional suppression.

Downsides of using emotional suppression and reappraisal

Emotional suppression is used after a person has already experienced the arousal of a particular emotion and suppresses any expression of that emotion. Research has found that while there may be a decrease in the expressive behavior, it does not decrease the subjective experience of the negative emotion and may in fact lead to an increase of physiological activation (Gross, 1998). Reappraisal can decrease the expressive and subjective signs of emotion but, surprisingly, still has physiological activation (Gross, 1998).

Being connected to your emotions leads to less stress and more satisfaction

It has commonly been thought in health care that suppressing one's own feelings or detaching from one's feelings is an effective, albeit less desirable, method for coping with the emotional toll of health care work with no negative consequences for the emotionally detached helper. Recent research has instead found that emotional suppression, repression, and attachment have negative effects for the clinician. In a large-scale study with physicians, Gleichgerrcht and Decety (2013) examined how poor emotional awareness and difficulties with emotional processing actually have negative consequences for the clinician. The researchers used the Toronto Alexithymia Scale, which consists of three subscales: (a) the difficulty describing feelings subscale; (b) the difficulty identifying feelings subscale; and (c) the externally oriented thinking subscale (measures the tendency to focus attention externally and avoid introspective thought). They found that physicians with no alexithymia had significantly higher compassion satisfaction scores than physicians with alexithymia and borderline alexithymia, as well as less burnout and secondary traumatic stress. Physicians with alexithymia or borderline alexithymia had significantly less perspective taking (the ability to adopt the point of view of others) and more personal stress than physicians with no alexithymia. Gleichgerrcht and Decety concluded that physicians who have difficulty identifying and describing their feelings as well as a tendency to focus their attention externally rather than on their own feelings tend to have increased levels of burnout and secondary traumatic stress with low levels of compassion satisfaction. Emotional detachment has exactly the opposite outcome than expected. *The ability to take the perspective of your patients and to have and emotional concern for them along with the ability to identify and process your own feelings is more likely to result in feeling satisfied about your work as well as having lower burnout and compassion fatigue.*

MINDFULNESS MEDITATION TO TRAIN OPTIMAL EMOTION REGULATION

Definition of clinician mindfulness compared to expert musicians

Ronald Epstein (1999) has articulated how a clinician who practices in a mindful way is practicing at the highest levels of the clinical professions. As he explains, "a mindful practitioner attends, in a nonjudgmental way, to his or her own physical and mental processes during ordinary everyday tasks to act with clarity and insight" (Epstein, 1999, p. 833). He or she is able "to observe the observed while observing the observer in the consulting room" (Epstein, 1999, p. 835). Epstein explains that this is very similar to what musicians have to master in their work. They must be able to perform their music while listening to it at the same time in order to make any adjustments or corrections necessary in the middle of a piece. They are aware of the technical aspects of playing a piece of music while also attending to the emotional expressiveness and musicality with a clear sense of the overall effect they are trying to achieve.

Examples of mindfulness in clinical practice

Likewise, a clinician has to be able to observe him- or herself and the patient while helping with the patient's problem. There is a kind of "peripheral vision" while doing the work—being open to what is difficult or unexpected and being ready to adjust accordingly. Another characteristic of the mindful clinician is the ability to do "processing" in which "the brain rapidly scans a wide array of perceptions, detects conspicuous features, and relegates some information to the background, all before the content of the perception is analyzed" (Epstein, 1999, p. 834). The clinician who is mindful is able to see the world as it is; the clinician approaches every situation prepared with tacit knowledge and experience but able to perceive the patient and the problem without bias, expectation, prejudice, or preconceived opinion. There is a curiosity about the unknown and a desire to understand what is happening more fully and as it really is. While the clinician has a great deal of knowledge, there is a way in which he or she has a kind of "beginner's mind" that is open to possibilities and new perceptions that allow for unique therapeutic solutions and even discoveries. There is a way, Epstein explains, that one welcomes rather than avoids uncertainty. "Difficult patients might then become interesting patients, unsolvable problems might become avenues for research" (Epstein, 1999, p. 836). There is a self-awareness and a humility to tolerate one's limits and blind spots. Clinicians know that they need to have the ability to observe and analyze themselves because their perception can be clouded by their own deficiencies, gaps in knowledge, or areas of "unconscious incompetence." There is a deep sense of connectedness with the other person who is the patient rather than a detached, more distant relating to the patient; this relational awareness allows for a deeper and more accurate perception of the person who is the patient. Finally, a mindful way of practicing is what lays the foundation for compassionate presence and insightful, active response to the patient's situation. Epstein (1999) eloquently describes this:

> *Self-knowledge is essential to the expression of core values in medicine, such as empathy, compassion, and altruism. To be empathic, I must witness and understand the patient's suffering and my reactions to the patient's suffering to distinguish the patient's experience from my own. Then I can communicate my understanding and be compassionate, to use my presence to relieve suffering and to put the patient's interests first. Perhaps lack of self-awareness is why physicians more often espouse these values than demonstrate them and why they tend to be less patient-centered and confuse their own perspectives with those of the patient in situations that involve conflict and strong emotions. (p. 836)*

Mindfulness is related to clinician well-being and better patient care

What is helpful about Epstein's description of mindful practice is that it lays out the importance of being able to reflect on your practice and yourself in that practice. There are a number of ways to achieve this. In training as well as practice, these might include journaling, processing interactions with mentors or colleagues, Balint groups, peer conversations, personal therapy, and so on. Mindfulness as a practice is being highly promoted as a way to achieve this. There is a great deal of evidence that has now accumulated to show the positive effects on clinician well-being (Shapiro, Astin, Bishop, & Cordova, 2005; Wilson, 2014) Many health care professionals are using this practice to deal with the stress of their work. Whether you try this practice or not for yourself, it is useful to examine what it is and how it works. In this way, as you create your own practices for maintaining balance, some of these principles may prove useful.

Overview of state of the field on mindfulness and clinical practice

Epstein (1999) has explained that mindfulness originated from the Buddhist philosophical-religious tradition and is being adapted in a pragmatic manner for use in dealing with the stresses of life and in psychological and medical treatment. The Western approach has historically separated the realms of cognition, emotion, memory, and action in the world, and it has become more evident that treating these realms as separate and distinct is not correct or even helpful. Approaches in the East as well as the phenomenological philosophical approaches of the West have viewed these realms as interdependent. Mindfulness practice has flourished, and research has corroborated its usefulness and effectiveness (Didonna, 2009). There is concern over the fact that distilling the pragmatic aspects from the original philosophical–religious context may have resulted in losing some important aspects to the practice, but research will continue sorting this out (Van Dam et al., 2017). There is also concern that this practice is being used in an overly outcome-focused manner (e.g., to increase productivity, competition) and that this is not in the spirit of mindfulness (Wilson, 2014). In any case, the sheer volume of research on mindfulness practice attests to the fact that training your mind is very possible and a powerful method to improve the quality of one's

life and one's work. For the purposes of this book, I would like to summarize an analysis of how mindfulness may be helpful to health care professionals. As I will describe later in this book, we now know it is important to help train the helping professional's brain (mind) to be able to do this difficult work and to do so in an effective and compassionate manner.

Mindfulness changes the attention deployment phase in emotion generation

Farb, Anderson, Irving, and Segal (2014) have provided an illuminating understanding of mindfulness practice by situating it in Gross's process model of emotion regulation. As seen in figure 10.2, mindfulness impacts emotional regulation by changing the attention deployment phase in emotion generation. When confronted with an emotion-provoking situation, mindfulness trains a person to accept the aversive emotional experience rather than avoiding it or distracting from it (Farb et al., 2014; Kabat-Zinn, 1982). Mindfulness trains

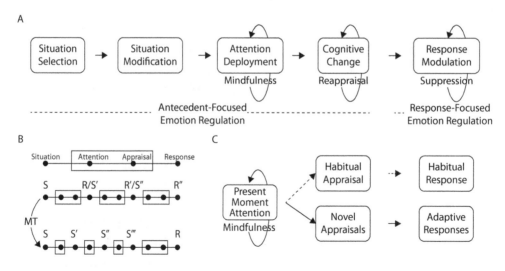

FIGURE 10.2 A process model account of mindful emotion regulation (Farb, 2014, p. 550).

a person to attend to the sensations of the present moment so that the focus is on the situation rather than automatically moving to the appraisal phase that then moves to the emotion response. As you know if you work in health care, you can quickly slide into automatic cognitive and emotional reactions based on habitual ways of thinking about a situation with a patient. Mindfulness training helps clinicians stay with a situation and their immediate awareness of it, which allows them to perceive the situation more accurately and to stay with this perception longer before moving to an automatic reaction that may not be helpful. Perceiving the situation in this way then allows for new ways to perceive what is happening and therefore new ways of responding to it.

Three components of mindfulness training

There are three central components of mindfulness training (Farb et al., 2014). First, one's intention in practicing mindfulness is essential. As Farb et al. explain, trainees' intention is to take responsibility for their reactions to stressful situations and enter a regular practice of noticing and restructuring cognitive habits. It requires a motivation and an expectation that this practice will benefit what they are doing. Second, mindfulness training trains attention in a meditation practice that emphasizes awareness of bodily sensations. This becomes the foundation for increasing awareness of all of one's experiences moment by moment, enabling a person to re-perceive the world. This helps create a psychological distance from what is occurring, in which whatever one is thinking or feeling is treated as a momentary, rather than permanent and unchanging, aspect of oneself or the situation.

This disrupts habitual ways of appraising a situation and allows new ways to interpret events and find more adaptive ways to respond to emotionally challenging situations. Third, having a nonjudgmental, accepting attitude is also essential in mindfulness training. A person approaches negative emotions with openness and curiosity rather than viewing them as unacceptable and an indictment of him- or herself. Automatic evaluations of one's sensations, thoughts, and feelings are disengaged; any thought, feeling, or experience is viewed as momentary. This attention to the present-moment sensation with an attitude of nonjudgmental acceptance "mutually support the gradual process of reconfiguring attention and cognition, extinguishing maladaptive patterns of reactivity, and introducing cognitive flexibility in the response to stress" (Farb et al., 2014, p. 554).

THE IMPORTANT ROLE OF POSITIVE EMOTIONS IN THE CLINICIAN

Options for dealing with the emotional toll of clinical practice

Clinicians want to do their helping work with a minimum of negative emotions and a maximum of positive emotions. They want to help patients and to continue helping others. But as a helping career unfolds, the emotional toll of the work begins to be felt, and this is when clinicians start acting in a way to lessen this toll. The options are to (a) not change anything externally or internally, just endure it as it is; (b) change the external stressors (e.g., do not work with challenging patients, work less); (c) change the inner emotional experience (e.g., repress or suppress your emotional experience, try to emotionally detach from patients); or (d) improve the positive experience of your work with patients. One way of doing this is cultivating and maintaining a compassionate caring attitude that is a crucial factor in healthier, balanced caring. This is the realm of the so-called positive emotions. Understanding how these function differently from the negative emotions is critically important.

Clinicians reminding themselves of their successes

In candid discussions of doing health care work, the most common stories are the very challenging, demoralizing situations and the extraordinary success stories. The extraordinary stories might be patient stories in which the persistence, commitment, and intelligence of the clinician brought about a positive patient outcome of some sort. Clinicians who try to maintain a positive attitude will often use the strategy of reminding themselves of these "successes" to "keep them going." One physician said, "With all the hassles in practicing medicine and difficult patients, I try to remember the good cases where I made a difference and the patient appreciated what I did." "I keep a file with all the thank you notes I have gotten over the years and I read them when I don't feel like working anymore."

New scientific research on positive emotions

Medical training and practice have often relied on simplistic and narrow understandings of what emotions are and how they function. This has not only crippled the ability to understand and help patients but also diminished the clinician's capacity to manage the emotional toll of patient care. In general, discussions in the helping professions have focused on the negative emotional toll of helping others, such as burnout, compassion fatigue, and secondary traumatic stress. Fredrickson (2013) has documented how for a century research has focused on studying the negative emotions and only recently begun seriously examining how positive emotions function in humans. In the past several decades, scientific research has tracked how positive emotions are very important in understanding how humans are able to be resilient and grow in the midst of difficult experiences. Balanced compassionate caring in the helping professions requires not only a management of the negative emotional experiences but also a cultivation of the positive emotional experiences that may undo the effects of the emotional toll and promote resilience and renewed energy to continue in this difficult work.

Undo hypothesis of positive emotions

Levenson (1988) proposed the undo hypothesis of positive emotions, in which positive emotions have an "undo effect" on negative emotional effects. Fredrickson and Levenson (1998) found that using the backdrop of negative emotional arousal, positive emotions have the ability to "undo" negative cardiovascular activation. Individuals with positive emotions could recover more quickly on cardiovascular measures. As Fredrickson (2013) describes the effect, "although positive emotions do not appear to 'do' anything to the cardiovascular system, when viewed against the backdrop of pronounced negative emotional arousal, the positive emotions clearly stood out in their ability to 'undo' lingering cardiovascular activation" (p. 10). The positive emotions of amusement and contentment were related to the fastest cardio-vascular recovery.

Fredrickson's broaden-and-build hypothesis of positive emotions

Fredrickson (2004, 2013), however, has described how "undoing negative emotions" is not, ultimately, the evolutionary function of positive emotions but the by-product of the *broaden-and-build theory* of positive emotions (figure 10.3). She explains that positive emotions have a different adaptive utility than negative emotions in terms of how our species has evolved. Negative emotions are adaptive in that these associated action urges drive behaviors that function to protect one's life. They function in a more short-term survival mode in which that human engages in some sort of fight-or-flight behavior as a result of some negative emotion. Positive emotions provide evolutionary adaptiveness in a more long-term timeframe. Her research has led her to conclude that positive emotions help build a person's resources for survival by broadening the person's scope of awareness in which he or she has "a wider array of thoughts, actions, and percepts than typical" (Fredrickson, 2013, p. 15). As she states,

> having a momentarily broadened mindset is not a key ingredient in the recipe for any quick survival maneuver. It is, however, in the recipe for discovery, discovery of new knowledge, new alliances, and new skills. In short, broadened awareness led to the accrual of new resources that might later make the difference between surviving and succumbing to various threats. Resources built through positive emotions also increase the odds that our ancestors would experience subsequent positive emotions, with their attendant broadened-and-build benefits, thus creating an upward spiral toward improved odds for survival, health, and fulfillment. (Fredrickson, 2013, p. 15)

Positive emotions provide an individual with a broadened awareness of possibilities in a particular situation and build internal

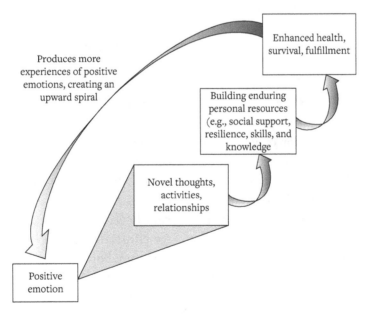

FIGURE 10.3 The broaden-and-build theory of positive emotions (Fredrickson, 2013, p. 16).

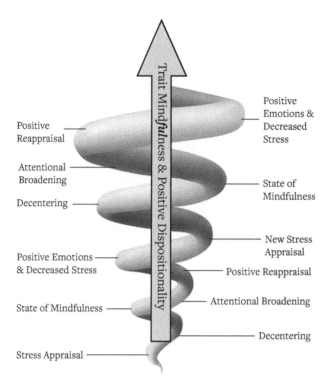

FIGURE 10.4 Upward spirals of positive emotions (Fredrickson, 2013, p. 35).

resources for future situations, with the added bonus that negative emotions are undone (figure 10.4).

Negative emotions are experienced more deeply than positive emotions in health care

Often the common conception of negative and positive emotions in medicine is that they are like the addition of negative and positive numbers. A − 1 + 1 = 0. With this kind of thinking, I need a positive emotion for every negative emotion that I experience in patient care. But oftentimes the experience of the negative in medicine is weighted heavily on the negative side, in which the negative is experienced more profoundly than the positive. The positives in health care may not be experienced as deeply as the negatives. As a result, clinicians often find it difficult to undo those negative emotional experiences. They might experience only fleeting moments of positive emotion in the midst of a typical day. The positives are not thought to be weighty enough to outweigh the emotional toll of the negatives. As a result, clinicians often try to detach from the negative experiences by suppressing, repressing, or avoiding situations that might bring about those negative emotions. The broaden-and-build theory of emotions has major ramifications for the emotional experience for clinicians because the positive emotions can somehow be experienced in a way that outweighs the negative emotions. Research that Fredrickson and others have done suggests that improving the way we experience positive emotions can increase their potential not only to undo negative experiences but to create more energy for compassionate caring.

Review of the research on how positive emotions broaden people's perspectives

Fredrickson (2013) has reviewed research both she and others have done to ascertain in which ways positive emotions tend to broaden an individual's thoughts, actions, and perceptions. Positive emotions tend to make people open to a wider array of possible actions. Testing the effects of the positive emotions of amusement and contentment, she found that these tended to broaden the scope of attention. Positive emotions led to people being able to list a wider array of possible actions compared to people in neutral or negative emotional states. Negative emotional states compared to the neutral states tended to narrow the repertoire of possible actions (Fredrickson & Branigan, 2005). People who had more genuine smiles during emotion induction tended to have greater increases in attentional flexibility and holistic processing (Johnson, Waugh, & Fredrickson, 2010). Other researchers have found that positive emotions broaden the scope of visual and semantic attention. Positive emotions were related to greater activation in the parahippocampal area, which was related to increased ability to perceive contextual surroundings of the visual image of a human face; negative emotions tended to narrow a person's field of view (Schmitz, DeRosa, & Anderson, 2009). In a driving simulator, positive emotions were related to increased steering performance and better task switching, especially when individuals encountered novel information. In the social domain, positive emotions were related to an increase of trust and the creation of more inclusive social categories rather than seeing people in terms of in-groups and out-groups. The own-race bias in face perception tends to disappear with the induction of positive emotions, and positive emotions are related to greater perspective taking and more compassion for a person from a different cultural background. Also, the positive emotions of joy and contentment were related to a more relaxed, open, and expansive physical posture, which she speculated is connected to a more expanded mindset having greater behavioral repertoires. Fredrickson (2013) also noted that positive emotions are distinguished from physical pleasures in that only positive emotions are related to increased awareness, but more research is required to confirm this.

Research for how positive emotions build resources for people

Fredrickson (2013) also has found substantial support for the build hypothesis within the broad-and-build theory of positive emotions. According to the theory, positive emotions lead to the development of resources that then place people on positive trajectories of growth. Research studies have found that an individual who experiences and expresses positive emotions more frequently than other people will tend to be more resilient, resourceful, and socially connected and have more optimal functioning. In the broad-and-build theory, "positive emotions, although fleeting, accumulate and compound over time in ways that incrementally build people's enduring resources" (Fredrickson, 2013, p. 25). Therefore, daily experiences of positive emotions would lead to increases in resilience over time and improved life satisfaction. It was also found that there is a reciprocal relationship between the experiences of positive emotions and psychological resource of broad-minded coping (the ability to step back from a current problem and approach it from a big-picture perspective). Fredrickson and Joiner (2002) found that positive emotions did predict increases in broad-minded coping over time and also that broad-minded coping led to increased positive emotions over time in an upward spiral fashion. In other research on positive emotionality, flourishing, and mindfulness, Fredrickson (2013) wrote,

> we found that people who flourish stand apart from their nonflourishing peers in the magnitude of the positive emotional boost they get out of every day pleasant events, such as helping others, interacting, playing, learning, and spiritual activity. These bigger "boosts" in day-to-day positive emotion forecast greater gains over time in the cognitive resource of mindfulness, which in turn predicts increased levels a flourishing in an upward spiral dynamic. (p. 26)

Physiologically, vagal tone predicted increases in positive emotions, and in turn, the increases in positive emotions led to increases in vagal tone. Vagal tone, the level of parasympathetic influence on the heart rate, is related to trait positive emotionality and physical and mental health. The experience of positive emotions, then, helps people become physically healthier. Fredrickson, Cohn, Coffey, Pek, and Finkel (2008) have been able to provide experimental support for the build hypothesis.

Definition of psychological resilience

Experiencing negative emotions occurs frequently in the work of helping others. To imagine that one could theoretically do this work without experiencing negative emotions is very unrealistic, yet helping professionals attempt this regularly by trying to detach emotionally from their patients, avoiding the most difficult patients, or trying to ignore the feelings that might erupt in the work of patient care. A more useful approach that fits what we have learned about emotions is to seek emotional management or emotional regulation, not emotional detachment. Given that negative things occur frequently in health care, the ability to bounce back from these negative experiences is essential to being able to do health care work for longer periods of time. The concept of psychological resilience is applicable in a very practical way to the experience of helping. In their review of the research, Tugade and Fredrickson (2004) define *psychological resilience* as "the ability to bounce back from negative emotional experiences and by flexible adaptation to the changing demands of stressful experiences" (p. 320). Resilience has been compared to the elasticity of metals. Some metals are hard and brittle. They do not have much "give" when they are bent, so they break. Other metals are more malleable and flexible; when bend, they do not break. (Tugade & Fredrickson, 2004; Lazarus, 1991). Going further with this metaphor, when some metals are bent, they remain in that bent position, whereas other types of metal spring back to their original shape after being bent and released.

Highly resilient people use positive emotions to recover more quickly from stress

In order to see what role positive emotions play in psychological resilience, Tugade and Fredrickson (2004) conducted a research study using psychological and psychophysiological methods. In one study, participants were told they had to prepare a three-minute speech in 60 seconds and then later found out they did not have to give that speech. Before the stressful task, higher resilient participants reported more positive mood, but there was no difference in negative mood between high- and low-resilient participants. When presented with the stressful task, participants with higher resilience tended to report more happiness and more interest (i.e., more positive emotionality). Those with high resilience also tended to have lower threat ratings of the stressful task. In terms of duration of cardiovascular reactivity (as measured by heart rate, finger pulse amplitude, pulse transmission times to the finger, pulse transmission time to the ear, and blood pressure), high-resilient individuals had a shorter duration of cardiovascular reactivity than low-resilient individuals. High-resilient people rebound faster from negative events. The researchers concluded that not only is resilience is a psychological phenomenon, it is embodied physiologically. They also found that the positive emotions and threat appraisal mediated the relationship between trait resilience and cardiovascular recovery. That is, having more positive emotions and appraising the stress as less threatening are how accelerated cardiovascular recovery occurs. Positive emotions and less threatening cognitive appraisals are two of the reasons high-resilient people recover more quickly from negative emotional arousal.

Low-resilient people can be more resilient with positive appraisal styles

But are people with low trait resilience doomed forever? Tugade and Fredrickson (2004) conducted the study again with the same stressful speech task, but this time after participants were given the instruction for the speech task, they were randomly assigned to view the task as a challenge or as a threat. In terms of

cardiovascular reactivity, when higher resilience individuals were encouraged to view the task as a threat, they still had faster cardiovascular recovery. Being told to view it as a threat did not diminish the recovery of the high-resilient people. However, as predicted, the low-resilient individuals who were encouraged to view this event as a challenge now had recovery times no different from the high-resilient individuals. This implies that training low-resilient people to have more positive appraisal styles can more effectively regulate their negative emotional experiences and help them recover faster from such experiences.

Highly resilient people use positive emotions for meaning making

Resilient people tend to find some positive meaning in a negative situation, such as learning important lessons of gaining some benefit. Tugade and Fredrickson (2004) conducted another study to find out if high-resilient individuals would have more positive emotionality and be more likely to find positive meaning than low-resilient individuals. In this study, participants had to write about the most important current personal problem they were experiencing and to do so in as much detail as possible, with all the thoughts and feelings they had about the experience. They were asked about the significance of the current circumstances, the long-term consequences, and what kind of sense they might make of these situations. They also completed a measure to assess how much they had found positive meaning in the situation. Even though high-resilient and low-resilient groups expressed equal levels of frustration about their problems, high-resilient individuals tended to report feeling more interest, eagerness, excitement, and happiness along with their high frustration about the task than low-re-silient individuals did. The researchers also found that, indeed, high-resilient individuals tended to find greater positive meaning in their problem situations. Furthermore, positive emotions were found to mediate the relationship between trait resilience and positive meaning making. That is, positive emotions appeared to be an important contributing part of the process leading to posi-tive meaning making. The compassion mindset is a way of generating and strengthening the pos-itive affect necessary to help the clinician find a balanced way to be emotionally engaged with the patient and to avoid empathy fatigue.

COMPASSION AS BUFFER AGAINST BURNOUT

What the most recent research seems to sug-gest is that the emotional toll that results from empathizing with patients all the time arises because this is empathy without the protective effects of a compassionate approach to working with patients. Compassion, in a sense, helps con-tain and redirect the empathic resonance with patients that is, in fact, better for clinicians as well as the patients. Klimecki and Singer (2011) have differentiated the constructs of empathy, compassion, and compassion fatigue and found that "a new integrative model arises that can account for mechanisms underlying compassion fatigue. This model suggests that, rather than compassion fatigue, it is empathic distress that underlies the negative consequences of care-givers who are exposed to others' suffering" (p. 370). An approach centered on compassion helps direct the empathy in a way that it does not emotionally burden and distress the clini-cian, as when a clinician is using an empathic approach without the protective (and ultimately more helpful) features of compassion.

Empathy can lead to clinician personal distress

As Klimecki and Singer (2011) explain, when a clinician empathizes with the suffering of a patient, this empathy can go in one of two directions within the inner life of the clinician. In the first direction, the clinician empathically resonates *with* the patient's suffering and vicar-iously experiences the negative emotions of the patient. This can often be felt as overwhelming and personally distressing to the clinician. Part of what occurs in this state of personal distress, according to Klimecki and Singer, is that there is not a clear distinction between the clinician self and the other person. The clinician identifies with the patient's feelings, what they call a state of *empathic distress*, and then tries to reduce that personal distress by withdrawing from the situ-ation. This withdrawal is not intended to harm the patient; it is a self-protective move on the part of the clinician.

Empathy can lead to compassion

The second direction of empathy is one that results in feelings of concern or compassion *for* the person suffering. It is other-oriented in that there is not a loss of the self–other dis-tinction and there is not an identification with that person's suffering. The clinician maintains awareness that it is the other person who is in a state of suffering. The clinician is able to emotionally regulate his or her own negative feelings and focuses on responding with feelings of concern for the patient. "In other words, the compassionate person has the capacity to help because he or she is not overwhelmed by dis-tress, but instead guided by feelings of concern, love, or affection toward the other" (Klimecki & Singer, 2011, p. 377).

Compassion fatigue should be replaced by the more accurate term empathic distress fatigue

The bottom line, it appears, is that it is not compassion that underlies the emotional toll in witnessing the suffering of others, it is empathy without the protective features of compassion. Klimecki and Singer (2011) propose that we no longer use the term *compassion fatigue* because the compassion is not causing the fatigue. It is a commonly used term in the helping professions that was introduced by Joinson (1992) and further developed by Figley (2002). *Compassion fatigue* refers to "a state of reduced capacity for compassion as a consequence of being exhausted from absorbing the suffering of others" (Klimecki & Singer, 2011, p. 369). Klimecki and Singer propose that the better term to describe this is *empathic distress fatigue*. The term *compassion fatigue* is in widespread use, and much research has been done on it that is quite important and valuable. The proposal of the term *empathic distress fatigue* instead of *compassion fatigue* does not negate this research. Rather, it is just a more precise term to describe what actually causes it and releases compassion to be actually the solution to the emotional toll problem, not the cause.

A compassionate mindset requires training, not simply a theoretical insight

Achieving a compassionate empathic concern and avoiding the automatic empathic resonance with personal distress pathway in working with patients is easier said than done. *A clinician has to train his or her mind to achieve this level of compassionate empathic response in a reliable and ongoing way in patient care.* Knowing this is the right approach is different than actually carrying out

this approach in a habitual way. The knowledge itself does not save us. I frequently have very busy and well-intentioned practitioners ask me to explain the difference between a compassionate empathic approach and the empathic resonance/personal distress approach, with the expectation that they can just flip into this mindset with the next patient. Like a new and hopeful prescription drug or a new way to do a procedure, the expectation is that a little reading and demonstration should be enough. But using a compassionate empathic approach is more like knowing what it takes for running a marathon and actually doing what it takes to run a marathon. You may know that to run a marathon you must be in very good physical condition, your running shoes need to be good, your body has to be well-nourished and hydrated, and so on. But to actually run a marathon, you have to actually condition yourself beforehand. Perhaps you build up to the long distance by doing progressively longer runs. As you do the longer runs, you work on training your mind to endure the long run and maybe the discomfort or pain that comes with it. This takes months of preparation. Once you have attained a certain athletic level, it becomes a regimen of maintaining your conditioning. The same is true with a compassionate empathic approach that helps buffer emotional stress and burnout. Clinicians have to train themselves to attain this state of compassion.

The challenge of attaining this level of compassionate clinical practice

In health care training and practice, however, we have two problems with attaining this level of compassion mindset. One is that we do not have a full and accurate sense of what compassionate care really is, beyond the simplistic, sentimentalist version we are given from our general society. The second is that we are just beginning to learn how to train this in clinicians. This book is a way of addressing both of these problems.

Approaches to training for a compassionate caring mindset

This realization that we need to train ourselves for this compassionate empathic approach is actually surfacing in diverse ways throughout health care. Certainly, Paul Gilbert's (2009, 2014) work on training the compassionate mind is very much focused on providing the background theory, evidence, and practices to develop this. Furthermore, a growing research literature on mindfulness and loving-kindness meditation (LKM) is helping chart this pathway. Klimecki and Singer (2011) concluded that

> accumulating evidence suggests that certain forms of meditation offer effective ways of circumventing compassion fatigue in caregivers by promoting an attitude of empathic concern and compassion that is associated with a skillful use of adaptive emotion-regulation mechanisms and a clear self-other distinction that makes one less vulnerable to the repeated experience of distress and suffering. (p. 379)

There are also many other approaches currently used in various pockets of health care practice that are helpful to developing this compassion mindset. In chapter 16 of this book, I summarize a number of these approaches.

Experiment comparing empathy training versus compassion training

Klimecki et al. (2013) experimentally tested whether compassion training can mitigate the negative emotional transfer in empathy. They sought to see both whether empathy and compassion had distinct neural characteristics and whether there would be participant reports of less subjective stress with compassion training versus empathy training. They constructed a prospective training study in which the experimental group was first trained in empathic resonance and later received compassion training. Measurements included the participants' affective experiences and blood oxygenation levels in repeatedly acquired fMRI measures, and these were collected after the empathy training and then again after compassion training while the participants watched high- and low-emotion videos. In the empathic resonance training, participants focused on resonating with the suffering depicted. Subjective and objective measures were taken after this training, and participants subsequently received compassion training that consisted of a contemplative technique from a secular compassion training program. The aim of the compassion training, according to Salzberg (2002), was to cultivate "feelings of benevolence and friendship in a state of quiet concentration" (cited in Klimecki et al., 2014, p. 873). It works by extending the caring feelings a person experiences with close loved ones to other human beings who are not close to the person. The guided contemplative practices first have the participant visualize a close loved one, then extend these same feelings and thoughts toward themselves, then a close person, a neutral person, a person in difficulty, strangers, and human beings in general.

Compassion training has distinct psychological and neural patterns compared to empathy

After empathic resonance training, participants reported increased empathic responses and increased distressing negative affect with both the high- and low-emotion videos. But after they received compassion training, the negative affect returned to the original levels, and there was an increase in positive affect. Furthermore, there were distinct patterns of neural plasticity. Watching the emotion videos after empathy training led to more activation in the anterior insula and anterior midcingulate cortex. These are regions of the brain connected to the empathy for pain network (Klimecki et al., 2014). Subsequent compassion training increased activations in a nonoverlapping brain network of the ventral striatum, pregenual anterior cingulate cortex, and the medial orbitofrontal cortex. These are networks associated with affiliation, reward, and positive affect. The researchers concluded that this suggests that

> the generation of compassion in response to distressing situations is distinct from other emotion regulation strategies, such as suppression or reappraisal, which involve an active downregulation of negative affect. Thus, the generation of compassion focuses on strengthening positive affect, while not ignoring the presence of suffering or changing the negative reality. (Klimecki et al., 2014, p. 877)

What is fascinating is that there was a differential pattern of brain plasticity with a relatively brief intervention. The compassion training was completed in a one-day, 6-hour training session. Participants practiced this an average of 5.7 hours on their own with at least 2 additional supervised training hours (Klimecki et al., 2013). The results suggest that longer-term brain training with compassion induction elements may increase this effect and be a way to buffer burnout.

Compassion training study showing neural changes and more altruism

Can compassion and altruism be trained? And does compassion training alter the brain's responses to suffering? Weng et al. (2013) compared one group that received compassion training to another group that received reappraisal training. Both interventions are means of training emotion regulation strategies that promote one's well-being. However, the goal of the compassion training was to increase empathic concern and the desire to relieve suffering, while the goal of the reappraisal training was focused on decreasing personal distress. Participants in the compassion training group practiced cultivating feelings of compassion toward four different targets, including loved ones, themselves, strangers, and difficult persons. Those in the reappraisal group practiced reinterpreting stressful events in order to decrease negative affect. Both groups practiced their respective trainings for 30 minutes a day for two weeks. The results were that individuals who received the compassion training tended to be more altruistic toward a person who was the victim of an unfair social interaction compared to the group that received the reappraisal training. Furthermore, the researchers found training-related changes in the participants' neural responses to suffering. Those in the compassion training group showed greater activation in the right inferior parietal cortex, the region that is part of the mirror neuron network. The compassion training group also showed greater increases in the dorsolateral prefrontal cortex. Weng et al. concluded that in the group that received compassion training, the frontoparietal executive control networks function to regulate people's emotions and increase their altruistic behavior. Those who received compassion training had decreases in reported arousal to images of suffering, but not those in the reappraisal training group. In short, compassion training appears to increase altruism and, at a neural level, helps a person be more sensitive to others' suffering while at the same time be less personally distressed by that suffering, thereby being more able to approach and help a person in need.

Compassion training compared to positive reappraisal

Engen and Singer (2015b) studied how a compassion emotion regulation strategy compares to a reappraisal strategy both in terms of the parts of brain respectively activated and what happens in terms of positive and negative affect. They compared how participants using a compassion strategy versus a reappraisal strategy experienced viewing a series of film clips of people in distress. In the compassion strategy condition, participants who had been trained in compassion-meditation technique used this to generate a caring and warm feeling of positive affect toward the individuals depicted in the film clips. Those in the reappraisal condition were asked to reinterpret what they saw by thinking that what was depicted in the film clip would turn out more positive than what was shown. The experimenters used this positive reframing approach to match the positive intention evident in the compassion strategy. Both reappraisal and the compassion strategy significantly reduced negative affect; but reappraisal was related to significantly less negative affect. In terms of positive affect, both strategies increased positive affect, but the compassion strategy was associated with significantly the most positive affect. Furthermore, the level of positive affect remained higher later for the compassion group, while the level of positive affect for the reappraisal returned to its baseline level (Engen & Singer, 2015a, 2015b).

Neural areas affected by compassion versus reappraisal

With regard to areas of the brain activated using fMRI, the compassion group showed increased activation in the medial and subcortical areas associated with positive affect (i.e., ventral striatum/nucleus accumbens, globus pallidus, midline cortical structures, ventromedial prefrontal cortex, rgACC) and areas connected to affiliative types of positive affect (i.e., bilateral midinsula), such as maternal love. For the reappraisal group, activation occurred in areas that are associated with cognitive control, working memory, and attention regulation (i.e., the frontoparietal network, which includes the ventral and dorsal prefrontal cortex, dorsal anterior cingulate, and TPJ/SMG areas). The compassion strategy appears to involve generating positive affect and does not alter the processing of the negative stimuli, while the reappraisal strategy uses cognitive control to regulate affect. There was more amygdala activity in the compassion group than the reappraisal group, suggesting that the compassion approach does not modulate the negative affective response as much as in the reappraisal group and instead generates positive affect.

Reappraisal versus compassion strategy with regard to sensitivity and empathy toward others

While reappraisal is effective in decreasing negative affect, the downside of reappraisal strategy is that this cognitive emotional regulation approach is associated with decreased sensitivity and empathy toward others. The compassion approach does not focus on decreasing the negative emotional responses but decreases empathic distress and maintains empathic connection with the suffering person. Connecting this to previous research, Engen and Singer note that the compassion approach has been associated with increased willingness to help others who are in need, and it also appears to increase clinician resilience. Compassion as an emotion regulation strategy does not appear to alter a person's exogenously triggered emotional reactions to stressors like reappraisal does. Instead, a compassion strategy is a volitional generation of an internal positive affective state (what Engen and Singer [2015a, 2015b] call a stimulus independent endogenous generation of positive affect) that enables a better emotional connection with the patient and also provides the clinician with a sense of satisfaction and fulfillment in working with that patient.

Research comparing talking about compassion versus mind training

Is talking about compassion care sufficient to change the practices of clinicians with their patients? Our training of clinicians in terms of compassionate caring often relies on formal discussions about caring in classes as well as informal discussions such as in clinical settings. We may get some information about this from a study done by Kang, Gray, and Dovidio (2015) in which they separated out the effects of discussing loving-kindness versus engaging in an LKM practice. As the researchers explain, discussions about cultivating compassionate attitudes toward self and others engages only logical and deductive aspects of thought processing, while actually practicing LKM "largely relies on individuals' direct experiences that involve more intuitive and non-propositional modes of affect processing" (Kang et al., 2015, p. 2). The researchers experimentally tested this by randomly assigning participants to two conditions

in which one group engaged in discussions about loving-kindness for six weeks, followed by six weeks in which they practiced LKM for at least 20 minutes a day for five days a week; this group was compared to another group that only practiced a meditation for at least 20 minutes a day for five days a week. What Kang et al. discovered is that discussions about having loving and compassionate attitudes resulted in participants having increased positive attitudes and decreased negative attitudes toward themselves, but this did not change their attitudes toward others. However, practicing LKM increased positive attitudes toward themselves as well as toward others. It also decreased negative attitudes toward themselves but, interestingly, did not change negative attitudes toward others. The combination of discussion and meditation did not differ significantly from the group that practiced meditation alone.

Compassion training requires an experiential discipline, not simply cognitive training

The bottom line is that if we are really serious about improving compassionate care in medicine, this may require clinicians to engage in some type of meditation practice over and above our academic discussions about the importance of compassionate care toward patients. As they say, talk is cheap. Discussing compassionate care is not sufficient to actually change how we feel toward our patients. The actual experience of doing compassionate caring practice is transformative. In many ways my point is, in a sense, not an original observation. Clinicians and teachers have for decades observed that knowing about something does not necessarily translate into actually implementing that knowledge. *What is important for our purposes is that actually integrating compassionate care into clinical practice may require some regular experiential discipline that engages the affective parts of the brain, not just the cognitive and logical parts.* When I have done continuing medical education workshops on compassionate caring in medicine, clinicians often ask for a summary of how compassionate caring benefits both patients and the clinicians, and because we are all pressed for time, they request information about how to change this. The fantasy is that the information itself will help improve not only the outcomes for patients but also how clinicians can feel better in their emotionally taxing work. At those times, I often feel as though the validity of everything I have said is in the balance. When clinicians walk away from a workshop and cannot immediately change how they practice and, more importantly, how they can feel better in their difficult work, it can cast doubt on this whole effort to improve compassionate care in medicine. The scientific information about the importance of compassionate caring both for patients and for the well-being of clinicians appears to be necessary for clinical practice, but the information alone is not sufficient to change that practice or to transform the inner experience of the clinician in a positive direction. Reading this book is one thing. Actually engaging in a regular, preferably daily, discipline of cultivating a medically compassionate mind appears critical.

CONCLUSION

Medicine has had an uncomfortable relationship with emotions and even a bias against them, positing that they did not perform a useful function in the practice of medicine. Medicine also did not keep up with the latest research on emotions and therefore did not train its clinicians with an up-to-date understanding of the role of emotions. As a result, rather simplistic notions of emotions were taught, and emotional detachment or detached concern became the ideal. It turns out that emotional detachment is not actually achievable; in addition, it is dangerous for both the patient and the clinician. Emotion suppression and reappraisal also have negative effects to both parties. Instead, emotion regulation or management is the key in working with patients. This requires the development of emotional intelligence in clinicians to use the emotional dynamics in the patient and in the clinicians themselves for the purpose of healing. Mindfulness meditation is a very effective means to achieve optimum emotion management. Furthermore, positive emotions function differently than negative emotions and provide the mechanism for how compassion is able to channel empathic resonance to lead to compassionate action rather than personal distress and withdrawal. Positive emotions broaden the attention and mental processing of the clinician as well as help build the internal resources of the clinician, especially with regard to psychological resilience. The compassion state does not ignore suffering or change the negative reality of it; instead, it generates and strengthens an internal positive state of concern for the patient that also results in the most satisfaction and fulfillment for the clinician as he or she responds to the patient. But this is a mental state that must be trained in order to be achieved and sustained. In short, the ability to manage both negative and positive emotions and the ability to generate positive compassionate emotional responses in patient care ultimately protects the clinician while engaging in the difficult emotional work of taking care of patients. With this more advanced understanding of emotions, empathy, and compassion, we are now ready to delineate the components of balanced compassionate caring in the next several chapters.

QUESTIONS FOR DISCUSSION

1. Describe a case in which you felt you demonstrated good emotion regulation with a patient who was suffering in some way.
2. How has this information on emotional intelligence and the key role of positive emotions changed your view of what you were implicitly and explicitly taught about emotions in medicine?

REFERENCES

Bennet, G. (1988). *The wound and the doctor.* London, UK: Secker and Warburg.

Cameron, C. D., & Payne, B. K. (2011). Escaping affect: How motivated emotion regulation creates insensitivity to mass suffering. *Journal of Personality and Social Psychology, 100*(1), 1–15.

Damasio, A. (1994). *Descartes' error: Emotion, reason and the human brain.* New York, NY: Putnam.

Decety, J., & Fotopoulou, A. (2015). Why empathy has a beneficial impact on others in medicine: Unifying theories. *Frontiers in Behavioral Neuroscience, 8,* 1–11.

Didonna, F. (Ed.). (2009). *Clinical handbook of mindfulness.* New York, NY: Springer.

Engen, H. G., & Singer, T. (2015a). Affect and motivation are critical in constructive meditation. *Trends in Cognitive Sciences, 20*(3), 159–160.

Engen, H. G., & Singer, T. (2015b). Compassion-based emotion regulation up-regulates experienced positive affect and associated neural networks. *Social Cognitive and Affective Neuroscience, 10*(9), 1291–1301. doi:10.1093/scan/nsv008

Epstein, R. M. (1999). Mindful practice. *JAMA, 282*(9), 833–839.

Farb, N. A. S., Anderson, A. K., Irving, J. A., & Segal, Z. V. (2014). Mindfulness interventions and emotion regulation. In J. J. Gross (Ed.), *Handbook of emotion regulation* (2nd ed., pp. 548–567). New York, NY: Guilford Press.

Figley, C. R. (2002). Compassion fatigue? Psychotherapists' chronic lack of self-care. *Psychotherapy in Practice, 58*(11), 1433–1441.

Fredrickson, B. L. (2004). The broaden-and-build theory of positive emotions. *Philosophical Transactions of the Royal Society of London Series B, Biological Sciences, 359,* 1367–1377.

Fredrickson, B. L. (2013). Positive emotions broaden and build. *Advances in Experimental Social Psychology, 47,* 1–53.

Fredrickson, B. L., & Branigan, C. (2005). Positive emotions broaden the scope of attention and thought-action repertoires. *Cognition and Emotion, 19*(3), 313–332.

Fredrickson, B. L., Cohn, M. A., Coffey, K. A., Pek, J., & Finkel, S. M. (2008). Open hearts build lives: Positive emotions, induced through loving-kindness meditation, build consequential personal resources, *Journal of Personality and Social Psychology, 95*(5), 1045–1062.

Fredrickson, B. L., & Joiner, T. (2002). Positive emotions trigger upward spirals toward emotional well-being. *Journal of Personality and Social Psychology, 65*(1), 45–55.

Fredrickson, B. L., & Levenson, R. W. (1998). Positive emotions speed recovery from the cardiovascular sequelae of negative emotions. *Cognition and Emotion, 12*(2), 191–220.

Gilbert, P. (2009). *The compassionate mind: A new approach to life's challenges.* Oakland, CA: New Harbinger.

Gilbert, P. (2014). The origins and nature of compassion focused therapy. *British Journal of Clinical Psychology, 53,* 6–41.

Gleichgerrcht, E., & Decety, J. (2013). Empathy in clinical practice: How individual dispositions, gender, and experience moderate empathic concern, burnout, and emotional distress in physicians. *PLoS ONE*, 8(4), e61526. doi:10.1371/journal.pone.0061526

Grillon, C., Quispe-Escudero, D., Mathur, A., & Ernst, M. (2015). Mental fatigue impairs emotion regulation. *Emotion*, 15(3), 383–389.

Gross, J. J. (1998). Antecedent- and response-focused emotion regulation: Divergent consequences for experience, expression, and physiology. *Journal of Personality and Social Psychology*, 74(1), 224–237.

Gross, J. J. (2002). Emotion regulation: Affective, cognitive, and social consequences. *Psychophysiology*, 39(3), 281–291.

Gross, J. J. (2014). Emotion regulation: Conceptual and empirical foundations. In J. J. Gross (Ed.), *Handbook of Emotion Regulation* (2nd ed., pp. 3–20). New York, NY: Guilford Press.

Gross, J. J., & John, O. P. (2003). Individual differences in two emotion regulation processes: Implications for affect, relationships, and well-being. *Journal of Personality and Social Psychology*, 85(2), 348–362.

Guggenbuhl-Craig, A. (1982). *Power in the helping professions*. Dallas, TX: Spring.

Harrison, R. (2017). Critical incident stress debriefing after adverse patient safety events. *American Journal of Managed Care*, 23(5), 310–312.

Hauerwas, S. (1986). *Suffering presence: Theological reflections on medicine, the mentally handicapped, and the church*. Notre Dame, IN: University of Notre Dame Press.

Johnson, K. J., Waugh, C. E., & Fredrickson, B. L. (2010). Smile to see the forest: Facially expressed positive emotions broaden cognition. *Cognition and Emotion*, 24(2), 299–321.

Joinson, C. (1992). Coping with compassion fatigue. *Nursing*, 4, 771–779.

Kabat-Zinn, J. (1982). An outpatient program in behavioral medicine for chronic pain patients based on the practice of mindfulness meditation: Theoretical considerations and preliminary results. *General Hospital Psychiatry*, 4(1), 33–47.

Kang, Y., Gray, J. R., & Dovidio, J. F. (2015). The head and the heart: Effects of understanding and experiencing lovingkindness on attitudes toward the self and others. *Mindfulness*, 6(5), 1063–1070.

Kennedy-Moore, E., & Watson, J. C. (1999). *Expressing emotion: Myths, realities, and therapeutic strategies*. New York, NY: Guilford Press.

Klimecki, O. M., Leiberg, S., Lamm, C., & Singer, T. (2013). Functional neural plasticity and associated changes in positive affect after compassion training. *Cerebral Cortex*, 23, 1552–1561.

Klimecki, O. M., Leiberg, S., Ricard, M., & Singer, T. (2014). Differential pattern of functional brain plasticity after compassion and empathy training. *Social Cognitive and Affective Neuroscience*, 9, 873–879.

Klimecki, O., & Singer, T. (2011). Empathic distress fatigue rather than compassion fatigue? Integrating findings from empathy research in psychology and social neuroscience. In B. Oakley, A. Knafo, G. Madhavan, & D. S. Wilson (Eds.), *Pathological altruism* (pp. 368–383). New York, NY: Oxford University Press.

Lazarus, R. S. (1991). *Emotion and adaptation*. New York, NY: Oxford University Press.

Levenson, R. W. (1988). Emotion and the autonomic nervous system: A prospectus for research on autonomic specificity. In H. L. Wagner (Ed.), *Social psychophysiology and emotion: Theory and clinical applications* (pp. 17–42). London, UK: Wiley.

Lief, H. I., & Fox, R. C. (1963). Training for "detached concern" in medical students. In H. Lief, V. Lief, & N. Lief (Eds.), *The psychological basis of medical practice* (pp. 12–35). New York, NY: Hoeber Medical Division.

Lifton, R. J. (1986). *The Nazi doctors: Medical killing and the psychology of genocide*. London, UK: Macmillan.

Lown, B. A., & Manning, C. F. (2010). The Schwartz Center Rounds: Evaluation of an interdisciplinary approach to enhancing patient-centered communication, teamwork, and provider support. *Academic Medicine*, 85(6), 1073–1081.

Maslach, C. (1982). *Burnout: The cost of caring*. Englewood Cliffs, NJ: Prentice Hall.

Maslach, C., Schaufeli, W. B., & Leiter, M. P. (2001). Job burnout. *Annual Review of Psychology, 52*, 397–422.

McCue, J. D. (1982). The effects of stress on physicians and their medical practice. *New England Journal of Medicine, 306*(8), 458–463.

McNaughton, N., & LeBlanc, V. (2012). Perturbations: The central role of emotional competence in medical training. In B. D. Hodges & L. Lingard (Eds.), *The question of competence: Reconsidering medical education in the twenty-first century* (pp. 70–96). Ithaca, NY: ILR Press.

Mitchell, J. T. (1983). When disaster strikes ... the critical incident stress debriefing process. *Journal of Emergency Medical Services, 8*, 36–39.

Mitchell, J. T. (2008). From controversy to confirmation: Crisis support services for the twenty-first century. *International Journal of Emergency Mental Health, 10*(4), 245–252.

Newton, B. W. (2013). Walking a fine line: Is it possible to remain an empathic physician and have a hardened heart? *Frontiers in Human Neuroscience, 7*(223), 1–12. doi:10.3389/fnhum.2013.00233

Palmer, S. (2017). *Supporting the emotional needs of staff: The impact of Schwartz Rounds on caregiver and patient experience*. Beryl Institute: White Papers.

Pennebaker, J. W. (1992). Inhibition as the linchpin of health. In H. S. Friedman (Ed.), *Hostility, coping, and health* (pp. 127–139). Washington, DC: American Psychological Association.

Richards, J. M., & Gross, J. J. (1999). Composure at any cost? The cognitive consequences of emotion suppression. *Personality and Social Psychology Bulletin, 25*(8), 1033–1044.

Richards, J. M., & Gross, J. J. (2006). Personality and emotional memory: How regulating emotion impairs memory for emotional events. *Journal of Research in Personality, 40*(5), 631–651.

Salovey, P., Detweiler-Bedell, B. T., Detweiler-Bedell, J. B., & Mayer, J. D. (2008). Emotional intelligence. In M. Lewis, J. M. Haviland-Jones, & L. F. Barrett (Eds.), *Handbook of emotions* (3rd ed., pp. 533–547). New York, NY: Guilford Press.

Salzberg, S. (2002). *Loving-kindness: The revolutionary art of happiness*. Boston, MA: Shambhala.

Schmitz, T. W., DeRosa, E., & Anderson, A. K. (2009). Opposing influences of affective state valence on visual cortical encoding. *Journal of Neuroscience, 29*(22), 7199–7207.

Shapiro, S. L., Astin, J. A., Bishop, S. R., & Cordova, M. (2005). Mindfulness-based stress reduction for health care professionals: Results from a randomized trial. *International Journal of Stress Management, 12*(2), 164–176.

Shiota, M. N., & Levenson, R. W. (2012). Turn down the volume or change the channel? Emotional effects of detached versus positive reappraisal. *Journal of Personality and Social Psychology, 103*(3), 416–429.

Slovic, P. (2007). "If I look at the mass I will never act": Psychic numbing and genocide. *Judgment and Decision Making, 2*(2), 79–95.

Spiro, H., Curnen, M. G. M, Peschel, E., & St. James, D. (Eds.). (1993). *Empathy and the Practice of medicine*. New Haven, CT: Yale University Press.

Srivastava, S., Tamir, M., McGonigal, K. M., John, O. P., & Gross, J. J. (2009). The social costs of emotional suppression: A prospective study of the transition to college. *Journal of Personality and Social Psychology, 96*(4), 883–897.

Stern, D. (1985). *The interpersonal world of the infant: A view from psychoanalysis and development*. New York, NY: Basic Books.

Tugade, M. M., & Fredrickson, B. L. (2004). Resilient individuals use positive emotions to bounce back from negative emotional experiences. *Journal of Personality and Social Psychology, 86*(2), 320–333.

Van Dam, N. T., van Vugt, M. K., Vago, D. R., Schmalzl, L., Saron, C. D., Olendzki, A., ... Meyer, D. E. (2017). Mind the hype: A critical evaluation and prescriptive agenda for research on mindfulness and meditation. *Perspectives on Psychological Science*, 1–26.

Västfjäll, D., Slovic, P., Mayorga, M., & Peters, E. (2014). Compassion fade: Affect and charity are greatest for a single child in need. *PLOS ONE, 9*(6), 1–10.

Weng, H. C. (2008). Does the physician's emotional intelligence matter? Impacts of the physician's emotional intelligence on the trust, patient-physician relationship, and satisfaction. *Health Care Management Review, 33*(4), 280–288.

Weng, H. Y., Fox, A. S., Shackman, A. J., Stodola, D. E., Caldwell, J. Z. K., Olson, M. C., ... Davidson, R. J. (2013). Compassion training alters altruism and neural responses to suffering. *Psychological Science, 24*(7), 1171–1180.

Wilkins, R. (Ed.). (1992). *The doctor's quotation book: A medical miscellany.* New York, NY: Barnes & Noble.

Wilson, J. (2014). *Mindful America: The mutual transformation of Buddhist meditation and American culture.* New York, NY: Oxford University Press.

Wuthnow, R. (1991). *Acts of compassion: Caring for others and helping ourselves.* Princeton, NJ: Princeton University Press.

CREDITS

"The zone between emotional detachment and emotional over-involvement in patient care."

Chapter Sections:

CHAPTER 11

The Model of Balanced Compassionate Caring

Question to consider before reading this chapter:

1. What do you think it takes to find the right balance between being emotionally detached with patients and being emotionally overinvolved with patients?

INTRODUCTION

In this chapter, I propose the model of balanced compassionate caring as a way to integrate the research of the previous chapters and to set the stage for the next part of the book, in which I provide the components for maintaining the balance between being, on one hand, detached (or negatively involved) with patients and, on the other hand, overly emotionally involved with patients. Here, I will briefly summarize the main findings of chapters 5 through 10 and integrate them with several diagrams starting with the healing effects of compassionate caring on patients, then representing that there is a continuum of clinician emotional involvement and how that continuum is related to effects on both the patient and the clinician.

THE BENEFITS OF COMPASSIONATE CARING BY CLINICIANS IN PATIENT CARE

Overview of variables representing facets of compassionate caring

In chapters 5 and 6, I presented the research that demonstrates how variables measuring different facets of compassionate caring are related to positive effects on patients. Compassionate caring variables included nonverbal behavior, communication skills of various types, emotional tone, and particular intervention styles. Other variables have included empathy, the patient care approach, and the quality of the therapeutic relationship. In chapter 6, I reviewed research on how communication skills in themselves are not enough to convey a genuine and caring relationship. Patients pick up the authentic caring intent from clinicians, and they can pick up on surface acting, being disliked by clinicians, and other aspects of what I called a caring veneer.

Overview of indirect and direct outcomes of compassionate caring variables

What has become evident at this early stage of research is that these compassionate caring variables do affect patient outcomes—both objective and subjective—and they do this through both indirect and direct pathways to those outcomes. Examples we reviewed included how these variables affect patients' willingness to disclose and discuss their symptoms, how well they understand the treatment plan, better diagnostic accuracy, and the likelihood that patients will adhere to the recommended treatment regimens. Compassionate caring increases patients' sense of safety with clinicians, making them physiologically and mentally calmer and more receptive to the treatment process. It helps them better manage their emotions and improves the social support they experience. They are more satisfied with their clinicians and the overall care. It is even related to fewer malpractice claims. Compassionate caring or its absence affects how motivated patients are to get better, and it leads to higher-quality health care decisions. There is even evidence that it can lead to improved efficiency in the clinic. Besides the subjective outcomes, we saw how compassionate care variables indirectly and directly are related to better medical outcomes.

Two ways a caring motivation benefits patients

Helping that is driven by a caring motivation benefits help recipients in at least two ways. First, the quality of helping is better. The helper who freely chooses to help and finds this personally meaningful is more likely to put more effort into the helping action and do so in a way that fits with what the recipient needed or wanted. It will matter to the caring helper that the help is received well, and so he or she will put more energy and attentiveness into it. Caring helpers are also more likely to express more care in the helping action and to be more enthusiastic about it. As a result, help recipients are more likely to feel more cared for, to experience increased benefit because of the way helpers treated them, and are more likely to feel grateful. Second, help recipients have improved outcomes from caring helpers because truly caring helpers will put more effort into the helping and therefore accomplish more than a less motivated helper who puts less effort into helping. Help recipients thus feel more care and support because the help they have received is from caring helpers who are personally invested in them and personally responsive to their suffering (Weinstein & Ryan, 2010).

Relationship between quality of compassionate caring and healing effect on patients

Based on this research, the graph in figure 11.1 conveys the relationship between the quality of compassionate caring, C^2, by the helping professional and the healing effect on patients or clients.

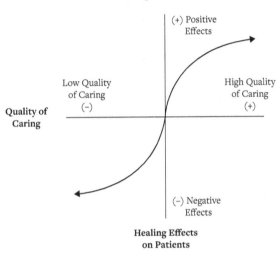

The Relationship between Quality of Clinician
Compassionate Caring
and Healing Effects on Patients

FIGURE 11.1 The relationship between quality of clinician compassionate caring and healing effects on patients.

All of these variables of compassionate caring have been combined into the quality of compassionate caring on the *x* axis as the independent variable, and all the indirect and direct outcomes have been combined as healing effects on patients as the dependent variable graphed along the *y* axis. While the exact slope of the curves is approximate, the effect of the quality of C^2 is such that it has increasingly positive or negative effects, then levels off in asymptotic fashion. In other words, in terms of positive quality of caring, its effects for the patient have rapidly increasing positive healing effects and

then tapers off. Thus, when compassionate caring is part of the way a technical procedure or intervention is done, it augments or amplifies its healing effects. For example, if you conduct an initial interview with a patient, as you "add" C^2 components such as a genuine caring attitude, being seated with an open posture, establishing rapport, and so on, the more the patient will feel comfortable and the better he or she will discuss his or her symptoms; this leads to getting better data from the patient, which then leads to a better diagnosis, increased motivation to follow your recommendation, and so on. But at a certain point, it is not as if more C^2 "adds" any more to the intervention. The same is true with the way a lack of C^2 leads to negative effects and outcomes for the patient. As the clinician has more and more negative behaviors and attitudes, it very quickly "contaminates" or undermines whatever procedure or intervention you are doing. For example, in your initial interview with a patient, as you increasingly act in a negative non-C^2 manner, the more it negatively affects the patient. If you do not establish rapport, or if you come across in a judgmental way, then this "contaminates" in the interview process: the patient becomes stressed and fearful, does not discuss the symptoms as freely, and becomes defensive and resistant. As a result, the clinician gets poorer data for diagnosis and treatment, and the patient is less motivated to follow treatment recommendations. At a certain point of treating a patient poorly, there is a leveling-off effect. When you treat a patient very negatively, it is not like a little more negative treatment is going to make it worse; it is already at its worst.

Given that we have examined compassionate caring variables in general, let us now consider specifically the effect of the clinician's level of emotional involvement with the patient and how that affects both the patient and the clinician.

THE BALANCED COMPASSIONATE CARING MODEL[1]

The balanced compassionate caring model describes how an optimum level of emotional involvement or engagement with a patient has positive effects both for the patient and the clinician. This is the *zone of balanced compassionate caring (C²)* that lies between being emotionally detached or neutral with a patient and being emotionally overinvolved with a patient. Being outside this zone has negative effects not only for the patient but also for the clinician. Interestingly, when we graph the effects of emotional involvement for the patient and then graph the effects for the clinician, the graph looks exactly the same. In the next two sections, I will present this model from the perspective of the effects on the patient and then from the perspective of the effects on the clinician.

EFFECTS OF CLINICIAN EMOTIONAL INVOLVEMENT ON THE PATIENT

Emotional detachment is a self-protective maneuver that may have been based in good intentions
In the previous chapters, I presented an analysis of the role of emotions and the idea of emotional detachment in clinical practice. One of the major concerns for clinicians is protecting themselves in the emotionally difficult work of clinical practice. The fear is that both the continual encounter with suffering in our patients and the emotionally grueling work of trying to help patients puts us at risk for burnout. Clinicians

for the most part enter the health professions because they want to relieve their patients' suffering, and they are passionate about this, compassionate about this. But after a time, many mute that enthusiastic desire into an emotionally detached approach, not because they no longer desire to help patients, but because many want to keep helping patients. Emotional detachment becomes a self-protective maneuver that enables clinicians to feel less pain from empathy fatigue and secondary traumatic stress; and, it becomes a way to stay in the marathon of a career in health care. The problem is that this does not work. That sincere desire to self-protect and endure in helping others with emotional detachment ends up harming the patients we love and harming ourselves as clinicians.

"Emotional detachment" is a metaphor or a word picture that is not scientific
Emotional "detachment" is a metaphor, but we literalize it into how emotions actually work. But we did not give ourselves a deeper and more scientific understanding of emotions and instead adopted a simplistic understanding that we perpetuate in the hallways of our hospitals. "Emotional detachment" is a metaphor, a word picture of a clinician disconnecting a pipe from the water flow, unhooking from being dragged by a car, or detaching our rope from being pulled down by another person. We "detach" from the emotions in that way. What was presented in chapter 10 showed how emotions cannot be separated out from the rest of our minds and bodies in so neat a fashion. From an evolutionary perspective, these emotions are in us because they are adaptive and have helped us to survive. As we looked at the science of emotion, we concluded

---

1   Special thanks to Dr. Robert White and Dr. Kathleen Kolberg for their feedback and suggestions for the diagrams and components.

that when we have achieved a state in which we are able to hang in with a very emotional situation, it is because we have learned emotion regulation or emotion management. "Emotional detachment" is our shorthand name for that ability. Without emotional arousal, we would not perform optimally; and with too much emotional arousal, we would be overwhelmed. Because of our upbringings, temperaments, and training, we learn how to channel our emotional arousal in very difficult situations into a focused, high-performance state not unlike what the best elite performers, test pilots, and warriors do.

The continuum from negative emotional involvement to overinvolvement

Now that we have a more accurate understanding of emotions, how would we draw the relationship between the emotional engagement

of the clinician and its effect on the patient? In figure 11.2, I offer a model of this relationship. On the x axis is the continuum of emotional involvement from being negatively involved with patients to being overinvolved, with the midpoint as being neutral or detached. *Negatively emotionally involved* means an attitude and/or behavior that is explicitly hostile to the patient. Examples include demeaning the patient, hitting the patient, abusing the patient, inflicting pain that is avoidable on the patient, and so on. *Neutral or detached* means that emotionally the clinicians has suppressed any emotional engagement or taken a solely objectifying attitude toward the patient just as one might have with chopping vegetables or changing a tire. *Emotional overinvolvement* refers to feeling more about, or doing more for, a patient than is necessary or prudent for what the patient's situation is. Examples would include calling a

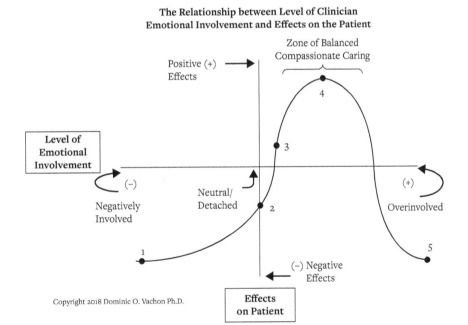

The Relationship between Level of Clinician Emotional Involvement and Effects on the Patient

Copyright 2018 Dominic O. Vachon Ph.D.

Thanks to Dr. Robert White M.D. for his suggestions in improving this graph

FIGURE 11.2 The relationship between level of clinician emotional involvement and effects on patient.

patient every time he or she needs to take medication, feeling like you have to solve all your patient's problems, giving your credit card to your patient, inviting your patient to stay at your home until he or she feels better, or habitually dwelling on your patients' suffering after you have left the clinic or expecting that you should feel everything your patient feels.

Effects of negative emotional involvement, detachment, and overinvolvement on the patient

What is the effect on your patient of being at various points on that continuum? On the y axis, the effects range from negative effects to positive effects. These can be defined widely from how the patient feels about how you are with him or her to the actual medical outcomes. Starting at point 1, when a clinician is negatively emotionally involved with a patient, this has very negative effects on that patient. The hostility, anger, or malignant motivation harms the patient. Point 2 is the emotionally detached clinician, and this is less harmful to a patient, but research suggests that it does not produce very good results. At point 5, when a clinician is overinvolved with a patient, it is very bad for the patient. Some examples include making the patient dependent on you so that when you are gone, the patient is not able to take care of him- or herself. The patient may not learn what needs to be done to take care of him- or herself because you have shielded him or her from learning from the experience.

Effects of being in the zone of balanced C^2

Now let us move to the *zone of balanced C^2* represented by points 3 and 4. Again, these curves are approximate descriptions of what we know from the research and clinical experience. Note that there is a range of emotional involvement that would be considered to be in the balanced

zone. As Larson (1993) explains, the intensity of emotional involvement can vary moment to moment with a patient; case by case in which you are involved differently with different patients; at different points in the same day or week; and by different points in your career. A different level is required by each patient in each unique situation. There is a range that is helpful to a patient. A novice clinician may not yet be very skilled in C^2, but his or her genuine caring and beginning competence has a positive effect, as represented at point 3. Or one clinician may have a level of emotional engagement with patients that is helpful, but if the clinician worked on his or her skills and mindset, this clinician could get even better results with his or her patients. For example, a clinician who does not have many health behavior change counseling skills may see limited change in his or her patients. But when that clinician learns motivational interviewing or stages of change counseling techniques, his or her results get better. Or maybe the clinician is somewhat reserved and does not get the best rapport early with a patient; but as the clinician improves that ability to establish rapport, then he or she would get better results in his or her patients. Point 4 would be the place of optimum emotional involvement that yields the best results possible in that patient situation.

EFFECTS OF HELPER EMOTIONAL INVOLVEMENT ON THE CLINICIAN

This then brings us to what the effect of emotional involvement has on the clinician. I have argued that both total emotional detachment and overinvolvement in helping someone have negative effects on the person helped but also on the clinician. However, there would seem to be an optimum level of emotional involvement which would have positive effects not only for the people helped but also for the clinician. In fact, the model for the practitioner effect of emotional involvement on the practitioner in figure 11.3 would be just like the one for the effect on the patient or client as seen in figure 11.2 There appears to be range of optimum emotional involvement, the *zone of balanced C²*, that has positive effects on the practitioner as well.

Analogy of the effects of too little or too much exercise

A helpful analogy about the positive effects of emotional involvement on clients or patients would be how exercise effects the person who exercises. Too little exercise leads to physical atrophy and numerous health problems such as heart disease and becoming overweight.

Too much exercise is also dangerous. It can lead to physical problems such as joint problems or other damage to the body. Yet there is a fairly wide range of exercise level which is beneficial to people. Furthermore, people differ not only in how much exercise is best for them but also in how that exercise is beneficial. Some people do daily vigorous walks and others do long runs. Some people get a lot of health benefits from vigorous walking while others, because of genetic or other factors, need a lot more than vigorous walking to obtain the same health benefit levels. In short, while there is a fairly wide range of exercise levels that are beneficial to a person, there is clearly a point at which exercise levels become insufficient or excessive. Furthermore, there are individual differences in terms of how physical exercise benefits people within this optimum range of exercise.

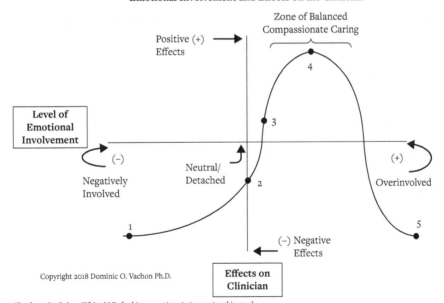

The Relationship between Level of Clinician
Emotional Involvement and Effects on the Clinician

Copyright 2018 Dominic O. Vachon Ph.D.

Thanks to Dr. Robert White M.D. for his suggestions in improving this graph

FIGURE 11.3 The relationship between level of clinician emotional involvement and effects on clinician.

Too little or too much emotional involvement is bad for the clinician

Clinician emotional involvement operates in similar fashion. The exercise of caring for another person has similar limits and possibilities. A lack of investment in the welfare of another person leads, as discussed previously, to emotional problems for the clinician and lack of a sense of personal accomplishment in the work as well as other negative effects. An excessive degree of involvement also leads to problems. Clinicians can become emotionally exhausted, especially as they encounter a multitude of tragic circumstances over which they have little control. In the optimum range, however, a number of positive effects for the clinician can result.

Optimal emotional involvement protects the clinician better than detachment

There are two ways in which optimal emotional involvement protects the clinician better than detachment. *First, an optimum or balanced level of involvement or care for a patient or client ultimately gives you better protection than excessive detachment or detached objectivity while also increasing your effectiveness (and therefore your personal satisfaction) in your helping of the patient.* Maintaining detachment is essentially a defensive maneuver. Detachment involves blocking out certain stimuli so that the clinician remains unaffected. Detachment might be likened to a knight in armor. The more armor you wear as a clinician, the more your psychological maneuverability decreases even though you are well protected. The very detached clinician puts so much energy into not being emotionally affected by what is going on that there is less energy to put into the action of helping the other person. This is not to say that the helper should not have defenses or self-protective skills. A positive image of this balance clinicians have to maintain is the image of a lifeguard saving a drowning person. People in panic can drown you not because they do not appreciate you, but because in their panic, they are not thinking of your safety or what is best for them; they are afraid of losing their lives. So, the lifeguard has to position him- or herself in a way that the drowning person cannot hurt the lifeguard but in which the lifeguard can also work to pull the person out of the water. Sometimes it is enough to throw a buoy from a boat to the person in the water and the rescue person does not have to enter the water. But sometimes the situation requires the rescuer to enter the water. The overinvolved clinician is like the lifeguard who approaches the drowning person from the front. In that case, the drowning person could drown the lifeguard. Likewise, the overinvolved clinician neglects to protect him- or herself from how other people's pain can consume him or her. The detached helper is like the lifeguard who would rather call out to the drowning person, telling him or her how to swim when what the drowning person really needs is someone to swim out to save him or her.

Study showing that optimal emotional involvement enables better emotional control and better attention to what is happening to the patient

Thus, caring about a patient is an active rather than defensive move. As Smith and Kleinman (1989) found in their research with how medical students manage their emotions, "moderate concern allows them to manage their own feelings *and* pay close attention to the patient" (p. 67). While the totally detached helper is putting most of his or her energy into emotional control, the optimally concerned helper needs fewer defenses because he or she is active in attending to the person needing help and is comfortable knowing what to do with personal feelings aroused in the helping situation. In fact, the optimally concerned helper has a wealth of data because he or she is connected to his or her own feelings and therefore is more likely to be effective in helping a person than a helper who has his or her feelings under rigid control.

Optimal emotional involvement allows the clinician to feel rewards of the work
A *second positive result of having an optimal level of concern for patients or clients is that the helper is more able to feel the rewards of the work.* The problem with excessive emotional detachment is that while feelings are controlled to protect the helper from negative feelings, the possibility of experiencing positive feelings emerging from the work is also prevented. Some support for this was found in a study I did on affect or emotional intensity in a sample of 257 registered nurses (Vachon, 1993). Affect intensity refers to the typical intensity that emotions are experienced by individuals (Larsen & Diener, 1987). That is, it refers to the degree to which an emotion is experienced, regardless of whether it is positive or negative. It was found that nurses had significantly lower affect intensity than the general population; that is, they tended to have a more even-keeled temperament in handling the diverse emotion-provoking events typical of nursing. But contrary to what was expected, affect intensity did not correlate with burnout. Instead, it appeared to operate as an amplifier for all emotions, negative or positive. A helper who experiences stressful events more intensely than another helper with lower affect intensity will feel the negative emotions more intensely than the helper with lower affect intensity. But it also means that positive experiences are felt more intensely by the helper. In fact, the study found that nurses with higher affect intensity had a greater sense of personal accomplishment on the job than did nurses with lower affect intensity.

Distancing emotional coping methods correlated with burnout
Supporting both of these points is a study by Doolittle, Windish, and Seelig (2013) in a sample of 173 internal medicine and medicine-pediatrics residents. Coping strategies that involve disengagement and objectification were found to be significantly correlated with emotional exhaustion, depersonalization, and not feeling a sense of personal accomplishment in their work. Specifically, those coping strategies were disengagement, denial, self-blame, humor, and venting. Coping strategies that appeared to protect residents against emotional exhaustion and depersonalization included acceptance, active coping, and positive reframing. Residents who used a more distancing coping strategy with patient suffering tended to be more burned out while residents who were more actively engaged with what they were experiencing tended to be less burnt out.

Study showing physicians themselves experience positive benefits in empathizing with patients
While it is common to think that physicians generally find empathizing with patients emotionally taxing, physicians actually have a very positive appreciation of empathy while knowing that it can be draining and exhausting. In an interview study of physicians from a number of specialties primarily working with cancer patients (i.e., oncology, palliative care, surgery, pulmonology, gastroenterology), Robieux, Karsenti, Pocard, and Flahault (2018) found that these physicians expressed a number of very positive benefits

to them beside benefits to patients. First, they described how being empathic is a source of pleasure and reward in doing clinical work. Second, they felt that empathy helped them do their work better in being able to identify their patients' needs, thus enabling them to be more successful in the care. Third, physicians also articulated how empathy was a coping resource for them. Rather than empathizing only being viewed as an emotional drain, many physicians noted how empathy helped them manage various clinical tasks; it also gave them meaning and made the work more interesting. In terms of how patients could be exhausting, they added how organizational constraints can be very taxing in terms of tasks and responsibilities demanded as well as the sheer quantity of the work expected. Rather than making clinical empathy the source of the problem in burnout, it is rather the unrealistic expectations of all the other things clinicians must do that is more the problem.

Clinical detachment and empathy with emotional resonance can both lead to burnout

Austen (2016) argued that choosing between clinical detachment and true empathy with emotional resonance is a false dichotomy. He succinctly summarizes what we know from the research as well as anecdotally that either approach at the extremes leads to burnout. Clinical detachment leads to a generalized emotional detachment from not only patients, but also our colleagues and loved ones. But empathy with emotional resonance at the extreme also leads to emotional exhaustion and to burnout. It is a no-win scenario, a catch-22, with either detachment or emotional resonance leading to burnout. *Either approach in the extreme is doomed to failure.* He recommends that we take care of that "true empathy" with better emotional support for all

clinicians using Schwartz Rounds, for example, and that we learn how to interpret the emotions that trouble us using, for example, reflective practices and clinical supervision. This is where our new science of compassion offers a way out of this no-win scenario because when we situate the "true empathy with emotional resonance" in the compassion mindset, this protects clinicians from burnout and allows them to stay emotionally engaged but not overwhelmed by their patients' distress. We now know that the practices Austen recommends work because they help clinicians find and sustain a compassion mindset.

Medical training must teach clinicians that managing and using emotions are an integral part of good clinical practice

A key component in maintaining an optimal level of concern for a client or patient is the ability not just to have feelings of concern for the person being helped, but also the skill of managing those feelings as well as the negative feelings that are typical in helping work. The option of emotional detachment is chosen by many helping professionals not because they are bad people, but because they have not been taught the skills of managing their negative emotions as well as using them, paradoxically, to improve the healing process. Because of the emphasis on objectivity in the sciences, the approach to feelings has been to discount them as not being integral to the helping process or to science. Subjectivity has been erroneously equated with irrationality or that it would necessarily interfere with science. The skill, then, of managing and using one's own subjective feelings in helping work has not been taught in medical schools or law schools. The helping professions have the potential to be much more satisfying if helpers learn how to "make friends" with the strong emotions they experience in their work rather than viewing these strong emotions as dangerous. One of the seven questions on the Mayo Clinic Well-Being Index is, "During the past month, have you worried that your work is hardening you emotionally?" (Dyrbye, Satele, Sloan, & Shanafelt, 2012). While the culture of the denial of the importance of emotions is still rampant in the medical professions, it is intriguing to see that a well-established measure of physician well-being answered by a simple yes or no is a marker of poor physician well-being.

Carmack's continuum of dysfunctional engagement to dysfunctional detachment

Carmack (1992) described balancing detachment and engagement as a continuum with one extreme representing *dysfunctional engagement* and the other extreme representing *dysfunctional detachment*. The goal is to balance the two extremes to find a functional balance. *Dysfunctional engagement* was found in one study in dealing with multiple AIDS-related losses as being overinvolved and overextended to the point that caregivers felt overwhelmed by the emotional needs and pain of others. Such individuals felt that they exceeded their own resources by being too involved for too long. *Dysfunctional detachment* was described as a state of being uninvolved or emotionally numb to an extreme degree. Such individuals reported feeling dissatisfied while being in such a state. They tended to feel helpless and depressed, reported engaging in more high-risk behaviors, had less social interaction, and tended to avoid new relationships. *Functional detachment* was described as having self-protection from being overly involved or feeling emotional pain but still caring. They tended to believe that self-protection was a valid and acceptable thing to do and that they should take time to recover and regenerate. This might include taking

physical time away or using cognitive methods like meditating and praying. Finally, *functional engagement* was characterized by feeling valuable to others while protecting themselves. Choice was a dominant theme; these individuals felt they were making a difference for others by choice and that they could manage their emotional involvement. They tended to help others within certain limits and experienced a sense of fulfillment in this work.

The subtle difference between functional detachment and functional engagement

What is interesting to note in Carmack's model is the subtle difference between *functional detachment* and *functional engagement*. While both would espouse good boundaries and self-protection, functional engagement has the element of focusing on the positive action while functional detachment focuses on the self-protection. This research was done before the current work on the science of compassion research, so it is noteworthy to see how functional engagement is very similar to the compassion mindset with its resulting compassion satisfaction.

Five themes that characterize highly functioning caregivers

But how does a clinician learn this delicate balance, and what does that balance look like within the clinician? There is not very much research on this question, and Carmack (1997) pursued this in a qualitative study of formal and informal caregivers. She found five themes that characterized this balance in highly functioning caregivers.

Focus on process, not outcome

First was a paradoxical way of believing in the potential for affecting the outcome but yet letting go of what the outcome turns out to be. These caregivers believed they could make a difference by their helping, but that they could not necessarily fix the situation or the people. They focused on what was under their control in the helping process, but also realized that the outcome was not under their control; that control is up to the choices of the person being helped or to other factors beyond anyone's control. There is a sense of accepting how limited one's ability is to change anything in others, but still doing everything that one can do to help. Carmack found that such caregivers had never been explicitly taught how to do this. Instead, they learned by making mistakes and suffering the consequences of being overinvolved. In order to survive, they learned this ability to let go of what is beyond their control. Furthermore, these helpers explained that this was something that required constant rebalancing over time or even within one day.

Be practical and conscious of choices in handling a situation

Second, maintaining consciousness and pragmatism was a common feature with high-functioning helpers. They tend to make conscious choices about what they can handle in a particular situation, keeping in mind what is necessary to manage their emotional states in order not to be overwhelmed by others' needs. They structure the helping in ways that are most manageable to them. They focus on the present rather than dwelling on the past or the future; they also focus on what is practical and possible in a given situation.

Be able to set and maintain limits and boundaries

Third, high-functioning helpers know how to set and maintain limits and boundaries on their involvement with others. In order to deal with ongoing demands and expectations, they planned what they needed to do in order to pace and protect themselves. Examples would include setting limits on how many hours one is working or establishing boundaries such as not giving one's home phone number to patients.

Self-awareness to continually adjust from excessive engagement or detachment

Fourth, in order to maintain balance, these caregivers continually were self-aware of where they were regarding excessive engagement or detachment. In doing so, these helpers can make regular adjustments if they go to one extreme or the other. If a helper notices that he or she is feeling numb, disengaged, angry, lonely or sad with patients, he or she can adjust for overdetachment. If he or she is feeling exhausted, feeling like he or she has to control everything, obsessing about particular patients, dreaming about a particular patient, not feeling clear in his or her judgment, or not wanting anyone around, then the helper realizes that he or she has tended to become dysfunctionally engaged.

Self-care practices

Finally, these helpers practiced good self-care. The self-awareness that operates in other factors is also used to detect when the helpers are stressed and must manage this stress. Every person will experience this uniquely, and the strategies to take care of oneself will also vary. This includes everything from time away, working on one's attitude, physical self-care, having a sense of humor, spirituality, being alone, or seeking support from others (Carmack, 1997).

Study on the three types of benefits of helping for helpers

There is very good evidence that helping others indirectly also benefits the helpers. Weinstein and Ryan (2010) reviewed the research literature and have found many ways in which helpers benefit from engaging in helping that is autonomous or freely chosen based on internal motivations. Helping can give *competence need satisfaction*, which is the satisfaction that comes from perceiving direct positive changes that come about from what helpers did. They may experience increased self-efficacy, feelings of usefulness, and feelings of involvement. Helping has *interpersonal or relatedness benefits* for the helper because helping others can lead the helper to feeling closer to others, experience greater cohesiveness with others, and gain positive responses from others. When help recipients experience a helper who is personally invested in doing good work for them and personally cares about what happens to the help recipient, the help recipient feels more grateful, which in turn becomes a source of satisfaction for the helper. Helpers experience what they called *autonomy need satisfaction* in which there is a sense of satisfaction from acting freely and expressing important internalized values. This has been found to be highly associated with well-being and happiness across cultures. When the helping is done because of external reasons (called *controlled helping*), there is less satisfaction in the helping. There is less autonomy need satisfaction because the helper does not feel personally responsible for the helping behavior. Helpers do not feel as much competence satisfaction in controlled helping because the helpers do not view the behavior as originating from them. Finally, there is less interpersonal or relatedness satisfaction because the helping behavior is attributed to the externals that brought about the action versus being attributed to an intrinsic care.

Source of clinician's motivation is key for clinician well-being

The source of the motivation for the helping is key for whether there are benefits to the well-being of the helper. Research has found that when helpers act out of an autonomous, freely chosen motivation, it is then that they feel greater well-being, more vitality, and higher self-esteem. The help action by itself was not related to these positive effects (Weinstein & Ryan, 2010). This is of major importance in the health professions. Simply doing the work that helps our patients, having the admiration of others, and getting paid for it are not enough of what it takes to get a sense of well-being in our lives. *The benefits to well-being come only when we truly care about the work and our patients. To detach ourselves from our caring motivation is nothing less than shortchanging not only our patients, but ourselves as clinicians. We are less happy overall when we are not personally invested in what we do for others.*

In conclusion, a case has been made that an optimal level of emotional involvement or concern for the patient is beneficial not only to the patient, but also to the clinician. Let us move now to defining what this optimal level of emotional involvement is in terms of what are the characteristics of balanced compassionate care.

CHARACTERISTICS OF BALANCED COMPASSIONATE CARING

Thus far we have considered the costs of chronic emotional detachment as well as chronic emotional overinvolvement. Both appear to be the results of an attempt to deal with the encounter of pain or distress in the people we help but relying on a concept of caring that is oversentimentalized, overemotionalized, overly gender stereotyped, and possibly spiritualized along an unbalanced bias. We have seen that most helping professionals operate with only a crude or simplistic understanding of caring, which therefore does little to inform the exact way to care in a helping relationship. There is a strong case already to be made that some type of affective connection with another person out of a caring stance is helpful both to the client or patient and to the helper. The next step, then, is to delineate the characteristics of caring in helping relationships that will provide a way to be in optimum emotional involvement or caring toward a client or patient.

The four components of the balanced compassionate caring model

Balanced compassionate caring entails four distinct components. First, balanced compassionate caring involves a certain internal attitudinal state in the helper. There are many helpers who are good at the behavioral aspects of balanced care such as taking care of themselves or setting good boundaries, but they lack the attitudes and awareness that can maximize the benefits of balanced care for the helper. Second, balanced compassionate caring involves certain behavioral components—that is, specific practices and skills that make the clinician compassion mindset sustainable. You can desire to be balanced in your caring and even have a good idea of what that means, but unless you make these desires concrete in your helping behavior, your behavior will not be balanced, and you will be at risk for emotional overinvolvement or excessive detachment. Third, balanced compassionate caring involves an underlying spirituality or philosophy of care in helping others. While this is, in a sense, an extension of the internal state of the helper, I have put them in their own section because they are more general than the specific attitudes in the internal state of the helper and involve the spirituality (or philosophy of life) of the clinician. Fourth, there are organizational and systemic factors that have an enormous impact on the practice of balanced caring by those who work within that organization.

A tool for self-assessment

It is important not to be unrealistic in your understanding of how compassionate caring can help you in patient care. For example, if you are working in an overwhelming situation, such as helping people after an earthquake in Haiti, compassionate caring does not mean you can indefinitely help others without food, water, and sleep for yourself. To be in a position of balanced compassionate caring, you would assess your attitudes, behaviors, and organizational culture, and change whatever factor that would be undercutting your attempt to be balanced in your caring for others. The list of the four factors of balanced caring can function as a checklist for you when you are trying to assess how well you are doing in your helping work or why you are experiencing difficulty in your work. Certain factors can have more impact than others, but all of them can contribute or detract from optimum balanced caring.

CONCLUSION

The model of balanced compassionate caring (balanced C^2) describes how there is an optimum zone of emotional involvement or engagement with a patient that results in the most positive outcomes for patients as well as has the most positive effects on the clinician's well-being. Medicine has often been fearful of what emotional engagement and a caring connection with patients entail because of concerns regarding emotional exhaustion and overinvolvement in patient care. Based on the research findings presented in chapters 5 through 10, we now know that there is an optimum range of emotional engagement with patients that lies between being negatively involved or emotionally neutral with patients and being overinvolved with patients. Being emotionally overinvolved with patients is bad for patients but so is being negative with, or emotionally detached from, patients. Likewise, being negatively engaged or emotionally detached with patients as well as being overinvolved with patients has negative effects on clinician well-being. Being in the zone of balanced C² actually provides better protection for the clinician than being emotionally detached and increases effectiveness with patients. Clinicians in the zone are also more likely to experience the rewards of their work, which, as we will see, is absolutely critical to buffer burnout. In chapters 12 through 15, the four components enabling the clinician to be in the zone of balanced C² will be presented, including the attitudes underlying and supporting the compassion mindset, the practices and skills that make the compassion mindset sustainable, the clinician's spirituality or philosophy of caring that enables him or her to survive and thrive in this work, and the organizational/systemic factors which support the compassionate caring of the individual clinicians.

QUESTION FOR DISCUSSION

1. Reflecting on your own personal experiences of giving or receiving care, what evidence do you find for the balanced C² model?

REFERENCES

Austen, L. (2016). Increasing emotional support for healthcare workers can rebalance clinical detachment and empathy. *British Journal of General Practice, 66*(648), 376–377.

Carmack, B. J. (1992). Balancing engagement/detachment in AIDS-related multiple losses. *Image: The Journal of Nursing Scholarship, 24*(1), 9–14.

Carmack, B. J. (1997). Balancing engagement and detachment in caregiving. *Image: Journal of Nursing Scholarship, 29*(2), 139–143.

Doolittle B. R., Windish, D. M., & Seelig, C. B. (2013). Burnout, coping, and spirituality among internal medicine resident physicians, *Journal of Graduate Medical Education, 5*(2), 257–261.

Dyrbye, L. N., Satele, D., Sloan, J., & Shanafelt, T. D. (2012). Utility of a brief screening tool to identify physicians in distress. *Journal of General Internal Medicine, 28*(3), 421–427.

Larsen, R. J., & Diener, E. (1987). Affect intensity as an individual difference characteristic: A review. *Journal of Research in Personality, 21*(1), 1–39.

Larson, D. G. (1993). *The helper's journey: Working with people facing grief, loss, and life-threatening illness.* Champaign, IL: Research Press.

Robieux, L., Karsenti, L, Pocard, M, & Flahault, C. (2018). Let's talk about empathy. *Patient Education and Counseling, 101*(1), 59–66.

Smith, A. C., & Kleinman, S. (1989). Managing emotions in medical school: Students' contacts with the living and the dead. *Social Psychology Quarterly, 52*(1), 56–69.

Vachon, D. O. (1993). *The influence of affect intensity, dispositional empathy, and emotional separation on the relationship between perceived stress and burnout in a nursing population* (Doctoral dissertation). Loyola University Chicago, Chicago, IL.

Weinstein, N., & Ryan, R. M. (2010). When helping helps: Autonomous motivation for prosocial behavior and its influence on well-being for the helper and recipient. *Journal of Personality and Social Psychology, 98*(2), 222–244.

"Often we hear about burnout, but increasingly we learn that burnout is not because we care too much. But because we wall ourselves off, and close off our heart, and close off our very source of love, and the human connectedness that give us the life-generating force for this work."

—Jean Watson

Chapter Sections:

CHAPTER 12

Attitudes for Balanced Compassionate Caring

Attitudes Underlying and Supporting the Clinician Compassion Mindset

Question to consider before reading this chapter:

1. What kinds of internal mental challenges do you have when attempting to maintain balanced compassionate caring in your work with patients and the health care system?

INTRODUCTION

To be in the zone of balanced compassionate caring (C²), we have to cultivate a number of attitudes that underlie and guide our actions. In many ways, most of this book is about these attitudes, especially what it means to be in a compassion mindset. What I have done in this chapter is discuss seven attitudes that are very important to maintaining balanced C². This is a practical list based on what emerges repeatedly from discussions I have had with clinicians about the attitudes that help them to be in that zone of balanced C². It covers the major attitudes; you may wish to add others. It is designed to be a way to self-assess how you are doing in each of these areas as a way to find that zone.

In many such lists, the attitudes for caring for patients are listed separately from the lists of the attitudes for clinician self-care. Here, they are one and the same. The attitudes that enable great patient care are the very ones that benefit the clinician. Not having these attitudes is harmful to the patient and to the clinician. At the end of each section, I will have a summary of the implications for how each attitude is relevant to patient care and to clinician self-care.

CARITAS ATTITUDE: COMPASSIONATE CARING ATTITUDE AS THE CORE DRIVING FORCE IN HELPING RELATIONSHIPS

Being afraid to care for patients robs them and you of the full power of caring

The foundation of balanced compassionate caring is most importantly the attitude of caring toward everyone with whom you work. The error most often made in medicine is to start with protecting ourselves from what we fear or find taxing in helping others. For years I did stress and burnout workshops with helping professionals and family caregivers until one day I realized that this approach had severe limitations to helping me really buffer burnout and become fully engaged and enriched by working with patients and clients. The error in this thinking is readily apparent if you compare it to other aspects of life. In athletics, if you spend all your energy on protecting yourself from being hurt and that becomes your main focus, then your performance in your sport will drastically suffer. In friendships and romance, if you put all your energy into not being hurt in those relationships, then it will take much longer to become closer to others. In the business world, if you spend all your time on not making mistakes and not taking any risks, it will interfere with your success in developing that business. In scientific research, if you always play it safe in your research proposals, worried about what others will think rather than really studying the phenomenon, then your work will automatically be destined for mediocre, forgettable results. Of course, the opposite is also true. A foolhardy risk-taking approach to sports, relationships, research, or business can be disastrous. However, protecting yourself from what

might happen in your venture does not teach you how to enter into the goal of that activity. Yet that is exactly what we often do in our helping professions when it comes to connecting with others. We may perform the technical part of the work well enough, but we adopt erroneous ideas about what it means to work with people without really examining those ideas. For example, "You should not get emotionally involved with patients"; "You don't have time to consider your patient's feelings or your feelings when you work with people"; "Going the extra mile for a patient will burn you every time"; "I don't care why you went into health care; you have to detach if you are going to survive."

A true caring attitude is beneficial both to patients and to clinicians

As discussed throughout this book, in medical training we typically do not really get trained to understand what it means to connect with a person in a way that would maximize the benefits to the patients and, paradoxically, what would actually help us do our work in a more fulfilling way. If you are more afraid of connecting with your patients and of how you might get depleted in working with your patients, you can count on mediocre results with your patients (and you will burn out anyway, as I will show later). An accurate understanding of what it means to help another human being is fundamental to the whole work of caring for others. In balanced C^2, it is vitally important that our attitude for connecting with others when we help them is based in an accurate notion of what it means to care for them. Paradoxically, an accurate notion of caring will provide not only the means to help people better but also will have protective elements already part of that caring process. In a study of resilience strategies of physicians, 67% of a diverse sample of

200 physicians reported that they experienced gratification from the doctor–patient relationship. They experienced a sense of meaning and efficacy in being personally invested in their patients, that what they did really made a difference to people. Often this personal investment is reflected in the patient's appreciation, and this becomes a source of renewal and strength for the physician (Zwack & Schweitzer, 2013). Really caring about patients is paradoxically related to physician resilience. But given what has been discussed earlier in this book, being able to keep experiencing the positive aspects of helping people is very important in being able to do well in this profession.

Definition of Caritas

Fundamentally, this attitude might be described by the Latin word *caritas*. Jean Watson explains that in its original sense, it means "to cherish, appreciate and give special or loving attention with charity, compassion, and generosity of spirit. Caritas is very fine and precious, and must be actively cultivated to be sustained" (Sitzman & Watson, 2018, p. 22; Watson, 2008). Wang (2005) explains that "compassion is the feeling that arises from the realization of the deeper reality that we are all connected, we are all one" (p. 104). The difficulty with scripted customer service approaches to helping patients and clients is that the script does not really help you with your attitude toward the person you are helping. But patients and clients can detect a scripted approach when it is not backed up with a caring attitude.

Caritas *as our fundamental core driving attitude*

Caritas is our core driving attitude in all that we do. To be in the zone of balanced C², we anchor ourselves in this way of being in such a way that even when things get tough, the attitude of *caritas* persists underneath. (Being in the clinician compassion mindset was summarized in chapter 4.) That is, whatever you do is grounded in this compassionate caring focus no different than a scientific researcher's mindset that is always focused on the quest for discovery even when there are setbacks. What often happens is that a *caritas* attitude is used intermittently. When a patient is difficult, the practitioner thinks, "Well, the caring approach is not working, so now let's try being tough." That is exactly the wrong approach. Rather, in moving to a "tough" strategy as a way to help a patient or client, the *caritas* attitude is always guiding and motivating what you are doing with another person. The same happens when a practitioner becomes discouraged by the suffering he or she witnesses or the failure of his or her work. He or she might think, "Well, I should not care so much because it is becoming too discouraging." Instead, a compassionate caring attitude provides a way of helping you understand what is happening in a way that you never suspend your *caritas* attitude; instead, you rely on it more deeply to find energy to care for those individuals.

Change *patient* to *the person who is suffering*

There has been criticism of using the word *patient* for a number of years because of the concern for how this can objectify those whom we help. This can be true. But what if we focused on the meaning of *patient* to help guard us against depersonalizing patients and to help keep us in the *caritas* attitude, the clinician compassion mindset. *Patient* comes from Latin, meaning "one who suffers." Imagine going through your day and every time you would have said "patient," you instead said "the person who suffers." For example, "I need to do a consult on 'the person who suffers' in room 219." "I have to see '20 people who suffer' this afternoon in clinic." When we are in touch with what our patients are going through, their suffering constellates in us in what we need to do. It keeps our priorities straight. When I bill the patient, if I said, "I need to charge 'the person who suffers' for the CABG I just did this morning," there is a way in which it keeps us accountable. It also alerts us to how hard this work can be. When I say, "I've seen many 'people who suffer' this week, and I really need a break," there is a way in which we may be more aware of how we need to take care of ourselves in this work.

Implications for maintaining balanced C²

In trying to find and maintain yourself in the zone of balanced C², this *caritas* attitude that drives the clinician compassion mindset process is the most fundamental of the balanced compassionate caring attitudes. The first part of this book has provided an extensive conceptual and empirical background for this. In staying grounded in the *caritas* attitude, we are in touch with the key force in helping our patients as well as being connected to the intrinsic motivation we have for being in this work. In addition, if we understand the nature of compassion, we will also be able to guard against being overly emotionally involved with patients and know what we need to do to take care of ourselves in this work.

BALANCED NOTION OF PERSONAL RESPONSIBILITY

A continuum from not feeling responsible at all to feeling excessively responsible for what happens to patients

A critical component of balanced compassionate caring is a balanced sense of personal responsibility. On one hand, it is obvious that if a helper has no sense of personal responsibility in helping another person, then the helping action will most likely not be successful. Clinicians, lawyers, teachers, and other types of helpers must have at least some personal investment in a particular case for anything positive to happen. On the other hand, an excessive sense of personal responsibility is also a problem in which the clinician feels he or she is completely responsible for what happens to the patient. With training and experience, clinicians become aware of how they can be effective agents of healing or change in other people's lives. With the knowledge and competence of a particular area of helping, clinicians know they can be key players in helping others get what they need or desire. But at least two temptations emerge for the clinician who comes to feel too responsible for the patient.

The trap of thinking that because you can be effective, you should always be effective

One temptation is the belief that because you can be effective in helping people, you come to the conclusion that you can and should always be successful in helping. But this does not always occur for a variety of reasons. Life is complicated, and it is unrealistic to take responsibility for all the variables that can affect a patient. Even though you might be of potential help, other unknown factors might interfere with your helping being successful. For example, you might know how to treat seizure disorders, but you will inevitably encounter types which are complicated by other medical problems or by seizure disorders not yet understood and studied. Also, patients bear responsibility for some of what happens; those we try to help are not passive in the process. They are not parts of a machine that will work if assembled by you correctly. Rather, they have a subjectivity that influences how your helping will be received and used. In fact, if they are passive, the help you offer probably will not work well at all. Patients need be active parts of the treatment process. If you treat respiratory problems of a smoker and he or she does not curb his or her smoking, your helping efforts will be limited even if you are an expert. If a person who has anxiety disorder does not become invested in learning how to think differently about his or her anxiety symptoms, then all your astute techniques and interpretations will not work for him or her.

Others may see you as more responsible than you should be

The second temptation is that those you help may hold you more responsible for their progress than you really can be and lay that expectation on you. The problem becomes magnified if you accept and buy into their unrealistic expectations of you. Even when they have done everything possible, helpers can be tempted to believe that they still did something wrong, that there was more they could have done. Also, as discussed in chapter 9 on the societal context of helping, the threat of lawsuits makes it difficult not to have an intense sense of personal responsibility for what happens because the legal system often seeks to hold a particular clinician or health care organization as completely responsible for negative outcomes. Clinicians have to work very hard to maintain a balanced sense of personal responsibility in spite of these unrealistic expectations.

We accompany people on their journeys, not do their journeys for them

An image that captures a balanced sense of personal responsibility is the one in which you imagine yourself as being a temporary companion to another person in his or her journey in life. As Carol Montgomery (1994) puts this:

> When working with clients in tragic or deplorable circumstances, our urge to help might cause us to take their life on as though it were our own. It helps to remember that we can never live another person's experience or pain, nor would that be helpful even if we could. Our ultimate responsibility is to respond with compassion and helpfulness. I like to think of myself as one person they meet by the side of the road during their journey through life. I can make a difference, but I can never take away or replace their particular journey. (p. 41)

Such a balanced sense of personal responsibility takes time to achieve. Most helpers experience both poles of excessive personal responsibility and insufficient responsibility at numerous times in their careers. Regular personal reflection on this issue as well as consulting colleagues, mentors, or supervisors can assist helpers in defining what a balanced sense of personal responsibility means for them with particular cases.

The effects on clinicians and patients of making a mistake

One of the most difficult challenges to maintaining a balanced sense of personal responsibility is when a clinician makes a medical mistake. Making a mistake is both bad for the patient who suffers from the mistake and for the clinician. When clinicians make mistakes, they hate increasing the suffering of patients who sought them out and trusted them. It can be also a devastating blow to the clinician's self-confidence, and he or she must work hard to work through the mistake and regain a sense of confidence. West et al. (2006) examined the influence that perceived medical errors have on internal medicine residents in a prospective longitudinal study. They found that residents who perceived themselves to have made a major medical error were more likely to feel depressed and burnt out; they also experienced a decrease in their quality of life. These residents in turn had higher odds of making a self-perceived error in the subsequent three months. Overall, 34% of the residents reported feeling that they made a major medical error. An adverse event is defined by the Harvard Medical Practice Study as "an injury that was caused by medical management (rather than the underlying disease and that prolonged the hospitalization and/or produced a disability at the time of discharge" (Brennan & Leape, 1991, p. 2). In a study of 1,463 physicians whose patients experienced an adverse event or a near miss (Harrison, Lawton, & Stewart, 2014), most physicians (76%) reported that it had affected them professionally or personally and that they experienced increased stress (74%), anxiety (68%), sleep problems (60%), and decreases in professional confidence (63%). Most of them (81%) worried about the potential for errors in the future. Most physicians complain of the lack of support from their organizations after such events have occurred.

The ability to help our colleagues when they make mistakes

The ability to work through having made a mistake is not only important in the likelihood that you may make a medical mistake, but that you will also most likely have to support another clinician who makes a medical mistake. In a study of internal medicine residents, West et al. (2006) found that 97% discussed perceived errors with at least one other person. Most commonly, 83% discussed it with another resident, 65% discussed it with a close family member or friend, and 54% discussed it with supervisory faculty. We need each other to process what

happened in mistakes and how we should proceed. It is devastating to us because we have aspired to learn a complicated profession to relieve suffering. We see a lot of perfectionism because we want to get it right and not hurt anyone. When we make a mistake, we need to help each other find a way to keep going and work through the feelings of failing our patients and our compassionate aspirations.

Being clear and realistic about outcome: curing as a subset of healing

A major difficulty many helpers have is that their helping does not always solve their problems or lead to a cure. For example, when working with people who have chronic medical problems, chronic psychological problems, or terminal illnesses, we need to determine the best outcome that is possible. It may be stabilization of the symptoms, slowing the progression of the disease, or maintaining the best possible quality of life given the chronic nature of a disease. So first, we need to be realistic about what outcome is possible. In hospice, for example, success will be defined by maintaining whatever quality of life can be achieved, controlling pain, and supporting the patients as they die. Our question always needs to be, "What is success in this particular case?" Second, success may not be cure or resolution, but rather helping someone maintain or cope with his or her situation as long as possible. As Montgomery (1994) and others have argued, curing is a subset of the larger caring enterprise. Healing is not always defined by cure; it is also defined by the realization of some other goal that is very meaningful for the patient or client.

The false dichotomy of curing versus caring—it's all caring!

I know several physicians who explain that in helping the patient with a terminal illness, the physician needs to move from curing to caring. This idea is taught generally with the best of intentions because these physicians are trying to explain that the physician should not withdraw from the patient when cure is no longer possible; this is because physicians do abandon their patients when *they* think they cannot do anything more. But the patients need that clinician's presence, support, and guidance about how to proceed. An aphorism commonly used in medicine is, "When the patient becomes terminal, you need to move from curing to caring." This is a reminder that our presence is still very helpful to our patients and that we should always keep in mind that even when we cannot facilitate a cure, we might be able to facilitate other things that are very helpful to the patient. But what is lost in this aphorism is that curing is part of caring as well. Montgomery (1994) explains that curing is conducted within a caring relationship. Even though the curing entails solving or removing the problem using one's knowledge or technology, the action of curing is an extension of the desire to respond to the patient's suffering. Curing is not an end in itself; it is part of the compassionate response. Whether cure is possible or not, all our actions are an attempt to respond to the patient's suffering in any way we can.

Osler on a way to think about making mistakes

We will make errors, and it is very important that we work on our attitude about errors because the cost is high if we let errors terminate our clinical self-efficacy. William Osler (in Osler, Hinorhara, and Niki, 2001) offered this advice about how we should approach when we make mistakes:

> Start out with the conviction that absolute truth is hard to reach in matters relating to our fellow creatures, heathy or diseased, that slips in observation are inevitable even with the best trained faculties, that errors in judgment must occur in the practice of an art which consists largely of balancing probabilities;—start, I say, with this attitude in mind, and mistakes will be acknowledged and regretted; but instead of a slow process of self-deception, with ever increasing inability to recognize truth, you will draw from your errors the very lessons which may enable you to avoid their repetition. (p. 122)

Not only is it important to keep learning from what goes wrong, but it is also important for clinicians to have the drive to keep moving forward. In her study of exemplary physicians, Helen Meldrum (2010) noted this as a theme among them:

> For people whose trajectory is founded on optimistic principles, failure is not part of their daily vocabulary. To consider a regretted action as permanent and unredeemed by subsequent learning would render them incapable of moving ahead. Because they believe that salvation for all lies in continued positive and pragmatic action, the demoralizing effects of caring something a failure are minimized. (p. 245)

While no one wants bad outcomes or mistakes, becoming better is a way of redeeming what has occurred for those patients who will follow.

Acknowledgment of personal limits and competency

The ability to have a balanced sense of responsibility for outcomes and for dealing with mistakes is the ability to know yourself well enough to realize your strengths and to understand and accept your weaknesses. This will shift with training, experience, and changing circumstances. In training and at the beginning of his or her practice, a clinician will face the challenge of not feeling very competent yet and of finding a way to practice that is safe for the patient. They have to avoid the temptation to do that which they are not yet competent to do by themselves. Sometimes this is internal pressure to do procedures they are not fully prepared to do; at other times it can be external pressure to do something they are not fully ready to do. There can also be the opposite problem in which the clinician underestimates him- or herself and does not fully realize how competent he or she is; the challenge here is to deal with the barriers of fear or whatever is blocking him or her from doing what he or she can really do. As one gets more experience and training, that sense of competent self-efficacy increases. But then the clinician faces a new challenge of becoming overconfident or lulled by routinization and must find practices to guard against that. Atul Gawande (2001) has addressed this so well in *The Checklist Manifesto: How to Get Things Right*, as has Jerome Groopman (2007) in *How Doctors Think*. Underneath all of this is the ability to separate your self-worth and your ego from an acknowledgement of your limits. Limits do not make you less of a person. Not understanding them leads you to do things that are dangerous or unhelpful. You are much more likely to be helpful when you know your limits.

Implications for maintaining balanced C²

A balanced notion of personal responsibility is absolutely critical to being in the zone of balanced C² both from the perspective of patients and of clinicians. When clinicians have a balanced sense of personal responsibility, patients can feel the clinicians' engagement and investment in helping them. Patients sense that the clinicians are using their trained competency and directing it toward them as individuals. If

patients feel their clinicians are detached, not invested in trying for the best outcome, they know they are at risk. On the other hand, if clinicians feel overly responsible for patients' outcomes, they may give these patients the mistaken impression that more is possible than is realistic. If the ideal outcome does not occur, the patient feels like it should have occurred. So clinicians who are realistic and balanced in the sense of responsibility assure patients that they will do the best that they can and that they are invested in bringing about the best possible outcome; but there is no guarantee about that outcome even though the clinicians did their best. Also, clinicians who make themselves overly responsible for the outcomes can cause patients to become passive; in many health issues, the patient must take responsibility for his or her part whether it be taking medication, instigating health behavior changes, doing physical therapy, and so on.

For clinicians, balanced notions of personal responsibility are vital to their personal well-being. As we have covered in earlier chapters, clinicians who do not take any responsibility for what is occurring are emotionally detached; this is bad not only for the patients but also for the clinicians. It may be a sign of burnout or dislike for a patient, but habitually staying in this detached mode is associated with lack of fulfillment and purpose in the work. If clinicians feel overly responsible for what occurs, they are adding a burden on themselves that is unrealistic and inappropriate. While we want clinicians who are very invested in the best outcome possible, we also want those clinicians to know that they are not omnipotent and omniscient. Failures, mistakes, and setbacks occur—and clinicians need to be able to bounce back rather than wallow in what they were not able to accomplish.

COMPASSIONATE EMPATHIC CONCERN VERSUS EMOTIONAL DETACHMENT OR EMOTIONAL ENGULFMENT

Balanced C^2 involves an internal stance of empathic concern embedded in the clinician compassion mindset that was presented in chapter 4. Since a great deal of this book is focused on that mindset and how empathy is part of that, it will not be repeated here. Instead, I will provide some selected information to supplement it with a view of how to be balanced in that empathy between being emotionally detached and emotionally engulfed in the patient's psychological state. As explained earlier, empathy is a neutral ability that can be used for good or ill. For the helping professions, it is the capacity to attempt to understand in cognitive and emotional terms what another person is experiencing and then express this understanding to that person. Empathy in the helping professions has as its goal the care of people in need. For our purposes, in order to distinguish the empathy that con artists and some salespeople use to manipulate others, we will use the words *empathic concern* to capture the intention of the caring professions.

Brief history of the term empathy

According to More (1994), the word *empathy* was coined in 1872 by a German philosopher of aesthetics, Robert Vischer. He used the term *Einfuhlung* ("feeling-into") to describe "the process by which a work of art can call forth an emotional response from the observer, a momentary fusion of subject and object" (More, 1994, pp. 20–21). Theodore Lipps brought this term into psychology and defined it as "the power of projecting one's personality into (and so fully comprehending) the object of contemplation" (Halpern 2001,

p. 75). As noted in chapter 3, empathy has been studied extensively, and there are several variations in how empathy and related terms are defined. Decety (2012), Halpern (2001), Hojat (2007, 2016), and Spiro, Curnen, Peschel, and St. James (1993) have done extensive reviews of empathy in the practice of medicine.

Empathic arousal increases the intrinsic motivation to help another person

What happens if empathic arousal is not part of your helping of patients? Would you still help the other person? The specific motivations of a person are a major predictor of helping behavior. Research has found that empathy leads to helping behavior because it increases autonomous motivation (i.e., internalized values of what is important to do) versus controlled motivation (i.e., feeling external pressure to help, seeking approval from others, and avoiding making others upset if one does not help). A controlled motivation is negatively associated with the willingness to help. Empathy arousal in this study was produced by having people to imagine what the suffering people were feeling, whereas low empathy was produced by telling people to be "as objective as possible," to "distance yourself emotionally from the person telling you the story," and to "try not to get caught up in imagining the other person's feelings" (Pavey, Greitemeyer, & Sparks, 2012, p. 686). Empathy-evoking experiences increase the autonomous intrinsic motivation to help another person. Without empathy, there is less likelihood of someone being motivated to help another person.

Empathic arousal motivates clinicians to help patients

This study is interesting for at least two reasons when it comes to working in medicine. First, as clinicians, the stirring up of our empathy gets us motivated to help our patients. When we are emotionally detached, objective, and distant, we are much less motivated to offer help. In fact, if we help for external reasons such as feeling pressured to help or to get approval or avoid criticism from others, the likelihood of being willing to help falls dramatically. One might argue that clinicians are "helping" all the time, often without being empathically engaged. In such cases, what is going on it that there is something that looks like helping is going on (e.g., I met with the patient, got information about him or her, assessed him or her, and offered some treatment), but the motivation to help him or her get *well* may be quite lacking. So, yes, you greeted the patient, interviewed him or her, diagnosed him or her, and gave him or her a prescription. But if you were not empathically connected to this patient, you would not make the good emotional connection that makes the patient feel safe. The patient would therefore not be very disclosive of his or her situation, which leads to poorer data for you to make a good assessment. Also, you would not be very motivated to notice subtle emotional cues of what is going on that might have a major effect on the diagnosis and whether your patient will feel engaged enough to even want to follow through on what you recommended. Some clinicians would argue back and say that they are engaged with their patients and would do high-quality work without being empathically engaged. But patients can detect a lack of emotional engagement. Patients tell story after story of clinicians who were not really invested in what is going on with them.

Motivation to help relies of internal value of helping

The second reason Pavey et al.'s research is interesting for our purposes is that autonomous motivation (as opposed to externally controlled motivation) relies on what your internalized values and goals are. If you do not have that internal value of helping because it is important in itself, then your empathic arousal would not lead to helping behavior. Maybe it would lead to self-protection and avoidance. For example, if I grow up without the intrinsic value that one ought to respond to suffering in others, then when my empathic arousal is stirred up, my focus will not be on helping others; it will be on taking care of myself alone. I might say, "That was terrible what happened to that person. I am going to make sure that does not happen to me." The motivation becomes using that empathic information of the other's suffering to focus on relieving my own distress.

Brain imaging study demonstrating empathy versus emotional engulfment

There is a great deal of literature on clinical empathy in medicine, neuroscience, nursing, psychology, and even philosophy. It is excellent literature, but it is complex with many terms related to empathy being used in completely opposite ways. For the purposes of this book, I am focusing on the inner experience of the clinician who is navigating the psychological territory between emotional detachment and emotion engulfment with patients. If we focus on what is happening in the brain with clinical empathy, it will help us with our goal of getting a practical handle on how to be balanced in empathy. An excellent example of this is a study by Jackson, Brunet, Meltzoff, and Decety (2006), who had research participants take one of three perspectives as they looked at pictures of the hands and feet of people in painful or nonpainful situations, such as being cut with a knife, having a toe under a heavy object, or having a finger caught in a closed door: (a) Self perspective (imagining it happening to them);

(b) Other perspective (imagining what it would be like for someone else); and (c) Artificial perspective (painful situation with a plastic limb).

Brain difference between "imagining what I would feel if I were my patient" versus "imagining what my patient feels"

In terms of ratings of pain, people who imagined the pain to themselves rated the pain as worse than when they imagined it happening to someone else; and, they were faster at rating pain when it happened to themselves. The fMRIs showed differences as well. In both the Self and Other conditions, the brain's pain network was activated (i.e., activation in the insula and the anterior cingulate cortex [ACC]) while it was not in the Artificial condition. But the pattern activation was different between the Self and Other conditions. In the Self condition, there was bilateral activation of the anterior insula, but it was only activated in the right hemisphere in the Other condition. There were different activations as well in the ACC, thalamus ACC, and the somatosensory cortex. The Self condition activated areas of the pain network related to sensory processes as well as the affective processes, whereas the Other condition was only in the affective processes. There was more activation in the ventral striatum (part of the limbic system and reward mechanisms), showing more affective processes were activated in the Self condition. Thus, there was more activation overall in the Self condition than in the Other condition.

The key to balanced empathy maintaining a clear distinction between Self and Other

What this study and others like it show is that empathy is a very different state than the sympathetic identification with another person's psychological state (Batson, Early, &Salvarani,

1997). When a clinician identifies too closely with what a patient is going through, this is akin to the Self condition in Jackson et al.'s study. This is what is called a self–other merging and leads to the clinician becoming emotionally overwhelmed and distressed. It is the difference between "imagining how you would feel if you were the patient" and "imagining how the patient feels." In true empathy, there is an activation of emotional processes in the clinician, but there is a sense of agency, meaning that this affective sharing or emotional resonance is regulated by a clear distinction between the patient and the clinician, and whose feelings are whose. If you experience empathic concern, you will be more likely to have an altruistic motivation and act to attempt to relieve the suffering of the patient. If you experience that sympathetic identification or merging with the patient's emotional state, you will experience both a mix of empathy for the other and personal distress; this, then, tends to lead to a more egoistic or self-centered motivation when you respond. This might include you withdrawing from the situation or helping someone while you are yourself in an emotionally distressed state. The latter is not attuned to what the patient really needs because you are really focused on helping your own internal distress and bad feelings (Batson et al., 1997). Merging yourself with the other (self–other merging) is not the mechanism by which empathy leads to helping. Rather, good self-other distinction underlies empathy-based altruism: "Empathic concern reflects an extension of value to include an interest in the welfare of the other, distinct from oneself, that is beyond self-interest" (Batson, 2011, pp. 159–160).

Connection to clinician compassion mindset

Recall how this connects with Klimecki and Singer (2011), who have also noted that empathic resonance with a patient can lead to empathic distress or to compassion for the person suffering. To be balanced between being emotionally detached from a patient and being emotionally engulfed or distressed by the patient, the keys, then, are to be in a mindset in which you are altruistically focused on understanding what the patient is going through and not losing the sense that this is your patient's experience—not yours. Recall the compassion mindset litmus test in chapter 4 when the staff person enters a room in which the patient has soiled him- or herself. One staff person was focused on his/her own distress: "Now I've got to clean up this patient!" The other was more rooted in the empathic mindset: *"Oh my gosh, how long has the patient been like this? Let's get you cleaned up."* You can imagine how the quality of helping would be different between the more self-focused motivation of the first staff person and the empathic-induced altruistic motivation of the second staff person.

The Davis dispositional empathy measure subscales showing the different facets of empathy

While there many measures of empathy, I will focus on one prominent example that captures much of what I have discussed above and how that has related to how one approaches patient care and the issue of clinician burnout. Davis (1983) proposed a multidimensional understanding of empathy that captures the cognitive and emotional dimensions of the empathic process. He argued that empathy is actually a set of four distinct constructs that are all concerned with reacting to the observed experiences of another. He developed the Interpersonal Reactivity Index as a measure of dispositional empathy comprising the four dimensions of empathy. The first is called *perspective taking*, which is the cognitive

understanding of the experiences of another; as Davis (1983) phrases it, it is "the tendency to adopt the point of view of other people in everyday life" (p. 117). The second is *fantasy empathy*, which is "the tendency to transpose oneself into the feelings and actions of fictitious characters in books, movies, and plays" (Davis, 1983, p. 117). This taps into the more imaginative and emotional aspect of empathy. Third is *empathic concern*, which is "the tendency to experience feelings of warmth, compassion, and concern for other people" (Davis, 1983, p. 117). Finally, *personal distress empathy* "taps one's feelings of personal unease and discomfort in reaction to the emotion of others" (Davis, 1983, p. 117); that is, it measures how one is affected by tense emotional or emergency situations.

Study of Davis dispositional empathy measure with nurses

In an effort to understand whether and how empathy might be related to burnout in a sample of hospital nurses, I did a study with 257 nurses of many different specialties and gave them tests of empathy, stress, and burnout; their affect intensity; and their ability to maintain emotional separation (Vachon, 1993). What emerged was that nurses who were high in fantasy empathy and personal distress empathy tended to be more emotionally exhausted than nurses who were lower in these two dimensions. But empathic concern was not related to emotional exhaustion, and it was nurses who were low in perspective taking who were more likely to be emotionally exhausted. Individuals high in fantasy empathy and low in empathic concern and perspective taking tended to have depersonalized attitudes toward patients. Furthermore, those who more likely to have an increased sense of personal accomplishment on the job were nurses low in personal distress empathy, high in perspective taking, and high in empathic concern—especially when there was a lot of stress on the particular hospital unit. Affect intensity (Larsen & Diener, 1987), a personality variable measuring how intensely people experience their emotions, acted like an amplifier for both negative and positive emotions. If nurses tended to be high in affect intensity, and if they leaned in a negative emotional direction, those emotions were intensified (like feeling personal distress); if they leaned in a positive emotional direction, those emotions (such as a sense of personal accomplishment) were intensified. If nurses were low in the ability to maintain emotional separation (Corcoran, 1983), their experience of stress was related to increased emotional exhaustion.

Empathy study with physicians and the "not losing a sense of yourself" empathy
McCleerey and Vachon (2007) replicated this study with a group of 145 physicians of various specialties, and a similar pattern of results emerged. Empathic concern and perspective taking were associated with less emotional exhaustion and depersonalization and a greater sense of personal accomplishment. Fantasy empathy is associated with increased emotional exhaustion, depersonalization, and decreased personal accomplishment. Personal distress empathy is associated with increased emotional exhaustion and depersonalization and a decreased sense of personal accomplishment. In a sense, I think of fantasy empathy and personal distress empathy as a "losing a sense of yourself" type of empathy and perspective taking and empathic concern as "not losing a sense of yourself" empathy. Fantasy empathy and personal distress empathy tap into the self–other merging discussed earlier, whereas perspective taking and empathic concern focus more the on the

other in the compassion mindset. The self–other merging with patients is related to increased burnout over time, whereas the clear distinction between self and other with empathic concern and perspective taking is associated with less burnout and a greater sense of personal accomplishment in the work with patients. In short, it is not feelings of compassion and the desire to understand the perspective of another that depletes the helper. In fact, these appear to be associated with energizing the caring professional. (We will examine the importance of this in recovery from burnout in chapter 16.)

Implications for maintaining balanced C²
The clinician compassion mindset is the vehicle for maintaining oneself in the zone of balanced C². Here we have used the research on empathic concern to provide a practical way of understanding how empathic concern is different from emotional engulfment or sympathetic identification with the patient. This is the compassion mindset that carries and directs empathic concern to be focused on the experience of the patient without losing a sense of oneself or becoming emotionally overwhelmed in the process. From the perspective of the patient, this is a clinician who is emotionally engaged with the patient but does not become overwhelmed by the patient's experience. The clinician is able to convey genuine caring that provides many therapeutic benefits. From the perspective of the clinician, this is being in the compassion mindset—this empathic concern in which the clinician is clear on self–other distinction and is altruistically focused on the experience of the patient (not the clinician). As we have discussed in chapter 10, it is this balanced stance between emotional detachment and emotional engulfment/distress that leads to the positive benefits to the clinician's well-being.

THERAPEUTIC PERSPECTIVE VERSUS DETACHED OBJECTIVITY (PERSON-CENTERED)

Emotionally challenging patient scenarios

Balanced C² entails an ability to gain perspective on challenging situations rather than the unrealistic expectation that one not be emotionally affected by what one encounters in helping others. Consider these scenarios or recall your own:

- A resident gets called to do an intake on a man who, once again, is being admitted to the hospital for complications secondary to this man not taking care of his diabetes. He is in DKA again. Everyone in the residency, the nurses, and the attendings all know his name.

- A woman presents to a medical office with multiple medical problems and severe pain. She is complicated medically and suffers in many ways. It is depressing for the nurses and physicians to work with her. It is still not clear how to help her beyond prescribing pain medications. She makes her doctors and nurses feel helpless, and it is discouraging to hear the many losses this woman has had to endure.

- You become aware that your patient is a drug seeker. You confront this patient when you find out he has been to multiple clinics and pharmacies obtaining prescriptions for the same drug. He yells at you, and tells you that this is not true about him and that he must have this medication to get through the day.

- A truck driver comes back to see you for severe back pain. Six months ago, you sent him to a surgeon for this severe back pain and did not hear anything further. The surgery was done, but it did not go well. The truck driver can no longer drive trucks, the company he worked for found a way to deny him financial disability support, and the surgeon did not want to see him after one follow-up visit. The insurance has not paid for as much of the surgery and follow-up care as he thought they would, but they are demanding payment and threatening to send him to collections. The truck driver is angry with you for sending him to that surgeon.

In all of these situations plus countless others, dealing with patient emotional reactions—whether precipitated by you, someone else, or extenuating circumstances—can be quite taxing on you. It can seem to be the right thing to go back to your science training for medicine, and believe that you need to be more objective and that would help you deal with it. After all, you think, you are more likely to find the correct medical answer if you adopt this objective attitude and not let your feelings "cloud your judgment," much less make you feel bad about the patient. However, there are a number of problems with this kind of thinking.

The problem with dispassionate objective approaches to patients

One problem is that this dispassionate approach to helping patients is exactly what you would not want if you were that person's patient and the likelihood of finding the best approach for that patient would actually decrease. This objective, emotionally neutral approach to the patient is actually related to the worst kind of medical care. I remember in a grand rounds we had with residents in which we discussed a very difficult case in which they were involved with a master physician. It was an "interesting case," as they say. As many of the physicians and nurses said later, "Please, may I never be an interesting case!" As the lab results were projected in front of all of us, the master physician used his Socratic method of teaching and said, "When you see lab values like this, they should bother you. You shouldn't be able to sleep tonight until you figure out what they are telling you about this patient's body." It was an incredible moment. If we all looked at this case as "interesting" in a detached manner, it would actually doom that patient. Why? Because what is needed is the motivation in those physicians, the drive, the emotional arousal pushing your wonderfully medically trained cerebral cortex to figure out what is happening to this patient.

What is therapeutic perspective with a patient?

The internal attitude in balanced caring requires a way to deal with one's negative emotional reaction to interactions with patients/clients. Montgomery (1994) sums this up very well when she states that

> in order to avoid becoming consumed by a client's pathology, hopelessness, or despair, we need to have access to a broader perspective that comes from our knowledge base, life experience, and experiences with other clients that serve as a source of hope and optimism. So, instead of maintaining therapeutic objectivity, we strive to achieve a therapeutic perspective. (p. 40)

The ability to gain a therapeutic perspective on a clinical situation is essential to balanced caring. For example, a drug addict becomes very angry with you for not prescribing opioid pain medications for him or her. An alcoholic is once again admitted for medical complications secondary to his or her drinking. Clinicians might

imagine that they could remain emotionally neutral in such situations, but anyone in practice knows this never happens. Physicians react to these situations by being angry at patients, belittling them with derogatory comments and labels behind their backs or even directly, or by becoming discouraged at doing the same things over and over for people like this. The consequences to physicians include everything from becoming more callous with everyone they meet, not trying to help patients with their core problems anymore, or becoming more negative in their interactions with this type of patient, which then guarantees that there will be no therapeutic progress.

How to put a situation in therapeutic perspective

What can help a physician maintain a sense of clinical engagement and compassionate care with a patient is to put the situation in therapeutic perspective. With the drug addict or the alcoholic, the physician keeps in mind that this is what addicted people do because their brains are physiologically intertwined with this substance. The purpose of therapeutic perspective is not to absolve the dysfunctional patient from responsibility or to stop challenging the patient toward health. It is a move that helps a clinician not take what is occurring personally. What the patient is doing makes sense given his or her illness, background, or situation. Back to the lifeguard example, if the person drowning is panicking and is acting in such a way that I as his or her rescuer might be drowned, the knowledge that "this is what drowning people do" helps me stay therapeutically engaged with the drowning victim. In other words, I know that even the most sophisticated person in a state of mortal fear can panic, and I plan for that by both protecting myself from harm and acting in such a way that helps the person without the unnecessary baggage of my taking the person's actions toward me personally.

How to distance yourself from pathology

If we find that we must distance ourselves from the pathology, Carol Montgomery recommends the following principle: "Sometimes we need distance, but when that happens we distance from the pathology rather than from the human person" (Montgomery, 1994, p. 40). In other words, we find a way to stay engaged with the person who has the pathology. Gregory Boyle has worked for over twenty years in a gang-intervention program in Los Angeles. He articulates how he and his colleagues view the men and women they help and the perspective that enables them to stay in the compassion mindset: "You stand with the belligerent, the surly, and the badly behaved until bad behavior is recognized for the language it is: the vocabulary of the deeply wounded and of those whose burdens are more than they can bear" (Boyle, 2010, p. 179). Working with addicts would be another example. Addicts can be very manipulative and hostile, so it makes sense that we would want to protect ourselves from them when they are in this state. If we start to dislike the person with the addiction, then we actually lower our motivation to do our best to help that person recover. However, if we think of this person being manipulative and hostile because the drug has changed his or her brain and personality, now we retain a compassionate connection to that person. This patient is not him- or herself. We protect ourselves from the disease, but we want to free the person. Referring back to the clinician compassion mindset process, gaining therapeutic perspective is a way of doing the compassion reset and recovery box in which we reframe what is going on with the patient as a way to stay engaged with the patient and motivated to help in some way.

Implications for maintaining balanced C²

Always considering patient situations from an attitude of therapeutic perspective is very important in balanced C² as a way of staying engaged with patients who are difficult in some way. From the patient perspective, if we become emotionally detached from such patients or even hostile toward these patients, we then lose the ability to be a force for change in these patients' lives. If these patients are negative and then we become negative, we are not able to be healing agents for those patients. Two negatives do not make a positive in this case. Clinicians must come from a positive caring perspective in order to have any hope for helping patients. From the clinician perspective, being able to continually get a therapeutic perspective on patients is one of the major ways we stay engaged with our profession's task and prevent falling into cynicism and negativity. Putting what is going on with patients in perspective is a way for us to keep in a problem-solving model in which we try to figure out why people are the way they are, make a game plan for how to approach the patient in light of that, and then implement that plan.

BEING CENTERED

Imperturbability means coolness and presence of mind under all circumstances, calmness amid storm, clearness of judgment in moments of grave peril, immobility, impassiveness, or to use an old and expressive word, phlegm. It is the quality which is most appreciated by the laity through often misunderstood by them;

and the physician who has the misfortune to be without it, who betrays indecision and worry, and who shows that he [she] is flustered and flurried in ordinary emergencies, loses rapidly the confidence of his [her] patients. (Osler et al., 2001, p. 22)

What are the typical circumstances in practicing medicine? It is a highly pressured, overscheduled environment with a wide variety of cases coupled with frequent interruptions, crises, and emergencies. This is a high arousal situation, and people who lack the training and experience would be overwhelmed and exasperated. With training and experience, you develop the ability to keep composed in these stressful situations.

Explanation of what it means to be "centered" in health care

What does it mean to be "centered" in a health care environment? Often, being centered is thought to mean being calm and relaxed, not rushed or stressed. Perhaps we should use a different phrase for clinicians because that description does not fit. Much of what we do counts on us being in a focused, high-arousal state. Let us consider what being centered might mean for us and start from scratch with what the image of being centered suggests. Physically, being centered would mean the way of being in which you are balanced—not tipping to one side or the other, and remaining grounded and stable. When you are walking on a railroad track or a balance beam, being centered would mean a kind of focused, emotionally regulated state that would enable you to stay on the railroad track or balance beam without falling. It you go too fast, you might get ahead of yourself. If you stay still, you are not getting anywhere. When you start falling off center, it takes energy to compensate and stay on the beam, and that interferes with

going forward because you have to regain your stability before you move forward. Being centered suggests that you are not off balance or easily thrown off balance. It suggests that you are pacing yourself so that you do not "get ahead of yourself" or "think about yourself too much."

Being centered as emotionally collected, focused awareness

Being centered for us does not mean a relaxed calm such as doing mindfulness meditation on the beach. Instead, it is an emotionally collected, focused awareness while doing something. There is an ability to concentrate even with distractions. There is an ability to manage strong emotions—yours, your patient's, and maybe even your colleagues'. It involves the ability to shift your mental state smoothly. For example, seeing different patients with a wide variety of presentations, shifting levels of analysis with a patient, dealing with between-appointment issues, listening to the patient, and doing electronic health records along the way. There is a sense in which you are present to where you are and the task at hand. If you are with a patient, you are emotionally present to him or her. You are not preoccupied with what you have to do later on or with whatever happened beforehand. You may have problems in your personal life, but you have put them aside for now with the promise that you will return to them later.

Centeredness as optimal emotional management and problem solving

Being centered, then, has at least two facets for us. The first is a mental state of optimum emotional management and problem solving. Neil Armstrong, the first person to set foot on the moon, was noted for his ability to remain composed under pressure. In training for landing the lunar module, one of the training vehicles malfunctioned—nearly killing him—and it was his ability to channel his perception of danger to ejecting from the vehicle just in time that saved him (Hansen, 2005). This is what it is like for us. We are "alarmed" by certain patient situations, but that "alarm" does not lead to becoming flabbergasted or paralyzed. In a code blue situation, we are not emotionally detached, doing the code as if we are folding laundry. We are invested in what we are doing and focused on giving all that we have for that situation. A Navy pilot told me that the Seal saying "Slow is smooth. Smooth is fast" was drilled into them in training. In a high-pressure situation, you have to pace yourself to do whatever you have to so that you do it right; and in doing so, you will be doing it the fastest and most efficiently it can be done (Roy & Lawson, 2015).

Centeredness as being fully present to the patient

The second facet to being centered is that we are fully present with the patient in the situation before us. One of the common problems in medicine is that clinicians often hurry to get the next thing for which they are behind. The patients pick this up. They feel it when our awareness is already on the next thing that we have to get to. The patients think, "Why can't I be the patient that you have to get to instead of being an unwelcome hassle in your schedule?" Also, being centered and fully present is stabilizing and calming for patients. If we are frazzled coming in to see patients, they pick this up and become more stressed because of our being stressed. Clinicians help change the perspectives of patients by being a centered presence that helps them feel safe and calmer, which then allows emotional processing and problem solving to go more smoothly.

Ways to help us cultivate and practice being centered

What helps us become centered in clinical work? The first thing is good training in learning how to be emotionally composed in high-stress situations. In many ways, health care training does this to us by default. You learn how to do it, or you wash out of the program. What we need is more intentionality in doing this. One of our flaws in medicine is that we think people just pick this up and that they should pick it up quickly. But this process goes better when we pay attention not only to what task has to be done but also to the process of how we are learning emotional regulation and being centered in clinical work. Second, we must have practices that train us not only to learn what this state is but also how to keep ourselves conditioned, just like we need to keep exercising regularly to stay fit. Many clinicians now use mind-training practices such as mindfulness (Kabat-Zinn, 2018; Shapiro & Carlson, 2017) and HeartMath (Childre, Martin, & Beech, 2000) to achieve this. Clinicians use prayer as a regular centering practice and a way to recover centeredness when they lose it. Clinicians also use rituals in clinical practice as a way to keep centered throughout their work. For example, because we wash our hands so much both before and after patient visits, it is easy to include a centering phrase or prayer as a way of letting go of what preceded that moment and intending to be fully present to the patients we are about to see (Larose, 2004; Watson, 2002).

Implications for maintaining balanced C²

Patient care is a high-performance situation that requires emotional composure in situations that most people would become overwhelmed by and find intractable. From the patient perspective, our ability to be centered allows us to manage our own emotions well so that we can be more therapeutically present to our patients. Our centered presence becomes a calming force in the encounter with the patient, who can then gain more clarity on what he or she may need to do. Our centeredness also enables us to think more clearly and efficiently so that we can solve problems more easily and creatively. From the clinician perspective, being centered is an important way of taking care of ourselves. We face very challenging emotional situations of all types in a single day. Being centered is a way of keeping our bodies from being excessively taxed, both physiologically and psychologically. In this way, we can be less exhausted and also more fulfilled in the work.

LIFETIME OF CARING AS A STORY WITH A SUCCESSION OF AWAKENINGS

What does it mean to view your health care career as a story?

To maintain a sense of balance in clinical work, it can be helpful for clinicians to look at their careers as a story with a succession of awakenings rather than as a static state achieved after medical school and remaining the same until retirement. When you view your health care career as a story or a journey, it changes how you imagine what is going on in it at any given point. As a story, your health care career is what led you into medicine, what you were like at the beginning of training, what training was like, what your early practice was like, and so on. There will be themes that emerge in terms of what you had to endure and how you overcame it. There will be a progression of insights, and you will find yourself later comforting those at earlier stages with your story of how you got through. When you view your career as a story, you have

now moved from viewing yourself as a static doctor (e.g., I am a doctor now and a doctor does this) to viewing yourself more dynamically. Viewing your career as a story enables you to frame struggles and setbacks as part of a process in which you will become something different afterward. You will find it to be a way in which you can identify when you are at the end of a "chapter" and at the beginning of another one. You will not expect yourself to stay the same, and you will come to expect that you will grow and have new insights about medicine and life itself.

Using the story of one's life in health care as a tool for clinician well-being

I have found the vehicle of viewing one's health care career as a story to be very helpful to all types of clinicians. With residents, we would begin residency with a retreat, with the highlight of the day being the new residents telling the story of how they got to the point of being residents. It was always remarkable to hear what had occurred in each person's life that led to this point of becoming a resident. It also changed how they viewed each other. Now, instead of judging each other by appearances or as "just an intern," they gained an appreciation for each other's journeys and the fact that they were going to be together for three years, going through an intense experience together. At the end of the third year, we would do the exercise again, except this time the task was to tell each other the stories of their three years of residency. "My residency was a story of _____." I have done similar retreats for physicians, nurses, ministers, and other clinicians in which the day is broken into different parts. We begin with what got them into this work. Later we move to the great moments in their work. Next, they tell stories of the hard things they are facing at the time of the retreat. Finally, we take time to consider how they want to approach going forward in the predicaments in which they find themselves. The exercise is a way to gain new perspectives on what is happening in their lives and also a way of "carrying the suffering" of their careers. That is, when you can articulate what your experience is and how it fits into the rest of your life, there is a way in which people feel encouraged because they have found their meaning, their quest, or their "dragon to slay."

Medical student dreams showing the psychological evolution of the physicians

There appears to be an unconscious developmental and emotional process in becoming a physician beyond learning facts and skills. Marcus (2003) examined the thematic progression of almost 400 dreams of medical students and residents. In the first year of medical school, the content of dreams tended to be about dissection or operations and information overload with frequent testing. The wish to heal is evident in a kind of hero-healer fantasy, but with risky and frightening scenes depicting students who are often overwhelmed with anxiety and helplessness, with the patient and the student being alone and emotionally abandoned. The scenes are often heroic and dramatic but with elements of fear, pain, and horror. The dreams tend to show a merger of the medical student and the patient, an identification with what is happening to the patient, but also indicating how the student is being brutally transformed or changed by the training process. One example of a first-year medical student dream showing this identification is evident in this dream: "There is a patient on a dolly. I am cutting out his heart. I then notice with alarm that his heart is still beating. I then pull down the sheet to look at the body. The body is mine" (Marcus, 2003, p. 373). Throughout the second year, the sense of internal suffering continues. For example, there is a deep sense of being overwhelmed about learning everything that is needed for patient care that moves often from an intense anxiety to a depressive resignation, and finally to feelings of anger at being tortured by the medical training process.

Dreams of medical students later in medical school

With the third year, the students have learned a tremendous amount, but they have not learned how to organize the information and do not have the experience to use it clinically. Again, there is a sense of being overwhelmed. There is the grandiose fantasy of wanting to learn everything and yet feeling humiliated by failure and the impossibility of being perfect. Marcus writes that there appears to be a narcissistic rage that emerges in the third year as a kind of psychological defense against the threats to self-esteem and failure to achieve these grandiose ideals. The new ideal is to imitate faculty by being more emotionally cold, unempathic, and unperturbed by difficult situations. There is a loss of the medical student's empathy around this time as the student's ideal shifts from being identified with the helpless patient to that of the image of sadistic, aggressive faculty. There is little identification with the patient by the fourth-year dreams. While the medical student is the patient in 18% of the first-year dreams, this only happens in 7% of the fourth-year dreams and is 0% by the second year of residency. The medical student as doctor occurs in 17% of first-year dreams, 38% in fourth-year dreams, and 80% of fourth-year resident dreams. Medical school is often experienced as sadistic, invasive, damaging, painful, traumatic, and with a loss of idealism and empathy.

Resident dreams

With residency comes the resurrection of a healing grandiosity. But interns are overwhelmed with the high number of work and on-call hours. There is again the need to learn an overwhelming amount of information with the anxiety of how to organize and use it. Dreams have a resurgence of the empathic mergers with patients: Both the resident and the patient are subject to invasive surgical and medical procedures. There are tremendous feelings of shame and inadequacy, of the impossibility of getting everything done, and of being alone in difficult circumstances. With second-year residency comes an increasing sense of mastery of medical skills and less vulnerability. As the physician becomes a third- and fourth-year resident, the tremendous responsibility feels easier to carry and not as personal, as is depicted in this fourth-year resident's dream:

> I was in the emergency room, presented with a woman in severe congestive heart failure; a left ventricular ejection fraction of 8 per cent. My reaction was very matter of fact: "Oh well, another patient with an ejection fraction of 8 per cent. I guess we should be able to handle this well, by now." This struck me as humorous during the dream, the matter-of-fact acceptance of the situation, and I woke up from the dream with a chuckle. (Marcus, 2003, p. 380)

Dreams as medical training ends

As medical training ends, dreams tend to show less anxiety and the ability to contain affect. The professional self emerges without the damage of the first few years. The dream images show an ability to carry responsibility and limited results without feeling humiliated. When failure occurs,

it moves from feeling guilt to feeling regret. There is a reemergence of hope and a reality-based idealism. The dreamer is less alone in these dreams and has peers and attendings who are present and sometimes helpful. There is more confidence, and there is a sense of being part of a professional group that provides a sense of sharing the burden of guilt. Aggression in dreams decrease. The empathic attitude is more flexible, realistic, and humane; there is a "self-presentation preserved uncontaminated by empathic feeling for patient's plight in a separate object representation" (Marcus, 2003, p. 380). Marcus notes that the emergence of aggression in the medical student dreams may function in a way to help protect the student to defend against feeling helpless and invaded. It may be motivating because of the responsibility to save lives. But because aggression is opposite the ideal of the gentle and empathic healer, this can create an inner turmoil that has to be resolved. Losing a sense of empathy may be a temporary part of this resolution. In the end, the physician is engaged in a kind of mourning process as the original grandiose ideals become more realistic and humbled by reality.

Dream study shows that clinical detachment is a temporary part of the transformation process

What is helpful in this study of medical-training dreams is that it is a unique way of articulating the grueling emotional developmental process of becoming a physician and how there might be a way in which, if it goes well, the clinician learns how to gain a self–other distinction in empathizing with patients and also learns how to try as hard as possible to help patients in their suffering without becoming overwhelmed. The sentimental ideals of the hero physician must become more realistic and a way to deal with failures—knowing that not everything has to be found in order to make it in this profession. One can see in this how a physician could get stuck or lost in the process. For example, the third-year loss of empathy makes sense if one thinks about how medical students have to find a way to get through the overwhelming amount of medical information and to navigate their own intense feelings. The emergence of aggression and cold detachment make sense as temporary defensive and adaptive maneuvers. The danger is that a medical student can get stuck there or when it emerges again in residency. Clinical detachment should be considered a temporary part of the inner journey of the clinician on the path to gaining a more mature emotional stance vis-a-vis the patient. What we have lacked in medical training is more time and sophisticated discussion of what that looks like. With the contributions of the science of compassion, we have more ability now to articulate what that mature clinical compassionate mindset looks like.

People become more compassionate toward others and to themselves as they age

Maturing as a helping professional will follow maturing as a person. Just because one may be less empathic and other-centered as a younger helping professional does not mean he or she is destined to remain that way. Neff and Pommier (2013) found that as people age, they become more concerned with the suffering of others as well as themselves. They noted that the ego-centrism of the college-age years declines and empathy increases in early adulthood. They found that with age, people tend to increase in empathetic concern, perspective taking, compassion for humanity, altruism, and forgiveness. They experienced less personal distress when faced with emotionally stressful situations.

Finally, they were more able to be self-compassionate. Neff and Pommier (2013) speculate that this occurs because of emotional maturity and that people understand more about life through their own experiences. "As individuals learn more about suffering and the causes of suffering with development, however, they may come to form a more unified understanding of compassion that generalizes to human beings more broadly, the self included" (Neff & Pommier, 2013, p. 172).

Study tracking satisfaction and burnout in physician careers

In a study of 7,288 physicians (Dyrbye et al., 2013), those who tended to be least satisfied with their overall career choice were physicians in the earliest part of their careers (1–10 years). Physicians were more satisfied in the middle part of their career (11–20 years), and most satisfied in their late career (21 or more years). In the earliest parts of their careers, physicians have the highest rates of work–home conflicts and the most difficulty resolving them in such a way that both work and home responsibilities are met. In terms of burnout, they have the highest rates of depersonalization. The middle parts of their careers tended to be the most productive but also the most exhausting. The middle career is when physicians are most likely to plan to leave medicine because of frustration (but not because of retirement). They tended to work more hours, had more on-call duty, were the most dissatisfied with their work–life balance, and had the lowest satisfaction with their specialties. In terms of burnout symptoms, middle-career physicians had the highest levels of emotional exhaustion and overall burnout. Late-career physicians tended to be the most satisfied and had the lowest burnout levels (Dyrbye et al., 2013).

Terminal connotation of the term burnout

One of the unfortunate consequences of using a term like *burnout* is that the image seems so final. The initial flame has "burnt out" like a torched building, a candle that no longer has any wax, an oil lamp that has exhausted its fuel, or a match that has already been struck. The image is not "blown out," in which case all that needs to happen is that the flame just has to be reignited. With burnout, the image is much more terminal. Burnout feels that way, too. When a clinician really experiences burnout, it does not feel like it will ever end. But as we will see in chapter 16 in more detail, burnout can actually be a time when clinicians reassess what led to that stage and figure out what they need to change to recover from burnout. When a clinician "burns out," he or she has two problems. One is that he or she has entered a state of exhaustion, cynicism, and discouragement. It is not easy to get the energy to recover from it. Second, not only does the clinician have to recover from burnout, he or she has to figure out what he or she did that got him or her there so that he or she can change it. Uygur (2012) found in her study of exemplary compassionate physicians that a period of burnout was common and the platform, in some sense, to recover a compassionate attitude that exceeded what they started with when they entered medical school. (More on this in chapter 16.) Perhaps we should change the term from *burnout* to *blown out* to convey that this is common among clinicians and often a time of transformation to a whole new level of being a clinician. While I doubt that we will now have a "Blown Out Inventory" as opposed to a "Burnout Inventory," it is important that we not take our images too literally. Burnout can be part of the lifetime of awakenings for the clinician.

Implications for maintaining balanced C²

From the patient perspective, when clinicians can view their careers as stories with a series of awakenings, clinicians are more engaged with what they are doing. Like climbing a mountain, they know to expect difficult parts, unexpected parts, and periodic beautiful views. Patients can feel it when clinicians are passionate about their work and have a desire to keep learning more and doing more for their patients. For clinicians, viewing their careers as stories with awakenings provides a way to get perspective on what is happening to them and what it means. It can provide a way to reflect on what is going on in their work and to signal when they are at a crossroads. Finally, knowing "what story you are in" is a way to carry the suffering or challenges you have in your own life that connects with your call and your purpose in being in a helping profession. With the expectation that it is a story with plots, themes, and chapters, you then open yourself to gaining insights about it.

AWARENESS AND USE OF THE WOUNDED-HEALER ARCHETYPE

A story of a physician with a wound that will not go away

In the three-minute play *The Angel That Disturbed the Waters* by Thornton Wilder (1998), the main character is a physician who goes to a healing pool to get cured of something that ails him. At one point he prays, "My work grows faint. Heal me, long-expected love; heal me that I may continue. Renewal, release; let me begin again without this fault that bears me down." Wilder never says what the physician's fault is. At one point the physician calls it an "old burden," "the flaw in my heart," and that it puts his "heart in pain." He also says it is like "nets in which my wings are caught" and it is a "sin into which all my endeavors sink half performed." Finally, it is something that makes him feel ashamed. Whatever this internal flaw or burden is, it is bad enough that he wants a cure for it, and he goes to a healing pool. Around this healing pool are very sick people accompanied by their attendants. What happens is that an angel comes periodically and stirs the waters of the pool, and the first one who gets in is healed. The sick people criticize the physician for being there—first, because he is a physician; secondly, because he does not look sick. When the angel comes, the physician argues with the angel about why he should get the cure. At a dramatic point in the play, the angel turns to the physician and says:

> Without your wound where would your power be? It is your very remorse that makes your low voice tremble into the hearts of [others]. The very angels themselves cannot persuade the wretched and blundering children on earth as can one human being broken on the wheels of living. In love's service only the wounded soldiers can serve. (Wilder, 1998, p. 74)

After saying this to the physician, the angel stirs the waters, and one of the other sick people jumps in and gets the cure. When he comes out of the water cured, he says to the physician, whom he knows:

> May you be the next, my brother. But come with me first, an hour only, to my home. My son is lost in dark thoughts. I—I do not understand him, and only you have ever lifted his mood. Only an hour ... my daughter, since her child has died, sits in the shadow. She will not listen to us. (Wilder, 1998, pp. 74–75)

What are the wounds of the wounded healer?

This story is one of the classic examples of what is called the wounded-healer archetype in which it is thought that the desire and the ability to help others is tied into having encountered one's own wound or illness. People who are helping professionals often speak of specific experiences that set them on the journey to work to heal others. It may have been an early illness in a close family member or themselves, the death of a loved one, a trauma, an ordeal that nearly does them in, or some profound encounter with an injustice such as prejudice or crime. People often speak of recurring internal issues, or suffering they incur from external situations, that create difficulties for them and humble them. Sometimes the clinician has an illness, a disability, or a condition in him- or herself that never goes away. Yet, somehow these old burdens and faults are part of the compassion that motivates the clinician and even gives him or her some of his or her healing ability.

Everyone has a "wound," and it has the potential to heal

In balanced compassionate caring, clinicians must learn how to both use and yet not be consumed by that which has "wounded" or "burdened" them. Some clinicians do not think they have one, but I have never met anyone who did not have a wound of some sort. To be balanced and effective in helping patients, clinicians have to be aware of what their "wounds" are, get a grip on these wounds and learn from them, and then they may be able to help their patients better than if they had not worked on it.

What is an archetype?

What do I mean by *archetype*? An archetype is a discovery made by C. G. Jung about certain universal patterns of behavior that occur in all humans. An archetype is a potential form of behavior, a basic schema in the human mind that becomes manifest naturally in a person's life (Jung, 1964). "These act like magnetic fields which, though unseen, arrange responses, emotions, and actions into specific patterns expressed in the form of symbolic images" (Ulanov, 1971, p. 50). They are themes or images that show up across cultures and throughout history. Although they may be expressed uniquely because they are expressed through the lens of a culture or historical period, humans have them in common. Examples are the Hero, the Great Mother, the Wise Old Man, the Wise Old Woman, the Trickster, or the Evil One. If you look across cultures throughout history, you will find the image of the wounded healer popping up as a shaman or healer in myths and healing practices (Halifax, 1988).

The myth of the wounded healer and how that connects to Hippocrates and the history of medicine

One of the most well-known images of the wounded healer is Chiron in ancient Greek mythology. Chiron was a centaur whose father was the Greek god Kronos and whose mother was the nymph Philyra. Chiron was abandoned by them but was adopted by Apollo, who gave him all his knowledge. Chiron became a great teacher to many gods, including Asclepius whom he taught the art of healing. Chiron was wounded in his knee by a poisoned arrow accidentally shot by his friend and mentor, Hercules. The arrow tip had been covered by the poisonous blood of the monster Hydra, and this gave Chiron a wound that was painful and would never heal. As the story goes, Chiron teaches Asclepius the art of medicine; Asclepius's symbol was the staff entwined by a snake, which we use today as a symbol of medicine. Asclepius, in turn, was the teacher of Hippocrates, whom we consider the Father of Medicine (Jackson, 2001).

How a clinician's "wound" can help him or her connect with patients

When a clinician has gone through some personal ordeal, encountered some kind of suffering or injustice, or experienced anything that could be called a "wound" or personal weakness, there is the potential for that clinician to use that experience therapeutically. When a clinician has suffered, no matter what the cause, there is a way in which that clinician can connect better with others who have suffered. That clinician knows what it is like to feel, for example, unsafe, vulnerable, or helpless. That clinician is grounded in what it means to be human, and this has the potential to make him or her more compassionate with patients. There is a way in which suffering and "wrestling" with one's wound can teach you and be a source of wisdom. Say a clinician is a recovered addict, is overweight, went through a bad relationship, or has been in a bad car accident. When a clinician meets patients with similar experiences, that clinician has a sense of what that psychological terrain is like. Their patients may be reacting differently, but still that clinician has a sense of what that experience does to a person and what it takes to go through it. At the very least, it protects the clinician from grandiosity. A clinician who believes he or she has no fault or no "wound" will have much less tolerance for humans who have flaws. But if a clinician can connect with his or her own suffering, then he or she is grounded in his or her humanity and able to use what he or she has learned there for the healing of others.

Having a "wound" does not automatically make you a wounded healer

However, simply having a "wound" is not enough to make you a wounded healer. It is very important that you have worked consciously with your "wounds," your issues, because not having done so can negatively affect your patient care. There is the danger that you perceive others through the lens filter of your own wound. You might assume, for example, that anyone who suffers thinks, feels, and behaves just like you would, especially with experiences or conditions like you had. Being unconscious about an unresolved issue or "wound" in your own life can interfere with your ability to help others effectively. A clinician may also be unable to help someone because he or she is overly focused on his or her own wound. For example, if a clinician has been the victim of some type of abuse or other trauma but has not worked through that experience, then it may interfere with the helping process. This is because that clinician is partially preoccupied with his or her own pain or tends to see others' issues only in terms of his or her own traumatized perspective. Another example would be a person who is an addict and has begun to recover. The addict may think he or she can help others but really cannot in the early stages of recovery. When he or she is more fully established in recovery, then he or she are able to help others more effectively. To be a wounded healer, a clinician must have named, worked with, mourned, and learned from his or her own wound.

In teaching, the best teachers are the ones who love to learn themselves

There is another aspect of the wounded-healer dynamic in which the degree to which a clinician is in touch with his or her woundedness, to that degree is the clinician better able to help the patient get connected to his or her inner healer. To explain this fully requires more detail than is appropriate for this book, but I will provide a few examples to demonstrate the dynamic. In teaching, it is often the case that the teacher who loves to learn is the best teacher. Students pick up that enthusiasm and start taking the initiative in learning themselves. That is, the teacher who is connected to his or her inner student inspires or influences students to be connected to their inner teachers. While this may sound rather mystical, it really is not. Think of the reverse scenario. Say that someone had a teacher who acted as if he or she knew everything and did not convey the sense of being a fellow learner as a teacher. Instead, the teacher puts him- or herself on the pedestal of power and knowledge. So what happens to the students? The students perceive themselves as below the teacher, and the classroom becomes an experience of feeling inferior, not good enough. If the teacher is very identified with being the all-knowing teacher, there is a way in which the students cannot imagine themselves ever being as good as that teacher. Therefore, they do not learn to take the initiative in learning because they are in a passive, one-down position (Guggenbuhl-Craig, 1982).

Clinicians who are in touch with their own problems are better able to help their patients heal themselves

The same is true with patients. Let me use doctors as the example. If a doctor is identified with being a doctor and not grounded in his or her humanity, then the patient will pick this up and not take as much responsibility for his or her own health care. The doctor who is grounded in his or her humanity knows what it is like to be sick, to not be in control (figure 12.1). That doctor knows, for example, that he or she has to watch his or her weight, too, deal with his or her own genetic health vulnerabilities, and also knows that he or she is human and doing the best he or she can

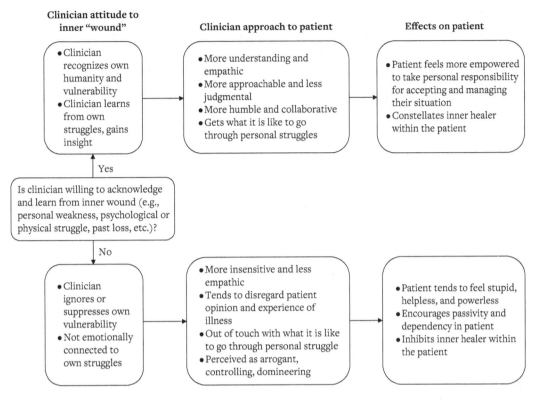

FIGURE 12.1 Wounded healer archetype.

to take care of him- or herself. Granted, we would expect physicians to be further along than patients on self-care and good health behaviors. But the physician who knows he or she is also a patient will convey the message to improve health behaviors in a way that encourages the patient to take more control of his or her own health—that is, to be a physician to themselves. If this seems too magical and nebulous, run the experiment on yourself in terms of how your patients tend to be with you compared to how patients are with an arrogant colleague, picking a colleague who does not seem grounded humbly in what it means to be human. Then run the experiment with you as the patient or the student and notice how this dynamic becomes evident (see Guggenbuhl-Craig, 1982; Groesbeck, 1975).

Examples of physicians who have experienced illness or trauma

I had a physician once who handled my questions about my condition very well. She had a clear sense of the systems of the body, and I finally asked her how she came to know body systems so well. She said to me, "I had cancer and I realized that medicine taught me how to take the body apart, but not how to put it together again." Some studies on physicians and nurses find negative effects on clinical practice if the clinician has not worked through the past "wound." But most find positive effects on clinical practice. Roberts, Warner, Moutier, Geppert, and Hammond surveyed 155 residents regarding the relationship between them having experienced personal illnesses and the residents' ability to have empathy and compassion for patients. In general, the residents believed that personal experiences of illnesses—either in themselves or their families—increased the compassion they had for their patients. Those who had personal experiences with physical or mental health problems during their residency believed more strongly that those experiences increased their capacity for empathy (Roberts et al., 2011). In a sample of 297 family physicians sent in an anonymous survey, 42.4% of women and 24.3% of men reported some type of personal abuse had occurred to them. These results are comparable to other studies of physicians asked about past histories of having gone through abuse. In terms of the effect on their clinical practices, these physicians said they were more comfortable screening their patients for trauma (Candib, Savageau, Weinreb, & Reed, 2012).

Other examples

In a sample of 361 physicians and medical students, Brady, Bambury, and O'Reilly (2015) found that 20% of them had a history of a personal illness, and 82% of that group said that this positively impacted their empathic ability with patients. Woolf, Cave, McManus, and Dacre (2007) found that 85.5% of newly qualified doctors (in a sample of 4,784) and 54.4% of medical students (in a sample of 749) reported having had significant personal illness experiences themselves or in close relatives or friends. In the short term, they reported this interfered somewhat with their learning and caused them to feel less prepared for their clinical jobs; they also tended to have higher levels of depression and anxiety. But in the long term, they seemed to have more empathy and be more patient-centered. In *When Doctors Become Patients*, Klitzman (2008) reported, "Frequently, personal experiences of illness reversed years of professional medical training. In facing the darkness of their own disease, these doctors often came to treat patients and to teach trainees better" (p. 257). But he noted that some physicians went too far in terms of "doing too much for patients" and then distancing themselves, struggling to find the right balance.

Implications for maintaining balanced C²

So how does the awareness and use of the wounded-healer archetype contribute to balanced compassionate caring? In terms of care for the patient, a clinician who is grounded in his or her humanity because of challenging personal experiences will be more likely to be emotionally engaged and empathic with patients. If the clinician has worked through and really learned from that experience, he or she will have a sense of what is doing too much for a patient. But if he or she is still "in the grip" of the wound, he or she may have more difficulty setting boundaries with patients. In terms of what this means for the well-being of the clinician, a clinician who has really engaged and learned from his or her own personal issues, illnesses, or problems is going to be more able to self-assess when he or she has a problem that needs to be dealt with; such a clinician will not be afraid of his or her own vulnerability. It will not scare the clinician that he or she is not perfect. But if a clinician is not grounded in his or her own humanity, he or she risks grandiosity and perfectionism.

CONCLUSION

To sustain the clinician compassion mindset and be in the zone of balanced C², it is very important that we are grounded in attitudes that act like rudders or the North Star in navigating troubled clinical waters. Among those is the *caritas* attitude, which is the constant driving force and motivation we bring to every situation. With this it is important that we have a balanced notion of our responsibility in between the poles of not being engaged with the situation to thinking we are completely responsible for everything that happens. It also means that we are realistic about outcomes. We bring the attitude of empathic concern—the compassion mindset—to all that we do, which is what enables us to be emotionally engaged but not emotionally engulfed in our work with patients. To stay engaged with challenging patient situations, we need the ability to frame and reframe situations from a therapeutic perspective instead of an ineffectual, detached, objective perspective. Being centered is the way we maintain our emotional composure to handle difficult situations optimally, to problem solve creatively, and to be a therapeutic presence for our patients. In term of our careers overall, it helps us to view our health care careers as stories with a series of psychological awakenings in our lives. This enables us to reflect regularly about ourselves in this work so that we may be open to what we need to do to take care of ourselves and to provide a meaningful perspective on what it means for us to be in health care.

QUESTIONS FOR DISCUSSION

1. In terms of these internal attitudes to maintain balanced compassionate caring, are there any others that you think should be added to your personal mindset?
2. Pick one of the attitudes and reflect on an instance that demonstrated the importance of that attitude for your work.

REFERENCES

Batson, C. D. (2011). *Altruism in humans.* New York, NY: Oxford University Press.

Batson, C. D., Early, S., & Salvarani, G. (1997). Perspective taking: Imagining how another feels versus imagining how you would feel. *Personality and Social Psychology Bulletin, 23*(7), 751–758.

Boyle, G. (2010). *Tattoos on the heart: The power of boundless compassion.* New York, NY: Free Press.

Brady, C., Bambury, R. M., & O'Reilly, S. (2007). Empathy and the wounded healer: A mixed-method study of patients and doctors views on empathy. *Irish Medical Journal, 108*(4), 125–126.

Brennan, T. A., & Leape, L. L. (1991). Adverse events, negligence in hospitalized patients: Results from the Harvard Medical Practice Study. *Perspectives in Healthcare Risk Management, 11*(2), 2–8.

Candib, L. M., Savageau, J. A., Weinreb, L., & Reed, G. (2012). When the doctor is a survivor of abuse. *Family Medicine, 44*(6), 416–424.

Childre, D. L., Martin, H., & Beech, D. (2000). *The Heart-Math solution: The Institute of HeartMath's revolutionary program for engaging the power of the heart's intelligence.* San Francisco, CA: HarperOne.

Corcoran, K. J. (1983). Emotional separation and empathy. *Journal of Clinical Psychology, 39*(5), 667–671.

Davis, M. H. (1983). Measuring individual differences in empathy: Evidence for a multidimensional approach. *Journal of Personality and Social Psychology, 44*(1), 113–126.

Decety, J. (Ed.). (2012). *Empathy: From bench to bedside.* Cambridge, MA: MIT Press.

Dyrbye, L. N., Varkey, P., Boone, S. L., Satele, D. V., Sloan, J. A. & Shanafelt, T. D. (2013). Physician satisfaction and burnout at different career stages. *Mayo Clinic Proceedings*, 88(12), 1358–1367.

Gawande, A. (2011). *The checklist manifesto: How to get things right*. New York, NY: Picador.

Groesbeck, C. J. (1975). The archetypal image of the wounded healer. *Analytical Psychology*, 20(2), 122–145.

Groopman, J. (2007). *How doctors think*. Boston, MA: Houghton Mifflin.

Guggenbuhl-Craig, A. (1982). *Power in the helping professions*. New York, NY: Spring.

Halifax, J. (1988). *Shaman: The wounded healer*. New York, NY: Thames & Hudson.

Halpern, J. (2001). *From detached concern to empathy: Humanizing medical practice*. New York, NY: Oxford University Press.

Hansen, J. R. (2005) *First man: The life of Neil A. Armstrong*. New York, NY: Simon & Schuster.

Harrison, R., Lawton, R., & Stewart, K. (2014). Doctors' experiences of adverse events in secondary care: The professional and personal impact. *Clinical Medicine*, 14(6), 585–590.

Hojat, M. (2007). *Empathy in patient care: Antecedents, development, measurement, and outcomes*. New York, NY: Springer Science + Business Media.

Hojat, M. (2016). *Empathy in health professions education and patient care*. New York, NY: Springer.

Jackson, P. L., Brunet, E., Meltzoff, A. N., & Decety, J. (2006). Empathy examined through the neural mechanisms involved in imagining how I feel versus how you feel pain. *Neuropsychologia*, 44(5), 752–761.

Jackson, S. W. (2001). Presidential address: The wounded healer. *Bulletin of the History of Medicine*, 75(1), 1–36.

Jung, C. G. (1964). *Man and his symbols*. New York, NY: Dell.

Kabat-Zinn, J. (2018). *Meditation is not what you think: Mindfulness and why it is so important*. New York, NY: Hachette Books.

Klimecki, O., & Singer, T. (2011). Empathic distress fatigue rather than compassion fatigue? Integrating findings from empathy research in psychology and social neuroscience. In B. Oakley, A. Knafo, G. Madhavan, & D. S. Wilson (Eds.), *Pathological altruism* (pp. 368–383). New York, NY: Oxford University Press.

Klitzman, R. (2008). *When doctors become patients*. New York, NY: Oxford University Press.

Larsen, R. J., & Diener, E. (1987). Affect intensity as an individual difference characteristic: A review. *Journal of Research in Personality*, 21(1), 1–39.

Larose, P. (2004). A blessing close at hand. *Home Healthcare Nurse*, 22(3), 200.

Marcus, E. R. (2003). Medical student dreams about medical school: The unconscious developmental process of becoming a physician. *International Journal of Psychoanalysis*, 84(Pt. 2), 367–386.

McCleerey, J., & Vachon, D. O. (2007, March 8). *The relationship between coping style, empathy, and burnout in a physician population*. Paper presented at Indiana Academy of Family Practice Research Forum, Indianapolis.

Meldrum, H. (2010). *Characteristics of compassion: Portraits of exemplary physicians*. Boston, MA: Jones and Bartlett.

Montgomery, C. L. (1994). The caring/healing relationship of "maintaining authentic caring." In J. Watson (Ed.), *Applying the art and science of human caring* (pp. 39–42). New York, NY: National League for Nursing Press.

More, E. S. (1994). "Empathy" enters the profession of medicine. In E. S. More & M. A. Milligan (Eds.). The Empathic Practitioner: Empathy, Gender, and Medicine (pp. 19–39). New Brunswick, NJ: Rutgers University Press.

Neff, K. D., & Pommier, E. (2013). The relationship between self-compassion and other-focused concern among college undergraduates, community adults, and practicing meditators. *Self and Identity*, 12(2), 160–176.

Osler, W., Hinorhara, S., & Niki, H. (2001). *Osler's "A Way of Life" & other addresses with commentary & annotations*. Durham, NC: Duke University Press.

Pavey, L., Greitemeyer, T., & Sparks, P. (2012). "I help because I want to, not because you tell me to": Empathy increases autonomously motivated helping. *Personality and Social Psychology Bulletin*, 38(5), 681–689.

Roberts, L. W., Warner, T. D., Moutier, C., Geppert, C. M. A., & Hammond, K. A. G. (2011). Are doctors who have been ill more compassionate? Attitudes of resident physicians regarding personal health issues and the expression of compassion in clinical care. *Psychosomatics, 52*(4), 367–374.

Roy, R. (with Lawson, C.) (2015). *The Navy SEAL art of war: Leadership lessons from the world's most elite fighting force.* New York, NY: Crown Business.

Shapiro, S. L., & Carlson, L. E. (2017). *The art and science of mindfulness: Integrating mindfulness into psychology and the helping professions* (2nd ed.). Washington, DC: American Psychological Association.

Sitzman, K., & Watson, J. (2018). *Caring science, mindful practice: Implementing Watson's human caring theory* (2nd ed.). New York, NY: Springer.

Spiro, H., Curnen, M. G. M., Peschel, E., & St. James, D. (Eds.). (1993). *Empathy and the practice of medicine.* New Haven, CT: Yale University Press.

Ulanov, A. B. (1971). *The feminine: In Jungian psychology and in Christian theology.* Evanston, IL: Northwestern University Press.

Uygur, J. M. (2012). *Understanding compassion in family medicine: A qualitative study* (Master's thesis). University of Western Ontario.

Vachon, D. O. (1993). *The influence of affect intensity, dispositional empathy, and emotional separation on the relationship between perceived stress and burnout in a nursing population* (Doctoral dissertation). Loyola University Chicago, Chicago, IL.

Wang, S. (2005). A conceptual framework for integrating research related to the physiology of compassion and the wisdom of Buddhist teachings. In P. Gilbert (Ed.), *Compassion: Conceptualisations, research and use in psychotherapy* (pp. 75–120). New York, NY: Routledge.

Watson, J. (2002). Intentionality and caring-healing consciousness: A practice of transpersonal nursing. *Holistic Nursing Practice, 16*(4), 12–19.

Watson, J. (2008). *Nursing: The philosophy and science of caring* (Rev. ed.). Boulder: University Press of Colorado.

West, C. P., Huschka, M. M., Novotny, P. J., Sloan, J. A., Kolars, J. C., Habermann, T. M., &Shanafelt, T. D. (2006). Association of perceived medical errors with resident distress and empathy. *JAMA, 296*(9), 1071–1078.

Wilder, T. (1998). The angel that troubled the waters. In A. T. Wilder (Ed.), *The collected short plays of Thornton Wilder* (Vol. 2, pp. 71–75). New York, NY: Theatre Communications Group.

Woolf, K., Cave, J., McManus, I. C., & Dacre, J. E. (2007). "It gives you an understanding you can't get from any book." The relationship between medical students' and doctors' personal illness experiences and their performances: A qualitative and quantitative study. *BMC Medical Education, 7*(50), 1–8.

Zwack, J., & Schweitzer, J. (2013). If every fifth physician is affected by burnout, what about the other four? Resilience strategies of experienced physicians. *Academic Medicine, 88*(3), 382–389.

CREDIT

"It's always further than it looks. It's always taller than it looks. And it's always harder than it looks."

—The three rules of mountaineering

"There have been joys too great to be described in words, and there have been griefs upon which I have not dared to dwell, and with these in mind I say, climb if you will, but remember that courage and strength are naught without prudence, and that a momentary negligence may destroy the happiness of a lifetime. Do nothing in haste, look well to each step, and from the beginning think what may be the end."

—Edward Whymper

Chapter Sections:

- ▶ Introduction
- ▶ Competence in the Skills and Interventions of Your Helping Profession
- ▶ Concrete Expressions of Caring Intent
- ▶ Being Able to Care for a Person Using Challenge and Confrontation
- ▶ Balance between Other-Care and Self-Care
- ▶ Energy Devoted to Self-Reflection and Analyzing Helping Interactions
- ▶ Ways of Dealing with Effects of Working with Individuals with Severe Problems
- ▶ Skill of Managing Emotions and Using Them for the Healing Process
- ▶ Effective Organizational and Practice-Management Skills
- ▶ Mind-Training Practices to Cultivate Compassion and Reduce Stress
- ▶ Conclusion

CHAPTER 13

Practices and Behavioral Skills

Practices and Behavioral Skills That Make
the Clinician Compassion Mindset Sustainable

Question to consider before reading this chapter:

1. What kinds of practices and skills do you think a clinician needs in order to be balanced in compassionate caring (C^2)?

INTRODUCTION

To be in the zone of balanced C^2, a clinician must have a number of skills and practices that the clinician cultivates and uses on a regular basis. In this chapter, I discuss nine skills and practices that help the clinician be in the zone of balanced C^2. While the attitudes and general approaches presented in chapter 12 provide the foundation for balanced C^2, we now consider what the clinician actually has to do to achieve this, both for the patient's benefit and for the clinician's well-being. Each of the skills and practices is simultaneously beneficial for the patient and the clinician. At the end of each skill or practice, I will briefly summarize how each skill and practice is relevant to patient care and to clinician well-being. This is a practical list based on clinical practice and research, but it is not exhaustive. Consider this list as a way to assess your ability to do each of these and how this affects your ability to be in the zone of balanced C^2.

COMPETENCE IN THE SKILLS AND INTERVENTIONS OF YOUR HELPING PROFESSION

The absurdity of distinguishing competence from caring

Competence in the profession or helping role you have is the very foundation of effective and balanced caring. Some people separate competence from caring, saying something like, "I didn't know what to do for the patient, but at least I cared about them." This kind of statement reflects the sentimentalized notion of caring, in which one is basically "being nice" and sympathetic. It implies that caring for people does not require much skill. It also suggests that people who have worked hard at mastering the skills for their type of helping work do not necessarily care about people. I have heard medical residents say things like, "I really don't know much about caring for people emotionally because I spent so much time studying medicine." When I hear this, I like to reframe it by saying that being competent in the skills of your profession is a significant part of caring for another person. To work from the opposite of this, if my physician has a caring manner but is not really competent in medicine, then he or she really does not care about me. This is like saying that if I need neurosurgery and one of my doctors says to me, "I read about brain surgery in medical school and I have seen it done once, so I would like to do the surgery because I care about you." If this doctor does not know how to do that surgery and still wants to do that surgery on me, then this doctor really does not care about me!

Compassion without competence is a cruel hoax

Once when I was giving a workshop on this topic at the University of Notre Dame, I happened to find this quote by Rev. Theodore M. Hesburgh C.S.C. on a plaque for the dedication of the Kresge Law Library on November 2, 1973:

> *May there be here a hunger for justice. May our students seek competence in the law since compassion without competence would be a cruel hoax upon those they serve. May they also realize that competence in the law without compassion leads the lawyer to use the law for other purposes than the works of justice, blinds him [or her] to the sad plight of persons who suffer injustice for want of a lawyer champion. (Bracketed text added for nonsexist language.)*

As the second part of Hesburgh's statement points out, it is possible to be competent in your profession or helping role and not really care about people; compassion is what directs that competence to the best interests of our patients. The remainder of the following characteristics of balanced compassionate caring address this. But the main point is that knowing the art and science of your profession or helping role lays the foundation for caring. To work on your competence in your specialty is to say that you care enough about the people you help that you learn everything you can in that specialty to help them.

> *While vocation may be a necessary condition for high-quality performance in many jobs, it is by no means a sufficient condition. Vocation does not guarantee skill. Someone who is effective in making patients feel truly "cared for" provides higher quality care than someone who performs his or her routines mechanically, all else equal. (Nelson & Folbre, 2006, p. 3)*

Would you rather have a smart doctor or a caring doctor?

Would you rather have a smart doctor or a caring doctor? This is a trick question. Think back to the cartoon in chapter 2 with the surgeon who comes out of the operating room and says to the loved one in the waiting room, "The nurses and technicians did all they could—I just wasn't into it." First, if I have the smartest and most technically competent surgeon in the world but that surgeon is "not into my problem," that technical competence means nothing. It does not ensure anything when it comes to my care. That surgeon may not like me, may be tired, may be preoccupied, or may be so full of him- or herself that he or she is not really paying attention to what is going on with my case. Second, if this is really a smart doctor, that doctor would know the latest research and the clinical wisdom that says that the internal caring attitude of the clinician, his or her communication skills, and his or her clinical compassion mindset have indisputable effects on every aspect of clinical care, from diagnosis to intervention and medical outcome—not just patient satisfaction. Third, being compassionately caring does not mean the clinician is less competent. A truly compassionate caring clinician has excellent composure, emotional regulation, and the ability to focus on exactly what a patient needs. As Sulmasy (1997) puts it, clinicians "cannot become so overwhelmed with emotional reaction to the pain of others that they are unable to render effective care. Competence remains the first act of compassion" (pp. 49–50).

Competence makes patients feels safe, which is a major way of expressing caring to a patient

There is another way in which the separation between caring and competence becomes absurd. As explained earlier in this book, caring should not be reduced to communication skills but should be concerned with ways patients pick up that they are safe with you and that you genuinely are interested in them and their problem. Salmon and Young (2009) point out that patients do not develop trust or feel cared for when they encounter clinicians who appear inexpert in their specialty. Patients feel cared for when they believe you have the capability of helping them and that you are interested in applying that capability to them. Hayes-Bautista (1976) found that there were at least three types of inadequacy on the part of the clinician that would lead to a patient wanting to terminate the relationship with him or her. One is *absolute inadequacy*, in which the patient comes to feel that the clinician is unable to handle some aspect of care judged by what the patient's expectation of what the clinician's actions should be. Second is a *change in competency*, in which the patient experiences the clinician as changing his or her approach in a negative direction or not being able to handle other issues as he or she did previous ones. I would add to this a patient concluding that his or her clinician has not kept up with the latest medical advances or that the clinician is not applying his or her skills as well as in the past (e.g., making more medication errors, missing diagnoses, hurrying through appointments in contrast to earlier experiences). Third, patients' evaluations of their clinician's competency can change in *comparison with other clinician's competencies.* Patients may find other clinicians who know more or have better treatment approaches. Or patients may discover another clinician who has the same knowledge but is more pleasant or kinder.

Learning organic chemistry and physiology are ways of demonstrating C²

When you learn medicine well, that is a way you are showing you care about patients. When you learn the basic sciences in the premedical years or general courses in medical school, or when you do years of residency and fellowship, these are all ways you are demonstrating that you really care about your future patients. When you keep current on your specialty and do continuing education, this is a way of demonstrating that you really care about your patients. When you remain curious about medicine, always think about why something worked or did not work, and maybe even do research on it, these are all ways you are demonstrating your commitment to compassion. Yes, it is very important that you learn good communication and patient care approaches. But compassionate caring should never be reduced to communication skills and bedside manner; it includes your tremendous competence that you are willing to give in a focused way for each patient you have.

The exercise of competence is important for physician well-being

Feeling that sense of competence is something that is important in physician well-being as well. Research has found that most resilient physicians experience gratification from their ability to treat people medically. Even in routine cases, the sense of self-efficacy and the experience of solving problems, applying oneself with discipline, and succeeding in complicated work is an important source of strength (Zwack & Schweitzer, 2013). This is not an emotionally disconnected clinician. This is someone who gains satisfaction and fulfillment in exercising his or her technical skills to the best of his or her ability.

Implications for maintaining balanced C²

To be in the zone of balanced C² requires that we realize that our competence is one of the primary ways we demonstrate our care. From the patients' perspective, learning our specialty as well as possible and staying current with the latest advances in our field is a way that we give our patients the best that we can. Focusing our competence on the particular patient in front of us is the primary way we show we are engaged with the patient, not detached and treating this patient as a nameless case. From the clinicians' perspective, realizing that our competence is the primary way we care keeps us from a nonsensical separation of caring from competence. Our caring shows through our competence, not in addition to it.

CONCRETE EXPRESSIONS OF CARING INTENT

Patients cannot tell if you care if you do not show them that you care

It is not enough to care about a person in your mind and heart. You have to show that you care by the way you act toward them. A clinician who has a caring attitude but does not express this concretely in his or her behaviors risks not being perceived as caring by the patient. A number of helping professionals will say something like, "I think my patients can just sense that I care about them, and it will just naturally show through my actions." This can be true, but I have also seen this backfire on clinicians. In my work with clinicians in training, I will observe them with their patients, and I know ahead of time about the caring attitude of many of those clinicians toward their particular patients. I know because they have told me. But then I have seen those very patients not experience that deeply felt caring. For example, very introverted or shy clinicians can be very competent and care deeply about people, but in their interactions, they simply do not say very much to their patients. Their greetings tend not to convey warmth and personal interest.

When their patients share emotional or physical concerns, they are met with little response from the clinician. The patient or client does not know what that lack of response means. Maybe my doctor is an aloof, arrogant person. Maybe he or she is thinking about something else and not my problem. Maybe he or she is the "quiet, caring type," but I cannot tell where I stand with him or her now. Maybe the lack of response means that my problem is really serious or overwhelming or irritating. In other words, lack of emotional expressiveness can make patients feel more tension and uncertainty when working with minimally expressive practitioners.

Very expressive clinicians can squelch patients

Very expressive clinicians can paradoxically run into the same problem. I have watched clinicians be very warm and talkative, use humor, and respond with many words to what patients said. But such clinicians can be so expressive and talkative that patients wonder if their clinician is really listening to them. I know for a fact that extraverts often have the ability to pick up a great deal of information from their patients or clients even though they are doing a lot of the talking. But the patient, especially if the patient is reserved or introverted, can wonder if the really expressive clinician is actually focusing on them. "My doctor is so talkative and friendly, but I feel like I have to get him or her to shut up for a little bit so I can fully talk about my worries." Or, "My nurse is always so perky and positive when she comes into my room, but then that makes me feel like hiding how bad I really feel today." In short, an overly expressive relational style can come across as uncaring and unhelpful when it dominates or squelches what the patient needs to express.

Caring attitude must be expressed in concrete actions

There have to be concrete signs of caring that allow your patients or clients to know that you care about them and that you are focused on them and their situation. One of the best quotes I have read that captures this is from Simone Weil (1951), who said, "The love of our neighbor in all its fullness simply means being able to say to him [her], 'What are you going through?'" (p. 64; bracketed text added for nonsexist language). The person being helped needs to have clear signs of your caring presence and your effort to help them in their pain. Asking about what the patient is going through, listening to the patient, supporting the patient with words and touch, and so many other clinician actions reflect the genuine care the clinician has for the patient.

Clinician communication consists of the content and relational cues

As discussed earlier in this book, Carol Montgomery has distinguished between the content and relational components in communication (based on Millar & Rogers, 1976). The content of the communication refers to what was said in terms of the objective meaning of the words spoken. The relational component refers to how the content is communicated, from which the person receiving the message can infer what kind of relationship this is. Montgomery (1993) quotes Watzlawick, Beavin, and Jackson (1967), who said, "If it is accepted that all behavior has message value, i.e., is communication, it follows that no matter how one may try, one cannot not communicate" (pp. 48-49). Montgomery (1993) adds, "This assumption is fundamental to the caring relationship, as all caregiving behaviors function as communication and, depending on the meaning created by the patient, will be interpreted as caring or as noncaring" (pp. 18-19).

Thus, it is important for clinicians to know not only the content of what they need to say to a patient but also how to convey that content. This will include things such as the clinician's non-verbal behavior, the timing of the message, the words chosen, the tone of the message, and overall how the delivery of the message is done. The difficulty, of course, as many communication theorists explain, is that what may be a caring relational tone for one person may not be exactly the same for someone else. The clinician must always assess what might or might not be perceived as a concrete expression of caring intent, and then self-correct accordingly to maximize the likelihood that the patient can infer the clinician's caring intent.

The vital importance of listening and considering the psychological state of the ill person

One of the best ways to assess the perception of patients is to be open to them and to listen. In the rush so many helping professionals experience in their work, it can be simpler just to give the raw truth or the bad news for efficiency's sake. Clinicians become accustomed to the raw truth of what needs to be done when people are having problems. They may have the "truth" or at least a good hunch, but a common error among clinicians is that they do not take the time to consider how to deliver the message. And then what happens is that it takes even longer to work through the issue because the patient has become defensive or shut down. As Connelly (1994) explains,

> although listening may appear mundane, it has a profound impact on every patient-physician relationship. Many problems arise when listening is not a priority of the physician—understanding does not occur, empathy is compromised, the therapeutic alliance may not develop, healing is minimized, and suffering

may result. Problems of caring, including ethical dilemmas and malpractice concerns can arise when doctor and patient do not relate to, or understand, one another. Inequities and conflicts occur when issues important to the patient, such as patient beliefs, values, family traditions, are deflected or are not taken seriously. When a patient refuses to accept the physician's suggested or prescribed means of diagnosis or treatment and the physician does not listen to the patient's reasoning, an ethical dilemma evolves. Many of these kinds of problems can be prevented or resolved by listening to the patient. (pp. 181–182)

A very important point to remember when working with people who are in some type of pain or distress is that when people are in such a state, they tend to regress. Normally calm and intelligent people can become irrational and emotional when their health or welfare is threatened. Veterinarians are actually some of the best teachers in this regard. The best ones are able to assess the kind of animal they have to work on, make a connection with it, and also just respect that an animal in pain may not react as it normally would. This is the optimum way to work with animals. Why would we not do the same or better with humans? Basically, you plan on people regressing when they are suffering and work in light of that.

Even toughness with a patient can come across as deeply caring

It is important to qualify the above, however, in terms of what people generally perceive as caring. I knew a psychologist who basically broke many of the rules a caring therapist would follow. That is, he asked blunt questions and objectively would be rated as rather intrusive and harsh when doing therapy with someone. Yet he had a very successful career. I said to him, "You break almost every rule I learned in how to be a therapist and yet your clients keep coming back to see you and they get better. Why is that?" He replied, "Because my clients know that I really love them, and that is why I am being tough with them." What appeared to happen is that his clients somehow knew he really cared about them and accepted his seemingly harsh comments as what they needed to hear to get better. They interpreted his toughness with them as a sign that he cared about them. I have witnessed the same dynamic occurring with all types of helping professionals.

Whether the clinician is caring becomes apparent over time

There are times when, objectively speaking, a clinician's behavior toward a patient appears uncaring or negative, but the patient does not interpret it in this way. Some patients or clients may even interpret a clinician's apparently negative concrete behaviors as positive. I have heard patients say things like, "I know Doc was really worried about me today because he really gave me a hard time." Some clinicians are abusive with patients or colleagues, and it is clear they are not interpreted as caring. It is interesting, therefore, how patients figure out how to interpret negative behaviors of the helper. When I have asked various groups of people about this dynamic, most often the answer is, "Over time, you can figure out who really cares about you. In fact, I've known doctors who acted like they cared about me, but later on I found out it was just an act." Others say, "You just kind of know if they care about you." In short, it is best that clinicians assume their intent will become apparent in time. But if you are a clinician with such negative helping behaviors, it would seem wise to assess if you can reliably convey your caring intent while persisting in what most would rate as negative helping behaviors.

Assume that patients can pick up your hidden feelings about them—because they can!

A general rule of thumb would be to make sure that you do indeed care about this patient with whom you are working so that this attitude forms the basis of your helping behavior. There are a multitude of subtle cues that help patients discern whether you really do care about them. Many clinicians make the fatal mistake of thinking that they can hide negative attitudes toward their patients, only to find that patients can intuit what their clinician really thinks of them. People who are in a vulnerable position can often reliably figure out whether they are safe and cared for with a person who is helping them. Patients who have chronic illnesses requiring them to see many types of clinicians learn the cues that indicate how caring those individual clinicians really are. Patients who have been maltreated in their lives become expert at "reading" their clinicians regarding whether they really care.

Practical involvement with patients, but doing the "least possible" at the same time

Being balanced in compassionate caring for others requires not only caring communication cues but actual practical involvement in the life of the person being helped. This involvement must be guided by avoiding the poles of excessive emotional overinvolvement on one end, which can foster dependency in the patient/client, and complete detachment on the other end, which can nullify helping interventions and even harm the patient/client. Montgomery (1994) explains that in order to avoid becoming overinvolved with a patient, the clinician should do the "least possible" (p. 40) in helping the patient. As uncaring as that sounds at first, the clinician should focus on empowering the patient to mobilize his or her own resources rather than caring for the patient in such a way that the patient becomes too dependent on the clinician. In the long run, this keeps the clinician from undercutting the patient's autonomy, and it also promotes a cost-effective approach rather than over-treating a patient.

How to assess the optimum degree of practical involvement

Discerning what is the optimum degree of practical involvement in helping another person is at times difficult. The extremes of complete detachment and overinvolvement are fairly straightforward. The ground in between those extremes can shift depending on the type of personality the patient/client has and where you are in the helping process with them. People differ in how they interpret your involvement with them. Very independent people who are resistant to being helped will be very sensitive to any loss of control when you help them. You will have to frame your help to such people as being respectful of their need to feel at least somewhat in charge of what is happening to them. In contrast, very dependent personalities will be anxious to rely on you for help, and you will have to set limits on this early in the helping process. The stage of the helping process is also a factor in the balance between detachment and overinvolvement. When people are in crisis, the clinician may be more directive and guiding. People in crisis need a kind of emotional container at the beginning so that they can start to figure out what to do in light of the crisis. As the helping process continues, they may need less emotional containment and direction. The clinician then needs to respond by moving more to the background in helping them.

Every specialty will define practical involvement differently

Every helping profession will have unique ways of defining what is the appropriate degree of practical involvement. Emergency room physicians and nurses will define their practical involvement differently than hospice physicians and nurses. For your clinical role, you must ask yourself what the goal of your help is and how you help people achieve that in an optimum way so that you are neither detached nor overinvolved. This is best done by discussion with similar colleagues of your specialty and can be informed by researching the outcomes of your type of involvement on your patients' lives. Were there things you should have done or facilitated that would have been more helpful to them? Were there things you did in helping them that later created problems for them?

Implications for maintaining balanced C^2

To be in the zone of balanced C^2, it is not enough to have a caring intention toward patients. There must be concrete signs of this in your behavior, your words, and your practical involvement over time with patients. From the patients' perspective, your actions and your expressiveness signal that you are not detached from the patient. On the other hand, the clinician must be careful not to do too much for patients, as this would foster dependency on the clinician and make patients feel like they are not as capable of taking care of themselves. From the clinicians' perspective, if we are detached or negatively oriented toward patients, we will have less fulfillment and have to deal with how our show of helping is actually duplicitous. If we are overinvolved, we risk exhausting ourselves and our loved ones, who have to put up with our overwork and preoccupation with our patients even after work is over; and if we persist in overinvolvement, we risk shortening our careers, which then deprives other patients of what we could have done for them.

BEING ABLE TO CARE FOR A PERSON USING CHALLENGE AND CONFRONTATION

Often, overly sentimentalized caring for others is reduced to simply "being nice." Many clinicians have difficulty challenging their patients because the occurrence of negative reactions by their patients makes clinicians worry that they are not being perceived as caring by their patients. This is worsened when the patient attacks the clinician and accuses the clinician of not really caring. But as Montgomery (1994) explains, confronting a patient can be a way of expressing concern. This may involve being direct, tough, or angry with a patient, as long as it is connected to a desire to express compassion for the patient, not from an abuse of power or a desire to punish. In order to make it possible to care for a patient, it may be necessary to set limits on patient behaviors. Being balanced in compassionate caring for others requires that we jettison an oversentimentalized notion of caring because it constricts the true scope of caring. Not to tell people of their erroneous notions or problematic behaviors is really not caring enough for them to warn them of something that will harm them in the future. It is critical that caring not be identified with "nice" feelings, because there are times when truly caring for someone can cause them some pain, and they may respond in a defensive or hostile way that makes us think we are not really caring about them.

A story about not caring enough to tell me the truth
Some time ago, I was in a well-known church for a service. It was a cool day, and I kept on my navy-blue nylon windbreaker. I was seated on the right side about two thirds of the way from the back of the church. The church was full, which means I was in front of a good number of people. About halfway through the service, I took off my jacket and noticed a kind of flaky white matter coming off of the jacket. I looked at the back of my jacket and found that dried bird droppings had made a large white swath down the back. I was embarrassed that I had not noticed it beforehand and that all those people behind me saw this. But then I thought, how come no one said to me, "Hey mister, you've got bird droppings on your back." On top of that, this was a Christian gathering that is supposedly built on the principle of loving others as Jesus taught. What were those churchgoers thinking? Some of them probably did not think they were obligated to do anything and were thinking, "What an idiot! He doesn't even realize what is on his back." Others were probably embarrassed for me and thought, "That poor man would be so embarrassed to find out he has bird droppings on his back. I would tell him, but I am afraid I would make him feel bad." The reality was that I felt even worse after I had gone through half the service in front of so many people on my side of the church. I would have been less embarrassed, though, if I had known earlier. I was also angry then that no one told me so that I could have been less self-conscious later.

Fear of patient negative reactions, either now or because I never told them the truth
People are often in helping roles because they like to help people, and that often means that they like to make people feel good as a result of that help. They also want to be thought of as helpful, caring people. Consequently, clinicians often filter their feedback to those they

help in order to avoid negative reactions from patients. One helpful statement clinicians can use to guard against this is to say to themselves, "What might my patients be upset with me about if years later they find out something about themselves they did not know and I could have at least brought it to their attention? What if I saw them again years from now and they asked if I had noticed this issue about them, but I did not care enough to tell them?"

Compulsive and sadistic confronting

Some clinicians err on the other extreme, however. They feel it is their duty to confront the patient about everything bluntly right away, with the motive of telling them the truth to help them. There is a compulsive and somewhat sadistic edge to this. They worry less about how the challenging is given and the appropriate timing. In these cases, the patients go away knowing some truth about themselves but are resentful or demoralized because of the way the clinician told them. The helping advice backfires, and some patients become even more resolved to keep continuing their negative health behavior. What happens to a large number of these patients then is that they end up focusing on that resentment or demoralization from how they were told instead of doing something to improve themselves. We have all heard stories about people who said that they changed as a result of some doctor or therapist confronting them in a tough way about some behavior they needed to change. But this "hit them with a hammer" approach does not often work. If it is not based on a true caring intent of the helper, then it can anger or discourage the patient. Furthermore, lots of times patients already know some truth about themselves that needs to be changed. For example, smokers can tell you it is unhealthy for them to smoke, and saying this over and over to a smoker is minimally effective. Instead, the caring helper must gauge when and how to challenge a person and understand how to facilitate behavior change, given the situation and the kind of person that patient is.

Example from doing trauma therapy

There are times in counseling and psychotherapy that the therapist needs to be ready to help a patient go through painful feelings and thoughts. When patients want to avoid an issue in themselves, our challenging them about it can feel uncaring, cruel, and threatening. A classic example is helping a patient with working through past trauma. For many survivors of trauma, it can be important for them to work through issues created by the trauma. They may have spent years trying to deny what has happened until they realize they need to face what happened in order to begin the healing process. Patients can often be resistant to do this work, and the therapist must help them work through this resistance. Then the therapist must help them tolerate often very uncomfortable feelings and troublesome thoughts. A good therapist understands that recovery from a number of problems necessarily involves a patient going through this, and the clinician must be able to continue accompanying the patient until the work is done. A therapist will be tempted to collude in avoiding these painful things or to be persuaded that going through some of this pain is enough and cut the therapy short before the healing is done.

Parenting and the need for the skill of caring confrontation and limit setting

A number of other examples highlight the helper's ability to continue accompanying people as they go through an unavoidable pain. Parenting children requires this ability. It is important that parents help children learn how to tolerate being frustrated with a problem they have and how to solve it themselves. A parent will be tempted just to solve it for the child to help the child be relieved of frustration. Another parenting challenge is what to do when a child has made a mistake and now must work through the consequences of that mistake. This ranges from a child who did not do his or her homework or stole something from a store to an adolescent or adult child who made poor romantic relationship choices or bad financial decisions. Many parents will tell you of the greater difficulties they faced when they spent a lifetime of rescuing their children into adulthood. Parents face the problem of entitlement in raising children in Western societies saturated with the media, and peers constantly giving children the message that they need this or that product and their needs should be met with little delay of gratification. Having all one's needs met soon and having a surplus has created a whole new set of problems now in which children have difficulty enduring long-term hardship or become easily overwhelmed when hardship occurs in their late adolescence and early adulthood. Parents, teachers, and other helping professionals are more and more recognizing the importance of setting limits and challenging self-indulgent materialism in order to raise healthier adults. This requires solid ego strength in parents and helping professionals and an ability not to be deterred by the negative reactions of these children.

Example from care for burn patients

Caring for burn patients provides a very powerful example of the need in some helping situations to hang in with patients when what you are doing to the patients causes them pain. Burn patients are already in great pain, and the treatments cause further pain. Nurses, therapists, and physicians in burn units have to find

a way to rely on the wider perspective that this treatment will ultimately be helpful and not to take personally the pain their patients suffer nor the negative emotional reactions they may have. Seasoned clinicians in burn units have learned how to do this rooted in a deep sense of caring that is not at all the sentimentalized "being nice" popular notion of caring.

Physical therapy and judging how much to put a patient in pain

Clinicians have to have good judgment about how much pain to put a patient through to achieve healing but not so much pain that it would cause unnecessary physical or psychological damage. What physical therapists do, I think, not only offers a concrete example but also a helpful image for other clinicians to use as a guidepost. When physical therapists are working with a patient with restricted range of motion in a joint like a knee or an elbow, they will extend the leg or the arm slightly past the point of pain and then retract the limb. Extending the limb too far too soon will damage the joint. It will also decrease patient trust, and the patient may not want to return. But not extending the limb enough will sabotage the potential healing that could occur.

The way you challenge a patient makes a major difference

With all these examples, it is not sufficient just to have the knowledge and technique of challenging patients or putting them through a necessary painful therapy. The *way* this challenge or painful therapy is done is critical to helping patients tolerate the pain in treatment and begin to heal. Patients might know they need to go through it, but the encouragement, humor, and coaxing of their caregivers helps them have the emotional strength to go through the painful procedure or challenge. Medical patients will tell you of the difference it makes when they have to go through a painful procedure at the hands of someone who has a caring manner and attitude versus someone who is detached or even rough with them. A caring atmosphere helps the patient endure more pain.

Implications for maintaining balanced C²
Being able to care for a patient using challenge and confrontation is one of the most important skills for being in the zone of balanced C². From the perspective of patients, not challenging patients about their negative health behaviors or other issues would be a sign of disengagement from them and not really caring enough about them to tell them the truth about themselves and what they are doing. If we are fearful of challenging them, we are not doing what is best for their well-being. On the other hand, if challenging or confronting is done out of a desire to punish or shame a patient and not a caring motivation, then this will have negative outcomes for the patient. From the perspective of clinicians, if we are fearful of challenging our patients because of their negative reactions, we probably do not have a solid understanding of compassionate caring. Our neutrality and passivity with patients suggest a failure in ourselves to be fully engaged with what healing requires. Our outcomes will be poorer and also suggest that we are not fully engaged with our professional responsibility.

BALANCE BETWEEN OTHER-CARE AND SELF-CARE

What kind of self are you giving your patient?
Caring for others requires the use of yourself to help another who is suffering or in some

difficulty. The work of caring requires emotional, mental, and spiritual energy. While there can be some type of reward either in terms of personal fulfillment, professional satisfaction, or monetary return, these come as a consequence of the work and do not change the fact that you have to invest yourself in the work of helping another person initially, and you may be affected by what is happening in the person you are helping. Elisabeth Kubler-Ross was a physician who did pioneering work on death and dying. Because of the very hard work she did, she has a great deal of credibility when she speaks of the importance of self-care:

> Healers must understand that love does not only mean love for others; it also means love for oneself. We must be aware of our limits and know when it is necessary to nurture ourselves. Each of us has different ways of nurturing. Some people need people; others need to be alone. We must strike a balance between what we do for ourselves and what we do for others, learning to receive as well as to give. For if we only give and never receive, we get out of balance. (Kubler-Ross, 1976)

Because we are the instruments of healing, if we are overly depleted, exhausted, bitter, or impaired, then we are not able to give our best to the patient. If we have not taken care of ourselves, then we run the risk of that interfering with our cognitive ability to think through a case, the emotional ability to maintain composure, and the physical ability to do what is necessary (e.g., spending hours doing surgery). We run the risk of not giving our patients the best that we can as well as harming them if we do not take care of ourselves. This is not only taking care of ourselves for what we need to do in the short-term, as in tomorrow or next week, but also taking care of ourselves so that we can give what we can as long as we can to our patients. That self-care also means taking care of ourselves in a holistic way in terms of our physical, psychological, and spiritual or existential needs.

Clinicians take better care of patients when they take care of themselves

When clinicians take care of their own health better, they are not only keeping themselves fit for very hard work but also improving the quality of the health care they provide. The obvious reason is that clinicians who have good self-care in terms of mind, body, and spirit are more able to notice, assess, and respond to the needs of their patients. What clinicians do in their personal lives in terms of health behaviors affects their patient care. Physicians' personal health practices in terms of smoking, alcohol use, eating more fruits and vegetables, and being physically active are often associated with counseling their patients to improve in these areas as well (Frank, Segura, Shen, & Oberg, 2010; Lewis, Clancy, Leake, & Schwartz, 1991).

Physicians tend not to assess themselves accurately

Physicians tend not to be very accurate at assessing their own well-being and their level of distress. In a study with 1,150 surgeons, Shanafelt et al. (2014) found that 89.2% of them thought that their well-being was at the same level or above other physicians. Only 13.6% thought that their well-being was average or below average compared to other physicians. The study revealed how poor surgeons' ability to subjectively assess their own well-being is. When the bottom 30% in terms of well-being were asked about how they would rate their own well-being, the majority, 70.5%, believed they were average or above-average. In fact, 24% of that these physicians thought they

were above average in well-being compared to other surgeons! Interestingly, of the top 30% in well-being, only 13.6% thought that their well-being was average or above average. The bottom line is that it appears clinicians are not good at self-assessing their well-being. But Shanafelt et al. (2014) did find that when those surgeons did an online self-assessment tool, 49.5% found the feedback somewhat to extremely helpful, and 46.5% said they were considering making at least one change in the areas of work–life balance, reducing fatigue, reducing burnout, or improving career satisfaction. This is hopeful but also disturbing, because half of these surgeons were not able to perceive benefit from this self-assessment or willing to make a change. However, the researchers did find a dose-response relationship with the feedback; those who were told that their well-being was lower than others were more willing to make a change.

Self-compassion is an important part of self-care

The ability to be compassionate toward oneself is an important part of self-care. Kristen Neff (2003) and others have done pioneering research on self-compassion. *She has found that the ability to have a self-compassionate frame of mind consists of the dynamic interaction of three components* (Neff, 2003).

Self-kindness versus self-judgment

First, one is able to be kind and understanding with oneself rather than judging oneself in a harsh critical way. With a personal flaw or inadequacy, one treats oneself in more of a supportive and benevolent way, rather than attacking and berating oneself. When life is difficult, self-compassionate people are able to soothe and comfort themselves. In being compassionate to oneself, it is not enough simply to refrain from being critical of oneself; one must also proactively be kind to oneself as well in order to comfort and soothe oneself.

Common humanity versus isolation

Second, one views oneself as part of a common humanity rather than being isolated from the rest of humanity. Self-compassionate individuals have the sense that all humans can make mistakes and are imperfect. When there are difficulties in life, they feel more connected to others because they are aware that all humans go through things like this. In examining their own flaws, there is the sense that this is part of the human condition. A person who is self-compassionate refrains from feeling isolated and goes the extra step of actively putting his or her imperfections in the context of the common human experience.

Mindfulness versus overidentification

Third, one is able to be mindful of one's experience—that is, aware and nonjudgmental of one's experience—rather than overidentifying with what is happening in one's experience. Mindfulness is the ability to be aware of one's present experience in a balanced way so that one is not ruminating on it but not ignoring it either (Brown & Ryan, 2003; Neff & Pommier, 2013). One can step out of one's experience and look at it with objectivity. Neff explains that mindfulness is a way of helping a person not overidentify with his or her own pain. "Overidentification" is when "one tends to ruminate and obsessively fixate on negative self-relevant thoughts and emotions, so that the mental space needed to be self-aware and self-compassionate is constricted" (Neff & Pommier, 2013, p. 161). This component requires not only that one not get carried away with the negative thoughts and feelings, but also that one be mindfully aware of what is occurring instead of ignoring or repressing what happened.

Self-compassion does not mean coddling or excusing oneself from responsibility

Overall, self-compassion is needed both when one is experiencing painful or difficult aspects of the external circumstances of one's life and when one is suffering from dealing with one's own inadequacies, mistakes, and failures (Neff & Pommier, 2013). Both of these types of situations are regular parts of being a helping professional. Sometimes the idea of self-compassion may come across negatively to health care professionals, especially in a medical culture that can be very critical, harsh, and berating. Self-compassion, however, should not be understood as coddling oneself or excusing oneself for responsibility for what one does or does not do. You can be a self-compassionate person who strives for excellence and quality in all that you do. It means, however, that you know that obsessively berating yourself really does not help your performance. In fact, it could interfere because you are dwelling on what went wrong and sapping your energy as you wallow in ongoing feelings of discouragement. Nor should it be understood as a Pollyannaish denial of the serious things that have occurred. It is, rather, a way of being in which one does the best that one can, but when things go badly, a self-compassionate approach works better for helping professionals than being self-destructive. This keeps a helping professional going in the quest to help other people far better than self-immolation.

Positive benefits of being self-compassionate

People who have high self-compassion tend to be have a higher satisfaction with life and to be less anxious and depressed. They tend to be more socially connected, less perfectionistic, and less self-critical. Self-compassion is also associated with being more emotionally intelligent and having better emotional regulation. Self-compassion helps a person regulate negative emotions and see them with clarity, allowing the person to work through them better than if he or she were not self-compassionate. Neff has argued that self-compassion appears to be an adaptive process that increases well-being and psychological resiliency. Instead of avoiding painful and distressing feelings or becoming overwhelmed by them, a person with self-compassion transforms the negative feelings to a more positive state. Self-compassionate people are able to clearly examine the situation and either take actions that respond appropriately and effectively to the situation or change themselves. They do not tend to suppress their emotions nor do they get carried away by them; instead, they have a balanced way of processing their emotions. (Neff, 2003)

Being more self-compassionate is related to being more compassionate to others

Many people commonly consider that being compassionate to yourself would undercut being compassionate to other people. The reality is that self-compassion is actually related to a greater other-focused concern. Neff and Pommier (2013) found that the greater the ability to be self-compassionate, the more likely people are to have more compassion for humanity, more empathic concern and perspective taking, greater altruism, and more forgiveness. They were also less likely to feel personal distress when encountering the suffering of others.

Self-compassion does not mean being passive or complacent about oneself

It is important to note, however, that self-compassion does not mean that one is passive and complacent about oneself, accepting lower standards for him- or herself. Instead of ignoring or disregarding their failings, the mindfulness aspect of self-compassion encourages individuals to see their failings clearly. It entails wanting to be healthy and having a better well-being, which means self-compassionate people will perceive and work to change behaviors that are harmful or unproductive (Neff, 2003).

Self-compassion is not the same as self-esteem

Self-compassion has some overlap with self-esteem but does not have some of the negative aspects of self-esteem. Self-compassion is moderately correlated with self-esteem, but research has found that these two constructs are measuring different psychological phenomena. People with high self-esteem would have some similarity with people high in self-compassion because people who have a higher sense of self-worth would tend not to be overly critical of themselves, feel isolated, or feel overidentified with their negative feelings. But one of the differences is that self-esteem has some correlation with narcissism, while self-compassion is not significantly correlated with narcissism. A number of people who have very high self-esteem can also be narcissistic or see themselves as better than others. People high in self-compassion would not be narcissistic or feel superior to others. People who are high in self-compassion would have a sense of self-worth that is based on being their authentic self, in contrast to feeling that self-worth is contingent on meeting certain standards or, for some people, based on subtle downward comparisons with others (Neff &Vonk, 2009). High self-compassion predicts feeling happy, optimistic, and positive more than self-esteem alone does. Self-compassion is related to more stable feelings of self-worth than self-esteem and fluctuates less relative to external circumstances. Neff and Vonk (2009) found that

> *for the majority of outcomes ... self-esteem offered no benefits whatsoever over and above those attributable to self-compassion. Thus, the degree to which people feel kind, connected, and centered when confronting personal adequacies may be more important for a healthy sense of self than merely judging oneself positively.* (p. 39)

People with self-compassion tend to have a sense of security and calmness when dealing with situations that might otherwise make them feel inadequate. Self-compassion is less contingent on receiving social approval, having successful performances, or being physically attractive. People high in self-compassion are able to embrace their weakness and their strengths without a need to defend their egos; they are able to admit any mistakes or shortcomings without defensiveness. Both self-esteem and self-compassion are linked to positive emotional states. But "self-esteem tends to be felt when things go right and self-compassion is more relevant when things go wrong" (Neff &Vonk, 2009, p. 42).

The importance of personal relationships in self-care

Self-care includes taking care of one's personal life, especially in terms of one's relationships. One's close relationships provide support for the work, but the work also affects one's relationships. Clinicians who practice good self-care realize this dynamic and know they must devote significant time and energy to having healthy and mutually satisfying relationships with their loved ones. When things are not going well in their personal relationships with one's spouse, partner, family, and any significant others, this will affect the well-being of clinicians as well as their patients. There may be a way in which clinicians take for granted the importance of the close personal relationships and do no invest in caring for these. They may not realize how much their spouse or partner, for example, does for them to enable their clinical careers. When both spouses or partners are involved in work and family, there is a delicate balance of time management and emotional investment that must be worked out. Clinicians may also not realize how the work exacts an emotional toll on them as well as on their close loved ones. If clinicians are chronically overworked, constantly distracted by work and patient issues, and always fatigued and irritable, this is risky not only for them but also for their loved ones. The loved ones pay a price also for the work that clinicians do. One's personal relationships are part of oneself, and this means self-care includes taking care of one's closest relationships.

The importance of leisure that gives physicians a different mental focus

Zwack and Schweitzer (2013) researched the resilience strategies of experienced physicians by interviewing 200 German physicians from a variety of practice settings, positions, and specialties who had low burnout scores on the Maslach Burnout Inventory. The sample included general practitioners, psychiatrists, and surgeons as well as other specialties. Among the resilience strategies they shared, leisure-time activity was emphasized by 79%. As a means to relieve stress, researchers found that while leisure activities such as sports relieved tension, what was also important was providing a different mental focus. Cultural activities provided a source of aesthetic pleasure and harmony, which was helpful. Having a serious hobby that they made special time for allowed physicians to feel a sense of inner freedom and joy independent of work.

Implications for maintaining balanced C²

Clinicians in the compassion mindset must use their whole selves to care for patients well. They need to use their intellect, cognitive processing skills, emotional intelligence, and physical conditioning to do this difficult work. They also rely on their worldview and their philosophy of life as they accompany patients through life-changing and life-threatening situations. This means that any problems in any of those areas will affect the clinician, who is the instrument of healing for patients. When all those areas are healthy and cared for, the clinician will be able to think, feel, and act optimally in caring for patients. Being balanced in one's life by taking care of oneself is essential for optimum patient care. From the clinician's perspective, good self-care enables him or her to be resilient and to do this work for a long time. Without it, a clinician will not be able to maintain him- or herself in this work. With good self-care, the clinician is able to be in the zone of balanced C², which will provide the basis for well-being and a fulfilling career.

ENERGY DEVOTED TO SELF-REFLECTION AND ANALYZING HELPING INTERACTIONS

In order to maximize therapeutic effectiveness with patients, clinicians must develop a practice of regular self-reflection and analyzing what is occurring in their interactions with patients. This enables us to maintain our ability to perceive our patients' perspectives, their suffering, and also how we as clinicians are helping or hindering the healing process. Furthermore, having a regular practice of, for example, always asking ourselves, "What did this patient teach me?" helps us continue to grow in our clinical judgment and wisdom as we progress through our clinical careers.

Clinicians paradoxically flee their emotions yet feel a desire to process them

In my experience, the medical culture has a paradoxical view of clinicians' emotions in treating patients. On one hand, clinicians often are promoting an emotional detachment in the culture, what is called "detached concern." They may engage in emotionally self-protective maneuvers such as negative humor or maintaining an appearance of self-assured brashness when it comes to difficult patient situations. On the other hand, clinicians informally want to tell stories about their experiences and what they went through. There is both implicitly and explicitly a desire to process the experience emotionally and seek support. They may deny that they are doing any "emotional processing" because of how this seems weak or soft. But I have seen on numerous occasions how even the toughest physicians wanted to talk about what just happened to them. The problem is that they may cut this off by making a cliché comment ("That's health care for you!"), blaming some favorite scapegoat, or making a disparaging remark about the patient. While this is understandable, there is a desire to process the experience as a way to get perspective on it, learn from it, and let it go. The problem is that physician and other clinician training does not typically model this well or train clinicians how to do this better for themselves and how to respond to each other more effectively. Healthy and effective organizations will find ways to promote effective emotional processing of difficult patient experiences, both informally and formally.

Individual self-reflection and analysis of helping interactions

Self-awareness is critically important in patient care because the clinician him- or herself is the instrument of healing with others. Self-reflective practices enable the healer to recognize and deal with any personal issues or needs that might be affecting one's perception of one's patient and the healer's motivation in helping that person. Being aware, for example, of what is leading you to be overinvolved with one patient and detached with another patient can be very important because of the potential damage each of these reactions can have on the patient. The intent to care for someone is a necessary but not a sufficient condition for actual caring to occur. It is easy to pick out the impersonal or the rude helper. But there are many times clients or patients are harmed because of the unconscious needs or problems of helpers. Balanced and caring helpers have done and continue to do work on exploring the unhealthy aspects of their personalities that contaminate their caring for others. Reflection and analysis of helping interactions can be necessary for effective healing to take place. Analyzing helping interactions can help healers understand covert or implicit factors that are important for healing to occur. Like detective work, analysis of the helping interactions can provide clues that help with the overall healing goal. It might have to do with relational factors that are interfering with the treatment process, such as multicultural factors. It might have to do with a unique presentation of a patient's problem that requires further analysis for more accurate diagnosis or better treatment.

Individual practices to promote self-reflection and analysis of helping interactions

There are various methods that assist helpers with self-reflection and analysis of helping interactions. These include personal reading, supervision, peer consultation, journaling, continuing education, and the use of personal psychotherapy. Medical culture typically does not promote a practice of self-reflection because time feels limited and self-reflection is often perceived as something to be indulged periodically and a luxury. Also, with the denigration of emotions, the subjective, and the psychological in medical culture, many clinicians come to think that it is not necessary to do this type of inner work. Clinicians may not even be aware that it is a useful practice. When it does not have a priority in training and because there are few positive examples of it, it is quite possible clinicians just never realized how beneficial it might be. When they experience how much they can learn by examining an individual case in depth or by meeting with a clinical supervisor to process strong emotional reactions they had with a patient, clinicians become aware of dynamics they did not realize were occurring in themselves and in the patient–clinician interaction. It is hard to know what you do not know. For many clinicians, it is an enlightening experience to become aware of these underlying dynamics, and many find that it makes their work with patients more effective, efficient, and satisfying. It can also be helpful to clinicians to participate in groups with colleagues that facilitate self-reflection and analyzing interactions with patients. Two examples common in health care organizations are Schwartz Rounds and

Balint groups. (These are described in detail in chapter 15.)

Research on the benefits of self-awareness practices

Nedrow, Steckler, and Hardman (2013) argue that in order to prevent burnout, physicians must increase their resilience by engaging in practical mental training. Creating thought patterns that cultivate physician resilience entails regular practice similar to physical strength training.

> Lifting weights requires learning techniques and proper form to build capacity and avoid injury. Failing to maintain that fitness can cause the muscles to atrophy. In the case of our minds, developing health patterns of thinking also requires regular and skillful workouts, or the mind reverts to its default mental and emotional states. (Nedrow et al., 2013, p. 28)

Nedrow et al. (2013) conclude that the key difference between those who suffer from burnout and those who have a healthy engagement in the practice of medicine is physicians' ability to have self-awareness of when their spirit in practicing medicine is weakening and to take steps to change this. Nedrow et al. advocate that resiliency training needs to occur in medical training. They suggest that resiliency consists of a triad of beliefs one uses to deal with the challenges within this profession. The first is engaging in self-care practices with regard to rest, nutrition, physical health, and social needs. The second is being grounded in one's values that give a sense of meaning or purpose in this profession and to align one's practice and all one's actions with that. Third, one needs a way to regularly have insight into one's behavior and underlying motivations. This is connected to practices that cultivate self-awareness on a regular basis. Not only does this apply to the clinician's life, it can also be applied more widely to gaining insight into others.

Research on the benefits of individual and group reflection

In terms of factors that facilitate compassion, research has found that individual reflection as well as reflection with peers helped resident physicians appreciate patients' perspectives, develop their confidence in caring for patients, and maintain compassion. Discussing this with peers provided emotional support and opportunities to realign with their personal values such as caring for vulnerable and underserved populations. The ability to maintain a balance between work and personal time has also been reported to be important to the ability to maintain compassion. Role models were also noted to help residents learn the ability to maintain work–life balance and to provide compassionate care to patients (Anandarajah & Smith, 2009).

Implications for maintaining balanced C^2

Practices to promote self-awareness and analysis of interactions with patients is what helps clinicians know whether they are in the zone of balanced C^2. To know if they are detached from a patient, unconsciously negative toward a patient, or overinvolved with a patient, clinicians need habitual practices to be able to notice this and to figure out why this is occurring. It is a good idea not only to do this regularly (e.g., weekly, monthly, after three months of working with a patient), but also to know how to do this very quickly after they become aware of some issue in themselves or in their patient interactions. Patients benefit because clinicians who are in the zone of balanced C^2 are giving patients the optimum effective level of emotional engagement.

Clinicians benefit because they have an ongoing way of assessing if they are out of that balanced C^2 zone and thus at risk for increased stress and burnout.

WAYS OF DEALING WITH EFFECTS OF WORKING WITH INDIVIDUALS WITH SEVERE PROBLEMS

To maintain balanced C^2, clinicians must have the skills to deal with how the most difficult or emotionally challenging patients will affect them personally. All patient care might be considered potentially stressful, but what I am focusing on here is working with patients with severe problems. This might include patients who are dying, severely chronically ill patients, burn patients, trauma patients, and patients who are the victims of terrible tragedies and violence. Other types of patients that are particularly emotionally difficult are patients who are suicidal, patient with personality disorders, patients who are perpetrators, and patients who have dementia. There are certainly other examples. The only commonality among these is that patients with these conditions can deeply affect clinicians. This is what is termed vicarious traumatization or compassion fatigue.

Each specialty and/or clinical role requires unique protective skills

Emotional detachment in a clinician is like a soccer player trying to play in a medieval knight's armor. It encumbers the clinician and interferes with effective helping. While the armor is protective, the more armor one has, the more one's maneuverability decreases. If a helper puts more energy into protecting him- or herself, then he or she will have less energy attending to the person needing help. With too much armor, the

clinician is bogged down under the weight of the protective gear. Overly defended clinicians tend to have less energy to do their clinical work, and the work itself is not satisfying. To stay with this analogy a bit, different sports require different types of protective gear. For football, various body pads, a helmet, and a mouthpiece are recommended. In fencing, one wears a padded jacket and a wire mesh mask. Shin guards are used in soccer but nothing else. Like different sports, different clinical professions also vary in terms of protective requirements. A therapist prepares differently to work with a psychotic patient in contrast to preparing to work with a client with career concerns. A nursing home worker adjusts a certain way when working with a patient with late-stage Alzheimer's compare to a patient who is seriously paralyzed. Physicians or nurses who treat burn patients must do different things to protect themselves from the emotional intensity of the work than when they work with less emotionally intense situations such as treating common ear infections. The key is to maximize maneuverability while protecting yourself. Each specialty and patient situation requires that those clinicians figure out what are the particular protective requirements for that specific type of work.

Adaptation process to becoming comfortable working with people in pain or distress

Learning to deal with the pain and suffering we cause patients

In treating patients, we often add pain and suffering to their illness. Sometimes the pain we cause is a necessary part of the process of healing. Examples are radiation and chemotherapy in cancer treatment, debridement of wounds, and pain as part of physical therapy. Other times the pain we cause is accidental or unintentional. We may prescribe a medication to which the patient has a severe allergic response or which cause severe side effects. As clinicians, we learn how to keep treating the patient in spite of the fact that we hurt them at times.

Case example from infra-low frequency neurofeedback therapy

One of the therapies I use with patients is infra-low-frequency neurofeedback, which is used to help with all sorts of conditions and many types of brain dysfunctions and instabilities, such as headaches, seizures, ADHD, anxiety, brain damage, and pain (Othmer & Othmer, 2016). In the method I use, the electroencephalogram (EEG) is used to train the brain toward optimum functioning. In the first phase of treatment, the clinician has to determine the optimum brain frequency to treat the patient. This is done systematically to find the frequency at which the patient feels alert, engaged, and fairly pleasant in the brain training. There are times when it is difficult to find this training frequency, which can create transient side effects. A patient can feel quite irritable, experience odd pains, become very sluggish, or experience other negative effects. The clinician is trained to interpret these side effects in terms of what training frequency the brain prefers. Within several sessions, this optimum training frequency is found, much like an optometrist has a patient look through a variety of lenses to determine the best one for clear sight.

Story of a patient telling me not to give up because of her pain

Years ago, there was one patient who was using neurofeedback for a particular type of pain. She had experienced relief using neurofeedback in the past, had stopped treatment, but then the pain returned and she sought treatment again. But the optimum frequency for her brain training had changed, and I spent more than the average number of sessions trying to find it. As I kept trying to find it, I became very discouraged, especially as I caused her uncomfortable side effects. Most of the time, I have no difficulty persevering, knowing that I will likely find the right frequency and appropriate brain sites for the electrodes in a couple of sessions. But this time I had lost my confidence after many sessions. One day, I told her that I did not think I could find the right frequency and that we should stop. It turned out to be a day in which the patient taught me something. She said something to the effect of, "Dr. Vachon, you have got to keep trying. You can't give up because I feel bad, because if you give up, we won't find what helps me feel better." Her earnest plea jolted me out of my discouragement. We kept going and eventually found the brain frequency that helped her.

The ability to cut people and inflict pain without hesitation

Physicians and all types of clinicians learn this emotional ability to keep treating patients even though they might increase their patient's pain and suffering in the course of the treatment. I have worked with residents who became overwhelmed by inadvertently harming a patient with a particular drug and became afraid to try another drug. It is an important part of the learning process for new physicians. On one hand, they need to know how what they do can really harm a patient. Their actions have tremendous consequences, and they learn to respect the power of the drugs as well as how vigilant and knowledgeable they need to be in treating patients. On the other hand, they need to know that they must find the courage and determination to keep trying despite setbacks, despite the pain they might have caused along the way. When I have asked clinicians about how they learned how to do this, after many years they cannot remember. It becomes basic to their practice. Of course, you have to keep going in treating. They do not realize how they have surpassed what nonclinical people can do. Using surgeons as one example, most people are not able to cut open another person's body and work inside it. This is part of the awesome psychological process that happens in clinicians through their initiation into their professions. Patients count on this emotional and cognitive ability in their clinicians not to be deterred by inflicting pain so that the patients might gain some relief and healing.

Being overwhelmed by patient pain versus not noticing patient pain anymore

There are two emotional poles the clinician has to navigate between. We have already discussed one, which is becoming overwhelmed and paralyzed after causing pain in a patient. The other pole is not noticing or acknowledging that the treatment has inflicted pain on the patient. Patients understand that pain can be part of the healing process. But if clinicians become so hardened that they do not prepare patients for it or acknowledge it when it happens, they risk alienating their patients and making them lose trust that their clinician really cares about them. They also risk not noticing what their patients need from them. One study found that even though physicians and nurses worked very closely with burn patients, they were not as likely to recognize the patient's pain cues compared to social workers who had less time with the patients (Baer, Davitz, & Lieb, 1970). Other studies have also documented that clinicians can

become less sensitive to their patients' pain the more experienced they become (Nagy, 1999).

Example from burn patients and wound debridement

There is very little in the research literature on how clinicians learn to make the psychological shift that in caring for patients they may also at time be inflicting pain. But there are a number of ways this shift can occur as well as how clinicians reconcile this for themselves. The little research I have found is on how health care staffs cope with inflicting pain on burn patients. Nagy (1999) did a qualitative study to learn what strategies 32 burn unit nurses use when they have to do procedures that inflict pain on adult and child patients. Patients describe the pain associated with wound debridement as worse than the burn itself (Perry, Heidrich, &Ramos 1981; Choiniere, Melzack, Rondeau, Girrard, & Paquin, 1989), and it is nurses who are most involved with doing this procedure. Nagy found that nurses had four categories of coping strategies: distancing from the patient's pain, engaging with the patient's pain, social support, and reconstructing the core role of being a nurse.

Distancing coping method

The distancing coping method was not so much an attempt to deny that the pain was occurring but to lessen the impact by adopting an emotional or physical distancing strategy. There were five types of strategies, and 94% of nurses used this at some point in their work: (a) "emotionally detaching oneself by switching off, tuning out, not dwelling on the pain, accepting the inevitability of pain, deliberately trying not to think of the patient as a person or by focusing attention on the procedure rather than the patient and the pain" (Nagy, 1999, p. 1429); (b) producing a kind of physical distance from the patient's pain by taking breaks from the procedure or the unit, or focusing one's attention on the long-term benefit of doing the procedure instead of the pain itself; (c) focusing on the long-term benefit of treatment rather than the pain itself; (d) decreasing feeling emotionally overwhelmed in doing the procedure by structuring it by, for example, maintaining active control of the situation rather than allowing the patient to have control; and (e) avoiding expressing negative feelings during the pain-inflicting situation but later "acting out" one's negative emotions by dumping them on colleagues, friends, or family. Sometimes this strategy becomes a way of obtaining social support and also a way of pulling themselves together emotionally.

Engaging coping method

The engaging coping method consisted of seven strategies in which one focused attention on the patient's pain rather than distancing; this was used by 59% of the nurses. These strategies include (a) preparing the patient for the painful situations by explaining to the patient each time why the nurse had to do something painful, which helps the patient understand and accept it, which in turn was a way that nurses could remind themselves why they were doing this; (b) working on improving one's knowledge and technical competence so that the situation was managed as effectively and efficiently as possible; (c) nurses sharing control with patients in managing the painful event by letting a patient pace the procedure and responding to patient requests for pain relief; (d) being able to use all possible procedures to relieve or reduce pain; (e) offering emotional support to the patient through soothing talk or cuddling children, which gives nurses a way to feel that they were helping patients and relieve the guilt associated with feeling helpless; (f) making the patient feel

physically comfortable after the procedure, which is a way of helping the patient and family members feel better emotionally; and (g) nurses making sure that they spend time doing non-painful activities with patients so that nurses are not only associated with inflicting pain.

Seeking social support

Seeking social support was a strategy used by 59% of nurses, in which they sought practical help, advice, debriefing, emotional help, or social companionship. This tended to be done mostly with colleagues but also families, friends, and counselors. It was noted that nurses expressed a great need for social support but that this was not always available.

Reconstructing the core role of being a nurse

Finally, 19% of nurses used a coping method that Nagy (1999) calls core role reconstruction. In having to inflict pain on a patient for a necessary procedure for burn rehabilitation, nurses have to reconcile their core image of self as caring for the patient yet having to cause extreme pain to the patient. This is an active reflective process of thinking through how doing painful procedures is necessary to healing the patient. Nagy (1999) references a nurse's comment as illustrating this:

> If you don't cause them that pain and if you don't do their dressings they're going to get septic and they could die on you, and that isn't doing the job; that's not looking after or caring for a person. ... So not putting up with it or not doing a proper job because you're upset or you can't cope, then you shouldn't be there. (p. 1431)

The engaging method as better than the other methods

Other clinicians would very likely have similar coping methods in dealing with times they have to cause their patient pain or suffering in the course of treatment. What is interesting from a compassion science point of view is how nurses felt the engaging method helped them increase the satisfaction they received from doing this type of work. Distancing provided self-protection from being emotionally overwhelmed and also gave nurses a sense of pride that they could do this work and be able to keep working there. But Nagy (1999) points out that there were costs to the distancing strategies. First, nurses who overuse this strategy can become less sensitive to patient pain and thus become less concerned about and aware of the pain they inflict in these procedures. Distancing can eventually desensitize clinicians to the needs of the patient. Second, distancing can create a cognitive dissonance within clinicians. On one hand, some nurses in this study felt a sense of accomplishment that they could control their emotions in this difficult work, but on the other hand, they were concerned about becoming emotionally hardened and calloused to what patients are experiencing. The engaging method is what allows nurses to match having to do difficult things to patients with their image of themselves as competent, caring clinicians. In turn, Nagy noted that some nurses found that the engaging method made the work seem easier and more successful because patients tended to be more cooperative; this in turn resulted in more satisfaction for those nurses.

Being "calloused" is actually a good thing

When a person first begins carpentry, there is a conditioning and seasoning process as he or she gains increasing skill working with wood. Besides the knowledge base that grows with experience, there is also a change in the woodworker's body as he or she adapts to working with wood and various tools. Most apparent is the development of callouses and specific muscles. At the beginning, it is easy to get splinters. But the body develops callouses over time that act as a protective skin layer, which in turns allows a person to work more easily with wood. If you take up carpentry, the first weeks getting back into shape sawing and manipulating the wood will transition to less muscle soreness and increased endurance to work whole days. It is still work; it takes energy and you may well be quite tired at the end of the day. But someone of comparable physical build and age could not keep up with you without that adapting process you have been undergoing. Simply put, you're in shape now and they are not. The same is true in the helping professions. There is an adaptation process for every type of helping work, enabling you to endure emotionally, physically, and intellectually all that is required for the type of work you are doing. We should probably change the negative connotation of being "calloused." Just as having callouses allows a carpenter to more fully engage the wood, so do we as clinicians develop psychological callouses to enable us to more fully engage our emotionally challenging patients.

Harper's stages of adaptation in working with patients who are dying

There is a lot of anecdotal information on how helping professionals adapt to a particular type of clinical work, but there is not much research literature on the topic. Below is one example from Bernice Harper's (1994) work on the adaptation process to working with people who are dying; it comes from her book *Death: The Coping Mechanism of the Health Professional*. Harper discovered stages in the adaptation process to become comfortable in working with patients who are facing death and dying.

Stage 1 is intellectualization, when the focus is on professional knowledge, understanding the new setting, becoming familiar with the way things are done, and providing tangible services. There is some anxiety and discomfort. In stage 2, called emotional survival, the health professional has more emotional involvement, often overidentifying with the patient's situation, and intellectualizes less. There is increased sadness, frustration, and guilt with more discomfort as he or she experiences the work as somewhat traumatic. Stage 3 is called depression; in this stage the health professional is coming to grips more with how he or she feels about death. There is a sense of mourning and grieving in this stage. Stage 4 is emotional arrival, in which the health professional has developed the ability to work with the dying patients and the families. There is a sense of competence, less concern about one's own death, and increased comfort doing this work. Stage 5 is the final stage, called deep compassion. Here the health professional gains self-awareness, self-actualization, professional satisfaction, and increased comfort doing this work. There is an increased ability to give oneself in the work, to accept death and loss, and to give self-respect and dignity to the person who is dying.

Knowledge of techniques to deal with compassion fatigue/vicarious traumatization

Clinicians need to be aware of how working with patients with severe trauma can have secondary effects on the psychological state of the clinician, in which the clinician will internalize the symptoms of the patients almost in mirrorlike fashion. This phenomenon has been called vicarious traumatization and secondary traumatic stress because it is as if the trauma the patient has experienced traumatizes the clinician who is working with that patient. *Compassion fatigue* is the common term used to describe this among all types of helping professionals who work with people who have experienced trauma (Figley, 1995). As Baranowsky (2002) explains,

> *compassion fatigue occurs when an individual becomes secondarily traumatized during exposure to traumatic incidents directly experienced and relayed by another. The reverberation of another's trauma in a caregiver's life can take the form of PTSD-like symptomatology that mimics the other's disturbances. … In addition, vulnerability to compassion fatigue becomes heightened when, caregivers are overwhelmed by unsupportive or emotionally toxic environments. (as cited in Figley, 2002, p. 157)*

There is a large body of research literature on compassion fatigue and interventions to prevent and treat it, which is beyond the scope of this book. For the purposes of this book, I will provide the overall model of how compassion fatigue relates to other concepts such as burnout and compassion satisfaction using Stamm's (2010) Professional Quality of Life Scale. I will then give an overview of common interventions used to help clinicians who experience this followed by an example of a very good study on treating these symptoms. I will then provide some concerns that have been raised about whether we should use this term *compassion fatigue* at all and substitute another term such as *empathic distress fatigue* in light of what the science of compassion has discovered about the true nature of compassion.

Stamm's Professional Quality of Life Scale of compassion satisfaction and fatigue

Stamm (2010) defines professional quality of life as "the quality one feels in relation to their work as a helper" (p. 8). Professional quality of life consists of compassion satisfaction and compassion fatigue, referring to the positive and negative experiences helpers have, especially when working with patients or clients who have experienced very stressful events or trauma. *Compassion satisfaction* refers to the positive aspects a clinician derives from helping others, feeling positively about colleagues, or one's ability to contribute to one's work setting or the greater good of society. *Compassion fatigue* refers to the negative aspects in the experience of helping others. Compassion fatigue consists of two parts: *burnout* and *secondary trauma*. *Burnout* refers to when helpers feel hopeless and have difficulties dealing with their work or doing their job effectively. In Stamm's model, burnout is characterized by feeling that one's efforts make no difference in outcome. The negative feelings associated with burnout usually have a gradual onset and are associated with work environments that have very high workloads or are nonsupportive. *Secondary traumatic stress* refers to the secondary exposure helpers experience when they work with people who have experienced extremely stressful or traumatic events. Like the posttraumatic stress disorder that people who have been exposed to trauma can have, helpers who work with such individuals can develop secondary traumatic stress

symptoms of feeling afraid, having difficulty sleeping, having intrusive images of what a patient or client experienced, or avoiding things that remind them of a patient's traumatic event. It has also been called vicarious traumatization (Pearlman & Saakvitne, 1995). The Professional Quality of Life Scale, developed by Stamm and her colleagues, measures the level of positive and negative effects helpers have experienced in their work.

Slatten, Carson, and Carson (2011) note that clinicians who are newer to this type of work are more susceptible to secondary traumatic stress. They recommend that newer clinicians have mentors or supervisors as an important way to teach them about what secondary traumatic stress is, how to lower the risk of this happening to them, and what to do if they do experience it. Some general things that can help include balancing a clinician's case mix so that he or she does not have too many severely traumatized patients at one time. Getting more training in stress management and coping techniques is helpful, as well as having colleagues who can be actively supportive and guide each other in managing this when it occurs (Slatten et al., 2011). As I will explain further below, having an accurate understanding of compassion will likely be the best protection or buffer for secondary traumatic stress. Below is a study that provides other examples of techniques to buffer compassion fatigue. Note how the results of this study connect well with the science of compassionate caring as presented in this book in terms of the ways the compassion mindset can itself be protective of the clinician. There is a great deal of research on this particular issue, and more is needed. In your particular specialty or clinical role, there is likely already an accumulated wisdom about how this might be done.

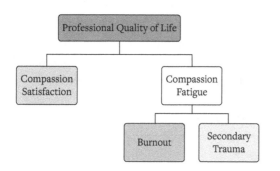

FIGURE 13.1 Diagram of Professional Quality of Life Scale (Stamm, 2010, p. 8).

Study of how exemplary oncology nurses avoid compassion fatigue

In a qualitative study of a sample of exemplary oncology nurses, Perry (2008) examined how they seemed able to avoid compassion fatigue. Three common themes emerged. *First, the nurses had established an emotional connection with their patients.* Nurses reported that they would look for similarities between themselves and their patients, discover something about their patients before they had the illness, and look for any way to meet patient needs in a positive way. Patients then became real people who might be like a member of their own family or even themselves, and this somehow motivated the nurses to focus more on the patients' needs than their own. Perry observed a positive cycle of caring that would energize the nurses. Doing something in a positive way that meets the needs of the patient can lead to a patient who responds positively to the nurse because the patient feels well cared for. The nurse then sees a sign that his or her caring had an effect, and this gives more energy to care for that patient. *Second, Perry found that these nurses were good at "making moments matter."* They regularly appreciated the privilege of being involved in the most intimate and important of patients' lives and were positively aware of the responsibility they had in helping patients. Relationships with patients were seen as gifts and opportunities to do meaningful work. Realizing that patient gratitude could be manifested in very subtle ways was another theme. *Third, exemplary oncology nurses had a "zest for life attitude" in which they brought a positive energy to their work* that was manifested in "a sense of humour, a playful spirit, a positive attitude, and a sense of self-confidence and self-awareness" (Perry, 2008, p. 90). Perry concluded that a decision to adopt a particular attitude was most likely rooted in core values by which nurses base their professional identity. She related that "nurses do not always have control over all aspects of their work environment, but they do have control over how they respond to those circumstances" (Perry, 2008, p. 90). These same dynamics are most likely operating among all types of exemplary helping professionals and caregivers.

Should we no longer use the term compassion fatigue?

There is a growing concern that we should no longer use the term *compassion fatigue* to describe this phenomenon of secondary traumatic stress in clinicians and that we should use the term *empathic distress fatigue* instead (Klimecki & Singer, 2011). There is no doubt that this phenomenon occurs in clinicians. The concern is that it does not occur *because* of compassion. In their extensive review of the research literature on compassion fatigue, Sinclair, Raffin-Bouchal, Venturato, Mijovic-Kondejewski, and Smith-MacDonald (2017) came to the following conclusions:

> *Suggesting that compassion is somehow the primary contributor to this phenomena is unfounded and detracts from the significant work-related issues and burnout faced by healthcare providers. If compassion was the underlying issue, one would expect that healthcare providers, particularly exemplary compassionate carers, would be particularly vulnerable to the effects of compassion fatigue. As a result of their so-called "chronic compassion," a collorary pandemic of "compassion fatigue" would ensue, making them among societies least compassionate individuals. Recent research, history and spiritual traditions suggest the opposite—increased opportunities to express compassion seem to sustain baseline compassion, mitigate work-related stress, and are beneficial for responders and recipients, within and outside of healthcare. (p. 21)*

As all the research reported in this book shows, secondary traumatic stress and burnout is more likely to occur not because of compassion, but because of not being in the compassion mindset. As we saw in the landmark study by Klimecki, Leiberg, Ricard, and Singer (2014), empathy training by itself results in increased negative affect and personal distress. When people are trained in compassion, that negative affect and distress decrease, and they have more positive emotions that carry and transform the empathic resonance to become a compassionate response. In their review of the research literature, Sinclair et al. (2017) found that *"there is no research demonstrating that exemplary compassionate carers are more susceptible to 'compassion fatigue'"* (p. 9; emphasis added). Clinicians in health care need to know that there is no research showing that compassionate caring is what burns people out. Yet that is what our medical culture believes and what it trains. Training clinicians to be in a compassion mindset and balanced C^2 is what most protects clinicians from burnout and secondary traumatic stress.

Implications for maintaining balanced C^2

To be able to be in the zone of balanced C^2, especially when working with severely ill and/ or traumatized patients, clinicians need to be aware of how they can be affected psychologically by engaging with patients in their suffering. There are unique protective strategies that vary by specialty in terms of how to do this, and there is also an adaptation process in which clinicians learn how to be compassionately engaged with their patients but not overwhelmed or distressed by that work. Patients benefit when clinicians know how to do this because it means that the clinicians will not be tempted to withdraw or to become overinvolved. Clinicians benefit because they have the tools to take care of themselves for

the long haul in this work when they can be in the zone of balanced C^2. In fact, it is the scientific understanding and practice of compassion itself that best leads to excellent patient care and clinician well-being.

SKILL OF MANAGING EMOTIONS AND USING THEM FOR THE HEALING PROCESS

The role of emotions has been a central theme in applying the science of compassion to clinical practice

The critical role of emotions has been a major theme of this book in applying the science of compassion to clinical practice. The empirical evidence for the impact of compassionate caring variables was reviewed in chapter 5; emotions are part of the mechanisms for how these variables are related to outcomes. The role of empathy is key in this process, which was discussed in the neuroscience of empathy as part of the compassion mindset process (chapter 2) as well as in models for explaining how empathic communication has both cognitive/action-oriented effects for the clinician and affective-oriented effects for the patient. Chapter 7 established the importance of clinicians training their subjectivity so that they can accurately perceive the emotional state of their patients and effectively use the biopsychosocial model. In chapter 6 the dynamics of the patient–clinician relationship and the role of subjective perception showed how emotions are central to the success or failure in work with patients. The driving force of motivation in chapter 8 also showed how this emotional process is what leads clinicians into this work and how they must attend to it to thrive in a healthy way in clinical practice. Chapter 10 was entirely focused on the role of emotions for the clinician. The fallacy of emotional detachment and the importance of emotional regulation and management for clinical work both for the benefit of patient care and for the well-being of the clinician were examined. Emotional intelligence is essential for patient care, as it involves the four competencies of having the ability to perceive emotions accurately (in the patient and in oneself); the ability to facilitate problem-solving and creativity; the ability to understand, analyze, and use emotional information; and the ability to manage and regulate emotions in oneself and in one's patients. Emotions are critical to the establishment of safety and trust in the patient–clinician relationship, and we saw how the polyvagal theory explained how this process occurs. In chapter 11, more evidence was given for how an optimal level of emotional engagement with patients is necessary for positive effects on patients and facilitating their healing process. The clinician needs to be comfortable with managing emotions and know how to use them to facilitate healing in patients.

Reclaiming emotion's integral role in clinical practice and research

One of the unfortunate and unnecessary results of the tremendous gains from the scientific method has been a denigration of the importance of emotions and subjectivity. Logical positivism and the pursuit of objective evidence has led to suspicion of emotional approaches and methods that focus on subjectivity. Because these approaches could not be easily measured or verified, they were excluded from many scientific analyses. Watson (1988), Howard (1986), Rychlak (1985), and others have offered very good arguments regarding the limits of the dominant research method paradigms and offered alternative paradigms more appropriate to the study of human subjectivity. Nevertheless, to those who are practitioners of various fields, the use of emotions in the healing process is considered a normal and essential component of helping patients/clients. For example, psychological change appears not to be possible unless there is some type of emotional arousal and transformation (e.g., most people know that smoking is bad for them; it takes some kind of motivational or emotional "push" internally and externally to help the knowledge lead to behavioral change). Scientists use emotions all the time in the quest for discovery using objective methods. They are "perplexed" by the problems, "determined" to find the solution, "driven" to find a cure, and "elated" to get positive results. I once heard an attending physician say to our residents, "When you get lab results like this, it should bother you; it should keep you up at night until you figure it out." In a study of what emotions physicians experience in emotionally challenging situations and how they emotionally regulate, Weilenmann et al. (2018) discovered that the physician's negative emotions can be experienced as ultimately positive and even correlated with physician well-being. Specifically, physicians might have unpleasant emotions as they picked up the irritation or nervousness of their patients, or they might feel stressed or insecure about their own performance with the patient or fear losing control over the session. But they found that these emotions helped the physicians to connect and bond with the patients. The result would be a positive shift in the patient interaction and the satisfaction that comes from being effective with a patient. Emotions are very important to the provision of care as well as part of the change process.

Balanced C² involves in-depth knowledge and skill in using emotions for the healing process.

Ways emotional intelligence, awareness, and engagement influence interactions with patients

Given that so much of this book has provided in-depth analysis of the integral role of emotions, I provide this list of ways that clinicians use emotions for the healing process.

Emotional connection: The clinician's emotional intelligence is what the clinician relies on to create emotional safety and rapport for patients. The emotional engagement of the clinician conveys the assurance that the clinician is invested in helping the patient with his or her problem. The emotional connection facilitates more complete disclosure by patients of their problems, which results in better data for diagnosis and treatment planning.

Symptom clarification: The clinician's emotional intelligence allows the clinician to consider the emotional context of symptoms presented by a patient, and this helps with the interpretation of those patient symptoms. The clinician is able to pick up on patient cues that enable a more complete assessment.

Biopsychosocial/holistic treatment: The ability to notice and explore emotional cues is the main way clinicians can use the biopsychosocial model. It enables the evaluation of psychosocial factors that influence the onset, maintenance, or healing of the medical condition.

Adherence to treatment regimen: The establishment of an emotional connection by a clinician with a patient underlies the increased motivation a patient has to follow through on treatment recommendations. Emotional sensitivity helps with addressing barriers to adherence and promotes investment in maintaining adherence.

Emotional support: Even at the most basic level, emotional support from clinicians is very helpful for healing and patient satisfaction. "Your illness is a challenge for you, and I recognize how it affects you and how you're dealing with it. You can count on me to do what I can to accompany you through it with my expertise and my desire to do the best that I can for you both as a patient and as a fellow human being." Emotional support has definite positive effects on patient outcomes.

Behavior change counseling: The clinician's emotional intelligence as well as emotional connection are what enable a clinician to help a patient change negative health behaviors. With this, the clinician has an emotional awareness of patient clues that help the clinician know what method would work best for behavior change. Behavior change only occurs with motivational transformation, which is grounded in emotional dynamics.

Referral: Emotional intelligence allows the clinician to be aware, when necessary, of a patient's emotional states that are signals that referral is needed. For example, when a patient needs assistance with severe emotional distress, intensive health behavior change, or concurrent mental disorders, the clinician is able to notice these needs and have the skills to facilitate referral.

Using clinical emotional reactions as data for understanding the patient: Well-trained clinicians learn how to read their own emotional reactions to patients as a way to give them more information about what patients are experiencing, and this provides more data for clinicians in assessing, treating, and supporting patients. This requires the ability of a clinician to distinguish personal countertransference issues (i.e., emotional reactions to patients that are related to my personal problems or issues) and countertransference reactions that are actually precipitated by the patient.

Clinician self-care: In order to deal with the stress of work in health care, a clinician must be aware of his or her own emotions so that he or she will understand what they mean and how to proceed. The clinician must not only be emotionally aware of but also comfortable with working through personal vulnerability and have the courage to address whatever is needed for balance in a very difficult profession. A clinician not being sensitive to patient emotional states strongly suggests the clinician is not emotionally connected to him- or herself and is therefore at risk for burnout, secondary traumatic stress, and compassion fatigue. Finally, following practices to maintain healthy emotional management leads to higher levels of composure in highly stressed situations.

How the clinician is part of the medicine
When medical students shadow clinicians on rotations, I instruct the students not only to notice the medical aspects of the clinical work but also to reflect on the question, "How is this clinician part of the medicine?" That is, what does the clinician do that is "medicinal" for the patient? This might include ways the clinician's therapeutic presence is beneficial in some way for the patient as well as clinician relational styles that have therapeutic effects on the patient. Balint (1972) was noted for talking about the doctor being the drug that is administered to patients:

> *In spite of our almost pathetic lack of knowledge about the dynamics and possible consequences of "reassurance" and "advice," these two are perhaps the most often used forms of medical treatment. In other words, they are the most frequent forms in which the drug "doctor" is administered. (p. 116)*

Implications for maintaining balanced C²
Being in the zone of balanced C² means that clinicians have the skill of managing emotions and using them for the healing process rather than viewing emotions as an interference with the practice of medicine. Following Damasio (2006), clinicians must realize the fallacy of separating cognition or reason from emotion. Cognition and emotion are intimately interconnected. Excellent clinicians realize this and rely on the emotional processes to help patients and to take care of themselves. From the patients' perspective, the skill of managing and using emotions for the healing process is fundamental to the balanced C² zone. The emotional engagement of clinicians is what facilitates an optimum clinical interaction. Clinicians are able to be aware of and navigate negative emotions in themselves as well as resist the temptation to be emotionally detached or neutral. They are also able to read the emotional material in themselves and in their patients so that they know how to calibrate themselves in working with patients and can maximize benefit to patients but not become overinvolved. From the clinician's perspective, the skill of managing and using emotions allows clinicians to find this zone of balanced C², which is critical for buffering dysfunctional helping and burnout and maximizing compassion satisfaction in the work.

EFFECTIVE ORGANIZATIONAL AND PRACTICE-MANAGEMENT SKILLS

Poor organizational skills have many negative consequences
Many a fine clinician has been undone by poor organizational skills. Balanced caring requires that the clinician be as freed up as possible to

attend to those he or she is helping. When a clinician gets behind on paperwork, dictations, returning phone calls, and getting the billing done, this becomes like throwing rocks in one's backpack while hiking up a mountain. First of all, dealing with poor organizational skills gets exhausting both for the clinician with bad organization and for those who "clean up" after that disorganized clinician. Second, not keeping up with organizational needs can distract the clinician from attending to the patient. When you are worried about how you are going to get all your paperwork done and make it home at a decent time, you may not be completely listening to the person in front of you. Also, lack of organization can make you resentful of the people you help, even though the situation is not their fault. Third, lack of organizational skills can alienate the people you help even if you do good work with them. When reports are not sent, letters not completed, billing not done, and phone calls not returned, these things begin to detract from the care that might have been felt in the helping interaction.

Not liking paperwork is not a good reason to devalue it

The common complaint among a number of helpers is that they are in the business to help others, but they are just not good at the "organizational stuff." In fact, they may say that things such as paperwork and so on "just are not as important as what I do for people." On one hand, this may be true. On the other hand, this kind of statement hints at a type of snobbery and a devaluing of "material things." Many a financial advisor has been amazed at the shambles the personal financial affairs are in for many well-paid helping professionals. To correct this, it is very important that such helping profession-als come to terms with this devaluing of the

material/organizational dimension and consider how to take care of themselves in this regard.

Health care organizations are responsible for how excessive documentation demands are harmful to clinicians

It is important, however, that the agencies and institutions who employ these clinicians not be exempt from their responsibility. As discussed in chapter 9 regarding the societal factors that can trump compassionate caring, the paper-work and EHR requirements have never been worse for many types of clinicians. Added to this are institutions or agencies that expect their physicians, therapists, or attorneys to have so many "billable hours" but do not give them enough time to do the necessary back-ground work or follow-up work. This leads to a number of negative consequences. One is that paperwork is simply not done or is done poorly. Money is lost, and quality of care can suffer. Second, clinicians come to resent this and basically look for ways out of that employ-ment situation. Third, unrealistic expectations of clinicians by the system that employs them contribute to their burnout.

Too much attention to documentation and billing is bad for patient care

The opposite imbalance is also possible. That is, the clinician might be overly attentive to orga-nizational demands. There are clinicians who are more focused on the paperwork than what is happening between them and their patients. They are already recording the visit and billing for it before they have really helped the patient. This can be a reflection of temperament, but it can also be an indication that a clinician does not really care about patients or that he or she is exhausted by the work and focusing on the "business" side of things is more rewarding. When the "business" appears to have primary emphasis in a clinician's behaviors, patients can perceive this as uncaring toward them. In short, for clinicians who make a living helping others, it is very important to maintain a balance between organizational needs and attending to the needs of the people they help.

Implications for maintaining balanced C²
Effective organizational and practice-management skills allow clinicians to be in the zone of balanced C² because these proactively manage the administrative and documentation requirements of the health care system. While these are considered to be hassles that take time away from actual patient care, our patients need us to keep good records and to submit what is needed for payment of services. If we do not do this because we dislike it or are not disciplined to do this, we may create more problems for our patients. Certainly, there is a major need to reform how documentation and bureaucratic demands have become excessive. But it will always be necessary to do this to some extent even under the best of circumstances. Clinicians benefit from having these skills well developed because it allows them to minimize the amount of time necessary to fulfill these requirements and not have to take large amounts of personal time to "catch up."

MIND-TRAINING PRACTICES TO CULTIVATE COMPASSION AND REDUCE STRESS

Mind training is necessary for optimum clinician performance
Clinicians need to train their minds in order to be consistently in the clinician compassion mindset and the zone of balanced C². The compassion mindset is a cognitive-affective-motivational state that is distinct from empathy, as we have seen in the research presented in chapters 3 and 10. As the research of Kang, Gray, and Dovidio (2015) suggested in chapter 10, compassion training requires an experiential training, not simply a didactic cognitive training, reading about it, or simply observing. Those are all helpful and important but not sufficient. Like any athletic or musical performance, it is one thing to learn about your sport or your musical instrument by reading about it and observing great performances, but to do your athletic or musical performance yourself requires that you have engaged in practicing it so that your whole brain and body have been conditioned for the performance.

Review of research on mind-training methods
Even though the research on applying the science of compassion is in its early stages, there is already evidence that confirms the effectiveness of various mind-training methods. Boellinghaus, Jones, and Hutton (2014) reviewed research with health care professionals on mindfulness techniques and the loving-kindness meditation (LKM) for cultivating self-compassion and compassion toward others. With regard to mindfulness techniques such as mindfulness-based stress reduction (Kabat-Zinn, 1990) and mindfulness-based cognitive therapy (Segal, Williams, & Teasdale, 2002), there is beginning evidence that it increases self-compassion. There is also some evidence for increased empathy, but there is some ambiguity in study designs about whether there may have been other contributing factors or a ceiling effect due to the already high empathy levels of the research participants. Qualitative studies showed increased self-compassion, self-awareness, compassion

toward others, ability to be present, ability to tolerate silences, and ability to be focused on client experiences and interpersonal processes.

Bornemann and Singer's ReSource model to break down the components of compassion

In understanding how one might engage in mind training for compassion, Bornemann and Singer (2013) offer what they call the ReSource model as a way to break down the different aspects of compassion. They propose that there are three components of compassion: *presence*, the *affective domain*, and the *cognitive domain*. *Presence* refers to those functions that prepare and stabilize the mind for the affective and cognitive aspects of compassion. To be in a state of compassion, one's mind needs to have good *attention* and *interoceptive awareness*. *Attention* requires that one be able to attend to the current situation and sustain that. The individual needs to be able to monitor him- or herself, resolve any conflicts in attention in favor of the intended object of that attention, and sustain that attention for long periods of time. *Interoceptive awareness* is the ability of individuals to perceive the internal state of their body. Listening to body signals such as muscle tension and the breath allows people to recognize their own feelings and the feelings of others.

In the *affective domain*, a person must have three skills to be in a state of compassion: "generating feelings of benevolence and warmth; accepting and being with difficult emotions; and generating prosocial motivation" (Bornemann & Singer, 2013, p. 183). First, *generating feelings of benevolence*, also called "opening the heart," is the ability to generate or be open to feelings of warmth, benevolence, and love toward oneself and others. Second, *accepting and being with difficult emotions* is the ability to regulate emotions

for the compassion state. Rather than downregulating negative emotions that would reduce our inclination to help (i.e., using suppression, distraction, or reinterpretation), compassion requires that a person notice and mindfully stay with the emotion as a way to understand what is happening and not become overwhelmed or distressed by it. From there, the person can adjust the emotional reaction in a more adaptive manner. Third, *prosocial motivation* refers to the ability to act in response to others. The person must be prepared to engage in altruistic action rather than withdraw or be passive.

In the *cognitive domain*, also called *perspective*, a person must be able to ascertain the internal and external perspectives. It consists of three subprocesses: metacognition, perspective taking on oneself, and perspective taking of others. *Metacognition* is the ability of individuals to think about their own thinking, to be aware of their thinking process. It includes viewing thoughts as mental events that may be connected to inner events like our feelings or body sensations, or outer events such as other people. *Perspective taking on oneself* is the ability to observe internal thoughts and feelings in order to understand what is occurring in oneself in relation to what is occurring externally; one is able to view oneself as a construction of a number of aspects in oneself—individuals have flexibility in how they view themselves. *Perspective taking of the other* is the ability to understand the thoughts, views, beliefs, or intentions of others (also called mentalizing or theory of mind). This is more cognitively focused rather than affective (Bornemann & Singer, 2013).

Overview of three types of meditation

Given these components and subprocesses of the compassion process, one can tailor the kinds of meditation or mind-training practices that would improve each of them. Ricard, Lutz, and Davidson (2014) noted the differences in three general types of meditation. One type is a focused attention meditation, in which the person concentrates on one's breathing and refocuses one's attention every time it wanders. This improves the ability to be focused and vigilant with less effort. A second, mindfulness meditation, which Ricard et al. call an open-monitoring meditation, observes inner and outer sensations and thoughts but does not get carried away with any of them. It is a state of detached focus that increases awareness and nonreactivity. It has been found to improve anxiety, depression, stress, ruminations, and pain among many other benefits. Finally, compassion and loving-kindness meditations (LKM) cultivate and strengthen benevolent feelings toward self and others who might be friends, strangers, or disliked people.

Choose your mind-training technique according to your goal

When selecting a mind-training technique, it is important to choose it by considering what your goal for it is. For example, Boellinghaus et al. (2014) point out that there are at least three significant differences between mindfulness and LKM methods. One is that mindfulness helps a person relate better to any experience, whereas LKM is focused on suffering. Second, mindfulness is directed toward general experience, and LKM is oriented toward oneself or other people. Third, mindfulness is more passive than LKM in that it focuses on nonjudgmental acceptance of present experience; LKM is an active meditation focused on the intention to offer concern to those who are suffering. Kok and Singer (2017) found that different meditation practices have different "psychological footprints." They examined changes in affect, metacognition, mind

wandering, and interoception after nine months of daily meditation training in four types of meditation: body scan, breathing meditation, LKM, and observing-thought meditation. Those who did the body-scan meditation had the biggest increases in interoceptive awareness. Those who did the observing-thought meditation had the greatest improvement in metacognitive awareness of their thoughts. The people who did LKM had increases in positive thoughts, warmth, and thoughts of others. The breathing meditation did not have unique effects, but the authors point out that this is a basic practice across many types of meditation. Despite the differences in meditation techniques, just doing meditation is related to increases in positive emotions. In a randomized control trial with 339 participants comparing mindfulness meditation with LKM, Fredrickson (2017) found both techniques led to relatively equal increases in positive emotions while negative emotions remained the same. The key factors were frequency and duration of doing the meditation. She found a dose-response such that the more often and the longer one did either practice, the more that person would have an increase in positive emotions.

Concerns about the overuse of mindfulness for clinicians

Mindfulness meditation was discussed in detail in chapter 10, so I will not review it again here. Mindfulness techniques have become very popular and have been recommended for a very wide range of conditions, with research documenting their wide-ranging effectiveness. However, there are a number of problems that have emerged in this popularity. One is that it has been recommended in a global way for clinicians to use to deal with stress, burnout, improved emotion regulation, and so on. However, the perceived faddish quality in how it is prescribed for everything at times irritates clinicians. The technique is often introduced and demonstrated in a watered-down fashion, which can lead to misunderstandings of the technique or resistance to using the technique because of how it is introduced to clinicians. Second, Van Dam et al. (2018) note that there is not a uniform definition of mindfulness, and the semantic ambiguity leads to a large number of meditation practices that are called mindfulness but are actually different types of meditation. Van Dam et al. encourage a more precise delineation and clarity of what all these techniques are. They also note that meditation techniques do not work uniformly well for all people and that there can be adverse reactions to using the techniques that those encouraging its use among clinicians should be aware of (Van Dam et al., 2018). In short, it is important to be careful in how we recommend these techniques with consideration to what the goal is, what the needs of a particular group of clinicians are, and how well we can introduce and practice these techniques in the stressed environments we work in.

LKM as an exercising of compassion capability

While LKM has been discussed in several chapters, it may be helpful to give more information about the mechanisms that lead to its positive results. There are a number of variations to LKM, ranging from those used in the Buddhist tradition to more secularized versions that are being used in research studies. According to Weng, Schuyler, and Davidson (2017), LKM appears to be a way to exercise compassion, just as we would do with muscles. In LKM, the meditator starts with someone for whom it is easy to feel compassion, then moves to him- or herself, to a neutral person, then a more difficult person. For each one of these target people, the meditator does three mental steps: (a) imagines a time when that person has suffered (*envisioning suffering*); (b) notices any thoughts, feelings, and sensations that arise when imaging that person suffering and doing so in a manner similar to mindfulness (*mindful attention*; i.e., nonjudgmental attention); and (c) cultivates feelings of care and concern for each target, repeating certain phrases like, "May they experience joy and ease" or "May they be free from suffering" (*cultivating compassion*). Notice how this mediation progressively builds on where it is easier to feel compassion to where it is more difficult. There is a kind of momentum that is built up to carry compassion to people outside one's "inner circle" and a way of challenging oneself to wish everyone freedom from suffering in the same way as one would wish this for a loved one or oneself.

Mental capacities changed by LKM

Weng et al. (2017) note in their review of this research that LKM creates certain neural states while in the regular meditation practice; these are then transferred to nonmeditative states, and this leads to improvements in prosocial behavior. They explain that LKM is a way to improve emotion regulation in the meditator. With the *envisioning suffering* step, the meditator is exercising greater empathic responses using visual and memory cues to understand another person both by affective sharing of what he or she might be going through and cognitive perspective taking. The meditator is increasing awareness of another's suffering. In the *mindful attention* step, the meditator is actually training him- or herself to have a decreased avoidance response to the suffering of the other. With a nonjudgmental acceptance of any thoughts, feelings, or sensations that arise in imaging that person, there is a way in which this trains the meditator to emotionally regulate the personal distress reactions that would normally lead to focus on oneself and avoidance of the suffering person. With the *cultivating compassion* step, there is a way in which one is mentally rehearsing greater approach responses or prosocial actions toward the suffering person. Using visualization, emotion-based strategies, and cognitive strategies, the meditator is strengthening their ability to appraise other differently (e.g., that the other's suffering matters to the meditator, the other person deserves compassion, and the meditator is able to cope with the other person's suffering) (Weng et al., 2017). Note how this would exercise many of the steps in the clinician compassion mindset process discussed in chapter 4.

How LKM changes neural states

There is growing research support for the model that Weng et al. (2017) have proposed. First, in terms of changes in neural states and increased empathic responses, various studies have found increased activation of the right inferior parietal cortex, which is part of the empathy network (Weng et al., 2013). LKM leads to increased visual attention to suffering cues (Weng, 2014). There is more activation of the amygdala, which is typically associated with a negative response, but with LKM it may mean that the suffering of another is more readily detected. Changes to the empathy neural networks have also been noted both in the meditative and nonmeditative states (Lamm, Decety, & Singer, 2011; Lutz, Brefczynski-Lewis, Johnstone, & Davidson, 2008; Mascaro, Rilling, Negi, & Raison, 2013; Zaki & Ochsner, 2012). There is evidence of decreased avoidance responses to suffering. Studies have shown an increased ability to regulate emotional arousal in response to suffering (Weng et al., 2013) and decreased avoidance responses (Ashar, Andrews-Hanna, Dimidjian et al., 2016; Ashar, Andrews-Hanna, Yarkoni et al., 2016; Klimecki et al., 2014; Rosenberg et al., 2015). Research has begun to show how LKM may increase actual prosocial behavior (Ashar, Andrews-Hanna, Dimidjian et al., 2016; Ashar, Andrews-Hanna, Yarkoni et al., 2016; Engen & Singer, 2015; Klimecki, Leiberg, Lamm, & Singer, 2012; Klimecki et al., 2014; Rosenberg et al., 2015; Weng et al., 2013).

Implications for maintaining balanced C^2

Clinicians who commit themselves to training their minds to be in a compassion mindset and to manage the stress of clinical work are more able to be in the zone of balanced C^2. Clinical work is so emotionally and cognitively taxing that clinicians need to devote time to training their minds to manage the stress of the work and to sustain a compassion mindset with all types of patients and circumstances. From the patients' perspective, clinicians who have trained and conditioned their minds for this work are able to be cognitively their best with patients and able to respond therapeutically to the needs of the patient. From the clinicians' perspective, training one's mind for this work enables clinicians to be able to engage in optimum emotional regulation and cognitive focus and therefore not be harmed themselves by being in a negative or detached emotional state or an overinvolved emotional state.

CONCLUSION

Caring intentions and attitudes are not enough to sustain the balanced C^2 that is optimal for patients and for the well-being of clinicians. Compassion is concretely expressed through our competence and the concrete ways we interact with our patients. Being an excellent clinician is like any other high-performance occupation that requires mental and emotional conditioning, self-care, discipline, and skills in managing difficult situations.

QUESTIONS FOR DISCUSSION

1. In terms of these skills and practices to maintain balanced compassionate caring, are there any others that you think should be added?
2. Pick one of the skills or practices and reflect on an instance that demonstrates the importance of that attitude for your work.

REFERENCES

Anandarajah, G., & Smith, M. (2009). Resident physicians' thoughts regarding compassion and spirituality in the doctor-patient relationship. In M. T. Evans & E. D. Walker (Eds.), *Religion and psychology* (pp. 307–316), New York, NY: Nova Science.

Ashar, Y. K., Andrews-Hanna, J. R., Dimidjian, S., & Wager, T. (2016). Towards a neuroscience of compassion: A brain systems-based model and research agenda. In J. D. Greene, I. Morrison, & M. E. P. Seligman (Eds.), *Positive neuroscience handbook* (pp. 125–142). New York, NY: Oxford University Press.

Ashar, Y. K., Andrews-Hanna, J. R., Yarkoni, T., Sills, J., Halifax, J., Dimidjian, S., & Wager, T. D. (2016). Effects of compassion meditation on a psychological model of charitable donation. *Emotion, 16*(5), 691–705.

Baer, E., Davitz, L. J., & Lieb, R. (1970). Inferences of physical pain and psychological distress: 1. In relation to verbal and nonverbal patient communication. *Nursing Research, 19*(5), 388–392.

Balint, M. (1972). *The doctor, his patient and the illness* (Rev. ed.). Madison, CT: International Universities Press.

Baranowsky, A. B. (2002). The silencing response in clinical practice: On the road to dialogue. In C. R. Figley (Ed.), *Treating compassion fatigue* (pp. 155–170). New York, NY: Brunner-Routledge.

Boellinghaus, I., Jones, F. W., & Hutton, J. (2014). The role of mindfulness and loving-kindness meditation in cultivating self-compassion and other-focused concern in health care professionals. *Mindfulness, 5*(2), 129–138.

Bornemann, B., & Singer, T. (2013). A cognitive neuroscience perspective: The ReSource model. In T. Singer & M. Bolz (Eds.), *Compassion: Bridging practice and science* (e-book, pp. 178–190). Saarbrücken, Germany: Max Planck Society.

Brown, K. W., & Ryan, R. M. (2003). The benefits of being present: Mindfulness and its role in psychological well-being. *Journal of Personality and Social Psychology, 84*(4), 822–848.

Choiniere, M., Melzack, R., Rondeau, J., Girrard, N., & Paquin, M. (1989). The pain of burns: Characteristics and correlates. *Journal of Trauma, 29*(11), 1531–1539.

Connelly, J. E. (1994). The empathic practitioner. In E. S. More & M. A. Milligan (Eds.), *The empathic practitioner: Empathy, gender, and medicine.* (pp. 171–188). New Brunswick, NJ: Rutgers University Press.

Damasio, A. (2006). *Descartes' error: Emotion, reason and the human brain.* London, UK: Vintage Books.

Engen, H. G., & Singer, T. (2015). Compassion-based emotion regulation up-regulates experienced positive affect and associated neural networks. *Social Cognitive and Affective Neuroscience, 10*(9), 1291–1301. doi:10.1093/scan/nsv008

Figley, C. R. (Ed.). (1995). *Compassion fatigue: Coping with secondary traumatic stress disorder.* New York, NY: Brunner/Mazel.

Figley, C. R. (Ed.). (2002) *Treating compassion fatigue.* New York, NY: Brunner-Routledge.

Frank, E., Segura, C., Shen, H., & Oberg, E. (2010). Predictors of Canadian physicians' prevention counseling practices. *Canadian Journal of Public Health, 101*(5), 390–395.

Fredrickson, B. L. (2017). Positive emotion correlates of meditation practice: A comparison of mindfulness meditation and loving-kindness meditation. *Mindfulness, 8*(6), 1623–1633.

Harper, B. C. (1994). *Death: The coping mechanism of the health professional* (Rev. ed.). Greenville, SC: Swinger Associates.

Hayes-Bautista, D. E. (1976). Termination of the patient-practitioner relationship: Divorce, patient style. *Journal of Health and Social Behavior, 17*(1), 12–21.

Howard, G. S. (1986). Dare we develop a human science. Notre Dame, IN: Academic Publications.

Kabat-Zinn, J. (1990). *Full catastrophe living: Using the wisdom of your body and mind to face stress, pain, and illness.* New York, NY: Dell.

Kang, Y., Gray, J. R., & Dovidio, J. F. (2015). The head and the heart: Effects of understanding and experiencing lovingkindness on attitudes toward the self and others. *Mindfulness, 6*(5), 1063–1070.

Klimecki, O. M., Leiberg, S., Lamm, C., & Singer, T. (2012). Functional neural plasticity and associated changes in positive affect after compassion training. *Cerebral Cortex, 23*(7), 1552–1561.

Klimecki, O. M., Leiberg, S., Ricard, M., & Singer, T. (2014). Differential pattern of functional brain plasticity after compassion and empathy training. *Social Cognitive and Affective Neuroscience, 9*(6), 873–879.

Klimecki, O., & Singer, T. (2011). Empathic distress fatigue rather than compassion fatigue? Integrating findings from empathy research in psychology and social neuroscience. In B. Oakley, A. Knafo, G. Madhavan, & D. S. Wilson (Eds.), *Pathological Altruism* (pp. 368–383). New York, NY: Oxford University Press.

Kok, B. E., & Singer, T. (2017). Phenomenological fingerprints of four meditations: Differential state changes in affect, mind-wandering, meta-cognition, and interoception before and after daily practice across 9 months of training. *Mindfulness, 8*(1), 218–231.

Kubler-Ross, E. (1976). *On death and dying: What the dying can teach doctors, nurses, clergy, and their own families.* New York, NY: Macmillan.

Lamm, C., Decety, J., & Singer, T. (2011). Meta-analytic evidence for common and distinct neural networks associated with directly experienced pain and empathy for pain. *NeuroImage, 54*(3), 2492–2502.

Lewis, C. E., Clancy, C., Leake, B., & Schwartz, J. S. (1991). The counseling practices of internists. *Annals of Internal Medicine, 114*(1), 54–58.

Lutz, A., Brefczynski-Lewis, J., Johnstone, T., & Davidson, R. (2008). Regulation of the neural circuitry of emotion by compassion meditation: Effects of meditative expertise. *PloS ONE, 3*(3), e1897. Retrieved from http://doi.org/10.1371/journal.pone.0001897

Mascaro, J. S., Rilling, J. K., Negi, L. T., & Raison, C. L. (2013). Compassion meditation enhances empathic accuracy and related neural activity. *Social Cognitive and Affective Neuroscience, 8*(1), 48–55.

Millar, F. E., & Rogers, L. E. (1976). A relational approach to interpersonal communication. In R. R. Millers (Ed.), *Explorations in interpersonal communication* (pp. 87–102). Washington, DC: Sage.

Montgomery, C. L. (1993). *Healing through communication: The practice of caring.* Newbury Park, CA: Sage.

Montgomery, C. L. (1994). The caring/healing relationship of "maintaining authentic caring." In J. Watson (Ed.), *Applying the art and science of human caring* (pp. 39–42). New York, NY: National League for Nursing Press.

Nagy, S. (1999). Strategies used by burns nurses to cope with the infliction of pain on patients. *Journal of Advanced Nursing, 29*(6), 1427–1433.

Nedrow, A., Steckler, N. A., & Hardman, J. (2013). Physician resilience and burnout: Can you make the switch? *Family Practice Management, 20*(1), 25–30.

Neff, K. D. (2003). The development and validation of a scale to measure self-compassion. *Self and Identity*, 2(3), 223–250.

Neff, K. D., & Pommier, E. (2013). The relationship between self-compassion and other-focused concern among college undergraduates, community adults, and practicing meditators. *Self and Identity*, 12(2), 160–176.

Neff, K. D., & Vonk, R. (2009). Self-compassion versus global self-esteem: Two different ways of relating to oneself. *Journal of Personality*, 77(1), 23–50.

Nelson, J. A., & Folbre, N. (2006). Why a well-paid nurse is a better nurse. *Nursing Economics*, 24(3), 127–130.

Othmer, S., & Othmer, S. (2016). Infra-low-frequency neurofeedback for optimum performance. *Biofeedback*, 44(2), 81–89.

Pearlman, L. A., & Saakvitne, K. W. (1995). *Trauma and the therapist: Countertransference and vicarious traumatization in psychotherapy with incest survivors*. New York, NY: Norton.

Perry, B. (2008). Why exemplary oncology nurses seem to avoid compassion fatigue. *Canadian Oncology Nursing Journal*, 18(2), 87–92.

Perry, S., Heidrich, G., & Ramos, E. (1981). Assessment of pain by burn patients. *Journal of Burn Care and Rehabilitation*, 2(6), 322–326.

Ricard, M., Lutz, A., & Davidson, R. J. (2014, November). The neuroscience of meditation. *Scientific American*, 39–45.

Rosenberg, E. L., Zanesco, A. P., King, B. G., Aichele, S. R., Jacobs, T. L., Bridwell, D. A., & Saron, C. D. (2015). Intensive meditation training influences emotional responses to suffering. *Emotion*, 15(6), 775–790.

Rychlak, J. F. (1985). A philosophy of science for personality theory, 2nd ed. Malabar, FL: Robert E. Krieger Publishing Company.

Salmon, P., & Young, B. (2009). Dependence and caring in clinical communication: The relevance of attachment and other theories. *Patient Education and Counseling*, 74(3), 331–338.

Segal, Z. V., Williams, J. M. G., & Teasdale, J. D. (2002). *Mindfulness-based cognitive therapy for depression*. New York, NY: Guilford Press.

Shanafelt, T. D., Kaups, K. L., Nelson, H., Satele, D. V., Sloan, J. A., Oreskovich, M. R. & Dyrbye, L. N. (2014). An interactive individualized intervention to promote behavioral change to increase personal well-being in US surgeons. *Annals of Surgery*, 259(1), 82–88.

Sinclair, S., Raffin-Bouchal, S., Venturato, L., Mijovic-Kondejewski, J., & Smith-MacDonald, L. (2017). Compassion fatigue: A meta-narrative review of the healthcare literature. *International Journal of Nursing Studies*, 69, 9–24.

Slatten, L. A., Carson, K. D., & Carson, P. P. (2011). Compassion fatigue and burnout: What managers should know. *Health Care Manager*, 30(4), 325–333.

Stamm, B. H. (2010). *The concise ProQOL manual* (2nd ed.). Retrieved from https://proqol.org/ProQOl_Test_Manuals.html

Sulmasy, D. P. (1997). *The healer's calling: A spirituality for physicians and other health care professionals*. Mahwah, NJ: Paulist Press.

Van Dam, N. T., Van Vugt, M. K., Vago, D. R., Schmalzl, L., Saron, C. D., Olendzki, A., ... Meyer, D. E. (2018). Mind the hype: A critical evaluation and prescriptive agenda for research on mindfulness and meditation. *Perspectives on Psychological Science*, 13(1), 31–61.

Watson, J. (1988). Nursing: Human Science and Human Care. New York: National League for Nursing.

Watzlawick, P., Beavin, J., & Jackson, D. D. (1967). *Pragmatics of human communication*. New York, NY: Norton.

Weil, S. (1951). *Waiting for god*. New York, NY: Putnam.

Weilenmann, S., Schnyder, U., Parkinson, B., Corda, C., von Känel, & Pfaltz, M. C. (2018). Emotion transfer, emotion regulation, and empathy-related processes in physician-patient interactions and their association with physician well-being: A theoretical model. *Frontiers in Psychiatry*, 9, 1–18.

Weng, H. Y. (2014). *Behavioral and neural effects of compassion meditation training* (Doctoral dissertation). Retrieved from ProQuest Dissertations and Theses database. (UMI No. 10185437).

Weng, H. Y., Fox, A. S., Shackman, A. J., Stodola, D. E., Caldwell, J. Z. K., Olson, M. C., ... Davidson, R.

J. (2013). Compassion training alters altruism and neural responses to suffering. *Psychological Science*, 24(7), 1171–1180.

Weng, H. Y., Schuyler, B., & Davidson, R. J. (2017). The impact of compassion meditation on the brain and pro-social behavior. In *The Oxford handbook of compassion science* (pp. 133–146). New York, NY: Oxford University Press.

Zaki, J., & Ochsner, K. (2012). The neuroscience of empathy: Progress, pitfalls and promise. *Nature Neuroscience*, 15(5), 675–680.

Zwack, J., & Schweitzer, J. (2013). If every fifth physician is affected by burnout, what about the other four? Resilience strategies of experienced physicians. *Academic Medicine*, 88(3), 382–389.

CREDIT

"Do not be daunted by the enormity of the world's grief. Do justly, now. Love mercy, now. Walk humbly, now. You are not obligated to complete the work, but neither are you free to abandon it."

—The Talmud 303

"Dedicate some of your life to others. Your dedication will not be a sacrifice. It will be an exhilarating experience because it is an intense effort applied toward a meaningful end."

—Dr. Thomas Dooley

Chapter Sections:

- ▶ Introduction
- ▶ The Spiritual and/or Philosophical Quests of Health Care Clinicians
- ▶ Research on Spirituality and Being a Helping Professional
- ▶ Awareness of Spiritual Risks and Rewards in the Encounter with Suffering
- ▶ Articulation and Reliance on a Spirituality of Caring/Philosophy of Caring
- ▶ Compassionate Caring as Gateway to the Transpersonal and/or Sacred Dimension
- ▶ Spiritual, Philosophical, and Meditation Practices to Endure and Transform the Encounter with Suffering
- ▶ Conclusion

CHAPTER 14

Spirituality or Philosophy of Caring

How Spirituality (or Philosophy) of Caring Helps the Clinician
Survive and Thrive Over the Course of a Health Care Career

Questions to consider before reading this chapter:

1. If you are agnostic or atheistic, how does your philosophy of life influence the way you are a clinician?

2. If you have a spirituality or religious affiliation, how does your spirituality influence the way you are a clinician?

3. From a philosophical or a spiritual perspective, how do you make sense of suffering and the response to suffering?

INTRODUCTION

To be in zone of balance C^2, it can be of great benefit to articulate how one understands the work of helping people who are suffering from the perspective of one's philosophy of life or spirituality. Clinicians find that they have to take care of themselves physically and psychologically for the emotional toll that results from working with suffering or difficult patients as well as the dysfunctional aspect of organizations and society. But the continual encounter with illness and suffering will challenge clinicians from an existential perspective. Clinicians will have philosophical and/or spiritual ways of understanding what is going on in the response to suffering, what their role is in that, and what the meaning of all of it is. In this chapter, I will begin by exploring the issue of philosophy or spirituality in the helping professions, followed by some research on this with clinicians. Then I will approach what this means for clinicians in four steps. First, clinicians need to assess what are the existential or spiritual risks and rewards of doing this work. Second, many clinicians benefit by articulating and relying on a spirituality or philosophy of caring. Third, many clinicians gain fulfillment from and energy for the work by experiencing compassionate caring as a gateway to the transpersonal and/or sacred dimensions. Finally, there are a variety of spiritual, philosophical, and meditation practices that clinicians use to help them endure and transform the ongoing encounter with suffering.

THE SPIRITUAL AND/OR PHILOSOPHICAL QUESTS OF HEALTH CARE CLINICIANS

Spirituality or philosophy helps many helping professionals in this work

Does a clinician's spirituality or religious beliefs help him or her deal with the emotional toll of being in a helping profession? Does having spiritual or religious practices help a clinician cultivate and maintain compassionate caring in encounters with human suffering? Or for those who are agnostic or atheist, does having a philosophy of life undergirding one's compassionate caring provide an added benefit to enduring the stress of helping work? As we have seen thus far in this book, specific attitudes and behaviors of balanced caring provide ways to maintain compassionate caring in practice and buffer against burnout. For a number of clinicians, this will be sufficient. However, many physicians, nurses, and allied health professionals find that their spirituality or their philosophies of life is a very important part of the ability to maintain compassion and cope with the physical, psychological, and existential challenges of being in a helping profession. While research on this subject is still in its early phases, having a spirituality or a philosophy of compassionate caring appears to be an important part of maintaining compassionate and balanced caring in the work of helping others for many people in helping professions. Working with people who are suffering can be painful. Does a spirituality or a philosophy of compassionate caring help you tolerate and engage this pain any better?

Many clinicians are not prepared spiritually or philosophically for helping work

A common scenario is that, over time, the clinician who deals with constant human pain or distress becomes discouraged. In addition to all the common ways clinicians get out of balance in their caring as described in the previous chapter, they also do not always have or take the time to assess how they are doing in encountering this constant human suffering. Working with people who are suffering takes an emotional toll on those who are helping them. People who go into helping work generally expect that this kind of work will be emotionally difficult, but this does not deter them from entering into or staying in helping professions. People in helping work often begin with the hope that this emotional toll will be surmountable for them and that the fulfillment which can come from a lifetime of caring will more than balance the emotional costs. Just as there is generally not a very sophisticated emotional training for people going into helping professions as discussed in previous chapters, there also does not tend to be a very sophisticated spiritual or philosophical preparation for the challenges of helping people who are suffering. Some clinicians have been fortunate to have a formation process that enables them to deal with the spiritual struggles that occur in helping work, but most have to find a way to develop this capacity while doing helping work. As Montgomery (1993) has explained, those who develop a "transcendent view of life" appear to fare better in this difficult work. This is discussed in different ways in various traditions and backgrounds, but they share a number of features in common. It is what I call a spirituality or philosophy of caring.

Definitions of spirituality of caring and philosophy of caring

A *spirituality or philosophy of caring is a way of living the life of a helper and healer in such a way that you are grounded spiritually (or philosophically) and in this way find strength to do this journey of helping and healing.* It includes spiritual and/or philosophical perspectives and practices that enable helpers to encounter suffering and difficulties yet be able to maintain and cultivate compassion as well as find psychological and spiritual renewal in this challenging work. It is an organized way of understanding the encounter with human pain and a way of viewing the activity of compassion as, first of all, worthwhile, and second, it provides of way to endure this encounter with human pain. A spirituality of caring (SOC) gives the clinician some way of breaking down, metabolizing, or transforming the toxic encounter with human suffering. It can provide a perspective on the meaning of that pain and the meaning of caring for people in pain. By incorporating the spiritual dimension, an SOC often involves how God, a higher power, divine force, or the life force is involved with what is happening in terms of the human suffering and the call to respond to this human suffering. Nontheistic religions or spiritualities may not have this reference to a divine being but nonetheless have a spiritual conception of what is occurring in the work of compassion. For those who prefer to avoid explicit spiritual language, it can be called a philosophy of caring (POC). Like an SOC, it is a philosophical perspective that helps helping professionals make sense of the suffering they encounter and allows them to continue in the work better than those clinicians who do not articulate for themselves some wider philosophical or spiritual perspective. Whether it is a POC or an SOC, they both contribute "to a deeper acceptance of what may appear to others as senseless, meaningless tragedy" (Montgomery, 1993, p. 114).

Observations of the emotional toll in residency training

Much of what I am referring to in this chapter is based on my own empirical observations both personally and professionally, as well as excellent research that is in its early stages. It is not a matter of some pious exhortation from a person with a spiritual worldview. I have seen clinical evidence of it in training and practice, and the research has been compelling. For over 10 years, I have been involved in training physician residents during their residency programs. As the director of behavioral medicine and caring science training, my role was to assist residents in improving their relational skills with patients, learning and applying behavioral medicine, and developing their abilities to take care of themselves in the emotional challenges of this work. I observed and accompanied many residents in a several-year journey from enthusiastic idealism to discouraged realism in clinical practice. Many residents were "like gold tested in fire" and it became my informal research to understand how certain residents successfully worked through this ordeal and sustained a positive caring spirit in this work. Furthermore, in my regular observations of their patient-relational skills, I could see an ability to keep working with patients in an engaged, personal, caring, and respectful manner—even when many of those patients were quite difficult or suffering terribly.

A topic not often discussed and the reasons why

I began to ask residents as well as attending physicians and other clinicians about what they were doing to help maintain this compassionate caring spirit. Such a question is not lightly asked or answered. A person's spirituality or philosophy of life is very personal and can make a person feel vulnerable when asked about it. When someone asks you this question, you do not answer fully when you think the other person will critique or ridicule what your spiritual or philosophical worldview is. In the secular operations of health care and medical science, this is not generally discussed because the fear is that it may not be respected and one will look down on the clinician with a particular spiritual or philosophical world-view. Some will respond that others will think them less intelligent or knowledgeable if they disclose what orients them spiritually or phil-osophically. Thus, clinicians often hide this so that no one will think less of them. Or, if the clinician's spirituality or philosophy is a minority one compared to the dominant spir-itualities or philosophies of that organization or group, whether religious or secular, that clinician may fear misunderstanding. So, no one talks about it.

Common patterns across spiritual traditions

When there is an atmosphere of mutual appre-ciation and respect, clinicians do talk about the spirituality or philosophy of life that helps them sustain and renew their spirits. When it was appropriate to ask the question about what was behind the positive perseverance and continu-ally caring approach to everything the clinicians did, I often heard what that spirituality or phi-losophy was and how they relied on it in a daily way. Asking this question of the residents who exemplified this from Mormon, Hindu, Jewish, Buddhist, Muslim, and Christian traditions, I discovered common patterns in how each cli-nician would deal with the difficulties he or she experienced, the tragedies he or she would wit-ness, and how the clinician would cultivate an ongoing, sincere desire to keep helping others. While they would get discouraged and despair periodically, the clinicians had a way of working this through.

Spirituality or philosophy of life is more than simply passively coping, but also transforming experience and facilitating growth

Many people in the helping professions have made the same observations. This is particularly true with those who encounter dying and death regularly in their work. As Carol Montgomery (1993) herself observed,

> caregivers are also challenged with a signif-icant personal experience of loss every time they get close to someone who dies. How they cope with this loss is greatly influenced by their philosophical and spiritual understand-ing of death. A spiritual understanding that allows for a sense of connection and conti-nuity within the cycle of life and death helps caregivers to transcend the personal expe-rience of loss. Those who do not have this spiritual resource may be personally devas-tated. (p. 114)

It is a coping method to have this transcen-dent perspective. While this can come across as a passive and escapist approach in terms of coping, it can also be quite active and problem focused. It is, as Pargament has described it, an *orienting system* (Pargament, 1997) in which clinicians are not simply coping; they are also transforming their experiences, growing as professionals and human beings, and effec-tively navigating very difficult experiences in a proactive manner. This benefits not only the clinician but also the patient. As Montgomery (1993) writes,

> the caregivers who experienced growth in response to this exposure were able to develop a transcendent view of life that would lend itself to a deeper acceptance of what may appear to others as senseless, meaningless tragedy. This is part of the broader perspective to which expert caregivers have access, which allows them to help their patients create new meanings that lend themselves to hope and healing. (p. 114)

Studies documenting the benefits of having an SOC in clinical work

Killian (2008) found that among therapists who work with trauma survivors, especially sexual abuse, spirituality was frequently reported to be a major part of their self-care routines. One of the main elements in its helpfulness was having a worldview of a larger force that is outside the individual and is ultimately in charge. This larger force guides them and works through them in helping these clients. Rather than making the therapists feel helpless, paradoxically this reliance on a larger force provides strength and support in doing this difficult work. Secondly, specific practices such as daily meditation were reported to be very helpful.

Compassionate caring is the common ground for all clinicians, and there are different paths to how clinicians make sense of their compassionate work

Compassionate caring is the common ground all clinicians share no matter what spirituality, religion, or philosophy they espouse. If the clinician is truly rooted in compassionate caring, that compassionate caring is the common language across all spiritualities, religions, and compassionate philosophies (e.g., compassionate atheism, compassionate agnosticism). With our colleagues, what we need from each other the most is to ensure that we are all united in the effort to benefit others and that we will help each other deal with the suffering we encounter, the quagmire of health care, and the challenges of our society. How we each conceptualize the work spiritually, religiously, or philosophically is secondary. But this is not to imply that because it is secondary it is not important to the work. *We each must have an orienting system and practice that enables us to endure the hardship of the work and also help us cultivate compassion.* Like

traveling to a particular destination, each traveler must find a particular path to get there. It is the nature of traveling that you must pick a path in order to get to a destination. There are many paths to the one destination. Everyone has a path—a worldview—for making sense of all of this. Whether you are conscious of it or not, whether it is well worked out or not, there is some way you are trying to make sense of what is happening to you and around you. While you might not hear about it or know how to talk about it, in the drive to your home, in moments catching your breath in the stairwell of the hospital, or from an intrusive thought about your work on your vacation, everyone wonders what it all means and what our purpose is in all of this.

Compassion is the common language of all spiritualities or philosophies of caring

It is not the purpose of this chapter to be concerned about which religious/spiritual/philosophical path is the "best." That is a task best left to theologians and philosophers if they think this endeavor is worthwhile or even possible. Arguing about which path is best does not, in my experience, produce any benefit. People are generally born and raised in a particular spiritual or philosophical tradition, and their spirituality evolves as they experience life and spiritually reflect on it. It is more fruitful when people of different spiritual or philosophical viewpoints share their perspectives with each other and learn from each other. Sometimes those discussions help individuals gain a deeper sense of their own traditions. Some individuals integrate the wisdom of other spiritual and philosophical viewpoints into their own. Nor is it my intention to say that it does not matter which path you take to practice compassionate caring. It does matter which one you take as long as it helps you cultivate compassion and provides a way for you to persevere in the helping work. This is not a relativistic or constructivist comment, but a practical one: religions, spiritualities, and philosophies can provide their adherents with the orienting worldview that facilitates compassionate caring. Upon closer and deeper examination, each of these paths can be found to share a common reality and common dynamics that point to this commonality of compassion. Compassion is the common language of healthy religion, spirituality, and philosophy of life. As we work together in health care with colleagues of diverse backgrounds and worldviews, compassion can be our common language as well in the shared desire to relieve suffering in others.

Karen Armstrong's research in the compassionate roots of religions and Greek philosophy

Religious historian Karen Armstrong (2007) has traced the origins of the world's major religions and found that their origins are marked by a reaction to the violence of their time, and the sages of that time emphasized a compassionate vision of what humans should be. Whether it be Confucianism, Daoism, Judaism, Hinduism, Buddhism, Islam, Christianity, or the philosophical rationalism of ancient Greece, the test for true religiosity of each one was the same: "if people's beliefs—secular or religious—make them belligerent, intolerant, and unkind about other people's faith," then that person has failed. "If, however, their convictions impel them to act compassionately and to honor the stranger, then they are good, helpful, and sound" (Armstrong, 2007, pp. 468–469). In her research, she found that the spiritual kernel of all religious doctrines was that they are all programs for compassionate action. She found that the sages of the Axial age (a period from about 900 to 200 BCE when the roots of the world religions were formed)

"put the abandonment of selfishness and the spirituality of compassion at the top of their agenda. For them, religion was the Golden Rule" (Armstrong, 2007, p. 468). Her final words to her book *The Great Transformation: The Beginning of Our Religious Traditions* are

> today we are living in a tragic world where, as the Greeks knew, there can be no simple answers; the genre of tragedy demands that we learn to see things from other people's point of view. If religion is to bring light to our broken world, we need, as Mencius, suggested, to go in search of the lost heart, the spirit of compassion that lies at the core of all our traditions. (p. 476, Armstrong, 2007)

Exercise to understand the legitimacy of all paths to compassion

In workshops, to illustrate the point that each spiritual path is a valid path of compassionate living, I have shown pictures of mountains and asked participants to tell me which one is their favorite mountain. Sometimes I try to get a bit of competitiveness going, asking people to argue why their mountain choice is better. Then I disclose to them that all the mountain pictures I have shown are actually the same mountain. The pictures were just from different perspectives. If I live on one side of that mountain, I can only have the view that I have. I may have been born on that side of the mountain and never could travel to see any other view. To climb that mountain, I may have only known the paths that were nearest where I live and the ones my elders knew and could pass on to me. But that does not mean your view is less that mountain or that the path from your perspective is less a path. They are both true. This is not relativism. This is the reality from different points of view. But I can only perceive that reality from the standpoint that I have and you can only perceive that reality from the standpoint that you have. Rather than arguing which path is better, our energy is better spent appreciating our respective perspectives especially since we have the common goal and common ground of compassionate caring.

Just because you can do God-talk does not mean you know how to integrate it into your work

It is important to note that simply having a religious affiliation, engaging in various religious or spiritual practices, or having a spiritual/philosophical perspective does not necessarily mean you are using this religiosity or spirituality/philosophy in your helping work. Clinicians may be able to do what I call "God-talk" or even pray, but that does not necessarily mean they have integrated this perspective with the work of helping. In my work with physicians and nurses, it is not unusual to see people being very devout in terms of religion or spirituality, yet not truly relying on this in day-to-day helping work. In an analogous way, a person might have a membership in a gym or own an exercise bike, maybe even use it occasionally, but it may not be very integrated in their day-to-day lives. A dietitian may be expert at teaching good eating practices to others but may not actually be living by these good principles in his or her own personal life. Like many other things in life, it is one thing to know what is good to do, and it is quite another to actually do it. Having a certain set of religious or spiritual beliefs or practices does not necessarily mean that these are integrated with a clinician's view of his or her work. Spirituality and religion can operate in a compartmentalized fashion for many clinicians and therefore not have much impact on indicators of well-being at work. But there is an added challenge in an SOC. As a clinician begins integrating and relying on his or her SOC in the

helping work, often the clinician is at a loss for exactly how to do this. While difficulties and tragedies happen in every person's life, a person who is in professional helping encounters a much higher quantity and intensity of suffering and difficulty in other people's lives. I began encouraging clinicians and students to articulate their spiritualities or philosophies of caring over 20 years ago, and I still remember a very faith-centered physician who said to me, "I'm not sure I know how to articulate my own spirituality of caring even though I am pretty religious. This is hard to do." These words have gripped me, as I know now that there are many clinicians who want to integrate their spirituality into their work but do not have a clear sense of how to do so. It can be very beneficial to our clinicians to help them facilitate what their POC/SOCs are in order to provide them with important ways to help them endure and navigate all that they encounter.

Most clinicians do not have the skills to grapple with difficult issues from a spiritual or philosophical perspective

Generally, people are not raised with the skills to grapple with an issue from a spiritual or philosophical perspective. In many ways, this lack of spiritual or philosophical reflective ability parallels what helping professionals encounter with the ideas of "caring" and "compassion" as they enter their helping careers. That is, helping professionals often maintain sentimentalized and simplistic notions of "caring" and "compassion" that do not carry much weight or are not very useful in very serious helping work. Just as helping professionals have to gain a much more sophisticated notion of compassionate caring in helping work, so, too, do caregivers have to have a more profound understanding of the spiritual and existential dynamics, risks, and rewards of helping work. Unless the helping professional has already suffered and spiritually/philosophically matured in a significant way before entering the helping profession, then he or she must find a way to accomplish this while being initiated into helping work—or do so later in his or her career after he or she has experienced burnout and even despair.

How it is difficult to reflect spiritually or philosophically with limited time and limited tools

Helping professionals often complain about the difficulty of achieving this. They complain about a lack of guidance and accessible wisdom for the things that they must encounter. For example, if you have not had much time or an opportunity to reflect on the meaning of life before you begin helping other people who are encountering threats to their lives because they are ill or even dying, then there is a great deal of pressure on you to come to terms with what life is all about. This is difficult to do when you are exhausted or have little time as you see one patient after another. Or maybe you have not reflected very deeply on what suffering is and why it occurs. Therefore, when you begin working with people who are suffering a great deal, you are now confronted with having to answer the question for yourself. Many people do not find that the teachings they received in childhood and adolescence are sufficient to help them navigate the serious life questions that they will encounter in working with people who are suffering. To deal with this, often helping professionals may simply avoid thinking about this and—giving into the temptation to be emotionally detached with patients—live a career disconnected in a sense from more deeply reflecting on their experiences. The religious teachings of childhood or those picked up here and there often do not seem very helpful. They smack of cliché, sentimentality, and naiveté. Often realizing that they have gotten only a juvenile understanding of their spiritual traditions, many professionals go back to their religious or spiritual traditions and ask new questions, reworking and deepening spiritual understanding of what is occurring in their lives. Many times, clinicians will seek out like-minded clinicians or mentors, readings, or conferences that enable them to grow in a spiritual or existential understanding of their experiences.

Religiosity and spirituality are empirically distinct

Religiosity and spirituality are two different things when it comes to their respective impacts on compassion. These concepts have been found to be empirically distinct from each other both in how people experience them and how they affect other aspects of their lives. Religiosity is defined more by identification with a particular religious institution, engaging in religious practices specific to that religion, and believing that belonging to a particular religion is most important in terms of living one's life. Spirituality is defined as self-identifying more in spiritual terms (not necessarily antireligious). Spiritual people would tend to say that spirituality is an important part of who they are and that it is important to attend to one's spiritual growth. They tend to say they have had transcendent experiences such as events in which they felt deeply connected to everything, in which all things seemed divine, or in which they somehow felt merged with a higher power or force. This group tends to have a questing orientation toward religion in which they are more willing to face religious questions and doubts (Saslow et al., 2013). While they are distinguishable constructs, they can be intercorrelated. Prayer and meditation are correlated with both religiosity and spirituality. Surprisingly, spirituality tends to be correlated with positive affect, but not religiosity. Neither spirituality nor religiosity is correlated with negative affect. Spirituality is related to the tendency to feel compassion, awe, and love; when religiosity is factored out in partial correlation, spirituality still predicts increased compassion and awe. Spirituality predicts increased love, but when compassion is factored out, it does not predict love. In other words, compassion appears to be the core of the spiritual experience. Religiosity is related to feeling compassion, but when spirituality is factored out, religiosity no longer predicts compassion. Religiosity is not correlated with awe and love. The conclusion the researchers reached was that, *"Spirituality is related to the emotional core of religion, whereas religiosity is related to the formalized rituals of religion"* (Saslow et al., 2013, p. 208).

Religion not necessarily associated with compassion

Religious motivation is not necessarily associated with compassion toward everyone. College undergraduates were given opportunities to help another person who either did or did not disclose that he or she was gay; and the help needed would either be for a behavior that might be seen as promoting the gay community (i.e., attending a gay pride parade) or not at all related to the person's sexual orientation (helping that person visit his or her grandparents). Batson, Floyd, Meyer, and Winner, (1999) found that undergraduates who scored highly on measures of devout intrinsic religion were less likely to help others who disclosed they were gay (even when the goal was as uncontroversial as helping

someone visit his or her grandparents) than when they did not know the sexual orientation of the other person. Rather than automatically promoting a universal compassion to everyone, there are times when intrinsic religion is associated with an antipathy toward a person whether they were engaged in a value-violating behavior or not.

Three ways of being religious: extrinsic, intrinsic, and quest orientations

What emerged in the Batson et al. (1999) study, however, was that individuals who viewed religion as a quest did not discriminate against the gay person. Allport and Ross (1967) first distinguished between an *extrinsic orientation* to religion and an *intrinsic orientation* to religion. Individuals with an extrinsic orientation tend to use religion for self-centered instrumental or utilitarian ends. They use religion "to provide security and solace, sociability and distraction, status and self-justification," in which the "embraced creed is lightly held or else selectively shaped to fit more primary needs." They turn to God "but without turning away from self" (Allport & Ross, 1967, p. 434). Individuals with an intrinsic orientation to religion view religion as an end in itself and other needs "are, so far as possible, brought into harmony with the religious beliefs and prescriptions" (Allport & Ross, 1967, p. 434). They internalize and truly live the religion. Batson (1976) found a third way of being religious: Rather than religion being a means to something or an end in itself, *religion is viewed as a quest*, "as an endless process of probing and questioning generated by the tensions, contradictions, and tragedies in their own lives and in society" (p. 32). People who view religion as a quest tend to be ready to face existential questions without reducing their complexity; they view religious doubt and questions as positive and more central to their religious experience, and they have an openness to change expecting that they will continue to question their religious beliefs and that these will grow and change (Batson & Schoenrade, 1991).

Religious quest orientation associated with being more attuned to victim's needs

Interestingly, there is some evidence that religious individuals with a quest orientation to religion are more attuned to what the needs of the victims are when helping them. Individuals who have a more intrinsic or end orientation to religion have a kind of rigid helping in which they helped victims according to what they presumed the victim's needs were, even when the victim was indicating needs that did not fit with that predetermined plan of helping. They formulated a particular interpretation of the situation and then tended not to be able to change that interpretation of what the victim needed. Individuals high in the quest orientation tended to be more tentative and able to respond to what the victims said they actually needed (Batson, 1976). There is also evidence that a quest orientation is related to posttraumatic growth. In a sample of individuals who had experienced a traumatic event, the openness to change dimension of the Quest Scale was related to positive changes and growth in dealing with the trauma (Calhoun, Cann, Tedeschi, & McMillan, 2000).

Religious quest orientation associated with being a compassionate clinician

While much more scientific study is needed, a number of things seem evident. First, the way in which a helping professional is religious is very important in this discussion about articulating an SOC. *Extrinsic religiosity* will not provide much inner support because it is not primary for the helping profession; it is directed toward some self-focused need other than the religion itself. *Intrinsic religiosity* would seem to provide more potential for inner support because the religion is an end in itself. But then comes this issue of whether the religion is more self-focused or compassionately focused. There is a way of practicing religion that may not be very helpful in terms of cultivating compassion, especially to people beyond your family and friends—beyond your tribe, so to speak. The professional code in medicine is to treat everyone who is suffering. Does your spirituality or religion help you do that? Second, how strong is the quest orientation in your religiosity or spirituality? It seems that a quest orientation to religion makes more sense in the helping professional's career. The encounter with great suffering is bound to generate questions and doubts about what one thinks of life. A quest orientation in a helping professional would fit very well in the sense that such a clinician would be more comfortable with facing constant, complex existential questions; and that being open to the questions that arise is considered a normal and a necessary part of the growth and insight experienced in the journey of the clinician. Living religion as a quest is more likely to lead to personal growth in the clinician. Most importantly from our patient's point of view, an other-focused and quest-oriented religiosity appears to be related to the clinician's ability to be truly attentive and flexibly responsive to what the patient actually needs.

Cautions about assumptions of another's religiosity or spirituality

It is very important to understand that this is not a critique of organized religion or that religious orientations are necessarily problematic. It is rather a finding of what the dominant motivation is in being part of an organized religion. A person in a particular religion who is high in religiosity and low in spirituality would be a person who is more identified with religion as a particular religion than as a method for spiritual growth. But it is also possible to be very identified with one's religion, with spirituality as the more dominant orientation. They might be very hard to distinguish from the outside, and so it would be a major error to assume a very religious person is not very spiritual or that a very spiritual person is not very religious. One way to think of this is that human beings are spiritual beings. Religion is a way this spiritual nature can be expressed. None of this should be taken as being critical of organized religion, and one should never assume a person is more (or less) spiritual because he or she is part of an organized religion. First, the assumption may be wrong because it is difficult to judge this as an outsider. Second, it is not helpful at all to judge another person in this way. What matters is that human beings are compassionate. What matters is that we work together to help others in our medical work. We must therefore allow and encourage each other to rely on the religious, spiritual, and/or philosophical practices that help us be the best we can be for our patients and for each other. It is also very helpful for us to learn from each other about the ways of thinking and the practices we bring to this question of cultivating and maintaining compassion in the face of suffering. In this way, we may learn of other practices that we may wish to add to our own practice; and in learning about other practices, we may be able to gain new insight and perspective in what we already practice.

What is needed from a POC/SOC

What exactly does a clinician need or desire from a spirituality or philosophy of compassionate caring? First, one would expect a spirituality or philosophy of compassionate caring to provide a way for a clinician to cope with the psychological and existential toll of helping work. It provides a way of understanding the work in terms of meaning, purpose, service, and a number of other spiritual dimensions. It provides a way to endure the strain of the ongoing encounters with challenging situations and a way to deal with the deep, big, or ultimate questions they evoke from a philosophical and/or religious/spiritual perspective. This is what we would commonly imagine when thinking about spirituality or one's philosophy in caring for others. Second, a spirituality (or philosophy) of compassionate caring not only might help the clinician keep going in the work, but also provides a way for the clinician to cultivate and maintain compassionate care toward others. From one perspective, a spirituality or philosophy of compassionate caring is focused on helping to take care of the clinician. But the nature of the work is such that focusing on how we clinicians feel is not sufficient. That spirituality (philosophy) of compassionate caring also has to be a source of energy and focus on caring for all people. While one might argue that all religions and spiritualities are intended to promote compassionate care among all people, the reality is that many practice their religions or spirituality in a more individualistic (e.g., "Am I doing the right thing?") or circumscribed manner (e.g., focused on one's family, in-group, or community) and only secondarily with all others. In clinical work, the primary focus is on extending compassionate care to all and secondarily to be concerned about oneself.

RESEARCH ON SPIRITUALITY AND BEING A HELPING PROFESSIONAL

Major study of spiritual and religious characteristics of US physicians compared to the rest of the population
Curlin, Lantos, Roach, Sellergren, and Chin (2005) compared the spiritual and religious characteristics of US physicians with the general population in a stratified random sampling of 2,000 physicians. With a response rate of 63% (1,125 physicians), they found that physicians were equally likely as the general population to have some religious affiliation and about the same percentage identified their affiliation as atheist, agnostic, or none (10.6% for physicians and 13.3% for the general population). Fifty-five percent of physicians said that their religious beliefs do influence their practice of medicine. In terms of differences with the general population, minority religions are overrepresented among physicians. Physicians are somewhat more likely to attend religious services regularly. They are somewhat less likely than the general population to say that they carry their religious belief into all their other dealings in life. Like the general population, about 50% self-identify as both religious and spiritual, but there are proportionally more physicians who self-identify as spiritual and not religious compared to the general population (20% vs. 9%). Physicians are somewhat less likely to "look to God for strength, support, and guidance" (48% vs. 64%), but significantly more likely to say they "try to make sense of a situation and decide what to do without relying on God" (61% vs. 29%). The authors concluded that, in general, physicians and patients therefore have different ways of relying on God as a way of coping and making decisions. With regard to specialties, family physicians and pediatricians tend to be more religious than other specialties (70% and over), while general internal medicine, anesthesiology, psychiatry, and radiology were somewhat less religious (from 48% to 52%).

Research shows that spirituality is definitely helpful for many clinicians
Research on the positive effects of integrating one's spirituality into the clinician's helping work is in its early stages. However, a number of studies suggest that spirituality does have positive effects on decreasing stress and burnout and improving the capacity for compassionate care toward patients. For many physicians, spirituality is viewed as integrally related to the ability to maintain compassion. Physicians sometimes choose this career based on spiritual beliefs focused on the centrality of compassionate action. While this may be the case, it has also been found that spirituality is not necessary for every clinician to have compassion; but that for quite a few, spirituality enhances compassion (Anandarajah & Smith, 2009). While much work remains in researching whether an integrated spirituality has an additive positive effect, it appears that, at least for some helping professionals, this is definitely the case. If it were to be found that spirituality has a clear additive effect on improving stress, burnout, and compassionate care, it would not necessarily be the case that all helping professionals should adopt a spiritual stance toward their work. A spiritual and/or religious worldview is a deeply personal thing that cannot be mandated and imposed from the outside. However, this does not rule out the fact that a POC/SOC that provides a sense of meaning and purpose might be very helpful in itself.

Good science must be aware of the bias both for and against the existence of the spiritual dimension

There is debate about whether the methods of science can be used to study the spiritual domain. There is a great deal of excellent research now that examines the positive effects of mindfulness meditation on decreasing stress and burnout among helping professionals (Luken & Sammons, 2016; Demarzo et al., 2015). Much of the research focuses on distilling the essential components in mindfulness meditation without the religious or spiritual beliefs that are part of its Buddhist historical roots. On one hand, it is thought that the spiritual beliefs and attitudes are not essential to the mechanism of how mindfulness meditation, for example, is able to benefit those who practice it. But they may prove essential for achieving the full effect of meditation. It is a good question worthy of scientific study. When it is demonstrated that a spiritual meditation practice is beneficial without the spiritual beliefs attached, Occam's razor applies in terms of taking the most parsimonious explanation of the phenomenon. But that does not necessarily mean that religion and/or spirituality is not additionally beneficial or that the spiritual domain does not exist. They still may be. Like the history of the philosophy of science demonstrates, the assumptions a scientist has can bias what is considered valid information. The secular scientist has an arguable point. A number of spiritual practices such as meditation can be explained without the use of spiritual concepts. Yet, it is hard to know what you do not know. It is hard to know (and accept) when your assumptions turn out to be wrong. Astronomers before Copernicus and Galileo assumed that the earth was the center of the solar system. That was considered good science—until they realized that the assumption was wrong. Newton's theories were considered the way the universe works—until Einstein and quantum theory. In the end, it is possible that the spiritual does exist. It is possible that the spiritual does not exist. It is an empirical question. If you are a good scientist, you should conduct your studies as if both are possible. The bias against the possibility that the spiritual domain exists is just that—a bias. A good scientist must be aware of assumptions, biases, and the limitations of one's instruments. The purpose of this chapter, however, is not to settle the question of whether spirituality "truly exists." But the beginning research is notable in terms of how a spirituality (or philosophy) of caring does appear to help clinicians cultivate and maintain compassionate caring in their work.

The attempt to derive a universal definition of spirituality

In their review of the literature, McSherry and Cash (2004) concluded that it is very difficult to derive a universal definition of spirituality. Instead, they developed a spiritual taxonomy to account for the diversity of definitions found in health care. They argue that there are no constant elements that are common when comparing individual views of spirituality. There is a way in which people individually tailor their own definitions of spirituality. They found that there appear to be two forms of spirituality. The first is based on religious and theocentric descriptors and is the form focused on belief in God and attendance at religious services. The second is what has been classified as a postmodern form of spirituality that

contains an infinite number of descriptors that may be phenomenological and existentially determined such as meaning and purpose in life, creativity, and relationships. They may also reflect the different values, beliefs and attitudes that guide and shape individuals from different world faiths that are not recognized in Judeo-Christian approaches. (McSherry & Cash, 2004, p. 157)

McSherry and Cash (2004) found that the continuum of definitions of spirituality range from one side as being based on religious and theistic beliefs to the other side as being based on secular, humanistic, existential, phenomenological, and mystical elements. Regarding a definition of spirituality, a consensus conference sponsored by the Archstone Foundation of Long Beach, California, in 2009, agreed upon the following *definition of spirituality*: "*spirituality is the aspect of humanity that refers to the way individuals seek and express meaning and purpose and the way they experience their connectedness to the moment, to self, to others, to nature, and to the significant or sacred*" (Puchalski et al., 2009, p. 887).

Palliative care research on how spirituality influences care of patients and learning from patients

In palliative care, physicians have reported that spirituality influences their holistic approaches to patients, increases their senses of fulfillment in the work, and helps them cope with the intensity and suffering witnessed on a daily basis. The sense of the spiritual enables them to care for all of their patients and families and have a sense of being part of something bigger than themselves. The physicians also reported that the spiritual perspective provided a framework in which they are able to learn from patients about life and dealing with difficulties (Seccareccia & Brown, 2009).

Spirituality is a protective factor against burnout in medical students and a positive coping method

Spirituality has also been found to be a protective factor against burnout in medical students.

In a study of 259 medical students, Wachholtz and Rogoff (2013) found that spirituality was associated with higher general life satisfaction and less anxiety, depression, and burnout. One of the spirituality measures included the Daily Spiritual Experiences Scale (DSES) (Fetzer Institute, 1999), which assesses how often an individual has a spiritual experience, such as feeling deep inner peace or harmony and having a sense of the transcendent, which may or may not include aspects of theistic religion. It also used the FACIT Spiritual Well-Being Non-Illness (FACIT Sp NI) scale (Peterman, Fitchett, Brady, Hernandez, & Cella, 2002) that assesses nonreligious spiritual well-being in coping with significant chronic stressors. It consists of two factors: a sense of meaning/peace in life factor and a faith factor that measures a sense that "things will be OK" as a result of spiritual beliefs. Higher levels of scores on the FACIT Sp NI scale and the DSES were associated with lower overall burnout and greater life satisfaction. In terms of whether spiritual coping is a positive or negative style of coping, the DSES was positively associated with adaptive coping and negatively associated with maladaptive coping. The FACIT Sp NI scale was positively associated with adaptive coping and not correlated with maladaptive coping. In multiple regression analyses, the spirituality measures predicted less burnout regardless of gender, year in medical school, mental health, adaptive and maladaptive coping, and life satisfaction. In a prospective study of 1,014 male medical students, lack of religious affiliation was identified as a possible precursor to alcohol abuse (Moore, Mead, & Pearson, 1990). In short, spirituality appeared to be an adaptive coping method that is correlated with less burnout, depression, and anxiety in medical school.

Spirituality helps decrease burnout in working with terminally ill patients

What clinicians experience while at work in terms of spirituality would be very relevant to this idea of an SOC. Holland and Neimeyer (2005) pursued this question in a study of burnout in working with terminally ill patients and their families. Eighty medical and mental health professionals were asked using the DSES how often they had everyday, ordinary experiences of spirituality (e.g., feeling close to God, grateful, blessed, experiencing God's love). The researchers found that those who had greater frequencies of daily spiritual experiences tended to report less physical, emotional, and cognitive burnout. Feelings of transcendence, connectedness, and being blessed were associated with less burnout, and this independently contributed to less burnout over and above other variables that were also related (i.e., demographic variables of age and education, amount of end-of-life training).

Palliative care physicians' spirituality helps with dealing with the work

In a qualitative study with palliative care physicians, Penderell and Brazil (2010) found that practicing palliative medicine had a major effect on their spirituality. The encounter with end-of-life issues made these physicians confront the issues of mortality all the time and as a result brought up spiritual issues in their own lives on which they were moved to reflect. Their own personal spirituality changed as a result—for example, being less spiritually rigid, being more comfortable with uncertainty, gaining insight about life, and leading to a reprioritizing of what they viewed as important in their lives. They often would be stimulated to think about how they relate to others, such as feeling more connectedness to others and the world. A number experienced the work as spiritually fulfilling and not burdensome from a spiritual perspective.

Palliative physicians with spirituality improved patient care practices and self-care

Penderell and Brazil (2010) found that palliative care physicians often used particular practices to help them in their work with patients. The physicians often used rituals or acts (e.g. breathing and centering practices, imagining how the divine is part of the patient meeting) to help them focus their attention on the patient or to prepare for difficult situations. Practices such as praying before seeing a patient or asking for guidance while washing hands were often used. Using spiritual readings would help them with how to be helpful to talk to patients and their families. Spirituality was reported to help these physicians be more open and receptive to the opportunities that might arise in care of their patients (e.g., being comfortable with spiritual concerns patients have). Spirituality was also reported to influence the self-care practices of palliative care physicians, such as journaling, as a way to reflect on the powerful experiences witnessed or of being energized to take care of themselves because of confronting mortality so much. The intensity of the work inspired many palliative care physicians to work on their spiritual lives more, to read about spirituality, and to seek out others to be able to discuss their spiritual experiences.

Spirituality related to higher QOL

Based on the World Health Organization's (WHO) definition of health and quality of life, the WHO developed a cross-cultural questionnaire on the quality of life called the WHOQOL–100. Quality of life (QOL) is defined by the WHO as "individuals' perception of their position in life in the context of the culture and value systems in which they live and in relation to their goals, expectations, standards and concerns" (World Health Organization Quality of Life Group, 1995, p. 1405). QOL in the area of spirituality is studied by using four questions related to personal values and an additional module called SRPB (spirituality/religiousness/personal beliefs). It consists of eight aspects called facets: spiritual connection; meaning of life; awe; wholeness/integration; spiritual strength; inner peace; hope; and faith. In a sample of health care workers in northern Italy, higher QOL scores on the SRPB work were associated with health care workers who consider themselves religious or very religious and those who report strong personal beliefs, especially personal values, wholeness, and hope. Poorer QOL was associated with individuals who reported less belief—whether it was spiritual, religious, or personal. Those who said they had stronger beliefs showed higher scores on wholeness and hope, and those who consider themselves more religious show higher scores on strength and inner peace (Boero et al., 2005).

Spirituality is related to better job satisfaction in hospice because of integrating spirituality

In a study of the relationship between spirituality and job satisfaction among hospice interdisciplinary team members consisting of nurses, home health aides, social workers, chaplains, and physicians, Clark et al. (2007) found that staff with strong spiritual beliefs were more likely to integrate their spiritual beliefs at work, tended to be more self-actualizing, and had a higher sense of job satisfaction. Interestingly, rather than a direct relationship between spirituality and job satisfaction, job satisfaction was more predicted by a model in which a staff member transforms one's spirituality into a process of integrating spirituality at work and self-actualization. *Spiritual integration* was defined as *"the degree to which one uses one's spiritual beliefs and values as resources to inform, guide, and/or shape their behaviors and decisions in the workplace"* (Clark et al., 2007, p. 1328). People high in spiritual integration reported integrating spirituality and work on a regular basis, felt able to integrate spirituality and work in their current positions, had meaningful discussions with coworkers about integrating the two, were able to integrate spirituality and work on decisions and actions that mattered most to them, and did not feel forced to compromise their spiritual or religious beliefs and values when making important decisions in their current positions. *Self-actualization* was defined as *"a set of needs to realize intrinsic personal happiness and inner satisfaction by engaging in metaphysical activities that are not related directly to or distant from the mundane and human needs of everyday life such as food, shelter, safety, security, respect, and self-esteem, etc."* (Clark et al., 2007, p. 1328). Clinicians who scored high in self-actualization would tend to report that they were able to give and receive love, were satisfied with their lives, set goals for themselves, were satisfied in the way that they used their abilities, were able to appreciate differences in others, tended to accept their life situations, and experienced high self-esteem. *In short, it is not simply having religious and/or spiritual beliefs that enables greater job satisfaction. Rather, it is the ability to integrate spirituality and self-actualization in one's work that improves job satisfaction. Simply having spiritual or religious beliefs is not sufficient in helping clinicians in their work. Clinicians must learn how to bridge their spiritual and religious beliefs with what they experience in their work in an intentional and regular way.*

Study on increased pain tolerance with spiritual versus secular meditation

It has become well documented that meditation has positive effects for people in general as well as specifically decreasing stress and burnout among health care professionals (Dobkin & Hutchinson, 2013; Shapiro, Astin, Bishop, & Cordova, 2005; Warnecke, Quinn, Ogden, Towle, & Nelson, 2011). Does spiritual meditation have an additive effect compared to secular meditation practices? Wachholtz and Pargament (2005) compared secular and spiritual forms of meditation to ascertain whether spiritual meditation was associated with additional beneficial outcomes compared to secular meditation and relaxation exercises. They randomly assigned 84 undergraduates to three groups to test this. There were no differences between the groups in terms of self-rated spirituality, religiosity, or prayer practice. In the secular meditation group, participants chose from four secular phrases: "I am content," "I am joyful," "I am good," and "I am happy." In the spiritual meditation group, participants chose from one of the four spiritual meditative phrases: "God is peace," "God is joy," "God is good," and "God is love." They were allowed to change the term "God" to a different word if it better described the center of their spirituality or religion. The relaxation control group was given the same instructions as the meditation groups in terms of physically comfortable positions and isolation but was not given instructions regarding what to do mentally during that meditation time. For two weeks, participants practiced their techniques for 20 minutes a day and completed an adherence diary recording their daily practices and whether they found these practices to result in positive effects. The researchers found that the spiritual meditation group had significantly less anxiety and better mood than the secular meditation and relaxation groups. The spiritual meditation group also reported more positive mood than the secular meditation and relaxation groups. In terms of the Existential Well Being Scale used to measure spiritual interactions between oneself and others, those in the spiritual meditation group had significantly higher existential well-being than those in the secular and relaxation groups. Those in the spiritual group also felt closer to God than the other groups. Those in the spiritual meditation group reported more daily experiences of a spiritual nature than the other groups. The authors speculated that the spiritual meditation group may have encouraged individuals to interpret daily events through a spiritual lens and/or that setting time aside to focus on one's spirituality may have facilitated more openness to subjective spiritual experiences.

Spiritual meditators could tolerate pain longer

The researchers also examined objective measures of pain tolerance and stress reactivity. Pain tolerance was tested with the cold pressor task to measure physiological and psychological reactions to pain. They measured pain perception, heart rate, and length of time that the research participants had their hands in a cold-water bath (36°F). There were no differences in pain perception among the three groups. There were no differences in heart rate. However, the spiritual meditation group kept their hands in the icy cold water nearly twice as long as the other groups. That is, while there were no differences in how much pain was experienced, the spiritual meditation appeared to increase the ability to cope with and tolerate pain. Why is it that spiritual meditation would lead to more improved mood, decreased anxiety, and an increased ability to tolerate pain? The authors speculated that one possibility is that the improvement in mood is what leads to better pain tolerance. The other possibility is that the spiritual meditation was a positive spiritual coping technique that itself enabled people to endure pain longer.

Theoretical pathways between pain and spiritual/religious coping

There is now a large amount of research which has found that religious and spiritual forms of coping are associated with positive health outcomes (Koenig, King, & Carson, 2012), and that such coping can predict psychological and physician outcomes beyond other types of coping (Hill & Pargament, 2003; McCullough, Hoyt, Larson, Koenig, & Thoresen, 2000). Reviewing this research, Wachholtz, Pearce, Koenig (2007) have proposed six potential pathways for how religious and spiritual practice and coping strategies may cause physiological and neurological changes that change the perception of pain (see figure 14.1). First, religious and spiritual coping may provide the person in pain with ways to make attributions about the meaning and purpose of his or her pain. This might change his or her perception of the situation and of the ability to cope with that pain. Such attributions might encourage the person and provide comfort, and examples of coping from the historical stories of those spiritual and religious traditions might provide ways that increase the motivation and ability to cope with pain. Second, religious and spiritual coping may increase the person's sense of control and self-efficacy to manage that pain. Third, religious and spiritual coping may provide a way to distract the person in pain, enabling him or her to tolerate pain longer. Fourth, being

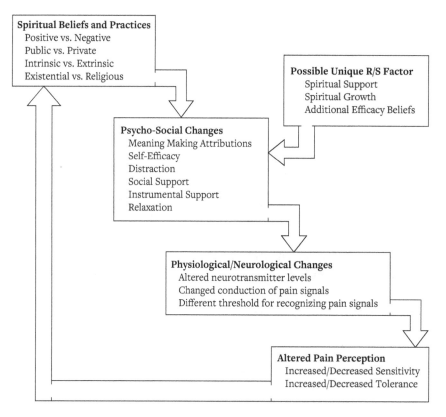

FIGURE 14.1 Potential pathways between spirituality and pain (Wachholtz et al., 2007, p. 315).

part of a religious or spiritual community can increase the social support for the individual in pain as well as provide instrumental and spiritual support; the person in pain also has the opportunity to provide support to others who might be suffering. Fifth, meditation and prayer practices may directly change the physiological experience of pain by, for example, calming the body. Sixth, there may be something unique about religious and spiritual coping that directly or indirectly changes the perception of pain. The person in pain may feel more connected to God and more supported by God, which encourages that person to use more active and adaptive coping, and to have increased self-efficacy to be open to ways of spiritually growing in this experience. Keefe et al. (2001) point out that spiritual experiences might encourage better self-care in which the person in pain follows through on prescribed medications, treatments, and exercise programs as well as taking time to rest and relax regularly.

Resident burnout and spirituality led to more personal accomplishment

Doolittle, Windish, and Seelig (2013) examined how resident physician burnout was related to their coping methods and spirituality. In a sample of 108 internal medicine and internal medicine–pediatrics residents at four affiliated programs, having more spirituality was related to having more of a sense of personal accomplishment in the work. Researchers used the Spiritual Involvement and Beliefs Scale (SIBS) (Hatch, Burg, Naberhaus, & Hellmich, 1998), which measures broad aspects of spirituality and practice. When the relationship between burnout and subscales of the SIBS were examined, a sense of personal accomplishment in one's work was positively correlated with the internal/fluid subscale, the existential/meditative subscale, and the humility/personal application subscale. The internal/fluid subscale reflected beliefs about understanding one's experiences in life through spirituality, personal growth, and evolving beliefs rather than measuring attendance or participation in formal religion. The existential/meditative subscale reflected existential beliefs about the nature of a spiritual force that influences one's life and the use of prayer/meditation. The humility/personal application subscale reflected the application of spiritual principles to one's life such as humility, apologizing when one has wronged another, telling someone when one is ashamed of something, solving problems using spirituality, and examining one's actions to make sure they are aligned with one's values. Interestingly, only the humility/personal application subscale was related to other dimensions of burnout in that individuals with higher scores on the humility/personal application subscale were less emotionally exhausted and less depersonalized in their work.

Interns' spirituality related to more personal accomplishment

Doolittle and Windish (2015) examined the relationship between the spiritual attitudes, coping strategies, and burnout with interns using the same scales and found that the SIBS was positively correlated with feeling a sense of personal accomplishment but not at all related to emotional exhaustion and depersonalization. In this sample, the two subscales that were correlated with increased personal accomplishment were the internal/fluid subscale and the existential/meditative subscale. Looking at both of these studies, what is notable is how these two subscales are related to only the personal accomplishment factor in burnout. Doolittle and Windish (2015) speculate that the internal/fluid subscale with its flexibility and sense of purpose in one's belief system and the existential/meditative with its belief in the usefulness of prayer and meditation "perhaps give support and meaning to the daily chores of patient care, thereby impacting personal accomplishment" (p. 4).

AWARENESS OF SPIRITUAL RISKS AND REWARDS IN THE ENCOUNTER WITH SUFFERING

Work in health care creates an existential pressure to answer spiritual and philosophical issues

My experience working with physicians, nurses, and other clinicians is that the concepts of spirituality and/or philosophy of life and the level of reflectiveness that clinicians typically have before they practice medicine is not at the level it needs to be when clinicians start engaging suffering patients regularly and encountering their own stress and burnout. This is also true for many other helping professions as well as other work that engages with life and death issues. Perhaps this is just true in general as people encounter the major difficulties one encounters in life. Childhood concepts of the spiritual and the typical training in one's faith to make sense of the spiritual challenges of this work do not provide the fully developed spiritual resources needed to develop a mature SOC.

The intensity of work in health care changes the clinician's understanding about life

The sheer intensity and quantity of difficult life experiences encountered in patient care is challenging physically and psychologically to clinicians. You have to learn how to see a large number of people in a relatively short span of time. You are required to adjust rapidly to the unique predicaments of each patient that you meet. You are helping large numbers of people,

each of whom is at some point encountering a life-limiting or life-threatening condition. Helping professionals have to learn how to physically gain the stamina to do this work for many hours at a time, and they have to learn how to adjust psychologically to witnessing patient suffering and difficulties to a degree most people never witness. In addition to being a physically and psychologically challenging adjustment process, it is also challenging spiritually. Even if a clinician does not use the term *spiritual*, the clinician is faced with experiences that will affect how the clinician sees life after he or she works with many people who are suffering. You do not look at life the same way. What people take for granted in life you do not take for granted anymore after doing this work. You know of the bad things that happen to people. No one is exempt from the sufferings of life. Someone who does not have a profession like this can get away with thinking that suffering does not occur that often; with imagining that the person suffering is somehow at fault; with thinking that the world is just and fair, or that it should be; or that looking at things positively will minimize the impact of suffering. When you are in a helping profession or similar work, you know that none of this is true. You have to confront the fact that tragedy is often senseless, undeserved, and can afflict people that are thought to be somehow less likely to suffer. Your illusions of life are shattered. What view of life do you have after that happens? That is the zone of the spiritual—or, if you prefer, the zone of your philosophical understanding of what life is all about.

While spiritually rewarding, work in health care challenges our thinking about life

There are likely both ordeals and blessings in the journey of the helping professional. A very important part of living our lives committed to helping others involves attending to how what we are doing is both dangerous and yet a powerful force making us live more deeply and responding to life with deeper love. Caring for others is a gateway to the sacred, but not in some sweet benign image of the spiritual we might have. It is both awesome and terrible, dangerous and yet full of blessing. On one hand, clinicians have the opportunity of accompanying people in many of the most significant events that can occur in a person's life. Patients and their loved ones often quickly rely on and trust the clinician. While a great responsibility, it is also a privilege granted to us. People shower us with gratitude for helping them, even when things go badly and they knew we did the best we could to help. We encounter everything about life, and, if we are even just a little open to it, we learn a great deal about life, what it means, and how fragile it is. We will go home and think about our lives differently because we have spent all day seeing how fragile it is; we come to value ours differently, our relationships differently, and we cannot help but think about life differently.

Spiritual costs as a result of compassion fatigue

Helping others who are suffering or who are difficult will challenge us in the deepest ways. It is possible to lose faith in humanity, in God (if you believe in God), and even in yourself. If you experience little success in your work or witness an overwhelming amount of tragedy, you may grow discouraged, be less optimistic about life, have less confidence in humanity, and wonder if what you are doing really matters. The effects of the continual encounter with suffering on the helper are real and they are dangerous. Over the past few years, we

have become very aware of the reality of compassion fatigue (Baranowsky, 2002; Figley, 2002).

Clinicians respond to patient suffering in many different ways

What are the options we have in the continual encounter with suffering? Some clinicians ignore it and approach the work in an emotionally detached manner. Perhaps they objectify the patients or somehow distance themselves from the patients. Clinicians at times anesthetize themselves with substances during or after work. Sometimes the encounter with suffering is so intense that clinicians are desperate to end their patients' suffering in any way possible. They may deny the futility and go to extensive measures to end the suffering. They may never leave the bedside in that they can do nothing else because they are gripped by someone's suffering. Or they may want to end the suffering by hastening death. Other clinicians have a perspective that allows them to be fully engaged with patients' suffering but not overwhelmed by it. They are moved by the patients' suffering, but they are able to accompany these patients without being irretrievably discouraged.

How physicians change as a result of practice

In terms of how physicians change as a result of practice, Fang et al. (2011) interviewed 27 Taiwanese physicians' terminally ill cancer patients and identified a number of ways these physicians changed. Physicians tended to change their ideas about life and death. They moved from viewing the dying process as shocking to viewing it as natural. They accepted death more readily than the general population and were not afraid of their own deaths. They reported less focus on wealth and fame and more focus on their families.

They tended to appreciate and be more content with what they had, valued life more, and realized how unexpected life and death are. They became more able to deal with loss because of patient deaths, and many said they became less likely to be tearful when this occurred, although others became more comfortable crying over the deaths of patients. Very compassionate and mission-driven physicians experienced existential doubts about their medical practices. They questioned the meaning of their work even though they worked with suffering patients to help them feel more comfortable, and they experienced feelings of loss with every patient death. In a study of 72 cancer surgeons at a major cancer treatment center, the rate of burnout was 42%, the prevalence of psychiatric morbidity was 27%, and the rate of potentially problematic alcohol use was 30% (Guest et al., 2011). Only one-third of the surgeons reported a high quality of life across physical, emotional, spiritual, and intellectual domains.

Study on physicians learning to navigate existential challenges and the ability to tolerate risk and responsibility

In a qualitative study about the existential experiences of physicians, Aase, Nordrehaug, and Malterud (2008) found that physicians described how the encounter with the deaths of all types of patients and horrible or shocking events early in their careers required that they learn how to cope with this in order to continue. This is what shaped their professional identities and led them to learn how to balance being close or distant with patients. What helped them was conversations with colleagues, loved ones, and friends. Quite a few physicians said they repressed their feelings to cope. The physicians described how their professional responsibilities were linked to feeling very vulnerable because of the decisions they had to make, the complexity and severity of illnesses, breaking bad medical news to patients, and the possibility of making mistakes. One physician was quoted as saying, "If you cannot tolerate the risk, you should never become a physician" (Aase et al., 2008, p. 768). What balanced this for them was being able to improve the conditions of their patients, making the work very gratifying and meaningful. However, not being able to "fix" problems made them feel powerless, and this was difficult to tolerate. While a number discussed the importance of mutually supportive colleagues, others disclosed feeling very isolated in dealing with tragedies in a medical culture that expected toughness and perfection because of its focus on prestige, pride, and competition.

Studies documenting the existential challenges of being in health care

Udo, Melin-Johansson, and Danielson (2011) interviewed surgical care staff and found a significant theme of existential distress and dilemmas among them in their work with cancer patients. Their existential distress consisted of feeling despair and isolation. Their dilemmas revolved around feeling powerless, sometimes identifying with patient suffering, and struggling to find how involved they should be with patients. In a study of palliative care clinicians, Chan et al. (2016) heard two basic themes: first, experiencing existential challenges because their assumptions about life and death were shattered; and second, dealing with major emotional challenges. They had to deal with their personal emotional reactions often related to death tapping into their own experiences of loss. They also had to deal with work-related emotional arousal when dealing with feeling powerless, overwhelmed, frustrated, pressured, or guilty. Clinicians, then, typically go through a process in their careers of rebuilding assumptions about life and death as well as meaning in life.

Five core challenges that affect the well-being of the compassionate caregiver

Halifax (2011) has proposed that there are five core challenges that affect the well-being of the compassionate caregiver: burnout, secondary trauma, moral distress, horizontal hostility, and structural violence. Halifax finds that the core challenges affecting caregivers are further intensified

> by the possible denial of death; the angst around pain, suffering, and death; the inability to discuss interventions and death; the inability to communicate about stresses in caregiving; workaholism, self-neglect, and perfectionism; guilt for avoiding or abandoning the dying individual; engaging in negative cognitive appraisal; and moral conflicts and distress. Caregivers also can experience a sense of futility that arises from patient demands, institutional demands, clinical errors, feelings of inadequacy, and interventions not benefitting patients. (Halifax, 2011, p. 147)

In so many ways, clinicians experience an emotional and existential toll in continually engaging with people who are suffering in every possible way human beings suffer. The constant exposure and engagement with that suffering intensifies the clinicians' own understanding of what life is about. There can be great rewards in the work in terms of fulfillment and meaning, as well as the experience of being able to help others who are suffering. There also can be increased insight and life perspective that comes from this work. But the sheer quantity and intensity impacts so strongly that clinicians will go through a process of adapting to this challenging lifestyle and must find a way to work through the suffering that they witness.

The body wants to heal itself

One of the awesome wonders of working in a profession of helping and healing is that you get to witness how the body heals itself. Our job is very humble in some sense. We set the conditions for the body to heal itself. True, we do have to figure out how the body is out of balance or lacking something to do what it normally does. But when we give the body what it needs, the body does the healing. When a bone is broken, we set the fracture and the bone heals itself. The body is geared toward healing itself. Whether it is a fracture or a wound, we facilitate the conditions for healing, and then sit back and often get to watch this amazing spectacle.

The mind is geared toward healing itself

What happens at one dimension of the human happens in a parallel way across any level that you study the human being. Just as we see healing at the level of bodily wounds and fractures, so do we see this at the psychological level. The mind wants to heal itself. People experience emotional setbacks, and that disturbance often sets in motion a process of reestablishing equilibrium and even growth in the face of difficulty. People who experience loss go through grieving and then bounce back. People encounter what feels (and often is) very overwhelming—like their lives are over in some sense. But after a day, a week, or some other length of time, they bounce back. With a good night's sleep, time to be alone or talk with trusted companions, or some way of reflecting on what has happened, people are often resilient. Not only do they bounce back, but often they have new insight into life and themselves; they grow in some way. A major setback at times becomes the major impetus to achieving something that dealing with the psychological wound set in motion. Some people who have these setbacks find the drive to create something new that benefits others. A person who loses a loved one to cancer goes on to enter a helping profession and helps others. A scientist turns his or her encounter with tragedy into scientific discovery that leads to a new drug or a new public health intervention that prevents or eases that condition for others. The phoenix rises from the ashes.

Human spirit, like nature, has processes to respond to injury

The human spirit likewise wants to heal itself. It wants to make itself whole. Whatever way you look at the human, there is evidence of this. Nature in general displays its mechanisms of healing, such as in how trees heal from scrapes in its bark to how salamanders regenerate lost limbs. There is no reason to think the spiritual dimension of the human being would operate any differently. The human being has an elegant mechanism for dealing with external attacks, toxins, dysregulation, infections, and damage. If healing is not completely possible, then nature has ways of trying to contain the damage and prevent it from destroying the whole organism. A tree, for example, responds to damage suffered to its bark by compartmentalization (growing a protective boundary around the wound to prevent infection or the spread of decay) or creating barrier zones (chemical and physical boundaries that keep the organisms of decay from spreading to the rest of the tree) (Shigo, 1989). The clinician who encounters suffering in another person can be, in a sense, wounded by that encounter. What processes are involved in both the injury sustained and the response to that injury?

Metaphor for how to ease physical pain

If you stub your toe on a table leg in the middle of the night, you would react in a certain way to that pain. You might groan and rub your foot to ease the pain. You might put ice on it or pretend it did not happen. You might say something invoking God, sex, or excrement. It is a silly example, but the point is, witnessing people in pain and suffering will affect us, and we will do something to try to relieve how the suffering makes us feel. Recall the automatic empathic resonance and the mirror neuron system discussed in chapter 3. As humans, we are constructed to empathize, to be affected by the suffering of another. But what do you do with the pain and suffering that you witness? What do you rub or apply on the wound, metaphorically speaking, to ease your pain? How do you make sense of, metabolize, or process it? What do you keep going back to in order to draw strength to do your work? What makes the work still worthwhile even though it makes you very sad or very angry? Now we turn to the articulation and reliance on a POC/SOC as one way that clinicians answer these questions.

ARTICULATION AND RELIANCE ON A SPIRITUALITY OF CARING/PHILOSOPHY OF CARING

Inevitable that we develop an SOC/POC

It is inevitable that a clinician develops a POC/SOC. As you encounter people who are suffering, you are confronted with what can happen in life. While we might try to distance ourselves emotionally and existentially from the suffering patient in front of us, at some level we realize that what happens to the humans we treat can happen to anyone—to our friends, to our families, and to ourselves. We might try to outmaneuver this empathic resonance with the suffering in front of us by coming up with a reason why this is not likely to happen to our friends, families, or ourselves. We might attribute the suffering to something that patient did to bring this condition about, or we tell ourselves that there is a quality we have or our loved ones have that makes this kind of suffering unlikely for us or our loved ones. Whatever cognitive move we make, the fact is that we have to come to terms with what we encounter in our patients and the people we help in general. We have to explain it, and that involves what our connection is with it. Over time, we develop a pattern of how we think about such situations. We begin to develop "theories" about the way life is and what our role is in life in general. The "theories" might be crude, inconsistent, simplistic, half-thought out, or a conglomeration of maxims we have about our experiences that may not really fit together, but nonetheless we use them to explain what we observe. Like it or not, as thinking beings with mirror neurons, we develop some conception of what all this hard stuff about life means. You are on spiritual ground at that point. Or, if you would rather, you are contemplating a philosophy about life.

SOC is like physiology of exercise

You already are using a POC/SOC! Do you know what yours is? Even if your POC/SOC is a loose stitching of various ideas or beliefs about life, it is still a spirituality or philosophy of life. The physiology of exercise is a perfect analogy for what is going on. The physiology of exercise explains and teaches us how various types of exercise benefit us. But it is not necessary to know any physiology of exercise in order to exercise. I can decide that I need to exercise, and so I begin walking 20 minutes three times a week. Or I can just start lifting weights. I do not need to know anything about the physiology of exercise in order to exercise, but that does not mean the physiology of exercise is not operating even though I am ignorant of it. I do my walk, and it benefits me in a certain way.

But just walking several times a week does not really give me the aerobic exercise I need. Maybe I do not get the nutrition I really need to help my body benefit from the exercise. Even if I do not know the underlying physiology of why this is, that does not change the truth about what is going on: my body does not have the nutrients that would help my exercise really benefit me, or only walking does not get my heart pumping as much as it should. The physiology of exercise is always operating whether I know it or not, and my exercise habits can be described in those terms as can what the state of my physiology is. Someone who observes me can characterize what the state of my physical conditioning style is. I have developed one even if it is not a very good or consistent one. This is what happens to many clinicians in terms of a philosophy or spirituality of how they view or imagine what they are doing regarding helping people and responding to suffering.

The more physiology of exercise I learn, the more the exercise benefits me

Continuing with this analogy, the more I know about the physiology of exercise, the more I can evaluate my exercise regimen and change it according to what my goals are. Maybe my physical trainer or physician listens to me describe that I walk 20 minutes a day three times a week and then says, "Well, it is good that you are doing some exercise, but you really are not giving yourself aerobic exercise. You really need to get your heart pumping more. And while your legs are getting a workout, you are not doing anything for your upper body." That feedback leads me to widening my exercise regimen. The more physiology of exercise I learn, the more I can improve how exercise benefits me. The same is true of articulating what my POC/SOC is. The more I learn about it, the more it can help me assess what I am doing and improve it.

Explicit SOC/POC is not necessary, but it is still operating

Is an explicit SOC/POC necessary? No. But that does not mean it is not operating. If a clinician says that he or she does not have a POC/SOC, it is just like when someone who exercises does not know anything about the physiology of exercise. Not knowing about it does not mean the physiology of exercise is not operating. The clinician who just does his or her work has an implicit philosophy or spirituality that is operating. Furthermore, just because I do not label things in a philosophical or spiritual way does not mean that philosophy or spirituality do not exist. In our society, spirituality or philosophy about life and caring is often seen as an optional accessory like what kind of jacket or hat I am going to wear. Just as people can imagine not having to wear a jacket or a hat, so too they imagine that if they do not think about the spirituality or philosophy of caregiving work, then it does not exist. But this is fallacious thinking. There is always an implicit way that you are viewing life, and it is reflected in your actions, thoughts, and feelings.

Articulating SOC is likely to be helpful

However, clinicians are not obligated to articulate what their POC/SOCs are. They can get by without the articulation process just as a person can exercise a certain way all their lives and never know what the strengths and weakness of that regimen are—until one day a lack of aerobic exercise and a good diet results in coronary artery disease. Or they might be lucky enough to have gained a good regimen of exercise with a good diet and good genes so that articulating the physiology of their exercise would not have added much to what they were already doing. But most of us can benefit by reflecting on what we are doing and adjusting it according to our goals. Articulating what your POC/SOC is will likely be helpful. It can help clarify what the meaning of your caring work is. It can help you figure out how to work through the exhausting parts of your work and do what you need to keep your spirit up. Getting clear about what this suffering and helping thing is about can help you figure out how to detoxify the encounter with pain, suffering, and evil. In the encounter with life's tragedies, you can figure out how to keep finding the energy to keep caring for other people and how to grow as a human being in the process.

Your SOC/POC affects your patients spiritually

A POC/SOC operates in every clinician whether he or she is aware of it or not. Moreover, how you care for others can affect them not only physically and psychologically; you can affect someone spiritually even though you do not think of yourself as spiritual. The way you treat someone can make him or her think there is no hope. Or, what you say and how you treat the patient might inspire him or her to reevaluate what his or her purpose in life is. The way you care for a patient or talk to a patient can add or detract to his or her motivation to keep working to get better or to do the best he or she can in the face of chronic illness or dying. You might not think of yourself as a deep or spiritual person. But what you do can affect others, negatively or positively, in a deep or spiritual way. It is worth figuring out what our spirit looks like because it is affecting our patients' spirits whether we intend it to or not.

Michael Meade and the three types of people

Michael Meade, storyteller and expert on mythology and what it teaches us, provides a glimpse of how a spirituality or philosophy of life can function in a person's life. He said that, roughly speaking, there appear to be three approaches to life. In the first approach, the person is thinking that he or she is here for himself or herself. Such a person goes through life and says, "I'm going to get mine." The second type of person discovers that there are ways to act in life in which he or she can do something for others and that he or she gets something back in doing this. This is a kind of win–win view of life. Meade notes that sometimes when things get difficult, people who use the win–win approach fall back to the "I'm going to get mine" approach. Finally, there is a third approach:

> *The third kind of person is the person whose vision has become clear and strong enough, is deep enough, awakened in themselves, that as the circumstances get more difficult, more full of threat, and more of great concern, they become more actively engaged and aware of and involved in the dream of their life. That when despair is present, their imagination, the vision of their life is greater … as if the brightness of their vision is intensified by the darkness of the circumstances. (Meade, 2003)*

Meade's description of the third type of person is an example of a POC/SOC.

SOC/POC is forged in the midst of clinical work

Typically, a POC/SOC is forged in the midst of clinical work. Rarely would a clinician have a fully evolved and stable SOC at the beginning of the clinician's career unless he or she had gone through other major life challenges beforehand that would have begun the process of formulating a POC/SOC earlier. Clinicians certainly get an initial formulation of an SOC from religious or spiritual instruction, role modeling, and study before getting into clinical work. But when a clinician fully engages regularly and intensely with patients, it is then that he or she encounters questions about life, meaning, suffering, and even evil that expose the limits of their previous spiritual or philosophical ideas about life.

Pargament's idea of an orienting system to help explain SOC/POC

A concept that helps explain how a POC/SOC works in the life of the clinician is Kenneth Pargament's idea of the *orienting system*. Pargament is a psychologist who has done extensive research on the psychology of religion and coping. He describes how human beings each rely on an orienting system to guide them in how to navigate and deal with life's difficulties. As Pargament (1997) explains,

> *we do not live totally at the mercy of stressful life events. In the face of crisis, we are guided and grounded by an orienting system. The orienting system is a general way of viewing and dealing with the world. It consists of habits, values, relationships, generalized beliefs, and personality. The orienting system is a frame of reference, a blueprint of oneself and the world that is used to anticipate and come to terms with life's events. The orienting system directs us to some life events and away from others. The orienting system is also the reservoir we draw on during hard times. Depending on the character of this system, it may be a help or hindrance in the coping process, for orienting systems are made up not only of resources but of burdens as well. Resources are attributes that are generally helpful in many situations. Burdens are attributes that are generally unhelpful. The orienting system also contains qualities whose value varies from situation to situation. (pp. 99–100)*

Every person has an orienting system that may or may not include religion/ spirituality

Every human being has an orienting system—a way of thinking about life and how to respond to it in light of that understanding. It is not necessarily religious or spiritual. A person can be raised with absolutely no exposure to religion or spirituality, but he or she still develops a way of understanding what life is and how one should navigate it. But one can see how religion and spirituality, if they are explicitly part of a person's life, can be an integral part of that person's orienting system. The same is true with the POC/SOC in a clinician's life. A clinician will develop a way of understanding what suffering is, what it means to help someone, why things happen the way they do, and what the meaning of this helping work is. Religion and spirituality can be a major influence in this orienting system for the clinician. But just because a clinician has a religion or spirituality does not mean this is necessarily helping to orient him or her in the helping work. As Pargament (1997) puts it, "It is important to note that the orienting system does not fully determine how a person will handle a stressful situation. It makes some methods of coping more available to the individual than others" (p. 106). The challenge for the clinician is that it requires extra effort and insight to use religion and spirituality to orient him or her through this difficult work.

SOC/POC is an orienting system to this life of helping

A spirituality or philosophy of compassionate caring is the orienting system on which a person in the helping profession relies in doing physically, psychologically, and spiritually demanding work. In doing this difficult work, this POC/SOC is how the clinician orients him- or herself to this work, a way of looking at this kind of work in general. What is this work about and why should I keep doing it? What discourages me about this work and what encourages me to keep going? What is my attitude about this work and how do I keep that attitude in healthy positive place?

A POC/SOC is my general attitude toward this work, my sense of the meaning of this work, the way I understand and deal with suffering, and why compassionate caring is the most fitting response. It is the way I orient myself to what happens in this work so that when things go badly, it guides me in how I should respond and keeps my spirit up.

Pargament and the concept of spiritual struggle

Kenneth Pargament has done extensive research on the role of religion and spirituality in coping with stress and trauma. His work can be applied readily to those who work in helping professions. He would describe the time when a clinician encounters the stress of the work taxing his or her previous spiritual concept as a spiritual struggle.

> Spiritual struggles are signs of spiritual disorientation, tension, and strain. Old roads to the sacred and old understandings of the sacred itself are no longer compelling. In their place, people struggle to reorient themselves and find a new way to the sacred or a new understanding of the sacred. (Pargament, 2007, p. 112)

Pargament has found that there are generally three types of spiritual struggles: interpersonal, intrapersonal, and tension between the individual and the divine.

What are the three types of spiritual struggles?

An *interpersonal spiritual struggle* involves "spiritual conflicts and tension with family, friends, and congregations" (Pargament, 2007, p. 112). An example of this would be an interaction with other people that violates what a person expects how people in a religious group should act. Or it might involve disagreements about doctrine or hypocrisy. An *intrapersonal spiritual struggle* would involve having doubt or uncertainty about one's religious tradition, questioning one's own spiritual purpose in life, or experiencing turmoil regarding an expected religious or spiritual virtue that conflicts with some desire a person would like to pursue. The third type of spiritual struggle emerges *when the person experiences tension with the divine.* A common example would be undergoing a critical life event that makes one wonder how an all-loving and all-powerful divine being could allow pain and suffering.

How spiritual struggles can lead to growth or deterioration

Spiritual struggles can be combinations of all three of these types and occur in all types of critical life events. They are not indications of weak faith or pathology. Indeed, Pargament notes how spiritual struggles are reported in great spiritual figures, and their stories are ones in which facing this spiritual turmoil becomes important in strengthening them. Spiritual struggles can be short-lived with the person returning to the previous spiritual pathway. Others can be quite serious and become a major turning point in a person's life, "a spiritual fork in the road that can lead to renewal, growth, and positive transformation in one direction, or despair, hopelessness, and meaninglessness in the other" (Pargament, 2007, p. 115). As Pargament has found, some empirical studies have found higher levels of personal growth as a result of spiritual struggles, and others have found them connected to increased anxiety and depression, poorer physical functioning, lower quality of life, increased relational distress, and even an increased risk for dying. People may experience spiritual emptiness or even abandon their spiritual or religious pathways.

Spiritual struggles test the spiritual orienting system and set the stage for potential spiritual transformation

Spiritual struggles set the stage for potential spiritual transformation. Pargament (1997) defines *spiritual transformation* as

> *fundamental changes in the place of the sacred or the character of the sacred in the person's life, and secondarily to a fundamental change in the pathways the individual takes to the sacred. Spiritual transformation can be difficult and painful. Furthermore, it is not always successful; some transformations lead to failure and decline.* (p. 116)

Spiritual struggles test the spiritual orienting system that the clinician has. How he or she imagines what this work is about, how to approach it, and how to keep going are challenged when the clinician encounters struggles from the work. For our purposes, it is important to note that this should not be seen as unusual in a clinician's career. The search for the sacred typically consists of a journey of spiritual struggle and transformation. As clinicians encounter the most difficult parts of being human, it should not be a surprise nor an indication of failure on the clinician's part that the spiritual understanding of what he or she encounters would be challenged. If the clinician does not use a spiritual perspective, a parallel occurs philosophically as the clinician tries to make sense of the difficult parts of life.

Spiritual orienting system can be inadequate

Thus, a clinician may have an orienting system that cannot sustain or metabolize the negative experiences of health care and have unhealthy religious or spiritual coping methods. Among people not familiar with spiritual and religious dynamics, there is the erroneous thinking that all religious and spiritual coping is considered acceptable and appropriate. In the spirit of political correctness, the thought is that if you have a particular religious or spiritual coping method, then it must be just honored and accepted as it is. But religious coping is not unlike other types of coping; it can be unhealthy as well.

Spiritual struggles and magnitude of stressor

Spiritual struggles are common after people have experienced all types of stressors including illnesses, disasters, trauma, and personal crises. The spirituality or religion that a person has used as an orienting system for dealing with life can be challenged because the person may encounter doubts about the orienting system vis-à-vis the difficulty he or she has experienced or because the stressor is more than he or she has ever encountered before. Pargament (1997) explains that vulnerabilities to failures in coping are a function of the magnitude of stressful life experiences and the strength of the orienting system. First, in terms of magnitude, a clinician can encounter a situation that becomes a kind of breaking point in his or her life. This could range from encountering human suffering in a major disaster, as a result of terrible poverty or violence, or in working with someone in terrible pain. It could also occur as a result of a cumulative effect of encountering suffering over a long period of time. If the clinician is also personally vulnerable in terms of undergoing personal stress in his or her own life, he or she can be even more vulnerable in encountering major suffering in others.

Spiritual struggles and insufficient spiritual orienting system

Second, the religious/spiritual orienting system a person has may be insufficient in helping the clinician deal with the stressors he or she encounters. Pargament (1997) describes several ways that religious orienting systems can be inadequate in helping a person encountering major stressors. These are *undifferentiated religion, fragmented religion, religious rigidity,* and *insecure religious attachment.* A *differentiated religious orienting system* is one in which a person is able to understand the complexity of living in the world and respond appropriately. The person has to be able to judge a situation accurately and then respond in the most fitting way to that situation. A differentiated system "equips the person with a broader repertoire of responses, more capable of coping with a wider range of life experiences" (Pargament, 1997, p. 342). A person who has an *undifferentiated religious orienting system* with a simplistic understanding of his or her own spiritual or religious tradition will lack the necessary ability to judge the situation in spiritual terms and be unable to respond accordingly. In other words, if an individual has only a cursory understanding of his or her religious or spiritual tradition—having only bits and pieces of the beliefs, practices, and guidelines of that tradition—the orienting system will provide little help in the face of major challenges. Pargament explains that this deficiency shows up especially when people encounter pain. The major religions have struggled to articulate and respond to the problem of pain and evil, and anyone who has studied them knows that there is no simple answer. Simplistic answers, he says, can make matters worse. People who are particularly vulnerable include believers who have an excessively passive submission that everything that occurs is part of God's plan, people who minimize or deny the problem of pain and suffering in the world, or believers who are preoccupied with suffering and sinfulness and are not able to see beyond it. While Pargament does not explicitly discuss how helping professionals use their religions/spirituality in helping work, it is to be expected that a clinician who has spent little time going beyond a cliché-ridden and simplistic philosophy of life or spirituality/religion could easily be overwhelmed in the encounter with great human suffering. *By definition, a helping professional's career is one of continual encounter with human pain and suffering. It is to be expected that when someone has a weakly developed religious or spiritual, or existential/philosophical orienting system, then any spiritual or existential/philosophical struggle which emerges will be more difficult to navigate.*

Spiritual struggles and fragmented spiritual orienting systems

A *fragmented religious/spiritual orienting system* also makes a person more vulnerable to failure in coping with major stressors. Pargament (1997) lists a number of ways in which a religious orienting system can be fragmented. He explains that as religion has become more of a private matter, problems can occur as people create their own mixtures of conventional and less conventional beliefs, practices, and experiences. This can lead to a piecemeal orienting religious system of beliefs and practices that may not make a coherent enough system to help one cope with spiritual struggles. Religious orienting systems also become fragmented as the religious belief and practice are not integrated into day-to-day behavior. When a person has not connected religious beliefs and practices with what happens in the complexities of life, one can only expect that religious orienting system will not be very effective in carrying the person through any struggle that he or she encounters. There can also be fragmentation between the religious motivation a person has and his or her religious practice. As Pargament explains,

there are problems when people are motivated to practice their religions for self-focused and unspiritual reasons rather than practicing their religions in order to be closer to God. He cautions, however, that a religious orienting system does not have to be perfect. As Pargament (1997) says,

> *few people have airtight, comprehensive religious orienting systems capable of responding to each and every exigency of living. Built into most religious perspectives, however, is a tolerance for some inconsistency and fragmentation. People can hold onto themselves and their religions, imperfect orienting systems and all. (p. 351)*

The problem with fragmented religion is well articulated by Pargament (1997):

> *But if there are too many holes and inconsistencies—if the religious realm is too disconnected from the secular, if practices are unrelated to beliefs, if motivations have little to do with practices—the orienting system loses its ability to guide the individual through troubled times. The religious beliefs prove empty, the institutions alien, and the rituals hollow. Fragmented as it is, religion becomes another burden in coping, for all it has to offer are piecemeal solutions to complicated problems. (p. 351)*

Spiritual struggles and religious rigidity

Religious rigidity also can make person vulnerable to failure in coping with major stressors. People who are religiously rigid tend to have a very clear and inflexible view of the world and very specific ways about how one should or should not live their lives. As Pargament (1997) explains, "the rigid religious system may be quite effective as long as it operates in a predictable, stable, and homogenous environment. Diversity and change, however, reveal the flaws in the system" (pp. 353–354). This is particularly true for our purposes in discussing what health care professionals encounter. Health care workers are ethically bound by the commitment to compassionate care and professionalism to help all people equally. They work with people from very diverse backgrounds and who run the gamut in terms of values and beliefs. Furthermore, situations and health care are commonly complex. A person who approaches life in an inflexible manner will have a great deal of difficulty operating in the world of health care.

Spiritual struggles and poor attachment history

Finally, Pargament argues that the *style of attachment a person has with God* can affect the strength of his or her orienting system and ability to cope with major stresses in life. Building on Bowlby's work on attachment styles with parents, the kind of attachment style people have with God can affect how they go through life. Like a child who has a secure attachment style with his or her parent, someone with a secure religious attachment perceives God as a secure base from which to explore various aspects in life. There is a confidence going out into life with the knowledge of a constant loving figure perceived as supporting him or her. Someone with a secure attachment to God would view God as generally warm and responsive toward him or her. God is viewed as knowing when to be supportive and protective, and when to let someone make his or her own mistakes. Such an attachment style might derive from the experience of a secure relationship with one's own parents, or a secure attachment with God might be a compensation for an insecure parental upbringing. People with insecure attachments to God often have developed this from insecure attachment styles with their own parents and seek out negative

substitutes that could be termed "false gods" to provide a sense of security. Examples of these would be addictions, getting into a codependent relationship, involvement with a cult, or religious dogmatism. Someone with an avoidant attachment style would view God as generally distant and impersonal, having little interest in his or her life and problems. They might feel that God does not care much about him or her—and may not even like him or her. Someone with an anxious or ambivalent attachment style with God would view God as inconsistent in reactions to him or her. Sometimes God would seem warm and supportive to his or her needs and sometimes not. The person thinks that God loves and cares about him or her but sometimes shows this love in ways that the person does not understand. Pargament reports research that finds that an insecure attachment style to God is associated with increased anxiety, depression, and loneliness; less satisfaction with life; poorer health; and less happiness (Pargament, 1997).

Religion has five key functions in daily living and dealing with crisis

From a psychological and spiritual point of view, religion has been found to have five key functions in daily living and in crisis. First, religion helps people in the search for meaning. It can provide a framework to understand and interpret suffering and difficult life experiences. Second, religion helps individuals achieve a sense of control in their lives. When individuals are heavily taxed by stressors in their lives, religion helps them find mastery and control in the midst of uncontrollable or irrational situations. Third, religion can provide comfort in the face of negative situations. These can be psychological coping strategies that help reduce the person's distress. From a spiritual perspective, the connection with a divine source can be a source of strength and calmness. Fourth, religion facilitates social solidarity and social cohesiveness among people. Members of a religion offer support, help, and fellowship to each other. From a spiritual perspective, feeling connected or close to a higher power also can provide a sense of intimate relationship that supports or encourages people. Fifth, religion can help people make major life transformations. While religion is often associated with being "conservational" (i.e., maintaining one's conception of meaning, closeness with God, control, etc.), religion can be the vehicle for helping people completely change their lives leaving behind their previous conceptions of what is of significance in their lives (Pargament, Koenig, & Perez, 2000).

Five functions of religion relate to variety of religious coping methods as well as how philosophies of life function in atheistic or agnostic coping

Using these five functions of religion, Pargament et al. (2000) described the wide range of religious coping that people use to deal with difficulties in their lives. As seen in the table listing the subscales of the RCOPE (the measure of religious coping; see table 14.1), coping methods can be described by how one finds meaning by some type of reappraisal of the stress, by finding some way to gain control in a situation, by gaining comfort and closeness to God, by finding support and intimacy with others and with God, or by finding ways of achieving a life transformation. As the authors point out, any type of coping can actually provide several functions. But this list of subscales is important because it shows the wide range of ways that people use religion and spirituality. One of the problems in the clinical world is that there is generally a narrow understanding

of how religion and spirituality function. By extension, for people who are agnostic or atheist, their philosophies of life will have similar functions that of course will not include a conception of the divine, for example. So, their philosophies of life will provide a source for reappraising stressors, finding a way to feel in control of a situation, having a way to feel comforted and soothed in the difficulties, having a sense of support, and finally, having a guide for transforming their lives.

Definitions of positive and negative religious coping

Coping methods can be positive or negative, even in religious coping. There is a misconception (probably relating to an earnest desire to be open-minded to others) that if it is a religious form of coping, then it must be positive. But this is not necessarily the case. In the study of measures of religious coping, Pargament and others have identified positive and negative religious coping methods that appear to have distinct and differing impacts on measures of physical and mental health. Positive religious methods "reflect the perception of a secure relationship with God, a belief that there is a greater meaning to be found, and a sense of spiritual connectedness with others" (Abu-Raiya & Pargament, 2012, p. 337). Negative religious coping

> is characterized by signs of spiritual tension, conflict and struggle with God and others, as manifested by negative reappraisals of God's powers (e.g., feeling abandoned or punished by God), daemonic re-appraisals (i.e., feeling the devil is involved in the stressor), spiritual questioning and doubting, and interpersonal religious discontent. (Pargament et al., 2011, p. 58)

Negative religious coping "involves expressions of the less secure relationship with God, a tenuous

TABLE 14.1 RCOPE Subscales and Definitions of Religious Coping Methods (Pargament et al., 2011 p. 56)

RELIGIOUS METHODS OF COPING TO FIND MEANING	
Benevolent Religious Reappraisal	Redefining the stressor through religion as benevolent and potentially beneficial
Punishing God Reappraisal	Redefining the stressor as a punishment from God for the individual's sins
Demonic Reappraisal	Redefining the stressor as an act of the Devil
Reappraisal of God's Powers	Redefining God's power to influence the stressful situation
RELIGIOUS METHODS OF COPING TO GAIN CONTROL	
Collaborative Religious Coping	Seeking control through a problem solving partnership with God
Active Religious Surrender	An active giving up of control to God in coping
Passive Religious Deferral	Passive waiting for God to control the situation
Pleading for Direct Intercession	Seeking control indirectly by pleading to God for a miracle or divine intercession
Self-Directing Religious Coping	Seeking control directly through individual initiative rather than help from God
RELIGIOUS METHODS OF COPING TO GAIN COMFORT AND CLOSENESS TO GOD	
Seeking Spiritual Support	Searching for comfort and reassurance through God's love and care
Religious Focus	Engaging in religious activities to shift focus from the stressor
Religious Purification	Searching for spiritual cleansing through religious actions
Spiritual Connection	Experiencing a sense of connectedness with forces that transcend the individual
Spiritual Discontent	Expressing confusion and dissatisfaction with God's relationship to the individual in the stressful situation
Marking Religious Boundaries	Clearly demarcating acceptable from unacceptable religious behavior and remaining within religious boundaries
RELIGIOUS METHODS OF COPING TO GAIN INTIMACY WITH OTHERS AND CLOSENESS TO GOD	
Seeking Support from Clergy or Members	Searching for comfort and reassurance through the love and care of congregation members and clergy
Religious Helping	Attempting to provide spiritual support and comfort to others
Interpersonal Religious Discontent	Expressing confusion and dissatisfaction with the relationship of clergy or congregation members to the individual in the stressful situation
RELIGIOUS METHODS OF COPING TO ACHIEVE A LIFE TRANSFORMATION	
Seeking Religious Direction	Looking to religion for assistance in finding a new direction for living when the old one may no longer be viable
Religious Conversion	Looking to religion for a radical change in life
Religious Forgiving	Looking to religion for help in shifting to a state of peace from the anger, hurt, and fear associated with an offense

and ominous view of the world, and a religious struggle to find and conserve significance in life" (Abu-Raiya & Pargament, 2012, p. 337).

Research on effects of positive and negative religious coping

Positive religious coping has been found to be correlated with fewer psychosomatic symptoms and more spiritual growth after experiencing a stressor (Pargament, Koenig, Tarakeshwar, & Hahn, 2004). It has also been related to a healthier psychological adjustment to stress (Ano & Vasconcelles, 2005) and less depression (Smith, McCullough, & Poll, 2003). Negative religious coping has been linked with "more signs of psychological distress and symptoms, poor quality of life and greater callousness toward other people" (Pargament, Feuille, & Burdzy, 2011, p. 57). In a national sample examining the links between spiritual struggles and symptoms of psychopathology, McConnell, Pargament, Ellison, and Flannelly (2006) found that negative religious coping was associated with anxiety, phobic anxiety, depression, paranoid ideation, obsessive-compulsiveness, and somatization. Negative religious coping is also associated with higher levels of anxiety and phobic anxiety after a recent illness.

Spirituality is not always helpful

Rather than being automatically an aid across the board for coping, spirituality is not always helpful. Reviewing the research on spirituality, Pargament (2007) concludes that

> all in all, these studies suggest that, without scope and depth, spirituality loses power. It may be unable to serve important psychological functions, and it may actually contribute to more psychological trouble. Not only that, a thin, fragmented spirituality can lead to still other spiritual problems, for the disparate bits and pieces of spiritual life may clash and

> collide, resulting in further dis-integration. (p. 156)

People start with conservational spiritual coping and then move to transformational spiritual coping if the conservational fails

When facing difficult experiences and experiencing spiritual disorientation, Pargament explains that people first try a conservational type of spiritual coping in which they try to protect and preserve their concepts of the sacred as they have known it. They try to hold on to their visions of the sacred as it has been (Pargament, 1997). In this type of coping, people try to reappraise what is occurring in a spiritual way and look for spiritual meaning. They may seek connections with others for spiritual support or for help. But when their concepts of the sacred can no longer be conserved as it was and they have exhausted every means of conserving it as it was, people then move to what Pargament calls transformational spiritual coping. Former ways of understanding the sacred and how to approach it fall apart. What is threatened is what we thought was most important in life, how we approached life's ultimate concerns (such as death, tragedy, and inequity), and how we might seek the sacred in that. The person has to go back to the drawing board, so to speak, on matters of philosophy of life or spirituality. Religious stories throughout history indicate how this has always been the case for humans.

> Every religious tradition has its exemplars of people who find themselves tested or lost in a real or symbolic wilderness. For 40 years, the Israelites wandered the desert of Sinai uncertain at times whether to return to Egypt, take up idol worship, or pursue the Promised Land. For forty days Jesus Christ lived in the wilderness and faced temptations by the devil. In moments of desolation, something of the sacred

is encountered, a new sense of direction and purpose emerges from the trials. (Pargament, 1997, p. 235)

What happens in transformational spiritual coping

Transformational spiritual coping is experienced as an emotionally painful time, and a person can no longer carry the load of what he or she experiences in life the same way this load was carried before. In such a time, people sometimes "find" religion and sometimes they "lose" religion. What was believed before becomes reorganized in a new way that in hindsight is viewed as a spiritual awakening or a deepening of understanding what their religious beliefs were all about in the first place. Or, one abandons the particular spiritual pathway he or she was on before and tries a completely different one. Perhaps it is a completely different spirituality, religion, or philosophy, or he or she integrates insights from other ways of thinking into an already developed belief system. Or, he or she may disengage from the search for the sacred or what is of significance to him or her (Pargament, 1997).

Transformational spiritual coping and spiritual disengagement

There are many ways people can go through transformational spiritual coping. As stated before, sometimes people *disengage from the spiritual altogether* when it starts falling apart. As Pargament (2007) explains, sometimes people disconnect from God or any sense of transcendence. They might lose interest in searching for the sacred, disconnect from their religious or spiritual communities, and no longer try to understand their experiences in a spiritual way. This might occur as a result of anger, or it might just fade away. It might signal the end of reflecting on things in a spiritual way for the

person, but Pargament notes that at times that anger and wrestling with the spiritual doubts and turmoil may be part of the transformation process itself. Living life from a spiritual perspective is like a journey that is a process of discovery, insight, and personal growth. Like a journey, there is a beginning, a middle, and an end. Sometimes it is smooth and pleasant; other times it is stormy, and it is not clear how it going to turn out.

Transformational spiritual coping becoming revisioning the sacred

Another way people undergo spiritual transformation is by *revisioning the sacred*. The images of the sacred that people have grown up with may no longer hold when encountering the suffering, injustice, and evil one witnesses in helping professions. Commonly, the belief in a loving, all-knowing, and all-powerful God is challenged when working with helping people in their difficulties. The understanding of God might shift to one of viewing the world as set in motion by God under its own scientific laws and human free will, and that God is accompanying humans as they make their life journey. Maybe the person had a view of God that was as a detached and punitive God, and that shifts to viewing God as a compassionate force. He or she might not bother with trying to understand God in any philosophical way (e.g., who is God, is God all-knowing and all-powerful, what is the substance of God) and instead focus on how God is experienced or operates in human life. The sacred might be revisioned by leaving a theistic view of the universe and instead viewing it in a nontheistic spiritual way.

Transformational spiritual coping by making sacred transitions

Another way people go through spiritual transformation is by what Pargament (2007) calls *sacred transitions*. These are rituals or rites of passage that "help participants view their life experiences from a new perspective, gain greater mastery over their emotions, and define themselves and their place in the community in a new light" (Pargament, 2007, p. 118). Funerals provide comfort, Pargament notes, but they also facilitate movement through a major life event. The participants take time in a funeral to mark that life is now different, honor the deceased, and begin to mourn the loss. Doing so then helps the participants to move on in life. Rites of passage such as the Native American sweat lodge can mark viewing life one way beforehand and then—through the prayers and rituals of the sweat lodge—go back into the world empowered or reborn in a different way, looking at themselves and at life in a new way. "Rites of passage announce the fact that ordinary time has been suspended and a process of transformation is underway in which an individual will be shepherded from one sacred place in life to another" (Pargament, 2007, p. 119).

Medicine and rituals and rites of passage

Medicine has many ways in which various rituals and rites of passage operate to help its healers and patients move through the process. For example, the giving of the white coat to the medical students, the pinning or the capping ceremony in nursing, the graduation, and the taking the oath of Hippocrates or Maimonides all function as ways to help clinicians mark that they are moving from one stage to another and that others should now recognize them in a different way afterward as having certain competencies and gifts to help the rest of us that they did not have beforehand. Washing hands before seeing a patient can be viewed as a spiritual or centering ritual in which a clinician symbolically marks the leaving of the patient one just saw to now engaging with a new patient. Whatever happened with the previous patient needs to be left behind (i.e., both that patient's bacteria and any psychological carry-over). The new patient now needs the healer to be completely focused on them with "clean hands and straight eyes," uncontaminated by what happened before and fully present to what this new patient needs.

Transformational spiritual coping and centering the sacred

Finally, another example of how people make spiritual transformations is by what Pargament (2007) calls *centering the sacred*. He explains that spiritual transformations are more than simple cognitive changes, but that all of a person's values and goals are reordered. "The sacred moves from a marginal position to the very center of the individual's life and definition of him- or herself" (Pargament, 2007, p. 122). For our purposes, a common example would be a person who approached life in a self-centered way but now dedicates him- or herself to living to relieve suffering in others. Pargament notes that centering the sacred is a three-step process. First, people become aware of the limitations of how they are approaching life. Second, they make the decision to change this. Third, they replace how they viewed life beforehand with this new spiritual reordering of their lives.

Decentering and recentering in clinicians' careers

Anecdotally, centering the sacred is commonly seen in the world of health care. There is certainly a decentering of the sacred, if I might play with Pargament's words. People enter health care with a view to dedicating their lives to others by using their intellectual gifts to relieve suffering. Medical students, for example, often become stressed and discouraged by all that they have to do. They may feel dehumanized by the training process and subtly pressured by the "hidden curriculum" to depersonalize their patients. The initial compassionate caring that was the center of their health care aspirations now moves to the margins of their imaginations. Yet often, it is this loss of the center of compassionate caring and the burnout that accompanies it that become the seeds for a "recentering" in the clinician's career. They renew their commitments to what health care is all about, often with a more mature understanding of what compassionate caring is. While not explicitly a "sacred process" or a "spiritual struggle," many clinicians do experience it as a spiritual process.

Evolution in spiritual understanding does not mean God does not exist

None of these descriptions should necessarily be taken as arguing that God is simply a human construction and that this construction is fictional and a helpful coping mechanism with a wonderful placebo effect. It might be argued that way. But it also might very well be the case that our understanding of God is an evolutionary process. For example, how I imagine God as a toddler is not going to be how I imagine God as an adolescent or an older person. Because one's concept of God changes does not mean God does not exist or that God changed. It can mean that one's understanding of God deepens as we mature and work through our experiences. In the end, it is an empirical question that is not the focus of this book. The fact is that humans engage life trying to understand what, ultimately, it is and they do this spiritually and philosophically. To discount whether the divine exists because of the way our spiritual understanding of it changes is

poor science. Our understanding of life evolves all the time. It does not mean what we knew before was wrong. It was the best we could understand at the time with the tools and ways of thinking we had. Early in our human history, we did not conceive that there might be thousands of galaxies in an expanding universe; we knew only that there were planets and a sun. But with the Hubble telescope, we now know that this solar system is part of a galaxy, and this galaxy is only one of many. What we knew early in our history was true, but it turns out to be only partially true. Our understanding has evolved. The same is possible for all things spiritual. We cannot know now what we will ultimately know later.

Viewing your work as a call or vocation is a type of spiritual or philosophical grounding

Many physicians and clinicians view the work in terms of having a call to do this work, a vocation. For them, the very nature of the work is grounded spiritually or philosophically from the very beginning of their careers. Puchalski and Guenther (2012) explain how viewing your work in the context of an inner call or vocation instead of just as a job provides the clinician with a deeper meaning for the work that is integrated in the whole of their lives.

> To be altruistic, clinicians must be able to remain true to their calling to serve and care for their patients. This is the foundation that gives clinicians the strength to override system requirements and pressures dictated by the economics of medicine and to use their professional knowledge and technical competence to act first and foremost in the best interest of individual patients. An understanding of one's vocation and ways to remain true to that call are critical professional development elements for clinicians who may be facing depression or burnout as they work within a system that

puts economics over patient care. (Puchalski & Guenther, 2012, p. 256)

Clinicians understand the ideas of "calling" or "vocation" in a number of ways. It may be a sense of being true to their talents—that is, that they are built for this work and they want to do it as a result. It may be a sense of purpose understood either from an atheistic or agnostic perspective, or from a religious perspective. For those from theistic spiritualities, it may be a sense of what God has called them to do and given the desire and aptitude to carry it out. The commonality among all these perspectives is that a call, a vocation, a purpose becomes a kind of psychological rudder or touchstone that helps orient the clinician in the direction he or she would like to go. When going through difficult times, it is a way of refocusing oneself or resetting one's approach to the clinical work. As Puchalski and Guenther (2012) put it, "The daily awareness, gratitude and celebration of our vocation, our calling, are perhaps the secret of restoration and re-creation" (p. 258). Reconnecting with what we think is our call reminds us of why we want to do what we are doing and how we wanted to do it. Puchalski and Guenther (2012) relate the following story that illustrates this point:

> One of my residents said that "from 6 p.m. to 6 a.m. I am a very spiritual person but not during the day." Once she reconnected with the reason she entered her profession, she began to integrate her deep inner self into her "work hours" and began to find greater meaning and joy in her daily life. (pp. 255–256)

Simple articulation not enough and danger of fast-food spirituality

While articulating what your POC/SOC is can be very helpful in buffering stress and burnout and cultivating compassion, the simple articulation of that spirituality or philosophy does not create the protective and energizing effects. It is not simply a concise summary with insightful quotes and wise principles that can be distributed at graduation or formulated after a brief workshop. The articulation is the result of wrestling and actively reflecting on what it is vis-à-vis your clinical experiences, and articulating it does not mean it will remain unchanged as your helping journey continues. To expect that in a relatively short period of time you can completely develop a mature POC/SOC is what I call the lure of fast-food spirituality. It is the expectation that with one action, with one concisely articulated spirituality or philosophy, you would get immediate positive results, that a particular spirituality or philosophy will look the same for every clinician or have the same effect for every clinician. Just as fast food can be quickly prepared but lacks the best nutrition, so too will a hastily formed or prepackaged spiritual or philosophical answer be unsatisfying and ineffective in the long run. It does not work when handed over to the young clinician as a formula. It is instead a commitment to a process of reflecting in a deep way about what is the wider perspective of this work and how one should continue in it.

SOC/POC is absolutely essential to working in health care

In our society, there is a sense that spirituality (or a life philosophy) is a kind of optional add-on to a person's life, like having a different coat or pair of sunglasses. That is, it is not absolutely necessary, and you could get through daily living without it. My experience is that having a POC or SOC is absolutely essential to surviving and thriving in this work. If you are working with suffering people and encountering the ills and evils of life on a daily basis, you are automatically existentially and emotionally confronted with what life is. We are at high risk psychologically if we ignore that part of ourselves that asks what the meaning of all this is and how should we act in light of that. How do we carry the load of all that we will experience in this work? While society has normalized not reflecting in a deep way on our experience, not to reflect on the spiritual or philosophical dimension of your work is not an option if you want to survive and thrive working in health care.

Superficial use of SOC/POC versus intentional and genuine use of SOC/POC

There is also the problem that clinicians can view getting a POC/SOC as somewhat like getting vitamins in order to avoid getting sick. The underlying motivation becomes a problem. The thinking is, "Well, I read in this book that if I get a philosophy or spirituality of caring, then I should be immune to stress and burnout in this work." The POC/SOC should be engaged to work through the existential and emotional challenges of the work, but we need to avoid using it as a kind of panacea or magic potion. Shuman and Meador (2003) addressed the problem of the use of religion in this more consumerist mentality:

> Modern American religion now abounds with prescriptions to help anxious consumers free themselves and remain free of the effects of disease and aging. The original concord between religion and medicine has been turned upside down. Whereas religion once taught its adherents to worship God, whether in sickness or in health, and to use medicine to live with the world and with one another in a way that encouraged that worship, religion now teaches its adherents to worship their desire for health and to use God—whomever that may be—to facilitate that desire. (p. 43)

A patient who has heard the research that religion is associated with improved health might adopt religion in a superficial manner in order to get the health benefits (e.g., praying daily, attending religious services). But this is not likely to be helpful because it is not really permeating the worldview or orienting system of the person. So, while a POC/SOC is likely to be helpful to the clinician's well-being, it must be rooted in a genuine intellectual and emotional wrestling with the experience of being a health professional, not a superficial attempt. The motivation for developing one's POC/SOC is very important in terms of your expectations for how this will help you. If the motivation to develop this is to avoid working with the challenging emotional, spiritual, and/or philosophical struggles of this work, then this is not likely to be helpful. The clinician will still experience this as a challenging work even with a mature POC/SOC. It is not an opiate or anxiolytic that deadens the perception of the pain of this work. It is more like the axiom "Lift with your legs, not with your back!" What you are lifting will still be heavy; the key is how you approach lifting that heavy object. Having a POC/SOC does not make you immune to difficulties and challenges, but it will make working through them more possible and more positive.

Using specific questions to articulate one's SOC/POC

As I became more clear that clinicians who were surviving and thriving in this work as well as maintaining compassion in their work with patients tended to be relying in some way on a POC/SOC, the challenge then became to try to articulate it. As one physician said to me, "I'm a pretty religious person, and I find this hard to find the words to describe how this works in myself." Clinicians who come from traditions where this is explicitly and regularly discussed have less difficulty. But most clinicians find that they have not really thought through how their SOC/POCs are integrated in their work. For many, it is compartmentalized. There is the spiritual side, for example, and the work side. Many are at a loss for how to integrate these philosophies. As a result, I have used the following sets of questions to help clinicians articulate what their POC/SOCs are. Table 14.2 lists questions for clinicians from atheistic and agnostic perspectives, and table 14.3 list questions for clinicians from religious and spiritual perspectives. Clinicians from nontheistic traditions may need to adjust the wording in either to describe their SOCs. My approach has been to have clinicians pick a few questions that are the most meaningful

for them and start there, not trying to answer all of them.

An Example of an SOC

An example of an SOC is useful at this point. My intention here is not to try to give a full-fledged POC/SOC, but to provide some outlines that might spark your own articulation. I have asked numerous clinicians and helping professionals about what helps them stay engaged with people who are suffering or difficult while maintaining a compassionate caring attitude. The responses are for another book. But one executive director of an organization helping people move out of generational poverty had found that articulating some of this for himself and his whole staff was very helpful. Their work involves a residential program helping people move out of generational poverty and other

TABLE 14.2 Questions That Will Help You Articulate Your POC

What literature, art, or philosophical writing provides you with information, guidance, or stories that help you make sense of and deal with the suffering you witness?
When you encounter suffering in your attempts to help others, what ideas or principles give you energy, renewal, and meaning for this work?
How do understand healing in the body and mind? What is your role in the healing process for others and what qualities do you need to have to optimize healing for others?
What keeps you from getting cynical in your work?
What helps you cultivate compassion to keep a positive energy to do your work?
What in your personal self-care practice helps sustain a caring attitude despite being exhausted, hurt, and discouraged by the suffering you encounter? (Not only intellectual sustenance, but emotional sustenance.)
What have you learned about life and yourself in the journey of your caring so far?
If you were to tell the story of your journey or career so far of helping someone/others who are suffering, what would it be?
What stories (e.g., from literature, movies, biographies/autobiographies) are you reminded of when you tell your story?
What have been the biggest philosophical questions or struggles you have had related to your work and how did you navigate those?

TABLE 14.3 Questions That Will Help You Articulate Your SOC

What in your sacred writings provides information, guidance, or stories that give you hope and inner strength in encountering suffering?
When you encounter suffering in your attempts to help others, what in your spirituality gives you energy, renewal, and meaning for doing this work in such a way that it keeps you from getting burnt out?
How do you understand healing in the body, the mind, and the spirit? What is your role in the healing process for others and what qualities do you need to have to optimize healing for others?
If yours is a theistic religion/spirituality, how is the divine involved in the healing process? How does the divine work in or through you? What is your connection with the divine in this work? What in your relationship with the divine helps you in this work?
What in your spirituality/religious practice keeps you from being cynical?
What in your spirituality/religious practice helps you to cultivate compassion to keep a positive energy to do this work?
What in your spirituality/religious practice helps sustain a caring attitude despite being exhausted, hurt, and discouraged by the suffering you encounter? (Not only intellectual sustenance, but emotional sustenance.)
What have you learned about God and yourself in the journey or career of your caring so far?
If you were to tell the story of your journey or career so far of helping someone/others who are suffering, what would it be?
What sacred stories are you reminded of when you tell your story?
What have been the biggest spiritual questions or struggles you have had related to your work and how did you navigate those?

difficult life situations. When I interviewed him using my often-asked question about what keeps his staff compassionate and what keeps them going, he stated there were three things. One, try to understand why people make the choices they make. When clients would make bad choices, staff would always approach them trying to understand that the choice that client made somehow made sense in that person's life—thus, not approaching them leading with judging and shaming. Instead, they had a process of always working from this point of view both in their private frustrations as well as in helping clients grow in their thought processes. Two, there are three divine attributes of change: (a) only God's grace can change people; (b) hold people to the truth; and (c) people do not change overnight. What this means is that in terms of what it takes for clients to change, the staff adopts the view that it is very difficult to change and that it is God who is working to help them both indirectly (e.g., through the staff) or directly. This seems to help staff stay realistic in terms of outcomes. But the staff also thought that this is balanced by holding people to the truth about themselves and working to help them be aware and accountable to that. Finally, the staff always reminds each other and the clients that it takes a lot of time for this kind of major change to occur.

And three, the executive director added that "in serving others, you cannot base your own well-being or try to meet your own needs through other people's choices." (Vanderveen, personal communication, 2016). While staff were trained and expected to function at their highest capacities, there is the idea that staff members' senses of selves had to be solidy independent of what the clients choose to do, and also that they worked on meeting their own needs and not depending on clients to make them feel better about themselves.

An example of a POC

An example of a POC by an agnostic physician focused on the starting point that all humans suffer and are interconnected. Rather than a hedonistic philosophy of "just meeting my own needs," he had the view that we all are happier when we try to help each other. Life is full of unfairness and tragedy, and this can befall any of us at any time. With just slight changes in the stories of our lives, the challenging patient in front of us could easily be ourselves. Being negative and self-serving does not seem to lead to feeling any happier or fulfilled while seeking to respond to the suffering of others does. Furthermore, he would say that you have to be realistic about what can be accomplished and content yourself with the fact that you did the best you could. There is much more that can be said about this philosophy of life. But this gives a sense of what this might be like.

COMPASSIONATE CARING AS GATEWAY TO THE TRANSPERSONAL AND/OR SACRED DIMENSION

When working with others during times of despair, vulnerability, and unknowns, we are challenged to learn again, to re-examine our meaning of life and death. ... From this place of deepening our humanity, we offer to our self, and those whom we meet on our path, our compassionate response for fulfilling our chosen life's work and calling. In encountering and facing death of self and others, we are in sacred space, touching the mystery of life itself, dwelling in the space of Infinity. (Watson, 2005, pp. 138–139)

Helping others often experienced as a self-transcendent or even sacred experience

How clinicians experience the actual helping encounter with patients is often experienced as a self-transcendent experience and, for those who have a spiritual worldview, a sacred experience. Thus far I have discussed the POC/SOC from the perspective of witnessing patient suffering and the challenge to the clinician of cultivating and maintaining compassionate caring in the continual encounter with human pain and suffering. We have examined how clinicians rely on a spirituality or a philosophy of life to deal with burnout and vicarious traumatization. However, many clinicians' experiences of what happens to them in the actual caring moments with patients lead them to describe those experiences as uniquely powerful, energizing, and inspiring. Puchalski and Guenther (2012) describe it in the following way:

Caring is not a one-dimensional function. It occurs within the context of the relationship of the caregiver in the care receiver. Out of that relationship the potential for healing arises. Whereas many see healing as unidirectional, from clinician to patient, it is actually bidirectional. We would describe that aspect of the clinical encounter as sacred—the sense of something greater than ourselves that is occurring during the parts of the clinical encounter that are poignant or perhaps moving. Clinicians talk of something hard to describe, but something that is perceived by both clinician and patient. (p. 254)

There is the sense, by both clinician and patient, that both are participating in something very special and that both clinician and patient are part of something bigger than themselves. In the following quote, there is the sense of participating in a special, energizing experience because of the mutuality shared between patient and clinician.

> In a busy practice, it's easy to concentrate on giving and to forget that your patients are a wonderful source of spiritual replenishment. One way to reconnect with the joy of practicing medicine is to take time to receive your patients' gifts. As you learn to experience your emotions, you'll begin to relish the love, appreciation and respect that many patients want to share with you. (Pfifferling & Gilley, 1999, p. 40)

Whether described in secular terms or spiritual terms, clinicians relate how the experience of working with patients is a privilege, a unique human experience, an encounter that elicits awe, and an experience that brings out unknown but welcome aspects of themselves as they work with patients.

Caring for another as flow experience

Clinicians may talk of a kind of flow experience in which they are able to say and do things for the patient in an effortless and exceptional way. They have the sense that while they have all the training and experience needed to help a patient in a particular situation, there are times when everything they know comes together in a way that flows easily and powerfully, and they are even astonished with the intuition and wisdom that comes out of their own mouths. This is true both for clinicians who have a spiritual worldview as well as for clinicians who do not. Even clinicians who do not especially look at things in a spiritual or philosophical way will make comments alluding to how certain encounters with

patients are extraordinary and make them feel good about being in these helping professions. "It affirmed why I went into this field." "I was my best self with that patient, and I loved how I could talk to them and helped them." "The time with that patient was like a high for me. Everything came together, and I felt like I even felt better about my life as I was helping my patient." "I lost track of time, and I was totally focused on what was going on with my patient." Hence, words like *transpersonal, transcendent*, and *awesome* are used. Sometimes, the clinicians feel like they operated at a higher level of skill than usual, as if injected with a performance-enhancing drug. No matter how this universal experience in caring for another is described, clinicians experience this as something that gives them fulfillment and the motivation to continue this work.

Helping Episodes Exercise

One way of helping clinicians and students become more aware of this potential transpersonal quality in caring is to have them do what I call the Helping Episodes Exercise. As described in chapter 6, when I am working with clinicians and students on becoming more deeply aware of what is happening psychologically with patients and in themselves, I ask them to use four questions to reflect on positive and negative experiences of giving help and receiving help.

Reflect on four different helping episodes in your life:

1. A time when you were the helpee, and it went well.
2. A time when you were the helpee, and it did not go well.
3. A time when you were the helper, and it went well.
4. A time when you were the helper, and it did not go well.

For each situation, the students or clinicians are to describe in a paragraph what the situation was and what went well or did not go well in that situation, and what they think were the reasons it went well or did not go well. Then I ask them to describe in a paragraph how they felt and thought during and after the episode, and, if they have a sense of it, how they think the other person in that episode felt. I ask them to describe their experiences in a phenomenological way—what it felt like, what their thoughts were like, how it felt physically, what their energy was like, what they imagined, what images or metaphors capture the experience, or whatever helps them explain that experience.

Intention for the helping episodes exercise

My intention for doing this exercise is not for spiritual or philosophical reasons. My main reason for having students and clinicians do this exercise is that they become more aware of how both helper and helpee experience positive and negative helping episodes. I am hoping that they connect how they felt giving and receiving help in both positive and negative helping episodes to later being in the helper role and how they can work to make the interaction as positive as possible for the person being helped. Given that clinicians trained in the sciences can undervalue the subjective experiences of both the clinician and patient (even regarding them as epiphenomenal and nonessential to the helping episode), this exercise gives them the opportunity to see how the subjective experience either in giving or receiving help affects how the helping interaction proceeds and how it affects both the patient and the clinician afterward. For example, if a patient has a positive experience in being helped by the clinician, he or she may feel more interest and motivation in following through on whatever may need to be done with regard to self-care. On the other hand, if a patient has a negative experience with a clinician (e.g., feels shamed, disliked, judged), then he or she may not follow through on what the clinician recommends that the patient does and be less likely to return for more helping assistance from the clinician.

Transpersonal themes that are commonly described with this exercise

Frequently, however, the students make statements that convey this self-transcendent or transpersonal quality of positive helping episodes. Typically, I group all the reactions to both positive and negative helping experiences, and the class examines the common themes of experiences. With positive experiences, one theme is feeling more energy, creativity, and renewal (e.g., "The room was filled with a special kind of energy that made me want to go out into the world and help everyone who I possibly could." "It was exhausting but incredibly rewarding." "Even though it was hard to help this person, I felt inspired and eager to help him." "Her energy was contagious, and she has helped me interact with other patients with more energy ever since.") Another theme is a deep sense of connection with others that is profound and transformative (e.g., "It felt like I was making a difference instead of just observing." "It made me feel that I was truly making a transformative impact on this person." "It was eye-opening for me because I ventured outside my comfort zone." "I was taken aback by how incredibly connected I could feel with someone I had exchanged so few words with."). There is often a theme of mutuality and learning from the helpee (e.g., "I was helping him but later realized my patient actually helped me." "We both benefited from the relationship." "I felt very grateful for how this experience shaped me in my work with others." "I had a better perspective on my own struggles.") Often there is a theme of profound peace, timelessness, and centeredness (e.g., "It gave me a feeling of peace and serenity that I was able to keep my composure regardless of the situation." "It felt like time was still and there was nothing else going on around us"). Sometimes, the experience was described in explicitly spiritual terms (e.g., "I felt that God had chosen me to care for this man, to teach me to treat everyone as if they are family." "I did not know how I found all the right words to say to my patient; it was as if God was helping me do the right thing." "I was completely humbled by her gratitude and her kind words, which gave me the spiritual fuel I needed to keep going"). Other regularly occurring themes include awe and amazement at either the courage of the helpee or fascination with how healing occurred; feeling honored to have helped someone and humbled to be a tool in improving someone's life; and gratitude for being in this helping work or for what happened to the helpee.

Importance of the positive experiences of the spiritual and transpersonal for clinician well-being

From a spiritual perspective, one could describe these experiences as sacred, connected to the divine, otherworldly, or even mystical. From a secular perspective, they could be described as peak experiences, flow experiences, being in the zone, feeling in awe of human beings, inspired by medicine, captivated by how the body works, or fascinated by the mysteries of life. It is not the point of this book to discuss whether there is a spiritual dimension. The point of this discussion is that there are powerful subjective experiences in being a clinician that can be very important in the way that a clinician conceives of his or her life work. As the research on physician resilience, compassion satisfaction, and the broaden-and-build theory finds, the ability to experience and maintain connection with the positive aspects of this work is critical to the well-being of the clinician. The spiritual or transpersonal perspective can be an important source of that positive wellspring. Sulmasy (1997) captures this dynamic in the following passage:

> To be joyful is to be attentive to the profound meaning of the privilege of serving the sick and to be grateful for that privilege. To be joyful is to be fascinated by people—in all colors, shapes, and sizes; of all sorts of temperaments; from all social strata—and to be conscious of how wonderful it is that God made them all and grateful that one has had the chance to meet so many on such intimate terms. To be joyful is to note the regenerative mysteries of the body, to understand something of how it all works, and to be grateful that one has been given the opportunity to nudge along the process of healing. To be joyful is to know that one has been gifted with hands and with a mind through which the healing power of the Spirit can be mediated and to be grateful for those gifts. To be joyful is to pour out the wine of fervent zeal and the oil of compassion day in and day out and to be grateful that the source of these liquors is inexhaustible. (p. 129)

Positive helping experiences as important for compassion satisfaction

Far from being a new idea, descriptions and discussions of the experience of helping another person abound in the clinical and spiritual literature. A number of theories of psychology have articulated and researched such encounters, such as transpersonal psychology, humanistic psychology, and existential psychology as well the discipline of philosophy. Spiritual and religious works also are filled with examples.

What is important for the purposes of this book is that being aware of and appreciative of such experiences can be very helpful for the clinician in strengthening a sense of fulfillment and meaning in this work. These experiences lift the clinician's spirit and become an ongoing inspiration for how to be engaged in the work. As we have seen throughout this book, dealing with negative feelings in patient care and preventing burnout is only part of the way helping professionals survive and thrive in this work. Recall Fredrickson's (2004) discovery of the broaden-and-build theory of positive emotions discussed in chapter 9. There can be increased energy and renewal that comes with noticing and appreciating the phenomenon of one human being in a vulnerable place being able to receive and be transformed by the help of another. Whether you delight in this from a scientific, philosophical, or spiritual viewpoint, the end result is still a sense of gratitude and wonder to be involved in this kind of work.

Jean Watson describes this as the transpersonal caring moment

Jean Watson has articulated and studied this phenomenon and called it the *transpersonal caring moment* that is manifest in an *actual caring occasion* between clinician and patient. Grounded in a deep commitment to the dignity and well-being of the patient, the clinician

> enters into the life space or phenomenal field of another person, is able to detect the other person's condition of being (spirit, soul), feels this condition in such a way that the recipient has a release of subjective feelings and thoughts he or she had been longing to release. (Watson, 2012, p. 75)

The clinician's centered and caring intentional presence helps the patient find and access his or her own inner healing resources to facilitate a healing process. Just as setting and casting a fracture sets the conditions for the body to heal itself, so does the caring presence of the clinician create the conditions for the patient's psychological and spiritual healing to occur. Such positive encounters appear to increase energy, possibility, and creativity in the patient. But it also seems to enhance both parties no matter who is the caregiver or who the recipient of care is. A sense of meaning and purpose is generated. There is often a sense of self-transcendence or having participated in something universal to humans that also might be called sacred.

Secular humanistic and spiritual understandings of peak helping experiences

Depending on your worldview, there are at least two pathways when a clinician encounters this kind of experience. One is a more secular, humanistic viewpoint in which the experience becomes a source of meaning and fulfillment. There is a kind of compassion satisfaction that helps the clinician maintain or even increase a compassionate caring motivation. The second is a more spiritual viewpoint that includes the first viewpoint and adds the notion that one has participated in a spiritual event and that the divine or a spiritual dynamic is somehow involved. Such clinicians may attribute what occurred as due to the healing action of the divine in whatever way they understand it. The ability to care is thought to be grounded in this spiritual source. As Montgomery (1993) puts it, "Caregivers draw on a greater source, one that sustains them and serves as a source of energy and self-renewal. The energy needed for caring is perceived to come from a greater source beyond the self" (p. 75). There can be the sense of being in tune with or collaborating with this divine source or as a life force. As Watson (2005) describes it,

> while we adhere to health and curing/caring and healing as our primary mission in this health care work, we also have to acknowledge honestly that we work within the great circle of life-death. This reality recognizes that we all share this common task of facing our humanity at a deep level, both personally and professionally. What we do is not without consequences, in that one way or another we are contributing to and co-participating with the web of life. … So, making and seeking meaning about understanding and deepening our view and appreciation for all of life is part of our human quest. (pp. 136–137)

When we become aware of the transpersonal aspects of our work, whether you describe it in spiritual or in experiential terms, there is sense of energy and renewal that can become part of what sustains you in this work. Sulmasy (1997) says it is what we all desire and that clinicians "can learn to see their patients as sacraments-doorways into the sacred" (p. 17).

Caring as gateway to the Divine

In addition to the transpersonal satisfaction that can come from compassionate caring, for many clinicians this connection with patients becomes a spiritual experience, a real connection with the divine. It can be one in which the clinician feels that the divine is working through him or her. For example, Nouwen (1992 said the mystery "is that we have been chosen to make our own limited and conditional love the gateway for the unlimited and unconditional love of God" (p. 37). This is the sense that the clinician is being used as an instrument by the divine. Some clinicians experience it in the opposite fashion, in which they feel they are encountering God in the suffering person. Paul Wright is a cardiologist who experienced a profound sense of burnout

and sought Mother Teresa of Calcutta to help him find his purpose again. In his recounting of this work with her in his book, *Mother Teresa's Prescription*, he writes at one point, "When I touch a human being who is poor, naked, sick, homeless, or thirsty, I am touching Christ in the distressing guise of the poor" (Wright, 2006, p. 112). Later he says, "I enjoy being a doctor now more than I ever have because I serve for *someone* rather than for *something*. Medicine is no longer just a business for me" (Wright, 2006, p. 112).

SPIRITUAL, PHILOSOPHICAL, AND MEDITATION PRACTICES TO ENDURE AND TRANSFORM THE ENCOUNTER WITH SUFFERING

> Often we hear about burnout, but increasingly we learn that the burnout is not because we care too much, but because we wall ourselves off and close off our heart and close off our very source of love and the human connectedness that gives us the life-generating force for this work. (Watson, 2008)

Difficult work requires conditioning

Any difficult work or activity that a person wishes to do excellently and over a long period of time requires regular and ongoing conditioning while the person is engaged in that work or activity. An elite athlete must continue to practice between competitions to stay in shape. An excellent singer continues to maintain and improve technique between performances, doing vocal exercises and getting voice lessons. Great performers do not "come out of thin air." They have capabilities that have combined with excellent training to get them to that level. But once they are at a high level, it is not as if they can relax and not practice anymore and expect to stay at that level. Even though they may take brief breaks, they know they cannot afford to stop practicing and expect to stay at that high level of performance. The same is true for clinicians who do the difficult work of working with people who are very sick and suffering. They must be physically able to endure long hours seeing many patients according to their specialties. They must be able to be mentally engaged and focused; every encounter requires a new set of circumstances in which they must assess and respond, accessing all the knowledge they have to help the person, which requires the highest levels of cognitive performance. Emotionally, they must be able to maintain composure in stressful situations, achieving an optimal level of arousal to attain peak performance in clinical situations. Underneath all of this, they must keep their spirits up, as we say. There must be a constant connection with one's purpose and mission so that one can stay motivated to keep doing this work and be able to bounce back from setbacks, mistakes, or tragic situations. This would be the zone of the POC/SOC.

The best clinicians have practices to maintain high levels of performance

The best clinicians have practices to help them stay at high levels of performance no differently than do musical performers, jet fighter pilots, elite athletes, or air traffic controllers. They will tell you of the practices they have to condition and maintain their physical bodies for the tasks they have to do, from nutrition and exercise to sleep. They will have ways that they stay cognitively sharp by practicing, doing simulations to be prepared for unexpected scenarios, and anything that keeps their brains firing at the best

level possible. Emotionally, they rely on their years of experience that gives them the confidence they can do this work while continuing to monitor and manage their emotional states by practicing, getting coached for any problems, and continuing to put themselves in challenging situations. What gets less explicit attention in medicine is what clinicians are doing to keep their spirits up.

Loehr and Schwartz's discussion of how high performance necessitates a high level of conditioning

In their book *The Power of Full Engagement*, Loehr and Schwartz (2003) explain how the key to high performance is managing energy rather than time. To do so requires having a set of practices to maintain a high level of conditioning. They note that being fully engaged in your work or activity requires drawing on four sources of energy: the physical, the emotional, the mental, and the spiritual. Our energy capacity can decline if we underuse or overuse it, so we have to balance how much energy we expend with energy renewal. Like elite athletes, if we want to improve our capacity, we have to train in a systematic way and push past our normal limits. The mental, emotional, and spiritual energy capacities are conditioned very much like how we increase our physical capacity:

> *Much as it is possible to strengthen a bicep or a tricep by subjecting it to stress and then recovering, so it is possible to strategically build the muscle of self-control. The same training regimen applies. Exercise self-control or empathy or patience past normal limits, and then allow time for rest and these muscles become progressively stronger. More reliably, however, we can offset the limitations of conscious will and discipline by building positive rituals that become automatic—and relatively effortless—as quickly as possible. (Loehr & Schwartz, 2003, p. 169)*

Positive energy rituals are very specific routines for managing physical, emotional, mental, and spiritual sources of energy, and it is these positive rituals that are key to helping us be fully engaged in our work at high levels of performance. Loehr and Schwartz (2003) use military training as an example:

> The more exacting the challenge, the more rigorous our rituals need to be. The preparation of soldiers for combat is a good example. ... Recruits are compelled to build rituals in every dimension of their lives—how they walk and how they talk; what time they go to bed and wake up; when and what they eat; how they take care of their bodies and how they think and act under pressure. This code of conduct makes it possible for them to do the right thing at the right time even in the face of the most severe of all stresses—the threat of death. (p. 171)

Clinicians develop rituals to maintain their high levels of performance. As clinicians mature, they discover through trial and error what they need to do to keep conditioned for clinical practice. When it comes to POC/SOC, clinicians have more of a challenge finding the positive rituals they need in that domain.

The neglect of explicit training in the four energy sources in medicine

It is always amazing to me in medical training how we do not explicitly address the training of these four energy sources. There is a way in which the grueling hours in residency training or surgical training can push clinicians to learn how to take care of themselves physically, for example, in order to do the work at high levels. But typically, clinicians are left up to their own personally created strategies to create the positive energy rituals to help them get the intermittent recovery needed for their very demanding jobs. We probably do a better job on teaching positive rituals on the physical

source of energy than we do on the other three sources. As I have discussed in this book, young clinicians do not get the best information or training on how to manage their emotional and mental sources of energy because of the way the hidden curriculum of medicine denigrates the subjective and the emotional realms. It is even worse with the spiritual source of energy. Interestingly, while Loehr and Schwartz state that the physical source of energy is important, they argue that the most significant and powerful source of energy is the spiritual for our motivation, our direction, and our perseverance. They define *spiritual* as

> the connection to a deeply held set of values and to a purpose beyond our self-interest. At the practical level, anything that ignites the human spirit serves to drive full engagement and to maximize performance in whatever mission we are on. The key muscle that fuels spiritual energy is character—the courage and conviction to live by our values, even when doing so requires personal sacrifice and hardship. Supportive spiritual muscles include passion, commitment, integrity and honesty. (Loehr & Schwartz, 2003, p. 110)

Practices that help people renew their spirits

Loehr and Schwartz explain that in order to renew our spirit regularly, we have to find ways to rest and rejuvenate, and we have to find ways to keep connecting with the values that are the most meaningful for us. This involves spiritual practices to keep connected to one's fundamental purpose or meaning. In our case, we are considering spiritual practices that help us cultivate compassion and be regularly reminded of how interconnected all human beings are and how we all want to avoid suffering and be happy. Loehr and Schwartz list simple practices such as being in nature, listening to music or an inspirational speaker, and reading inspirational writings. Other practices include meditation, yoga, prayer, and reflection. But they advise that we not limit our possible spiritual practices because there can be other ways that people can achieve rejuvenation and a reenergized reconnection with our values (Loehr & Schwartz, 2003).

Five types of spiritual practices

What I like about Loehr and Schwartz's explanation of the spiritual source of energy is that this applies well to both people with explicitly spiritual backgrounds as well as people who prefer a more secular understanding of their particular purpose or values in life. Their descriptions of how it takes a regular practice to keep reconnecting with what our deepest values and mission are fits very well with what the POC/SOC is for clinicians. Taking this a step further, I have developed a typology of spiritual/ philosophical practices among clinicians that are used to endure and transform the suffering that is encountered. These are not meant to be exhaustive but rather to provide examples that may assist in helping you identify your own practices and how they function in your work. Also, the same practice can fall under different types depending on how the clinician uses that practice, or they can fall under multiple types simultaneously.

Practices for cultivating compassion

The first type is *practices for cultivating compassion*. Spiritual practices—in a number of traditions as well as secular philosophies—specifically focus on training the mind to be more compassionate. A prime example is the Loving-Kindness Meditation (LKM) in the Buddhist tradition. In this particular meditation practice, the person begins with loving-kindness wishes toward the self or benefactor, and then as if extending outward in a series of concentric circles, extends these wishes to a friend or loved one, a neutral person, a difficult person, and finally to all living beings. (There are slight variations in the meditation with both traditional Buddhist and secular versions.) The exact wishes vary among different versions of this meditation, but one example is the four wishes taught by Sharon Salzberg (Salzburg, 2002; Salzburg & Goldstein, 2001): May I (you) be free from danger. May I (you) be happy. May I (you) be healthy. May I (you) live with ease. After wishing these for oneself, one then extends these wishes toward a benefactor, a person who has been very kind to you and helped you in some way. These same wishes are extended next to a friend or loved one. As one has cultivated these very positive wishes to people about whom one finds it easy to wish loving-kindness, the meditation then moves to a neutral person, then a difficult person, and finally all living beings without exception or distinction. As one does this regularly, it has the effect of training the mind to approach anyone in a spirit of loving-kindness. In a sense, it increases the capacity to be compassionate and even resilient in all that one encounters. The Dalai Lama (1981) describes it in this way:

> There are various positive side-effects of enhancing one's feeling of compassion. One of them is that the greater the force of your compassion, the greater your resilience in confronting hardships and your ability to transform them into more positive conditions. [The Dalai Lama goes on to describe one effective practice for cultivating compassion.]
>
> I also think that the greater the force of your altruistic attitude towards sentient beings, the more courageous you become. The greater your courage, the less you feel prone to discouragement and loss of hope. Therefore, compassion is also a source of inner strength. (pp. 76–77)

While the compassion meditations in Buddhism such as LKM are very well known and studied, there are spiritual practices in each of the world religions that are also compassion meditations—even though they may not be called that explicitly. They are recognized by being spiritual practices of wishing or urging compassion and kindness toward others such as loved ones, strangers, difficult people, and people who are rejected or oppressed. They may promote a sense of the dignity of all humans and advocate for social justice. There is often a component of having compassion toward oneself as linked to having compassion toward others—for example, the Golden Rule, which appears in similar forms throughout all religions: Do to others as you would have done to you. There is often an assumption of the interconnectedness of all living beings. It is typically encouraged that compassion meditations are to be done regularly within a calming or centering technique (e.g., comfortable posture, relaxed body and breathing). Hofman, Grossman, & Hinton (2011) have done research on compassion meditation practices and found that, in general, they are associated with enhancing unconditional, positive emotional states of kindness and compassion. They tend to increase positive affect and decrease negative affect. They may reduce stress-induced subjective distress and immune response. They may also enhance activation of brain areas that are involved in emotion processing and empathy.

Research on the effects of contemplative meditation

People who practice contemplative meditation (i.e., Tibetan Buddhism, Theravada Buddhism, centering prayer, yoga, and mindfulness) tend to be higher in measures of empathic concern, perspective-taking empathy, compassionate altruism toward strangers, empathy-based survivor guilt (guilt over being better off than others), agreeableness, conscientiousness, openness to experience, and the general factor of personality (a global measure of resilience and effective social functioning). They tend to have more positive personality traits and better psychosocial functioning. Compared to nonmeditators, they score lower on depression, empathic distress, neuroticism, and omnipotent responsibility guilt (i.e., that one is responsible for the happiness and well-being of others). The more intensely one practices meditation and the longer one meditates is associated with greater altruism, especially toward strangers; they also appear to have more positive personality traits and better psychosocial functioning. If the goal of the meditation was specifically other-focused (i.e., to benefit all sentient beings) as opposed to self-focused (e.g., focused on being relaxed or calm, becoming enlightened), there was a significantly increased cognitive empathy, higher compassionate altruism toward strangers, and positive personality characteristics as well as significantly lower proneness to negative emotions, less empathic distress, and less separation guilt (i.e., the belief that one will cause loved ones to suffer if one separates and leads his or her own life or differs from the loved ones in some way) (O'Connor et al., 2015).

Comparison of religious and secular motivations for meditation practice

Does it matter if a meditation practice is based in religion? Overall, there appear to be general positive benefits with all meditation practices. Those who use religiously based meditation practices and mindfulness meditations all tend to score higher on altruism toward strangers than nonmeditators. But those who are specifically religiously based practitioners tend to have more altruism toward strangers, higher conscientiousness, and greater resilience than secular meditation groups. These practices included Tibetan Buddhism, Theravada Buddhism, and centering prayer. There was no difference between the religiously based and secular meditators in altruism toward family and friends. Religiously based meditators also appear to have less depression, empathic distress, neuroticism, and omnipotence guilt (i.e., that one is responsible for the happiness and well-being of others) than the secular meditation practices of mindfulness and yoga (O'Connor et al., 2015). The effects from the practice of yoga need to be researched further because this type of meditation may be practiced by people with a religiously based intention and this study did not distinguish these motivations (O'Connor et al., 2015). One would expect that if yoga is practiced so that it is connected to a religion, the positive effects would increase. Also, while there is a significantly higher percentage of religiously based meditators who explicitly endorse other-focused goals compared to secular meditators, it is interesting to note that there were a significant number of religiously based meditators who endorsed more self-focused goals and a significant number of secular meditators who endorsed other-focused goals. *It appears, then, that we should not assume all religiously based meditation is altruistically focused; nor should we judge secular meditations as automatically self-focused. While a religious motivation appears to add something unique to the meditation practice, the nature of that motivation may not be automatically compassionately oriented.* More research is needed to confirm this. But one should refrain from judging the quality of another person's meditation practice from an external spiritual or secular label.

Other practices besides meditation can cultivate compassion

There are other practices besides meditation that would also function in cultivating compassion. An important practice to help cultivate and maintain compassionate caring in ourselves is to regularly ask ourselves what our patients are teaching us. As Hatem (2006) puts it, "Daily, we are allowed access to the intimate stories embedded in our patients' life-and-death issues. Emotional fatigue often becomes the distorting prism that prevents a clear understanding of the privileges of doctoring, but the lessons are there, ready for our reflection" (p. 300). This can be done from both spiritual and secular perspectives.

Patient care as a spiritual or philosophic practice in itself

While we have focused on the spiritual and philosophical practices that help clinicians maintain a compassion mindset, some physicians viewed the work with patients as itself a spiritual practice to maintain compassion. That is, one might choose to work with a particularly vulnerable or difficult patient population as a means to deepen one's own spirituality. The work with patients might make him or her feel more connected with spiritual purpose; it may also be a way to keep improving the self, or a way to give to others who are less fortunate. Anandarajah and Roseman (2014) quoted a physician who works in a prison with rapists and killers: "Because if I could bring compassion to a killer or a rapist or an arsonist or a pedophile, then I considered that the highest form of my job" (p. 19). They noted the possibility that, for some clinicians, this is not at all connected with participation in religious things like prayer, but that the act of caring for underserved or difficult people is a way of participating in a larger goal or a path to goodness itself. Finally, rather than looking at the spiritual in a unidirectional way (i.e., spirituality enhances compassionate action or compassionate action increases spirituality), there is, rather, a synergistic circular effect in which the desire for purpose and meaning enhances compassionate action, but the involvement with patients deepens the sense of meaning and purpose, energizing the clinician further (Anandarajah & Roseman, 2014). In his book *What If I Am You? The Mysticism of the Physician-Patient Relationship*, Klauer (2016) reflects on patient care from the assumption that we are all one and how that would change how one approaches patient care if that is the case.

Practices of deep reliance on sacred or philosophical writings, prayer, and ritual

The second type of practice used among clinicians is *practices of deep reliance on sacred or philosophical writings, prayer and ritual*. First, in terms of sacred writings, these practices often involve reflecting on one's experiences with patients with a variety of goals. One may be to gain insight into suffering and the interconnectedness of all humanity. It may be to draw inspiration from exemplary individuals in one's spiritual tradition to help with dealing with challenging people or with maintaining one's spirit in ongoing hardship or challenges in one's work. Or it may be to place one's particular experience with a clinical situation or emotional/cognitive state, and gain insight or encouragement from the parallels between one's experience and a similar one in those sacred writings. There may be a way in which the meditation on specific passages or sacred stories in one's tradition may facilitate emotional processing such as grieving setbacks, finding hope, or affirming resolute determination to continue. From atheistic and agnostic perspectives, there are a number of texts reflecting on humanistic philosophy that become a way to be inspired and motivated for service to others and the world.

Prayer and ritual as a way of connecting to the divine for assistance

Prayer and ritual are also methods clinicians use to maintain or cultivate a compassion mindset for the long haul in taking care of people who are suffering or otherwise presenting a challenge. There are two facets to these practices. One facet is that it may function as a way for the clinician to connect with God in the hope of gaining assistance in helping patients. It may be to ask for help in helping particular patients. It may be praying for wisdom, courage, emotional composure, patience, support, or skill in order to help patients more effectively. It may be to ask for God to help the patient in a particular way.

Prayer and ritual used to maintain balance, composure, and energy

The second facet of prayer and ritual is the way these spiritual practices assist the clinician in keeping balance, finding strength, or engaging in self-reflection. When done in a spiritual context, clinicians may be placing themselves and their helping work as part of the ongoing call from the divine to care for all people. It can be done outside of patient care or while doing patient care as a way to maintain equilibrium and a compassion mindset with patients. Or it may be a way to protect oneself from certain dangers or emotional hazards of being in a helping profession. For example, Moore notes that people in helping professions can be tempted to grandiosity because of their powerful skills or because of how patients project on clinicians special status, power, or superhuman qualities: "When people turn you into a god or goddess, it tends to make you more crazy, not less" (Moore, 2003, p. 92). Moore explains that prayer is not necessarily to be pious or nice, but because it is a survival technique to deal with one's potential grandiosity as well as all the positive and negative projections patients place on you as a clinician (e.g., it is your fault that everything is going poorly, that you have special healing powers). When that occurs, prayer can be a way of connecting with the divine as a way to filter or protect oneself from what people place on you. As Moore (2003) puts it, "You can take that energy that is coming toward you and, through your prayer, pass it on. 'Here,' you say, 'this is really yours, Lord. Take it. It belongs to you'" (pp. 95–96). In this way, clinicians can buffer themselves both psychologically and spiritually against the negative behaviors and energy from patients.

Prayer and ritual to stop dysfunctional ways of thinking and encourage mindfulness

Prayer and ritual may also be a way of getting ourselves to stop dysfunctional ways of thinking and be mindful of what is happening to us in the pressures of clinical work.

> There is a story in Zen circles about a man and a horse. The horse is galloping quickly, and it appears that the man on the horse is going somewhere important. Another man, standing alongside the road, shouts, "Where are you going?" and the first man replies, "I don't know! Ask the horse!" This is also our story. We are riding a horse, we don't know where we are going, and we can't stop. The horse is our habit energy pulling us along, and we are powerless.
>
> If we cannot stop, we cannot have insight. (Nhat Hanh, 1989, p. 24)

Mindfulness meditation can be very helpful in this regard by having a way to observe one's thoughts as a way to expose cognitive distortions in ourselves. (See the discussion of mindfulness meditation in chapter 10.)

Prayer and ritual to remind oneself that one is part of a larger mystery or force

Prayer and ritual can also be a way in which some clinicians remind themselves that they are part of a larger mystery, power, or force, and thereby gain inner strength. Some clinicians, for example, might think of themselves as instruments of God's compassion rather than in control of all outcomes. From a nontheistic perspective, a clinician might think of him- or herself as part of the force of compassion in general. Nhat Hanh describes how one can connect oneself to something greater than oneself that allows one to have more capacity to encounter and transform suffering.

> Because of its immensity, the river has the capacity to receive and transform. The river doesn't suffer at all because of a handful of salt. If your heart is small, one unjust word or act will make you suffer. But if your heart is large, if you have understanding and compassion, that word or deed will not have the power to make you suffer. You will be able to receive, embrace, and transform it in an instant. What counts here is your capacity. To transform your suffering, your heart has to be as big as the ocean. Someone else might suffer. But if a bodhisattva receives the same unkind words, she won't suffer at all. It depends on your way of receiving, embracing, and transforming. If you keep your pain for too long, it is because you have not yet learned the practice of inclusiveness. (Nhat Hanh, 1989, p. 198)

Whether from a theistic or nontheistic perspective, the connection a clinician feels to this larger force or entity assists the clinician to feel stronger and more resilient in the face of difficulty because they are not alone.

Prayer and ritual as a way to experience God's support

Finally, there is also the sense that as a clinician relies on, stays connected to, the divine in this work, there is a way in which God provides support in that work. Theologian John S. Dunne has articulated the experience many clinicians have of experiencing strength by relying on God. He explains that a table, for example, is potentially a support for me to lean on. But it does not support until I actually lean on the table; it is then that I feel the support of the table (Dunne, 1978). Many clinicians experience a dynamic like this in their own careers in which they relied on the divine—however they conceived of it—and experienced additional strength because of it. Indeed, 12-step AA programs capture this dynamic with Steps 2 and 3:

> 2. Came to believe that a Power greater than ourselves could restore us to sanity.
> 3. Made a decision to turn our will and our lives over to the care of God as we understood Him. (Alcoholics Anonymous, 1972, pp. 25, 35)

Practices of active engagement with suffering

The third type of practice used by clinicians is *practices of active engagement with suffering*. These are practices in which working with the suffering of others or oneself leads to insights or attitudes that are helpful in energizing a person to do compassionate work. Facing and engaging suffering rather than denying or avoiding it allows clinicians to engage the reality of human life. But paradoxically, this has the effect of deepening commitment and drive. Attempting to explain how this occurs is beyond the scope of this work. My task is simply to relate how, for some clinicians, this describes how they manage to keep up their spirits in very difficult work. Clinicians from the Buddhist tradition engage the suffering of all people as a way to realize our common humanity and to discern the sources of our suffering. As a person comes to know one's suffering, one can be on the path to be free from it (Nhat Hanh, 1989). This type spiritual practice encourages the person to engage his or her own suffering as a way to be helpful to others. This is an example from the Christian tradition:

> It is in the face of apathy in ourselves that compassion becomes less and less possible for us. While it is appropriate to speak of degrees of coping healthily with suffering, the logic of the conclusion is irresistible. If we are not able to feel our own suffering and consequently to utilize resources for healing, the possibility of compassion slips away from us. If I cannot feel my own suffering, there is no chance that I will be able to feel your suffering: That is, to suffer with you, to have compassion. (Purves, 1989, p. 91)

This example from French philosopher and mystic Simone Weil also emphasizes the importance of deeply engaging the suffering of a person who is afflicted and attending to that suffering being a sign of love of one's neighbor.

> The love of our neighbor in all its fullness simply means being able to say to him: "What are you going through?" It is a recognition that the sufferer exists, not only as a unit in a collection, or a specimen from the social category labeled "unfortunate," but as a man [or woman], exactly like us, who was one day stamped with a special mark by affliction. For this reason it is enough, but it is indispensable, to know how to look at him in a certain way. ... This way of looking is first of all attentive. The soul empties itself of all its own contents in order to receive into itself the being it is looking at, just as he [she] is, in all his truth. ... Only he [or she] who is capable of attention can do this." (Weil, 1951, p. 115)

Practices of connecting to the mythic or story grounding of your life as a clinician

The fourth type of spiritual or philosophical practice is *practices of attending to the mythic or story grounding of your life as a helping professional*. This approach, as part of a POC/SOC, imagines the work of helping within a mythological perspective. Clinicians who use this approach will, for example, look to myths and stories from ancient times for wisdom that previous cultures and societies had for making sense of suffering and for providing guidance in how to forge ahead in difficult, worthwhile work. Mythological adventures are typically stories of how the hero goes through trials and adversity to reach a particular goal or destination (Campbell, 1968). Like real life, the myths are stories of people who encounter both outside challenges and issues they must battle within themselves. The great myths are a myriad of stories of struggles that may end in success or failure (Pargament, 1997). In this way, they mirror in an archetypal manner what all of us go through. In reading and reflecting on these myths and other stories, clinicians can get insights and perspectives into their own life journeys.

Using the power of story to understand your life and work

Simply asking yourself as a clinician about the story of your work and career can be a powerful tool when examining what is going on in your life and then using that as a way to live the kind of story you want to live. In *The Power of Story: Change Your Story, Change Your Destiny in Business and in Life*, Loehr (2007) offers an excellent example of this approach:

> By "story," then, I mean those tales we create and tell ourselves and others, and which form the only reality we will ever know in this life. Our stories may or may not conform to the real world. They may or may not inspire us to take hope-filled action to better our lives. They may or may not take us where we ultimately want to go. But since our destiny follows our stories, it's imperative that we do everything in our power to get our stories right.
>
> For most of us, that means some serious editing.
>
> To edit a dysfunctional story, you must first identify it. To do that, you must answer the question: In which important areas of my life is it clear that I cannot achieve my goals with the story I've got? Only after confronting and satisfactorily answering this question can you expect to build new reality-based stories that will take you where you want to go. (p. 5)

Mythological approaches to gain perspective on one's journey as a clinician

Others find it helpful to reflect on their journeys and inner experiences using the work of Joseph Campbell (1968), who devoted his entire career to examining the myths of all cultures and historical periods and found that the journey of the hero shows up in all cultures with common themes (called the monomyth). The monomyth typically has these successive steps. The hero experiences a call to adventure. There is often a refusal of that call, but also the appearance of helpers and mentors who help the person find his or her way. There are always trials that nearly kill the person but also strengthen him or her to face some major quest or battle. The hero meets that challenge and many times returns to his or her point of origin with benefits for the home tribe or people. In our case, the clinician is the hero of his or her own myth. Campbell offers this famous quote that he based on his study of the myths in terms of what they might suggest for how we approach the future. It seems quite applicable to the ways many of us experience health care.

> We're in a free fall into future. We don't know where we are going. Things are changing so fast and always when you are going through a long tunnel anxiety comes along. And all you have to do to transform your hell into a paradise is to turn your fall into a voluntary act. It's a very interesting shift in perspective, and that's all it is. Joyful participation in the sorrows, and everything changes. (Campbell, 2005)

Initiation myths and the shamanic journey

Michael Meade is well known for his recounting of the myths and ancient stories as ways to convey ancient wisdom about life. Clinicians can juxtapose their lives next to those ancient stories and myths as a way to gain insight and guidance for how to survive and thrive in the pursuit of learning how to heal and then living a life facilitating healing for others (Meade, 2012). This approach often has the theme of asking yourself what your life is calling from you, and that there is a purpose for which you have been built and brings fulfillment in your life. Meade observes that there are three phases of initiation: separation from one's current life, going through an ordeal, and then returning to the community. While he speaks of these about life in general, it fits particularly with clinicians who are initiated into healing: they feel called to leave their lives as they were, they go through the ordeal of training and the psychological trials of practice, and then they return to the community with the gifts they have received from that ordeal. Nixa (2017) does this similarly relying on Native American spirituality. In any case, this type of practice can be done from both spiritual and secular perspectives by clinicians in which the great stories and myths are used to reflect deeply on the personal experiences of caring for patients.

Practice of participating in the mystery of suffering and the compassion of the divine or connection with what is greater than oneself

The fifth type of spiritual practice is *practices of participating in the mystery of suffering and the compassion of the divine or connection with what is greater than oneself.* In this type of practice, the clinician views his or her experience as a helping professional as participating somehow in the way the divine is working toward the relieving of suffering. That is, the clinician's work is an extension of this divine compassion. The clinician, therefore, is not alone in this work and can rely on being part of this larger mission and energy. This is an example from Presbyterian theologian Andrew Purves (1989):

> If the ministry of compassion is a participation in the ongoing compassion of Jesus Christ ... it comes as no surprise to discover that suffering is also to be understood in the same way, as a participation in the suffering of Christ. In fact, to participate in Christ's suffering, and therefore to share in his life and power, is the counterpoint of the participation in Christ's compassion. (p. 103)

Simone Weil (1909–1943), a French philosopher, political activist, and mystic theologian, wrote a great deal about suffering and affliction and how God is involved in both the person suffering and the person offering compassion.

> In true love it is not we who love the afflicted in God; it is God in us who loves them. When we are in affliction, it is God in us who loves those who wish us well. Compassion and gratitude come down from God, and when they are exchanged in a glance, God is present at the point where the eyes of those who give and those who receive meet. The sufferer and the other love each other, starting from God, through God, but not for the love of God; they love each other for the love of the one for the

other. This is an impossibility. That is why it come about only through the agency of God. (Weil, 1951, p. 151)

Practices that promote spiritual or philosophical reflection on the work of helping

The sixth type of practice is *practices that promote spiritual or philosophical reflection on the work of helping.* Puchalski and Guenther (2012) provide a number of examples of spiritual or reflective practices that include participation in a spiritual community, consulting spiritual directors or mentors, having friends or groups in which one can have deeper conversations, meditation, prayer, reading from a sacred text, gratitude practices, retreats, reflective writing, engaging in the arts, appreciating beauty, exercise, studying fields different from our own expertise, having hobbies, and being able to have a sense of humor. The practice of spiritual direction or spiritual companionship is one in which the clinician (either individually or in a group) works with a person trained to help the clinician reflect on his or her experience (Morneau, 1992). All of these can function as ways to help cultivate one's capacity for compassion. They can also be understood as falling under the types of practices listed above in terms of providing personal renewal and perspective. The practices can be done individually or in groups. The benefits are many, ranging from gaining insight, having the support of like-minded colleagues, processing difficult experiences, or speculating about the meaning of the work.

CONCLUSION

Many clinicians rely on a spirituality or a philosophy of caring (SOC/POC) as a way to maintain and cultivate compassion in the work of helping and healing others. It provides an organized way of spiritually or philosophically understanding

the encounter with human pain and provides a perspective on the meaning of that pain and suffering. It also provides a perspective on what it means to be compassionate to people who are suffering. It provides the helper with some way of breaking down, understanding, metabolizing, or transforming the toxic encounter with human pain as well as how one might bounce back from the hardship of this work and keep going. While many clinicians do not have any explicit POC/SOC, I would argue there is always an implicit one that is operating. There are advantages when a clinician can articulate and rely on an explicit POC/SOC. The following quote seems fitting for people involved in the helping profession who might experience the work as an ordeal. It captures many of the themes of this chapter.

> *My child, when you come to serve the Lord, prepare yourself for trials. Be sincere of heart and steadfast, undisturbed in time of adversity. Cling to God, do not forsake the Lord; thus will your future be great. Accept whatever befalls you, in crushing misfortune be patient. For in fire gold is tested, and worthy people in the crucible of humiliation. Trust God and God will help you; make straight your ways and hope in the Lord. (Ecclesiasticus 2:1–6)*

In terms of being in the zone of balanced C^2, a POC/SOC might provide guidance in terms of the best way to be involved with patients. It would give a sense of what the clinician's role is between being too detached and too involved. From the clinicians' perspectives, the SOC/POC provides a way of reminding clinicians of their purpose, which reminds them to stay engaged with patients even when they are really suffering or very difficult. Ideally, the SOC/POC also stresses how they need to care for themselves in the work and provides them with coping methods to metabolize and transform the suffering clinicians witness.

REFERENCES

Aase, M., Nordrehaug, J. E., & Malterud, K. (2008). "If you cannot tolerate that risk, you should never become a physician": A qualitative study about existential experiences among physicians. *Journal of Medical Ethics*, 34(11), 767–771.

Abu-Raiya, H., & Pargament, K. I. (2012). On the links between religion and health: What has empirical research taught us? In M. Cobb, C. Puchalski, & B. Rumbold (Eds.), *Oxford textbook of spirituality in healthcare*. New York, NY: Oxford University Press.

Alcoholics Anonymous. (1972). *Twelve steps and twelve traditions*. New York, NY: Author.

Allport, G. W., & Ross, J. M. (1967). Personal religious orientation and prejudice. *Journal of Personality and Social Psychology*, 5(4), 432–443.

Anandarajah, G., & Roseman, J. L. (2014). A qualitative study of physicians' views on compassionate patient care and spirituality: Medicine as a spiritual practice? *Rhode Island Medical Journal*, 97(3), 17–22.

Anandarajah, G., & Smith, M. (2009). Resident physicians' thoughts regarding compassion and spirituality in the doctor-patient relationship. In M. T. Evans & E. D. Walker (Eds.), *Religion and psychology* (pp. 307–316). New York, NY: Nova Science.

Ano, G. G., & Vasconcelles, E. B. (2005). Religious coping and psychological adjustment to stress: A meta-analysis. *Journal of Clinical Psychology*, 61, 461–480.

Armstrong, K. (2007). *The great transformation: The beginning of our religious traditions*. New York, NY: Anchor Books.

Baranowsky, A. B. (2002). The silencing response in clinical practice: On the road to dialogue. In C. R. Figley (Ed.), *Treating compassion fatigue* (pp. 155–170). New York, NY: Brunner-Routledge.

Batson, C. D. (1976). Religion as prosocial: Agent or double agent? *Journal for the Scientific Study of Religion*, 5(1), 29–45.

Batson, C. D., Floyd, R. B., Meyer, J. M., & Winner, A. L. (1999). "And who is my neighbor?": Intrinsic religion as a source of universal compassion. *Journal for the Scientific Study of Religion*, 38(4), 445–457.

Batson, C. D., & Schoenrade, P. A. (1991). Measuring religion as quest: 1. Validity concerns. *Journal for the Scientific Study of Religion*, 30(4), 416–429.

Boero, M. E., Caviglia, M. L., Monteverdi, R., Braida, V., Fabello, M., & Zorzella, L. M. (2005). Spirituality of health workers: A descriptive study. *International Journal of Nursing Studies*, 42(8), 915–921.

Calhoun, L. G., Cann, A., Tedeschi, R. G., & McMillan, J. (2000). A correlational test of the relationship between posttraumatic growth, religion, and cognitive processing. *Journal of Traumatic Stress*, 13(3), 521–527.

Campbell, J. (1968). *The hero with a thousand faces* (2nd ed.). Princeton, NJ: Princeton University Press.

Campbell, J. (Host). (2005). *Sukhavati: A mythic journey* [DVD]. United States: Mystic Fire Video.

Chan, W. C. H., Fong, A., Wong, K. L. Y., Tse, D. M. W., Lau, K. S., & Chan, L. N. (2016). Impact of death work on self: Existential and emotional challenges and coping of palliative care professionals. *Health and Social Work*, 41(1), 33–41.

Clark, L., Leedy, S., McDonald, L., Muller, B., Lamb, C., Mendez, T., ... Schonwetter, R. (2007). Spirituality and job satisfaction among hospice interdisciplinary team members. *Journal of Palliative Medicine*, 10(6), 1321–1328.

Curlin, F. A., Lantos, J. D., Roach, C. J., Sellergren, S. A., & Chin, M. H. (2005). Religious characteristics of US physicians: A national survey. *Journal of General Internal Medicine*, 20(7), 629–634.

Dalai Lama, H. H. (1981). *The power of compassion* (G. T. Jinpa, Trans.). San Francisco, CA: Thorsons.

Demarzo, M. M. P., Monero-Marin, J., Cuijpers, P., Zabaleta-del-Olmo, E., Mahtani, K. R., Vellinga, A., ... Garcia-Campayo, J. (2015). The efficacy of mindfulness-based interventions in primary care: A meta-analytic review. *Annals of Family Medicine*, 13(6), 573–582.

Dobkin, P. L., & Hutchinson, T. A. (2013). Teaching mindfulness in medical school: Where are we now and where are we going? *Medical Education*, 47(8), 768–779.

Doolittle, B. R., & Windish, D. M. (2015). Correlation of burnout syndrome with specific coping strategies, behaviors, and spiritual attitudes among interns at Yale University, New Haven, USA. *Journal of Educational Evaluation for Health Professions*, 12, 41. doi:10.3352/jeehp.2015.12.41

Doolittle, B. R., Windish, D. M., & Seelig, C. B. (2013). Burnout, coping, and spirituality among internal medicine resident physicians. *Journal of Graduate Medical Education*, 5(2), 257–261.

Dunne, J. S. (1978). *The reasons of the heart: A journey into solitude and back again into the human circle.* Notre Dame, IN: University of Notre Dame Press.

Fang, C. K., Li, P. Y., Lai, M. L., Lin, M. H., Bridge, D. T., & Chen, H.W. (2011). Establishing a "physician's spiritual well-being scale" and testing its reliability and validity. *Journal of Medical Ethics*, 37(1), 6–12.

Fetzer Institute & National Institute on Aging Working Group. (1999). *Multidimensional measurement of religiousness/spirituality for use in health research: A report of the Fetzer Institute/National Institute on Aging Working Group.* Kalamazoo, MI: John E. Fetzer Institute.

Figley, C. R. (Ed.). (2002). *Treating compassion fatigue.* New York, NY: Brunner-Routledge.

Fredrickson, B. L. (2004). The broaden-and-build theory of positive emotions. *Philosophical Transactions of the Royal Society of London Series B, Biological Sciences*, 359(1449), 1367–1377.

Guest, R. S., Baser, R., Li, Y., Scardino, P. T., Brown, A. E., & Kissane, D. W. (2011). Cancer surgeons' distress and well-being, I: The tension between a culture of productivity and the need for self-care. *Annals of Surgical Oncology*, 18(5), 1229–1235.

Halifax, J. (2011). The precious necessity of compassion. *Journal of Pain and Symptom Management*, 41(1), 146–153.

Hatch, R. Burg, M. A., Naberhaus, D. S., & Hellmich, L. K. (1998). The spiritual involvement and beliefs scale. *Journal of Family Practice*, 46(6), 476–486.

Hatem, C. J. (2006). Renewal in the practice of medicine. *Patient Education and Counseling*, 62(3), 299–301.

Hill, P. C., & Pargament, K. I. (2003). Advances in the conceptualization and measurement of religion and spirituality: Implications for physical and mental health research. *American Psychologist*, 58(1), 64–74.

Hofman, S. G., Grossman, P., & Hinton, D. E. (2011). Loving-kindness and compassion meditation: Potential for psychological interventions. *Clinical Psychology Review*, 31(7), 1126–1132.

Holland, J. M., & Neimeyer, R. A. (2005). Reducing the risk of burnout in end-of-life care settings: The role of daily spiritual experiences and training. *Palliative and Supportive Care*, 3(3), 173–181.

Keefe, F. J., Affleck, G., Lefebvre, J., Underwood, L., Caldwell, D. S., Drew, J., ... Pargament, K. (2001). Living with rheumatoid arthritis: The daily role of daily spirituality and daily religious and spiritual coping. *Journal of Pain*, 2(2), 101–110.

Killian, K. D. (2008). Helping till it hurts? A multimethod study of compassion fatigue, burnout, and self-care in clinicians working with trauma survivors. *Traumatology*, 14(2), 32–44.

Klauer, R. G. (2016). *What if I am you? The mysticism of the physician-patient relationship: The dream* (Vol. 1). North Charleston, SC: CreateSpace.

Koenig, H. G., King, D. E., & Carson, V. B. (2012). *Handbook of religion and health* (2nd ed.). New York, NY: Oxford University Press.

Loehr, J. (2007). *The power of story: Change your story, change your destiny in business and in life.* New York, NY: Free Press.

Loehr, J., & Schwartz, T. (2003). *The power of full engagement: Managing energy, not time, is the key to high performance and personal renewal.* New York: Free Press.

Luken, M., & Sammons, A. (2016). Systematic review of mindfulness practice for reducing job burnout. *American Journal of Occupational Therapy, 70*(2), 1–10.

McConnell, K. M., Pargament, K. I., Ellison, C. G., & Flannelly, K. J. (2006). Examining the links between spiritual struggles and symptoms of psychopathology in a national sample. *Journal of Clinical Psychology, 62*(12), 1469–1484.

McCullough, M. E., Hoyt, W. T., Larson, D. B., Koenig, H. G., & Thoresen, C. (2000). Religious involvement and mortality: A meta-analytic review. *Health Psychology, 19*(3), 211–222.

McSherry, W., & Cash, K. (2004). The language of spirituality: An emerging taxonomy. *International Journal of Nursing Studies, 41*(2), 151–161.

Meade, M. (2003). *Holding the thread of life: A human response to the unraveling of the world* [Book on CD]. United States: Mosaic Audio.

Meade, M. (2012). *Fate and destiny: The two agreements of the soul* (2nd ed.). Seattle, WA: Green Fire Press.

Montgomery, C. L. (1993). *Healing through communication: The practice of caring.* Newbury Park, CA: Sage.

Moore, R. D., Mead, L., & Pearson, T. A. (1990). Youthful precursors of alcohol abuse in physicians. *American Journal of Medicine, 88*(4), 332–336.

Moore, R. L. (2003). *Facing the dragon: Confronting personal and spiritual grandiosity.* Wilmette, IL: Chiron.

Morneau, R. F. (1992). *Spiritual direction: A path to spiritual maturity.* New York, NY: Cross.

Nhat Hanh, T. (1989). *The heart of the Buddha's teaching.* New York, NY: Broadway Books.

Nixa, J. (2017). *The lost art of heart navigation: A modern shaman's field manual* (2nd ed.). Rochester, VT: Bear.

Nouwen, H. J. M. (1992). *In the name of Jesus: Reflections on Christian leadership.* New York, NY: Crossroad.

O'Connor, L. E., Rangan, R. K., Berry, J. W., Stiver, D. J., Hanson, R., Ark, W., & Li, T. (2015). Empathy, compassionate altruism and psychological well-being in contemplative practitioners across five traditions. *Psychology, 6*(8), 989–1000.

Pargament, K. I. (1997). *The psychology of religion and coping: Theory, research and practice.* New York, NY: Guilford Press.

Pargament, K. I. (2007). *Spiritually integrated psychotherapy: Understanding and addressing the sacred.* New York, NY: Guilford Press.

Pargament, K., Feuille, M., & Burdzy, D. (2011). The Brief RCOPE: Current psychometric status of a short measure of religious coping. *Religions, 2*(1), 51–76.

Pargament, K. I., Koenig, H. G., & Perez, L. M. (2000). The many methods of religious coping: Development and initial validation of the RCOPE. *Journal of Clinical Psychology, 56*(4), 519–543.

Pargament, K. I., Koenig, H. G., Tarakeshwar, N., & Hahn, J. (2004). Religious coping methods as predictors of psychological, physical, and spiritual outcomes among medically ill elderly patients: A two-year longitudinal study. *Journal of Health Psychology, 9*(6), 713–730.

Penderell, A., & Brazil, K. (2010). The spirit of palliative practice: A qualitative inquiry into the spiritual journey of palliative care physicians. *Palliative and Supportive Care, 8*(40), 415–420.

Peterman, A., Fitchett, G., Brady, M., Hernandez, L., & Cella, D. (2002). Measuring spiritual well-being in people with cancer: The Functional Assessment of Chronic Illness Therapy-Spiritual Well-Being Scale (FACIT-Sp). *Annals of Behavioral Medicine, 24*(1), 49–58.

Pfifferling, J. H., & Gilley, K. (1999). Putting "life" back into your professional life. *Family Practice Management, 6*(6), 36–42.

Puchalski, C., Ferrell, B., Virani, R., Otis-Green, S., Baird, P., Bull, J., ... Sulmasy, D. (2009). Improving the quality of spiritual care as a dimension of palliative care: The report of the consensus conference. *Journal of Palliative Medicine, 12*(10), 885–904.

Puchalski, C. M., & Guenther, M. (2012). Restoration and re-creation: Spirituality in the lives of healthcare professionals. *Current Opinion in Supportive and Palliative Care, 6*(2), 254–258.

Purves, A. (1989). *The search for compassion: Spirituality and ministry.* Louisville, KY: Westminster.

Salzberg, S. (2002). *Loving-kindness: The revolutionary art of happiness.* Boston, MA: Shambhala.

Salzburg, S., & Goldstein, J. (2001). *Insight meditation workbook.* Boulder, CO: Sounds True.

Saslow, L. R., John, O. P., Piff, P. K., Willer, R., Wong, E., Impett, E. A., ... Saturn, S. R. (2013). The social significance of spirituality: New perspectives on the compassion-altruism relationship. *Psychology of Religion and Spirituality, 5*(3), 201–218.

Seccareccia, D., & Brown, J. B. (2009). Impact of spirituality on palliative care physicians: Personally and professionally. *Journal of Palliative Medicine, 12*(9), 805–809.

Shapiro, S. L., Astin, J. A., Bishop, S. R., & Cordova, M. (2005). Mindfulness-based stress reduction for health care professionals: Results from a randomized trial. *International Journal of Stress Management, 12*(2), 164–176.

Shigo, A. L. (1989). *A new tree biology: Facts, photos, and philosophies on trees and their problems and proper care* (2nd ed.). Durham, NC: Shigo and Trees.

Shuman, J. J., & Meador, K. G. (2003). *Heal thyself: Spirituality, medicine, and the distortion of Christianity.* New York, NY: Oxford University Press.

Smith, T. B., McCullough, M. E., & Poll, J. (2003). Religiousness and depression: Evidence for all main effect and the moderating influence of stressful life events. *Psychological Bulletin, 129*(4), 614–636.

Sulmasy, D. P. (1997). *The healer's calling: A spirituality for physicians and other health care professionals.* Mahwah, NJ: Paulist Press.

Udo, C., Melin-Johansson, C., & Danielson, E. (2011). Existential issues among health care staff in surgical cancer care: Discussions in supervision sessions. *European Journal of Oncology Nursing, 15*(5), 447–453.

Wachholtz, A. B., & Pargament, K. I. (2005). Is spirituality a critical ingredient of meditation? Comparing the effects of spiritual meditation, secular meditation, and relaxation on spiritual, psychological, cardiac, and pain outcomes. *Journal of Behavioral Medicine, 28*(4), 369–384.

Wachholtz, A. B., Pearce, M. J., & Koenig, H. (2007). Exploring the relationship between spirituality, coping, and pain. *Journal of Behavioral Medicine, 30*(4), 311–318.

Wachholtz, A., & Rogoff, M. (2013). The relationship between spirituality and burnout among medical students. *Journal of Contemporary Medical Education, 1*(2), 83–91.

Warnecke, E., Quinn, S., Ogden, K., Towle, N., & Nelson, M. R. (2011). A randomised controlled trial of the effects of mindfulness practice on medical student stress levels. *Medical Education, 45*(4), 381–388.

Watson, J. (2005). *Caring science as sacred science.* Philadelphia, PA: Davis.

Watson, J. (2008). Caritas Meditation [CD]. Boulder, CO: Watson Caring Science Institute.

Watson, J. (2012). *Human caring science: A theory of nursing.* Sudbury, MA: Jones & Bartlett.

Weil, S. (1951). *Waiting for God.* New York, NY: Putnam.

World Health Organization Quality of Life Group. (1995). The World Health Organization Quality of Life Assessment (WHOQOL): Position paper from the World Health Organization. *Social Science and Medicine, 41*(10), 1403–1409.

Wright, P. A. (2006). *Mother Teresa's prescription: Finding happiness and peace in service.* Notre Dame, IN: Ave Maria Press.

CREDIT

> "I want to be in the room where it happens."
>
> —From the musical *Hamilton*

Chapter Sections:

CHAPTER 15

Organizational/Business/Systemic Factors

How Organizational/Business/Systemic Factors Can Make or Break the Individual Clinician's Compassion Mindset

Questions to consider before reading this chapter:

1. How do you imagine that an organization can enable or inhibit compassionate caring among its staff?

2. How does an organization create and maintain a compassionate caring corporate culture among its staff?

INTRODUCTION

One of the essential components of helping clinicians be in the zone of balanced C^2 is the organizational culture and the systemic factors in which the clinicians work. In fact, the organizational culture is one of the strongest influences on both what the quality of the patient care will be like and what the long-term well-being of the clinicians will be. There are four characteristics of an organizational that is a strongly positive atmosphere for the clinicians. First, a compassionate caring ethic permeates the entire corporate culture. Second, the leadership supports, protects, and cultivates the caring mission. Third, there is a strong expectation and practice of collegial support in the organization. Finally, the organization must have self-reflective and self-correcting organizational practices to maintain its C^2 culture.

Analogy of the toxic building infecting employees

Clinicians will have difficulty sustaining compassionate caring in a negative organizational culture. It is no different than working in a toxic or sick building. Individuals can take great care of themselves physically and psychologically—taking optimum care of their body and mind. Perhaps they are above average in performance of their skills. They are strong and resilient, excellent at what they do. But put those people to work in a sick building, and in a short amount of time they will become physically ill and have great difficulty performing. Perhaps there are chemical or biological contaminants in the ventilation system that subtly infect everyone who works there. The way you begin detecting it is by noticing a pattern of previously high-performance employees deteriorating after beginning to work in that building. That is exactly what occurs in health care organizations. Competent and caring professionals come to health care work idealistic, driven, and full of potential. In certain organizations, they deteriorate and burn out. In other organizations, they thrive and seem to gain energy and momentum to help others.

Organization's culture a better predictor of burnout than the individual

Most often when focusing on compassionate caring, people focus on the individual. Why did that doctor burn out? What was wrong with him or her? What vulnerability did he or she have that he or she was not tough enough to make it? The clinician is analyzed in an individual manner in terms of burnout or effectiveness. But it turns out that the culture of an organization is a much better predictor of the burnout and the loss of caring than individual characteristics of the clinician. Christina Maslach and Michael Leiter (1997), internationally recognized pioneer researchers on burnout, warn that we should be very careful about blaming the health care professionals for the burnout:

> As a result of extensive study, we believe that burnout is not a problem of the people themselves but of the social environment in which people work. The structure and functioning of the workplace shape how people interact with one another and how they carry out their jobs. When the workplace does not recognize the human side of work, then the risk of burnout grows, carrying a high price with it. (p. 18)

Individually oriented interventions less effective than systemic interventions

Periodically, I am asked to help hospital units with their ability to compassionately care for patients and with their burnout. Occasionally, I will be asked to do a talk or a workshop lasting anywhere from an hour to half a day to "raise the morale" and "improve the staff attitudes." If that is the only intervention that is planned for that unit, I decline to do the talk. Without a systemic approach to compassionate care in an organization, it is unlikely to be successful. If there is a negative culture in the organization, it will be difficult for the clinicians not to have that affect them in how they treat patients.

> When the culture of an organization diverges from the core principles of relationship-centeredness, the practitioner is forced to engage with patients in a manner sometimes quite different from how he or she is treated. The energy and enthusiasm that a practitioner brings in to the consultation with a patient is profoundly influenced by the practice and the larger organization's values and integrity. (Beach, Inui, & Relationship-Centered Care Research Network, 2006, p. S6)

There are numerous studies documenting that empathic and compassionately caring interactions with patients lead them to be more satisfied with that patient care, to feel more trust and safety with the clinician and disclose more complete information enabling a more accurate diagnosis, to be more adherent to the treatment recommendations, to have better medical outcomes, and to be less likely to make malpractice claims. Yet the current health care delivery method seems in direct conflict with this because of time pressures to see more patients; less time for patient interaction because of documentation requirements and EHRs; and less reimbursement for many procedure codes, especially for those in which the emphasis is on prevention or verbal consultation. Health care organizations create cultures that somehow try to resolve this tension. The organization's leadership will make decisions about what it expects its clinicians to do and the manner in which they do it. Clinicians may complain when one side of the other is over- or underemphasized. But clinicians do not always consider becoming more direct advocates for compassionate care models of delivery. As Halpern (2014) explains it, "When physicians and nurses as well as patients see the value they derive from empathic interactions, they may join with other advocates in seeking new models of healthcare with less stringent constraints on the time they have with their patients" (p. 310). It is then that those who lead the organization have an opportunity to create a culture that is good both for the patients and for the clinicians.

Individual compassion mindset may not be sufficient to withstand all the negative stressors of health care work

One of the obvious temptations with a book like this is that those who manage others may use these characteristics of balanced caring with the sole intention of increasing productivity or patient satisfaction scores. This book can be used for yet another customer relations program by mandating a compassionate caring attitude. The other problem is that when clinicians are emotionally exhausted or burned out, we engage in blaming of the victim: "If you had been using your mindfulness or compassion meditation practices, you would not have been so emotionally exhausted." There are two problems with this. First, organizational culture is essential for the long-term support and cultivation of compassionately caring staff and may have contributed to a toxic climate for the clinicians no matter how well they were engaging in their self-care practices. Second, helping work is hard work that has risks and hazards that accompany it, and those risks are there even if we have positive organizational cultures. In our society, we engage in the same kind of thinking with physical health, in which we somehow blame the person for an illness. "It is your fault you got a cold because you did not rest enough, wash your hands well, or take your vitamins." Maybe that is true, but maybe you got the cold because you were exposed to colds all day in the clinic. Like any hard work, even though it is very worth doing, it is still taxing on the physiological, psychological, and spiritual systems of the human person. We should not think that a compassionate mindset and balanced caring practices will immunize clinicians from all negative consequences. Perhaps how flu vaccines are created is a useful analogy. Every year the vaccine is created based on a careful selection of which influenza viruses are expected to spread in the coming year. Sometimes, calculated prediction is successful, but other times it is not, because a viral strain spreads that was not predicted. Often, however, even if the vaccine is not perfectly matched to combat the viral strains that will predominate in the coming year, having the vaccine can mitigate the symptoms to some extent. In short, if you do nothing to prepare yourself or to maintain yourself in the strenuous emotional work of compassionate care, you can definitely expect that it will go poorly for you more quickly than for someone who has conditioned him- or herself for this work. But even if you have perfectly conditioned yourself for the work, it is still a work with risks and unexpected occurrences that can have some effect on you.

The responsibility of organizations for the causes and repair of the moral injury to clinicians

In chapter 8, I discussed how the dysfunctions and profit-focused motivations of health care organizations can be experienced as a moral injury to clinicians. Because clinicians have to satisfy many different demands from patients, insurance companies, the government, their health care organizations, and their own internal understanding of what it means to provide very good health care to patients, clinicians experience not being able to deliver the health care they believe they should as a betrayal to the patients and to their intrinsic compassion-centered motivation. Shay (2011) has emphasized that there is an institutional context to moral injury. He defines moral injury in military service as being present when:

> (1) there has been a betrayal of what's right (2) by someone who holds legitimate authority (3) in a high-stakes situation. When all three are present, moral injury is present and the body codes it in much the same way it codes physical attack. (p. 183)

Shay emphasizes what he calls *leadership malpractice* in moral injury essentially because leadership gives the commands that undercut the motivations and moral sensitivity of those who serve in that organization. He argues that

the institutional source of moral injury must be addressed in order to improve this situation. So healing this moral injury requires not simply therapeutic interventions for the individual but "education, advocacy, and institutional reform" (Wiinikka-Lydon, 2019, pp. 178–179). Many in health care are warning us that what is happening to clinicians is not simply burnout and lack of resilience, but moral injury as the result of the competing and chaotic demands of our health care system. Talbot and Dean (2018) warn that leadership must have the wisdom and courage to address this in a systemic way, not simply using individually focused interventions like physician wellness programs or mindfulness meditation workshops. As they put it, "We need leaders who recognize that caring for their physicians results in thoughtful, compassionate care for their patients, which ultimately is good business" (par. 15). What is needed is leadership that protects and advocates for their intrinsically motivated compassion-centered clinicians rather than treating them as objectified replaceable business assets when they are depleted and burnt out.

Preparation for working in health care

As health care is currently, there are more dysfunctional organizations than healthy ones. As David Graber (2009) summarizes his analysis of it, "Most hospitals assert a commitment to empathy and patient dignity in their mission or vision statements, yet do little to support these among their staff and in the organizational environment" (p. 528). So while the best answer to the problem is a system-wide organizational intervention, we have to do the best we can until that happens; we transfer to a healthier organization, keep going until we collapse and end our careers, or arm ourselves with self-numbing detachment and cynicism and wreak havoc on our patients, our families, and ourselves. The first step in dealing with this problem is knowing that health care is very much a "sick building" right now and to prepare for that. When we welcomed first-year physician residents to the beginning of their three years of residency, I would make sure at some point to say to them in our orientation retreat, "Health care is a sick system; we have to help you not get sick in it."

COMPASSIONATE CARING ETHIC PERMEATES THE ENTIRE CORPORATE CULTURE

Compassionate caring is typically viewed in terms of individual episodic interactions with patients. However, cutting-edge research has clarified that an organizational cultural approach to compassionate caring is the best way to support compassionate caring interactions with patients and the best way to buffer burnout and increase the well-being of all the staff of that organization. The Beryl Institute has offered a definition of the *patient experience* as *"the sum of all interactions, shaped by an organization's culture, that influence patient perceptions, across the continuum of care"* (Wolf, Niederhauser, & LaVela, 2014, p. 8). In their review of the literature on the construct of patient experience, Wolf et al. (2014) note that we are prone to divide health care organizations into component parts and distinct efforts by various staff that patients may or may not directly experience. However, patients experience the organization as a whole when they use health care. Their experience is based on all the interactions they have with both clinical and nonclinical staff through direct and indirect means. For example, patients may have direct interactions with everyone from the receptionist and cafeteria cashier to the nurses and physicians. Indirectly, there are many interactions that patients never see that affect their experience, such as the staff members who ensure the cleanliness and safety of all aspects of the health care organization, those who support the clinical staff, and those in administrative roles. All of those interactions influence the kind of experience that the patient has. But Wolf et al. explain that the patient experience is not simply captured by patients' satisfaction with the health care they are receiving, but also by what the patient and loved ones go through physically, emotionally, and socially when they are involved with a health care organization. More than level of satisfaction, the patient experience answers the question, "What was it like for the patient to receive care from this particular organization, and how did that affect them?"

The service-profit chain

There is a great deal of literature articulating the importance of corporate culture and how it is manifested in how an organization operates. Businesses in general know that the quality of the products and the profitability of a company are directly related to the internal culture of the organization: the values and norms that permeate everything from how employees are recruited and trained to how they are managed and held accountable. Service industries such as restaurants, banking, and airlines know that they are more likely to succeed when they make the customer primary and have employees who are engaged and highly motivated in serving that customer. Heskett, Jones, Loveman, Sasser, and Schlesinger (2008) in the *Harvard Business Review* call this the service-profit chain, which is described succinctly in the following passage:

The service-profit chain establishes relationships between profitability, customer loyalty, and employee satisfaction, loyalty, and productivity. The links in the chain (which should be regarded as propositions) are as follows: Profit and growth are stimulated primarily by customer loyalty. Loyalty is a direct result of customer satisfaction. Satisfaction is largely influenced by the value of services provided to customers. Value is created by satisfied, loyal, and productive employees. Employee satisfaction, in turn, results primarily from high-quality support services and policies that enable employees to deliver results to customers. (p. 119)

How health care is different than typical customer service

What is unique to health care is that the service is provided in response to human suffering or the prevention of human suffering. In typical service industry organizations or in any business, profitability is seen as linked to good customer service in selling a product. Whether the employee is a flight attendant, a bank representative, or a food server, businesses expect their employees to treat people kindly because this leads to better customer satisfaction and better sales. But the manner in which the service is given is not necessarily considered integral to the product being sold. *In health care, we believe the manner in which the service is given is beyond simple customer service, especially if we believe that compassionate caring is the foundation of what we are doing for patients.* We would like to think typical service industry employees really mean it when they ask, "Did you find everything you were looking for today?," or that they are really empathizing with us when they say something like, "That must be so hard on you and your family that your refrigerator broke down." Now sometimes the person saying those things really does mean them. But the typical consumer now is aware that employees are trained to say certain things and act certain ways when serving the consumer, so consumers do not necessarily expect genuineness in those remarks. In health care, frankly, the same methods in customer service are applied in staff training. But a "faked caring attitude" has more critical negative consequences in caring for the health of human beings. The bottom line is that, as a patient, my life is going to feel much more secure if you, the health care person, really do care about me. If you really care about me, you are going to invest more of yourself in my health condition, be more vigilant about my condition, and make fewer errors; and if something goes wrong, it is going to matter to you what happens to me.

Professional practice models help get all the health care staff on the same page in terms of philosophy of care and caring behaviors

Health care organizations generally realize that, ideally, they have to get all their employees on the same page when it comes to how they are going to deliver their care to patients. The best health care organizations will adopt a professional practice model that articulates the manner in which the whole system will work together to provide care to patients; and because health care is about responding to or preventing suffering in patients, professional practice models typically articulate a theory or philosophy of caring that they would like all their staff to believe in helping patients—that is, a theory or philosophy that explains why being patient-centered really matters for patient outcomes and why my clinical relationship with patients (and my colleagues) is essential for their care and also my own well-being as a clinician.

All the actions of the staff, then, should flow from this common understanding of caring for patients.

Professional practice models explained in more detail

The bottom-line profitability and success of a company depends on how its employees feel about their work and the company. Health care organizations generally understand (and periodically forget) the linkage between employee satisfaction and engagement and the outcomes in terms of the patient experience. There are many approaches to creating and maintaining a positive culture in which all staff work together as a team to take care of patients. Health care organizations will use techniques from the service industry, or what are called *professional practice models*, which are models of care specifically designed for health care. As articulated most often in nursing, but ideally applied to the whole organization, these professional practice models typically include five elements: (a) specified professional values that underlie nursing practice and training; (b) a description of how professional relationships should proceed; (c) the structure and process for how patient care is delivered by the staff; (d) the management approach in terms of the structure and process of how decisions are made and operations are conducted; and (e) how staff are compensated and rewarded for their contributions to patient care, the organization, and their profession (Hoffart & Woods, 1996). Common models of caring practice include the patient-centered approach (Mead & Bower, 2000; Stewart et al., 2003), relationship-centered caring (Tresloni & Pew-Fetzer, 1994), relationship-based caring (Koloroutis, 2004), Watson's theory of caring (Watson, 1988, 2012), and the Planetree model (Frampton & Charmel, 2008). There are also many consulting organizations that specialize in helping health care organizations with improving their organizational culture and quality of the patient experience. All of these models have a great deal of commonality in their approaches. The reality in health care is that organizations either adopt a specific professional practice model or particular patient care philosophy, or organizations blend components of various models into their own unique care model. In many cases, organizations have had successive organizational cultural efforts in order to create a unified understanding and approach to high-quality patient care.

While there is little research on how organizations facilitate compassionate caring, there are many efforts to do so in actual practice

In a review of research literature on compassion and the design of organizational systems, Crawford, Brown, Kvangarsnes, and Gilbert (2014) found that there was little attention to how organizations can systemically facilitate increased compassionate engagement throughout the organization. Instead, the focus is typically an individualistic one focusing on the clinician's training, the individual clinician's actions, and the organization stressing individual accountability for how the health care services are delivered. In actual practice, however, health care organizations devote a great deal of effort to trying to increase the caring attitudes and behaviors of their staffs, measure this any number of ways, and track how this improves the overall effectiveness and success of their organization. Much of this wisdom never makes it into the research literature, but that wisdom and experience is encountered and noticed all the time in the work of health care. Dedicated and innovative individuals or small groups will often lead efforts to change the culture of their individual units or clinical practices. When staff members who know other models of care or patient care philosophies come together, they generally find a great deal of common ground. People in health care want patients treated the best they can be treated. They know that the more a staff is genuinely motivated to care for patients and the more they can work out how to work together for the welfare of patients, the better the patient care will be. Several genuinely caring employees in an organization will not be as effective in patient care compared to an organization in which most, if not all, of the staff are genuinely dedicated.

Definition of compassion applied to organizations

If we use the definition of compassion in chapter 2 and apply it to organizations, compassionate caring is demonstrated in a health care organization when staff notice suffering, when they feel or are empathically moved by the suffering, and when they respond to that suffering. *From a systemic perspective, how does that organization through its culture and practices enhance or impair the ability of staff to notice, feel, and respond to suffering?* Rewarding and recognizing compassionate behavior fosters a climate in which staff are more likely to notice suffering and respond to it, want to engage with someone who is suffering, treat the suffering person in a holistic way, and customize or tailor the response to what the suffering person actually needs. It also adds to the satisfaction of doing this good work. The suffering may be not only what the patient and his or her loved ones are experiencing, but also what fellow staff may be suffering, either because of what is happening in the workplace or in their personal lives. Organizational practices that compassionately support staff help them cope with the stress and trauma of the work,

increase their resilience, increase their psychological engagement with the work, help them feel more connected to the organization, and make them more likely to reciprocate and extend compassionate behavior beyond themselves, which in turn helps them continue to detect, feel, and respond to the suffering they encounter (McClelland & Vogus, 2014). All of this leads to greater patient satisfaction because the care is much better attuned to patients' suffering and needs.

Research study on how rewarding and acknowledging compassion improved HCAHPS

If a health care organization explicitly rewards compassion in the organization and extends compassionate support to the employees, will it make a difference in patient perceptions? McClelland and Vogus (2014) addressed this question by examining whether certain compassion practices would make a difference on hospital HCAHPS scores (which stands for Hospital Consumer Assessment of Healthcare Providers and Systems). They assessed practices in which a hospital rewarded compassion or compassionately supported its staff. The five practices were using recognition awards of employees who had shown care to patients and families; recognition programs for employees who had helped each other; formal compassionate employee award programs (e.g., DAISY Award, awards for clinical staff, awards for support staff); the extent that the hospital provided pastoral care to its staff; and whether the hospital had support sessions for departments dealing with things such as trauma, crisis events, workplace stress, or conflict. The researchers looked at two indicators of patient perceptions of care quality on the HCAHPS: the overall hospital rating and the likelihood of recommending that hospital. Based on results from

269 nonfederal acute care US hospitals, they found that compassion practices were significantly positively related to top-box hospital ratings and the likelihood of recommending the hospital. This positive predictive relationship held even after the researchers controlled for the technical quality of the care (e.g., hospital readmissions) and the organization quality (e.g., Magnet status). These practices implemented by hospital management were related to patients having more positive perceptions of the hospital. When hospitals reward employees for showing compassion and when leadership provides support for employees, this reinforces that compassion is considered most important within the organization. These practices also are responses to the suffering of staff in the workplace (e.g. burnout, stress in patient care), which helps ameliorate some of the emotional toll that work in health care can cause. Quint Studer (2008) has an excellent way to summarize this:

> A workplace comprised of satisfied employees just feels different, and better. It feels better to employees and it feels better to customers. That's one big reason leaders should care about employee satisfaction. Satisfied employees tend to go the extra mile to please customers. Happy customers not only keep coming back, they refer friends, family, and business associates—and your company prospers. (p. 145)

Compassion organizing in organizations

Dutton, Workman, and Hardin (2014) describe a process in organizations called *compassion organizing*, in which individuals notice, feel, and respond to suffering in a coordinated way with other individuals in the organization. *Compassion organizing* is the "collective response to a particular incident of human suffering that entails the coordination of individual compassion in a particular organizational context" (Dutton, Worline, Frost, & Lilius, 2006, p. 61).

It is a particular capability of the organization to extract, generate, coordinate, and calibrate resources toward someone who is suffering. Dutton et al. (2006) are reluctant to label an organization as compassionate because they argue that this is not a static quality but a capability that may or may not be tapped in all situations. It is a dynamic quality that unfolds in a particular social architecture of the organization, depending on the actions of human agents in a particular situation with emergent processes that result from collective action.

Dutton et al.'s study of compassion organizing

Compassion organizing has been discussed in terms of how organizations respond to unexpected suffering either outside the organization (e.g., a disaster or emergency in the community) or inside the organization (e.g., staff member whose house burned down, illness or other hardship in colleague's family). In a study of how a large business school employing 135 full-time staff and 140 full-time faculty responded to a fire in an apartment building where some of its students lived, Dutton et al. (2014) analyzed the sequence of events and proposed a model of how compassion becomes organized within an organization. A diagram of this model is shown in figure 15.1. A pain trigger, an event that signals human pain, is what initiates the compassion organizing process. Compassion activation is the way that the pain trigger gains the collective attention of a group and becomes a social reality. The social architecture of an organization is "the amalgam of social networks, values, and routines that structure an organization and that constrain and enable individual action" (Dutton et al., 2014, p. 74). It is the social architecture of an organization that influences whether the collective attention of the members is called to the pain and how feelings of empathetic concern spread and lead to a response.

Three sets of factors underlying compassion activation and mobilization
There are three sets of factors in this social architecture that underlie the activation and mobilization of compassion: shared values,

routines, and networks. *First, there are shared values of what people in the organization feel is important and that generate the expectations of how they should act.* In this case, it was that people are important as people (more than their professional identities), that they should express their humanity in the face of suffering, and there is a sense that they should treat each other like

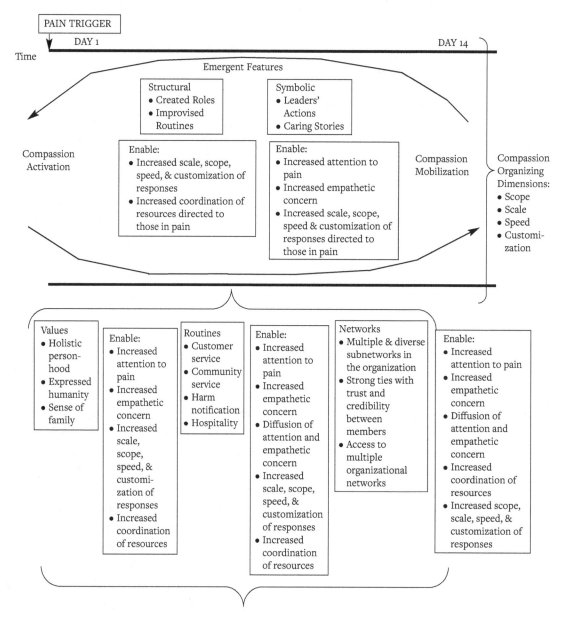

FIGURE 15.1 The process of compassion organizing (Dutton, 2014, p. 83).

family. *Second, organizations have routines that are "well-grooved scripts" for coordination and action.* In this case, there was a structure for providing services to students, a network already established among students for community service, and an email communication system that was used to notify everyone in the community about a severe harm or loss that had occurred. *Third, there were subnetworks throughout the organization that had strong credibility and trust so that any request for help would be considered legitimate.*

How compassion activation leads to compassion mobilization

The shared values, routines, and networks function together to increase the ability of everyone to notice and collectively attend to the pain trigger; elicit empathic concern among the group; increase the scale, scope, speed, and customization of the response; and coordinate the resources to direct them to those who are in need. *Compassion activation* consists of how the noticing of the suffering spreads among the members of the organization. *Compassion mobilization* is how that activation leads to how the organization coordinates and delivers a response to those who are suffering. Compassion activation and mobilization become a kind of mutually reinforcing engine in organizing the compassion, and there are structural and symbolic factors that emerge in the process. The emergent structural features are unofficial and informal roles that individual staff take on to facilitate the response (e.g., someone who has useful knowledge about this type of crisis, a particular skill that is uniquely helpful in this situation) and also improvised routines that are modifications of the normal work routines in order to respond to the suffering. The symbolic features involve the symbolic actions of the leaders or the stories about how others are responding, which inspire

others and makes everyone feel good about what they are doing. These emergent features facilitate increased attention and empathic concern as well as energize the response (Dutton et al., 2006).

Applying compassion organizing to health care organizations

While this case example of compassion organizing is not a health care organization, I find that the description of the process of activation and mobilization depicts what we do in health care organizations all the time. One might argue that this process is only relevant to disasters or misfortunes in the community or among fellow staff. Or one might argue that responding to patient suffering becomes so routine in health care that we do not get activated that much by "ordinary" patient suffering. But I would respond that this is an indicator of whether we have become exhausted and burned out as a group. Our work is a constant cycle of all of us working together, noticing and attending to suffering, being moved by it, and responding to it according to the actual needs and urgency of the people suffering, and paced by all the other demands we have to juggle at the same time. If we have become numb to each other's suffering, then it is a sign that our culture needs help.

Study of compassion behavior among hospital staff

Lilius et al. (2008) conducted several studies examining compassionate behavior among the staff of a hospital; that is, they examined how staff responded to the suffering they witnessed in each other and what the consequences of that were. In one study, they tracked how often this occurred at work and from whom the staff experienced compassion. In general, the staff reported that they received compassionate responses from their coworkers more often than from their supervisors. It also occurred significantly more in administrative or outpatient units than it did in medical/surgical units. The researchers did not know why this occurred but speculated that perhaps there were different "feeling rules" in which self-reliance and resilience in a medical/surgical unit decreased the compassionate responses to fellow staff. But what they discovered in general is that experiencing compassion at work is associated with more positive emotion and that this leads to increased affective commitment to the organization. They concluded that experiencing compassion at work has a kind of cumulative and long-lasting positive effect on an organization.

Types of suffering among hospital staff

In a second study with 239 hospital staff, Lilius et al. (2008) studied the types of suffering that occurred in the staff, which colleagues responded and how they responded, and what the consequences of doing this were for the workplace. In terms of the types of suffering among colleagues, the largest category was illness of oneself or a loved one (44%). Other categories were the death of family member or friend, a colleague's personal problems (e.g., divorce, finances, family problems), interactions with patients, and work stress in the hospital (e.g., uncivil behavior, work injury). In terms of which colleagues responded, most of the time it was several coworkers or the whole unit who responded (80%), 10% a single coworker responding, and 7% only the supervisor responding. The ways in which compassion was expressed were giving emotional support, giving time and flexibility, and offering material goods. Giving emotional support was the most common compassionate action. In terms of giving time and flexibility, this involved colleagues or supervisors covering shifts, giving time for recovery, or taking time to help out the coworker. While the action itself can be helpful in terms of getting time off, the symbolic nature of action is also a boost for the suffering coworker.

The emotional consequences of compassionate actions among colleagues

In terms of the emotional consequences of compassionate actions among colleagues, most of the time this resulted in feelings of empathic understanding; feeling positive emotions like joy and encouragement; or feeling calm, comforted, or relaxed. Compassionate action also decreased negative emotions such as anxiety, sadness, shame, or fear. Finally, employees appeared to engage in making sense of the meaning of compassion at work. Individuals tended to improve the way they viewed themselves, such as feeling more able to be themselves at work and being more able to manage their pain. Employees tended to make inferences about how good relationships are at work and how they can be trusted and relied on. Finally, compassionate acts among coworkers led to inferences about how positive it is to work with this organization, how good the organization is to work for, and how the organization exemplifies these positive values. When compassionate actions are lacking, it led to employees feeling disconnected from their coworkers and almost feeling like the lack of compassionate response was an aggressive action, and it decreased their commitment to the organization. Far from hurting the workplace, internal compassionate acts boost how employees see themselves, each other, and the organization. They lead to strong positive emotions that in turn lead to better outcomes in the workplace. As Lilius et al. (2008) put it, *compassion represents a form of personal connection that we rarely notice in work organizations and is usually invisible in any formal sense. This is because if compassion "works," it allows people to heal and recover, generating little if any interruption to the normal flow of action and leaving little visible trace of its deep impact. (p. 211).*

LEADERSHIP SUPPORTS, PROTECTS, AND CULTIVATES A CARING MISSION

Leadership must protect the compassionate caring of staff

Organizations have to protect the compassionate caring of their staffs. Health care organizations are often engaged in trying to promote a culture of compassionate caring. But there are many things that can undercut the already existent compassionate caring of a staff, both within and outside the organization. In an organization, managers, departments, and even single individuals can wreak havoc on the morale and the caring attitudes of the staff. It is a favorite topic of leadership to push staff to be caring and promote a positive patient experience. This is very good for patient satisfaction and very good for business. But if the staff is pressured to be more caring while other management or departments push efforts that oppose this, then the caring attitudes are more difficult to sustain. For example, if a very punitive approach is used for any number of things, such as a department not meeting a certain goal or measure, writing staff up for relatively minor issues, or a management style that is heavy on the criticism and light on the compliments, then this negative atmosphere overpowers the efforts to promote a more positive atmosphere. Another example would be when an administrator, manager, or director berates staff groups or individuals in

an excessively shaming or negative manner. There is also a problem when certain staff are rewarded financially, in promotion, or otherwise for high productivity in assembly-line medicine while other staff who have handled difficult, time-consuming situations are not recognized or rewarded in the same organization. Of course, there needs to be methods of holding staff accountable for organizational goals, and there needs to be consequences if staff are not doing their part—for example, when a clinician has a pattern of being rude to patients. A compassionate caring culture is harmed by a lack of consistency in the organizational culture in terms of what behaviors or attitudes are actually rewarded or punished and the manner in which this is done. Accountability methods, incentive mechanisms, and management styles have to be examined for how the compassionate caring is protected within the organization. Furthermore, to create a truly compassionately caring corporate culture, leadership needs to meet regularly with all types of staff in formal meetings as well as informal hallway conversations to learn what clinicians are actually going through and what they need. Leadership is most effective when it is collaborative with its clinicians in decision-making and empowering of its clinicians to create the best care possible (Beeson, 2009; Cara, Nyberg, & Brousseau, 2011). As Beeson (2009) put it, "Great leaders create a shared vision that connects to the hopes, dreams, and aspirations of physicians and the entire healthcare workforce to make a difference, save lives, and be a part of something extraordinary" (p. 2).

Staff needs to be protected from outside risks and dangers

The compassionate caring spirit of staff also needs to be protected from outside risks and dangers. When staff are maltreated or abused by patients, the organization has to find ways to help support and safeguard its staff. Emergency department staff are particularly aware of this. With an obligation to see and treat all patients who come, emergency staff must deal with many difficult types of situations. They will tell you of entitled, manipulative, and rude treatment by patients and their loved ones and the lack of appreciation that is commonly experienced from patients. As our society works through a period of time with increased fragmentation of civility and respect for helping professionals (although schoolteachers and food servers will vouch for this as well), this problem will only get worse before it gets better. This can include not only rude and entitled verbal behavior but also violent behavior, with patients threatening and hitting staff. Organizations increasingly must find ways to protect and support staff. That protection and support can be providing the emotional and instrumental support for staff who must deal with difficult patient situations. Are individual staff members left to deal with these alone? Do they have supervisory or collegial support? Have they been given the skills for dealing with certain situations? Are staff given an opportunity to recover from difficult situations? Do particular staff become saddled with more difficult situations more often than other staff, and if so, how are they supported and compensated? Is there security readily available in dangerous situations? More and more, however, our society will have to address this issue in order to protect the helping professions. This includes legal protections from frivolous malpractice claims that take a major emotional toll on clinicians, even when the claim is not likely to be substantiated. There is nothing like getting sued to curb a clinician's desire to be helpful. It is demoralizing when a clinician is berated in public (e.g., in the news or online)

but is not able to respond. Hence the common phrase in the helping professions, "No good deed goes unpunished!" What do our organizations (as well as our community and society) do to protect the caring attitudes and behaviors of our staffs?

External forces diffusing responsibility and pressuring clinicians not to treat patient holistically

One of the consequences of our increased specialization and complexity of the health care system is a diffusion of responsibility. As we each focus on our piece of the body or a bodily system according to our specialty or our role, there is less emphasis on examining the person as a whole. We are each busy enough as it is with our particular slice of the patient; there are time pressures as all the documentation has to be filled out properly for reimbursement, and there is not much incentive to analyze the patient as a total system. For one thing, there is not much financial incentive to treat the patient as a whole person, and second, it is not easy to take the time and energy to do so. It is easier just to do one's piece in the assembly line of medicine. In fact, what has happened is that there has been a kind of entropy of thinking energy when it comes to thinking through a patient's medical problem. It is not that clinicians are not capable of thinking through a problem systemically; they had to do it at least in medical school and residency. But as one is in practice with all the pressures both at work and at home, there is actually more incentive to just stay focused on one problem and try to ignore the rest unless it forces our attention. With all the time and financial pressures clinicians face, there has also been more incentive to do the simple, straightforward cases and to distance oneself from the more complex cases. Leadership needs to be aware of this tendency toward diffusion of responsibility and compartmentalization and work to foster a systemic norm of shared responsibility, teamwork, and holistic thinking.

Leadership can undercut the compassion mindset

Leadership must be very aware that the tone it sets and the way it frames its discussions within the organization can either encourage a compassionate caring mentality among its staff or actually undercut the very attitude necessary for quality health care. Leadership generally acknowledges and desires that its staff care about the quality of its services and that it is perceived as compassionately caring. The bottom line is that being perceived this way is good for business, and so it will want a staff that exemplifies compassionate caring. It desires a staff that has a compassionate mentality or is in the compassion mindset described in chapter 4. Inadvertently, however, leadership can actually subvert the brain dynamics that make the compassion mindset of the clinician possible.

Compassion mindset can be switched off by threat-based or competitive mindsets

Recall from chapter 3 how, rather than compassion being a single emotion or cognition, Paul Gilbert (2009) found that compassion is a "major pattern generator in our brains" (p. 192) in that it brings together and organizes specific motivations, competencies, and attributes that result in compassion. Based on evolutionary biological and neuroscientific evidence, Gilbert notes that our minds work in patterns; and when a person's mind is in one pattern, it makes it hard for another pattern to generate. As he explains,

different patterns in our brain turn different systems on and off. You can't feel relaxed and frightened or angry and loving as the same time. You can switch between them, of course, but you can't feel them simultaneously. One pattern negates another. (Gilbert, 2009, p. 77)

Compassion is a mindset or mentality that organizes our motivation, attention, emotions, and behavior in a specific way geared toward our goals and the kind of relationship we have with a person we are helping. In stressful health care environments, it is easy to fall into threat-based or competitive mentalities that organize our mental processes in different ways that undercut a compassionate mind (Crawford, Gilbert, Gilbert, & Gale, 2011).

How health care staff can fall into a threat-based mentality

Health care personnel can fall into a threat-based mentality when they are pushed into a production-line mentality or a culture in which time pressure or cutting costs dominate over quality of care. This is not to say that efficiency and financial viability are not very important elements to sustainable health care organizations. What it does mean is that we have to be careful of the overall tone we set in health care cultures because that tone can push the staff into mentalities that tap into more primitive brain systems that are concerned more with being threatened and self-protection than with a compassionate mentality. Crawford et al. (2011) analyzed the language used in health care organizations on the discourse regarding cleanliness with regard to infection control. They found a paucity of compassion mentality discourse that would frame the efforts for infection control and cleanliness in terms of compassionate intent, like *caring*, *helpful*, and *supportive*; instead, there was a dominance of production-line language.

Care was framed more as a product or process. While one might argue that the focus on nursing actions and interventions is ultimately about care quality, the point is that the overall emotional tone can send your health care staff psychologically and neurologically into a mode of self-protection if they feel threatened, or aggression and intense reward-seeking if they feel too competitive. These are antithetical to a compassionate mentality. If leadership frames the internal discussion and organizational tone in such a way that staff feel threatened or mainly competitive, staff will have difficulty keeping the compassionate brain pattern dominant.

Study of compassion language being used in the context of a threat dynamic

Crawford et al. (2011) examined staff understandings of compassion in two acute psychiatric units and found that compassionate language appeared in the context of a threat dynamic. For example, when they examined how the compassionate word *giving* was used, they reported

> it is noteworthy that a number of mentions of giving are to do with what practitioners can't give—time, a better service and the like. There's also a kind of moral imperative in some cases: "should be giving". The practitioners have a sense of what they should be doing, but they are unable to act on it, and are thus demoralized. (Crawford et al., 2011, p. 11)

Words reflected a distancing from emotional language regarding relationships with patients; words like *kind, warm, friendly, respectful,* and *calming* were rarely used. Language was more institutional in referring to patients and staffs as homogenous groups rather than individuals and persons. A production-line mentality was evident, "where 'us and them' framings apply in processing individuals through a health care service" (Crawford et al., 2011, p. 12). There tended to be a "heightened concern for managing and processing people to reach targets amid personnel or other resource shortages" (Crawford et al., 2011, p. 13).

Pressures for efficiency in patient care

"I wish I could care more for my patients, but there's just not enough time, and I've got a focus on the more important stuff." It is generally agreed among clinicians that compassionate caring in patient care is preferred not only by patients but by the clinicians themselves. However, a large number of clinicians argue that especially in financially pressured times, with multiple institutional strictures dictating the practice of medicine, there is no time for caring and compassion. It is argued that compassionate caring takes too much time and decreases efficiency. Clinicians commonly worry that if they engage the patient more personally, this will lengthen the patient visit because the clinician has to engage in more conversation than is "necessary" to address the presenting problem. Another fear is that if clinicians address the emotional concerns the patient has connected to his or her illness or other medical problem, there is no telling what emotional material might come forward and make it difficult to do a briefer visit. At times, in residency training programs, when resident physicians take too much time with patients, they might be told to "quit the chatting and cut to the chase" regarding the patient's problem. All of this is argued in terms of efficiency and profitability as well as the purported desire to treat as many patients as possible. But if we analyze this a bit further, we may find that the appeals to efficiency can sometimes be cover for pressure to cut corners in health care.

Motivations for efficiency

Efficiency is the quality of getting as much as possible done with the least amount of effort expended. This allows us to accomplish more of our goals with the most economical use of our resources. This is a worthy goal for almost anything in our lives. The issue is really about what our goals are. If we look at this layer by layer in health care, the first layer is the goal of taking care of the patient according to the standards of good medical practice. We want to be able to treat as many patients as possible in the best possible manner as efficiently as possible in order to keep costs down and be able to help more people. If we are inefficient, our patients have to wait longer in their waiting room, and we go home later because we have not gotten our work done. The second layer is the goal of making a living practicing medicine. Health care organizations must operate in such a way that they can continue to survive and we as clinicians can make a living and support ourselves and our loved ones. Efficiency is necessary in order that resources are wisely used and costs are kept down so the practice can survive and the clinician can make a living. But there is a third layer that can dramatically affect the other two layers, and that is the goal of an increased profit margin. There is no general agreement about what is an appropriate profit margin. But generally, health care organizations and clinicians want to make as much money as can be made in this ostensibly noble work. In the history of American health care, this desire to make as much money as possible is what led to the rise of managed care. Clinicians and hospitals were not able to regulate their own charges, which led to the rise of increased accountability and regulation (Starr, 1982). Coupled with this is the industrial ethic of innovation to accomplish whatever results we want more quickly and with fewer resources. In making a piece of furniture, for example, the goal is to use as few screws and as little glue as possible. But there is a limit to how few screws and how little glue you can use to build a piece of furniture. At a certain point, the quality of the furniture will decrease as cheaper materials and too few screws are used. In many ways, this is the story of the car industry. Of course, the cheapest furniture and cars are important because a lot of people can only afford these. But when something is built too cheaply, it is no longer worth it to buy that particular car or piece of furniture. At this point, we would say that quality is being sacrificed because too many corners were cut. At a certain point, it is no longer efficiency that is the guiding principle in cutting corners, but making more profit.

Self-deception in health care regarding efficiency versus cutting corners

In health care, we often engage in self-deception about efficiency versus cutting corners. It is a rare instance when a health care organization or clinician voluntarily decreases fees. Pharmaceutical companies are a classic example of this. While certain drugs may be more efficiently made with lower costs, it is not always the case that the patient pays less for them. Generally, health care organizations charge the maximum of what the market can bear. When a particular profit margin is selected and particular levels of salaries are set, these become nonnegotiable in many ways. At this point it, is not the quality of patient care that guides the process but the level of profitability that is being sought. Certainly, clinicians want to be able to say that care is not being compromised, that care is always safe and at a therapeutic level. But what we witness regarding compassionate caring is that it is considered a threat to efficiency when really it is cutting corners in order to achieve maximum profitability that is the overriding motivating force.

Leadership mechanisms to support, protect, and cultivate C² culture

For an organization to have a compassionate caring culture, its leadership must support, protect, and cultivate it. Leadership sets the tone by whom it hires and fires. What kind of people are sought in terms of their skills and attitudes? When clinicians and other staff are brought on board, they are oriented and trained according to the mission and values of the organization. Organizations differ in what they consider their organizational values and objectives and how these are to be cultivated among the staff. To hold staff accountable for those values and objectives, an organization must find ways to measure whether and how well those values and objectives are implemented in patient care and the way the organization is operated. It has to consider how staff are rewarded for successfully achieving those values and objectives and what is to be done to hold accountable staff who have failed to reflect those values and objectives. Leadership must also invest in supporting those values and objectives. Using tools such as professional practice models, the leadership facilitates all its staff being on the same page in terms of understanding the mission of the organization and how this is implemented. Ongoing training and supervision provide avenues for improving the compassionate caring culture. While the attitudes and skills of individual staff members are important, ultimately it is leadership that holds the greatest influence on the culture of an organization.

COLLEGIAL SUPPORT

Clinicians are trained to think they are alone in patient care

A very important way to keep balance in caring for others is to have good support from others in doing this work. Paradoxically, many people in helping professions feel alone when they are working with patients. First, the journey to become a helping professional is an individual one. As a medical student or a law student or whatever role you are being trained to do, you spend thousands of hours by yourself studying and writing. When you begin seeing patients, most often you are thrown in by yourself and then report back to a supervisor or attending physician. Second, as you begin to do the work of your profession after you are fully trained, you may be part of a larger staff, but often you are alone in the room with the patient. Depending on your role, you perform your duties alone with the patient, and no one may directly know what happened between the two of you. You alone write the narrative of what happened with that patient, and your word is often believed over the patient's. Generally, you alone are held responsible for what happened in the consulting room, and you alone might be sued if the patient feels he or she was not treated according to the expected standard of care. As a result of this training experience and the individual day-to-day interactions with patients, you may not only feel alone in the work but also have the expectation that this is the way it is supposed to be. Therefore, seeking support would be felt as out of the norm or reserved only for the most difficult or stressful times.

Contrast with military emphasis on success through teamwork

It is ironic that helpers would view themselves as working alone when soldiers in the military are constantly required to think of themselves as part of the unit in executing some action. When soldiers are trained, they are trained to work as part of the team and reprimanded if they are not working together with the rest of the unit or if their individual performance negatively affects the whole group. They also practice various maneuvers, both simple and complex, over and over together so that in the chaos of battle, they know their individual roles and how they need to act for the success of the whole unit. When their training is over, they continue rehearsing various difficult scenarios together with endless drilling. In actual battle, success is thought to depend on how well the various units execute the overall battle plan, whether in defense or offense. From the ancient Spartans to the modern-day sailors on aircraft carriers, the individual warrior works for the benefit of the whole army, not by him- or herself. Through this emphasis on team, the soldier has the sense of being supported and backed by the whole group. In health care, often clinicians have to operate alone and do not have the explicit sense of being on a team unless they make a special effort to develop it.

Must shift to viewing yourself as part of a team that supports you

Collegial support among helpers occurs in a number of ways. The first is in the actual work together. Certain helping roles are explicitly set up with a group working together. For example, in surgery the surgeon cannot act alone. He or she must work together with an anesthesiologist and at least one surgical assistant. Some participants on surgery teams might feel they are isolated while working with the others, but the best surgery teams experience a dynamic flow with each other, even with emotional support being shared as they go through a difficult surgery together. But many helping situations are not so explicitly perceived as a group working together. The nurse goes alone to check on the hospital patient; the physician sees the patient alone; the therapist sees one client after another

hour after hour, hardly talking to anyone else; and the teacher spends most of the day with the students and has little conversation with other teachers. While your group may be the exception, most helping professionals imagine themselves as being alone. To achieve more balance in caring for people, clinicians first need to change how they imagine themselves working, from being alone to being part of a larger group. For example, if you are working with the often-challenging patient who has borderline personality disorder, you might want to work with this patient in collaboration with other clinicians, such as the psychiatrist and other mental health personnel. You may be alone in the consulting room, but you would want to be regularly talking with each other about what is happening with that patient and what role each of you can play.

Fellow staff are witnesses to what you have to go through

Up to this point, I have focused on just the supportive function of viewing yourself as sharing the workload together. Closely tied to this, of course, is the emotionally supportive part of collegial support. When you talk with other colleagues, you know what is going on with each other and can offer support in difficult situations. You become the audience or witnesses to the drama that you are living in helping a particular person; and, just like an actor is energized by the audience, you become energized in working with your patients/clients because you know your colleagues will be interested in what has happened so far.

Intellectual as well emotional aspects to collegial support

In addition to the emotional supportive function colleagues can offer each other, there is also the cognitive or intellectual supportive function of social support. You come out of the patient room and run into one of the other staff. The staff member asks you how you are doing, and you respond by telling him or her about a difficult patient. You "vent," as it is commonly called. The staff person empathizes with you. Emotional support occurs. But then something more often occurs. The staff person asks you a thought-provoking question or gives a different perspective; maybe he or she has some knowledge or "pearls" that might be helpful to you. Or you explain what is going on with the patient, and as you explain this to your colleague, it becomes clearer to you what is going on and what you need to do about it. Many helpers who work alone will formalize this kind of support by making sure they meet regularly with other colleagues so that they can receive emotional and cognitive support.

Collegial support protects the clinician from grandiosity

When helpers work alone, often the concern is that they can become demoralized in working with difficult people or with people in pain. But the other occupational hazard is grandiosity. Helpers can be tempted to think that they can only rely on themselves. For many helpers, it can seem that all they have is themselves, alone there in the room with the patient or client. Montgomery (1994) comments,

> it is important to keep in mind that, unlike curing, caring is a social creation not an individual achievement. Therefore, we need to think of ourselves as part of a larger team or network when providing care. Otherwise we might be seduced into an over-inflated sense of our own importance. (p. 41)

The more isolated a practitioner becomes, the more there can be a risk of thinking you have all the answers. In helping roles in which the helper is often alone, there is no one to challenge him or her about their ideas. If you stop talking with people who are your professional peers, if you stop reading the journals and books of your profession, and if you stop participating in quality continuing education, you run the risk of developing a "God complex." As you embark on your clinical career, it can feel exhilarating to be free finally of all the supervision you endured in your training program, especially if it was grueling or abusive. It is not unusual for medical residents of a particular specialty to think they are done being supervised by attending physicians; now they are the teachers, and they do not have to listen to anyone else. This becomes the perfect setup for having gaps in your knowledge and not even knowing you have these gaps. Believing you no longer have much to learn from other staff (and not necessarily just your professional colleagues, but any person on the staff) sets you up for arrogance. Being arrogant is distinct from being very sure of yourself in your work. Patients like clinicians who are confident in their competence. They get nervous when a clinician is arrogant because they know that anyone who acts like he or she knows it all has bought into self-deception, and the patient is likely the one who will pay the price for it. Being an active, mutually supportive member of a team protects you from grandiosity.

Clinicians paradoxically flee their emotions yet feel a desire to process them

In my experience, the medical culture has a paradoxical view of clinicians' emotions in treating patients. On one hand, clinicians often are promoting an emotional detachment in the culture, what is sometimes called "detached concern." They may engage in emotionally self-protective maneuvers such as negative humor or maintaining an appearance of self-assured brashness when it comes to difficult patient situations. On the other hand, clinicians informally want to tell stories about their experiences and what they went through. There is both implicitly and explicitly a desire to process the experience emotionally and seek support. They may deny that they are doing any "emotional processing" because of how this seems weak or soft. But I have seen on numerous occasions how even the toughest physicians wanted to talk about what just happened to them. The problem is that they may cut this off by making a cliché comment ("That's health care for you!"), blame some favorite scapegoat, or make a disparaging remark about the patient. While this is understandable, there is a desire to process the experience as a way to get perspective on it, learn from it, and let it go. However, clinician training does not typically model this well or train clinicians how to do this better for themselves and how to respond to each other more effectively. Healthy and effective organizations will find ways to promote effective emotional processing of difficult patient experiences, both informally and formally.

Schwartz Rounds

A common way many health care organizations embed a practice to help their staffs emotionally process difficult material in the work is Schwartz Rounds. Begun in 1997 by the Kenneth B. Schwartz Center and piloted at Massachusetts General Hospital, Schwartz Rounds are now conducted at hundreds of health care organizations throughout the world. Typically, they are one-hour facilitated discussions among all health care staff, who discuss their clinical experiences with each other. Topics can be thematic (e.g., impact of patient violence on clinicians, dealing with making mistakes) or a difficult patient

case in which three or four clinicians from various roles will each present their experience on the same case, followed by the discussion and sharing of similar experiences in the audience. The audience includes any clinical role, administrators and management, dietary, security, and so on. The focus is on the mutual sharing of emotional experiences in challenging clinical situations. It has been found that Schwartz Rounds improve compassionate care for patients by helping health care staffs reinforce the importance of compassionate care and their shared purpose. By sharing their experiences with each other, health care staffs gain increased appreciation and support of each other's roles, improved teamwork, and decreased stress, all of which improve the culture of the organization and the quality of patient care (Goodrich, 2012; Lown & Manning, 2010; Palmer, 2017).

Balint groups

Another formal way health care organizations facilitate collegial support is through Balint groups. Balint groups are small groups of practicing physicians, residents, or even medical students who discuss the relational and emotional aspects of a challenging patient case facilitated by one or two clinical facilitators. The groups were begun by Michael Balint (1972), who viewed the personality and emotions of the physician as a diagnostic and therapeutic tool in the patient–physician relationship. Typically, one physician will present a challenging case for 10 minutes, after which participants imagine the experiences of each person in the case (e.g., the physician, the nurse, the patient, the family member), and the group works on what may be the sources of the difficulty in that case. Balint groups help clinicians improve their empathic ability, their ability to become more aware of both clinician and patient contributions to difficult interactions, and their understanding of transference and countertransference issues. Examples of cases include difficult patient relationships, an incurable patient, role confusion, value conflicts, and witnessing injustice (Torppa, Makkonen, Mårtenson, & Pitkälä, 2008). Residents who are trained in Balint groups report increased communication skills, abilities, and confidence in the psychological aspects of medical care (Ghetti, Chang, & Gosman, 2009; Mahoney et al., 2013; Turner & Malm, 2004) and in physician self-awareness and awareness of patient reactions (Ireton & Sherman, 1988). They also can help with preventing compassion fatigue and burnout (Benson & Magraith, 2005). Participants have been found to feel an increase in their sense of control and work satisfaction and also in their ability to work with psychosomatic patients (Kjeldmand, Holmström, & Rosenqvist, 2004).

Venting versus getting perspective on difficult experiences

Venting has a bad connotation in health care. When an organization or clinical group sets up an opportunity for the clinicians to discuss difficult patient situations, compassion fatigue, or burnout, there is usually someone who will say that venting, just talking about your feelings, is a waste of time. In this they are absolutely correct. However, there is a difference between venting and processing an experience in order to get perspective on it. Venting does not provide a change in perspective. It can seem to provide some emotional relief, but the clinician does not grow in the process. In fact, there are people who continually vent like this, complaining in victim-like fashion of what they went through, seeking in a masochistic way the pity of others or a martyrdom in feeling sorry for themselves. (We see it in patients frequently,

too.) In working with clinicians on developing the skill of effective emotional processing of challenging clinical situations, I use the image of a typical coffee cup with a handle. If the cup had no handle, it would be hard to hold it if it contained very hot liquid. You would want to put the cup down right away. The same is true when we have emotionally difficult experiences in health care. They can be so uncomfortable or unpleasant that we want to distance ourselves from them as quickly as possible. Psychologically, when we put our thoughts and feelings about our experiences into words, we are able to get perspective on them—"get a handle on them," as the saying goes. As a person puts his or her experiences into words, especially when trusted others are listening, that person can view the situation from another perspective, get an insight about the situation, or discover something. But at the most basic level, there is a way in which articulating your experience is calming. This is rooted in developmental psychology (Kennedy-Moore & Warson, 1999; Pennebaker, 1990; Rimé, Herbette, & Corsini, 2004).

The vital role of collegial support in staying in the zone of Balanced C^2

From the patient care perspective, collegial support enables a staff to have the energy and drive to provide high-quality C^2 for patients. Staff who have good collegial support do not feel alone in facing challenges, because they rely on each other as an emotional and intellectual resource. This support for clinicians gives them energy to engage the patient with more enthusiasm and commitment. From the clinician perspective, an atmosphere of collegial support enables clinicians to maintain balance by allowing colleagues to use each other to keep from being emotionally detached or negative and from being overinvolved with patients.

Collegial support is not only a supportive feedback function that creates an atmosphere of innovation and continuous improvement; it is also a way an organization can recognize and reward exemplary staff members.

SELF-REFLECTIVE AND SELF-CORRECTING ORGANIZATIONAL PRACTICES

Maintaining a compassionate caring organizational culture is a constant balancing effort. Health care is always dealing with change. Administrators who may have been the major advocates and protectors of the compassionate culture may leave the organization, and it may not be clear who will fill that role with new executives. Insurance changes, Medicare and Medicaid changes, new governmental policies or regulations, and economic changes may affect the operations of health care organizations and require reorganization of the business, layoffs, and changes in procedures. Key managers or staff who were leaders in championing the organization's compassionate culture may turn over shift roles, leaving a kind of vacuum where they were. There may be a change in the type of patients coming to a unit or practice that may create new pressures or problems for that staff, who may have to readjust or deal with the new stressors (e.g., the closure of a nearby hospital that shouldered a high number of patients without resources, and now your hospital has to deal with these patients), or something like the current opioid abuse and overdose epidemic may heavily tax the compassionate capacity of an organization. To maintain a balanced compassionate caring organizational culture, an organization has to have in place self-reflective and self-correcting practices to be able to detect when there is a problem in the organizational culture and correct for it.

The cultural transformation of Cleveland Clinic

Toby Cosgrove (2014), president and CEO of the Cleveland Clinic, tells the story of how a student told him that even though the Cleveland Clinic had excellent results for mitral valve surgery, her family decided not to bring her father there because they heard the Cleveland Clinic "had no empathy" (p. 109). She then asked, "Dr. Cosgrove, do you teach empathy at Cleveland Clinic?" (Cosgrove, 2014, p. 109). Cosgrove realized that in the quest for technical excellence, the clinic had lost the human dimension of the care. So, beginning in 2006, he and his colleagues led a cultural transformation of the Cleveland Clinic to improve the "patient experience." They made major changes in the physical components of care (e.g., building space, food) and the service-related components, which included how their caregivers communicate with their patients and how they conduct themselves professionally. In 2007, the Cleveland Clinic established its Office of Patient Experience and appointed its first chief experience officer. In the years since, the clinic has become one of the leaders in delivering excellent patient-centered care, treating the whole patient and achieving the best clinical outcomes possible with the highest patient satisfaction.

Practices to cultivate a culture of compassionate caring in an organization

In terms of practices that cultivate a culture of compassionate caring, Dewar and Nolan (2013) found that having regular conversations among patients, families, and staff as well as regular conversations among the staff are very important. Periodically asking patients and families for feedback on what staff behaviors are perceived as caring helps staffs become clear on what behaviors to continue doing and what behaviors to change. But it is also important, the researchers found, to have the entire staff regularly engaging in conversations about caring in order to achieve compassionate, relationship-centered care in everyday practice. These can be discussions at regular staff meetings, but the preferred dynamic is one in which staff have brief discussions about this and check in with each other about how they are doing. These conversations involve times when staff can problem solve difficult and complex situations, as well as times when staff share what is working well in terms of caring. The researchers call these "appreciative caring conversations," (p. 1248), which is an approach based on appreciative inquiry that has staff talk about positive examples of successful caring and then examine what enabled that caring to occur. This promotes shared learning among staff, whereby successes are analyzed to ascertain how to repeat them, just as a staff might analyze a mistake or negative event to learn from it. The appreciative approach has the advantage of also celebrating caring successes, rewarding what is desired in the organizational culture, and providing a means for promoting collegial support (Dewar & Nolan, 2013).

Dewar and Nolan's seven Cs of caring conversations

Dewar and Nolan (2013) created a model called the seven Cs of the main elements of these caring conversations: (a) being courageous enough to ask questions about the work, taking risks, facing uncertainty directly, and being assertive about changing established practices; (b) being able to connect emotionally with patients, families, and other staff and being interested in each other's feelings and experiences; (c) being curious about others' experiences as a way of not making assumptions and looking for alternatives ways of doing things; (d) being collaborative in that all the staff as well as the patients and families foster a sense of involving others in decisions, working together for shared goals, and having shared responsibility for what happens; (e) considering others' perspectives, in which staff explore others' points of view, acknowledge differences, and are able to discuss these differences openly; (f) compromising, seeking consensus, and having a sense of mutuality in the work; and (g) being celebratory, whereby staff show each other regularly that their contributions are valued and take time to notice what is working well and why it is working well.

Compassion capability

Compassion capability is defined as *"the reliable capacity of members of a collective to notice, feel, and respond to suffering"* (Lilius, Worline, Dutton, Kanov, & Maitlis, 2011, p. 874). In their research with organizations, Lilius et al. (2011) found that there are practices within an organization that build a collective capability for compassion. Organizations have routines or recurrent activities that cultivate certain types of connections and understanding among staff, and this enables specific collective capabilities. Lilius et al. (2011) found seven practices that appear to cultivate this compassion capability: acknowledging (noting other's efforts, articulating another's strengths, recognizing and honoring other's contributions), addressing issues directly, bounded playing, celebrating, collective decision-making, help offering, and orienting (figure 15.2).

Case example of compassion capability

In one of their studies, Lilius et al. (2011) observed and interviewed 26 members of a health insurance billing unit. This unit was

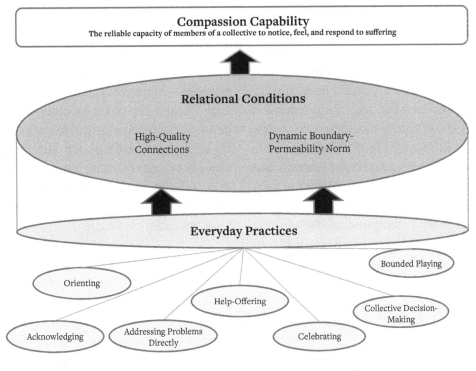

FIGURE 15.2 Compassion capability (Lilius et al., 2011, p. 882).

known as a high-performing group in terms of collecting revenue from the insurance companies faster than most other organizations, and it had just a 2% turnover compared to 25% in the entire health system and a higher turnover rate in medical groups in general. The unit was not involved in direct patient care but was observed to have a high degree of collective compassion among its staff. That is, they tended to have a shared awareness and understanding of when a staff member was going through a hard time, fellow staff empathically shared the suffering person's experience, and there was often a collective response to that person. There were many instances of major compassionate responses to particular "pain triggers," such as family deaths, personal illness, caregiving for elderly parents, and a number of other hardships. But there were also regular minor compassionate responses, such as offering support to each other, making

donations, hospital visits, doing errands for others, checking in with fellow staff to find out how they were feeling, and many other helpful gestures. Finally, the unit was engaged in ongoing altruistic ways with the community (e.g., providing money or goods to those in need, responding to difficult circumstances in the community).

Dealing with organizational burnout

Quadruple aim in health care, improving the work life of staffs

In 2008, Berwick. Nolan, and Whittington proposed the triple aim as what was necessary to improve the US health care system. These three aims were improving the health of populations, improving patients' experience of care, and reducing the per capita costs of health care for populations. More recently, however, it has become very clear that burnout among all health care professions threatens to undercut accomplishing the triple aim. Bodenheimer & Sinsky (2014) proposed that we should have the quadruple aim instead, which adds the fourth aim of improving the work life of all those who work in health care. In a sample of 6,880 physicians in the United States, burnout and dissatisfaction with work–life balance worsened from 2011 to 2014. Over half (54.4%) reported at least one symptom of burnout in 2014, compared to 45.5% in 2011. Satisfaction with work–life balance declined from 48.5% to 40.9% (Shanafelt, Hasan, et al., 2015).

Seven drivers of burnout and engagement: the twofold approach to improve these

Shanafelt and Noseworthy (2017) identified seven drivers of physician burnout and engagement: (a) workload and job demands; (b) efficiency and resources; (c) meaning in work; (d) culture and values (i.e., personal and professional values, unit and organization culture, larger health care system); (e) control and flexibility; (f) social support and community at work; and (g) work–life integration. Each of these drivers are influenced by individual factors, work unit factors, organizational factors, and national factors. The key to effective work in reducing clinician burnout and sustaining engagement is a twofold approach. First, an organization has to accurately assess which of the structural and functional drivers is operative in a particular situation and at what level it needs to be addressed (i.e., the individual, work unit, larger organization, or societal level). Second, it takes steps to strengthen the individual resiliency of its staff (Swensen, Kabcenell, & Shanafelt, 2016). The Mayo Clinic uses a physician engagement model that it calls the listen-act-develop model. The listen phase

consists of actively listening to frontline physicians' concerns to identify and understand the specific burnout drivers. The act phase involves empowering physicians to develop and implement remedies to the top burnout driver in their work area. The develop phase involves selecting and developing physician leaders to work on improving engagement and burnout. This model is not viewed as a one-time intervention; it is repeated as a continuous cycle of improving performance continuing to address burnout drivers as they arise (Swensen et al., 2016).

Organizational interventions to reduce physician burnout more effective than individual approaches

Organizational interventions to reduce physician burnout appear to be more effective than individual approaches. In a meta-analysis of 19 studies of controlled interventions using only measures of burnout as the outcome measure, Panagioti et al. (2017) found that, in general, interventions appeared to lead to significant but small reductions in burnout (equivalent to three points on the Emotional Exhaustion subscale of the Maslach Burnout Inventory). When the researchers examined if the intervention was physician directed versus organization directed, they found that interventions directed at the organizational level led to medium significant improvements in burnout, whereas interventions directed at physicians individually led to small significant improvements in burnout. Individual physician-directed interventions included mindfulness-based techniques, improving communication skills, coping skills and stress reduction education, and self-care (e.g., individual and group exercising). Interventions directed at the whole organization might be schedule changes or simple reductions in workload. More complex organizational interventions involved improving teamwork and job control, improving communication among health care staffs, and making structural changes. The researchers concluded that this is evidence that we should consider burnout to be rooted at the organizational systemic level. In line with Maslach and Leiter (1997), burnout is more the result of unhealthy organizations than primarily the clinician's deficiency.

Potential negative consequence of interventions to improve compassionate caring

Any intervention to improve compassionate caring in clinicians must be careful of the implicit message communicated to clinicians by the way that intervention is done. For example, a program on improving physician resilience must guard against suggesting that physician burnout is the physician's fault or deficiency (Panagioti et al., 2017) and that if the physician could be more resilient and more caring, then he or she would not get burned out and patients would get better care.

> When individually focused offerings are not coupled with sincere efforts to address the system-based issues contributing to burnout, this approach is typically met with skepticism and resistance by physicians ("they are implying I am the problem"). In this context, the response to well-intentioned "resilience training" is frequently a cynical one ("you only want to make me more resilient so you can further increase my workload"). For this reason, it is important that such individual offerings are part of a broader strategy that demonstrates that the organization is also doing its part to address issues in the system and environment. (Shanafelt & Noseworthy, 2016, p. 141)

Both organizational and clinician-focused interventions are necessary

In thinking about improving the level of compassionate caring among clinicians, it appears much more likely that organizational, system-wide interventions are much more likely to be effective than individually focused interventions. This is not to say that clinician-focused interventions are not worthwhile. In their systematic review and meta-analysis of 37 cohort studies and 15 randomized trials for preventing and reducing physician burnout, West, Dyrbye, Erwin, and Shanafelt (2016) found that even reductions of one or two points on burnout measures can be very helpful and lead to significant reductions in adverse outcomes. There is clear evidence that both individual clinician-focused and organizationally focused interventions improve physician burnout. West et al. believe that both types of interventions are necessary.

Two misconceptions that prevent organizations from taking systemic action to promote physician well-being

Shanafelt & Noseworthy (2017) found that there are two misconceptions that prevent organizations from taking systemic action to promote physician well-being. One is that efforts to cultivate physician well-being will be in conflict with other objectives of the organization. However, working on physician well-being will actually help with the achievement of the other objectives of the organization. The second misconception is that physician well-being interventions will be too costly. The researchers found that such interventions can be cost neutral and that small investments in programs to improve physician well-being can have significant impact.

Mayo Clinic's nine organizational strategies to improve physician well-being

In their successful experience at the Mayo Clinic with promoting physician well-being, Shanafelt and Noseworthy (2017) identified nine organizational strategies that help achieve this. First, the organizational leadership has to acknowledge the level of physician burnout and then show physicians that it cares about this and would like to take steps to improve it. This is followed by assessing what the problems are. The organization should then regularly measure physician well-being and burnout, just as the organization has with other performance metrics such as financial performance, patient volume, and patient satisfaction. Second, the leadership behavior of the physician supervisor has a great deal of impact on physician well-being. In a study with 2,800 physicians at the Mayo Clinic, researchers found that 47% of the variance in physician satisfaction and 11% of the variance in burnout was predicted by physicians' ratings of their work unit supervisors (Shanafelt, Gorringe, et al., 2015). Also, the researchers found that it was very important that these leaders know what motivates the individual physicians reporting to those leaders and what their unique talents are. Shanafelt et al. (2009) found that the risk for physician burnout is much lower if clinicians spent at least 20% of their work on the area they found the most meaningful to them. Every 1% decrease under 20% is associated with increased risk for burnout. But interestingly, there was a ceiling effect at 20%; that is, there was not as much added benefit in terms of burnout if physicians did more than 20% of what they found most meaningful.

Third to fifth organizational strategies

The third organizational strategy is to develop and implement interventions that are targeted rather than general. Shanafelt and Noseworthy (2017) emphasize that the most effective interventions result by solving the drivers of burnout at the local level. It works best that leadership uses participatory and collaborative methods to address the drivers for burnout at the local level

rather than using general solutions that might not fit the particular work unit and specialty. The fourth strategy is to help cultivate community among the clinicians. The organization should look for ways to promote peer support among clinicians, whether it be a designated space such as a physician lounge or time set aside and organizationally protected for clinicians to talk with each other about their experiences, the meaning in their work, and dealing with stress and burnout. Fifth, it is important to examine how the physicians' work is rewarded and incentivized. Every model has its drawbacks, and the organization has to find the one that works best in each situation. Shanafelt and Noseworthy note that individual productivity is only narrowly improved by a particular physician's skill, efficiency, and experience. In a practice environment that is equally efficient, the way productivity or revenue is increased is by shortening patient visit time, ordering more procedures and tests, or working longer. The researchers note that shortening patient visit time and making money by ordering more procedures and tests negatively affects the quality of care. But working longer increases the risk for burnout. They therefore recommend other models, such as having productivity incorporate patient satisfaction or other quality measures, using a salaried compensation model, providing more flexibility to allow for better work–life integration, and providing protected time for the clinician to pursue what is more personally meaningful.

Sixth and seventh organizational strategies

The sixth strategy to promote engagement and reduce burnout is for an organization to make sure that its actions align with its values and that it continuously works to strengthen its culture. Organizations need to examine the factors that are influencing their culture, periodically engage in system-wide self-appraisal to assess how well the actions of the organization are aligned with the values of the organization, and keep finding innovative ways to help keep the values alive in the organization. The seventh strategy to improve physician well-being is to work to promote work–life integration and flexibility in when and how clinicians work. Work–life integration can be addressed by examining options for decreasing hours (and adjusting compensation accordingly). Many organizations are also finding ways to increase flexibility in when clinicians work to fit better with the other demands in the clinician's life, including when certain life events (e.g., illness or death in one's family, birth) occur.

Eighth and ninth organizational strategies

The eighth strategy is for an organization to provide resources to promote self-care, deal with distress, and improve well-being and resilience. The important thing is to make sure that such programs are part of a broader organizational strategy, not piecemeal or subtly blaming clinicians for not being more able to deal with the drivers of burnout. Finally, the ninth strategy is to advance the science of reducing burnout and promoting engagement by working to do that in one's organization as well as funding or supporting this work in all of health care.

Mayo Clinic's success in improving burnout using systemic approaches

The Mayo Clinic has made important innovative initiatives in improving physician engagement and preventing burnout. Shanafelt and Noseworthy (2017) describe how the burnout rates of Mayo Clinic physicians increased from 2011 to 2013, to the point that they were just as bad as the national average for physician burnout. The Mayo Clinic implemented a systemic organizational intervention to reduce burnout and improve engagement for all staff, not just physicians. While physician burnout rates nationally increased from 2011 to 2014, the Mayo Clinic's physician burnout rates decreased by 7% (Shanafelt, Gorringe, et al., 2015). While the clinic is quick to say that a third of its physicians are still experiencing serious burnout, its efforts at the systemic level indicate that the systemic approach is the most effective one.

Dealing with burnout and emotional contagion in an organization

Emotional contagion among staff

It is important to remember that the emotional toll that comes from working with patients is only one driver of burnout for clinicians. Yet in the hallways of medicine, we often overattribute burnout to the stress of working with patients. In fact, clinicians may be quite self-protective of their emotions when it comes to interactions with patients (Airagnes et al., 2014). However, the emotional reactions we receive and give each other on health care teams are actually a major source of the emotional dynamics in providing care, yet this is not usually considered. Clinicians will vent with each other about particular patients, the health care system, the organization's leaders, other clinicians, or particular situations. Other clinicians are our safe zone. We feel more comfortable engaging in sharing how we feel with each other, venting about what is happening, and even making fun of patients in a way we would never want anyone outside our circles to hear.

Burnout is contagious among health care staffs

Individuals on a health care staff can "catch" burnout from each other like a virus. In a study of 507 general practitioners, Bakker, Schaufeli, Sixma, and Bosveld (2001) found that the number of burnout complaints by colleagues predicted emotional exhaustion, which in turn predicted depersonalization and reduced personal accomplishment in the work. Burnout complaints were measured by the answers to two questions: "According to you, how many of your colleagues are 'burned-out'?" and "How many of your colleagues complain that they have physical or psychological problems carrying out their work?" (Bakker et al., 2001, p. 89). But the researchers also measured an individual personality difference called "susceptibility to emotional contagion," (p. 89) in which higher scores indicate the physician is more susceptible to picking up the negative feelings, attitudes, and behaviors of their colleagues. The researchers found that emotional contagion made an independent contribution to predicting burnout. The more susceptible the physician was to emotional contagion, the more this predicted that physician's emotional exhaustion in addition to the number of perceived burnout complaints among colleagues.

Positive and negative emotions are contagious among health care staffs

Recent research has found that there is an emotional contagion process for both positive and negative emotions among health care staffs. As you many recall from chapter 2, emotional contagion through the mirror neuron system is our tendency to automatically and unconsciously mimic and synchronize with the facial expressions, postures, vocalizations, and movements of the person with whom we are interacting. From an evolutionary biological point of view, this automatic ability to absorb other people's emotions is adaptive because this emotional attunement facilitates our communication, increases our sense of affiliation with other

people, and helps us prepare others for action such as in fearful situations (Hatfield, Cacioppo, & Rapson, 1994). In the compassion mindset process, clinicians automatically mirror the emotions of their patients; of course, the concern is that this potentially increases the emotional toll on clinicians working with patients in the whole spectrum of human tragedy and triumph. But this same process is occurring among health care staffs: We are automatically absorbing our colleagues' emotions. The emotions of our colleagues can be negative or positive. Negative emotions can become part of the job demands of our work, and positive emotions can become part of the job resources of that work environment. In a health care environment, the sheer quantity and intensity of those negative and positive emotions is manifest not only with patients but in all the many interactions with health care staffs.

Job demands–resources model of burnout

Another model of burnout besides the Maslach Burnout Inventory, with its dimensions of emotional exhaustion, depersonalization (cynicism), and personal accomplishment, is the job demands-resources (JD-R) model of burnout (Demerouti, Bakker, Nachreiner, & Schaufeli, 2001). Burnout in JD-R results from the interaction of two independent factors: exhaustion and disengagement. Exhaustion results from job demands that can overtax the worker. Job demands are "those physical, social or organizational aspects of the job that require sustained physical or mental effort and are therefore associated with certain physiological and psychological costs (e.g., exhaustion)" (Demerouti et al., 2001, p. 501). The more the demands there are, the more the physiological and psychological costs are. In order to survive and thrive in a work situation, individuals rely on job resources. Job resources are "those physical, psychological, social, or organizational aspects of the job that may do any of the following: (a) be functional in achieving work goals; (b) reduce job demands at the associated physiological and psychological costs; (c) stimulate personal growth and development" (Demerouti et al., 2001, p. 501). If there are insufficient resources, the person may eventually psychologically withdraw or disengage from the work.

Negative emotions are part of job demands, and positive emotions are job resources

In a work situation, negative emotions such as anger become part of the job demands of the work, and positive emotions become part of the job resources. Recall from chapter 10 how negative and positive emotions function differently in humans. In the broaden-and-build theory of positive emotions, positive emotions broaden the thought–action repertoire of a person and build physical and psychosocial resources. Negative emotions narrow the thought–action repertoire of the person and deplete the physical and psychological resources (Fredrickson & Branigan, 2005). So, if we automatically and unintentionally capture our colleagues' emotions, positive or negative, that emotional contagion becomes part of the mix for the experience of working in health care.

Physicians and nurses absorb emotional contagion differently

Petitta, Jiang, & Härtel (2016) tested the relationship between emotional contagion and burnout in a health care setting. With a sample of 252 nurses and 102 physicians in three different hospitals, they examined how these caregivers absorbed joy and anger from leaders, colleagues,

and patients. The researchers found that nurse and physician burnout was, indeed, associated with the emotion contagion the caregivers absorbed from leaders, colleagues, and patients. But the peculiar thing is that the sources of the emotional contagion affected nurses and physicians differently. Physicians tended to absorb joy and anger from their colleagues, but not so much from patients and leadership; and the burnout was manifested more as exhaustion and cynicism. Nurses tended to absorb joy and anger from their interactions with colleagues, patients, and leaders; burnout was manifested more by cynicism and not so much by exhaustion.

Why physicians and nurses absorb emotional contagion differently

It is not clear how the effects of emotional contagion map differently in terms of sources and burnout effects between nurses and physicians. The authors offer some ideas. One is that nurses are required to engage in teamwork more and have to coordinate a great deal with supervisors, physicians, other staff as well as patients. Compared to physicians, they have to work more closely for longer periods of time with each group. Interestingly, nurses reported not absorbing anger from their colleagues so much; the researchers believe this might be due to the fact that the teamwork and team spirit may overshadow the negative feelings from their fellow staff. The researchers speculated that physicians had more limited social interactions relative to nurses and that their sphere of mutual influence is more with colleagues.

Health care staffs are less aware of and less protected from staff emotional contagion

We should be careful about drawing major conclusions from this study in terms of which sources of positive and negative emotions are likely to be absorbed by nurses and physicians. A number of health care organizations have work structures that might promote much more interaction among leaders, physician and nurse colleagues, and patients than was seen in this study. However, what is much more clear and crucial for our purposes is that emotional contagion is not just a factor in patient care; emotional contagion plays a major role in burnout, and its source includes our colleagues and our leaders. Yet we are less aware of it, and we absorb each other's joy and anger without the same "filter" and "protections" that we use with patients. With patients, we have a particular protocol for how we should manage our emotions. Even when we manage our emotions with patients badly, we still are using methods to suppress or regulate the emotional contagion from our patients. But our "windows are wide open" when it comes to each other on the health care team. This is where the culture of the organization becomes so important. What is the tone we strive for in each unit? How do we process difficult patient situations or tumultuous organizational issues or politics with each other?

Clinicians need to be aware of emotional contagion from colleagues

Let us recall what happens in the compassion mindset process and apply it to emotional contagion among ourselves as clinicians. In the compassion mindset process with patients, we encounter the emotional state of our patients through the automatic mirror neuron/bottom-up empathy processing. We are not conscious of this generally. Milliseconds after our neocortex receives this emotional contagion signal, we rely on our top-down empathy processing to categorize and manage the emotional exchange we have had. The more

self-aware and mindful we are, the more we may be able to notice that we have absorbed the other's emotion and process in a conscious, more deliberate manner using different methods of emotion regulation (Petitta et al., 2016). With our colleagues and leadership, it becomes important that we are mindful of what we are absorbing from each other and more deliberately manage these in a healthy manner so that a source of anger does not automatically become a forest fire of negativity throughout the work group.

The importance of self-reflective and self-correcting practices for balanced C^2

Health care organizations are complex entities that are always changing as they adapt to various circumstances. To operate effectively in a balanced C^2 zone, an organization has to build in mechanisms to reflect on itself and assess how it is doing relative to its mission. Then it needs to systemically implement changes to correct for any deficiencies. From the perspective of patients, an organization that regularly self-assesses and self-corrects will likely be providing high-quality care. From the clinicians' perspective, an organization's ability to self-assess and self-correct is the most effective way to protect clinicians from the drivers of burnout and enable them to be in the zone of balanced C^2.

CONCLUSION

The organizational culture is the most powerful long-term force in providing high-quality compassionate caring to patients. In an organization in which the caring ethic permeates the entire organization and in which leadership supports, protects, and cultivates C^2, clinicians will be enabled to work with patients in an optimally engaged manner without being pressured to be detached or even negative with patients. For clinicians, this C^2 culture and leadership takes care of its clinicians in a systemic way. It is also an organization that fosters collegial support, which also buffers burnout and enhances compassion satisfaction. Finally, an organization in the zone of balanced C^2 has mechanisms to assess itself and to self-correct in a systemic manner.

QUESTIONS FOR DISCUSSION

1. What are examples of these organizational balanced C^2 characteristics that you have witnessed in organizations in which you have been trained or employed?
2. What positive and negative examples of collegial support have you experienced or observed in an organization in which you worked?

REFERENCES

Airagnes, G., Consoli, S. M., De Morlhon, O., Galliot, A., Lemogne, C., & Jaury, P. (2014). Appropriate training based on Balint groups can improve the empathic abilities of medical students: A preliminary study. *Journal of Psychosomatic Research, 76*(5), 426–429.

Bakker, A. B., Schaufeli, W. B., Sixma, H. J., & Bosveld, W. (2001). Burnout contagion among general practitioners. *Journal of Social and Clinical Psychology, 20*(1), 82–98.

Balint, M. (1972). *The doctor, his patient and the illness* (Rev. ed.). Madison, CT: International Universities Press.

Beach, M. C., Inui, T., & Relationship-Centered Care Research Network. (2006). Relationship-centered care: A constructive reframing. *Journal of General Internal Medicine, 21,* S3–S8.

Beeson, S. C. (2009). *Engaging physicians: A manual to physician partnership.* Gulf Breeze, FL: Fire Starter Publishing.

Benson, J., & Magraith, K. (2005). Compassion fatigue and burnout: The role of Balint groups. *Australian Family Physician, 34*(6), 497–498.

Berwick, D. M., Nolan, T. W., & Whittington, J. (2008). The triple aim: Care, health, and cost. *Health Affairs, 27*(3), 759–769.

Bodenheimer, T., & Sinsky, C. (2014). From triple to quadruple aim: Care of the patient requires care of the provider. *Annals of Family Medicine, 12*(6), 573–576.

Cara, C. M., Nyberg, J. J., & Brousseau, S. (2011). Fostering the coexistence of caring philosophy and economics in today's health care system. *Nursing Administration Quarterly, 35*(1), 6–14.

Cosgrove, T. (2014). *The Cleveland Clinic way: Lessons in excellence from one of the world's leading healthcare organizations.* New York, NY: McGraw-Hill Education.

Crawford, P., Brown, B., Kvangarsnes, M., & Gilbert, P. (2014). The design of compassionate care. *Journal of Clinical Nursing, 23*(23–24), 3589–3599.

Crawford, P., Gilbert, P., Gilbert, J., & Gale, C. (2011). The language of compassion. *Taiwan International ESP Journal, 3*(1), 1–16.

Demerouti, E., Bakker, A. B., Nachreiner, F., & Schaufeli, W. B. (2001). The job demands-resources model of burnout. *Journal of Applied Psychology, 86*(3), 499–512.

Dewar, B., & Nolan, M. (2013). Caring about caring: Developing a model to implement compassionate relationship-centred care in an older people care setting. *International Journal of Nursing Studies, 50*(9), 1247–1258.

Dutton, J. E., Workman, K. M., & Hardin, A. E. (2014). Compassion at work. *Annual Review of Organizational Psychology and Organizational Behavior, 1*(1), 277–304.

Dutton, J. E., Worline, M. C., Frost, P. J., & Lilius, J. (2006). Explaining compassion organizing. *Administrative Science Quarterly, 51*(1), 59–96.

Frampton, S. B., & Charmel, P. A. (Eds.). (2008). *Putting patients first: Best practices in patient-centered care.* San Francisco, CA: Jossey-Bass.

Fredrickson, B. L., & Branigan, C. (2005). Positive emotions broaden the scope of attention and thought-action repertoires. *Cognition and Emotion, 19*(3), 313–332.

Ghetti, C., Chang, J., & Gosman, G. (2009). Burnout, psychological skills, and empathy: Balint training in obstetrics and gynecology residents. *Journal of Graduate Medical Education, 1*(2), 231–235.

Gilbert, P. (2009). *The compassionate mind: A new approach to life's challenges.* Oakland, CA: New Harbinger.

Goodrich, J. (2012). Supporting hospital staff to provide compassionate care: Do Schwartz Center Rounds work in English hospitals? *Journal of the Royal Society of Medicine, 105*(3), 117–122.

Graber, D. R. (2009). Organizational and individual perspectives on caring in hospitals. *Journal of Health and Human Services Administration, 31*(4), 517–537.

Halpern, J. (2014). From idealized clinical empathy to empathic communication in medical care. *Medicine, Health Care and Philosophy, 17*(2), 301–311.

Hatfield, E., Cacioppo, J. T., & Rapson, R. L. (1994). *Emotional contagion.* New York, NY: Cambridge University Press.

Heskett, J. L., Jones, T. O., Loveman, G. W., Sasser, W. E. Jr., & Schlesinger, L. A. (2008, July-August). Putting the service-profit chain to work. *Harvard Business Review,* 118–129.

Hoffart, N., & Woods, C. Q. (1996). Elements of a nursing professional practice model. *Journal of Professional Nursing, 12*(6), 354–364.

Ireton, H. R., & Sherman, M. (1988). Self-ratings of graduate family practice residents' psychological medicine abilities. *Family Practice Research Journal, 7*(4), 236–244.

Kennedy-Moore, E., & Watson, J. C. (1999). *Expressing emotion: Myths, realities, and therapeutic strategies.* New York, NY: Guilford Press.

Kjeldmand, D., Holmström, I., & Rosenqvist, U. (2004). Balint training makes GPs thrive better in their job. *Patient Education and Counseling, 55*(2), 230–235.

Koloroutis, M. (Ed.). (2004). *Relationship-based care: A model for transforming practice.* Minneapolis, MN: Creative Health Care Management.

Lilius, J. M., Worline, M. C., Dutton, J. E., Kanov, J. M., & Maitlis, S. (2011). Understanding compassion capability. *Human Relations, 64*(7), 873–899.

Lilius, J. M., Worline, M. C., Maitlis, S., Kanov, J., Dutton, J. E., & Frost, P. (2008). The contours and consequences of compassion at work. *Journal of Organizational Behavior, 29*(2), 193–218.

Lown, B. A., & Manning, C. F. (2010). The Schwartz Center rounds: Evaluation of an interdisciplinary approach to enhancing patient-centered communication, teamwork, and provider support. *Academic Medicine, 85*(6), 1073–1081.

Mahoney, D., Brock, C., Diaz, V., Freedy, J., Thiedke, C., Johnson, A., & Mallin, K. (2013). Balint groups: The nuts and bolts of making better doctors. *International Journal of Psychiatry in Medicine, 45*(4), 401–411.

Maslach, C., & Leiter, M. P. (1997). *The truth about burnout: How organizations cause personal stress and what to do about it.* San Francisco, CA: Jossey-Bass.

McClelland, L. E., & Vogus, T. J. (2014). Compassion practices and HCAHPS: Does rewarding and supporting workplace compassion influence patient perceptions. *Health Services Research, 49*(5), 1670–1683.

Mead, N., & Bower, P. (2000). Patient-centredness: A conceptual framework and review of the empirical literature. *Social Science and Medicine, 51*(7), 1087–1110.

Montgomery, C. L. (1994). The caring/healing relationship of "maintaining authentic caring." In J. Watson (Ed.), *Applying the art and science of human caring* (pp. 39–42). New York, NY: National League for Nursing Press.

Palmer, S. (2017). *Supporting the emotional needs of staff: The impact of Schwartz Rounds on caregiver and patient experience* (White Paper, Beryl Institute).

Panagioti, M., Panagopoulou, E., Bower, P., Lewith, G., Kontopantelis, E., Chew-Graham, C., ... Esmail, A. (2017). Controlled interventions to reduce burnout in physicians: A systematic review and meta-analysis. *JAMA Internal Medicine, 177*(2), 195–205.

Pennebaker, J. W. (1990). *Opening up: The healing power of expressing emotions.* New York, NY: Guilford Press.

Petitta, L., Jiang, L., & Härtel, C. E. J. (2016). Emotional contagion and burnout among nurses and doctors: Do joy and anger from different sources of stakeholders matter? *Stress and Health, 33*(4), 358–369. doi:10.1002/smi.2724

Rimé, B., Herbette, G., & Corsini, S. (2004). The social sharing of emotion: Illusory and real benefits of talking about emotional experiences. In I. Nyklíček, L. Temoshok, & A. Vingerhoets (Eds.), *Emotional expression and health: Advances in theory, assessment and clinical applications* (pp. 29–42). New York, NY: Brunner-Routledge.

Shanafelt, T. D., Gorringe, G., Menaker, R., Storz, K. A., Reeves, D., Buskirk, S. J., ... Swensen, S. J. (2015). Impact of organizational leadership on physician burnout and satisfaction. *Mayo Clinic Proceedings, 90*(4), 432–440.

Shanafelt, T. D., Hasan, O., Dyrbye, L. N., Sinsky, C., Satele, D., Sloan, J. & West, C. P. (2015). Changes in burnout and satisfaction with work-life balance in physicians and the general US working population between 2011 and 2014. *Mayo Clinic Proceedings, 90*(12), 1600–1613.

Shanafelt, T. D., & Noseworthy, J. H. (2017). Executive leadership and physician well-being: Nine organizational strategies to promote engagement and reduce burnout. *Mayo Clinic Proceedings, 92*(1), 129–146.

Shanafelt, T. D., West, C. P., Sloan, J. A., Novotny, P. J., Poland, G. A., Menaker, R., ... Dyrbye, L. N. (2009). Career fit and burnout among academic faculty. *Archives of Internal Medicine, 169*(10), 990–995.

Shay, J. (2011). Casualties. *Daedalus, 140*(3), 179–188.

Starr, P. (1982). *The social transformation of American medicine.* New York, NY: Basic Books.

Stewart, M., Brown, J. B., Weston, W. W., McWhinney, I. R., McWilliam, C. L., & Freeman, T. R. (2003). *Patient-centered medicine: Transforming the clinical method* (2nd ed.). Abingdon, UK: Radcliffe Medical Press.

Studer, Q. (2008). *Results that last: Hardwiring behaviors that will take your company to the top.* Hoboken, NJ: Wiley.

Swensen, S., Kabcenell, A., & Shanafelt, T. D. (2016). Physician-organization collaboration reduces physician burnout and promotes engagement: The Mayo Clinic experience. *Journal of Healthcare Management, 61*(2), 105–127.

Talbot, S. G. & Dean, W. (2018, July 26). Physicians aren't 'burning out.' They're suffering from moral injury. *STAT.* Retrieved from https://www.statnews.com/2018/07/26/physicians-not-burning-out-they-are-suffering-moral-injury/

Torppa, M. A., Makkonen, E., Mårtenson, C., & Pitkälä, K. H. (2008). A qualitative analysis of student Balint groups in medical education: Contexts and triggers of cases presentations and discussion terms. *Patient Education and Counseling, 72*(1), 5–11.

Tresloni, C. P., & Pew-Fetzer Task Force. (1994). *Health professions education and relationship-centered care.* San Francisco, CA: Pew Health Professions.

Turner, A. L., & Malm, R. L. (2004). A preliminary investigation of Balint and non-Balint behavioral medicine training. *Family Medicine, 36*(2), 114–117.

Watson, J. (1988). *Nursing: Human science and human care.* New York, NY: National League for Nursing.

Watson, J. (2012). *Human caring science: A theory of nursing.* Sudbury, MA: Jones & Bartlett.

West, C. P., Dyrbye, L. N., Erwin, P. J., & Shanafelt, T. D. (2016). Interventions to prevent and reduce physician burnout: A systematic review and meta-analysis. *Lancet, 388*(10057), 2272–2281.

Wiinikka-Lydon, J. (2019). Mapping moral injury: Comparing discourses of moral harm. *Journal of Medicine and Philosophy, 44,* 175–191.

Wolf, J. A., Niederhauser, D., & LaVela, S. L. (2014). Defining patient experience. *Patient Experience Journal*, 1(1), 7–19.

CREDITS

"It's hard, but I wouldn't want to be doing anything else."

—A quote from many clinicians I have known

"What good is a path that doesn't carry us to the edge of our capacity and then beyond that place? A true calling involves a great exposure before it can become a genuine refuge."

—Michael Meade

"It's all right if you grow your wings on the way down."

—Robert Bly

Chapter Sections:

CHAPTER 16

Recovering Compassionate Caring in Your Career and Constellating the Compassion Mindset

Questions to consider before reading this chapter:

1. When a person has a setback in his or her life, what do you think it takes to recover from that?
2. What have you witnessed in health care settings in terms of clinicians who appear to be burned out and those who appear to have enthusiasm and fulfillment in their work?

INTRODUCTION

Most of us will experience burnout in health care. My own journey to writing this book began 24 years ago when I came home and told my wife, who is also a clinician, "I hate my patients." All the things I had done before and even my research on empathy and burnout did not immunize me from going through it myself. I went back to the drawing board to figure out what happened and what I could do to get motivated to help patients again and not feel so discouraged and cynical. After I had done that, I then worked alongside physicians, nurses, and therapists for many years and witnessed how many of them had gone through something similar or were just entering a time of burnout. Some did not seem to recover. Others did recover and became better clinicians and people than they were before they burned out.

In this chapter, we explore how clinicians can recover from burnout and constellate the compassion mindset. There is much research and many books on burnout, and I will not try to summarize all those valuable approaches. My focus here will be on what appear to be guiding principles we should use in that recovery process, and then to consider how we might constellate (or reconstellate) the compassion mindset. I use the word *constellate* to suggest that, like the stars, when the various constituent aspects of compassion are in place, the constellation that I call the compassion mindset comes into view.

RECOVERING COMPASSIONATE CARING: THE BRIEF ANSWER

The pressure for a two-minute answer

"What's the bottom line on recovering from burnout and staying compassionate in a crazy health care system?" When I get this question, it is usually from a stressed clinician who genuinely wants to know the answer and does not have a lot time to hear the answer. In residency training, I mastered the ability to give two-minute didactics on clinical issues. I knew that if I went past the two minutes, the resident would start fidgeting and give me signals that I was giving too long of an answer. On one hand, I wanted residents to understand that I was compressing hours of training and experience on a particular topic and giving them this pearl in two minutes! There is no way they can really hope to understand a particular issue of patient care with any depth in two minutes, but often it was enough to get them through a particular patient situation. On the other hand, I was sympathetic to their predicament. These residents were being thrown into complicated situations without enough training, especially when it came to communication issues, psychological issues, and dealing with their own emotions. So, I would accept that this was what we had to do, and I would do my best to give the best guidance I could. But with this question, I know that the two-minute answer will not be enough to turn the tide on a burnout process that has dimmed the light of compassionate care in their health care journey.

The two-minute answer

Here is my two-minute answer. We have to work in a crazy health care system with challenging patients in a culture that has unrealistically high expectations for what health care can do, and it's probably going to get worse before it gets better. It's a system that frustrates our patients and a system that is grinding up clinicians. We also have a lot of people who want to make a lot of money off of the way it is, so there is a lot of resistance to improving it. And there are a lot of people who don't care about compassion; they just care about their profits. On top of that, we sent you to medical school and did not give you everything you needed for this work. We gave you a sentimentalized notion of compassionate caring and a primitive understanding of how to work with your patients' emotions and your own emotions. And this is hard, emotional work. Emotional detachment does not work, and if you try to do it, you will hurt your patients and yourself. The first thing you do when your compassion has burned out is realize that this happened to you and that you have to find again what drew you into medicine and rebuild it. What we know from the research is that it is not enough to control negative emotions. That will not be enough to get you through a lifetime of this work. You need to get a deeper understanding of what compassionate caring really is and then protect and cultivate your positive emotions in health care. You'll never get rid of the negative. To recover your compassionate mindset, you have to train yourself mentally, emotionally, and spiritually, just like if you were an elite athlete. A philosophy or spirituality of caring is likely to help you, but the religion or philosophy you grew up with is probably going to need to be overhauled. Then work with your brother and sister clinicians, administrators, and other advocates to help create organizations that protect and cultivate compassionate caring. This is a lifelong process. But once you reconnect with compassion in your life, you will get the energy to keep doing this.

The longer answer

Now for the longer answer. In this chapter, I will provide a summary of a number of approaches to recovering a compassion mindset. I will begin by discussing the typical pathways for compassion over a clinician's career.

CAREER TRAJECTORIES AND THE LOSS OR RECOVERY OF COMPASSIONATE CARING

The typical progression of compassionate caring in a clinical career

The reality of being a clinician is that most likely you begin your health care career with some initial level of idealism about what the helping professions are and that you have a good level of compassionate motivation to enter these professions. Your personal statement will most likely articulate that you "really want to help people," "want to give back to others what you've been given in your life," "feel called to help others," "want to relieve suffering in the world," and "desire to make the world a better place." Your application will most likely be a testimonial and verification of this compassionate motivation by the volunteer work you have done, a list of work and research experiences, the courses you have taken, and a number of letters by credible recommenders who will vouch for your intellectual ability and altruistic motivation. Then you get into a professional training program and may begin with a great deal of enthusiasm. But at some point in training or later practice, that initial compassionate promise begins to fade. Whether it is because of the "hidden curriculum" that erodes it, stressful and difficult course experiences that make you focus only

on surviving, or demoralizing experiences with patients or trainers, that initial level of compassionate caring begins to decline. If it does not happen early in your training, then it may happen in residency. If by some good fortune you have been spared an unhealthy training program and had positive experiences in early practice, then the collapse of your compassionate attitudes may happen later in your clinical practice, caused by burning out in patient care, being ground up in a dysfunctional health care system, or having to balance your career with major problems in your personal life.

Collapse of compassion as a normal phase in a clinical career

The important thing to remember in the quest to learn balanced compassionate caring is that typically your career path will entail a loss of compassion at some point and that this is normal. For reasons that have been explained in this book, it is practically inevitable that this collapse of compassion will occur within your career. Helping professions are likely to exact an emotional toll, and training programs rarely prepare their graduates well enough to manage that very well. Frankly, even if you had a program that did train you on handling the emotionally difficult parts, we would not expect that you could master this right away. There is a learning that happens in the formal academic training, and there is a whole different learning that occurs with actually doing the work. Add to this that our conceptions of compassion and caring are naive and undeveloped going into training, and training programs do not typically offer more mature conceptions of what compassionate caring is. Rather than engage in some victim-thinking about how inevitable and awful this situation is, it seems better to enter this journey of being a health care professional just knowing and accepting that you will encounter a time of crisis when all your idealism and compassionate motivation seems lost and you have come to dislike the patients you were going to heal in your application, as well as despise the institution of health care on top of that. *Just expect that this crisis, this "burnout," will occur in your career. Perhaps it will happen a couple of times. Accept that it will happen. But view it as a part of the normal development of the helping professional, a potential transitional phase with the possibilities of transformation, stagnation, or disintegration.*

Graphing three common trajectories of compassionate caring in a clinician's career

In most helping careers, there is an initial compassionate idealism and enthusiasm that may increase at first. But at some point, like a marathon runner "hitting the wall," clinicians will experience a loss of that compassionate attitude. It comes as a surprise to most clinicians because most think they will be different, they will be stronger and more caring than the others who have faltered. It often happens in medicine as medical students begin to see patients (Hojat et al., 2009). Or it may happen in residency or early practice. It will happen at least once and maybe several times in a career. Jane Uygur (2012) conducted a qualitative study with family physicians to understand their ideas, perceptions, and experiences of what influenced their capacity for compassion at various points in the training and practice. She interviewed residents, physicians who had been in practice less than 5 years, and physicians who had practiced more than 10 years (from 10 to 40 years). She found a typical pattern of compassion from an initial increase in medical school, then a dramatic decline often occurring in later medical school or residency, and then, in this particular sample, a steady increase in compassionate capacity that surpassed their initial levels. That trajectory is represented in what I have labeled the recovery and amplification of C^2 (i.e., compassionate caring). With her permission, I adapted the graph from her study and added two other trajectories to represent physicians who have a partial recovery of C^2 and the loss of C^2. While her original study was with exemplary family physicians, when I have shared her graph with other clinicians of other specialties, they draw out their C^2 trajectories that are slight variations on these three curves. Some have had several times when their level of compassionate attitude went very low and then recovered. While most "bottomed out" in residency, others had their bottoming out later in their careers. While we do not know at this time how those trajectories may vary by country of practice, specialty, gender, and so on, these curves articulate the journeys of many clinicians I know.

Loss of C^2 trajectory

In the loss of C^2 trajectory, the clinician has lost the initial level of compassionate attitude and likely sunk to a level lower than that at which he or she started. This is a place that is dangerous ground. With this often comes a state of severe demoralization. It is manifested in a number of ways: depression, anxiety, acting-out behavior, substance abuse and addiction, anger problems, suicidal thoughts, marital problems, or declining work performance. Many factors play into how bad this time is, including the clinician's previous psychological history, social support, how negative the setting is, and the clinical experiences that preceded this breakdown of compassion.

Partial recovery of C² trajectory

In the partial recovery of C² trajectory, the clinician has the initial enthusiasm and commitment to compassionate caring, and this increases in the early years of clinical training. But then the clinician loses this attitude and sinks to a point lower than when he or she entered training. This might happen anytime during a career, but often we hear of it happening in later medical school or early practice. Of course, this could happen much later in a career as well. But in this trajectory, the clinician somehow recovers some of his or her compassionate caring attitude to a level similar to that in the early stages of his or her career. However, the partial recovery suggests that this attitude is not as good as it could be and that the clinician struggles with it in some way.

Recovery and amplification of C²

In the recovery and amplification of C², the clinician has the initial high level of enthusiasm and commitment to compassionate caring and has an increase in this in the early stage of training. But then there is a loss of this level of compassionate caring to a level lower than when he or she first began. But in this trajectory, the clinician recovers compassionate caring, and it is amplified beyond what it was at the beginning of training.

Uygur's research on the decline and recovery of compassion in physicians

This last trajectory developed by Uygur's (2012) research led to her discovery of what she calls the *compassion trichotomy*. It would seem applicable across specialties in terms of what is one of the ways compassion can be recovered. First, let me summarize what she found. In her sample of physicians, Uygur discovered that while these physicians reported a major decline in their sense of compassion during training, they also reported that they

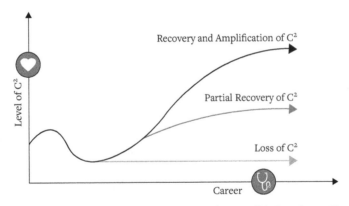

Medical Career from Application, Medical School, Residency, to Clinical Practice over Time

Level of Compassionate Caring (C²) over 3 possible career trajectories:
1. Loss of C²: Initial good level of C² followed by loss of C² some time during training, residency, or early practice, then continuing throughout career.
2. Partial Recovery of C²: Initial good level of C² followed by loss of C² some time during training, residency, or early practice, then partial recovery.
3. Recovery and Amplification of C²: Initial good level of C² followed by loss of C² some time during training, residency, or early practice, then followed by full recovery and amplification of C².

FIGURE 16.1 Level of C² over three possible career trajectories (Adapted with permission from Uygur, 2012).

regained it and that it evolved over the course of their careers. Physicians said the motivation for compassion tended to decrease during training. They had to learn an incredible amount of material, and the emphasis of that material was biomedical. As they learned their new roles and responsibilities while learning medicine, they had increased stress and time pressures, often struggling to find time to meet the basic needs of eating and sleeping. With more clinical experience and a clearer sense of their role, this biomedical emphasis became more holistic. They found that only a relatively small part of their work was directly curing patients, and their attitude about how this changed was often attributed to having to help patients with chronic medical issues. They discovered that patients experiencing a caring attitude while working on medical issues was helpful to them. With good outcomes related to this caring attitude, physicians wanted to keep using it. Physicians who could not accept that they could not control and cure everything became more frustrated, while those who shifted from the illusion of control to supporting patients were happier.

Components of regaining compassion in physicians' careers

In terms of feeling the capacity for compassion, Uygur found that physicians described how it takes mental and emotional energy to engage in a compassionate way with patients. The lack of physical, mental, and emotional well-being tends to make it difficult to focus and care for patients. Mental health problems, personal problems such as with finances or personal relationships, and other life stressors could interfere with the emotional energy and focus needed to do compassionately caring patient care. Physicians had to learn how to achieve a work–life balance in order to improve the capacity to care. But interestingly, Uygur discovered a reciprocal relationship between energy and compassion. "While compassion required an initial output of energy from the physician to engage with and focus on the patient, compassion energized and fueled physicians in their work" (Uygur, 2012, p. 85). As physicians matured in their work, their understanding of what it means to be compassionate changed, and they became more empathetic over time. Uygur (2012) found that as medical students, they had an idealistic desire to help people, but their "lack of life experiences at this early stage in their careers made it difficult for them to empathize with their patients" (p. 93). *Pity* would describe their feelings for their patients better than *compassion*. Along with this was the medical culture of emotional detachment and depersonalization that discourages having a compassionate attitude and emotionally connecting with patients. There was also a self-protective emotional detachment that occurred in order to cope with the suffering and death they witnessed. However, as time went on, many physicians became more empathic as they had continuity with their patients. They became more able to control their own emotions with patients and able to be more consciously intentional in being empathic with patients, rather than being more reactive and overwhelmed in their work with patients. Most importantly, Uygur found that what increased empathy and compassion in physicians was their own life experiences, such as death, illness, and parenthood. However, she reported that not all physicians became more empathetic over the course of their careers. Physicians described other physicians who continually blocked their own empathy, with the result that they did not get to know their patients as people, nor did they enjoy working with them. Those physicians became caught up in the routine and monotony of their work.

The compassion trichotomy

Engaging in a compassionate caring way with patients takes mental effort and emotional labor. It is work. But contrary to the way clinical work has often been portrayed, it is not a one-way route of energy depletion. Paradoxically, it can generate energy for the helper. In her qualitative study of compassion in family medicine physicians, Uygur (2012) found a reciprocal dynamic between compassion and energy that she called the *compassion trichotomy*, a cyclical process among *connection* with patients, *motivation* for compassion, and *capacity for compassion*. Physicians discussed how *connection* with patients often made them feel energized by patient care. They felt good about making a difference, which gave them a sense of meaning. This increased their *motivation* to be compassionate with other patients and increased their felt *capacity* to be compassionate. With that increased sense of capacity, they increased their desire and skills to connect with their patients. The cycle then repeats itself as increased connection leads to deepening of the motivation and then an increase in capacity (figure 16.2).

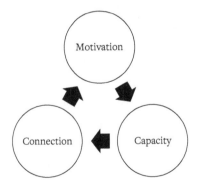

FIGURE 16.2 The compassion trichotomy (Uygur, 2012).

How did compassion evolve over the career?

What did a fully evolved compassion progression look like from the early years to later years? The physicians had limited abilities or time for *connection* at the beginning of their careers, but their clinical experience increased their ability to connect with patients, including the difficult patients. Their *motivation* at the beginning was more biomedical and shifted to being more holistic/biopsychosocial. They were trying to survive residency and meet their basic needs such as eating and sleeping. Over the course of their careers, their *motivation* shifted from an emphasis on curing to caring when they realized that only part of their work involved curing; many more patients required them to help them over long periods of time, such as those with chronic illness. Their *motivation* also shifted from an emphasis on control to support. These physicians discovered that so much is not under their control and that supporting patients to the best that they could was a better attitude. As their motivation evolved, their *capacity* developed. At the beginning, a culture of emotional detachment diminished their empathy. But they grew in becoming comfortable with their own feelings and dealing with emotions in their practices. Physicians reported that there were a number of sources for that capacity: innate aspects of their personality; what they learned in their individual upbringing and how their families handled emotions; spiritual factors that made them more open to emotions and compassion; and learning about compassion in various roles in their lives, such as individual experiences, volunteering, teaching, and personal experiences inside and outside their homes (Uygur, 2012).

Becoming intentional about the compassion trichotomy in your life path

This compassion trichotomy provides one way clinicians can recover compassion in their careers. Uygur's study conveys how this unfolded in her sample, but the dynamic is implicit, and the events that helped physicians may have been a combination of intentional choices to grow and fortuitous circumstances (e.g., a good mentor or attending physician, family influences, significant others who helped them, powerful life experiences that challenged their thinking). One way, then, to recover and maintain compassionate caring in your career is to be more conscious of and intentional with this dynamic. The compassion trichotomy becomes a kind of flywheel in our lives in which we are mindful of what our connections are like and what we might learn in them. What we learn deepens our motivation for compassion and our understanding of it. With that increased insight and energy, our capacity for compassion increases. It is the dynamic that Francis W. Peabody described in his famous quote from 1927:

> *Time, sympathy and understanding must be lavishly dispensed, but the reward is to be found in that personal bond which forms the greatest satisfaction of the practice of medicine. One of the essential qualities of the clinician is interest in humanity, for the secret of the care of the patient is in caring for the patient. (p. 882)*

Clinicians hate losing their compassion and want to recover it

While there is much to be concerned about in terms of the loss of empathy and compassion documented in studies of clinicians in their early careers, Uygur's study illustrates that this is not necessarily what will happen for the rest of their careers in health care. Not all clinicians remain with a deficit in compassionate care if they happen to have lost it while in training or in practice. Many go back to the drawing board on what it means to have compassionate care in their practices. In a state of burnout, compassion fatigue, or whatever you want to call it, there is certainly the option of giving up and either leaving the profession or continuing to practice and inflicting your unhappy, uncompassionate self on all your patients for the rest of your career. But other clinicians do not want to see themselves continue this way. They do not like to see themselves treating patients in depersonalized, inadequate ways. They do not like to see how they are not the caring people they used to be. They do not like to see how their patients are getting poorer care (if they have the courage to really look at their effect on patients). They are unhappy with their cynicism and emotional suppression. Their loved ones get tired of them being this way because they are not unhappy only at work; their foul inner emotional state is sensed at home and with friends. What happens is that many clinicians rebuild compassionate care in themselves again on their own or with the help of others who have previously recovered from this compassion deficit and burnout.

The dangers of habituating to the positive aspects of our work

Helping professionals who help people in the worst of situations can come to take for granted how wonderful the work they do is. This is true in any profession. You can become an excellent car mechanic, and solving car problems can become routine. You lose a sense of wonder about your work and the achievement that your skill level represents. In helping professions, people who are suffering and vulnerable often open up automatically to their helpers. While a therapist might say to him- or herself, "Here's another depressed person I've got to do an intake on," for that person it may be the result of a long road to see that therapist, and the person is now fully disclosing that suffering. In medicine, we encounter people at the most difficult of times in their lives, and we can become accustomed to another critical surgery, another intubation, another death. Not only do we become desensitized to how difficult these things are, we can forget how incredible the work we get to do is. Somehow, helping professionals have to find a way to keep from becoming numb to how wonderful the work they do is. We need to be careful when we say to ourselves, "It's just my job." "It's just what I do." There can be a way that we devalue what we are doing and short-circuit a way to keep being rejuvenated in our work.

CONVERGENCE OF RESEARCH ON THE IMPORTANCE OF AUGMENTING POSITIVE FACTORS TO BUFFER BURNOUT AND RECOVER COMPASSIONATE CARING

To thrive in this difficult profession, not merely survive, clinicians must attend to and cultivate the positive aspects of doing this work. To prevent burnout, to achieve satisfaction and fulfillment, and to recover compassionate caring as the foundation of helping work, it is absolutely necessary to work on maintaining and cultivating the positive resources within clinicians and in health care work environments. What is fascinating from a scientific perspective is that different lines of research are all converging on this common theme. Research on physician job satisfaction, physician resilience, emotional regulation, and compassion all affirm the importance of

devoting regular and focused energy to nurturing the positive aspects as well as dealing well with the negative. Epstein (2014) notes that the literature on physician well-being has tended to focus on maintaining work–life balance by protecting time away from work. He proposes that while this is important, we should also be examining how to bring more joy to work of medicine. As he puts it, "The opposite of burnout is engagement, being fully present in one's work and deriving meaning and nourishment from it, even in moments of conflict, unhappiness, tough decisions, and difficult tasks" (Epstein, 2014, p. 282). A growing number of researchers and clinicians have also noted the limits of only an empathy approach and the importance of a compassion approach. As Epstein (2014) summarizes this, "in contrast to empathic reflection, enacted compassion appears to be associated with a sense of reward, meaning, and purpose. This view suggests that compassion is nourishing to the healer as well as the patient" (p. 283). There is now a convergence of thinking and research on the importance of compassion in medicine and its positive role for patient care and for clinician well-being. In the next several sections, I will highlight some of the research— first on physician satisfaction, then physician resilience, and finally compassion satisfaction. I will then discuss some general guidelines on individual and organizational interventions to help clinicians recover compassionate caring in their careers.

CLINICIAN SATISFACTION

What makes physicians happy?
Scheurer, McKean, Miller, and Wetterneck (2009) reviewed 97 studies from 1970 through 2007 that quantitatively assessed physician

satisfaction or identified factors associated with physician satisfaction. Reporting on the Community Tracking Study physician survey, physician satisfaction was generally high and stable from 1996 to 2001, around 80% for both primary care physicians and specialists. The percentage of primary care physicians who reported being very satisfied went down from 42% to 38%, with no significant decline for specialists. Several other studies found modest declines.

Age, gender, and specialty factors in physician satisfaction

Intrinsic factors of physician satisfaction are factors that are not changeable, such as age, gender, and physician specialty. In terms of age, there is a weak association with age when it is analyzed as a continuous variable. When it is analyzed by age groups, there is a U-shaped association; the youngest and oldest physicians are most satisfied, although this was not found in some studies of primary care physicians. There is the possibility that the higher satisfaction among older physicians may be due to fewer satisfied physicians leaving the profession. In terms of gender, Scheurer et al. (2009) reported that it was difficult to make any clear conclusions because of the heterogeneity of satisfaction measures and confounding variables. They reported that they did not find overall gender differences in the national studies, the Physician Worklife Study and the Community Tracking Study. However, the Physician Worklife Study did reveal some differences in certain aspects of satisfaction. Women physicians tended to report more satisfaction with their relationships with colleagues and patients but reported less satisfaction regarding pay, autonomy, resources, and community relationships. In terms of race,

Scheurer et al. did not find many studies examining this and recommended more research in this area. Of the five studies they found, four studies found no differences, and one study found lower satisfaction among minorities in a sample of preventive medicine physicians. In terms of physician specialty, pediatricians tend to have the highest satisfaction, and general internal medicine tends to have lower satisfaction. Again, the reviewers noted a difficulty in making generalization based on the heterogeneity of the studies.

Extrinsic factors in physician satisfaction

In terms of extrinsic factors, job demands pertain to workload, work stress/pressure, and work hours. Nine of the 10 studies found that increased job demand is associated with more dissatisfaction. Regarding workload, interestingly, physicians tend to be dissatisfied when there is too much or too little work. Of the few studies they had, most found dissatisfaction to be moderately associated with on-call frequency. The reviewers concluded that, in terms of subjective factors, dissatisfaction tends to be found when there is an imbalance between the expected stress and the experienced stress, pressure, or workload. But there is less of an association with workload when satisfaction is analyzed by the objective work hours or workload. Regarding part-time versus full-time status, there are not many studies. Two of the three studies did not find any relationship, but one found there was more satisfaction with full-time status. In terms of job control and autonomy, most studies found a strong association between satisfaction and having control over aspects in the workplace. Having positive interactions and support with colleagues is moderately associated with physician satisfaction.

Amount of time spent on the most meaningful work buffers burnout

Indirectly, it is showing more and more in research that staying connected to the deep satisfaction of practicing medicine is critical to the well-being of clinicians. But there are even studies showing this directly. Shanafelt et al. (2009) asked physicians in a large academic medical center what was the most meaningful part of their work. Of the 465 physicians who responded, 68% said that it was patient care, 19% said it was research, 9% said it was education, and 3% said it was administration. But that was not the main finding of the study. With 34% of the sample meeting the criteria for burnout, the researchers were able to analyze what factors contributed to burnout and satisfaction in the work. They found four factors that predicted burnout: spending less than 20% of one's time on what was the most meaningful activity to that physician, being over 55 years old, being a generalist, and the number of hours the physician works a week. The biggest predictor was the first factor. If a physician could spend more than 20% of his or her time on what was most meaningful to him or her, the odds of burnout would significantly decrease.

What keeps physicians going?

While many studies on physician satisfaction focus on what makes them unhappy, stressed, and burned out, there are some studies that examine how physicians sustain compassionate approaches despite the barriers to this in the current problems of medical practice. Branch et al. (2017) researched this question by studying the responses of 68 faculty physicians who had previously completed an intensive program on medical humanism about what motivates them to teach and practice humanistically and what the barriers to doing this were. About half

were from primary care specialties, and the rest were from all types of specialties. There were five themes that emerged about what motivated them. First, the most commonly mentioned theme was that they identified with the humanist values of compassion, respect, integrity, excellence, altruism, and service summed up in the phrase, "It is who I am" (Branch et al., 2017, p. 2322). Second, they desired to provide the kind of care they or their family would want. Third, they loved the connection they experience with patients and reported that the satisfaction of this connection was rewarding and protected them against burnout. Fourth, being a role model and wanting to pass on these values was a major motivating factor for them. Fifth, they were able to sustain themselves by "being present in the moment" (Branch et al., 2017, p. 2324). When they were with patients, they brought their full attention and presence to the person in front of them and let the external stresses go to the background for that period of time.

Barriers high-performing physicians experience and what helps them

When asked what the barriers were to practicing humanistically, the physicians in the Branch et al. (2017) study reported first, not having enough time because of things like documentation, phone calls, insurance, too much to do, and "the system." Second, feeling stress was a barrier, which included all the time factors but also things like feeling fatigued, challenging patients, psychosocial patient problems, feeling demoralized, organizational hassles, and work pressures. Third, the culture of medicine was a barrier, with its "hidden curriculum" of medical training, the business culture of the organization, or "a kind of hidden bureaucratic curriculum of the practice" (Branch et al., 2017, p. 2324); and in this culture was a staff cynicism and negativity toward humanistic values. Fourth, the final type of barrier was called an "episodic burnout and discouragement" (Branch et al., 2017, p. 2325). Interestingly, the researchers noted the very low rates of burnout in this group of physicians that appeared to be connected to their passion for these humanistic values. This is the way they think of themselves at their core as physicians, and it "sustained" them through all the barriers. Despite this sustaining core identity, the researchers noted that the physicians were still experiencing a great deal of turmoil and stress and did not have enough collegial support. As Branch et al. (2017) put it, "physicians portrayed themselves as isolated individuals heroically placing their fingers in the dike and hoping that their individual humanism would save the day" (p. 2327).

CLINICIAN RESILIENCE

Definition of resilience

Jackson, Firtko, and Edenborough (2007) define resilience "as the ability of an individual to adjust to adversity, maintain equilibrium, retain some sense of control over their environment, and continue to move on in a positive manner" (p. 3). They define workplace adversity "as any negative, stressful, traumatic, or difficult situation or episode of hardship that is encountered in the occupational setting" (Jackson et al., 2007, p. 3). On the basis of a literature review on resilience in the face of workplace adversity, Jackson et al. propose five specific self-development strategies to help build this personal resilience: (a) building positive nurturing professional relationships and networks, (b) maintaining positivity, (c) developing emotional insight, (d) achieving life balance and spirituality, and (e) becoming more reflective.

Correlates of clinician resilience

In a review of 13 studies of resilience in primary health care professionals, Robertson et al. (2016) concluded that resilience is a multifactorial and evolutionary process in which positive adaptation emerges from discrete personal traits and experience. In the ongoing encounter with stress, the health care professional continues to perform well, is able to adapt to changing circumstances, and is also able to maintain a sense of professional and personal fulfillment. The traits of having high self-determination, high persistence, and low harm avoidance appear to provide the foundation of resilience. The level of workplace demand (i.e., the volume, intensity, and controllability of the workload), along with external supports both at work and outside work, also affect resilience. Several studies indicate the importance of personal meaning, sense of purpose, and vocation in resilience. But Robertson et al. caution that it is not clear whether these drive resilience or result from being resilient.

Study on four themes characterizing physician resilience

Jensen, Trollope-Kumar, Waters, and Everson's (2008) research found four themes that characterized physician resilience: (a) attitudes and perspectives, (b) balance and prioritization, (c) effective practice management style, and (d) supportive professional and personal relationships.

Attitudes and perspectives

First, resilient physicians tend to have attitudes and perspectives in which they value the physician role and have self-awareness. In terms of valuing their physician role, they have a sense of meaning because of the contribution they are able to make in people's lives. They find ways to maintain their interest and commitment to their role.

They also have an acceptance of the demands of the work but find ways to organize their lives so that they can manage this. In terms of self-awareness, they gain a sense of their expertise, along with having realistic expectations in the work. They are able to accept themselves and their personal limits with humility and are able to forgive themselves for errors they have made.

Balance and prioritization

Second, resilient physicians seek balance and prioritization in their professional and personal arenas. In their professional arena, they prioritize by being able to set limits, saying no, and being willing to initiate changes or restrictions in their practices. They also prioritize continuing professional development using four strategies: (a) they focus on emphasizing the education they need by focusing on what they need for their patients and letting other material go, (b) they schedule professional development such as scheduling it a year in advance or allotting half an hour a day to read journals, (c) they seek out peer learning by directly asking colleagues or relying on practice-based small groups that also indirectly provide professional support, and finally (d) they teach others as a way to keep stimulated in their role and staying current. In the personal arena, resilient physicians are able to honor themselves by making sure they take care of themselves by setting limits, taking regular time out for recreation and exercise, and scheduling regular vacations before they really need them. Also, taking time to reflect on the philosophical questions that arise in practice and relying on their spirituality helps them gain perspective.

Effective practice management style

Third, having an effective practice management style is a common characteristic shared by resilient physicians. They recognize the business aspects of their practices and will address time planning, systematic patient scheduling, and making sure paperwork is regularly done. They tend to be conscious about what level of workload they want to have and learn how to restrict other professional responsibilities. They make sure they hire quality staff who will create a smoothly running office. They know how to delegate tasks and how to create a team among the staff. They often are in group practices that provide collegial support, call coverage, and mentorship. They have chosen the best payment system for their practice with regard to billing and payment. They have good technology and computing for records and communication but are able to set limits on things such as email after hours.

Supportive professional and personal relationships

Fourth, resilient physicians have developed good professional and personal support. For professional support, they have a group of peers they can rely on to discuss stressful issues and difficult cases. They have consultants to whom they can refer when they cannot manage certain issues in patients. They also tend to have multidisciplinary teams that provide additional support in patient care. In terms of personal support, they have prioritized having supportive partners, family, and friends. They realize personal support is essential but that it is easy to lose if they do not put time and energy into it. Interestingly, it was also found that resilient physicians had their own family physician to have someone to help them with their health or stresses, as well as to avoid getting into the problem of treating oneself or one's family members.

Criticism of the idea of physician resilience

Even though I have reported some of the research on clinician resilience, it is important that we put the whole idea of clinician resilience in perspective. Physicians and other clinicians are some of the most resilient people one will ever know. One has to have an incredible amount of resilience to become a clinician in the first place. We should not conclude that because we become burned out and discouraged that it was because were not resilient. As Schwenk (2018) put it, "While appropriate in moderation—resilience is a worthy trait in all careers and lives—it is a fine line between promoting resilience and blaming physicians for being too weak to cope in the face of unrelenting pressures" (p. 1544). Many clinicians are resentful about being told to just practice mindfulness and be more resilient. They feel that society and the business of health care have taken advantage of their resilience, and there is only so much that they can take of this. Rebekah Bernard (2016) argued this in her article "To Prevent Burnout, Physicians Need Less Resilience, Not More." She made the point that physicians really want to take care of patients, but over the years they have accommodated so many reimbursement and administrative requirements that it has taken them away from the patient care that is the most important reason for the whole work. What is more important is that we protect the core of compassionate caring in our clinicians and be realistic about the personal and systemic factors that bury that core.

THE ROLE OF COMPASSION SATISFACTION

Another avenue to recovering compassion in your career and maintaining it is to look at and use the research on compassion satisfaction. In examining some of these studies, one again can notice the dynamic of positive emotions

explained by Barbara Fredrickson (2004) in chapter 10. What is helpful for our purposes here is to review some of the research in terms of what qualities are associated with compassion satisfaction. While the research is still in the early stages, it already provides guidance for the kinds of qualities clinicians can cultivate in themselves to increase their compassion satisfaction.

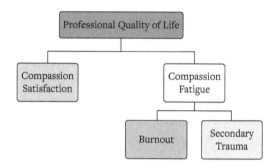

FIGURE 16.3 Diagram of Professional Quality of Life Scale (Stamm, 2010, p. 8).

As discussed in chapter 13, the field of the helping professions now recognizes that professional quality of life is not simply the level of burnout a clinician has or does not have. Professional quality of life is "the quality one feels in relation to their work as a helper" (Stamm, 2010, p. 8). As seen in figure 16.3, it includes the negative experiences helpers have under *compassion fatigue*, which is further described as consisting of *burnout* and *secondary trauma*. The positive experience helpers have when working with patients or clients is called *compassion satisfaction*. Its importance is described in the following way:

> *Not all health care workers engaged in traumatic or emotionally demanding work fall prey to the stressors of their practice. The motivation of these workers to provide social support and care to others is driven by the satisfaction derived from the work of helping others. It can be concluded then that compassion satisfaction*

is a vital part of being emotionally fulfilled by one's work in the human services field. (Slatten, Carson, & Carson, 2011, p. 326)

Compassion satisfaction is the positive sentiment the clinician has in empathically connecting with patients and the feeling of achievement in providing care. It refers to the positive aspects a clinician derives from helping others, feeling positively about colleagues, or the clinician's ability to contribute to his or her work setting or the greater good of society. Compassion satisfaction contributes to a sense of well-being as a helper who has an increased sense of self-efficacy and fulfillment in helping work. Such people feel more invigorated in their work and are energized further to contribute helping others who need care (Stamm, 2010; Slatten et al., 2011; Zeidner & Hadar, 2014). Compassion satisfaction also acts as a buffer against the negative consequences of working with people who have experienced trauma. Higher levels of compassion satisfaction in clinicians are related to decreased compassion fatigue, secondary traumatic stress, and burnout (LaFauci Schutt & Marotta, 2011).

Major study of compassion satisfaction with physicians

Gleichgerrcht and Decety (2013) examined compassion satisfaction in a very large study with 7,584 physicians. They found that physicians with higher levels of compassion satisfaction tended to be those who were high in empathic concern, perspective taking, and altruism. Physicians who were motivated to help a person in need or distress while being able to distinguish their patients' feelings from their own could experience positive emotions in helping patients. Physicians who experienced higher personal distress and who were more alexithymic (difficulty

describing feelings, difficulty identifying feelings, and externally oriented thinking) tended to have more compassion fatigue and less compassion satisfaction. Thus, those physicians who had difficulty with emotionally regulating their negative emotions and who had difficulty identifying and describing their emotions were more prone to the burnout symptoms of emotional exhaustion, detachment, and a low sense of personal accomplishment. But physicians with the desire to help others along with the ability to regulate one's own feelings and maintain a self–other distinction mentally were more able to be compassionate and to have a sense of satisfaction in that.

Compassion satisfaction associated with more effective coping and emotional intelligence

We need to change our outdated notions that detachment and suppression of the emotional life in the physician are considered more scientific or necessary for emotional survival in the medical professions. Clinicians who have higher levels of emotional intelligence and healthy emotional regulation abilities are happier and give much better patient care. In a study of 93 physicians (across various specialties) and 89 mental health practitioners (psychiatrists, psychologists, and social workers), Zeidner and Hadar (2014) examined predictors of compassion satisfaction. They found that emotional competencies (trait emotional intelligence and ability-based emotion management), positive affect, and problem-focused coping significantly predicted compassion satisfaction. Clinicians who are emotionally intelligent exercise better emotion-management skills, whereby they can regulate their own emotions and deal effectively with the emotions of their patients.

The exercise of these emotional competencies enhances the experience of satisfaction with the work. Furthermore, the researchers speculate that the experience of compassion satisfaction in turn feeds back into increasing positive emotional states, which has been found to increase the clinician's cognitive flexibility and creative ideas in treating patients as well as increase the coping abilities and internal resources of the clinician (Fredrickson, 1998; Keyes & Haidt, 2003). Zeidner and Hadar also found that this emotional competency was associated with increased levels of problem-focused coping. More than that, problem-focused coping mediates the relationship between emotional competency and compassion satisfaction. *Mediates* means it helps explain or provide the mechanism for how emotional competency predicts compassion satisfaction. This is interesting because in our medical culture that downplays emotional competence, it is often thought that being problem focused is characteristic mainly of the nonemotional aspects of clinicians. This study showed that emotionally intelligent people tend to select more effective coping methods that lead to more adaptive results, what Zeidner and Hadar (2014) call "emotional intelligence in action" (p. 94). Highly emotionally intelligent clinicians can read the situation and themselves more accurately and select the most appropriate problem-focused strategies. Rather than using emotion-focused (focused on relieving their own emotions) or avoidance coping (wanting to escape from or deny the situation), highly emotionally competent clinicians are more engaged in the situation and can emotionally handle being engaged in the situation. This experience of successfully exercising their competencies in helping another person is fulfilling—hence, compassion satisfaction.

Improving empathy and emotion-management skills can increase compassion satisfaction

In short, another route to recovering and maintaining compassion satisfaction is developing empathic concern and perspective-taking ability; putting energy into improving one's emotional intelligence and ability to regulate emotions seems to be a kind of buffer against compassion fatigue. Working on one's ability to identify and describe one's emotional experience and being comfortable working with emotions would also be skills to keep developing. Improving one's emotional competencies lays the foundation to successfully managing one's own emotions and the patients' emotions. *It makes sense that physicians who have difficulty with emotions in general would not be as satisfied in medicine—because emotions are a central part of the illness experience, and physicians hate not doing something well.* If they are not good at reading and managing emotions, it makes sense they would want to avoid them or detach from them. But when that happens, the possibility of feeling compassion satisfaction decreases as well. To improve a clinicians' compassion satisfaction, then, one route would be to help clinicians get the skills to work with emotions, both their own and their patients'. When they feel more competent managing these emotions, the work will become more enjoyable, and compassion would be likely to be recovered and maintained.

Emergency room physicians with the highest compassion satisfaction

Surveying United Kingdom National Health Service emergency physicians, Dasan, Gohil, Cornelius, and Taylor (2015) found that compassion satisfaction decreased somewhat in the first 10 years of practice but then increased after

20 years. The researchers speculate that this may due to a survivor bias, in which the more unhappy and burned-out physicians have left this work. A third of the physicians reported that the work stress had contributed to them being irritable with patients and colleagues and reduced their standards of care. A third reported that the stress had led to mistakes that were potentially harmful to a patient, and 11% reported that they did make mistakes that harmed a patient. Those physicians who were most fatigued reported more perceived lack of control and/or less support at work. Those who were more satisfied had strategies that helped them maintain or regain control at work, such as physical activity that gave them time to destress and to think, or a five-minute tea break when they were becoming irritable. Support from colleagues (including fellow physicians, secretaries, porters, and cleaners) was often mentioned as key to reducing or preventing stress and compassion fatigue, while those who were fatigued did not mention support or reported how poor team relationships negatively affected them. Having variety in the work, such as having a split between clinical and managerial roles, helped. Being motivated to provide good patient care under pressure, whether the patient was seriously ill or not, characterized a number of the most satisfied physicians.

Factors associated with compassion satisfaction in trauma therapists

In a study with 104 therapists specializing in treatment of survivors of trauma, particularly sexual abuse, Killian (2008) found that social support, especially from friends, family, and community, was highly predictive of compassion satisfaction. In fact, it was the most significant factor, along with having a reasonable number of work hours and feeling an internal locus of control at work. Being able to debrief or process what happens in clinical care with people who understand this work is very helpful. A colleague in the same field knows what the work is like, what patients are like, and why it is stressful. No time is needed to explain the overall work to such a colleague. It can be done formally in team meetings but also in relatively brief conversations in the hallway or some other removed area in the hospital or clinic (Killian, 2008).

RECONNECTING OR STAYING CONNECTED TO THE POSITIVE DIMENSIONS OF CLINICAL PRACTICE

The positive experience of compassion is a by-product of helping, not the primary goal

What emerges over and over again in research even from quite different theories or models is that somehow the clinician needs to have some positive experience in the work. It might be called compassion satisfaction, engagement, personal accomplishment, fulfillment, or positive emotion. This should not be understood as the clinician needs to be rewarded for his or her work. We all know clinicians who receive a lot of rewards in terms of money, respect, or fame for their work but are not happy in clinical work. This positive experience of the compassionate caring mindset is not what the clinician seeks for helping others; what the clinician seeks first and foremost is responding to suffering. Actually, when a clinician primarily seeks the positive rewarding feeling in helping others, it short-circuits the compassion mindset, because the clinician's own needs are primary; it is a self-focused helping. "I help you so that I can feel good about myself." The positive experience of the compassion mindset is a kind of by-product of the compassionate response, yet it plays an important role in the "engine" of compassion. Clinicians say things like, "I hate how people suffer, and I want to be there to lessen their suffering." "I found that I had the capacity to help people, and I don't want to turn away." It is a paradoxical willingness to notice and be moved by another's suffering, to enter that suffering person's world because you hate what suffering does to people—it does not make you feel good. Yet responding to the suffering in the attempt to alleviate it is a positive experience.

Neurophysiological and psychological mechanisms for the role of positive emotions have been presented throughout this book

This book has presented the psychological and neurophysiological mechanisms for how positive emotions result from the compassionate mindset and how those positive emotions in turn energize clinicians as well as broaden and build their inner resources. Recall the experiment by Klimecki, Leiberg, Ricard, and Singer (2014), in which the research participants were given empathy training and viewed videos of suffering—they reported increased distressing negative emotions. When they received some training in gaining a compassionate mindset, they experienced an increase in positive emotions (e.g., wanting to be helpful), and their negative emotions returned back to their baseline. The positive aspects of being in a compassionate mindset do not erase the negative feelings, but they seem to help the clinician carry the suffering of the others differently. Barbara Fredrickson's (2004) theory on how positive emotions work differently than negative emotions to broaden and build a person's inner resources and resilience is an important

explanation for their role in compassionate work (see chapter 10).

To begin recovery, clinicians must articulate and work through their emotional pain

In their work helping physicians recover from burnout and find well-being again, Pfifferling and Gilley (1999) articulate this connection between feeling emotional pain and how it can affect a sense of joy in clinical practice:

> To start healing, it's necessary to admit that there's been a lot of pain. Along with it, there's likely to have been a lot of frustration, anger, sadness, loss and even fear. Admitting that we have these feelings is one key to recapturing joy. When we suppress pain, frustration, anger and fear, we simultaneously incapacitate our ability to experience peace, love, excitement, enthusiasm and joy. Because our emotions are integrally related, it's impossible to disable some without handicapping them all. No body parts exist without function (even though there are some we can survive without). Our emotions are the same. Paralyzed emotions are just as dangerous to our health as an atrophied limb. (p. 38).

The first step in recovering from burnout and reconstellating the compassion mindset is to get in touch with and articulate all the negative feelings and thoughts. This requires a willingness to tolerate this state for a while and to do a kind of grief work, grief work because there is a part of you that has died or been lost.

Retreat process with other clinicians to recover

Reconnecting with the positive aspects of your work can be accomplished in many ways. In retreats we have had with physicians and nurses, the reconnecting with the positive experience of the clinical work is an important part of the retreat. In the past, we had work retreats that were focused only on having the group articulate and problem solve the sources of our stress and burnout. These were limited in their success. When we integrated a reconnecting with what they love about the work, it was much more effective. We called one the Journey of the Physician from Ideality to Reality or some variation on that title, depending on the type of clinicians or staff group that we had. Whether they had been in practice for many years or in residency, we would take time near the beginning of the day to ask the participants why they became physicians, nurses, and so on. The first time we did this, we were not prepared for how much clinicians would share about why they aspired for their particular profession or how they ended up in their specialty. Often, they told stories of how they became aware of a deep desire to help people. It might have been loving science and solving problems, and then discovering how meaningful it is to use this love to help people who are suffering. Often the story was one of personal pain because of a loved one or even themselves who went through some significant injury or illness; this experience gripped them in the dynamic of wounded healer. From there in the retreat, we might move to "the great moments in healing" that they had experienced. Later in the retreat, we would then move to what has not been going well in their professional work, the problems they experience at the clinic or in the hospital. Depending on the type of retreat, this might move into problem solving or simply just grieving the disillusionment or discouragement they feel. As we ended these retreats, we would allow time to reflect on the whole retreat but never try to resolve all the issues or "make it all better." Yet almost every time, there was a renewed spirit both individually and collectively. The combination of reconnecting to what clinicians loved about the work and what the reality has been, all shared with colleagues in the safe and supportive atmosphere, brought new energy and creativity to respond to what is not going well in a work setting. Looking back at years of doing these kinds of retreats, I see how they came straight out of the broaden-and-build theory of positive emotions that Barbara Fredrickson (2004) articulated.

Optimum recovery occurs when the organization has a systemic plan for recovery of C²

It is very important in attempts to help clinicians recover their compassionate caring mindset not to do these "interventions" without having a wider organizational plan. The administrator who reluctantly supports time for a retreat but does not have a wider plan to create a supportive and engaged clinical work environment is not likely to help things for the long term. As I discussed in chapter 15, an organizational commitment to creating a compassionate caring culture with a variety of practices and interventions is much more likely to be effective.

The choice we must make if we do not have organizational support

Sometimes, however, individuals want to recover the compassion mindset in their profession but do not have an organization that will support this effort. While we know that the biggest predictors of burnout are a toxic organizational culture and a poor supervisor, at those times we are left with a choice about what to do to take care of or neglect the soul of our caring. A while ago I encountered an elderly clinician who had clearly lost the soul of his caring for some time. He was emotionally detached, cynical, and grumpy; he was really smart, but he was a curmudgeon. Some of his patients would privately tell me how they did not like to see him because his detachment and self-focus were not helpful to them. I had two insights as a young clinician at the time. One was that patients really can pick up when we have become negative. The other was that I could become just like this elderly clinician, a bitter detached clinician doing perfunctory clinical work; and I did not want my patients or my friends saying this about me.

The courage to do this for yourself no matter the organizational situation

When you are faced with the fact that you work in a system too sick to renew itself and that you are on your way to getting sick right along with it, but you do not want that, then you have to make a radical and courageous move to recover it for yourself. Our compassionate core is precious and needs care. It is what helps our patients the most and what energizes us to continue this work. Clinicians who are on the recovery and amplification curve of C^2 in figure 16.1 are often clinicians who had to do this on their own, without the best situation, training, or organization. It usually begins with disillusioned clinicians declaring to themselves that they will not allow this to continue to a complete loss of compassion for the rest of their careers. In what follows, I will summarize some of the ways that clinicians piece together to recover the soul of their caring.

Stories on how clinicians flipped back into the compassion mindset

When I have asked individual clinicians to tell me the story of how they recovered compassion in their work, I have heard many different ways, but all have the theme of somehow flipping them back into the compassion mindset. One of those ways is that these clinicians often decide they are going to teach. If their colleagues are going to practice in a soulless way, they are going to make sure the next generation gets a better shot at it. So, they teach a class, let students shadow them, take medical students, or invite residents to shadow them. Clinicians practice better medicine when they have students with them. The students bring out the best self in the clinician. In fact, when organizations and individual clinicians refuse to teach at all (usually under the excuse that it gets them too far behind or they lose money), I become suspicious that they do not like the way they might appear to those students, and so they stop wanting to teach. In asking clinicians to help me with teaching or mentoring students going into health care, I have had physicians and nurses regularly thank me for asking them and express to me that they hope I ask them again. A number who teach will actually directly tell the students that teaching keeps them in touch with what is important in medicine. While it takes time, it is an investment in the clinicians of the future and a way for physicians to keep themselves connected to what they love about medicine.

Recovering the compassion mindset in volunteer work

Another type of activity that seems to help clinicians who want to recover their compassion is taking time to give their skills away, such as volunteering in a clinic for homeless people, disaster relief, and going on a medical mission trip. Freed of the pressures of documentation and reimbursement requirements, they seem to get a direct experience of the compassionate caring mindset that renews them. They come back, sometimes from physically working extremely hard, with a renewed awareness of why they are really in health care, that this compassionate caring is what is most fulfilling. This should not be considered as a sole intervention or as the only thing you need to do.

Usually, what happens is that clinicians have this experience and then readjust their priorities afterward, either by changing the way they work or changing the place where they work.

Research study on decreased burnout after mission trips

Campbell et al. (2009) tracked burnout levels for a group of mostly physicians and nurses who went on volunteer short-term mission trips to South America. Before the trip, most were in the moderate range of burnout in terms of emotional exhaustion, depersonalized attitudes toward patients, and a reduced sense of personal accomplishment. After the trip, their levels of burnout decreased and continued to improve even six months later. Specifically, emotional exhaustion significantly decreased, and the sense of personal accomplishment (PA) increased. Depersonalization showed a decrease, but it was not statistically significant. As the researchers put it,

> the major finding of this study is counter-intuitive: that medical personnel who are emotionally exhausted, have an impersonal response towards their patients, and lack of sense of PA (moderately burned out) benefit by working hard with numerous patients in an international context. (Campbell et al., 2009, p. 635)

The researchers speculated that the reasons for the change may include a revitalization that occurred with these professionals feeling that they were making a difference and being appreciated by patients with high needs. Perhaps they gained a renewed perspective on their own lives and situations, getting back in touch with what they love about medicine or increasing a sense of meaning in the work. Whatever it was, they left a stressful environment in which they complained of lacking control over personal time, feeling pressured to see more patients in less time, dealing with administrative hassles, and having too much time on call. Yet they returned to that same environment with the same stressors, and they viewed it differently; this effect lasted even six months later.

Your intention in doing volunteer work is key

The potential booby trap in this type of recovery attempt is that it has to be an activity that engages your compassion primarily. That is, if you say, "I am going to volunteer at the homeless shelter in order to make myself feel better," what we know about the neuroscience of compassion is that the compassion mindset will not get constellated. If giving to another person is primarily motivated as a way to help ourselves, then it is not really compassion and does not make us feel better. It has to be something that brings us out of ourselves and back in touch with the interconnectedness of all human beings and the desire to relieve all beings from suffering. One's intention in going on a mission trip is an important factor in whether it will help with clinician burnout. There are a variety of reasons clinicians go on mission trips, and they may not be related to genuinely altruistic intentions. Clinicians may go on mission trips in order to portray a public compassionate persona to gain admiration, prestige, or some other social gain. Health care organizations might require or pressure their clinicians to go on mission trips or do volunteer clinics, and this would obviously not be conducive to burnout prevention. Going on a mission trip can be a form of escaping or seeking adventure and so will not result in the recovery of compassion mindset. Also, an intriguing question is that while there is usually a plethora of local opportunities for work with high-need patients who cannot pay for the services, why is a mission trip considered more desirable? We all know clinicians who actively avoid local patients who cannot pay for services or patients who are profoundly suffering. What makes a clinician view a mission trip as a worthwhile endeavor, but not doing similar work in one's own setting or community? There are a number of possible answers, but for our purposes, being honest and self-aware about our own intentions is a critical factor in whether volunteering or mission work leads to a rejuvenation of compassion.

The need for long-term organizational and individual interventions

While there is pressure in the field to have short-term interventions to decrease the high rates of burnout, in the end, it is a long-term systemic issue requiring changes in how we train clinicians, how we organize clinical practice at the organizational level and the societal level, and how we help clinicians realize that surviving and thriving in medicine requires an ongoing commitment to maintain personal well-being in this work. This is no different from what happens with our patients. We can give a medication for a high cholesterol or hemoglobin A1c in the short term, but we encourage our patients to make lifestyle changes and think long term to manage their illnesses better. Some patients think a cholesterol medication is a way to keep eating as much red meat as they want. But changing habits gives the patient more life. With clinicians, this means that we need to condition our minds for a marathon, not a series of hundred-meter dashes. What is being affirmed in recent research from diverse professions is that if you want to survive and thrive in a clinical profession, the clinicians who are faring the best are those who are engaging in a regular mind-training practice that centers the clinician, enables emotional regulation, focuses cognitive abilities, and cultivates a compassionate caring approach to patient care.

How many clinicians discover this process of compassion recovery on their own?

As Uygur's (2012) research suggests, clinicians who recover their compassion are often figuring things out as they go. Unless clinicians are fortunate enough to have a mentor or colleague who has gone through this, they must piece together a strategy for how to recover from burnout and refind the compassion to animate their work. More and more clinicians are sharing their experiences of doing this both informally among colleagues or in writing, retreats, and conferences. For example, many clinicians have relied on Rachel Naomi Remen's work, such as *Kitchen Table Wisdom* (2006) and *The Human Patient* (1980). Paul Wright (2006) shared his recovery from burnout through his work with Mother Teresa. There are many physician writers who are discussing more healthy ways to view and practice medicine, such as Robin Youngson's book, *Time to Care: How to Love Your Patients and Your Job* (2012). Danielle Ofri helps clinicians reclaim the importance of emotions in her books *What Doctors Feel: How Emotions Affect the Practice of Medicine* (2013) and *Medicine in Translation: Journeys with My Patients* (2010). Ronald Epstein also provides a way to practice medicine that reclaims the compassionate core of medicine and discusses the helpfulness of mindfulness in *Attending: Medicine, Mindfulness, and Humanity* (2017). James Doty discusses the way the study of the science of compassion has transformed his perspective as well in *Into the Magic Shop: A Neurosurgeon's Quest to Discover the Mysteries of the Brain and the Secrets of the Heart* (2016).

As I explained in chapter 1, we are living in a paradigm shift to a compassion-centric paradigm in health care, and these writings are an indication that this is well underway.

Problem of perfunctory use of mindfulness interventions

Many medical, nursing, and mental health training programs are now implementing some type of self-care or stress-relieving practice. The specific practices taught are often chosen based on the particular experiences and expertise of those supervising the training. What is needed now is a wider understanding that provides the context for what we are doing with specific practices. For example, mindfulness meditation practices are most commonly being taught, especially as a growing body of research has documented the positive benefits to helping professionals. Yet there is a range of ways that mindfulness practices are done, and as occurs with any popular practice, there is a way in which core tenets of mindfulness become watered down or lost in the variety of ways it is taught and practiced. To the frustration of mindfulness experts, the mindfulness practices become used in a perfunctory manner, or the full potential of the practices is never fully realized because of limited knowledge about the practices.

Single interventions like mindfulness meditation must be part of a larger context for training and compassion recovery

Many clinicians are attesting to the benefits of practices like mindfulness meditation, but there is a way in which practices like these can be simplistically prescribed to the helping professional. "You need to start doing mindfulness; it really helped me be less stressed." "When I started doing yoga stretching exercises every day, I got so much more energy, and I was less bothered by the stresses of the day." So, your training program, hospital unit, or clinic starts a mindfulness training program or a yoga class for the staff. Is this helpful? Of course. But we need now to move a step further in training and clinical practice to understand that we need more than a single, simplistic, stress-relieving practice. It is really part of a mind training that is needed for this kind of work, ideally in an organizational culture that protects, cultivates, and supports a compassionate caring mindset. Clinicians have haphazardly stumbled onto this for many years. But we still need to understand that, just as we are training the minds of young clinicians by having them learn huge amounts of facts, develop the ability to problem solve clinical cases, and practice particular techniques, so do we need to devote time in training them what to do with their emotions and thoughts while doing this difficult work. We need to train their minds more completely than only training medical facts or how to do a particular therapy or surgery. We cannot train the mind with more facts. We must train the mind as it becomes pressured by more stresses and gorged by more facts. In that way, the mind can carry those stresses better and use those facts more beneficially.

Individual clinician interventions can be misused by administrators

There is a great danger, however, that this argument to maintain composure through the many hassles of the health care system will be misused by administrators—for example, to blame you for not being able to roll with the hassles. On one hand, a clinician can be a prima donna who tends to engage in "victim thinking" and whining. Humans do that. But on the other hand, administrators must be careful of making the mistake illustrated by the punchline "Floggings will continue until morale improves." Unfortunately, that is exactly the way many organizations work—and floggings do not increase compassion in an organization. Everyone bears responsibility to do the best that he or she can in a situation but also to always examine processes and problems to look for new ways to help a health delivery system be more efficient and positive. Those who have the power and the ability to influence health care systems must commit themselves to listening to what is occurring on the front lines of health care delivery and work to make it better. Those on the front lines of health care delivery must also be willing (as well as given the opportunity) to articulate and analyze recurring hassles and advocate for change.

Interventions should not focus only on preventing negative feelings and mental illness

Preventing yourself from having negative feelings does not mean you are thriving in your career. Preventing burnout does not mean you are functioning well as a clinician. One of the main themes of this book is that in order to prevent burnout, you need to combine a way to address the negative experiences you have but also cultivate the positive aspects of your work and your life. There has been much concern over the high levels of depression, addiction, and suicide among physicians compared to many other groups in society. This has led to important work in helping physicians be able to notice mental illness in themselves and have the courage to treat it. This happens particularly if there is a suicide among one of your colleagues. There can be very good and important organizational efforts to help clinicians recognize and seek help for mental disorders both in themselves and in each other. The problem is that focusing only on mental disorders among clinicians is only half of the answer. Decreasing the amount of mental illness does not mean we are increasing the overall mental health of clinicians.

Study of wellness-promotion practices

In a qualitative study of 130 primary care physicians, Weiner, Swain, Wolf, and Gottlieb (2001) found five types of wellness-promotion practices. First, they found a wellness-promotion practice that they called "relationships," in which physicians made sure they were spending time and involved with family, friends, and colleagues or involved in the community. Second, "religion or spirituality" was another theme; this included prayer, religious services, and involvement in religious activities. Third, there were "self-care practices" that included good nutrition, exercise, vacation, hobbies, meditation, avoiding drugs and alcohol, getting help for personal problems, or changing unhealthy relationships. Fourth, another set of wellness practices was called "work," in which physicians reported deriving satisfaction and/or meaning from their work, limiting their practice, and choosing a type of medical practice that fit them best. Finally, the fifth theme of wellness-practices was called "approaches to life." This included a general philosophical outlook and a specific way of implementing this outlook. Examples were responses such as maintaining a balance in one's life, being positive, and focusing on success. The key unifying idea was balancing various aspects of one's life. Physicians also completed a psychological well-being measure, and what emerged was that "approaches to life" was significantly more related to higher levels of psychological well-being than any other theme. What is affirmed in this study is that some philosophical outlook about how to balance one's life is most related to psychological well-being; and within the other themes, one can see the elements of the importance of meaning, religion, and spirituality.

Research on improving burnout and patient-centeredness with physicians

Krasner et al. (2009) tested a program that appears to be very useful in helping physicians. The researchers did an 8-week intensive course with 70 primary care physicians that was 2.5 hours a week, with one 7-hour retreat. There was then a 10-month maintenance phase in which they met 2.5 hours a month. The intensive course included mindfulness meditation training of various types (e.g., body scan, sitting meditation, walking meditation, and mindful movement). They reflected and wrote on a topic a week, then met together. Topics included being aware of unpleasant experiences during patient visits, clinical experiences that demonstrated perceptual biases and filters, burnout, meaning, boundaries and conflict management, self-care, and being present to suffering in end-of-life care. The researchers used an appreciative inquiry approach, examining successful work with difficult patient situations. The results were that these physicians reported significantly less burnout and improved well-being. Their overall mood and emotional stability improved. They also improved in using patient-centered approaches with increased perspective-taking empathy and psychosocial assessment. This study is useful for our purposes because it shows how a number of interventions combined together with the collegial support of the program is a way to help clinicians recover from burnout and become more patient centered.

PARALLEL INSIGHTS FROM THE INZOVU CURVE

Application of compassion science research in the memorial of the Rwandan genocide

We have relied on compassion science research to understand what it means practically for clinicians to stay in a compassion mindset. As we saw in the earliest chapters of this book, the empathic resonance in encounters with suffering can lead to personal distress in the clinician, which results in clinician withdrawal or conflicted care for the patient, or it can lead to a compassion response. In thinking about burnout in clinicians, there is a way in which they have become exhausted and demoralized in this work. In this chapter, we consider how they might recover, and we have used the science of compassion to examine this. Interestingly, the creators of the memorial of the Rwandan genocide were faced with the challenge of creating a museum that would not leave the visitors demoralized and paralyzed at the end. They used this same compassion science research to help visitors move more toward a compassion mindset when they left.

How to help visitors through the memorial of the Rwandan genocide

The Kigali Genocide Memorial houses the remains of 250,000 Rwandans who were killed in the genocide of 1994. The memorial is built with the intention of being an antidote to genocide and "teaching us and moving us to ensure we will never again be detached and complicit" (Calali, 2014, p. 3). One of the concerns in creating this museum was that visitors would have a profound emotional experience when learning about the 1994 genocide, but such a profound emotional experience does not necessarily transform the visitors. The UX for Good worked with the Aegis Trust, the organization that built and operates the memorial, to design the museum in such a way that it could help move the visitors from having this overwhelmingly negative emotional experience to one in which they would be hopeful and inspired to act on behalf of the victims of the genocide. Using the research of Tania Singer and Olga Klimecki (2014) on the difference between empathy and compassion, the UX for Good and the Aegis Trust developed the Inzovu Curve (figure 16.4) as a model for how to help visitors to the museum make this shift from being emotionally moved (and possibly numbed) to taking compassionate action.

Witnessing suffering can lead to either personal distress or compassionate action

As explained in more detail elsewhere in this book, Singer and Klimecki (2014) concluded

from their research that encountering suffering leads to an empathic resonance with the pain of the victims. But empathy does not automatically lead to compassionate action and is quite likely to lead to personal distress in the observer. When encountering the overwhelming negative experience of others, the observer may become emotionally distressed and unable to manage those feelings or may become emotionally detached and suppress those feelings. In either case, what results is paralysis and inaction. Compassion is the other pathway that is connected with a desire to lessen or eliminate the other person's pain. As I have described in this book, the compassionate response requires a particular mindset that typically requires mental practice to achieve.

The Inzovu Curve was the model used to help visitors to the memorial make this shift from overwhelming negative feelings to compassionate action. Because the curve looks like the elephant's trunk, it is given the name Inzovu,

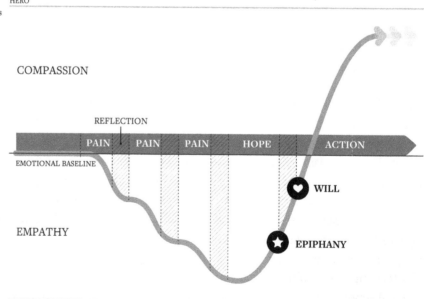

The Inzovu Curve is a model that maps specific designed activities to the emotional response of the individual experiencing them.

It's defined by three aspects:

1. THE EMOTIONAL EXPERIENCE
Each individual has a completely personal baseline that is a neutral starting state. The vertical axis then maps below the line the intensity of empathic response, down to the potential burnout or shutdown; and above the line the intensity of compassionate disposition.

2. THE EXPERIENCE STAGES
The central sequence represents the various stages of the lived experience: pain, reflection, hope and action.

3. THE TWO KEY MOMENTS
There are two key moments in the process from awareness to action: the epiphany and the will.

FIGURE 16.4 Inzovu Curve.

which is the Kinyarwanda word for *elephant*. The Inzovu Curve describes four aspects through which curators guide museum visitors. First, visitors move from their emotional baseline to some level of intense empathic response that could easily lead to emotional distress or detachment. Visitors see and hear the tragic account of the genocide, which can trigger an emotional reaction. Second, visitors are given opportunities to reflect on what they have learned. The space of the museum is set up with time for visitors to decompress and think about what they are experiencing. This can be done by having to walk through empty spaces or have moments just to collect their thoughts between exhibitions. Third, visitors are then told about the heroes in the genocide, the normal people who saved others or did other positive things. This brings about hope and helps create a shift in the painful reflective state of the visitor. Fourth, the hope encourages action, in which each person is encouraged to act in some positive way as a result.

The key moments of epiphany and will on the Inzovu Curve

As noted in the Inzovu Curve, there are two key moments that occur: epiphany and will. *Epiphany* is defined as "the moment where the person is able to create a personal connection to the experience of genocide and following recovery" (Calali, 2014, p. 10). Visitors are encouraged to reflect on what has happened and on their own lives, with the understanding that this kind of tragedy can occur again. The moment of *will* is the point at which visitors are able to think of an action they can do to help humanity and have the motivation to do so. This is in some ways similar to what clinicians need to do when they recover from burnout. In mourning what has happened to them and in going back to the

drawing board, there is a way in which clinicians have an epiphany or awakening about their situation. As clinicians work on their compassion again, they find their desire again to respond to illness and suffering.

WHAT HAPPENED TO MY LOVE OF MEDICINE, AND HOW DO I GET IT BACK?

Throughout this book, I hope you have noticed how distinct research disciplines have all pointed to how compassionate caring for the patient comprises the love of medicine. We have explored the various ways that have contributed to the love of medicine getting buried. The image is important. Did it get "lost," "burned out," or "buried"? Based on all of this research and my own experience accompanying clinicians, I think the appropriate image is "buried," with the allied image of "losing the connection to our fuel source." It is still there. To recover it, we need to dig through what has disconnected us from our source and get back in touch with what we desired in the first place. I offer these steps to summarize what all of the research in this book suggests about how we recover compassionate caring in our careers and be in the compassion mindset.

Step 1: Ask yourself what happened to your love of medicine

The first step in recovery is to ask yourself what happened to your love of medicine. What happened to your connection with this compassionate caring? It will take courage and a willingness to be honest with yourself. It will likely not feel very good, and it will be important to hang in with the negative thoughts and feelings that will arise. You may be intensely frustrated, angry, hurt, and sad for what has happened in your career and what has happened to you in your life. You may literally need to grieve what you feel you have lost and what you have become. Paradoxically, there may be something rather liberating in doing this as you articulate how you are doing right now in this work.

Step 2: Go back to the drawing board of your work and life

Once you have gotten a grip on how bad you feel and that you do not want to be this way anymore, then you will need to go back to the drawing board to figure out how this all happened and what you need to repair and transform to get reconnected with your passion and compassion. If you are burned out (i.e., exhausted, cynical and depersonalized, feeling very unfulfilled), then you have two problems: you need to deal with the burnout first and then deal with what got you burned out. You may end up solving both of these simultaneously, but as with your patients, you need to treat the symptoms and then figure out the underlying problem, do the surgery, the physical therapy, and the lifestyle changes to treat both the problem and what got you to having this problem. It could take time and a variety of methods to heal the burnout and correct what got you to this point. There are many wonderful resources for this, and you should pick the ones that resonate with you. While there are generalizations that can be made about clinician burnout, you got to yours in a unique way, and you will need to find what it is that you need to be able to reconnect. All of the books and programs for stress and burnout are tools and resources. This is all about reconnecting with your source for this work, and by definition, nothing outside you can dictate what you need to do internally.

Step 3: Be open to reflecting on and transforming your assumptions about life

When you have gone through burnout, there is a way in which you may end up questioning a lot of your assumptions about everything, including the meaning of your work and your life. Many clinicians and researchers really emphasize the importance of reflecting on and working on your philosophy of life, what your meaning and purpose in life is. In chapter 14, I used the two terms *philosophy of caring* and *spirituality of caring* to discuss this. But whether you come from a spiritual perspective or an atheistic/agnostic/ humanistic perspective, recovering compassion in your career requires reexamining your assumptions about life and your work. There are many ways to do this, but the main thing to keep in mind is to be open to new ways of thinking. Allow yourself to doubt, to question, and to explore new ideas and ways of being. Be open to synchronicity—the meaningful coincidences that may occur. When people allow themselves to be in a state of asking new questions and seeking new answers, there is a way in which they notice things that they never noticed before. It is important to tolerate a period of intellectual, psychological, and existential uncertainty so that a new way of being can emerge in which you will be happier and more energized to reengage this work.

Step 4: Consult your council of elders

It can be very helpful to talk to people who know you well and who care about you to help you figure out what happened to you and encourage you to do what might be helpful to you in getting reconnected to the compassionate core of your profession again. Some people use the phrase "your personal board of directors," which gets at this same basic idea of people who function as a corporate board with you as the corporation.

I prefer the phrase "council of elders" because "board of directors" connotes that you are a product, and the focus is on making you successful (i.e., profitable). "Council of elders" would be those people whom you choose that know you well and want what is best for you as a person, not as a product or a success object. These are often the mentors and advisors in your life who care enough to tell you what they see in you and who would share any concern with you of what might harm you or help you. They might be certain members of your family, your spouse, your partner, former teachers, spiritual directors or companions, counselors, friends, or whoever is an advocate for you as a person and who desires what is best for you. In this process of reconnecting with what matters to you, consulting them helps provide clarity and perspective on yourself.

Step 5: Find what makes your love of medicine primary again and organize your life around that

Whatever it is that you love in medicine, it is important that you protect and cultivate it. This will differ for each person, and you will need to navigate the circumstances that you have to do this. You may not be able to change things overnight, but you can make concrete steps to do the things that reconnect you with what you love and give you energy for it. It might include changing some part of your job or even changing your job. It might be adding something such as volunteer work, teaching, research, mission work, or some other avenue that allows you to get back to what drew you into this profession or represents what that call or motivation has become now. These are ways to help you flip back into the compassion mindset and give you more energy because it puts you back in touch with the meaning and fulfillment of what you do. It might also include various practices that

you would incorporate to cultivate this, such as periodic retreats, continuing education, keeping up in your field, or learning new things. While the practice of regular and planned vacations is part of this, you need time off that is intentionally designed for personal reflection and discernment. For some people, this is time set aside every day, perhaps connected to a meditation practice, journaling, and so on. Others feel the need for periodic retreats either individually or with like-minded others to recover from the past year, reflect on what happened, and renew for the coming year.

Step 6: Connect regularly with other passionate, compassionate people in health care

Getting together regularly with colleagues to freely discuss your experiences working with patients and the health care system is a high priority in reconnecting with the love of medicine and then sustaining it. You will notice in health care how this kind of thing emerges spontaneously and in all sorts of different forms. It may be the formal Schwartz Rounds, Balint groups, or some type of meeting at which clinicians can talk openly and honestly about what is going on. It may be informal ones that appear to be leisure focused but are actually indirect ways clinicians get together to support each other and regain perspective (e.g., poker night, book or journal club, friends you know at conferences you regularly attend).

Step 7: Expect the negative, and make the positive love of medicine challenge the outside systemic problems and the internal barriers in yourself

As you do these steps or some variation, it is not like you will become blissfully unaware or numb to the chaos of the health care system and our society. The negatives of health care will still persist, but you will have the desire to do the best that can be done. I found it very interesting in Singer and Klimecki's (2014) study of empathy and compassion training that after compassion training, the negative affect was still there to some extent, but it was the generating of positive affect that transformed the experience. I feel like I lived that study long before I ever heard about it. When I began reconnecting with what I loved about patient care and this work, the negatives of difficult patients and exasperating organizational issues were still there, but I was different. Whenever you stay close to what it is that you love about this work, there is a renewed energy to do this work. "I wouldn't want to be doing anything else." "I found that I had the capacity, and I didn't want to turn away." There is a drive that for some period of time, you want to be in that "fight," in that "struggle." It may even take the shape of advocating for change in which you and others push to reform whatever you can when it comes to patient care, the health care system, and our society. It becomes what is worth spending your life on.

CONCLUSION

In this chapter, I have focused on the recovery of compassionate caring as the core driving force and source of energy for the clinician. It is very common that clinicians will experience the loss of this compassionate caring. While some clinicians may never recover it, many turn this burnout into an opportunity to transform how they understand compassionate caring as essential to patient care and as essential to their wellness as clinicians.

QUESTIONS FOR DISCUSSION

1. How would you describe your career trajectory so far in terms of C^2 using the adapted graph by Jane Uygur in figure 16.1?
2. What are sources of your compassion satisfaction at this point in your training or practice?

REFERENCES

Bernard, R. (2016, September 13). To prevent burnout, physicians need less resilience, not more. *KevinMD.com*. Retrieved from https://www.kevinmd.com/blog/2016/09/prevent-burnout-physicians-need-less-resilience-not.html

Branch, W. T., Weil, A. B., Gilligan, M. C., Litzelman, D. K., Hafler, J. P., Plews-Ogan, M., ... Frankel, R. M. (2017). How physicians draw satisfaction and overcome barriers in their practices: "It sustains me." *Patient Education and Counseling*, 100(12), 2320–2330.

Calali, D. (2014). *The Inzovu Curve booklet. Revision 5.* UX for Good, Insight Labs, Aegis Trust. Retrieved from http://www.inzovucurve.org

Campbell, C., Campbell, D., Krier, D., Kuehlthau, R., Hilmes, T., & Stromberger, M. (2009). Reduction in burnout may be a benefit for short-term medical mission volunteers. *Mental Health, Religion and Culture*, 12(7), 627–637.

Dasan, S., Gohil, P., Cornelius, V., & Taylor, C. (2015). Prevalence, causes and consequences of compassion satisfaction and compassion fatigue in emergency care: A mixed-methods study of UK NHS consultants. *Emergency Medicine Journal*, 32(8), 588–594.

Doty, J. R. (2016). *Into the magic shop: A neurosurgeon's quest to discover the mysteries of the brain and the secrets of the heart.* New York, NY: Avery.

Epstein, R. M. (2014). Realizing Engel's biopsychosocial vision: Resilience, compassion, and quality of care. *International Journal of Psychiatry in Medicine, 47*(4), 275–287.

Epstein, R. (2017). *Attending: Medicine, mindfulness, and humanity.* New York, NY: Scribner.

Fredrickson, B. L. (1998). What good are positive emotions? *Review of General Psychology, 2*(3), 300–319.

Fredrickson, B. L. (2004). The broaden-and-build theory of positive emotions. *Philosophical Transactions of the Royal Society of London Series B, Biological Sciences, 359*(1449), 1367–1378.

Gleichgerrcht, E., & Decety, J. (2013). Empathy in clinical practice: How individual dispositions, gender, and experience moderate empathic concern, burnout, and emotional distress in physicians. *PLoS ONE, 8*(4), e61526. doi:10.1371/journal.pone.0061526

Hojat, M., Vergare, M. J., Maxwell, K., Brainard, G., Herrine, S. K., Isenberg, G. A., ... Gonnella, J. S. (2009). The devil is in the third year: A longitudinal study of erosion of empathy in medical school. *Academic Medicine, 84*(9), 1182–1191.

Jackson, D., Firtko, A., & Edenborough, M. (2007). Personal resilience as a strategy for surviving and thriving in the face of workplace adversity: A literature review. *Journal of Advanced Nursing, 60*(1), 1–9.

Jensen, P. M., Trollope-Kumar, K., Waters, H., & Everson, J. (2008). Building physician resilience. *Canadian Family Physician, 54*(5), 722–729.

Keyes, C. L., & Haidt, J. (Eds.). (2003). *Flourishing: Positive psychology and life well lived.* Washington, DC: American Psychological Association.

Killian, K. D. (2008). Helping till it hurts? A multimethod study of compassion fatigue, burnout, and self-care in clinicians working with trauma survivors. *Traumatology, 14*(2), 32–44.

Klimecki, O. M., Leiberg, S., Ricard, M., & Singer, T. (2014). Differential pattern of functional brain plasticity after compassion and empathy training. *Social Cognitive and Affective Neuroscience, 9*(6), 873–879.

Krasner, M. S., Epstein, R. M., Beckman, H., Suchman, A. L., Chapman, B., Mooney, C. J., & Quill, T. E. (2009). Association of an educational program in mindful communication with burnout, empathy, and attitudes among primary care physicians. *JAMA, 302*(12), 1284–1293.

LaFauci Schutt, J. M., & Marotta, S. A. (2011). Personal and environmental predictors of posttraumatic stress in emergency management professionals. *Psychological Trauma: Theory, Research, and Policy, 3*(1), 8–15.

Ofri, D. (2010). *Medicine in translation: Journeys with my patients.* Boston, MA: Beacon Press.

Ofri, D. (2013). *What doctors feel: How emotions affect the practice of medicine.* Boston, MA: Beacon Press.

Peabody, F. W. (1927). The care of the patient. *JAMA, 88*(12), 877–882.

Pfifferling, J. H., & Gilley, K. (1999). Putting "life" back into your professional life. *Family Practice Management, 6*(6), 36–42.

Remen, R. N. (1980). *The human patient.* New York, NY: Anchor Books.

Remen, R. N. (2006). *Kitchen table wisdom: Stories that heal* (10th ed.). New York, NY: Riverhead Books.

Robertson, H. D., Elliott, A. M., Burton, C., Murchie, P., Porteous, T., & Matheson, C. (2016). Resilience of primary healthcare professionals: A systematic review. *British Journal of General Practice, 66*(647), e423–433. doi:10.3399/bjgp16X685261

Scheurer, D., McKean, S., Miller, J., & Wetterneck, T. (2009). US physician satisfaction: A systematic review. *Journal of Hospital Medicine, 4*(9), 560–570.

Schwenk, T. L. (2018). Physician well-being and the regenerative power of caring. *JAMA, 319*(15), 1543- 1544.

Shanafelt, T. D., West, C. P., Sloan, J. A., Novotny, P. J., Poland, G. A., Menaker, R., ... Dyrbye, L. N. (2009). Career fit and burnout among academic faculty. *Archives of Internal Medicine, 169*(10), 990–995.

Singer, T., & Klimecki, O. M. (2014). Empathy and compassion. *Current Biology, 24*(18), R875–R878.

Slatten, L. A., Carson, K. D., & Carson, P. P. (2011). Compassion fatigue and burnout: What managers should know. *Health Care Manager, 30*(4), 325–333.

Stamm, B. H. (2010). *The concise ProQOL manual* (2nd ed.). Pocatello, ID: ProQOL.org.

Uygur, J. M. (2012). *Understanding compassion in family medicine: A qualitative study* (Master's thesis). University of Western Ontario.

Weiner, E. L., Swain, G. R., Wolf, B., & Gottlieb, M. (2001). A qualitative study of physicians' own wellness-promotion practices. *Western Journal of Medicine, 174*(1), 19–23.

Wright, P. A. (2006). *Mother Teresa's prescription: Finding happiness and peace in service*. Notre Dame, IN: Ave Maria Press.

Youngson, R. (2012). *Time to care: How to love your patients and your job*. Raglan, New Zealand: Rebelheart.

Zeidner, M., & Hadar, D. (2014, July). Some individual difference predictors of professional well-being and satisfaction of health professionals. *Personality and Individual Differences, 65*, 91–95.

CREDITS

"Who must do the hard things? Those who can. And who must do the impossible things? Those who care."

—Carolyn Payton

CHAPTER 17

Conclusion

Every day I hear someone in health care being absolutely disgusted with the way some patients are, how ridiculous the documentation requirements are, how much the computer dominates our clinical work, and how chaotic the health care system is. We are burning out at a terrible rate, and we are losing colleagues. I also hear patients who feel like they are on a health care assembly line with clinicians who are in a hurry to get to wherever they need to go next. Patients complain about being quickly prejudged based on all the bad patient experiences that clinician has had. Patients are worried to go to the hospital without someone to watch over them to protect them from all the mistakes that are possible when their health care is divided among many different people, all of whom seem like they have other things they have to do.

So, the temptation is to protect ourselves more and distance ourselves, especially emotionally. Yet, as Jean Watson says, when we do that, we cut ourselves off from the very source of our energy for this work. Our fears, our competitiveness, our concern about making enough money all threaten to trump our compassionate caring mindset. We imagine that perhaps this is no longer possible, given "the way things are." But what we know now is that we humans are built for compassion. It has been the secret of our success as a species that we look out for each other, notice each other's suffering, are moved by that suffering, and act to help each other in that suffering. We clinicians sign up for even more and devote our whole careers to this most beautiful quality of being human. We end up being in the thick of it and encounter more about the sad and troubling things of being human than most people do. While disgusted with "the way things are," we want to do something about the suffering we witness, we want to reach out and help using the skills we were given. We have the capacity, and we do not want to turn away. Cutting ourselves off from compassion makes us less happy, less fulfilled, and less helpful in doing the very thing that matters to us: helping other people.

The science of compassion has revealed that our past understanding of compassionate caring was sentimentalized and emotionalized. The reality is that compassion is a specific mindset that involves cognitive, emotional, motivational, and behavioral components. Rather than being considered to be just being nice and having a good bedside manner, compassionate caring is actually the focused and personalized attention of one's technical competence on what the patient's needs are. It involves the courage and openness to notice what a patient is going through, to empathize with that patient, and to respond in any way possible within the limits of our role to help alleviate or prevent suffering.

While we *know* the right answers for patient care, we are not *doing* those answers. We know that treating our patients in a compassionate caring way is very good for them not only because they feel better when we treat them this way, but also because the medical outcomes are actually better. When we are in our clinician compassion mindset, it makes a difference to our patients. They feel safe with us. They can sense that we are pulling all our smarts and skills together and focusing all of that on how we can help this particular person in front of us. They come to trust us, even when our communication skills are not the best, because they sense we are "into it," that their particular problem matters to us and we are

going to do whatever we can to help them with that. Our patients come to feel safe with us, and they tell us everything we need to know. Our warmth and cognitive investment actually lead us to get better "data" from them, and we can make a much better diagnosis. We know that getting to know them in a whole way, in a biopsychosocial way, is much more likely to help them than if we only looked at them in a reductionist, biomedical way. Because we get to know them in this more complete way, we have more information about how this illness or injury happened and what it is going to take to help them get through it. Our interventions are going to be more sound. We are going to know how to support them and how to challenge them in a way that is most likely to be effective. Because they know of our compassionate caring commitment to them, they are much more likely to listen and follow through on what they need to do than if we treated them in an emotionally detached, technical manner. Compassionate caring makes a huge difference in what happens to our patients.

We are clearer on why we are not doing those answers. As we have examined in this book, we set up clinicians for failure. In medical school or whatever helping professions training program they were in, we demanded having the brightest and most caring students we can get. Once we have them, we inundate them with so much information that they wonder if they can survive. But then we teach them to devalue that caring part of themselves. We give them sentimentalized or clichéd understandings of caring and compassion that work well in marketing but cannot help them manage what they are going to face. We give them the best and latest advances in medicine, but we teach them simplistic, outdated notions of how to manage their emotions or deal with the emotions of their patients. We have tremendous potential in teaching about emotional intelligence and emotional regulation, but we do not give them this in their training "because there are more important things to teach." Our devaluing of the subjective dimensions of clinical medicine reveals that we are still operating out of Cartesian dualism and distorted understandings of what "objectivity" means. Working with patients is technically and emotionally very hard. We train the technical very well, but we assume clinicians can "just pick up" the emotional and the interpersonal skills they need on the side. We set them up to be half-good clinicians. We set them up to fail. We know how to train people to deal with the interpersonally and emotionally difficult aspects of this work—but we do not generally give our student clinicians this. Some of us do not even know that this capability even exists.

What is amazing is that what we thought were causing the problems in medicine are actually the solution. When our burnout levels are as high as they are now, we can see how it shows up in the way we are with patients. We have less energy for our patients, less patience for our patients, and emotionally we just try to make it through the day. This leads us to attribute the cause of the burnout to the patient care when actually patient care is what we like doing the best. We falsely attribute the compassionate connection with our patients and the emotional labor in health care to be the cause of the stress and burnout. So, we stop being compassionate and move to a more emotionally detached clinical care to protect ourselves. It makes sense that we would do this. But we actually do not feel any better when we do this. And it is literally killing us to practice like this. What must be our priority is keeping the compassionate caring central to

whatever we do. Both as individual clinicians and as organizations, our ability to be in the compassion mindset allows us to experience the deep satisfaction that results from reaching out to prevent and relieve illness and suffering in our patients. It is what we are built to do. It is why we sacrificed so much in order to have the opportunity to practice our specialty. To cut off our emotional connection to our patients and to ourselves and to sabotage the compassion mindset are surefire ways to make us eventually very unhappy and discouraged in this work.

The future will be the best of times and the worst of times in health care. We are clearer that we must train our new clinicians to deal more holistically with patients in the twenty-first century, patients whose poor health conditions are more than ever before related to negative health behaviors. In our medical schools and other health professions training programs, in the MCAT, in the ACGME competencies, et cetera, at least on paper we know we need to select and train future clinicians with a stronger ability to assess and treat patients using the biopsychosocial model. Medical advances will continue at their rapid pace, and neuroscience and biology will continue to vanquish mind–body dualism with all the problems this model of human nature has created. However, just as we are getting a better perspective on how clinicians should be trained now, including the science of compassion, we face an age of depersonalization and dehumanization as people are viewed more as economic objects. Just as we will train our clinicians from a more compassion-centric paradigm in which being a smart doctor necessarily means you are a compassionately caring doctor, they will face an age in which the value of relationship is being redefined and possibly diminished by our transition to the electronic age. Just as we are attempting to train our clinicians to be more relational, more comfortable with emotions and using these for the healing process, they will be working with people who have a diminished ability to relate interpersonally. There will be more attachment problems, and patients may value compassionate connection less than they do now, even though strong relational skills will be absolutely necessary in order to help patients of the future improve their health behaviors. We are going through a time in which there is a breakdown of family and community relationships, a decrease in societal cohesion, and difficulty valuing face-to-face interactions that are the best way to help human beings become aware of themselves and their blind spots about their health behaviors. It is a time with increased rudeness, a decrease in the ability to appreciate human service, a massive drug abuse problem, an increased sense of entitlement, and a population becoming less educated.

It appears that we will have more reasons than ever not to be compassionate and will be more likely to burn out. With all the challenges listed above, it will be much easier to treat patients in a detached manner. Already we have patients who do not want to discuss with us how they are not taking care of themselves and preferring a quick fix with their overblown expectations of the advances of medical science. If the business concerns continue to shape what medicine will become, we can be assured that our clinical staffs will be more objectified, as will our patients. It will be easier to treat people in compartmentalized ways because looking at humans in more holistic and preventive manners is not valued or reimbursed. We will know that compassionate caring is better for both the patient and the clinician, but it may be very difficult to sustain the clinical compassion mindset when health care is organized through a business/economic paradigm rather than a compassion-centric paradigm.

What we know, however, is that if we do not generally work within a compassionate caring mindset, our patients will get poorer medical care, and we as clinicians will wither and die because we have betrayed the way our physiologies and our psychologies are built for compassion. We have already been living that experiment in which we thought it was possible to treat patients with emotionally detached, biomedically reduced, compartmentalized care. But our patients are faring worse, our economic costs are higher, and we have never been more burned out than we are right now. Why would we want to continue this emotionally detached, reductionistic approach within organizations that promote assembly-line production in medicine and dehumanizing management styles to the detriment of the compassionate spirit of their clinicians? We have already seen the effects of such an approach. Our clinicians do not stay long, and those health care organizations tend to fail.

Yet we know it can be different because we are seeing organizations that realized that a compassion-centric organizational culture actually is more efficient, that there is less staff turnover, patients get better care, clinicians are able to feel more fulfilled in their attempts to prevent and relieve suffering, and the organization is more profitable. Practicing compassion-centric medicine is what we know is the best medicine based on all the scientific study we have. Not practicing in this way is outdated medicine. The best way to give patients the best care and to support our clinicians is for whole organizations to work toward creating cultures in which compassionate caring permeates every facet of the organization. The biggest predictor of burnout is the culture of our organizations. Individual interventions such as those focused on a single unit or department, a group of clinicians, or individuals can be somewhat helpful but not as helpful as when a whole organization does it.

About 24 years ago, I came home and said to my wife that I had started hating my patients; that I dreaded each hour and pushed myself through acting as competent and caring as I could be. I had done research on how empathy was actually related to less burnout. I thought I had a spirituality of caring that would protect and sustain me through the challenges of making a life helping people. But that did not immunize me from becoming aggravated by my patients or discouraged by the "system." My wife said to me, "Well, honey, you've got a problem. Because your patients need you to love them to get better. Right now, you don't." From there, I went back to the drawing board, physically, emotionally, intellectually, and spiritually. When I could admit that I had gotten disconnected from the soul of compassionate work, that I was becoming the kind of clinician that I had detested, it was then that my recovery of compassion could begin. That recovery is how I discovered many of the things that are written in this book and began the practices to restore balanced compassionate caring in my life. In working with physicians and nurses, I discovered that many of them had gone through this or were going through this. There were many residents who had said to me after several years, "I used to be an idealistic caring physician, but I don't feel like I'm caring anymore." I discovered that many clinicians had gone through or were going through becoming disconnected from the call to compassionate work. Through their experiences, I learned how some recovered compassion in

their lives and how some did not. With the tremendous advances that have come in the science of compassion, it is more clear what happens to us as we do this work and what we need to do to recover and reengage in the work of preventing or responding to illness and suffering.

I remember that shortly after I had recovered the compassion mindset in my life, I noticed how the patients and the system were just as I had left them. The patients were still in terrible predicaments, trying to recover from terrible trauma, or simply desiring to stay alive. The patients were still difficult, still manipulative, still unreasonably demanding, or still entitled. The negatives in clinical care were still all the same. But I had changed. Even though the negatives were the same, I had a renewed desire to be there doing the best I could to help them. My fascination with how to help people get better had returned. My ability to keep my composure and work with very challenging people was again a worthwhile endeavor. It motivated me to go learn the skills that would make me better at it. It also motivated me to make sure I spent time with people who love this compassionate work just like I did—where we could share what we had learned in difficult cases and what we were going through in doing this work. And I realized that I had to do a much better job of taking care of myself so that I could take better care of others. The problems were the same; I was different. I was "into it" again.

When I was faced with a difficult decision in my life, one of my teachers stopped me in the middle of my complaining and said, "Dom, what are your priorities?" The question jolted me into recognizing who I really was and what really mattered to me. I was discouraged and fearful. But the timing of that simple question was perfect. Very soon after he asked me that question, I knew what really mattered to me and what kind of person I wanted to be. In medicine, we do better if we start and stay centered in our priorities. Everything else should orbit around those priorities. Compassionate caring is our central organizing principle. Whenever we make compassion less central, our patients suffer, and so do we.

Dominic Ovide Vachon, MDiv, PhD

August 1, 2018

Author Credentials

Dr. Dominic O. Vachon, MDiv, PhD, is the John G. Sheedy MD Director of the Ruth M. Hillebrand Center for Compassionate Care in Medicine in the College of Science at the University of Notre Dame. The mission of the Hillebrand Center is to advance the application of the science of compassion at every level of medical education and practice in order to transform clinician well-being and patient care and restore the spirit of compassion in healthcare. The Hillebrand Center for Compassionate Care in Medicine collaborates with many local and national efforts to foster compassionate care in medicine and the helping professions. Vachon is Professor of the Practice in the Preprofessional Studies Department at the University of Notre Dame. He teaches courses including Compassionate Care in Medicine, Medical Counseling Skills, and Spiritualties of Caring in the Helping Professions. He does research on the internal mental and emotional processes of the clinician compassion mindset in patient care, clinician communication skills, and innovations in medical training applying the science of compassion. He is also a national speaker in the area of maintaining balanced compassionate caring in the helping professions.

Vachon was the director of Behavioral Medicine and Caring Science Training at Saint Joseph Regional Medical Center's Family Medicine Residency Program beginning in 2000. He continues to be involved in the training of physician residents for patient–physician communication and professionalism. He teaches medical students as Volunteer Clinical Faculty for the Indiana University School of Medicine in South Bend, Indiana. He provides continuing education programs and retreats for physicians and nurses as well as other medical professionals in training. He consults with organizations that wish to promote more caring attitudes and behaviors in their staffs as well as programs to help health care staffs deal with compassion fatigue and burnout. He is also a practicing psychologist specializing in neurofeedback therapy.

He graduated from the University of Notre Dame in 1980 with a bachelor's degree in psychology and philosophy. In 1985 he earned a Master of Divinity from the University of Notre Dame. In 1993 he earned a PhD in Counseling Psychology from Loyola

University, Chicago. He did a postdoctoral scientist–practitioner fellowship in psychology at the University of Notre Dame. Over the past 25 years, he has taught medical students, physician residents, undergraduates in the Preprofessional Department, and graduate students in the Psychology and Theology Departments.

Index

CPSIA information can be obtained
at www.ICGtesting.com
Printed in the USA
FSHW011024030221
78269FS

9 781516 540082